THE 9/11 BACKLASH:
A DECADE OF U.S. HATE CRIMES
TARGETING THE INNOCENT

By Nicoletta Karam

Beatitude PRESS

BERKELEY, CALIFORNIA

A Beatitude Press Book.
Berkeley, CA 94703
Beatitude Press, Est. 1976
Cover design by Chris Cass

First edition: September 2012

Karam, Nicoletta
        The 9/11 Backlash : A Decade of U.S. Hate Crimes Targeting the Innocent / Nicoletta Karam − 1st ed.
                p. cm.
Includes endnotes.
ISBN (electronic copy) 978-1623095390
ISBN (print copy) 978-1478230953

Contents : 9/11 Backlash Deniers and the Diversity of Hate Crime Victims and Perpetrators − Bias Attacks and Xenophobia Before 9/11 − The Arab, South Asian, and Muslim Victims of the September 11, 2001 Terrorist Strikes − Backlash Assaults, Sept. 2001 to Sept. 2011 − Backlash Attacks at Mosques, Gurdwaras, Hindu Temples, Synagogues, and Churches, Sept. 2001 to Sept. 2011 − Backlash Hate Crimes at Schools, Sept. 2001 to Sept. 2011 − Backlash Attacks at Work, Sept. 2001 to Sept. 2011 − Backlash Hate Crimes at Homes, Sept. 2001 to Sept. 2011 − Backlash Death Threats, Sept. 2001 to Sept. 2011 − Post-9/11 Kills of Muslims, Sikhs, Arabs, and South Asians − Why Backlash Hate Crimes are Undercounted − Steps to Curb Backlash Bigotry − August 5, 2012 Wisconsin Sikh Temple Shooting.

1.War on Terrorism, 2001 − Moral and ethical aspects. 2. September 11 Terrorist Attacks, 2001 − Influence. 3. Muslims − United States. 4. Arab-Americans − Crimes Against − United States. 5. Sikhs − Civil Rights − United States. 6. Islamophobia − United States. 7. Hate Crimes − United States. I. Title.

HV6431.K264 2012

The 9/11 Backlash:
A Decade of U.S. Hate Crimes
Targeting the Innocent

"When the Nazis came for the Communists, I remained silent; I was not a Communist. When they locked up the Social Democrats, I remained silent; I was not a Social Democrat. When they came for the Trade Unionists, I did not speak out; I was not a Trade Unionist. When they came for the Jews, I remained silent; I was not a Jew. When they came for me, there was no one left to speak out." – Pastor Martin Niemoller

This book is dedicated to the 9/11 backlash victims and their relatives, who came from diverse ethnic, racial, and religious backgrounds. It is also for all the brave Americans – including many celebrities – who spoke out against intolerance, urging their fellow citizens not to attack people of other faiths.

About the Author:

Nicoletta Karam graduated with honors from Swarthmore College, where she was an editor of the *Phoenix* and a correspondent for the *New York Times*. She has a degree in Arabic from the University of Alexandria, Egypt, and a Ph.D in American history from Brandeis University, where she taught history, English, and literature courses. Her 2005 dissertation, "Kahlil Gibran's Pen Bond: Modernism and the Manhattan Renaissance of Arab-American Literature," explores how early 20th-century Middle Eastern immigrant writers used the liberating clash of Oriental and Occidental worldviews to reformulate their values and institutions in the U.S. In the past, Nicoletta Karam worked as a Research Fellow at the Institute of Women's Policy Research in Washington, D.C. She has also assembled exhibits on women's history for the San Francisco Public Library and other Bay Area venues. She is currently a writer-in-residence for Shoestring Players, an Oakland-based theatre group. Most recently, she adapted three Mark Twain short stories for the stage, to the delight of Bay Area audiences.

Abstract:

Many journalists and news commentators deny the existence, length, and intensity of the wave of intolerance that began immediately after 9/11 and continued for years afterward. This book is an attempt to document that this backlash did occur, and was much worse and much longer in duration than many Americans realize. In the years following 9/11, many ethnic Americans and immigrant residents were affected by a surge of hate crimes triggered by the terrorist strikes and the concomitant 'War on Terror.' This book argues that the 9/11 backlash was fueled by 20th-century Islamophobia and Hinduphobia, coupled with local and federal authorities' long-standing unwillingness to acknowledge the reality of hate crimes or handle them with the gravity they deserved. These factors created a "perfect storm" of xenophobia that swept through the U.S. after the terrorist attacks and continued to affect diverse minority communities for more than a decade.

Chapter one establishes the need for this book, discussing how reporters and pundits often dismissed or trivialized the bias component of attacks taking place in the aftermath of 9/11. This introductory chapter also explores the incredible ethnic and religious diversity of both bias crime victims and perpetrators. Bigots in the U.S. targeted neighborhood Middle Easterners, Arab-Americans, Muslims, Sikhs, Hindus, South Asians, Africans, American blacks, Latinos, Jews, Asian-Americans, bearded white men, and ethnic-looking European immigrants. Other vulnerable communities were also singled out. Fundamentalist Christian leaders Jerry Falwell and Pat Robertson blamed the terrorist strikes on the ACLU, feminists, gays and lesbians, and the pro-choice movement. Because most U.S. citizens belong to at least one of these groups, the majority of Americans were scapegoated by at least someone in the aftermath of 9/11. Americans who ate at targeted ethnic restaurants or shopped at minority-owned stores were also endangered by bias-motivated attacks. Almost as diverse as the backgrounds of victims, the perpetrators came from a variety of racial, religious, and ethnic groups. Assailants included Christian Caucasians, African-Americans, Latinos, Jews, and Asian-Americans. Post-9/11 attacks in the U.S. were committed by community members of different ages, genders, educational backgrounds, and nationalities.

Chapter two provides an overview of pre-9/11 bias attacks targeting Muslims, Arabs, Sikhs, and South Asians, arguing that poor local and federal response to 'Dot-buster' assaults, mosque arsons, and other 20th-century hate crimes created an environment in which post-9/11 xenophobia was permitted to flourish. To understand the cultural context in which these bias attacks were occurring, this section includes a brief overview of American films that disseminated pernicious stereotypes of foreigners. Chapter three acknowledges the South Asian, Christian Arab, and Muslim victims of the terrorist strikes in order to challenge nativist interpretations of 9/11, a tragedy which affected people from scores of different countries and religious backgrounds.

Subsequent chapters explore different dimensions of the decade-long backlash, demonstrating how news commentators routinely minimized the severity of post-9/11 hate crimes and local and federal investigators repeatedly denied that hate crimes were taking place in their jurisdictions. Chapter four discusses physical assaults that began on September 11, 2001 and continued for years afterwards, often spiking on or near each anniversary of the terrorist strikes. Chapter five examines post-9/11 vandalism attacks and arsons at mosques, Sikh prayer centers, and Hindu temples. On occasion, synagogues and immigrant-friendly churches were also targeted. Chapter six investigates backlash incidents on academic campuses, showing that students and instructors were frequently physically assaulted or mistreated. Chapter seven explores 9/11 hate crimes targeting minority employees in their workplaces, establishing that taxi drivers, 7-Eleven convenience-store clerks, and gas station attendants were particularly vulnerable. Chapter eight delves into bias-motivated attacks on minority residences in the aftermath of the terrorist strikes. Chapter nine examines death threats and verbal attacks after 9/11. Chapter ten discusses killings linked to the backlash. Each of these middle chapters begins in the immediate aftermath of 9/11 and covers hate crimes in the decade that followed. These chapters also include a discussion of Islamophobic and Hinduphobic television programs and films that fueled American nativism and coincided with the timing of bias attacks.

Chapter eleven investigates 75 reasons why hate crimes against Muslims, Arabs, Sikhs, and South Asians are undercounted in the U.S., focusing on the unwillingness of many minority victims to report attacks to minimally-sympathetic local and federal authorities. This chapter also delves into the problematic ways in which hate crimes are tabulated. When Indian Sikhs are mistaken as Saudi Muslims, it is difficult for American governmental record-keepers to figure out how to fit the crime into a single-bias category (i.e., was it an anti-Sikh, anti-Muslim, anti-South Asian, anti-Arab, anti-Indian, or anti-Saudi hate crime?) Chapter twelve offers 75 solutions to problems raised by the backlash in the hopes of creating a more tolerant U.S. This section questions the efficacy of specific 'War on Terror' federal policies and proposes strategies to end post-9/11 discrimination, such as the widespread racial profiling of airport travelers.

The book ends with a discussion of the August 5, 2012 massacre at a Sikh temple in Wisconsin, demonstrating that hate crimes against minorities are continuing to take place more than a decade after the terrorist attacks.

CONTENTS

CHAPTER ONE:

9/11 BACKLASH DENIERS AND THE DIVERSITY
OF HATE CRIME VICTIMS AND PERPETRATORS

My most vivid childhood memory is of a poem. My father was engrossed in a Constantine Cavafy anthology and suddenly began reciting, "Waiting for the Barbarians."[1] This literary work tells the story of a town anxiously awaiting invasion by oncoming barbarian hordes. I remember being frightened by my dad's dramatic narration, visualizing Cavafy's barbarians in minute detail.

On September 11, 2001, I felt as if Cavafy's mythical barbarians had suddenly sprung to life and descended upon American soil. Like the traumatized townspeople in the poem, Americans began fearfully anticipating the barbarians' return.

Americans were deeply affected by the events of 9/11, spending years looking for traces of terrorism in every suspicious package, unattended bag, and inbound flight. Many frightened people began seeing Osama bin Laden in every ethnic-looking face they encountered, targeting innocent people in suburban shopping malls, school playgrounds, and ball parks. This is the story of these hate crimes.

The scope of 9/11 backlash attacks is difficult to measure because many victims never came forward. As a result, it is impossible to determine the exact numbers of murders, assaults, death threats, and vandalism cases unleashed by the wave of xenophobia triggered by the terrorist strikes. In many instances, bias-crime victims were more willing to report attacks to community groups instead of to local police or federal authorities, creating disparities in the numbers of crimes recorded by different agencies.

The FBI defines hate crimes as those motivated by "prejudice, hatred or advocacy of violence against victims because of their race, religion, sexual orientation, ethnicity, or disability."[2] In cities throughout the country, police officers and government officials reported huge spikes in bias crimes in the month following the attacks on the World Trade Center and Pentagon.[3]

Experts giving testimony on October 11, 2001 at the U.S. Commission on Civil Rights estimated that the most serious backlash crimes in the first 30 days included 80 assaults and several deaths.[4] Hate crimes took a variety of forms, including: murders, arsons, bombings, aggravated assaults, batteries with handguns, attacks with pepper spray, stonings, motor vehicle assaults, vandalism, mob violence, lootings, bomb threats, school closings, workplace violence, religious attacks, and harassment. In the first month after the terrorist strikes, the *New York Times* reported that 80 bias crimes took place in New York City alone.[5] Finding one U.S. event particularly significant, the *Manchester Guardian* reported that on September 12, 2001, the Los Angeles-based Museum of Tolerance was closed.[6]

What is particularly noteworthy about the 9/11 backlash is the incredible diversity of its victims. Bigots in the U.S. targeted neighborhood Middle Easterners, Arab-Americans, Muslims, Sikhs, Hindus, South Asians, Africans, American blacks, Latinos, Jews, bearded white men, and ethnic-looking European immigrants. Other vulnerable communities were also singled out. Fundamentalist Christian leaders Jerry Falwell and Pat Robertson blamed the terrorist strikes on the ACLU, feminists, gays and lesbians, and the pro-choice movement.[7] Because most U.S. citizens belong to at least one of these groups, the majority of Americans were scapegoated by at least someone in the aftermath of 9/11. Americans who ate at targeted ethnic restaurants or shopped at minority-owned stores were also endangered by bias-motivated attacks. For example, on September 13, 2001, a Utah bigot set fire to a Pakistani restaurant in a backlash attack, putting the lives of racially-diverse diners and employees in jeopardy.[8]

Almost as varied as the diversity of their victims, the perpetrators came from numerous racial, religious, and ethnic groups. Assailants included Christian Caucasians, African-Americans, Latinos, Jews, and Asian-Americans. Bias attacks were committed by Americans of different ages, genders, and educational backgrounds.

Many immigrant residents were so frightened by the intensity of the backlash that they decided to return to their countries of origin. Naturalized Americans also considered leaving the U.S. Bassam Mahdawi, editor of an Arabic newspaper in Anaheim, told the *New York Times* that many ethnic and religious minorities were so afraid of hate crimes that they felt compelled to emigrate, even though it meant giving up their businesses and removing their American-born children from their schools.[9] Mahdawi observed that terrified ethnic Americans and immigrants sometimes resorted to selling their possessions at a loss so they could flee the U.S. One Lebanese man was so frightened that he decided to forgo a $15,000 deposit on a new American home in order to return to the Middle East, where he felt safer.[10]

Along with Muslims and Middle Easterners, Sikhs were profoundly affected by the 9/11 backlash and the inflammatory media coverage of the terrorist attacks. Across the U.S., South Asians were outraged that CBS repeatedly aired montages of the Twin Towers collapsing next to a news clip of a bearded, turbaned Sikh being hauled off a train in handcuffs, after another traveler reported him as a possible terrorist.[11]

Anyone who looked "foreign" suddenly became a threat. Shortly after 9/11, a *Los Angeles Times* poll found that 68% of all respondents and 63% of African-Americans supported the racial profiling of Arabs in the U.S.[12] One CNN/*USA Today* Gallup survey conducted a few days after the World Trade Center strikes determined that about half of Americans agreed that Arabs – even U.S. citizens – should have to carry special identification and undergo special security checks before boarding a plane.[13] The same poll also uncovered that 32 percent of Americans believed that Arabs living in the U.S. should be subjected to special surveillance similar to the experiences of Japanese-Americans after the attack on Pearl Harbor.[14]

Remembering the World War II. internment of Japanese-Americans, some Arab-Americans and Muslims worried that they might be put in camps. Community organizations were particularly alarmed by the inflammatory remarks made by U.S. Civil Rights Commissioner Peter Kirsanow at the Commission's July 19, 2002 meeting in Detroit.[15] At this gathering, Kirsanow predicted that if there was another terrorist strike and the perpetrators came from the same ethnic group that attacked the World Trade Center, America's commitment to civil rights would be abandoned.[16] He told the audience that he anticipated a groundswell of public opinion in favor of more stops, detentions, and racial profiling. He also raised the possibility of mass detention camps for Arab-Americans and American Muslims, predicting a return to Korematsu, the Supreme Court decision that sanctioned the internment of more than 110,000 Japanese and Japanese-Americans during World War II.[17] Kirsanow's words attracted considerable attention in newspapers like the Albany *Times Union* and the *Milwaukee Journal Sentinel*, prompting civil rights groups and members of Congress to call for his removal.[18] Prior to accepting President George W. Bush's nomination on December 6, 2001 to a six-year term on the Human Rights Commission, Kirsanow was a practicing attorney and founding member of the conservative organization, New Black Leadership. Many civil rights activists in America were disturbed that any governmental official, especially an African-American representative on a human rights organization, could make such alarming statements. An editorial in the *Arab American News* highlighted the significance of Kirsanow's comments, seeing them as a warning from the Bush Administration to ethnic communities, conveying the message that minority groups needed to remain silent on the suspension of civil liberties and the looming Iraq War, or face governmental persecution similar to the past experiences of Japanese-Americans.[19]

One Muslim woman shared her fears about internment with the *Washington Post,* telling the newspaper that she was comforted that her blond son Zaki could escape persecution by passing for white if the U.S. government began rounding up Muslims.[20] South Asians and Middle Easterners opted to change their names to avoid being treated as second-class American citizens. The *San Francisco Chronicle* reported that after 9/11, a Muslim woman went to the New York Department of Health to change her son's surname from Mohammed to Smith, hoping it would protect him from community Islamophobia.[21]

Internment fears were exacerbated by articles in the *Los Angeles Times* and other prominent newspapers publicizing a controversial 1986 Immigration and Naturalization Service proposal about the logistics of putting Arab-Americans in internment camps in Oakdale, Louisiana in the event of increased tensions with the Middle East.[22] On the first anniversary of 9/11, the *New York Times* reported that members of the Wednesday Club, a Lebanese social group in Dearborn, nervously joked about the possibility of playing cards at an internment camp in Louisiana.[23] In response to concerns about putting Arabs and Muslims in U.S. relocation centers, many Japanese-Americans, recalling their own experiences of internment, acted to protect the civil liberties of their fellow citizens.

On occasion, post-9/11 governmental announcements and policies conveyed the message that Muslim-Americans were a threat to their neighbors. Instead of cautioning against racial scapegoating, Attorney General John Ashcroft called on the U.S. population to form a 'National Neighborhood Watch,' and thanked Americans for calling in hundreds of thousands of tips about suspicious U.S. residents.[24]

As a result of this increased scrutiny, many South Asians, Muslims, and Arab-Americans began limiting their movements. In response to post-9/11 hate crimes and threats, many organizations cancelled cultural events. In Orange County, the annual Arab American Festival in Garden Grove, expected to draw 30,000 attendees, was cancelled. In San Francisco, the Arab Film Festival was postponed. In Virginia Beach, the Punjabi Society of Hampton Roads decided not to hold its annual festival at Old Dominion University. Discussing this cancellation, group president Jagdish Singh told the *Virginia Pilot* that the event could not take place because South Asians in the area were too afraid to go out in public.[25]

Many terrified immigrants and minority Americans avoided traveling to scarcely-populated rural areas, fearing they would be particularly vulnerable in these places. A few weeks after the terrorist strikes, Pakistani immigrant Dr. Liaquat Husain told the Albany *Times Union* that he was dismayed that he and his wife Khalida had become the object of post-9/11 scrutiny, enduring the stares and whispers of hostile people when they walked around a local farmers' market.[26] Worried about their safety, the Muslim couple decided to cancel trips to small towns and the Adirondacks, places they enjoyed traveling in the past.

Middle Easterners and South Asians began altering their dress in the U.S. Leila Al-Marayati, a spokeswoman for the Muslim Women's League, told the *New York Times* that the sense of being under siege was so great that some of their members began exchanging their Islamic head scarves for hats and turtlenecks.[27] Sikhs also changed their appearance. The *Washington Post* reported that racially-motivated attacks caused Sikh-American Jaswinder Singh Sidhu to replace his religiously-mandated turban with a Yankees baseball cap.[28] Although he knew that strict Sikhs might call for his excommunication, he felt compelled to abandon his *dastaar* because his family members were afraid it would cause him to be attacked by bigots.[29]

While many immigrants stopped going out in public to avoid becoming targets, minorities who maintained their usual routines occasionally faced overt discrimination in their neighborhoods and their communities. Shortly after 9/11, the *Rocky Mountain News* reported that a Tunisian man in Denver was refused seating at a restaurant because he looked too Middle Eastern.[30]

Minority workers also felt the effects of the 9/11 backlash. In the months following the terrorist attacks, the U.S. Equal Employment Opportunity Commission received so many allegations of illegal bias against Muslim, Middle Eastern and South Asian workers that it created a new category, Code Z, to track these cases. In March 2002, EEOC Chairwoman Cari Dominguez told the *Washington Post* that she was shocked by the hundreds of complaints her agency received, noting that the upswell in bigotry was unprecedented.[31] Other local and state workplace discrimination agencies also experienced a dramatic increase in new cases.

Minority-owned businesses were often financially crippled by the 9/11 backlash. Naz 8, a Bay Area movie theatre specializing in Bollywood and Afghan film, experienced a 50% decline in revenue since many movie-goers were afraid that the building might be targeted.[32] Other ethnic businesses suffered even more precipitous declines. In Anaheim, Travel Plus, an agency specializing in booking pilgrimages to Saudi Arabia and South Asia, was particularly hard-hit. In the first three months after the terrorist strikes, revenues tumbled to approximately 5% of pre-9/11 levels.[33] Travel agent Fahim Kaiser told the *Orange County Register* that business had decreased so dramatically because Muslims were reluctant to travel in such a hostile climate.[34] Although Travel Plus survived the recession, other smaller agencies catering to Muslim travelers went out of business.

3

U.S. governmental policies also increased the unease of Arab-Americans and Muslims. In a *Times Union* article, Moustafa Bayoumi lamented the erosion of civil liberties in the U.S., including the monitoring of libraries and bookstores, the fingerprinting of Arab visitors entering the country, and the arrest and detention of immigrants.[35] Bayoumi noted that many attorneys and judges were uncomfortable about what was transpiring, particularly the Bush administration's position that American citizens could be detained indefinitely without charges or counsel if they were declared to be enemy combatants.[36] Because governmental officials refused to release the names of many immigrants in custody, Former Secretary of State Warren Christopher likened their fate to the 'disappeared' of Argentina in the 1970s.[37]

In response to governmental assaults on civil liberties and hate crimes taking place throughout the country, U.S. Senator Daniel Inouye of Hawaii told the *Yakima Herald-Republic* that the racist treatment of Arab-Americans in the aftermath of 9/11 was comparable to the experiences of Japanese-Americans during World War II.[38]

Other concerned citizens spoke out in defense of Arabs and Muslims in the U.S. Members of the Japanese American Citizens League publicly expressed their outrage when Asian-American syndicated columnist and FOX news commentator Michelle Malkin defended the U.S. government's decision to put Japanese-Americans in internment camps during World War II., and hinted that it might be necessary to do the same to people of Middle Eastern origin in response to the World Trade Center attacks. In her 2004 book, In Defense of Internment: The Case for 'Racial Profiling' in World War II and the War on Terror, Malkin argues that Americans' civil liberties should not be viewed as sacrosanct in wartime.[39] Contradicting the findings of American historians and the conclusions of an official U.S. government commission, Malkin contends that the federal government made a rational decision when it ordered the internment of Japanese immigrants and Japanese-Americans living on the West Coast.[40] Malkin acknowledges that she was inspired to write the book because of criticism of the Department of Justices' efforts to root out terrorists in the aftermath of 9/11.[41] She also maintains that criticism of the internment of Japanese-Americans during World War II. unfairly limited the options of the federal government in combating terrorist groups in the U.S.[42] According to the *Seattle Post-Intelligencer*, Malkin suggests that liberal activists used the story of the World War II. internment of Japanese-Americans as a trump card to challenge President Bush's policies, from 'innocuous' FBI interviews to the more extreme decision to incarcerate suspects at Guantanamo Bay.[43] Malkin claims that by defending the internment, the U.S. government could have more latitude in fighting America's current domestic enemies.[44] Justifying internment policies and civil liberties infringements, she argues that the suspension of Constitutional protections is preferable to being killed by terrorists.[45] Some pundits and ideologues embraced Malkin's book, writing positive reviews in newspapers like the *New York Sun*.[46] Despite the book's favorable reception in right-wing circles, historians and civil rights groups were outraged by her reasoning. The Japanese American Citizens League was particularly incensed, telling the *Denver Post* that Malkin's book was a desperate attempt to impugn the loyalty of Japanese-Americans in the 1940s as a means of justifying the mistreatment of Arab and Muslim Americans in the wake of the terrorist strikes.[47]

In the aftermath of 9/11, Arabs, Muslims, Sikhs, and South Asians began flying the American flag to express their patriotism and to shield themselves from nativist attacks. Amolak Singh, a South Asian Sikh, told the *San Francisco Chronicle* that he repeatedly received threats after 9/11, and used the flag as a means of advertising his loyalty to the U.S.[48] Other Bay Area minorities began using red, white, and blue lawn chairs and articles of clothing as a means of protecting themselves from the wrath of area xenophobes.[49]

Although Sikhs, Muslims, Christian Arabs, and Hindus were painfully aware of the hate crimes terrorizing their communities, many Americans refused to acknowledge that these events were taking place. Newspapers across the U.S. published articles denying a problem existed. For example, former mayor Richard Riordan and David Lehrer claimed that no dramatic spike in hate crimes occurred after the terrorist attacks. In their May 8, 2003 *Los Angeles Times* article, "We Can All Just Get Along: A Major Hate Crime Backlash Against Muslims and Arab-Americans Failed to Materialize Despite Ominous Warnings," Riordan and Lehrer argue that the predicted 9/11 backlash never occurred.[50] Although they acknowledge that there were some isolated incidents of bias, they claim that there was no big upsurge in hate crimes and that Americans almost never took their anger out on Arab-American grocers, Pakistani cab drivers, or neighborhood mosques.[51]

Journalists, scholars, and educators also repeatedly denied the existence or the scope of the 9/11 backlash. In her October 3, 2004 on-line article, "Fake Muslim Hate Crimes," columnist Michelle Malkin calls attention to a small handful of fabricated hate crimes and uses them to challenge the credibility of other reported bias attacks.[52] Some mainstream news reporters joined Malkin and other conservative commentators in questioning the true scope and duration of the 9/11 backlash. On July 24, 2005, the *Richmond Times-Dispatch* downplayed the frequency of Islamophobic hate crimes, claiming that anti-Muslim incidents were few and far between in the U.S.[53] Other newspapers also reinforced the false belief that the backlash was merely a small blip on the cultural landscape. On September 9, 2006, as the five-year anniversary of the terrorist strikes approached, the *Deseret Morning News* printed journalist Deborah Bulkeley's article, "Muslims in U.S. See Little 9/11 Backlash."[54]

Years later, newspapers continued to perpetuate the myth that a significant backlash never took place. On August 26, 2010, the *New York Post* suggested that a substantive wave of hate crimes never happened, writing that although anti-Islamic incidents rose in 2001 in response to 9/11, they fell flat soon after and remained so low that they were virtually nonexistent for the better part of the decade.[55] Other papers expressed similar views. On August 27, 2010, the *Corpus Christi Caller Times* reported that there was no anti-Muslim climate in the U.S., and that the predicted anti-Islam backlash never occurred in the nine years following 9/11.[56] News commentators also challenged the existence of the 9/11 backlash. In an August 30, 2010 article, "The Supposed Anti-Muslim Backlash Among Americans is Mostly a Myth," syndicated columnist Jonah Goldberg denied the existence of a wave of hate crimes targeting American Muslims.[57] Other journalists voiced the same opinion. In a December 8, 2010 op-ed, "The 'Islamophobia' Myth," Jeff Jacoby challenged the prevalence of anti-Muslim hate crimes in the U.S., and the existence of high levels of Islamophobia in the country.[58]

American textbooks also ignore the reality of the 9/11 backlash. In August 2009, Michael Romanowski published the results of his study on the treatment of the terrorist strikes in American history and civics textbooks.[59] According to Romanowski, the books failed to make a connection between post-9/11 patriotism and the scapegoating of minority communities in the U.S., which he likened to the experiences of Japanese-Americans after Pearl Harbor.[60] He contends that because of these omissions, American schoolchildren were left with the impression that no surge in bigotry took place after the terrorist attacks.

This book is an attempt to document that this backlash did occur, and was much worse and much longer in duration than many Americans realize. In the years following 9/11, many ethnic Americans and immigrant residents were affected by a wave of hate crimes triggered by the terrorist strikes and the concomitant 'War on Terror.' This book argues that the 9/11 backlash was fueled by 20th-century Islamophobia and Hinduphobia, coupled with journalists' and local and federal authorities' long-standing unwillingness to acknowledge the reality of bias crimes or handle them with the gravity they deserved. These factors created a "perfect storm" of xenophobia that swept through the U.S. after the terrorist attacks, victimizing diverse minority communities for more than a decade.

This book explores this backlash in its historical context. Chapter two provides an overview of pre-9/11 bias attacks targeting Muslims, Arabs, Sikhs, and South Asians, arguing that poor local and federal response to 'Dot-buster' assaults, mosque arsons, and other 20th-century hate crimes created an environment in which post-9/11 xenophobia was permitted to flourish. To understand the cultural context in which these bias attacks were occurring, this section includes a brief overview of American films that disseminated pernicious stereotypes of foreigners. Chapter three acknowledges the South Asian, Christian Arab, and Muslim victims of the terrorist strikes in order to challenge nativist interpretations of 9/11, a tragedy which affected people from scores of different countries and religious backgrounds.

Subsequent chapters explore different dimensions of the decade-long backlash. Chapter four discusses physical assaults that began on September 11, 2001 and continued for years afterwards, often spiking on or near each anniversary of the terrorist strikes. Chapter five examines post-9/11 vandalism attacks and arsons at mosques, Sikh prayer centers, and Hindu temples. On occasion, synagogues and immigrant-friendly churches were also targeted. Chapter six investigates backlash incidents on academic campuses, showing that students and instructors were frequently physically assaulted or mistreated. Chapter seven explores 9/11 hate crimes targeting minority employees in their workplaces, establishing that taxi drivers, 7-Eleven convenience-store clerks, and gas station attendants were particularly vulnerable. Chapter eight delves into bias-motivated attacks on minority residences in the aftermath of the terrorist strikes. Chapter nine examines death threats and verbal attacks after 9/11. Chapter ten discusses killings linked to the backlash. Each of these middle chapters begins in the immediate aftermath of 9/11 and covers hate crimes in the 10 years that followed. These sections also include discussions of Islamophobic and Hinduphobic television programs and films that fueled American nativism and coincided with the timing of bias attacks.

Chapter eleven investigates 75 reasons why hate crimes against Muslims, Arabs, Sikhs, and South Asians are undercounted in the U.S., focusing on the unwillingness of many minority victims to report attacks to minimally-sympathetic local and federal authorities. This chapter also delves into the problematic the ways in which hate crimes are tabulated. When Indian Sikhs are mistaken as Saudi Muslims, it is difficult for American governmental record-keepers to figure out how to fit the crime into a single-bias category (i.e., was it an anti-Sikh, anti-Muslim, anti-South Asian, anti-Arab, anti-Indian, or anti-Saudi hate crime?) Chapter twelve offers 75 solutions to problems raised by the backlash in the hopes of creating a more tolerant U.S. This section questions the efficacy of specific 'War on Terror' federal policies and proposes strategies to end post-9/11 discrimination, such as the widespread racial profiling of airport travelers. The book ends with a discussion of the August 5, 2012 massacre at a Sikh temple in Wisconsin, demonstrating that hate crimes are continuing more than a decade after 9/11.

Although a small handful of high-profile backlash assaults made the national news, local newspapers often refrained from covering hate crimes taking place outside of their districts. Consequently, the majority of Americans have no knowledge of the extent of these bias-motivated attacks, or how many went unreported in local or national newspapers. Immigrant Americans, on the other hand, had access to ethnic news sources, non-English television programs, and community grapevines, giving them a more comprehensive picture of the scope and duration of these post-9/11 hate crimes.

In the weeks and months following the World Trade Center strikes, ethnic newspapers kept their readers informed about the backlash in North America and on other continents, documenting how post-9/11 xenophobia endangered minorities in many parts of the world. In Canada, Muslims experienced 30 to 40 hate crimes in the immediate aftermath of the 9/11.[61] Houses of worship were also targeted. For example, a suspicious fire gutted a Hindu temple in Hamilton, a town located west of Toronto, a few days after the Twin Towers fell.[62]

Minorities were also targeted in Europe. In England, Muslims were assaulted in many parts of the country. In a particularly vicious attack, three white men brutally pummeled an Afghan taxi driver in West London, screaming slurs referencing 9/11, kicking him repeatedly, and leaving him paralyzed from the neck down.[63] In other cities, Muslim women were singled out by bigots. In Wiltshire, a 19-year old woman wearing a hijab was hit over the head with a metal baseball bat.[64] London's central mosque was evacuated after a bomb scare, and Islamic prayer centers were attacked in other European countries.[65]

The 9/11 backlash also swept through other continents. In Brisbane, Australia, a group of bigots threw rocks at a school bus full of Muslim children, and an arsonist tried to burn down a Lebanese church in retaliation for the attacks on the World Trade Center and Pentagon.[66]

Whereas many Western newspapers and news programs downplayed the frequency and severity of post-9/11 hate crimes, many Middle Eastern and South Asian media stations devoted extensive coverage to these bias attacks. I was staying at a hotel in Alexandria, Egypt, on September 11, 2001, and learned of the terrorist strikes from a Sudanese bellman. Because my colloquial Arabic was marginal at the time, I listened attentively to Egyptian television news broadcasts and tried to piece together what, exactly, had taken place. Since I knew no one who spoke English, I spent the next two days curled up in my hotel room, trying to determine whether it was wise to venture outside. I finally went to a nearby internet café where I learned that my family members were safe. I had been particularly concerned about my dad, who was in Greece after having visited me in Egypt. His September 11, 2001 return flight from Athens to New York to San Francisco had been canceled, so he was stranded in Europe. My Lebanese-American cousin Melissa, a United Airlines flight attendant, was alive but shaken by 9/11, since her former roommate was one of the crewmembers killed on Flight 93. Although friends and family members were concerned about my safety in Egypt, I was more worried about them, seeing so many Arabic news reports of hate crimes taking place in American cities.

Because I had satellite access to about a dozen Arabic news channels from the Middle East and Africa, I saw firsthand the extensive international coverage of these crimes. At times, some of the news stories seemed to be motivated by ant-Western sentiment, undermining America's reputation as a tolerant country. The outpouring of international sympathy for the U.S. government diminished somewhat after George W. Bush made the mistake of declaring a "crusade" against America's attackers, since this somewhat innocuous English word is understood in Arabic to mean "a Christian holy war to slaughter Muslims."

News agencies throughout South Asia also devoted extensive media coverage to post-9/11 bias attacks. Since Sikhs were frequent targets, India's news networks called attention to the viciousness of the backlash. Sikhs in India protested American hate crimes, prompting Prime Minister Atal Bihari Vajpayee to write to President Bush about the safety of Indian nationals and American Sikhs in the U.S.[67] Bias assaults also made the news in other parts of Asia. On September 19, 2001, the *Oregonian* reported that Intel engineer Mohammed Haque had to calm his panic-stricken mother in Bangladesh, who worried about his well-being after hearing so many international news reports about attacks on bearded Muslims in the U.S.[68]

Since American nativists were often too ignorant to know the difference between South Asians and Middle Easterners, they ended up targeting immigrants from many countries and religious backgrounds. Before exploring how different ethnic and religious communities were affected by the 9/11 backlash, it is important to understand the different theological beliefs, cultural traditions, and historical experiences of these groups.

SIKHS

Although they are neither Muslim nor Arab, Sikhs were repeatedly scapegoated in the aftermath of the attacks on the World Trade Center and Pentagon. According to the *San Francisco Chronicle*, at the time of the terrorist strikes, there were approximately 22 to 25 million Sikhs worldwide, with approximately 300,000 to one million living in the U.S.[69] Sikhs comprise approximately 10% of the Indian-American community, five times the proportion in India.[70] Sikh immigrants began coming to the U.S. in the 1880s, finding employment as lumber mill operators, farm hands, and railroad workers. In the 19th and early 20th centuries, Sikhs settled in California, Arizona, and the Pacific Northwest. Many Punjabi farm laborers worked in the Sacramento, San Joaquin, and Imperial Valleys, where they were called "Hindus" by growers. Because early 20th-century Sikh immigrants were barred from bringing their families, many of these men ended up marrying Mexican women. In the decades following the 1924 passage of a U.S. immigration restriction law, the numbers of Sikhs coming to America dwindled. In the second half of the 20th century, coinciding with the easing of immigration restriction, Sikhs once again began coming to the U.S. in large numbers. In 2001, the *Los Angeles Times* estimated that there were approximately 25,000 Sikhs in the California Bay Area, and 10,000 in the agricultural communities in Yuba City, Marysville, and Sacramento.[71]

Sikhs are monotheists, and believe that all religions share the same God. Their faith maintains that people of different races, religions, and sexes are all fundamentally equal. Founded 500 years ago, Sikhism has become the world's fifth largest religion. Practitioners are encouraged to work hard and earn an honest living, meditate on God's name, and share rewards of labor with others. The word "Sikh" is derived from the Sanskrit word for "disciple," and practitioners of this faith follow the teachings of ten gurus who lived from 1469 to 1708.[72] These Sikh prophets emphasize "seva," or selfless service towards others.

In Sikhism, the place of worship is called a "gurdwara," which literally means "a door to the teacher." In keeping with the faith's emphasis on service and charity, people are fed and educated for free at the temple.

Women can perform any religious ceremony and can lead the congregation in prayer. The Sikhs have no priests or religious hierarchy. To connote the equality of all believers, all Sikh men are named "Singh" (meaning "lion") and all women take the name "Kaur" (meaning "princess"). All Sikh men are "Singhs," but not all Singhs are Sikhs.

The Sikhs' holy book is the Sri Guru Granth Sahib, which teaches that contributing to the welfare of others is a sacred duty and that helping the less fortunate is a moral imperative. Sikhs believe that humans cannot claim immunity from the results of their actions. Through effort and perseverance, Sikhs believe that they can practice honesty, compassion, generosity, patience, and humility.

There are five outward articles of faith:[73]

Kesh   –   uncut hair covered by a turban;
Kirpan –   a small sword symbolizing divine justice, used only in defense;
Kara   –   a metal bracelet that is a reminder of the Sikh's responsibility to faith and bondage to truth;
Kanga –   a comb that serves as a reminder to always be neat; and
Kaccha –   special underwear that is a reminder of a Sikh's responsibility to family.

Of all of these outward symbols of faith, "kesh" is perhaps the most noticeable. For Sikhs, unshorn hair is a symbol of spiritualism and devotion to God. Turbans are mandatory for men and an option for women, who tend to wear head scarves. Turbans, also known as "dastaars," are a symbol of the fundamental equality of all believers and are intended to make Sikhs more visible to help those in need. The turban is also supposed to deter Sikhs from committing immoral actions, since a wrongdoer will make the whole community look bad. Touching the turban can be viewed as an insult akin to challenging someone's faith. According to the *Fresno Bee*, approximately 99% of turban-wearing men in the U.S. are Sikhs.[74] Some younger Sikhs have abandoned the turban, but still wear the kara.

Although the first Sikh prophet Guru Nanak emphasized the harmony of Hinduism and Islam, Sikhism is not an offshoot of either faith. Sikhism rejects caste distinctions, superstitions, fasting, pilgrimages, worship of the dead, and veneration of idols. Like the Sufi mystics of Islam, Sikhs stress singing and music as a path to enlightenment. Sikhism shares with Hinduism a belief in transmigration and karma but rejects the Hindu ideal of ascetic withdrawal in favor of active service.

HINDUS

Like Sikhs, Hindus are neither Muslims nor Arabs; nevertheless, they were also targeted in response to the World Trade Center strikes. There are between one and two million Hindus in the United States, and most are of Indian origin. According to the Hindu American Foundation, Hinduism is the world's oldest living religion, consisting of hundreds of spiritual and philosophical traditions practiced throughout Asia for more than 5,000 years.[75] Although Hinduism lacks an identifiable beginning in history, a central founder, or a main authoritative scripture, its traditions emphasize tolerance and pluralism. Hinduism preaches respect for other faiths, accepting diverse traditions as legitimate. Practitioners believe that it is a mistake to insist that there is only one true and meaningful path to God. Because of this theological commitment to pluralism, practicing Hindus do not have a history of proselytizing or conquering foreign lands in the name of religion. Hindus believe in the divinity of all beings, and view all organisms as manifestations of God. Like Buddhists, they ascribe to the notion of the transmigration of souls, claiming that all creatures are reincarnated according to their deeds in a previous life. If a person lived virtuously, he or she will be reborn into a higher caste. If a person lived dishonorably, he or she will be born into a lower caste, or might even be reincarnated as an animal. For this reason, many Hindus are vegetarian, and eating beef is prohibited. Through good deeds, a Hindu can improve his or her karma.

MUSLIMS

Along with Sikhs and Hindus, Muslims were frequent victims of the post-9/11 backlash. According to the *Christian Science Monitor*, there were between six and seven million Muslims in America in September 2001.[76] Around the time of the terrorist strikes, some State Department officials predicted that Islam would soon become the second-largest faith practiced in the U.S.[77] Muslims are monotheists, and worship the same God as Jews and Christians. Although they accept the Hebrew Scriptures and the New Testament as sacred books, they maintain that God's message in these texts was somewhat obfuscated by their human authors. Muslims believe that God spoke to Mohammed directly, and that this last and final prophet transcribed God's exact words in the holy Quran.

There are five pillars of Islam:

1) a declaration of faith, in which Muslims declare that there is only one God and Mohammed is his (last and final) prophet;
2) daily prayer, performed five times a day;
3) fasting during the month of Ramadan;
4) alms to the poor, focusing on feeding the hungry and giving charity to orphans;
5) a pilgrimage to Mecca at least once in a lifetime.

Muslims view Moses, Abraham, Jesus, and Mary as holy figures, but reject the notion that God took human form and lived on earth as his own son. Many Muslims regard the Christian belief in the trinity – God the Father, Son, and Holy Ghost – as a challenge to monotheism, and maintain that God, being eternal, could not have died on the cross.

A central holiday for Muslims is "Eid," a Thanksgiving-like celebration commemorating the end of Ramadan. As part of "Eid," Muslims traditionally sacrifice livestock to commemorate God's mercy in allowing Abraham to substitute a ram in place of his favorite son, whom Muslims identify as Ishmael.

Orthodox Muslims refrain from drinking, gambling, and eating pork, viewing these activities as forbidden. Since the Quran encourages Muslim women to dress modestly, some Muslim women wear the hijab, a head scarf. In some parts of the world, conservative Muslim women wear the niqab, a face and hair veil. Within Islam, there is considerable debate about whether the hijab is a religious requirement. Some feminist Muslims question the necessity of veiling, suggesting that what is in women's heads is more important than what is on them.[78] Even among women who wear the hijab, there is some disagreement about the ideal age at which girls should begin the practice.

Although the Quran doesn't prohibit men from shaving, some devout Muslims wear a beard because the Islamic prophet Mohammed wore one and encouraged believers to do the same. Many Muslims consider growing their beards more of a custom than a mandatory religious duty.

There are two main sects of Islam: Sunni and Shia. Like Protestants and Catholics, these sects have historically been at odds. The schism began after Mohammed's death, with some of his followers (Sunnis) declaring that Abu Bakr, the father of the prophet's wife Aisha, was the legitimate successor. Sunnis believe that the Muslim community should choose religious leaders by collective consensus, not by male lineage. Shias disagree with Sunnis about the man who should be recognized as the spiritual head of Islam after Mohammed. Shias believe that God wanted the prophet's cousin and son-in-law Ali to function as the leader of the faith, followed by his direct descendents. Shias revere Ali, who was married to Fatima, the daughter of Mohammed and his first wife Khadijah. The disagreement between followers of Abu Bakr and Ali eventually escalated into war. The rift became even more acute after Ali's son Husayn was killed near the Iraqi town of Karbala, causing Shias to regard this site as a particularly holy place. Along with disagreeing about Mohammed's rightful successor, the two main Islamic sects have other ideological differences. Shia Muslims place more importance on the "Hadith," the sayings of the prophet Mohammed. Sunnis regard it as blasphemy to consider this a holy book, although they revere Mohammed as a wise man whose aphorisms should be followed closely.

The two main Muslim sects also disagree about whether Islam should be hierarchical. The majority of Shias believe that the spiritual qualities of Mohammed are shared by 12 of his successors, Ali and other holy imams who are immaculate from sin and human error. Minority groups of Shias, the Ismailis and Zaidis, dispute the lineage of the imams. In addition to believing in exalted spiritual guides, Shias turn to other imams as leaders of the faith, regarding them like priests or rabbis. In contrast, Sunnis feel that having religious leaders is antithetical to Islam's emphasis on equality. Since the Arabic word, "imam," literally means "in front of," any Sunni practitioner leading the prayer at the mosque becomes the "imam" for the day. Shias and Sunnis also disagree on the minimum time interval between the five daily prayers and the position of the arms during worship. Druze practitioners constitute a separate Islamic sect that many consider to be an offshoot of Shia beliefs. Along with other Muslim groups, Sufis believe that the Mahdi will appear at the end of times to bring about a just society. These practitioners embrace the mystical side of Islam and emphasize a personal approach to God. Although Sufism exists throughout the Muslim world, it is perhaps most visible in the whirling dervishes of Turkey.

Muslims are perhaps the most ethnically and racially-diverse religious group in the U.S., with practitioners from Asia, Africa, Europe, Latin America, and the Middle East. The first African Muslims came to America on slave ships, and some literate Muslim slaves challenged Antebellum stereotypes of Negro inferiority.[79] Because of religious oppression, many 18th and 19th century American Muslims were compelled to abandon their religious tradition and adopt Christianity, causing them to disappear from most historical records. For much of the 20th century, immigration restriction limited the numbers of Muslims entering the U.S. After 1965, sizeable numbers of Sunni and Shia Muslims immigrated to America from Pakistan, India, Bangladesh, Somalia, Sudan, Bosnia, North Africa, and the Middle East.

Because of the diversity of Muslims in the U.S., bias crimes against these worshippers are often difficult to categorize. Investigators are often unsure about whether a specific victim was targeted because of his or her faith, ethnicity, race, or national origin.

NATION OF ISLAM

Other religious communities in America were also affected by the 9/11 backlash. The Nation of Islam describes itself as an African-American religious movement founded by Wallace D. Fard Muhammad in Detroit in July 1930. From 1931 to 1975, the organization was run by Elijah Muhammad, but it splintered after his death. The theological doctrines embraced by Nation of Islam practitioners differ considerably from those of orthodox Muslims, who follow the Quran closely. Sunni and Shia Muslims believe that there is only one God, and Mohammed was his last prophet. Followers of the Nation of Islam regard Wallace D. Fard as the long-awaited Messiah of the Christians and the Mahdi of the Muslims. They also believe that Elijah Muhammad was a prophet sent by God to preach about the incarnation of Fard. Whereas traditional Muslims observe Friday as their special prayer day, Nation of Islam members generally attend Sunday prayer services. Unlike traditional Muslims, who believe that the Quran supersedes other holy texts, Nation of Islam members embrace a wider array of holy writings and follow a different translated version of the Quran. They also think that this holy book was revealed to black scientists, instead of to the prophet Mohammed by the Angel Gabriel. Sunni and Shia Muslims maintain that all human beings were created equal, and should be judged on their conduct instead of their skin color. The Nation of Islam preaches racial differences, claiming that blacks, the original race, are superior to whites, who were created by their darker-skinned human predecessors. Because of the organization's controversial beliefs and anti-Semitic public statements proclaiming the racial superiority of blacks, the Southern Poverty Law Center declared the Nation of Islam to be an American 'hate group.'

In 1995, the *New York Times* estimated there were only about 10,000 members of the Nation of Islam, a small fraction of the more than 3 million African-American Muslims in the U.S. at that time.[80] In 2010, the

Nation of Islam estimated that it had between 20,000 and 50,000 members. Despite being relatively few in number, Nation of Islam practitioners were disproportionately subjected to hate crimes and police brutality before and after 9/11.

Just as particular religious groups were affected by the 9/11 backlash, certain ethnic groups also came under fire.

ARAB-AMERICANS

Many Arab-Americans are of Lebanese or Syrian origin, tracing their ancestry to Christian families who fled Ottoman occupation in the late 19th and early 20th century. Because the U.S. Census has traditionally counted Arab-Americans as 'whites,' it is difficult to know the precise size of this ethnic community. Governmental surveys of Arab-Americans and other Middle Eastern ethnic communities are not particularly reliable, since many minority residents are hesitant to disclose their national origin to federal demographers. Some journalists have estimated that more than 70% of Arab-Americans are Christians, with significant numbers of Catholic, Greek Orthodox, and Protestant practitioners.[81] There are also more than 600,000 Copts in the U.S., most of whom are of Middle Eastern origin.[82] In the days after the terrorist strikes, Michael Meuner, president of the U.S. Copt Association, contacted the White House and Congress, asking for added protection and closer attention to the security needs of members of his faith.[83] During the most acute stage of the 9/11 backlash, some Copts in Los Angeles, New York, and New Jersey opted to cover the Arabic script spelling out the names of their churches out of fear that this lettering would cause them to be targeted by angry bigots.[84]

Whereas early Arab immigrants to the U.S. were primarily Christians, more recent arrivals were more likely to be Sunnis and Shias, particularly among families entering the country after 1965. Many of these more recent immigrants came from Syria, Jordan, Palestine, North Africa, and the Gulf. Overall, Arab-Americans are perhaps the most religiously-diverse ethnic group in the U.S. Since they come from more than 20 countries throughout the Middle East and North Africa, Arab-Americans are also a culturally-diverse community.

Arabs speak several different dialects of Arabic. Just as Latin gave birth to disparate languages (Italian, French, Spanish, and Portuguese), seventh-century Arabic (fusha) generated separate dialects (Egyptian, Moroccan, Gulf, and Levantine Arabic). In many schools in the U.S., these modern dialects are taught separately, as an elective to supplement classical Arabic, the written language. Because contemporary Gulf Arabic is closest to "fusha," its speakers are generally regarded as the most eloquent, having the best grasp of the language of the Quran. Since Arabic dialects have distinct vocabularies, grammatical structures, and letter pronunciations, Middle Easterners sometimes have trouble understanding one another. In some instances, educated Arabs use "fusha" as a "lingua franca," or speak colloquial Egyptian, since movies and songs have disseminated this dialect throughout the region. On occasion, linguistic differences impede easy communication among Arabic populations in the U.S. Rather than see Arabic immigrants as a culturally, religiously, and linguistically-diverse community, American bigots lumped them all together in the aftermath of the terrorist strikes.

OTHER AFFECTED COMMUNITIES:
PERSIANS, AFGHANS, TURKS, SOMALIS, SUDANESE, AND ETHIOPIANS

Along with ethnic Arabs, other immigrant groups were victims of post-9/11 hate crimes. Although Iranians are not ethnically Arab and speak Persian Dari (Farsi) instead of Arabic, these immigrants and their descendants were occasionally targeted by bigots. In response to American intolerance and international tensions, many Iranians in the U.S. choose to call themselves Persians, in reference to the ancient name of their country of origin. A 2008 survey conducted by Zogby International estimated that approximately 50% of Iranian-Americans had experienced discrimination personally, or knew a Persian community member who had been singled out or unfairly profiled in the U.S.[85] Many respondents reported experiencing employment discrimination, social harassment, and heightened scrutiny at airports. Unassimilated Persian immigrants were more likely to report discrimination than their more Westernized counterparts.

Although small numbers of ethnic Persians arrived in the U.S. in the early 20th century, Iranian immigration increased dramatically after the overthrow of the Shah. At the time of the 1979 Iranian Revolution, there were approximately 50,000 Persian students in the U.S. Rather than return to their homelands, many of these international students opted to remain in America. In Iran, the overwhelming majority of citizens are Shia Muslims. Because Persian religious minorities were particularly likely to emigrate, Iranian immigrants came from a wide range of religious backgrounds. Persian-Americans include Muslims, Jews, Christians, Bahais, and Zoroastrians. A large percentage of Iranian-immigrants also describe themselves as non-religious. Since the U.S. Census has historically counted Iranian-Americans as 'whites,' it is impossible to obtain precise figures on the size of this ethnic community, particularly since many Persians are reluctant to disclose their national origin to U.S. governmental surveyors. Some researchers have estimated that there are approximately 500,000 to 1.5 million Persian-Americans in the U.S., with large numbers in the Los Angeles area.

Like Iranians, Afghani immigrants spoke Persian Dari. Many also knew the Pashto and Uzbek languages, as well as many local dialects. Unlike many other North African demographic populations, they are not ethnic Arabs. Afghans are predominantly Shia Muslims, but the ethnic community also includes hundreds of Jewish families living in New York. Although some Afghans immigrated to the U.S. in the early 20th century, the majority arrived after the 1979 Soviet invasion of Afghanistan. Although they belonged to a different ethnic population and Islamic sect than the 9/11 hijackers, Afghans were frequently singled out during the backlash, particularly in American cities where they were highly-concentrated. Unassimilated Afghan immigrants were especially likely to be targeted.

Along with other North Africans, the U.S. Census historically considered Afghan immigrants as 'whites.' As a result, the precise size of this ethnic group is unclear. According to the *Boston Globe*, there were approximately 125,000 to 200,000 Afghanis living in the U.S. in 2001, and about 40,000 residing in the Bay Area.[86] Because of the large numbers of Afghan residents in Fremont, California, the city was nicknamed "Little Kabul." Many Afghan immigrants also settled in Texas, Illinois, Florida, and New York.

Turkish immigrants were also scapegoated in the aftermath of 9/11, even though they have had a particularly long history in the U.S. Between 1820 and 1920, approximately 1.2 million Ottoman subjects came to America, but ethnic Turks comprised only a small minority of these immigrants, who included many Arabs. Because of problematic record-keeping, there is no precise ethnic breakdown available. Some social scientists have estimated that most Ottoman immigrants were fleeing religious and ethnic discrimination, and that only about 15% were Muslims coming to America to improve their economic prospects. During the Great Depression, many ethnic Turks left the U.S., returning home aboard ships sent by Mustafa Kemal Attaturk. After World War II., Turkish immigration to America resumed in large numbers. Because the census historically counted Turkish-Americans as 'whites,' there are no reliable figures on the size of this demographic population. Some researchers have estimated that by the early 21st century, there were between 190,000 and 500,000 Turkish Americans and immigrant residents in the U.S.

African immigrants were also affected by the 9/11 backlash. Although they were not ethnic Arabs, Somalis were occasionally confused with Taliban terrorists. Some Somalis moved to the U.S. in the early 20th century, but the majority came during their homeland's civil war, which began in the 1990s after the overthrow of dictator Mohamed Siad Barre. According to the U.S. Census, there were 35,760 Somalis living in the U.S. in 2000. Others have maintained that the actual Somali population is more than three times this number, noting that many members of this ethnic community are reluctant to disclose their national origin to census surveyors. There are sizeable numbers of Somalis residing in Minnesota, especially in Minneapolis and St. Paul. There are also large populations in Lewiston, Maine, Columbus, Ohio, and Washington, D.C.

The 9/11 backlash also affected Sudanese refugees, who are not ethnically Arab. In the 1990s, Sudan erupted into civil war, with the predominantly-Muslim Northerners fighting Christian Southerners. During this conflict, Sudanese immigrants of both faiths came to the U.S. to escape religious persecution, wartime dangers, and financial devastation. Although Northern and Southern Sudanese were at odds in Africa, immigrants from both regions were lumped together by American bigots during the 9/11 backlash.

American nativists also targeted other African immigrants in the aftermath of the terrorist strikes. Ethiopians in America came from diverse religious backgrounds, and included Orthodox Christians, Muslims, and Jews. Although many of these immigrants were fluent in Amharic, others spoke Oromo and dozens of dialects belonging to the Semitic, Cushitic, and Afro-Asiatic language families. Although Ethiopian immigrants were not ethnic Arabs, they were often confused with Taliban terrorists and harassed in cities where they were highly concentrated: D.C., New York, Los Angeles, and Atlanta.

To understand why such diverse communities were scapegoated after 9/11, it is important to view these hate crimes as an extension of 20th-century crimes against 'suspect' American communities. In the years prior to the terrorist strikes, American nativists frequently lashed out at Muslims, Christian Arabs, Sikhs, and Hindus, seeing their presence as a threat to the country.

CHAPTER TWO:

THE HISTORICAL ROOTS OF THE BACKLASH –
BIAS ATTACKS AND XENOPHOBIA BEFORE 9/11

The wave of hate crimes unleashed by 9/11 can best be understood in its historical context. Without knowing the roots of this bigotry, it is difficult to understand the virulent nativist response to the terrorist strikes. This chapter establishes that 20th-century Islamophobia and Hinduphobia functioned as the ideological foundation of the September 11th backlash. In the decades prior to 9/11, American police detectives and federal agents failed to launch thorough investigations of bias attacks targeting Middle Easterners and South Asians, giving the green light to bigots.

This chapter begins with a discussion of pre-9/11 hate crimes targeting black Muslims, South Asians, Arab-Americans, and Middle Eastern immigrants in the U.S., establishing that xenophobia affecting these communities pre-dated the terrorist strikes. This chapter also explores late-20th century attacks at American mosques, revealing the deep roots of Islamophobia in America. Because local and federal investigators often failed to acknowledge the bias component of these crimes, many Arabs, Muslims, and South Asians lost faith in the American justice system and became reluctant to report many of the attacks that took place in the aftermath of the terrorist strikes. The chapter ends with an overview of 20th-century movies that demean Arabs, Muslims, and Hindus, contributing to a climate of bigotry that allowed the 9/11 backlash to flourish.

Although Middle Eastern and South Asian communities in the U.S. have been targeted by nativists throughout the 20th century, poor tracking has limited the appearance of these crimes in the historical record. Governmental monitoring and recording of bias attacks did not begin in earnest until relatively recently, with the passage of the U.S. Hate Crimes Statistics Act of 1990. This legislation defines bias attacks as "crimes that manifest evidence of prejudice based on race, religion, sexual orientation, or ethnicity, linking where appropriate the crimes of murder, non-negligent manslaughter, forcible rape, aggravated and simple assault, intimidation, arson, and destruction and damage or vandalism of property."[1] The legislation was later modified to include Americans with disabilities. The FBI has long attempted to segregate bias-motivated attacks into discrete categories based on race, religion, and ethnicity/nationality. This method of tabulation is problematic because it overlooks the fact that many hate crimes are simultaneously motivated by more than one factor. Because of faulty record-keeping, many bias crimes against Muslims, Arabs, and South Asians have been hidden from history.

PRE-9/11 CRIMES AGAINST BLACK MUSLIMS

American hate crimes against black Muslims date back to the 18th century, when African followers of Islam were forced to come to America on slave ships. Allen Austin's comprehensive book, <u>African Muslims in Antebellum America: a Sourcebook</u>, contains hundreds of primary source documents revealing the experiences of this victimized community.[2] Muslim slaves were exposed to the same whippings, lynchings, and sexual assaults as other enslaved Africans. Like other non-Christians, they were coerced into concealing or abandoning their traditional religious practices and adopt the religion of their owners. Since slaves were prohibited from reading, Muslims could not access the Quran or expose their children to their holy book. Christian families compelled Muslim slaves in America to abandon their religious practices, making them celebrate Christmas and attend church on Sundays, instead of observing Ramadan and praying at mosques on Fridays. Muslim slaves were not permitted to maintain their religious dietary practices and were sometimes compelled to eat pork or go hungry. Because they had to obey or be killed, Muslim slave women in early America were auctioned off naked in public, although their religion emphasized modesty in dress.

In the mid-19th and early 20th centuries, some black Muslims voluntarily came to the U.S. These immigrants experienced the same legal and social mistreatment as other dark-skinned Americans. Like other blacks in the U.S., they feared the KKK and other hate groups, particularly the ones that practiced lynching.

Throughout American history, bigots often targeted orthodox black Muslims as well as members of the Nation of Islam. In the early 1960s, the *New York Times* reported that prison rights activists began filing lawsuits to curb the abuse of black Muslim inmates in California, Alabama, and Maryland, citing over 100 incidents of religious mistreatment.[3] During this period, dark-skinned Muslims were also targeted in American neighborhoods, especially if they were politically active. In his autobiography, Malcolm X discussed some of the hate crimes he experienced, first as a Nation of Islam convert and later as a follower of orthodox Islam. On February 14, 1965, his house in Queens was firebombed with Molotov cocktails at 2:45 a.m., when he and his family members were asleep.[4] He was eventually gunned down in a hate crime by Nation of Islam followers who were upset about his religious conversion. His co-religionists were also killed in bias crimes. According to the *New York Times*, Kenneth Morton, Benjamin Brown, Leon Ameer, and James Shabazz were other black Muslims who were beaten, shot, and killed in hate crimes during the late 1960s and early 1970s.[5]

Throughout the second half of the 20th century, Muslims were frequently targeted in American prisons. The *New York Times* reported that on July 11, 1976, a Sunni Muslim imam was gang-beaten by Attica guards after he objected to their sacrilegious handling of his Koran.[6] Inmates who witnessed the brutal hate crime launched an eight-day protest strike in response, corresponding with the time the victim spent hospitalized.

Although the U.S. civil rights movement curtailed the frequency of some bias attacks, African-American Muslims continued to be targeted in the late 20th century. In Pennsylvania, a vandal badly defaced a public portrait of Malcolm X at Swarthmore College in the spring semester of 1991.[7] The assailant slashed the painting repeatedly with a knife, threw it on the ground, and covered it with cigarette butts and empty beer bottles. According to the *New York Times*, African-American and Muslim students on campus were particularly upset by the bias-motivated vandalism, seeing it as an attack on their presence at the school.[8]

Hate crimes targeting black Muslims also took place at other colleges. In March 1992, racist flyers aimed at black and Muslim students were tacked up on bulletin boards and slipped under office doors at Saddleback College in Southern California.[9] Vandals also defaced posters advertising Black History Month events organized by the Black Student Alliance and the Muslim Student Union. College president Constance Carroll told the *Orange County Register* that the flyers and the vandalism were part of a larger pattern of racial harassment on campus, characterizing them as hate crimes targeting vulnerable students.[10]

Throughout the 1990s, members of the Nation of Islam were frequently affected by bias-motivated attacks. Since this religious group had its own newspapers, practitioners were kept informed about hate crimes affecting their community. The *Amsterdam News* reported that Rikers Island guards allegedly beat Nation of Islam inmate Anthony Cook on July 19, 1992, before he was transferred to court.[11] According to his attorney, Majied Mannan, Cook argued with guards after they denied his request to use the bathroom, telling him he had no need of a toilet to urinate or defecate. When Cook continued to protest, the guards allegedly gang-beat him, calling him "Nigger Muslim," "Saddam," and "A-Salaami-bacon."[12] Following the beating, a judge refused Cook's request to have his multiple bruises photographed. According to Cook, other Muslim inmates were terrorized by guards, fed pork, denied medications, and prevented from obtaining evening meals when they returned to Rikers Island from court.[13] One prisoner, Shadyk Abdul Muhammed, claimed to have been beaten so many times that he opted to remain in his cell all day in order to remain safe from prison authorities.[14]

Nation of Islam newspapers also published news of bias crimes targeting their ministers. According to the *Bay State Banner*, Rodney Muhammed was awarded a cash settlement on March 11, 1993 after being roughed up by prison guards in Boston.[15] Throughout the 1980s and early 1990s, Mohammed often visited the prison and delivered religious sermons, which were attended by hundreds of inmates. Although Muhammed had been ministering for years and presented the proper identification to authorities, he was assaulted by bigoted prison guards. Describing this ordeal, Muhammed told the *Bay State Banner* that authorities at the Suffolk County jail threw him to the floor, handcuffed him, and kneed him in the back.[16]

They then brought him to the Boston police headquarters, where he was booked and released on his own recognizance. Muhammed claimed that his assault was part of a larger pattern of prison staff members' harassment of Muslim prisoners and clergy, noting that on many occasions the guards would confiscate Qurans, lie to prisoners that sermons were cancelled, or bring inmates late to religious services. As a result of his mistreatment, Muhammed stopped ministering at the prison.

Sometimes, even black guards mistreated African-American prisoners if they took issue with their religious beliefs. Mosheh Ben-Abraham, a security officer for the Cuyahoga Metropolitan Housing Authority, claimed that he was beaten by a black guard who heard his Hebrew name and mistakenly assumed that he belonged to the Nation of Islam.[17] This incident took place in Cleveland on September 13, 1996, after Ben-Abraham was arrested on suspicion of drunk driving. According to the *Call and Post*, a jail guard allegedly entered the holding cell and assaulted Ben-Abraham, accusing him of being a follower of Farrakhan.[18] Ben-Abraham was then taken to MetroHealth Medical Center, where he got stitches above his eye. Rather than confess to his excessive use of force, the guard filed charges against Ben-Abraham, accusing him of resisting arrest and assaulting an officer.

Along with experiencing police and prison guard harassment, members of the Nation of Islam were subjected to cyber hate crimes. In the aftermath of the October 16, 1995 'Million Man March,' a computer hacker broke into the Nation of Islam's home page and defaced it with hate messages. The hacker changed the name of the religious web site to the "Bigots of Islam Homeboy Page," and referred to the group's recent political demonstration as the "million Moron March," asserting that participants prayed to "some goofy god that does not exist."[19] The hacker also suggested that Nation of Islam practitioners were murderers who were willing to kill to achieve their objectives.

Bigots also targeted orthodox black Muslims in the U.S. Because they belonged to both racial and religious minority communities, investigators sometimes had difficulty determining why, exactly, a hate crime occurred. In 1997, skinheads in Denver shot Senegalese Muslim hotel housekeeper Oumar Dia, who later died from his wounds.[20] Jeannie Van Veklinburgh, a nurse's aide, was also shot when she tried to help Dia.[21] Although she survived, she became paralyzed from the waist down. At the funeral, Dia's friends and family members recited Muslim prayers and spoke out against the hate crime. To this day, detectives remain unsure about whether Dia was targeted primarily because of his black skin, his Senegalese heritage, or his Muslim faith.

In New York, another black Muslim was shot and killed. In February 1999, police officers opened fire on unarmed Amadou Diallo, riddling his body with bullets and killing him instantly.[22] In the aftermath of this unwarranted shooting, Amadou Diallo's parents – Saikou and Kadiatou – spoke out at rallies and community meetings about police brutality and officers' unfair treatment of minority community members. Since Dia's father was an eminent Islamic scholar, he often discussed how he drew on his faith to survive the pain of his son's death.

PRE-9/11 CRIMES AGAINST SOUTH ASIANS

Like African Muslims in America, South Asians did not have the option of concealing their ethno-racial heritage in the U.S. when nativist sentiment escalated. Many South Asians arrived in North America at the end of the 19th and the beginning of the 20th century. These immigrants came to the U.S. seeking employment, enticed by Indian newspaper ads placed by lumber businessmen looking for workers. South Asians experienced racism and discrimination because of their dark skin and distinctive clothing. Nativists occasionally assaulted, humiliated, and verbally harassed Sikhs and Hindus.[23] For example, in September 1907 in Bellingham, Washington, a mob of approximately 500 white men ambushed South Asian lumber mill workers, beating one of them and stripping off his turban. According to the September 5, 1907 issue of the *Bellingham Herald*, local police responded to this incident by rounding up and detaining hundreds of South Asian workers, to maintain the peace.[24]

South Asians also faced employment discrimination on railroad construction sites. In some instances, Sikhs were forced to shave their beards and abandon their turbans if they wanted to find employment. Some

Sikhs found conditions a little better working on farms in the Imperial Valley. As American politicians passed Asian exclusion measures and laws prohibiting Asians from owning land, many South Asians and "white Asiatics" began questioning whether the exclusionary legislation applied to them. In 1923, the Supreme Court case, *U.S. vs. Bhagat Singh Thind*, denied the right of South Asians to become naturalized Americans.[25] This case was brought by a Sikh man who maintained that he should be entitled to legal privileges afforded to whites because South Asians were ethnically Aryan. In their ruling, the Supreme Court rather arbitrarily drew a line in the middle of Arabia and declared that anyone who came from the area west of it could become naturalized Americans, and that those who came from the east of it were Asiatics and therefore ineligible to become U.S. citizens. This decision switched the racial designation of Indian immigrants in the U.S. from "white" to "Asiatic."[26] In the 1920s, American government also enacted comprehensive immigration restriction, cutting off South Asians and other Asiatics from entering the country.

As the Eugenics movement grew, South Asians and other immigrant communities faced escalating hostility in the U.S. Because segregated America divided community members into two categories – blacks and whites – South Asians sometimes presented a problem to Americans accustomed to operating within binary racial frameworks. Shamshere Singh, who was born in 1930, told a *Providence Journal* reporter some of the challenges he experienced living as a South Asian in the U.S.[27] In the 1950s, he was invited to a Washington wedding attended by politicians and dignitaries. The day before the ceremony, he and the other guests were invited to a beach resort. Because of his skin color, he was barred from swimming. The next day, he found himself seated at the wedding beside then-Vice President Richard Nixon.

For much of the 20th century, school bullies targeted South Asian children. Sikhs were frequently singled out by bigoted classmates who touched their patkas and called them derogatory names like "turbie." Recalling his own experiences with pre-9/11 xenophobia, Mandinder Singh told a *Little India* reporter that he was constantly harassed while attending primary school in Chicago, remembering that he was so traumatized that he would get off the bus and begin weeping.[28]

In the 1970s, South Asians were sometimes mistaken for Iranians and attacked in response to the hostage crisis. Surinder Singh told *Little India* that he was heckled everywhere during this period, even though he didn't wear a Sikh turban.[29] He eventually cut his hair so that he would be less conspicuous while racial tensions were so high.

Between 1985 and 1993, South Asians living in New Jersey became ethno-racial targets of the Dot-busters, a gang who announced they were going after women wearing bindis.[30] These gang members, who came from Hoboken and Jersey City, began harassing or attacking anyone who looked Indian or Pakistani, regardless if they wore saris or jeans. For several years, the 15,000 South Asians living in the Garden State were terrorized by these neighborhood thugs.

In July 1987, a Dot-buster gang member anonymously published the following letter-to-the-editor in the *Jersey Journal*, expressing the group's hope to drive South Asians out of Jersey City:

> *I'm writing about your article during july [sic] about the abuse of the Indian People. Well, I'm here to state the other side. I hate them, if you had to live near them you would also. We are an organization called Dot-busters. We have been around for two years. We will go to any extreme to get Indians to move out of Jersey City. If I'm walking down the street and I see a Hindu and the setting is right, I will hit him or her. We plan some of our most extreme attacks such as breaking windows, breaking car windows, and crashing family parties. We use the phone books and look up the name Patel. Have you seen how many of them there are? Do you even live in Jersey City? Do you walk down Central avenue and experience what its [sic] like to be near them: we have and we just don't want it anymore. You said that they will have to start protecting themselves because the police cannot always be there. They will never do anything. They are a week [sic] race physically and mentally. We are going to continue on our way. We will never be stopped.*[31]

Many Dot-busters were teenagers of Latino descent, and viewed the new immigrants as a threat to their employment opportunities. Some South Asian journalists saw a connection between Dot-buster attacks and New Jersey newspaper coverage of financially-prosperous South Asians, who were being heralded as a model minority group. During the Dot-busters' reign of terror, reporters were publicizing the findings of the 1980 census, which showed that of the 400,000 Indians in America, 11 percent of the men and 8 percent of the women were physicians.[32] The survey also found that 17 percent of Indian men were engineers, architects, or surveyors, making them one of the most educated and affluent ethnic groups in the U.S. The Dot-busters did not limit their attacks to affluent Hindu professionals, targeting South Asians of different socio-economic levels and religious groups.

On September 12, 1987, teenage assailants viciously attacked two Indian students at the Stevens Institute of Technology in Hoboken. According to *India Abroad*, the Acevedo brothers picked up Syed Hasan, slammed him against a door, and hit him with a metal bar; they also punched and kicked him for about five minutes.[33] The assailants also beat Vikas Aggarwal senseless, hitting him in the face and striking him from behind with a baseball bat.[34]

The same month, the Acevedo brothers participated in other hate-motivated assaults. Along with two other teens, they attacked Navroze Mody, a 30-year old Parsee and manager from Citibank, after he left Hoboken's Gold Coast Café with a friend. While bludgeoning Mody's head with bricks on September 27, 1987, the four assailants allegedly chanted, "Hindu! Hindu!"[35] Four days later, Mody died of the multiple skull fractures he sustained during the beating. Mody's four attackers were acquitted of murder charges on April 3, 1989, but were convicted of assault and sentenced to prison terms ranging from six months to ten years.[36]

In response to his son's death, Jamshid Mody filed a lawsuit alleging that Hoboken law enforcement officials were indifferent to crimes directed against the Indian American community. Mody argued that if the police had aggressively pursued and apprehended the Acevedo brothers after they attacked Aggarwal and Hasan, these two batterers would not have been free to murder his son. On April 24, 1991, the District Court in Newark threw out this discrimination suit.

Along with Navroze Mody, other South Asians were attacked in New Jersey. A group of assailants seriously injured Kaushal Sharan, a Camden resident who had been a physician in India and was in the process of getting licensed in America.[37] In September 1987, 28-year old Sharan was assaulted in front of a firehouse while walking home from his brother's residence, where he had spent the evening typing résumés for a residency position. Sharan's assailants hurled racial epithets while they beat him unconscious.[38] Five years after the attack, in September 1992, Thomas Kozak, Martin Ricciardi, and Mark Evangelista were indicted on civil rights charges for their involvement in the assault.[39] In January 1993, a jury was unable to reach a unanimous verdict. In May 1993, one of the accused assailants was acquitted. The Justice Department declined to retry the other two men, citing prosecutorial difficulties caused by the police's shoddy handling of the assault after it occurred. Although Sharan's assailants were not convicted, the case was significant because it was the first time federal prosecutors upheld the civil rights of a South Asian victim.[40]

While South Asian crime victims were pursuing justice, Indian community members continued to be targeted by Dot-busters and other New Jersey bigots. On April 8, 1992, Dr. Babu Patel was assaulted in Jersey City by ten white youths shouting racial slurs and derogatory comments. During the attack, one of Patel's assailants kicked his car tires and told him, "Go back to your own country!"[41] The attacker then maced him and struck him, leaving him bleeding from a head wound.

At the height of the Dot-buster attacks, South Asians were sometimes afraid to take out the garbage or walk alone on the street. Alita Masson told *India Abroad* that the South Asian community was terrified by community xenophobia, and demanded that authorities take action to protect vulnerable community members.[42]

In addition to the Dot-busters, who were centered in Jersey City, another racist gang, the Lost Boys, emerged a few years later in Middlesex County.[43] These gang members also terrorized South Asians, yelling out racial slurs and threatening them with physical harm. Although many Indians had lived in New Jersey for decades, the upsurge in racial harassment during this period caused some Hindus, Muslims, and Sikhs to move to other parts of the country, afraid for their safety.

South Asians on the West Coast were also victimized by hate crimes. In April 1990, an Indian family in Los Angeles received a phone call telling members of the household that they would be killed unless they returned to South Asia.[44] The same month, another Indian family in the same city found hate literature on the windshield of the car, which was parked in the driveway. South Asians in Northern California were also targeted. In September 1990, Indian and Pakistani families living in a condominium complex in San Leandro, California found swastikas painted on their garage doors.[45] Along with residences, bigots also targeted houses of worship used by South Asian community members. Teenagers vandalized Hindu temples in Martinez and Fremont in 1990, terrorizing congregants who were predominantly from India.[46]

In many school districts, South Asian children were singled out by bullies. In Walnut Creek, Pakistani children were harassed at their school by their classmates, who called them "Khaddafys."[47]

Throughout the 1990s, South Asians were occasionally attacked by Americans who mistook them for Arabs. For example, in early 1991, 25-year old Sumeet Singh was returning to his taxi at San Francisco international airport when a bigot shouted that he should go home to Iraq.[48] Shortly thereafter, Singh discovered that someone had spray-painted the rear window of his vehicle. Singh's attackers presumed he was Middle Eastern, not realizing that he was actually a Fijian Indian. Responding to news of late 20th century bias cases like Singh's, Mukesh Advani, president of the Indo-American Bar Association, noted that bigots often attacked Indians out of anti-Arab bias, conflating the two ethnic groups.[49]

Hate crimes became more frequent as Middle Eastern tensions escalated. According to *India-West*, the gurdwara in Fremont, California received over 25 harassment reports from Sikhs around the time of the Gulf War.[50] As nativism grew in the U.S., South Asians continued to be singled out in Northern California. In a January 1991 incident, two young men threatened to kill 30-year old Gurtej Singh while he was walking in a Hayward park.[51] Indian Christians in the area were also victimized in racial incidents.[52]

South Asian Muslims across the U.S. were increasingly scapegoated after Iraq invaded Kuwait. The Husseins of Fremont, California were repeatedly targeted during this period, apparently because of their surname. In a 1991 interview, Mehdi Hussein told *India-West* that the harassment intensified as the overseas situation worsened.[53] On occasion, bigots phoned the family in the middle of the night, making ethnic slurs at 3:00 a.m. Some of these callers acted as though they were calling Saddam Hussein's house, telling Mehdi Hussein to put the dictator on the phone so that they could discuss Iraq with him.[54] After the threatening calls escalated in frequency to the point that they were coming in on a daily basis, the Husseins contacted the Fremont police. Rather than take meaningful action, the responding officers suggested that the family obtain an unlisted number or get the phone company to run a trace.[55] Although the harassment eventually abated, the family continued to be wary of community intolerance.

Other South Asian families in California were also targeted around the time of the Gulf War, presumably by bigots who confused Hindus and Sikhs with Arab Muslims. In Hayward, an arsonist set fire to an Indian family's car and garage, where a child was doing homework.[56] In the aftermath of the bias-motivated arson, the homeowners became terrified of follow-up attacks. South Asians in Southern California were also affected by Gulf War nativism. In Orange County, an Indian family was terrorized by vandals who mistakenly thought they were Arabs. The assailants broke into the home, stole a computer, and wrote anti-Arab death threats in foot-high letters, urging the South Asians to leave the neighborhood.[57]

Orange County Human Relations Commissioner Rusty Kennedy acknowledged that Gulf War jingoism led to racial scapegoating, and noted that investigators had difficulty documenting the frequency of bias-motivated attacks. In a March 1991 article in the *Orange County Register*, he estimated that only 5% to 10% of these wartime hate crimes were ever reported to police or federal authorities.[58]

In some instances, South Asians were killed in apparent hate crimes. In 1993, Srinivas Chirukuri, a graduate student from Las Vegas, told investigating officers that two men set him on fire, presumably because of his actual or perceived ethnicity.[59] He eventually died as a result of his extensive burns.

During this period, South Asians were occasionally assaulted by law enforcement personnel. In 1993, Dr. Rajnish Mehra, a University of California finance professor, and his wife Neeru were roughed up by the police after they were forced to leave an Amtrak train following a disagreement concerning whether it was necessary for them to move their luggage to accommodate other passengers when there were numerous open seats in the car. *India-West* reported that during this incident, the officers used racial epithets and caused physical injury to the couple.[60] When South Asian community members learned of the police misconduct, many questioned the efficacy of reporting bias crimes or discrimination experiences to unsympathetic law enforcement officials.

In the mid- and late 1990s, South Asians continued to be attacked in the U.S. *Asianweek* reported that in November 1997, a 14-year old Indian immigrant student was beaten and hospitalized by his racist classmates in Union City, California.[61] On the bus to James Logan High School, the Sikh student was harassed by two other boys, who jeered at his turban, poured cologne on him, and told him he smelled bad. The bus driver did not intervene to stop the harassment. When the Sikh boy got off the bus, the bullies followed him and physically assaulted him. According to vice principal Donald Montoya, the police filed a report but did not classify the assault as a hate crime.[62] Following the attack, the Sikh boy remained so terrified for his safety that he returned to school without his dastaar and with his hair shorn, even though this was a violation of his faith. The inability of school administrators to protect vulnerable minority students made them lose faith in the system, eroding their willingness to report future attacks.

South Asians were also targeted at work. In January 1998, *Asianweek* reported that Yogesh Sagar, a security guard at Fisherman's Wharf in San Francisco, was midway through his night shift when three white men and a white woman began calling him "Akmed" and heckling him with anti-Arab slurs.[63] Once Sagar spoke, their taunts turned anti-South Asian. The three men then attacked him, punching him in the left eye and shattering his glasses. One of the assailants pounded him on the back, causing him to fall on the ground. In response to his injuries, the group laughed and ran off. Following the attack, Sagar told journalists that he was particularly angry that the police report failed to indicate that the crime was motivated by ethnic or religious bias.[64]

South Asians were also assaulted and beaten in other parts of the country in the late 1990s. In Pittsburgh, Pennsylvania, a gunman shot Sandip Patel, paralyzing him from the waist down, and murdered another South Asian.[65] During the same rampage, the assailant also shot a Jewish woman and an African-American community member.[66] Because all the gunshot victims were minorities, community members believed the shooter had acted out of bias.

During the same time period, New York bigots occasionally attacked South Asians. In one particularly brutal hate crime that took place in Queens, three men assaulted teenager Rishi Maharaj, beating him on the street and ordering him to get out of Richmond Hills.[67] Maharaj's assailants eventually received convictions for assault.

South Asians were particularly vulnerable in some New York neighborhoods. Throughout 1999, bigots repeatedly targeted Indian and Pakistani men near 90th St. and 95th Avenue. In the summer of that year, a South Asian man was harassed and beaten by white men in their late teens or early 20s. This victim, identified simply as "Swinder" to protect his identity, told the *News India-Times* that the hate crime was not his first encounter with community bigotry – his car had been repeatedly vandalized when he parked it in the area.[68] In the same neighborhood, a gang of white youths viciously assaulted construction worker Bhajan Singh when he was walking near Rockaway Blvd.[69] A third South Asian man, identified in the same article as "Parmjit," was attacked on August 27, 1999 by two assailants who threatened him with a gun and a knife before robbing him.[70] South Asian community residents also reported that their school-age children were harassed and beaten up on several occasions by bigots, who often congregated in the local park between 88th and 89th St.[71] Many Indians and Pakistanis in the area were dismayed that police officers were doing so little to protect them, undermining community confidence in the cops.

On occasion, vandals targeted South Asian homeowners. On November 24, 1999, an Indian family was subjected to a disturbing hate crime in East Meadow, Long Island. At the time of the attack, the Jaspars had been living in America for more than 18 years and considered the U.S. their home. While they were leaving to see their two young sons off to school, Amarjit Jaspal, 42, and his wife, Sarabjit Kaur, 36, realized that vandals had damaged their cars and flattened their tires.[72] The *News India-Times* reported that the assailants scratched death threats on the Toyota Camry, writing, "kill all that is not White" and "Hitler rule."[73] The vandals also damaged the Mercury Sabal, drawing a swastika and writing "Kill all Hindu Indians."[74] The hate crime ruined the family's Thanksgiving, making them feel unwelcome in the neighborhood. Police promptly investigated the hate crime, and arrested 18-year old Robert Seaman the same day.[75]

At the time of the vandalism, there were about 14 other houses owned by Indians or Pakistanis on the block, interspersed with houses owned by whites. In an interview with the *News India-Times*, Sarabjit Jaspal reported that neighborhood race relations had been strained prior to the menacing vandalism, and that children from white families were unwilling to play with her sons Karanjit, 11, and Sanjit, 16.[76]

In the months prior to 9/11, South Asian students were frequently harassed at American schools. A February 2001 article in *Hinduism Today* claims that bullies in the U.S. often taunted Hindu children, with much of the harassment centering on their distinctive clothing, vegetarianism, and religious beliefs.[77] On many occasions, Hindu students reported that their classmates ridiculed their bindis, making gun gestures with their hands and pretending to shoot them in the head. Other Hindu children reported that they had been approached by classmates who denigrated their beliefs, telling them that they would burn in hell for all eternity unless they converted to Christianity. By failing to stem this misconduct, teachers and administrators were fostering an environment of intolerance.

It is difficult to determine the precise numbers of anti-Hindu and anti-Sikh bias attacks that took place during this period because no official statistics exist. Rather than having a separate category for hate crimes affecting these groups, the FBI lumped them under "anti- other religions" category in their annual reports. Civil rights and religious organizations have requested that the FBI make the necessary changes so that authorities can keep track of crimes directed against these minority religious communities.

Like their Hindu and Sikh classmates, Muslim South Asian students were also targeted by bullies. In June 2001, a group of bigots attacked Ali Khan in front of Brooklyn's Lafayette High School. During the assault, the assailants pummeled his body with chains. Discussing this bias crime, Ali's father, Pakistani immigrant Sajjad Khan, told the *New York Post* that his teenage son was targeted because he was a South Asian Muslim.[78]

PRE-9/11 HATE CRIMES AGAINST ARAB-AMERICANS, MIDDLE EASTERN IMMIGRANTS, AND MOSQUES

Unlike African Muslims and South Asians, many Arab-Americans constitute an "invisible" minority in the U.S. Whereas many Muslims and South Asian immigrants experienced overt prejudice and discrimination in America, the first wave of Arab immigrants had more positive assimilation experiences. These Ottoman subjects arrived in the U.S. between 1880 and 1924 from what is now Lebanon and Syria. They were overwhelmingly Christian, and left their homeland to escape religious persecution and ethnic oppression. Because of their olive skin, these "Syrians" (as they called themselves at the time) were usually considered "ethnic whites" in segregated America.

Although many Syrian immigrants successfully blended into American communities, nativists occasionally spoke out against these Semitic newcomers. In an 1888 article, "Masters of Mendicants," a *New York Times* journalist claimed that Syrian Arabs, "the most filthy of immigrants," were "infesting the cities."[79] This same reporter warned the American public to be on guard against this foreign menace, referring to them as "dirty, ragged, shiftless Arabs without stockings, their hands in their pockets… puffing away at cigarettes, which they roll up themselves from tobacco they managed to beg from their fellow immigrants."[80]

In response to widespread xenophobia, some writers challenged nativist rhetoric aimed at Syrians and other Caucasian Asiatics. In a November 15, 1909 *New York Times* editorial, Carl Hansmann argued against excluding Arabs and other "Asiatic Whites" from citizenship, suggesting that doing so "would disqualify fully one-half of the members of the Caucasian race from the right to naturalization."[81]   Hansmann also maintained that many of America's recent immigrants were not so racially-distinct from other whites: "It is well known, both historically and scientifically, that the Caucasian race is of Asiatic origin, and that a large part of the inhabitants of Western Asia are members of the Caucasian race, including Armenians, Syrians, Persians, Hindus, and others, likewise many of the inhabitants of Mediterranean Africa."[82]

In the early decades of the 20th century, politicians increasingly worried that "swarthy" immigrants would pollute the gene pool and weaken the fabric of the country.   Many Arab-Americans began Anglicizing their names in order to assimilate.

Despite immigration restriction and xenophobia, many Middle Eastern immigrants were treated as "whites" in segregated America. In the South, Arab immigrants were permitted to ride in the front of buses and be served at "whites-only" lunch counters. Like other Mediterranean immigrant communities in the U.S., they occasionally experienced ethnic discrimination. In 1920, a political candidate in Birmingham, Alabama circulated a xenophobic flyer asserting that Arab-Americans should be stripped of their voting rights: "They have disqualified the negro, an American citizen, from voting in the white primary. The Greek and Syrian should also be disqualified. I DON'T WANT THEIR VOTE. If I can't be elected by white men, I don't want the office."[83] Also in the 1920s, a Syrian family in Marietta, Georgia was targeted by bigots, who dynamited their home.[84] The perpetrators were presumed to be members of the KKK.

One of the most serious anti-Arab crimes was the 1929 killing of an immigrant couple in Lake City, Florida, a crime denounced as a "lynching" in Arab-American newspapers.[85] Grocer Nicholas Romey, his wife Fannie, and their two children were one of two Syrian-American families living in the Southern town. What made their extra-legal shootings so unexpected was the couple were assimilated Americans – they had become citizens in 1916, and had lived in Valdosta, Georgia prior to moving to Florida. According to newspaper accounts of the attack, Fannie was shot multiple times and killed by sheriff's deputies after she refused to comply with Southern police Chief John Baker's request that she remove produce from a display outside the grocery store.[86] Her enraged husband was then taken into custody by deputies, who allowed the prisoner to be removed from his cell by a mob who subsequently riddled his body with bullets. Two black men incarcerated at the time that the mob took Romey claimed to have seen nothing.[87]

Arabic newspapers were outraged by the killings, with *As-Shaab* reporting, "The Syrian is not a negro whom Southerners feel they are justified in lynching when he is suspected of an attack on a white woman. The Syrian is a civilized white man who has excellent traditions and a glorious historical background and should be treated as among the best elements of the American nation."[88] Since Arab-Americans were treated as "honorary whites" in the South, many were worried that speaking out against racial injustice would jeopardize their standing in the community. My father, who was born in Louisiana in 1929, told me that members of Shreveport's large Lebanese Catholic community were afraid that they would be targeted by Klan violence if they challenged the racial status quo. Because the KKK was active in the South, Maronite Arabs worried about anti-Catholic community prejudice. Many first-generation immigrants joined Syrian social clubs where they played dominoes and ate ethnic foods, but still enjoyed the social privileges accorded to white Southerners.

Despite occasional instances of attacks and harassment, most early Middle Eastern immigrants had positive assimilation experiences. The first wave of Arab immigrants arrived at the beginning of the century. Most of these Christian newcomers married European-Americans and blended into predominantly-white or integrated neighborhoods. Most Arab-Americans are descendents of this first wave of immigrants, which is why this ethnic group is mainly Christian. Because of immigration restriction and the Great Depression, the numbers of Middle Eastern immigrants dropped precipitously, beginning in the 1930s.

In the mid-1960s, new waves of Arab immigrants came to the U.S. Many of these Middle Easterners were Sunni and Shia Muslims, and were less likely than their Christian immigrant predecessors to assimilate. Because some of the newcomers wore Islamic attire, they became more likely to be victimized than their Christian predecessors.   During the 1970s and 1980s, particularly when tensions in the Middle East escalated, assimilated Arab immigrants were frequently targeted by nativists.

On some occasions, Arabs in the U.S. were singled out by Americans who mistakenly thought they were Iranians. *The San Diego Union Tribune* reported that Lebanese immigrants were repeatedly cursed, harassed, and challenged to fights in response to the seizure of the U.S. embassy in Tehran.[89]

Hate crimes against Arab-Americans became increasingly frequent in the 1980s. One of the most infamous hate crimes was the October 11, 1985 murder of Alex Odeh, the Southern California director of the American-Arab Anti-Discrimination Committee. Odeh was killed by an explosion which took place as he was opening his Santa Ana office. According to the *Boston Globe*, the suspects were Jewish Defense League members who fled to the West Bank Jewish settlement of Kiryat Arba under Israeli government protection.[90]

Some scholars have argued that international politics and media stereotyping contributed to a rise in anti-Muslim sentiment in the U.S. According to University of Chicago history professor John Woods, Islam emerged as the new international enemy following the collapse of Communism.[91] Writer and documentary film maker Jack Shaheen also recognized that Islamophobia surged after the Cold War ended, arguing that Americans replaced the red threat with the green threat, namely fear of the Islamic religion.[92]

Like their South Asian counterparts, Arab-American and Middle Eastern immigrants experienced hate crimes during the Gulf War. According to the *Orange County Register*, physical assaults against Arabs took place in Michigan, New York, New Jersey, and the District of Columbia.[93] According to a 1990 report from the Los Angeles County Commission on Human Relations, the Iraqi invasion of Kuwait may have been responsible for a more than 400% increase in anti-Arab hate crimes, compared to the previous year.[94] Arab-American organizations estimate that the jump was even steeper nationally, approaching 900%. According to a *Los Angeles Times* article, Latinos, Armenians, and other minority groups were occasionally targeted in California during the Gulf War by bigots who confused them with Arabs.[95] At a conference addressing Gulf War hate crimes, Latino actor Edward James Olmos spoke out against bias attacks, noting that the international conflict seemed to give Americans permission to start hating Muslims and Arabs.[96]

During the Iraqi invasion of Kuwait and the Gulf War, Arab-American and Muslim businesses were targeted throughout the U.S. A Cincinnati grocery store owned by Arab-Americans was bombed twice the same week.[97] Arsonists also attacked an Arab-American delicatessen in Los Angeles and an Iraqi-American's grocery store in El Cajon.[98] In San Diego, an Arab-American food market received death threats.[99]

As war tensions escalated in the U.S., American mosques were frequently attacked. *The San Diego Union* reported that in 1990, arsonists destroyed the Islamic Center in Quincy, Massachusetts, which was built by families from Lebanon who worked in the shipyards in the first and second World Wars.[100] Other houses of worship were also targeted around the time of the Gulf War. In Tulsa, a bigot shattered a mosque's windows during a prayer service for peace.[101] Houses of worship were also attacked in California. Hundreds of Muslims attending Friday prayer services at a San Diego mosque were shocked by the discovery of a crude homemade firebomb on the premises.[102] During this period, the same Islamic center also received numerous threatening and vulgar phone calls, causing some hijab-wearing women to be too terrified to leave their homes to attend religious services or go shopping. Islamophobia was also present in other parts of California. A mosque in San Jose decided to take down its sign in 1991, afraid it might attract vandals.[103] Islamophobes also made their presence known in other states. In Michigan, bigots threatened to bomb Detroit Muslims.[104]

As Gulf War tensions escalated, minority students were increasingly singled out at schools and universities. Throughout the country, Arab-American children faced discrimination on American campuses. *The San Diego Union* reported that neo-Nazi skinheads at Valhalla High School in El Cajon harassed Iraqi-American students in January 1991.[105] In other states, college students were targeted. At the University of Texas, racist posters were hung depicting a Middle-Eastern man with the caption, "Wanted Dead or Alive: Any Arab."[106] In many parts of the country, religious schools were attacked. In February 1991, the *Orange County Register* reported that an Islamic campus in Tulsa, Oklahoma was vandalized.[107]

During this period, ethnic organizations received death threats. In early 1991, authorities arrested Kurt Haber, a 60-year old Beverly Hills construction engineer, for threatening to bomb the offices of the American-Arab Anti-Discrimination Committee.[108] Haber was apprehended after an electronic device traced the call back to him.

Instead of devoting adequate resources to protecting ethnic communities under siege, federal investigators increased the racial profiling and governmental harassment of minority citizens. In response to problems overseas, the FBI interrogated Arab-Americans without probable cause, including elected officials and civil servants. Wadie Deddeh, a longtime state senator from Bonita and San Diego, was one of the thousands of Iraqi-Americans interrogated by federal investigators.[109] They also interviewed San Diego city clerk Chuck Abdelnour simply because his father was Lebanese.[110]

Along with their disappointment that federal agents failed to treat them fairly, targeted minority groups were frustrated by the unsympathetic decisions of American judges. At times, hate crime victims had a difficult time receiving financial compensation for their losses. The *Journal Star* reported that on August 2, 1991, vandals desecrated a mosque in Peoria, Illinois.[111] Although the perpetrators broke all the windows, ransacked the building, and wrote a racial slur on the wall, a Tazwell County judge dismissed a lawsuit by the Muslims Association of Greater Peoria seeking $1,000 from the assailants to repair the damage. These types of legal outcomes made minority community members reluctant to look to the legal system for justice.

During this period, Iranian-Americans were frequently targeted. On March 14, 1992, bigots trashed the office of USC professor Iraj Ershagi, causing approximately $30,000 worth of destruction. *The Los Angeles Times* reported that vandals broke Ershagi's computers and scrawled racist graffiti and death threats on the walls, including, "No Scuds, Never Again," "No More Hostages," and "Death to Hezbollah."[112] They also poured motor and battery acid over his office equipment and destroyed his research papers. Ershagi, an Iranian-American who immigrated to the U.S. in 1966, felt he was singled out because he was active in the Muslim community and encouraged campus discussions on the Gulf War. Because he specialized in petroleum and chemical engineering, he participated in school-sponsored forums about oil production in the Middle East and its connection to the invasion of Kuwait. The attack made other campus minorities reluctant to speak publicly on sensitive political topics.

Police often failed to take anti-Muslim hate crimes seriously. In March 1992, on successive evenings, teenage attackers hid behind a six-food high wooden fence and hurled dozens of stones and snowballs at worshippers on their way to Ramadan services at a West Springfield mosque in Massachusetts. On March 25, 1992, six of these young assailants injured several congregation members, hitting one man in the head. Although the perpetrators unequivocally attacked Muslims en route to worship at their mosque, police opted against treating the assaults as a serious matter. West Springfield Detective Sgt. Paul Finnie told the *Boston Herald* that he and other police officers did not regard the repeated stonings of Muslims outside the mosque as a bias attack.[113] He maintained that the youths were too young to understand the meaning of a hate crime, and speculated that the Massachusetts courts would fail to hold the six perpetrators accountable for their actions.[114] As Finne predicted, the U.S. attorney's office failed to investigate the matter thoroughly, and ended up charging the assailants with simple vandalism.

Dr. Kimat Khatak, president of the mosque, told the *Boston Herald* that more serious charges were warranted since the youths had deliberately targeted Muslims.[115] He worried that congregation members would remain vulnerable as long as authorities failed to punish community members who singled them out. Talal Eid, the director of the Islamic Center of New England in Quincy, was similarly outraged that the hate crime perpetrators were given a slap on the wrist for their involvement in what he considered a serious attack.[116]

This was not the first bias-motivated incident at the mosque. When the religious site was under construction seven years before, vandals broke 18 windows, causing $4,000 in damages.[117] After this incident, mosque leaders chose not to press charges against the three young assailants, and paid the repair costs out-of-pocket. On another occasion, racial slurs were carved in wet cement in the front of the building.[118] In yet another attack, an arsonist set the house of worship on fire, causing nearly $500,000 worth of damage and leaving the congregation without a place to pray.[119] This ongoing community harassment made mosque officials especially disappointed that the police and the district attorney were unwilling to file hate crime charges after the 1992 Ramadan attack.

Bias assaults against Muslims spiked after the February 26, 1993 bombing of the World Trade Center. During the ensuing backlash, New York Muslim taxi drivers were frequently threatened or attacked by customers.[120]   In response to the surge in Islamophobia, some cabdrivers opted to cover up their identification and photo so customers would not spit at them or assail them with profanities.

Along with physical assaults, Arab-Americans were subjected to other manifestations of xenophobia. In the fall of 1993, officials in Natchez, Mississippi planned a "National Security Exercise" involving a mock terrorist strike by the faux group, "Arabs Against Americans."[121]   After officials from the American Arab Anti-Discrimination Committee (ADC) objected to the use of Arabs as the bad guys, Natchez's mayor apologized and Mississippi planners changed the faux terrorists' groups' name to "Anyone Against America" when the military exercise was conducted throughout the state.[122]

Throughout 1994, arsonists repeatedly attacked Islamic centers and houses of worship. In September, a nearly-completed mosque in Yuba City was deliberately burned down.[123]   The following month, a Brooklyn mosque was seriously damaged by a fire.[124]

Arabs, Muslims, and South Asians in the U.S. were also attacked in response to the April 19, 1995 Oklahoma City bombing, particularly after journalists, television reporters, and radio commentators falsely claimed that Middle Easterners were responsible. In the first week after Timothy McVeigh killed 168 adults and children at the Alfred P. Murrah federal building, there were approximately 138 media reports mistakenly fingering Islamic fundamentalists as the culprits.[125]

In the immediate aftermath of Oklahoma City, news programs and radio shows inflamed Islamophobic sentiments. After a caller questioned why Muslims were being blamed, New York's WABC talk show host Bob Grant threatened to put the man against the wall and execute him, alongside area Muslims.[126]

In the first 72 hours after the Oklahoma City bombing, there were at least 300 documented hate crimes directed against Muslims in the U.S.[127]   In New York, Arab-Americans received numerous death threats. In Brooklyn, Muslim shop owners were informed that that their businesses would be bombed and their families would be killed.[128] Muslims were also beaten in the streets.[129] The Council on American Islamic Relations estimates that the hundreds of hate crimes they documented during this period were but a small fraction of the total, since only 10% of the 1500 mosques in the U.S. responded to their 1995 survey about anti-Muslim bias attacks in the aftermath of Oklahoma City.[130]   Since this survey was distributed exclusively to Islamic houses of worship, non-practicing Muslims, Arab-American Christians, Sikhs, and Hindus were excluded from victim totals, suggesting that the scope of this backlash was considerably more extensive.

In the wake of the Oklahoma City bombing, Muslims of all ages – including small children - were targeted by religious bigots. The Cleveland *Plain Dealer* reported that at a suburban Muslim day care center, a teacher and her 60 young students were terrorized by a passing motorist who threatened to kill them before throwing a fake bomb at them.[131]   College students were also harassed in different parts of the country. According to the *Pittsburgh Post-Gazette*, two men accosted Indiana University of Pennsylvania students and accused them of being complicit in the April 19, 1995 plot.[132] The bigots then attacked one of the students, Mumtaz Mahmood.[133]

According to the *Boston Globe*, a particularly tragic hate crime happened in Oklahoma City the day after the bombing.[134]   On the morning of April 20, 1995, 26-year old Suhair Al Mosawi was seven months pregnant, sitting in her sunny one bedroom apartment and playing with her two children, ages two and three.[135]   Minutes after her spouse Saidi left for work, she heard some men pounding on the door and shouting obscenities, cursing Muslims and Islam. Worried about her safety, Suhair wondered who the assailants were and why they were targeting her family. Because she and her husband emigrated from Iraq in 1992, she was unsure if she was being singled out because of her race, religion, or national origin.[136] As the banging intensified, she worried that the attackers would break down the door and enter the apartment. While she was praying to God for assistance, the attackers hurled bricks through her windows, making a noise that she thought were gunshots.[137] Some of the shattered glass hit her and her toddlers, who started to scream. Afraid for her life, she took her children into the bathroom inside the bedroom and locked the door. Suhair desperately tried to calm and comfort her children, even though she was petrified herself.

In the midst of the attack, she began to feel dizzy and realized she was bleeding profusely.[138] She remained in the bathroom, hovering in terror for about an hour until she was sure that the door pounding and rock throwing had stopped. She then crawled helplessly to the phone and managed to page her husband, who arrived to find her unconscious in a pool of blood beside their two hysterical children.[139] He immediately called 911, and accompanied her to Oklahoma City's Mercy Hospital to be treated for her uncontrollable bleeding. On the way there, Saidai told Suhair to remove her hijab because he feared that American doctors might refuse to treat her if they found out she was Muslim.[140] After several hours in the intensive care unit of the hospital, the doctors informed her they had to deliver the baby immediately or both she and the infant would die. With Saidai weeping beside her, the physicians delivered a stillborn little boy.[141] The distraught parents buried "Salam" four days later.

Based on the types of bricks used in the attack and the assailants' knowledge of the family's residence, Saidai Mosawi wondered if his construction site co-workers were responsible.[142] Concerned about his family's safety, he decided to move out of Oklahoma City, particularly since the perpetrators had not been apprehended.

In the aftermath of the Oklahoma City bombing, mosques across the country received death threats. In Quincy, Massachusetts, a caller told the Islamic Center that the building would be blown up in 15 minutes.[143] Talal Eid, the center's religious director, was frightened by the call, although the police did not find a bomb. The call was particularly alarming because many Muslims remembered a previous 1990 arson attack on the center, which caused significant damage to the facility.

Other American mosques also received menacing messages. In Richardson, Texas, a mosque was subjected to 10 threatening phone calls.[144] The Islamic Association of North Texas was similarly targeted. In Cedar Rapids, Iowa, an imam answered a 3:00 am menacing call promising to get him in retaliation for the April 19, 1995 bombing.[145] In Los Angeles, an Islamic relief organization was repeatedly threatened, with one caller screaming that Muslims were murderers responsible for the Oklahoma City destruction.[146]

On occasion, threats escalated into violent attacks. The *Tulsa World* reported that an Oklahoma gunman shot at the Stillwater mosque in retaliation for the bombing of the Alfred P. Murrah federal building.[147] Youseif Sherif, the Libyan-born chairman of the Stillwater Islamic Society, later forgave the mosque assailant and arranged for him to come to the house of worship to apologize to the Islamic community.[148]

The backlash to Oklahoma City was also felt in other states. In North Carolina, an April 26, 1995 suspicious fire destroyed the Islamic Center in High Point.[149] Congregants assumed the blaze was a deliberate attempt to intimidate them, and they began worrying about their safety. Muslim worshippers were also targeted in other parts of the country. In Indiana, a gunman shot at the Masjid al-Fajr, the Mosque and Islamic Center of Greater Indianapolis.[150] This May 1995 attack damaged the house of worship, which had been established in 1971. One bullet pierced a window in the prayer area before penetrating the wall. Another bullet hit the dome at the top of the mosque. Earlier the same day, the mosque received a menacing message on its answering machine. The threat and the gun attack frightened worshippers, particularly since the mosque housed a school serving 40 children. Worshipper Ismail Abdul-Aleem told the Indianapolis *Recorder* that the mosque attack may have been triggered by inaccurate media reports blaming Muslims for the Oklahoma City bombing.[151]

Muslims were also targeted in Illinois. On June 6, 1995, a Springfield mosque was burned down. According to the *New York Times*, police officers refused to conduct a thorough investigation of the crime, even though fire marshals pointed to arson and acknowledged the smell of gasoline.[152] Although the mosque's next door neighbors reported that they had been woken up by the sound of motorcycles and men's voices in the parking lot directly before the midnight blaze, police detectives openly speculated that congregants had burned down their own mosque. Without any evidence to support this conclusion, Tony Sacco, Sangamon County's chief of detectives, told the *New York Times* that local Muslims were likely responsible for setting their house of worship on fire, since he had difficulty believing other community members were capable of committing such a crime.[153]

The morning after the fire, Muslims in front of the building were harassed by locals. The *New York Times* reported that three carloads of young men drove by the burnt mosque, hooting, hollering, and laughing, while congregation member Maryam Mostoufi was talking to reporters about the fire.[154]

Area Muslims were dismayed that authorities chose not to investigate the Springfield mosque arson as a hate crime, particularly since neighborhood bigots had repeatedly targeted the house of worship in the years prior to the attack. On numerous occasions, worshippers entering the building were subjected to slurs. In 1992, Muslims discovered a blue swastika on a telephone poll in front of the mosque.[155] For three years, city employees failed to cover up the anti-Muslim vandalism, sending worshippers the disturbing message that they would not be protected in their own neighborhood. Despite the presence of the menacing graffiti, the gasoline-induced fire, and public jeers at worshippers, police investigators failed to classify the mosque arson as a bias attack. Springfield Fire Marshall Cliff Garst told the *State Journal Register* that the fire was not necessarily bias-motivated because there was no obvious hate element.[156] After their mosque was destroyed, Springfield Muslims were forced to hold services on the wood floors of the Jefferson elementary school gymnasium.[157]

After the Springfield mosque fire, the Muslim community members were disheartened that local politicians and community leaders failed to come to their assistance. Dismissing the seriousness of the torching of the Islamic prayer center, state senator Larry Bomke told the *New York Times* that he saw no connection between the swastika outside the mosque and the burning down of the Muslim house of worship.[158] Rather than denouncing community Islamophobia, radio commentators blamed congregants for stirring up class resentments. Springfield's popular talk show host, Don "One-Eyed" Jackson, suggested that local Muslims were to blame for angering the community by parking $30,000 luxury cars in front of $20,000 houses.[159]

In October 1995, Illinois Senator Paul Simon inspected the charred remains of the mosque. The *State Journal Register* reported at the time of the visit, the mosque remained a wreck of its former self, with a gaping hole in the roof, melted vinyl siding, blackened religious books on a shelf, and the scent of ashes permeating the building.[160]

Despite the attention Senator Simon brought to the case, the Springfield police refused to step up their investigation efforts. Congregation member Mohamed Adil Rahman told the *State Journal Register* that he was disappointed that no one had been arrested, and that investigators were treating the attack as a cold case.[161] Rather than concentrate on community members who heckled worshippers, police investigators asked three members of the mosque to submit to a polygraph test in case they were involved in instigating the arson. The congregants refused, viewing the request as ridiculous and insulting. In response, Chief Deputy Tony Sacco declared that the investigation could not go forward until mosque officials complied with his request that they take polygraph tests.[162] This kind of police insensitivity made hate crime victims reluctant to rely on the legal system for justice.

Because many local and federal authorities were slow to respond to anti-Muslim hate crimes, mosque attacks continued to occur throughout the U.S. In Alabama, vandals severely damaged a Huntsville mosque on July 16, 1995.[163] During this early morning incident, perpetrators ripped apart Islamic books, damaged computers, and trashed facility equipment. Even more destructive attacks took place in other parts of the state. In Tuskegee, an arsonist destroyed an Islamic prayer center.[164]

Mosques were also targeted in other parts of the country. In Reno, Nevada, an Islamic Center was trashed by vandals. According to Rafik Beekun, faculty advisor of the Muslim Student Association at the University of Nevada, the perpetrators took all the Islamic books from the bookshelves and threw them all over the floor of the campus prayer space.[165] The hate crime upset congregation members, who worried about their safety in the area.

Mosques continued to be attacked throughout 1996. In Greenville, South Carolina, an arsonist set fire to an Islamic house of worship. The perpetrator was later apprehended by police and charged with the crime.[166] The same year, mosques were targeted in other states. In Pennsylvania, an arsonist set two garbage cans ablaze and set them against the sides of the Islamic Society of Greater Harrisburg in July 1996.[167] Following the arson, Steelton Muslims cleaned up the damage and beefed up security at the targeted prayer center.

Because many police departments failed to take hate crimes seriously, many victims stopped reporting bias-motivated threats, assaults, and vandalism to authorities. Federal investigators also neglected to track these attacks. Throughout the 1990s, the FBI refused to create a separate category for hate crimes against Arab-

Americans and Middle Easterners in the U.S., categorizing them as crimes against whites. Because of local and federal investigators' apathy and insensitivity, hate crime victims often reported bias attacks to community groups instead of law enforcement agencies. Whereas CAIR received hundreds of reports of anti-Muslim hate crimes in 1995, the FBI registered a total of only 29 incidents in the entire U.S. during the same year.

Because of the volume of information it was receiving, CAIR was able to ascertain that some ethnic groups might be particularly vulnerable. For example, in its 1997 report on anti-Muslim hate crimes, the organization found that 43% of victims were Arabs or Arab-Americans, 25% were African Americans, and 17% were from the Indian Subcontinent.[168] Muslims of European heritage made up 8% of bias crime respondents. The data showed that 81% of the reported hate crimes occurred in the 14 states with the highest concentrations of Muslims: California, New York, Illinois, Pennsylvania, Virginia, Maryland, Minnesota, Michigan, Ohio, North Carolina, Florida, Tennessee, Texas, and Georgia.[169] CAIR also recorded significant numbers of anti-Muslim hate crimes taking place in D.C.

Since FBI agents were receiving just a handful of the hundreds of anti-Muslim hate crimes being reported elsewhere, federal investigators were unable to ascertain which community members were most at risk and how the government was best able to protect them. In the 1990s, some authorities began acknowledging that Muslims seldom informed local and federal agencies of bias attacks. During this period, James Mulvhill, an assistant attorney general for New Jersey, told the *Bergen County Record* that he suspected that there was a gross underreporting of hate crimes against the Muslim community.[170]

To improve their record-keeping, some cities began including a "check-off" box so police officers would have an easier time tabulating crimes motivated by bias.[171] San Francisco witnessed a huge spike in police reports of hate crimes just by making this paperwork change. For some areas, this became a mixed blessing, since more conscientious urban areas began looking more intolerant than they actually were. For example, San Francisco documented 290 prejudice-related crimes in 1995, whereas Santa Clara County - an area with twice the population – reported only 47.[172] Statewide the same year, 435 counties (out of a total of 750) reported no hate crimes whatsoever, including in areas with large numbers of migrant workers like Vallejo and Napa. In many instances, Muslims remained more likely to report attacks to community groups instead of to governmental agencies. In the year after the Oklahoma City bombing, the San Francisco chapter of CAIR received over 40 reports of bias incidents and attacks targeting Bay Area Muslims, but California agencies recorded only eight anti-Muslim hate crimes for the entire state during the same period.[173]

One of the most bizarre anti-Muslim incidents occurred in Aurora, Colorado, after four KBPI radio station employees stormed into a mosque in March 1996 while performing a "prank" during a live broadcast. According to the *Denver Post*, Joseph Teehan, William Jones, Dean Brian Myers, and Roger Dale Beaty barged into the Islamic prayer center and began playing the national anthem on a trumpet and bugle.[174] The radio station orchestrated the disruptive mosque visit after Denver Nuggets guard Mahmoud Abdul-Rauf refused to stand for the national anthem at the beginning of basketball games. In response, the NBA suspended Abdul-Rauf, but later reinstated him after he agreed to stand and pray during the anthem.

During the disc jockeys' invasion of the mosque, Teehan, the radio show's producer, wore a turban and a T-shirt featuring Abdul-Rauf.[175] When worshippers asked the intruders to stop playing music and leave the mosque, the radio employees laughed. They also tried to put headphones on a worshipper in the middle of prayer in order to interview him against his will during the live broadcast. Explaining why the radio station employees' actions were so offensive, mosque spokesman Mohamed Jodeh told the *New York Times* that the intruders desecrated the house of worship by dressing like clowns and symbolically shoving the national anthem down their throats, suggesting that worshippers were unpatriotic and anti-American.[176] Jodeh claimed that the radio employees' actions were designed to foster racial, ethnic, and religious prejudice in the minds of their listeners. Congregants also faulted the KBPI employees for wearing shoes and playing music in the mosque, although these practices were prohibited.

Despite the seriousness of their offenses, the KBPI radio show personnel were charged with disorderly conduct, a misdemeanor, and unlawful conduct, a petty offense. Area Muslims were disappointed that the radio station employees were not charged with ethnic intimidation or committing a hate crime. Congregation member Mohamed Bashir Kharrubi told the *Denver Post* that more serious charges were warranted, since the mosque intrusion undermined the safety of worshippers.[177] In the immediate aftermath of the incident, radio station administrators suspended the DJs indefinitely without pay, but refused to fire them.

Inspired by the radio show's the unwelcome visit to the house of worship, men in a pickup truck drove around the mosque's parking lot, blaring the offensive KBPI broadcast and disrupting a board meeting. Although many Denver residents were supportive of area Muslims, others blamed mosque congregation members, claiming that they brought the situation on themselves by practicing an odious faith.[178] According to the *Denver Post*, the mosque received threatening calls promising more intrusions like the one committed by the radio DJs.[179]

The following year, American Muslims were disturbed by another strange incident. In March 1997, a mentally-disabled man in Albany told others that he was an Arab terrorist. Claiming to have a bomb, he threatened to kill himself and others in the downtown area. In response, Albany *Times Union* writer Genghis Khan expressed his disappointment that anti-Muslim stereotypes were so ubiquitous that they were capable of reaching a man with limited abilities to hear and communicate.[180]

The same year, bigots occasionally targeted Arab-American residences. In San Francisco, two Iraqi-American families were driven out of a housing project in 1997. According to the *San Francisco Chronicle*, the victims were repeatedly assaulted, robbed, and harassed at the 250-unit Alice Griffith housing project, which was inhabited primarily by African-Americans.[181] In a particularly serious incident, a vandal broke into one of the Iraqi-occupied apartments and stole a kidney dialysis machine used by two sick children.[182] In response to the racial and religious harassment, the Asian Law Caucus brought a lawsuit to protect Arab-American and Asian-American families at the housing project.

Anti-Muslim hate crimes persisted as the decade drew to a close. On occasion, bias attacks took place in prominent locations. Beginning in the mid-1990s, CAIR received permission to display a crescent and star at various New York landmarks, including Grand Central Terminal, the lobby of the Empire State building, and Kennedy International Airport. U.S. governmental officials also designated one day a year to be "Muslims' Day," a new secular national holiday. On December 19, 1997, in honor of "Muslims' Day," the National Park Service invited artist Mohamed Said Ouafi to display a ten-foot tall Islamic symbol on the Ellipse, the area between the Washington monument and the Lincoln memorial.[183] Ouafi created the lime green crescent moon out of plywood and added a large orange star hanging from the top. That evening, Ouafi went with a friend to look at his crescent and star, and found it lying about 300 feet away, ripped and tossed near a trash can. After picking the artwork up, Ouafi discovered a red swastika spray-painted on it. Police sergeant Joe Cox told the *New York Times* that he was surprised by the anti-Islamic vandalism, especially because Christmas trees and Jewish menorahs had been on display for more than 20 years without incident.[184] On January 4, 1998, Arab and Muslim groups erected a new star and crescent near the White House to replace Ouafi's trashed exhibit.

Many Muslims found the vandalism particularly painful because the crescent and star was the first time an Islamic symbol joined Christian and Jewish religious displays on the Ellipse. In response to the vandalism, then-President Bill Clinton told the *Washington Post* that the hate crime was an act of bigotry that struck at the heart of what it meant to be an American.[185]

Discussions of the hate crime often downplayed its seriousness. The *Houston Chronicle* reported that many Americans were debating whether the vandalism was committed by kids on a lark or by adults acting out of anti-Muslim bias.[186] The title of a December 1997 article from the *Fort-Worth Star Telegram* also raised the possibility that the incident was nothing more than a practical joke: "Swastika Spray Painted on Islamic Symbol: Police are Investigating Whether Vandalism to the Crescent Star was Done as a Prank or as a Hate Crime."[187]

Meanwhile, mosque attacks continued. In January 1998, the Islamic Center of Fort Collins, Colorado was desecrated in the predawn hours after at least two vandals carried a concrete parking curb from the mosque's parking lot and slung it through the building's glass entryway, shattering the door and bending its steel frame.[188] Approximately $1,000 damage was done to this mosque, which had also been vandalized in April 1996 when assailants shattered the center's windows. Fort Collins Police spokeswoman Rita Davis told the *Denver Post* that the initial investigation failed to produce any suspects.[189] Mosque executive committee member Dean Mulla was particularly upset that the mosque attack coincided with Eid el-Fitr celebrations at the conclusion of Ramadan, undermining congregants' sense of security.[190] Hundreds of worshippers regularly attended services at the targeted mosque, which was also a worship center for international students from Colorado State University.

In the late 20th century, xenophobes occasionally protested the construction of Islamic schools in the U.S. In 1998, town residents of the D.C. suburb of Ashburn took issue with a community proposal to build an Islamic school for the children of Arab diplomats and businessmen. According to the *Wall St. Journal*, opponents of the project distributed flyers warning of foreigners from terrorist-aligned Muslim countries roaming the neighborhood while Americans were at work.[191] Alarmists also gave sermons, circulated petitions, and wrote letters-to-the-editor denouncing the school, despite the fact that the same group of Saudi educators had operated a similar K-12 school in nearby Fairfax County since 1984. At that Saudi-run academy, more than half of the students and most of the teachers were American citizens. In addition to following the Virginia educational curriculum, the Fairfax school offered classes in Arabic and Islamic studies. Muslims in the D.C. area were disturbed by the virulence of the opposition to the proposed Auburn school, wondering why others found it so threatening.

Muslims were also harassed or intimidated in New York. In Bensonhurst, bigots in their early 20s shouted racial slurs at members of the Al Badr mosque in February, 1998.[192] As a result of this harassment, some congregation members became afraid to attend services.

In other states, Muslim worshippers confronted more extreme forms of intimidation. In the spring of 1998, members of Austin's Islamic Community were disturbed to discover that a bigot had mounted the heads of four goats or sheep on the fence behind their central mosque near the University of Texas. Commenting on this attack, Mehmet Tanis, a spokesman for the Greater Austin Islamic Center, told the *Austin American Statesman* that he was surprised that the perpetrator went through the trouble of obtaining and arranging the animal heads in order to intimidate congregation members and desecrate a house of worship.[193] Austin police investigating the case declared that the incident was either a possible case of criminal mischief or a hate crime showing bias against Muslims. Community members thought it was ridiculous that local law enforcement officers were unable to realize that the attack was clearly a hate crime. Because the center held five daily prayer sessions and ran an elementary school, mosque officials were concerned about the safety and well-being of worshippers and students, particularly since the mosque had been previously vandalized with graffiti. Some Austin residents were concerned that the mosque attack received practically no media attention, pointing out that a hate crime involving severed animal heads was undoubtedly newsworthy. In a June 3, 1998 letter to the *Austin American Statesman*, Richard Cardona expressed his dismay that the paper devoted minimal coverage to the story, giving it no online copy and poor print placement.[194]

In other parts of the country, immigrants were targeted by Islamophobes. In Nebraska, bigots attacked pedestrians who looked Middle Eastern. The *Lincoln Star-Journal* reported that on June 14, 1998, a knife-wielding bigot attacked two Arabic-looking men.[195] At the time of the assault, the pedestrians were walking near 27th and Holdredge St. in Lincoln when the assailant suddenly jumped out of a car and demanded to know why they were in the U.S.[196] He then slashed them with his blade.

The following year, mosque attacks continued. On March 5, 1999, intruders in Minneapolis attacked the Masjid al-Huda. Discussing this hate crime, the *Star Tribune* reported that on Thursday night, shortly before Friday religious services, arsonists set two separate fires to the non-descript stucco building.[197] The first blaze was set on the ground floor at approximately 2:45 a.m. and went out within the hour. The second one, which began in the basement at 5:00 a.m., gutted the building. As a result of the intentional destruction, the religious center was reduced to a blackened hull of charred wood, broken glass, and waterlogged carpets, which had been installed less than a month before the attack. At least one firefighter was injured extinguishing the blaze.

According to center president Mustafa Hammida, the arsonists attempted to burn religious books in the mosque's library by igniting a bundle of rugs they stuffed between shelves.[198] While surveying the damage, officials were dismayed by the gaping hole in the roof, the dangling wires, the blackened walls, and the scorched pulpit in the prayer hall.[199] They were also forced to look for a temporary site to hold services until their mosque could be rebuilt. Local Muslims were unable to rely on insurance to cover the exorbitant costs of rebuilding the facility, which had been erected in 1951. Hammida told the *Star Tribune* that the attack deprived the congregation of a prayer center and religious school.[200] Since the building also functioned as a cultural center, area Muslims were left without a place to gather and celebrate holidays.

Authorities looked into the mosque attack, complying with a federal law mandating the investigation of any suspected arson at any house of worship in the U.S. Fire inspector Rick Nelson determined that an accelerant was used and two men were seen leaving the crime scene in a newer white van at the time of the first fire. [201] Hesham Mahmoud, an Egyptian immigrant who worshipped at the mosque, told the *Star Tribune* that he sometimes heard hecklers harassing congregants and threatening to burn down the building.[202] He also reported that the mosque's windows had been vandalized on previous occasions.

Fire investigators told the *Minneapolis Star Tribune* that although they were unable to ascertain whether anything had been stolen, they suspected that the fire could have been intended to cover-up a burglary of the mosque's ransacked office inside the Islamic Cultural Community Center.[203] It is curious that authorities were willing to speculate that the fire was set to mask a burglary even though there was no evidence that anything was missing. Apparently, these investigators dismissed the possibility that the two deliberately-set fires at the Islamic prayer center were hate crimes.

Also in 1999, a mosque was targeted in Colorado. On May 12, Littleton police spotted a suspicious vehicle parked in front of the Colorado Islamic Center. To avoid the authorities, the driver sped off in his car. Officers eventually apprehended the suspect, who declared that he was an enemy of the Islamic nation, intent on taking care of business.[204] Law-enforcement personnel discovered loaded weapons and bomb-making materials inside the man's car, including 9 mm semi-automatic pistols, a high-powered rifle, a loaded shotgun, bomb-making equipment, several knives, and hundreds of rounds of ammunition.[205]

A few days later, a mosque was targeted in Illinois. In the early hours of May 15, 1999, vandals attacked the Islamic Foundation's Villa Park mosque. The assailants caused $4,000 to $5,000 in damage by hurling large concrete slabs, rocks, and milk bottles through the windows of this religious center, located in an upper-class suburb of Chicago.[206] Many community members denounced the vandalism, including representatives from Christian, Jewish, Zoroastrian, and Bahai congregations.

According to the Arlington Heights *Daily Herald*, the mosque had also been attacked on several previous occasions, with passing motorists shouting ethnic and racial slurs at worshippers, telling them to return to India.[207] Muslim women walking in the vicinity of the mosque were also singled out by religious bigots yelling rude comments.

Police Chief Ron Ohlson told the *Daily Herald* that the mosque's six smashed windows were located at the building's entrance and in the prayer hall area.[208] A surveillance tape captured a man exiting from the passenger side of a white van or SUV and approaching the main doors of the prayer center shortly before the attack took place.[209] Although mosque officials viewed the destruction as a hate crime, police disagreed, contending that there was no evidence that it was a bias-motivated. Although they were contacted by police, the FBI refused to get involved with the investigation. Disregarding the deliberate vandalism to the house of worship, federal agents declared that there was no evidence that the mosque attack was a hate crime. In an interview with the *Daily Herald*, FBI spokesman Ross Rice explained that his agency did not believe that the arson was instigated by bias because there was no note or phone call by a hate group claiming responsibility.[210] Because of their unwillingness to investigate the mosque attack, the FBI did not explore whether the white van or SUV involved in the Villa Park vandalism was the same vehicle involved in the Minnesota mosque arson a few months previously. The FBI also failed to investigate if it was merely a coincidence that both mosques were attacked shortly after they had been renovated.

A few months later, assailants once again targeted the Islamic Foundation's mosque, a religious facility that included a prayer hall, Islamic school, book store, and activity center. During this attack, a giant concrete block was thrown through the window of the religious center, which had just been repaired and refurbished.[211]

Mosques were also singled out in other parts of the country. In June 1999, a burning car tire was found in the predawn hours in front of the Pullman Islamic Center in Washington state. A bush between the street and the sidewalk had also been set on fire. Rather than recognize that the arson was likely bias-motivated, the Vancouver *Columbian* reported that the deliberately-set fire at the mosque did not appear to be a hate crime.[212]

Muslim homeowners were also targeted prior to 9/11. In August 2000, Joshua Hass plead guilty to painting swastikas and other white supremacist symbols on an Egyptian man's home in California.[213] In November of the same year, Hass was sentenced to ten months in federal prison for the hate crime. Unfortunately, other bigots were not deterred by this outcome, and continued to target Muslims throughout the U.S.

In the fall of 2000, the Islamic Center of Southern California was repeatedly vandalized. According to the *Los Angeles Times*, on October 26, two black swastikas were painted on the entrance, desecrating the house of worship. Underneath the graffiti were the words, "Zion go."[214] A vandal also scratched anti-Semitic words on the mosque's glass doors, proclaiming, "Jews get out."[215] Based on the content of this graffiti, the hate crime perpetrator may have mistakenly assumed that the mosque was a Jewish synagogue. It is also possible that the vandal intended to frighten Muslims and Jews simultaneously.

The same mosque was attacked repeatedly in the days following the vandalism. *The Los Angeles Times* reported that on October 29, an assailant threw a rock through the glass door when worshippers were gathered in the front prayer area.[216] In early November, vandals kicked open and ransacked the guard station in the center's parking lot, smearing the window with blue paint. The mosque's van was also damaged with paint and graffiti.[217] Worshippers were particularly worried about the safety of their children because some of the vandalism was near the jungle gym used by Muslim preschoolers. In response to the repeated attacks, staff members tightened security at the facility, which included a school for 105 students from kindergarten to sixth grade. Police acknowledged that the mosque attacks were motivated by bias, and investigated the incidents as hate crimes.

In other parts of the country, Muslims exiting mosques were assaulted by strangers. In Sparks, Nevada, two white teenagers lurking outside a mosque took a baseball bat and severely beat two Muslims who had just finished Friday night prayers in March 2001. The attack at the northern Nevada Muslim Community Center gravely injured both victims. Eltag Mirghani, a Reno physician from Sudan, suffered head injuries so severe that he was listed in critical condition at Washoe Medical Center.[218] The other victim, Muhammad Sanad, a Reno engineering consultant from Egypt, suffered a broken arm resulting from his attempts to shield his head during the beating. Police Lt. Ken Lightfoot told the *San Diego Union Tribune* that the assailants attacked the Muslim men suddenly, walking up to them and striking them with the bat without warning.[219] After many swings, the attackers dropped the bat and ran from the scene. Once the white perpetrators were apprehended, they claimed that robbery was the motive for the brutal attack. Because hate crimes are associated with lengthier prison sentences, it is curious that police and journalists quickly took these violent assailants at their word, instead of probing the possible bias motivation of an assault targeting two African Muslims on mosque grounds after Friday night prayers. Many worshippers viewed the brutal beatings as hate crimes, particularly since the house of worship had received several calls before the attack asserting that the mosque taught filth.[220]

In the months preceding 9/11, hijab-wearing Muslims were routinely singled out by bigots. In March 2001, a veiled woman and her six-year old daughter were attacked in Bloomfield Township, Michigan. The *Detroit News* reported that while the victim and her child were sitting in their car at the drive-through lane of a McDonald's restaurant, employee Rebecca Gibson pounded on the vehicle, broke the windshield, and tried to bend the wipers in half, screaming at the Muslim patrons to leave the country.[221] Although four of Gibson's co-workers witnessed the attack, they failed to call for help. Because none of the McDonald's employees or customers came to her assistance, the victim used her cell phone to contact the police herself, after frantically trying to calm her terrified daughter. According to Bloomfield Township Chief Jeff Werner, Gibson was charged with malicious destruction of property for the damage done to the Muslim woman's car.[222] Area Muslims felt that hate crime charges were also warranted. In response to the incident, CAIR officials in Michigan asked that the McDonald's restaurant issue an apology to the victim and offer culturally-sensitive emergency response training to its employees.

The same month, the *Arab American News* reported that vandals targeted the Islamic Center of Southern California and two mosques in Canada.[223] The newspaper also listed mosque attacks in Michigan, Indiana, New Jersey, Colorado, Illinois, and Georgia.[224]

On occasion, bigots attacked Muslim prayer centers on college campuses. The weekend of April 20, 2001, intruders desecrated Georgetown University's Muslim prayer room, a space used by hundreds of students and faculty members. Owas Balti, president of the Georgetown Muslim Student Association, told *India Abroad* that trespassers broke into the room and vandalized it.[225] Campus security officials had no suspects in the crime.

In other parts of the country, anti-Muslim attacks were even more violent. On June 19, 2001, a Tennessee gunman targeted worshippers at an East Memphis mosque, wounding one person.[226] The attack happened at the Masjid al-Noor, as worshippers were starting their 4:30 a.m. prayers. The assailant shot 26-year old Najah Abdul Kareem as he approached the mosque. While the injured Kareem ran up the driveway and into the building, the shooter fired at Danish Siddiqui, president of the University of Memphis Muslim Students' Association.[227] The attacker then shot repeatedly at the locked doors of the mosque, which was located near the University of Memphis.

Discussing this hate crime, worshipper Omar Amer told the Memphis *Commercial Appeal* that he and other worshippers scattered for safety as soon as they heard the shotgun blasts.[228] He called 911, but was forced to lay down the phone when the gunfire got closer. He then hid in the bathroom, praying to God for protection.[229] The gunman continued firing at the mosque entrance, trying repeatedly to shoot his way through the locked doors until he ran out of bullets. When police arrived at the scene, they arrested Brent Fong, who was standing on the sidewalk in front of the mosque carrying the 20 gauge Mossberg shotgun he used in the rampage.[230] Once Fong was apprehended, the injured Kareem was taken to Regional Medical Center where he was treated for shotgun wounds to his pelvis.

According to the Memphis *Commercial Appeal*, Fong and other members of the community had harassed Muslim worshippers on previous occasions, throwing dirt on them, chasing them with dogs, and smoking marijuana in front of the mosque.[231] Rather than assume that the gunman acted out of bias, the FBI chose to reserve judgment on the matter. Special agent Kelli Sligh reported that the FBI was monitoring the situation, looking at the facts to see if the case was a hate crime directed against a religious institution.[232] Congregation members were dismayed that the FBI was reluctant to acknowledge that the mosque shooting rampage was a bias attack, particularly since the religious institution had a documented history of bigotry-motivated abuse.[233]

PRE-9/11 MOVIES THAT DEMEAN ARABS, MUSLIMS, AND SOUTH ASIANS

To understand the zeitgeist in which hate crimes were taking place, it is important to appreciate the role that early 20th-century cinema played in disseminating harmful stereotypes of Arabs, Muslims, and South Asians. According to the American Psychological Association, only about 5% of all hate crimes are committed by members of organized hate groups.[234] The APA also determined that bias attacks are committed by people who have been given explicit or implicit permission to hate members of other ethnic and religious communities.[235] Throughout the 20th century, movies that depicted Arab Muslims as misogynistic terrorists gave audiences implicit permission to regard Middle Easterners as nefarious villains, contributing to an atmosphere of intolerance in which hate crimes thrive. In his comprehensive and ground-breaking book, Reel Bad Arabs, film critic Jack Shaheen analyzed 950 20th-century American movies that stereotype Arabs and Muslims.[236] In many of the films, Arabs were depicted as hook-nosed savages who attempted to kill Christian protagonists and rape blonde women. Since Arabs are Semites, Shaheen characterized these derogatory cinematic stereotypes as components of a new manifestation of anti-Semitism.[237] According to Shaheen, these 20th-century film caricatures of Arabs resemble an earlier version of intolerance in which Jews were depicted as the incarnation of evil.[238]

After viewing hundreds of movies, Shaheen concluded that many Hollywood costume designers relied on an "instant Ali Baba kit" to assemble stock Arab characters, adorning the men with fake beards, checkered burnooses, worry beads, exaggerated noses, curved daggers, scimitars, and nargilehs.[239] The female characters were frequently costumed with conservative black chadors, hijabs, belly-dancing outfits, balloon pants, see-through veils, and jeweled navels. Shaheen convincingly argues that Arab stereotypes pervade American movies, teaching audiences to fear Middle Easterners and Muslims as dangerous enemies. What follows is an overview of some of the movies Shaheen discusses in his path-breaking book, coupled with some of the films analyzed by Tim Jon Semmerling in his study, 'Evil' Arabs in American Popular Film.[240]

Twentieth-century American movies capture the enduring nature of Islamophobia in the U.S. According to Shaheen, the plot of the 1920 film, *Son of Tarzan*, contains some of the earliest negative cinematic portrayals of Muslims.[241] In this film, the British-born hero and his son Korak kill Arabs involved in a child slavery ring. At the beginning of the film, the evil Ben Kahour shoots Captain Jacot's wife and abducts his daughter Jeanne into slavery. Ten years later, Jeanne has become accustomed to her life as the Arab's slave, waiting on him in obsequious fashion and filling his nargileh with tobacco. Although the movie heroes rescue her, Ben Khatour and his men capture her again, along with Tarzan's wife, Jane. To punish Jeanne for attempting to escape, the Arab villain declares that he has sold her to Hamid the black.[242] He then makes an unsuccessful attempt to brand her. Korak comes to her rescue, killing the evil sheikh before being captured himself. In retaliation for killing their leader, the Arab villains spear Korak, tie him up, and attempt to set him on fire. After watching this film, American audiences are left with the impression that Arabs are villainous barbarians who abuse and enslave women.

Films from the 1930s include even more sinister depictions of Middle Easterners. Shaheen notes that in the 1931 movie, *Beau Ideal*, Arabs kill Western legionnaires.[243] Instead of depicting Islam as a religion of peace, the film associates the faith with murderous violence. Stereotypical Arabs bring weapons into a mosque, and scream out that they should kill in the name of Allah.[244] Another character in the movie is Zuleika, a half-Arab dancer who shocked American audiences with her aggressive sexuality, bad manners, and anti-Christian sentiments. When Otis, the Western protagonist, rebuffs her unsuccessful seduction attempts, she spits in his face and calls him a Christian dog.[245] Brown-skinned Arab characters in this movie also plot a religious massacre targeting all Christians.[246]

Shaheen reported that approximately one-third of the 950 films he reviewed involve a lecherous, brown-skinned Arab preying upon an unwilling white woman.[247] Like Americans' racist worries about black men raping fair-skinned women, these movies entertain audiences by exploiting their miscegenation concerns. Many of these films were released when racial tensions in America were particularly high. According to Shaheen, the 1956 film, *Abdullah's Harem*, takes place in a fictitious land ruled by a sexist, self-indulgent tyrant.[248] Abdullah amuses himself with electric trains, belly dancers, and slave girls. For much of the movie, he pursues Ronnie, a European model who resists his persistent and unwelcome advances. At one point, Abdullah's assistant makes misogynistic statements, comparing women to flowers that needed to be changed constantly.[249] When Abdullah and Ronnie are on board a yacht, he makes an unsuccessful attempt to rape her. He then insults her by referring to her as a comely devil sent to destroy him.[250]

American films also feature Arabs and Muslim Sudanese as white slavers. Shaheen notes that in the 1964 film, *East of Sudan*, British Christians are pitted against black Muslims and Arabs.[251] The movie, set in the 1880s, repeatedly shows Sudanese Muslims committing religious hate crimes. In one scene, they desecrate a Christian grave by tearing down a cross. The movie also suggests that blacks in power can't be trusted, showing an African prince attempting to sell white women to the Arabs. The movie's dialogue also emphasizes that dark Muslim men are sexually obsessed with white women.[252]

Arabs also appear as heartless villains in the 1967 film, *Follow That Camel*. In his analysis of the film, Shaheen observes that Middle Easterners are referred to as dogs and monkeys.[253] One of the villains in the movie is Abdul, a misogynist who is missing his front tooth. Despite having 12 wives, he is sexually obsessed with Lady Jane, a white woman, and attempts to take her against her will to the El-Nookie oasis.[254] After swarthy Middle Easterners force her into a tent, legionnaires rescue this white damsel in distress. In several scenes in the film, Arab characters are depicted as primitive buffoons. In one scene, an Arab gunman shoots a clock, prompting a Western observer to comment that the Arabs were unable to cope with technology.[255]

In the early 1970s, many films also disseminated harmful images of South Asians and Indian culture. In the 1973 film, the *Golden Voyage of Sinbad*, Anglo actor John Law plays Sinbad, appearing in the film with a turban, beard, and long sword. The movie contains troubling images of Hindu villains. In the trailer, Sinbad is shown fighting a "six-armed goddess of evil." By transforming a traditional Hindu deity into a Hollywood movie villain, the film teaches American audiences to associate non-Western faiths and South Asians with malevolence.

Negative racial and religious stereotypes also appear in movies released in the early 1970s. In his book, 'Evil' Arabs in American Popular Film, critic Tim Jon Semmerling argues that images of the Arab "Other" in popular films often shed light on Americans' cultural, economic, and political anxieties.[256] Semmerling contends that the demon from the *Exorcist* is a manifestation of the Occidentalist's fear of the Orient.[257] Semmerling maintains that the film's Iraq prologue links the evil in Regan's bedroom to the nefariousness of the Middle East.[258] The film turns Iraqi archeological artifacts into demonic relics, making Americans fear them as sources of evil. This movie was released in the U.S. on December 26, 1973, when Americans were concerned about political relations with the Middle East and OPEC's oil embargo.

Other films from the 1970s feature the stereotype of the Muslim Arab terrorist. Semmerling argues that the movie, *Black Sunday*, explores Americans' Orientalist fear by showing Arab terrorists creeping into the U.S. to launch an attack.[259] In this 1977 film, Palestinian villains have infiltrated Los Angeles, Miami, and the District of Columbia. These Arab Muslims attempt to kill the American president and murder 80,000 civilians attending the Super Bowl. The film's protagonist is Israeli antiterrorist fighter David Kabakov, played by Robert Shaw, who has come to protect the vulnerable U.S. Like Westerns that pit heroic cowboys against savage Indians, the Israeli and American characters battle the Arab savages. Semmerling points out that the movie intertwines real and fictitious events and people, so that American audiences lose track about what parts of the film are imaginary.[260] He also draws attention to the movie's conflation of sexuality and violence, discussing a bedroom scene in which two of the sociopathic terrorists make a cassette recording of their nefarious plans after making love.[261]

Semmerling maintains that throughout the movie, the Palestinian terrorist Dahlia uses her sexuality as a weapon and a shield.[262] In one scene, Kabakov opts against shooting her when he sees her naked in the shower. He later realizes that his mercy was a mistake, since she proves to be one of the most dangerous of the Arab assassins, plotting to use a lethal blimp to kill American spectators at a football stadium. She also uses the cloak of her femininity when she kills an Israeli agent, who sees her nurse's uniform and unwisely turns his back on her in the elevator. Near the end of the film, Kabakov ends up shooting her and re-routing the blimp so that no American lives are lost. According to Semmerling, the end of the movie shows the masculine, civilized Western world conquering the feminine, savage Orient.[263]

Other American movies from the 1970s also depict Muslims as heartless monsters. The 1978 film, *Midnight Express*, depicts Turks as cruel villains, suggesting that other Middle Easterners are just as savage as Arabs.

Islamophobic movies continued to entertain American audiences in the 1980s. The 1985 movie, *Jewel of the Nile*, includes offensive stereotypes of Muslims. The film's villain, Sheikh Omar, lusts after blondes, and makes unwanted sexual advances at Joan Wilder, played by Kathleen Turner. Shaheen observes that although the movie is supposed to take place in modern Arabia, the characters ride on camels instead of driving in cars.[264] In the course of movie, Turner's character is taken hostage by incompetent Arabs who are unable to use their own weapons. Shaheen takes issue with this movie's use of derogatory language like "towel-head" and for including anti-black scenes, including one involving dark-skinned women performing an offensive Hawaiian disco dance.[265]

The 1987 movie, *Ishtar*, also perpetuates negative stereotypes. In this film, Omar and his Arab colleagues find a map that claimed that there was another prophet of God who was Mohammed's contemporary. Along with its extensive use of ethnic and religious slurs, this movie suggests that Muslims are violence-prone individuals. In one scene, an Arab knifes Omar in the gut. In other parts of the film, Moroccans are depicted as dishonest people who live in unclean conditions and eat unappetizing food. According to Shaheen, Dustin Hoffman and Warren Beatty received "Golden Pit" awards from the National Ethnic Coalition of Organizations for their participation in this racist movie.[266]

In the late 1980s, Arab and Muslim movie characters continued to be depicted as violent terrorists, intent on killing American civilians. In the 1988 action film, *Terror in Beverly Hills*, Arab terrorists kidnap the U.S. President's daughter, Margaret, during a shopping spree in Southern California.[267] They also abduct the wife and son of a LAPD officer. Throughout the movie, Palestinian and Arab-American villains are portrayed as heartless misogynists who target helpless women. One of the Middle Easterners ties Margaret to a chair, spits in her face, and attempts to rape her.[268] Arabs are also portrayed as being anti-black. At one point in the film, a terrorist kills a sympathetic African-American police officer. In response to this crime, another villainous character comments that his blood-thirsty comrade Abdul enjoys committing murder.

Similar stereotypes resurfaced in the 1990s. The 1994 film, *True Lies*, depicts Palestinian Muslims as heartless terrorists intent on killing Americans. In this movie, Arabs possess nuclear weapons, and detonate one in Florida. They also mistreat and assault women, and take an African-American community member hostage. Shaheen observes that in one scene in the movie, Tom Arnold's character Gib cheers up Arnold Schwarzenegger's depressed character Harry by telling him that he will feel better once they catch and beat the hell out of the terrorists.[269] None of the film's main actors voiced any misgivings about being in the racist film. Discussing her starring role, Jamie Lee Curtis expressed her difficulty understanding others' objections, commenting that the script was simply funny.[270]

Other movies released the same year contain equally-damaging cinematic portrayals. In the film, *In the Army Now*, army reservists kill Libyan terrorists before they are able to implement their plan to use chemical weapons. Shaheen observes that the plot emphasizes that Arabs are pitiless villains, capable of turning the skulls of the heat-stroke victims into ashtrays.[271] He also points out that like many other movies, the dialogue employs gibberish instead of actual Arabic, making the villains seem even more sub-human.

Some Islamophobic films suggest that gender differences disappear when male and female American soldiers join together in defeating Arab enemies. In the 1997 film, *GI Jane*, Demi Moore's character Jordan O'Neil proves her worthiness as a warrior when she joins other SEALS in a mission to kill Libyan Arabs. As a result of her participation in this bloody mission, the female protagonist was able to prove to her unit that she was just as capable of killing Arabs as any other American SEAL. In this film, the white protagonist bonds with a black member of her unit, suggesting that American soldiers of different genders and races can find common ground killing Middle Easterners.

Other American movies also feature Arab villains. Semmerling argues that the 1999 movie, *Three Kings*, perpetuates Orientalist stereotypes.[272] This movie takes place in the Middle East, after the U.S.-led coalition forces declared victory in Desert Storm. Semmerling maintains that the Arab characters in the movie are portrayed as threatening to America, even though U.S. forces have already won the war.[273] Semmerling suggests that the movie uses the classic war story genre to allow audiences to feel better about the regeneration of American militarism.[274]

Movies with even more dastardly Muslim characters were released shortly before 9/11. In the 2001 movie, the *Point Men*, Amar Kamil, a villainous Arab played by Vincent Regan, murders Israeli agents, a plastic surgeon, a nurse, and a sympathetic blonde woman.[275] The Arab sociopath is eventually killed by Israeli agents before he implements his plan to kill his own half-brother. By reinforcing racial stereotypes of Arabs as terrorists, films repeatedly exposed American audiences to the xenophobic message that Middle Easterners and Muslims were bent on destroying innocent Westerners. These movies gave audiences implicit permission to hate ethnic and religious minorities living in the U.S.

CHAPTER THREE:

ARAB, MUSLIM, AND SOUTH ASIAN
VICTIMS OF THE TERRORIST STRIKES

Although Middle Easterners, South Asians, and African Muslims were frequent targets of U.S. bigots throughout the 20th century, attacks against these communities escalated considerably on and after 9/11. Rather than acknowledge that the terrorist strikes affected people from around the world, American pundits framed the attacks on the World Trade Center and Pentagon as an exclusively American tragedy, setting the stage for xenophobes to lash out at immigrants. This chapter investigates some of the minority victims of 9/11 as a means of undermining nativist interpretations of the terrorist attacks.

There were 372 innocent foreign nationals killed on September 11, 2001, representing approximately 12% of the total.[1] These victims included Bangladeshians, Ethiopians, Indians, Pakistanis, Jordanians, Lebanese, and Malaysians.[2] According to U.S. governmental researchers, the 9/11 victims came from more than 50 different countries.[3] An April 2002 New York City Department of Health report determined that India was the country with the third largest number of September 11th fatalities, after the U.S. and the U.K.[4]

American and British citizens killed or injured in the Twin Towers included ethnic Middle Easterners and South Asians, living primarily in New York and New Jersey. In addition to the innocent minorities and foreign nationals who perished in the attacks, Arab-Americans, Middle Easterners, South Asians, Muslims, Sikhs, and Hindus were among the thousands of World Trade Center and Pentagon workers who fled from the targeted buildings, sustaining physical injuries, lung damage, and emotional trauma. The firefighters, paramedics, and police officers who were killed or seriously injured on 9/11 also came from different ethnic, racial, and religious backgrounds. Despite the diversity of the victims, many Americans opted to view 9/11 through parochial lenses. Frustrated that minority victims were being overlooked, Shabbir Ahmed, a Bangladeshi-American who lost family members at the World Trade Center, reminded the *Washington Post* that many ethnic communities were affected by the terrorist strikes.[5]

The *News India-Times* reported that scores of South Asians were killed on 9/11, including: Sushil Solanki, 35, a computer operator; Anil Shivhari Umarkar, 34, an operations broker; Deepika K. Sattaluri, 33, a consultant; Vishnoo Ramsaroop, 44, a janitor; Dipti Patel, 38, a data systems engineer; Sankara S. Velamuri, 63, an auditor with the New York State Department of Taxation and Finance; and Mohammed Salahuddin Chaudhury, 38, a waiter at the Windows on the World restaurant.[6]

These victims left behind heart-broken relatives. Chaudhury came to New York from Bangladesh in 1987. Although he usually worked in the evenings, he took a day shift on September 11, 2001 because doctors told him that his pregnant wife would likely deliver their second child later that day. Chaudhury was killed working on the 106th floor of the South Tower. The *Washington Post* reported that in the months following the terrorist strikes, Chaudhury's first child, a five-year old daughter, kept asking when her father would return home.[7]

The emotional devastation that many of these families experienced was compounded by the xenophobia that swept the U.S. in the aftermath of the hijackings. Mohammed Chaudhury's brother-in-law, Masud Qurashy, told the *Post* that their family's grief was exacerbated by their fears of backlash hate crimes.[8]

Taimour Khan was a 29-year old commodities trader for Carr Futures who worked in the North Tower.[9] He was born in the U.S., and grew up in Woodbury, New York, where he was captain of the high school football team. According to the London *Independent*, Khan was extremely popular at school, even though his family members were the only Pakistanis in the neighborhood.[10] After moving to Manhattan, he developed a wide group of friends and enjoyed going to nightclubs. He considered himself an American above all else. Although he was somewhat ambivalent about religion, he honored Islam's focus on the family. His uncle, Arshad Khan, told the *Independent* that Taimour remained extremely close to his relatives, visiting his mother weekly and taking her to the best restaurants.[11] Taimour Khan's sister Zara spent the week after 9/11 roaming the streets of Manhattan, giving out small sheets of paper with her brother's photo and a contact number. She told the *Boston Globe* that she weathered stares from hostile people as she frantically searched hospitals and rescue sites for her brother, looking for news of him or his co-workers from the 92nd floor.[12]

Other Muslims were victims of the 9/11 tragedy, including: Abdoul Karim Traore, Abdu Malahi, Abdul K. Chowdhury, Amenia Rasool, Boyie Mohammad, Ehtesham U. Raja, Jemal Legesse Desantis, Karamo Trerra, Khalid Shahid, Michael Baksh, Mohammad Ali Sadeque, Mohammed Jawara, Mohammed Shajahan, Mon Gjonbalaj, Nasima H. Simjee, Nizam A. Hafiz, Nurul Huq Miah, Sarah Khan, Shabbir Ahmad, Shakila Miah, Shakila Yasmin, Simon Suleiman Ali Kassamali Dhanani, Syed Abdul Fatha, Touri Bolourchi, and Zuhtu Ibis.

Christian Arabs were also killed in the Twin Towers. According to MSNBC, Jude Moussa, a 35-year old Lebanese bond trader, was killed on 9/11.[13] He had been working in the North Tower when American Airlines Flight 11 crashed into the building, killing him and 656 other Cantor Fitzgerald employees.[14] Moussa left Lebanon in 1984 to escape the civil war and study in the U.S. A few years later, his Christian relatives emigrated as well, settling in the Caribbean. Moussa's parents, Yvette and Joseph, were proud of their son, who had worked at his job since 1998. On the morning of 9/11, Moussa called his family, as he did at least once a day, sending his mother and niece Sophie kisses over the phone.[15] Because they were so close, his parents were devastated by his death. His mother suffered a nervous breakdown and had to be repeatedly hospitalized for depression. She told reporters that nights were the hardest time of the day since she was often flooded with images and memories of her son.[16] His father was so overwrought that he lost his faith in God.[17] To find comfort in more familiar surroundings, Yvette and Joseph Moussa moved back to Lebanon. Jude Moussa's brothers, who remained abroad, were also shaken by his horrific death.

Scores of other innocent minorities were killed on 9/11, including members of the same ethnic communities scapegoated in the backlash: Alok Agarwal, Amarnauth Lachhman, Anette Andrea Dataram, Anil Bharvaney, Asad Samir, Ashraf Ahmad Babu, Avnish Patel, Azam Ahsan, Babita Guman, Bernard Mascarenhas, Deepa K. Pakkala, Ganesh Ladkat, Gopalakrishnan Varadhan, Goumatie Thackurdeen, Jayest Shah, Joseph Mathai, Jumma Haque, Jupiter Yambem, Kalyan Sarkar, Kiran Gopu, Krishna V. Moorthy, Kum-Kum Girolamo, Mukul Agarwala, Narendra Nath, Nitin Parandter, Omar Namoos, Pendalaya Vamsikrishna, Prem Nath Jerath, Qasin Ali Khan, Rajesh Khandelwal, Rajesh Mirpuri, Rena Sam-Dinnoo, Ricknauth Jaggernauth, Robert Talhami, Samad Afridi, Shashi Kiran Kadaba, Shreyas Ranganath, Sita Sewnarine, Suresh Yanamadala, Swarna Chalasani, Talat Hussain, Tariq Amanullah, Valsa Raju, Vinod K Parakat, Waleed J. Iskandar, and Yusuf Saad.[18]

Many Muslim-Americans looking for loved ones at Ground Zero were accosted or threatened by their fellow citizens. While searching for a missing colleague, Moukhtar Kocache, a curator at the lower Manhattan cultural council, told the *Washington Post* that he was verbally attacked by an irate man who threatened to bomb him, demanding that he return to his country of origin.[19]

Durreen Shahnaz, a pregnant New Yorker of Bangladeshi ancestry, spent 9/11 trapped in her smoky office lobby near the Twin Towers. The *Washington Post* reported that when she went to inscribe a goodwill message on a memorial canvas near Ground Zero, she was greeted with threatening anti-Muslim comments.[20]

Some victims' families were unable to attend funerals because they were barred from traveling on airplanes. The *Post-Standard* reported that after Rahmie Salie and her husband Michael Theodoridis were killed on American Airlines flight 11, their Muslim family members were prohibited from flying to their memorial services.[21] At the time of her death, Salie was a 28-year old observant Muslim from Sri Lanka who had lived in the U.S. for more than ten years. She married her college sweetheart Michael Theodoridis, who converted to Islam, and was seven months pregnant with her first child when the couple boarded the doomed flight traveling from Los Angeles to Boston.[22] They were killed when their hijacked plane hit the North Tower. Many of their family members were unable to attend the memorial because their names were put on watch lists. Salie's uncle was already on a U.S.-bound flight from Tokyo to attend her memorial service in Boston when the plane was called back to the gate and he was hauled away by police.[23] In response to this racial profiling, Salie's mother, Haleema Salie, called attention to the diversity of the World Trade Center victims, telling the *Independent* that the terrorist attacks harmed people from different religious backgrounds.[24]

Some Muslim family members of 9/11 victims attempted to address community Islamophobia. The *Orange County Register* reported that Arefe Simjee, a respiratory therapist from Westminster, spoke out at a 9/11 memorial, reminding other mourners that innocent Muslims were also killed in the attacks.[25] At this gathering, Simjee told the crowd that her 38-year old cousin, Nasima Simjee, died in the World Trade Center's South Tower.[26]

Undocumented workers from South Asia and the Middle East may have also been injured or killed in the 9/11 attacks. The *Independent* reported that illegal aliens were working in the vicinity of the Twin Towers, and may have inhaled smoke or been hit by the falling debris.[27] If their friends and family members were also undocumented, these New Yorkers might have been hesitant to risk deportation by reporting missing or injured loved ones.

Muslim-Americans were among those who died attempting to assist World Trade Center victims. On September 11, 2001, Mohammed Salman "Sal" Hamdani, a 23-year old laboratory technician, was traveling to work as a research assistant at Rockefeller University when the first hijacked plane crashed. Because Hamdani was an emergency medical technician, the *New York Times* speculated that he was probably killed after taking it upon himself to climb aboard an ambulance and rush to the burning Twin Towers to help his fellow Americans.[28] His mother Talat told the *Times* that her son had driven an ambulance to earn money for school, and always helped others in an emergency.[29]

According to the *New York Times*, Sal Hamdani was born in Karachi, Pakistan, and moved to Queens with his parents when he was a year old.[30] His father worked as a store owner, and his mother became an English teacher, working with middle school students in Jamaica, Queens. His two younger brothers were born in New York. Sal Hamdani played football in high school, and spent his free time mastering video games and reading science fiction. A June 2001 graduate of Queens college, he read the Quran five times a day, loved *Star Wars* movies, and drove a navy-blue Honda Civic with the license plate "YungJedi."[31] His neighbor Mrs. Fuchs, recalled that he was always helpful to others, shoveling her walkway in the winter.[32] He was a part-time graduate student at New York University, and was working towards becoming a doctor.[33] He never got the chance.

Rohy J. Shalabi, president of the Arab-American Bar Association of Illinois, told the *Los Angeles Times* that the 9/11 rescue workers came from diverse backgrounds, and included Arab and Muslim firefighters and police officers.[34] For example, Ashraf Sabrin, an EMT in Arlington, belonged to one of the firefighting companies that rushed to the burning Pentagon to save lives.[35]

Muslim Americans, Arab-Americans, and South Asian Americans were also among the thousands of volunteers who contributed their time and expertise in the aftermath of 9/11. The American India Foundation helped collect $1 million to help children orphaned by the terrorist strikes. South Asians also provided emergency care to victims' relatives. Dr. Anand Pandya coordinated the psychiatric care of families and patients of the World Trade Center attacks, counseling grieving and suicidal family members.[36] Pandya worked alongside Linda Chokroverty, the acting director of the Child and Adolescent Care, helping the sons and daughters of 9/11 victims.[37] While assisting families affected by the terrorist attacks, Pandya and Chokroverty reported feeling vulnerable because of their South Asian looks.[38]

Rather than acknowledge the diversity of 9/11 victims and relief workers, many Americans focused their anger and rage on area minorities.

CHAPTER FOUR:

BACKLASH ASSAULTS,
SEPT. 2001 TO SEPT. 2011

Although World Trade Center victims came from all races, ethnicities, and religions, bigots began blaming and assaulting innocent South Asians, Sikhs, Muslims, and Arabs almost immediately after the Twin Towers fell. This chapter explores the backlash beatings and attacks that began on September 11, 2001 and continued for years afterwards, often spiking on or near each anniversary of 9/11.

Even before the media began to speculate about which groups might be responsible for the terrorist strikes, Americans began targeting Middle Easterners and South Asians, including those who were born in the U.S. or were naturalized citizens. Perhaps the first victim of a 9/11 backlash hate crime was Amrik Singh Chadwala, a Brooklyn-raised financial consultant who was singled out by his fellow Americans simply because he wore a turban. The *Washington Post* reported that on September 11, 2001, he took a cab to the World Trade Center and saw smoke coming from the North Tower.[1] As he was exiting the cab, he saw the second plane crash into the South Tower. Watching debris flying through the air and smoke filling up the streets, he began wondering about the fate of his friends and colleagues in the targeted buildings. The *Washington Post* reported that as Chadwala began to follow the crowd, two young men wearing t-shirts and jeans began screaming at him to take off his turban.[2] He crossed the street, but the men followed, calling him a terrorist, using profanities, and repeating their demands that he remove his dastaar.[3] He began to panic when the men became even more hostile and he realized his cell phone wasn't working. When he broke into a jog near Broadway and 52nd St., the three men began chasing him.[4] After running about four blocks, he darted into the Broad St. subway station and took the first train, without knowing where it was going. He exited at the next station on Court St. in Brooklyn and felt everyone staring at him. Terrified about getting beaten up by enraged Americans scapegoating nearby minorities, Chadwala ducked into a hair salon, took off his turban, and put it into a briefcase.[5] When he arrived home, he put his dastaar back on, vowing never to remove it in public again. At that moment, he began reflecting on the enormity of the World Trade Center tragedy and the loss of his close friends, who worked inside the destroyed buildings. In a September 26, 2001 article in *Asianweek*, Chadwala expressed his dismay that in addition to being frightened of the terrorists, he was terrified of being killed by his fellow Americans.[6]

Singh was not the only Sikh targeted in New York on September 11, 2001. According to the *Boston Globe*, a group of young men attacked 66-year old Attar Singh Bhatia, beating him with a baseball bat and shooting him in the forehead with a pellet gun.[7] The assault occurred outside the Richmond Hills gurdwara, where Bhatia had gone to pray after the terrorist strikes. Also in Queens, another Sikh was beaten by assailants wielding chairs.[8]

The same day, South Asians were targeted in other parts of the U.S. The *Tulsa World* reported that Naveed Alam, a 28-year old Pakistani, was badly beaten and kicked by three men in Broken Arrow, Oklahoma, on the evening of September 11, 2001.[9] The assault took place as he attempted to visit a friend working at a Quik Stop convenience store. Police speculated that the beating, which lasted three to five minutes, was in misplaced retaliation for 9/11. Alam's assailants hit him over the head and repeatedly kicked him in the face and body, causing him to hemorrhage and lose five lower teeth.[10] The beating, which broke his jaw in three places, caused his face to swell and turn purple. Alam underwent surgery at Tulsa Regional Medical Center, where he was listed in fair condition. His girlfriend, Dollie Leon, told the *Tulsa World* that they were overwhelmed by the support they received from community members horrified by the backlash crime.[11] Strangers brought flowers and a Tulsa dentist called to offer his services, accurately guessing that Alam lacked both health coverage and dental insurance.[12]

On occasion, enraged Americans assaulted African immigrants in response to 9/11. A mere 13 hours after the World Trade Center strikes, six men in metro Atlanta attacked Simon Machar, a 22-year old

Sudanese refugee living in Clarkston. According to the *Atlanta Constitution*, the men jumped Machar and tried to stab him while accusing him of killing Americans in New York.[13] During the beating, one of the assailants took a two foot by four foot board off the apartment sign and threw it at the window of Machar's room in the Le Carre Apartments, shattering the glass. Machar finally escaped after another Sudanese refugee came to his assistance. To prevent further attacks and to show support for their adopted homeland, Machar and his Sudanese roommates put a U.S. flag in their shattered window, and urged other refugees to do the same as a means of expressing solidarity with grieving Americans.[14] Many Sudanese refugees in Atlanta contributed money to the Red Cross in support of the victims, even though these donors were recent immigrants who did not yet have jobs. Machar told the *Atlanta Constitution* that the attack terrified him, especially because it triggered recent traumatic memories of Sudan's civil war. Machar though his assailants might have mistakenly presumed he was Muslim, not realizing he was a Christian from Southern Sudan.[15] Machar appreciated the opportunity to start over in America, but was disappointed that the U.S. was not as tolerant as he had hoped.[16] Another Sudanese refugee, Garang Malou, told the newspaper that the Atlanta attackers were targeting all foreigners as a means of expressing their rage over 9/11.[17]

Many minorities in America saw a connection between backlash assaults and the media's racist coverage of the terrorist strikes. South Asians in America were particularly outraged by news footage pertaining to the arrest of Sher J.B. Singh, a 28-year old software engineer, for possession of a kirpan on September 12, 2001. Singh, a Sikh American who had a full beard and wore a green turban, was traveling home to Virginia after trying to set up a telecommunications company in Boston.[18] Born in New Delhi to an Indian Air force pilot and an English literature teacher, Singh became an American citizen in 1998. Although Singh's wife Hermani Kaur urged him to postpone traveling until the 9/11 backlash abated somewhat, he decided to proceed with his return trip, boarding Amtrak train no. 173 at Boston's South Station.[19]

As the train stopped in Providence, federal agents and local police crossed the platform with bomb-sniffing dogs. According to the *Providence Journal*, officers with guns drawn singled out Singh, pressed him against the train, handcuffed him, and asked him about his residency status.[20] While he was being interrogated, spectators lunged at him and promised to kill him in retaliation for 9/11. Instead of taking action against the angry onlookers who threatened Singh's life and physical safety, one officer joined in the verbal abuse, taunting the victimized South Asian and asking him about Osama bin Laden.[21]

When authorities asked Singh if he had a weapon, he volunteered that he had a three-inch kirpan, the religiously-mandated small knife he and other Sikhs carry to fight injustice. After confiscating this blade, officers hauled Singh away, charging him with possession of a concealed weapon.[22] They then detained him for six hours, insensitive to how the media would blow the event out of proportion and unfairly link Sikhs and South Asians with the 9/11 hijackers.

The police also arrested another Sikh and a Pathan at the same train station, but detained Sher Singh for the longest time. While he was in custody, Singh was fingerprinted, strip-searched, and asked about his appearance. The police also kept possession of his kirpan. Discussing the loss of his religiously-mandated knife, Singh told the *Washington Post* that it was akin to depriving a Christian of a cross.[23]

Singh challenged the validity of the charges, which were later dismissed. After being cleared, he spoke publicly about his mistreatment at the hands of xenophobic police officers, and began devoting considerable time to fighting anti-Sikh bigotry during the backlash.

Singh and the other Providence travelers were not the only minority commuters racially profiled by law enforcement officials in response to the terrorist strikes. According to the *Washington Post*, New York police officers searched the bags of three Sikh men in Grand Central Terminal in the aftermath of 9/11.[24] In another incident, Dr. Prathap Chandram, a heart surgeon from Charleston, West Virginia, was manhandled and handcuffed by police.[25] By viewing South Asian and Middle Eastern community members as potential terrorists, authorities were fueling a climate of xenophobia in the U.S. Many activists saw a connection between the racial profiling of immigrants and the scapegoating of minorities by bigots.

In the days after 9/11, South Asians, Arabs, Afghanis, and Africans were targeted in all parts of the country. The *Washington Post* reported that Mustafa Nazary, an Afghan-American, was attacked in a vicious hate crime.[26] According to the *Post*, Nazary began realizing that Islamophobia was surging in his adopted country after hearing a radio commentator propose that the U.S. nuke the Middle East in response to the terrorist strikes.[27] Nazary, a naturalized citizen who lived in the U.S. since the age of 12, put American flags on his bakery delivery van, to express his patriotism and show community members that he was a loyal citizen. On September 14, 2001, Nazary was on Edsall road in Alexandria, listening to Bush memorialize the World Trade Center victims on the radio, when Michael Johnson drove his vehicle up to the minority driver and asked him if he was from Afghanistan. The irate driver then followed Nazary's delivery van two blocks into a shopping center parking lot and attacked the Afghan-American, beating him and punching him in the head.[28] At the time of the assault, Johnson weighed 350 lbs., making him twice as heavy as his victim. Although Nazary sustained serious head injuries, his assailant received only 60 days in jail after being convicted of this vicious felony hate crime. The judge even allowed Johnson to leave prison on the weekends. Nazary told the *Post* that his assailant's lenient sentence made him feel like a second-class citizen in his own country.[29]

Minorities were also attacked in backlash hate crimes on the West Coast. According to the *San Francisco Chronicle*, two software engineers were assaulted while walking South of Market at 11:30 p.m. on September 14, 2001.[30] As Sean Fernandes and Robin Clarke were crossing Townsend and Brannon streets, a group of men and women began shouting racial epithets at the two men, telling them that they didn't like Arabs.[31] One of the men then singled out Sean Fernandes, calling him a dirty Arab. Although the assailants assumed that Fernandes was a Muslim from the Middle East, the 26-year old was actually a Catholic of Indian and Hispanic heritage. His friend, Robin Clarke, was a white man from Australia. In the course of the attack, the assailants punched both men before stabbing Clarke with a screwdriver.[32] The assailants then fled from the scene in a blue Mustang coupe. Clarke's injuries were so severe that he was listed in critical condition. Clarke spent more than a week in the hospital, recovering from surgery. Fernandes told the *New York Times* that he was deeply shaken by the bias-motivated attack, adding that he had lived in the U.S. for eight years without incident prior to 9/11.[33]

Hispanics in Texas were also beaten up during the 9/11 backlash. On September 15, 2001, a mob jumped a Latino man exiting a night club in Southeast Houston. During the beating, the nine assailants shouted racist remarks and made comments about Osama bin Laden. Ralph Marsh, an officer in the Houston Police Department's Criminal Intelligence Division, was disturbed by the crime, telling the *Houston Chronicle* that it was a horrific example of racial scapegoating.[34]

In the days following the terrorist strikes, Sikhs continued to be physically assaulted in many parts of the U.S. On September 16, 2001, Kent residents Jagit Gill, 40, and his father-in-law Santokh Singh, 60, were attacked near Eugene, Oregon. Gill told *India Abroad* that he simply greeted a woman at the Gettings Creek highway rest area when she started screaming at them, making derogatory comments and calling them terrorists.[35] The 54-year old woman, Shari Margaret Mitchell, then knocked over their tea, slapped Gill, and tried to take off Singh's turban.[36] Several other motorists confronted Mitchell as she drove away. Responding officers chased her for some time before she was apprehended. Oregon state troopers and jailhouse deputies reported that Mitchell continued to make bigoted comments about the two Sikhs when she was in custody.[37] Police eventually determined that she attacked the South Asian travelers because she thought they were Muslims responsible for the terrorist strikes. Officer Susan Hardy told the *Oregonian* that Mitchell admitted to making racist comments and ordering the South Asian men to go home, because they weren't wanted in the country.[38] Gill characterized the attack as the worst experience he had in the 13 years he lived in the U.S.[39] He described the psychological trauma as being worse than the physical pain. He was also disturbed that his father-in-law, who had been in the country for three months, had such an unpleasant introduction to the U.S.

According to the *Register-Guard*, Mitchell claimed that the inflammatory television coverage of the 9/11 attacks and the news media's demonization of the terrorists prompted her to lash out at others.[40] Her attorney Russell Barnett mounted an insanity defense, claiming that she thought she was meeting Osama bin Laden in a rest area. Lance County Deputy District Attorney Paul Graebner challenged this argument, maintaining that her claims of mental illness were fabricated and that she should be punished for being a violent bigot.[41]

On December 7, 2002, a six-member jury convicted Mitchell of second-degree intimidation and physical harassment, misdemeanor offenses. Mitchell was eventually sentenced to 30 days in jail and five years of probation for these minor crimes. According to prosecutor Paul Graebner, Mitchell was only charged with misdemeanor offenses because her victims suffered no injuries.[42] Sikh activists questioned why local prosecutors were unwilling to recognize that Mitchell caused physical injury to the two men, since he had struck Gill and forcibly attempted to remove Singh's turban. Discussing the sentence, Lane County Circuit Judge Ted Carp told the *Register-Guard* that Mitchell's sentence was intended to discourage bigots from acting on their xenophobia.[43] Gill, a store manager in Kent, told *India Abroad* that he was pleased that Mitchell was given jail time for her outrageous conduct.[44] Other community members were disappointed with Mitchell's light sentence, feeling a stiffer penalty was warranted since she physically assaulted two South Asians out of bias.

The day after Jagit Gill and Santokh Singh were attacked in Oregon, a 20-year old Boston University student from Saudi Arabia was stabbed by a group of men in Massachusetts. The *Boston Herald* reported that on Saturday night, September 16, 2001, the victim and his friends were attending a 9/11 fundraiser at Club Nicole, a Back Bay nightclub.[45] Early Sunday morning, as the student and one of his friends were waiting for the others to fetch a car, four or five assailants jumped them and stabbed the BU student twice in the arm, and once in the back with a four-inch knife blade.[46] Because the student's wound was bleeding profusely, his friends drove him to a nearby hospital to be treated. The puncture wound in the back was the most serious, and it missed the young man's kidney by only four inches. The victim's brother reported that the assailants used profane language and shouted an anti-Arab slur during the attack.[47]

The victim's brother, who had recently graduated from MIT, told the *Boston Herald* that he was devastated by the hate crime, wondering if the city was still a safe place for international students and other minorities.[48] He also reminded the newspaper that on the evening of the attack, Club Nicole patrons – many of whom were Arabs – had been privately raising money for Red Cross disaster relief, to help the families of the terrorist attacks. In an interview with the *Boston Herald*, Mayor Thomas M. Menino voiced his outrage at the Club Nicole attack, expressing his hope that the perpetrators would be arrested and prosecuted to the fullest extent of the law.[49]

Minorities were also targeted in the Midwest. The September 19, 2001 issue of the *Plain Dealer* reported that the Cleveland FBI office was investigating 34 post-9/11 attacks in the city, including one in which an enraged bigot beat up a man for the crime of looking Arabic.[50]

On occasion, Americans intervened in heroic fashion when they saw minorities being scapegoated. According to the *Pittsburgh Post-Gazette*, Hannah Mumma, a political science major at Pitt University, came to the aid of fellow student Humar Ahmed when he was assaulted by a white man on September 19, 2001.[51] Mumma, a Korean-American who had been adopted and brought to the U.S. at age two, had just finished her waitressing shift at the Spice Island Tea House in Oakland, Pennsylvania. She was walking along Atwood St. towards Dawson St. when she saw a beating in progress. Ahmed's white assailant, David Hardwig, was making racist comments as he repeatedly kicked and punched the Pakistani-born engineering student. Mumma told the *Pittsburgh Post-Gazette* that she heard Hardwig threaten to kill his victim as well as demand to know if he was from Afghanistan.[52] Realizing that a hate crime was taking place, she began screaming at the bigot, imploring him to stop the assault. Rather than listening, he shoved her aside and resumed the bias-motivated attack. Although other witnesses initially failed to come to her aid, Mumma's intervention eventually prompted a man in a nearby apartment building to grab Hardwig and wrestle him off of Ahmed. Mumma then called 911 as Hardwig fled. Reflecting on the hate crime, Mumma suggested that Ahmed's assailant may have made the erroneous assumption that racial minorities were incapable of being American citizens.[53] The *Pittsburgh Post-Gazette* reported that Mumma's mother was disturbed by the attack, simultaneously frightened and proud of her daughter's heroics.[54]

Ahmed, who had lived in the U.S. since he was three, told the *Pittsburgh Post-Gazette* that the assault made him constantly vigilant whenever he went out in public.[55] He also began carrying a cell-phone, at his mother's insistence. Ahmed was appreciative of Mumma's help and the outpouring of interfaith support he received. To educate others about hate crimes, Ahmed began discussing his bias-motivated beating at community meetings and rallies, to make others aware of the intensity of the 9/11 backlash.

To the relief of area minorities, Hardwig eventually turned himself into police, in the hopes of receiving more lenient treatment. He was arraigned at that Allegheny County Court on December 5, 2001 on charges of ethnic intimidation, simple assault, and making terrorist threats.

Along with Muslims, Sikhs continued to be targeted throughout the country. The September 28, 2001 issue of *India Abroad* described a post-9/11 hate crime in which a white assailant attacked Jasbir Singh, an Indian American Sikh, in downtown Chicago.[56] The perpetrator escaped when witnesses came to Singh's aid.

In response to the hate crimes, many Sikhs, Muslims, and Arabs felt that they needed to purchase and display American flags and red, white, and blue paraphernalia, so bigots would not assume they were terrorist sympathizers. The *San Francisco Chronicle* reported that a few days after 9/11, Sikhs began flying American flags out of a mixture of patriotism and fear.[57] Newspapers in other states also found that minorities were using the stars and stripes to protect themselves against community bigotry. Amarjit Singh, a Sikh man, told the *New York Daily News* that he successfully used an American flag to calm down an angry bigot who interrogated him in Queens.[58] When the man approached him in a menacing manner and asked about his loyalties, Singh pointed to an American flag on his car to ward off an imminent attack.

SEPTEMBER 2001 ATTACKS ON MUSLIM WOMEN

In the aftermath of the terrorist strikes, Muslim women wearing the hijab were targeted throughout the U.S. In West Virginia, a group of white men approached a group of young Syrian women walking down Morgantown's High Street shortly after 9/11. The assailants first surrounded the women and then attacked them. Discussing the assault, West Virginia University student Sohail Chaudhury told the *Gazette-Mail* that the white men ordered her and her friends to take off their veils, accusing them of using their religious headwear to conceal guns.[59] When the women failed to comply, the assailants tried to pull off their hijabs. The attack finally ended when by-standers came to the women's assistance.

Muslim women were also singled out in Illinois. The September 13, 2001 issue of the *Chicago Defender* reported that two local women wearing religious headwear were assaulted in a post-9/11 hate crime.[60] The attack worried area Muslims, who began restricting their movements in public.

On occasion, Muslim women were attacked in California. In one incident, a young Persian woman was assaulted on September 14, 2001. The hate crime occurred at a Los Angeles Café, where she was eating lunch with a friend who jokingly called her an Arab. Another woman overheard the comment, asked the Muslim woman if she was indeed an Arab, and punched her in the eye.[61]

Other hate crimes in the state were even more brutal. The *Los Angeles Times* reported that three men attacked a local woman wearing a hijab at a La Miranda parking lot.[62] During the assault, they called her a terrorist and yanked off her veil. They also slapped, bit, and kicked her.

Muslim women in Massachusetts also experienced backlash hate crimes. The *Patriot-Ledger* reported that an assailant at a subway station attacked a local Muslim woman soon after the terrorist strikes.[63] During the assault, the vigilante tugged on her head scarf, conveying the message that Muslims were not welcome in the area.

In many instances, anti-Muslim attacks were particularly vicious near the epicenters of the terrorist strikes. The *Washington Post* reported that in the D.C. area, an assailant with a bat severely beat up a Muslim woman on September 19, 2001.[64] The hate crime victim worshipped at a mosque in Falls Church, where Muslims were mourning the loss of friends and family members who died in the demolished buildings. According to the *Post*, one member of the congregation lost a niece and nephew on 9/11.[65]

SEPTEMBER 2001 ATTACKS ON SIKH WOMEN

Along with veiled Muslims, Sikh women who wore religious headwear were frequently targeted during the 9/11 backlash. On September 16, 2001, Gurpreet Kaur was attacked in Eagan, Minnesota. The Sikh American had just left Rainbow Foods and was walking to her car when a group of teenage boys followed her, pushed her against her vehicle, and began beating her. Kaur told the *Minneapolis Star Tribune* that one of the assailants punched her in the stomach and elbowed her in the back.[66] The assailants left no doubt in her mind that her attack was in response to 9/11, telling her that it was what her people deserved.[67] Because of her turban, she wasn't sure if the attackers recognized that she was a woman. Kaur, who was originally from Bethlehem, Pennsylvania, reported that her assault shook her faith in America, making her feel like an alien in her own land.[68]

Dastaar-wearing Sikh women were also attacked in California. On September 30, 2001, Swaran Kaur Bhullar was stabbed while sitting in her convertible in Miramar. On the afternoon of the attack, the 52-year old South Asian left her house and was driving to her family's video store to work the evening shift. She told the *Los Angeles Times* that she felt happy during her commute, anticipating a pleasant day of doing business.[69] Shortly after she stopped at a traffic light at the north gate of the Marine Corps Air Station, two men on a black motorbike pull up next to her and yanked her door open.[70] According to the *Daily News*, one of men shouted that he was going to slash her throat in retribution for what she had done to them.[71] When Bhullar heard these words, she crouched defensively under the steering wheel, raising her elbows to protect her neck.[72] The attackers stabbed her twice in the head before speeding away upon hearing an approaching car. Bleeding profusely from her wounds, she drove to her store to get help, too frightened to ask roadside strangers for assistance. Her customers saw her disheveled appearance and helped her get into the store. She was taken to a local hospital, where physicians closed and sutured her head wounds.

Bhullar, who had emigrated from Kenya in 1988, was certain she was the victim of a backlash crime. Because of the assailant's words, she was convinced she was targeted because the men saw her turban and mistakenly associated her with the 9/11 hijackers. Despite evidence to the contrary, investigating officers refused to acknowledge the bias component of the attack. According to the *San Diego Union Tribune*, detective Sharlene Ramirez publicly speculated that the stabbing was likely a result of road rage, instead of backlash bias.[73]

Because the assault was so sudden, Bhullar told the *Los Angeles Times* that she was unable to give investigators a detailed description of her attackers, noting only that they were male adults and that one of them had red hair.[74] She was unable to get the motorcycle's license plate. When no witnesses came forward, police offered a $1,000 reward, hoping it might generate new leads.

A year after the attack, Bhullar continued to be shaken from the stabbing. She told the *Los Angeles Times* that she stopped taking carefree drives with the windows rolled down and the doors unlocked.[75] Worried that her attackers might return and try to kill her again at the same traffic light, her daily commute became a source of acute anxiety. She also became excessively concerned about Sikh friends and family members, cautioning them to lock their doors and windows when driving in the area.

According to the *Los Angeles Times*, Bhullar was appreciative of the community support she received after her attack, particularly a letter signed by 300 members of a neighborhood church.[76] She was also grateful of the responsiveness of the local police. Although she continued to view the U.S. as a beautiful country, she remained concerned that South Asians were becoming too terrified to wear ethnic clothing in public. Although Bhullar was the first 9/11 backlash victim in San Diego County, there were scores of other incidents in that area in the weeks following her stabbing. The *Los Angeles Times* reported that a year after 9/11, only two of the 93 reported crimes were close to being solved.[77]

POST-9/11 ATTACKS ON CHILDREN AND TEENS

On occasion, 9/11 backlash victims included small children. In many states, minority youths were targeted by bigots. In West Seattle, an eight-year old Muslim girl was assaulted by a 19-year old man who pushed her off of her bike and told her to go back to where she came from.[78] Genuinely confused, the little girl asked the man why he wanted her to go back to California.[79] According to the publication *Colorlines*, the attack left the girl with a large scar on her face.[80]

Other Muslim children were also singled out in the aftermath of the terrorist strikes. The Center for the Prevention of Hate Violence reported that at the height of the 9/11 backlash, two Muslim boys were jumped on their way home from school.[81]

Muslim teenagers were also targeted. On September 16, 2001, a 16-year old Somali girl was assaulted at a gas station in West Seattle. The attack began when three white men pulled their car up alongside her and began screaming at her. According to police statements in the *Columbian*, the men shouted that they hated the Muslim girl's religion and proclaimed that she should be evicted from the U.S.[82] They then pulled a knife and cut the bottom of her dress.[83] Some news sources reported that the underage victim was also stabbed by her assailants.[84] When she broke free and ran into a store for help, the attackers drove off.

On occasion, Sikh teenagers were singled out during the 9/11 backlash. For example, the September 18, 2001 issue of the *Boston Globe* reported that two Sikh teens were assaulted with paintball guns in the aftermath of 9/11.[85]

SEPTEMBER 2001 VEHICULAR ATTACKS

Along with bias-motivated physical assaults, minorities were attacked by angry motorists during the 9/11 backlash. These assailants used their vehicles as weapons, attempting to crash into or run over Muslim and Sikh community members. The *Richmond Times-Dispatch* reported that on the same day as the terrorist strikes, Amandeep Singh Sidhu, a Norfolk-born business analyst at the Department of Defense, was run off the road in Northern Virginia by an enraged driver who mistakenly associated the Sikh driver with Taliban terrorists.[86]

In other states, nativists in cars scapegoated Arab immigrants. On September 13, 2001, Abdul Mohammed, a sophomore at the College of Staten Island, was targeted near the campus, when he was attempting to cross Richmond Road. The Yemeni student saw a car approaching, and noticed the driver shaking his fist and pointing a finger at him. The driver then started speeding up and coming right at him, deliberately trying to run him down. Mohammed told the *New York Daily News* that he relied on his physical conditioning as a soccer player to jump out of the way of the oncoming vehicle, which was driven by a skinhead.[87] This racist incident upset his CSI soccer teammates, including those mourning friends or family members killed on 9/11. For instance, Mitchell Poormand, a midfielder with a Syrian mother and Iranian father, lost an uncle in the World Trade Center attacks.[88]

In the days that followed, hostile drivers continued to vent their rage at American minorities. Because of their visibility, Muslim women who wore hijabs were often targeted by other motorists. In Huntington, New York, an enraged man attempted to run over a Pakistani woman in the aftermath of 9/11.[89] According to police reports, Adam Lang, a drunken 75-year old man, revved his car engine for several minutes outside the Walt Whitman mall before driving directly at a Muslim woman waiting on the sidewalk. The *San Francisco Chronicle* reported that the woman survived by jumping out of the way and entering a nearby store in an attempt to escape her attacker.[90] Lang followed her and threatened to kill her for destroying the U.S.

Sikhs were similarly targeted. On September 16, 2001, two truck drivers used their vehicles to threaten Dr. Rajwant Singh, president of the Sikh Council On Religion and Education. While making dangerous maneuvers on Capital beltway 495, they nearly caused an accident, practically driving Singh off the road.[91] At the time of the incident, Singh, a resident of Fairfax, Virginia, was en route to donate blood to help victims of the terrorist strikes.

Sometimes, drivers with guns attempted to shoot Sikh motorists in the aftermath of the terrorist strikes. On September 19, 2001, 21-year old Satpreet Singh was traveling from Frederick, Maryland to Mechanicsburg, Pennsylvania, when a bigoted motorist began harassing him. *India-West* reported that Singh had just started driving on a sparsely-populated highway north of Route 15 when he noticed a blue pickup truck tailgating him.[92] The white male driver, wearing sunglasses and a baseball hat, began making obscene hand gestures at Singh, giving him the finger. Singh told *India-West* that he decided to ignore him, hoping to defuse the situation by continuing to drive.[93] According to Singh, the other motorist then made a threatening gesture with his hand, pretending to shoot him with a gun. Frightened by the non-verbal death threat, Singh accelerated, changing lanes and passing a 16-wheeler ahead of him. Blocked by another car in the right lane and the pickup truck on the left, Singh was forced to slow down. When Sikh realized that the pickup driver had rolled down his window and was pointing a rifle at him, he began frantically accelerating. The Sikh heard a shot, and saw the other driver reverse directions on the road. The 21-year old web designer told the *Washington Post* that he was considerably shaken after the incident.[94] Frederick police investigated the shooting as a likely bias-crime, triggered by the victim's South Asian appearance.

South Asians were also singled out in North Carolina. In mid-September, an enraged motorist tried to run down a South Asian man in an apparent backlash attack. According to the *Wall St. Journal*, Madhusudan Natarajan, a 29-year old neurobiologist from Plainsboro, was exiting a grocery store when he noticed a man in a car glaring at him.[95] As Natarajan approached his car, the man suddenly swerved towards him intentionally, as though he meant to hit him. In response to the incident, Natarajan decided to shave his beard at his fiancée's urging, worried that other nativists might try to harm him because he was of Indian ancestry.[96]

Some South Asians were targeted by enraged drivers on more than one occasion. The *Boston Globe* reported that Singh Khalsa, a therapist and yoga trainer, was attacked twice by motorists shortly after 9/11.[97] In each instance, a car with several men deliberately tried to run him off the road.

Along with South Asians, Latinos and other olive-skinned people were targeted by bigoted motorists who mistook them for Arabs or Muslims. According to the *Los Angeles Times*, a Hispanic man was attacked in the Antelope Valley by two white construction workers from Lancaster in a post-9/11 crime.[98] On September 28, 2001, 20-year old Mark Martin and his uncle, 34-year old Timothy Martin, tailgated 47-year old Gerald Pimental on the Antelope Valley Freeway and repeatedly bumped his vehicle.[99] Once Pimental arrived home, he fumbled with the key and decided to run to the rear of the house, where he smashed a window and climbed inside. The assailants kicked in the front door and entered Pimental's residence, attacking him while pejoratively referring to him as an Iranian.[100] Pimental then ran next door and asked his neighbors to call 911. Realizing his 15-year old daughter was upstairs in his home, Pimental ran back to his house and grabbed a baseball bat to defend his child against the intruders.[101] The two men overpowered Pimental and began beating him with their fists. The police arrived on the scene, and arrested the two assailants. According to the *Daily News*, an investigating officer concluded that the suspects were motivated by bias after conducting an interview confirming that the assailants thought Pimental was a Middle Easterner responsible for the terrorist strikes.[102]

Latinos were also attacked in other parts of California. The *Los Angeles Times* reported that in San Dimas, six men in a car pulled a Hispanic man out of his car and threatened him at gunpoint for being from the Middle East.[103] When the victim addressed them in Spanish, they realized he was not an Arab and left him alone.

AND THE ATTACKS CONTINUE...

In the weeks and months following 9/11, hate crimes continued taking place in many regions of the country. The *Los Angeles Times* reported that at approximately 8:20 p.m. on October 1, 2001, an arsonist threw a Molotov cocktail at a window of a hotel room occupied by an Arab-American guest.[104] Police determined that the assailant targeted the victim because of his ethnicity, and followed him to determine where he was staying. The window screen prevented the bomb from entering the man's room at the Country Inn and Suites in Ontario, California.

Arab-Americans were occasionally assaulted in New Jersey, a state with a high Middle Eastern and Muslim population. According to the October 3, 2001 issue of *Asianweek*, Charles Harvey, a 23-year old man from Hamilton, shouted ethnic slurs at an Arab-American man and his son.[105] New Jersey police reports noted that the father used his cane to defend himself against the attacker, who demanded money from the pair while threatening them with a knife. Harvey was later charged with aggravated assault, robbery, and weapons offenses.

In some instances, hate crimes took place in crowded public places. Inside a bar in the northern part of Costa Mesa, California, assailants viciously beat an Arab man on October 7, 2001. Police sergeant Dale Birney told the *Orange County Register* that the attack was clearly a 9/11 backlash hate crime, since the perpetrators made several references to 'Arabs' and 'Afghanistanians' during the assault.[106]

Sikhs continued to be targeted by bigots in the fall of 2001. The *Richmond Times-Dispatch* reported that Amandeep Singh Sidhu, the same defense analyst who was targeted by an angry motorist in Northern Virginia shortly after 9/11, was subjected to other hate crimes in the area.[107] In one particularly disturbing incident, a bigot at a restaurant flipped a table onto his lap.[108] As a turban-wearing Sikh, Sidhu was also bothered when a Richmond restaurant that he and his family often patronized suddenly started requiring patrons to remove any headwear as a condition to being served.[109]

South Asians were also singled out in Southern California. The *Los Angeles Times*, *India-West*, and the *Orange County Register* reported on the brutal beating of an American-born man of Asian Indian ancestry outside an Anaheim karaoke bar.[110] On October 20, 2001, "Sundeep," a physical therapist who worked at USC's hospital, was celebrating his 27th birthday with friends and family members.[111] As the birthday party guests exited the establishment at around 1:00 a.m. Sunday, they were approached by a group of Asians, around 18 to 21 years old, who were possibly of Korean descent. The nine trouble-makers, including two girls, began taunting Sundeep, his relatives, and his friends, making derogatory slurs about Middle Easterners.[112] The abusive youths then assaulted the South Asians, who were approaching their respective cars in different parts of the parking lot. The assailants first attacked Sundeep's brother-in-law, knocking off his visor and hitting him in the face when he tried to pick it up.

Sundeep told *India-West* that when he begged the assailants to stop, they jumped him and the others, punching them repeatedly in the face and head.[113] When he finally managed to get away, he realized that the two young women were threatening his wife, using profanities and accusing her and the others of being from the Middle East.[114] At this point, Sundeep realized that his attackers were blaming them for 9/11. To protect his spouse, he pulled her behind him. The assailants then uttered additional ethnic slurs about Middle Easterners.

One attacker approached Sundeep from the back, hit him in the face, and knocked him to the ground, punching him repeatedly.[115] He felt an enormous pain, realizing he had begun to bleed profusely. While blood was drenching his clothes, another attacker pounced on him. He attempted to stagger to his feet, but his attackers punched him in the ribs and kicked him behind his head. In the course of this vicious beating, the assailants shattered Sundeep's jaw, damaging it so severely that it had to be wired shut for seven weeks.[116] To interrupt the assault, Sundeep's sister yelled that the police were on their way. At this point, the attackers ran to their cars and drove off.

The *Orange County Register* reported that Sundeep was out of work for two months because of his extensive injuries, which prevented him from taking care of his patients at the hospital.[117] Months after the attack, he continued to have major fractures in his jaw, hardware in his mouth, and facial muscle spasms. The beating also destroyed the nerves to his teeth, causing a loss of sensation.

Sundeep told the *Los Angeles Times* that the ferociousness of the 9/11 backlash shocked and disturbed him, making him fear for his life in his own country.[118] By raising public awareness about his assault, he hoped that law enforcement officials would make solving backlash hate crimes a departmental priority.

Many South Asians were outraged that the police were investigating the attack as a felony assault instead of as a bias crime, particularly since anti-Arab ethnic slurs were used during the attack. Sgt. Rick Martinez told the *Los Angeles Times* that investigating officers had not been able to ascertain what triggered the fight, and hoped to someday unearth the motive of the gang-beating.[119] Area minorities were disturbed by the police's inability to understand that the crime was motivated by post-9/11 hate.

Mary Anne Foo, the executive director of the Orange County Asian and Pacific Islander Community Alliance, told *India-West* that she was dismayed that Asian perpetrators attacked the South Asian group.

She described the beatings as a heinous crime made even more shocking by the fact that the assault was committed by minority perpetrators.[120] To help Sundeep and the other victims of the attack, Ken Inouye of the California Association of Human Relations offered a $1,000 reward for information about the attackers and another $1,000 to cover some of the victims' extensive medical expenses.

Despite news stories urging tolerance, hate crimes continued to occur. On one occasion, a minority reporter was attacked while covering the 9/11 backlash. Pakistani journalist Haider Rizvi was beaten in New York, where he was interviewing hate crime victims. *The New York Times* reported that Rizvi, a self-described atheist, was exiting a Pakistani-owned grocery store on Fifth Avenue when three men surrounded him and began hassling him.[121] They asked him if he was from Pakistan, and compared him to Osama bin Laden. The men then began kicking and punching the reporter until he lost consciousness.[122] When he woke up at New York Methodist Hospital, he realized that he was missing his front tooth, which had been knocked down in the attack.

Instead of abating, the backlash continued in the months and years following 9/11. On occasion, black assailants targeted African immigrants. The November 17, 2001 issue of the *Atlanta Inquirer* reported that two African-American men assaulted two Sudanese refugees because of their Muslim-sounding names.[123] Civil rights organizations were dismayed that area minorities were attacking immigrants instead of promoting tolerance.

ASSAULTS, 2002

While hate crimes were taking place across the U.S., Americans were being entertained by television programs and movies depicting Middle Easterners and Muslims as villains. In her essay, "Representations of Arabs and Muslims in Post-9/11 TV Dramas," Evelyn Alsultany takes issue with shows with Islamophobic characters and plot lines.[124] Other scholars have challenged cinematic depictions of Arabs in the aftermath of the terrorist strikes. In his book, Guilty, Jack Shaheen analyzed hundreds of movies released after 9/11 and found that many of these films depicted Arabs and Muslims as dangerous criminals.[125] According to Shaheen, these Islamophobic and racist movies perpetuated harmful stereotypes of vulnerable ethnic communities. For example, he notes that in the Jackie Chan movie, *Gen Y Cops*, Asian heroes fight evil Arabs.[126] In one scene, the swarthy villain Achmed and his henchmen pay $400 million for a destructive robot. Their dastardly schemes unravel when the Gen-Y cops appear and kill the Arab criminals. This movie aired on television in the U.S. on February 23, 2002, and was released on DVD later that year.

On occasion, even X-rated movies employed Middle Eastern villains. According to Shaheen, the porn movie, *Mummy Raider*, released in the U.S. on June 8, 2002, suggests an "Arab-Nazi" connection by showing a rampaging Middle Eastern monster attempting to revive Hitler's legions from the dead.[127] At the conclusion of the film, the protagonist Misty foils the Arab mummy's destructive plans.

The same summer this Islamophobic movie was released, Crystal Ali-Khan, a 24-year old mother of three, was attacked by an enraged Anglo woman. Immediately prior to the assault, Ali-Khan had gotten out of her car to buy hay fever medicine at a pharmacy near her Southwest Houston home. Ali-Khan told the *Houston Chronicle* that she had just left her vehicle when the Anglo woman abruptly body-slammed her, twisting her hijab into a strangulation hold and limiting her ability to breathe.[128] Ali-Khan told her attacker that she would be facing a lawsuit if she didn't release her immediately. The Anglo woman responded that she would not be prosecuted for the crime because she was a Christian.[129] During the assault, the Anglo woman compared Ali-Khan to the 9/11 terrorists.[130] The police eventually arrived and took an incident report. Area Muslims were frightened by the attack and concerned that Ali-Khan might lose her children to state custody because she had momentarily left them unattended. Judy Hay, a spokeswoman for Children's Protective Services, confirmed that her agency was investigating Ali-Khan since Texas state law prohibits leaving children under seven unsupervised in a motor vehicle.[131]

In the months after 9/11, hate crimes took place in Mississippi. The Memphis *Commercial Appeal* reported that many of Mississippi's 2,000 Muslims experienced backlash-related problems, including being pelted with food in public settings.[132] Many minority members were dismayed that authorities were not doing more to stem the abuse.

In other parts of the country, public officials took action to curb the 9/11 backlash. In Nebraska, a hate crime against a Muslim man in Omaha prompted Governor Mike Johanns to proclaim October 3, 2002 "Stop the Hate" Vigil Day. [133] Clergy members, activists, and students congregated at the state office building to express their outrage over post-9/11 hate crimes. The *Omaha World* reported that at this event, community members spoke out about the anti-Muslim assault and other bias-motivated crimes in the state, including an attack on a Pakistani business owner who was beaten and verbally abused because of his race.[134]

A 2002 report conducted by the Center for the Prevention of Hate Violence documented numerous post-9/11 bias attacks targeting American minorities. On one occasion, a vandal threw a rock through a Somali woman's living room window.[135] In another incident, an enraged driver attempted to run a Muslim woman off of I-295.[136]

ASSAULTS, 2003

The 9/11 backlash intensified shortly before the beginning of the Iraq War. According to the *Washington Post*, Muslims were physically assaulted in California, Georgia, New Jersey, and South Carolina in the six weeks before the start of this international conflict.[137]

On occasion, the attacks were incredibly brutal. In Yorba Linda, California, a mob of white supremacists severely beat up Lebanese-American teenagers and injured several of their friends. According to the *Orange County Register*, the hate crime took place on February 22, 2003, when Rashid Alam, his brother, and some friends met at San Antonio Park with the intent to go bowling.[138] Before they knew what was happening, a mob suddenly attacked them. The *Los Angeles Times* reported that Rashid Alam was pummeled by approximately 20 teens, many of whom were armed with bats, beer bottles, screwdrivers, and a golf club.[139] Witnesses reported that the assailants shouted white supremacist slogans as they stripped off their t-shirts, and at least one of the attackers had a swastika tattoo.[140] Michael Tinio, a neighborhood resident, told the *Los Angeles Times* that he saw the assailants surround Rachid Alam and beat him severely.[141] The mob finally stopped brutalizing Alam after one of the attackers repeatedly jumped up and down on the boy's head, stomping him so violently that it looked like he was being killed.[142] According to the *Los Angeles Times*, witnesses reported that the white supremacist attackers used numerous anti-Arab racial slurs and profanities during the beating, calling the brothers 'camel jockeys' and 'Arab pieces of shit.'[143] After this attack, Alam was left with a fractured jaw, bruises around his eyes, shattered facial bones, and two metal plates in his cheeks.[144]

Ignoring detailed witness statements to the contrary, Sgt. Jack Conklin told the *Los Angeles Times* that there was no conclusive proof that assailants shouted 'white power' slogans or used anti-Arab slurs during the attack, although he acknowledged that some of the 20 assailants had white supremacist ties.[145] Conklin also challenged witness statements that weapons were used because bats and clubs were not recovered at the scene. Witnesses were puzzled by Conklin's specious conclusion, pointing out that the fleeing assailants left with the golf club and baseball bats before the police arrived.

The victims' relatives saw a connection between the attack and a rise in anti-Arab sentiment resulting from the escalating conflict in Iraq. Ahmed Alam, the victim's father, was disturbed that authorities tried to minimize the incident and prevent the family from speaking about what happened. He told the *Los Angeles Times* that a detective instructed him to remain quiet about the incident pending the outcome of the investigation.[146] Conklin defended the police officer's request that they hide the beating from public view, maintaining that the case's low profile facilitated the investigation.[147] Questioning the veracity of this explanation, many Southern California Muslims and Arabs became convinced that the police were minimizing the attacks and dismissing witness accounts because they realized that such horrifying hate crimes would bring unwanted national attention to the city. Despite police attempts to keep the attack under wraps, the vicious beating became a central topic of discussion at Esperanza High School in Anaheim, where some of those involved attended class.

Alam's father, who owned an Arabic and English language newspaper in the city, became increasingly outraged by the police handling of the case and investigators' failure to alert others about the unprovoked attack against his sons and seven of their friends.[148] Members of the Arab community were also outraged at the police's failure to charge the assailants with a hate crime, arresting only two of the 20 perpetrators a few days after the beating and charging them with misdemeanor assault.

The Alam brothers filed a lawsuit in Orange County Superior Court against four of their assailants and the parents of the violent minors. In this suit, the Lebanese-American brothers demanded compensatory and punitive damages for battery, assault, and civil rights violations. Rashid Alam told the *Orange County Register* that he hoped that his attackers would be held accountable for their actions, reminding the public that he should not be considered a terrorist simply because he was an Arab Muslim.[149] Los Angeles newspapers did not release the names of the minor defendants or any of the parents who were included in the Alams' suit. Although the white supremacist youths were seen gang-beating the Arab-American teens in front of witnesses, at least one of the defendants' parents disputed the Alams' version of events.

The Alam family's attorney, Federicko Castelan Sayre, told the *Orange County Register* that the February 22 attack demonstrated how vulnerable Muslims and Arabs were in the U.S.[150] Sayre, who represented Rodney King in his civil suit against the LAPD, characterized Alam's injuries as being more severe than King's.

One of the white supremacists involved in the attack had gotten into a fight with Rashid Alam the previous summer, according to Mohamed, the victim's 18-year old brother.[151] Some of the defendants named in the suit had participated in an August 2002 altercation with Mohamed Alam after they stole his watch.[152] At the time of this theft, they were caught on videotape spouting racial epithets against Arabs and Muslims while holding up the stolen timepiece.[153] Alam's attorney regarded this videotape as evidence of the attackers' anti-Muslim and anti-Arab bias, viewing the bigotry-motivated robbery and the brutal beating as part of the ongoing 9/11 backlash. Family members were outraged that police were attempting to use this previous attack to suggest that the vicious February 22nd hate crime was somehow provoked or part of an ongoing feud between rival teen gangs.

Speaking through his reconstructed jaw at the Anaheim office of CAIR, Rashid Alam told the *Orange County Register* that he remained traumatized by the attackers who stomped on his head, beat him with golf clubs, and stabbed him with a screwdriver.[154] Along with the insomnia and psychological damage, he also continued to feel excruciating pain from his severe physical injuries, noting that he was still unable to have lateral movement in his jaw months after the attack.[155] His surgeons told him that the beating was so vicious that he was lucky that his long-term injuries weren't far worse.[156]

The Alams' civil suit was filed shortly after Sgt. Jack Conklin submitted the Brea police's findings to the District Attorney's office. Conklin told the *Orange County Register* that his office determined that the beating was a felony assault that involved a hate crime.[157] Members of the Arab and Muslim communities wondered whether Southern California media coverage of the vicious beating played a role in the police's decision to change the charges from misdemeanor to felony assault, and acknowledge the bias motivation of the perpetrators.

Muslims were also targeted in other parts of the country. In Irving, New Jersey, a Pakistani man and his sons were attacked at a Pathmart parking lot.[158] According to the *Star-Ledger*, the assailants knocked the Muslim father on the ground, kicking him in the head, abdomen, and groin.[159] During the attack, the assailants screamed obscenities about Islam, called him a terrorist, and demanded that he return to his own country. Because of the nature of the insults, minority community members viewed the attack as part of the 9/11 backlash.

Attacks continued in the summer of 2003. In Florida, a bigot stabbed an Iraqi-American and called him an Iraqi terrorist.[160] The assailant was later charged with committing a bias assault. Hate crimes also took place in other states. In Pennsylvania, three teenage boys beat up an eight-year old Muslim child. During the attack, they called him 'Saddam Hussein's helper,' and ordered the boy to go back to Iraq.[161]

Throughout the 'War on Terror,' Sikhs were frequently targeted by bigots who associated them with the 9/11 mastermind. On occasion, newspaper employees insensitively reinforced the misperception that Sikhs were associated with al-Qaeda. In October 2003, political cartoonist Carol Lay depicted a Sikh as "Randy bin Laden, Osama's no-good cousin."[162] News of the racist drawing reached South Asia, angering Indians abroad. After United Sikhs organized a protest petition signed by thousands, Lay issued an apology for her hurtful picture.

The same month, a 67-year old Sikh was viciously beaten in Carteret, New Jersey. According to WCBS TV, an assailant knocked Ajit Singh Chima on the ground and punched him repeatedly in the head in late October, 2003.[163] The perpetrator did not steal anything. Many area South Asians saw a connection between the attack and the surge in xenophobia that began after the Twin Towers were destroyed. Some community members were reminded of the Dot-buster crime spree that terrified area residents in the late 1980s and early 1990s.

While post-9/11 hate crimes were taking place, American audiences were watching movies with Middle Eastern villains. In the 2003 movie, *Fire Over Afghanistan*, a thuggish, misogynistic Afghan sadist is shown violently raping Kris, an attractive Western journalist.[164] The film concludes when Captain Walker uses his Black Hawk helicopter to kill the nefarious Afghan villains. Some viewers were alarmed that the movie was fueling Islamophobic sentiment and a climate of bigotry in American neighborhoods, especially since bias attacks were occurring with alarming frequency.

ASSAULTS, 2004

During the Iraq War, veiled Muslims were attacked in many parts of the U.S. In Tampa, Florida, three people assaulted a Muslim girl wearing a hijab in the spring of 2004. According to the *Palm Beach Post*, one of her assailants told her to leave the country.[165] Vicious attacks also took place in Illinois. In Springfield, a knife-wielding assailant stabbed a Muslim woman. The May 3, 2004 issue of the *Washington Post* reported that she was wearing a hijab at the time of the attack.[166]

In Freeport, Illinois, a Muslim convert was assaulted in June 2004. The woman was sitting in her car at a stop sign when she was approached by two women and one man, who asked her for a light. Responding to her veil, the strangers then started kicking her car and shouting anti-Muslim slurs and profanities, instructing her to leave the country.[167] When she got out of her car, her assailants pulled off her head scarf and began punching her repeatedly in the head. After the assault, one of the woman's attackers was charged with misdemeanor battery. Many community members thought that more serious charges were warranted in response to the vicious bias-motivated assault.

Muslim women were also targeted in New York. The *Buffalo News* reported that on July 24, 2004, two white assailants tried to run over two Muslim teenage sisters who wore hijabs.[168] At about 7:45 p.m., two white females in a car threatened and chased Suna and Muntaha Shafie in Buffalo. During the attack, the assailants yelled anti-Muslim and ethnic slurs at the two teens. The driver then accelerated toward the two girls. According to Buffalo police reports, the driver ran over the toes of one girl after she pushed her sister out of the way. As a result of this vehicular assault, the injured girl needed medical treatment to deal with the extensive swelling. Dr. Khalid Qazi, president of the Western New York chapter of the Muslim Public Affairs Council, told the *Buffalo News* that the victims were shocked by the unprovoked attack, since the girls had no previous problems with anyone in the neighborhood.[169] Qazi added that because of escalating Islamophobia in the U.S., many Muslim hate crime victims were becoming increasingly reluctant to draw attention to themselves by contacting police or visiting a hospital.

Muslim men were also attacked the same summer. On June 30, 2004, a white man shouting racial slurs attacked a Muslim shopper of Middle Eastern descent outside of a San Diego grocery store. According to the *San Diego Union-Tribune*, the attack began at about 1:45 p.m. when the white man, who was about 25 to 30 years old, pulled up alongside the Muslim man in Ralph's parking lot on Mira Mesa Blvd. The assailant then punched the victim in the face several times, cutting his lip and knocking out his front tooth. The attacker also shouted anti-Arab racial slurs and used profanity, telling the victim to get out of the country.[170] Ibrahim Hooper, a spokesman for CAIR, told the *San Diego Union-Tribune* that he saw a connection between foreign affairs and domestic hate crimes, noting that spikes in bias attacks often corresponded with increased tensions overseas.[171]

While Muslims were being assaulted, American audiences were being entertained by Muslim and Middle Eastern movie villains. In the 2004 movie, the *Manchurian Candidate*, Denzel Washington's character, Captain Ben Marco, guns down attacking Iraqis during the 1991 "Liberation of Kuwait." Film critic Shaheen was particularly disturbed by a scene featuring a menacing Arab woman in black, arguing that the character made no sense in terms of plot.[172] Nefarious Arab characters also appear in other movies released the same year. In Raptor Island, navy SEALS fight stereotypical Arab terrorists and man-eating dinosaurs.[173] Other movies also portray villains in Middle Eastern dress. The 2004 film, *Flight of the Phoenix*, features desert-dwelling Muslims who ride camels, hide their faces with headscarves, and work as unscrupulous arms merchants.[174] These xenophobic movies transmit the cultural message that non-Westerners should be regarded with hatred and suspicion.

During the summer of 2004, Sikhs were occasionally attacked by bigots who mistook them as Muslim Arab terrorists. One of the most vicious hate crimes took place in New York on July 11, 2004. On that afternoon, Rajinder Singh Khalsa, 50, and Gurucharan Singh, 51, were going to tea at Singh's Tandoori Express restaurant on 101st Ave.[175] As they were walking on Lefferts Blvd., they were verbally harassed and beaten by drunken men attending a christening party at the Il Palazzo di Villa Russo Restaurant. The incident began when two inebriated women attending the gathering began making disparaging remarks about the Sikhs' turbans. Khalsa and Singh responded by explaining that their religious headwear was an important part of their Sikh faith.[176] Their drunken male companions came out and joined in the abuse, mocking the South Asians. According to *India Abroad*, the attack escalated when one of the men pointed to Khalsa's turban and asked him to give him back his curtain.[177] Khalsa once again tried explaining the religious significance of their dastaars, but the restaurant patrons continued the verbal taunting, referring to the religious headwear in derogatory fashion.[178] The men then demanded that the Sikh men take off their turbans and go back to their own country. In response to the harassment, the Sikhs called 911 at about 5:30 p.m.

At this point, the restaurant patrons jumped the two Sikhs. The drunken men knocked Singh's turban on the ground and punched him in the face.[179] When Khalsa tried to intervene, two of the assailants, Salvatore and Nicholas Macelli, attacked him as well, hitting him so hard that he fell to the ground. Khalsa told the *New York Daily News* that his assailants punched him two or three times, causing injuries so severe that he felt the earth moving around.[180] The men continued hitting Khalsa in the face and kicking him in the body until he blacked out. Because the police still hadn't arrived 19 minutes after the initial 911 call, a bystander made a second emergency call at 5:49 p.m., to report that the attack was still in progress. Because the police were still absent from the scene, Villa Russo maitre d' Kim Delucia and her boss intervened with the five men beating up Khalsa, who by this time was collapsed on the ground. By the time the police finally showed up 34 minutes after the first 911 call, the drunken assailants had already fled the scene in two cars.[181]

Khalsa was unable to receive prompt medical attention because it took the ambulance 49 minutes to respond to the first distress call. Paramedics eventually took Khalsa to Jamaica Medical Center. According to Queens District Attorney Richard Brown, Khalsa suffered multiple fractures to his left orbital bone, nose, septum, and sinus. A CAT scan showed that Khalsa had complex fractures so severe that he needed facial reconstruction surgery to help him breathe.[182] The attack also left him with blurred vision, and compromised sight in one eye. Responding to the attack, Khalsa expressed outrage that the intoxicated restaurant patrons assumed he was a terrorist simply because he wore a turban.

Community groups recognized that the assault was a post-9/11 hate crime. Interfaith groups, such as the American Jewish Christian Muslim Alliance, viewed the attack as part of the ongoing backlash, reminding the public that the Sikh victims had nothing to do with the terrorist strikes. The organization also informed the public that Khalsa solicited blood donations to help World Trade Center victims.[183]

The assailants were later apprehended and charged after seven witnesses picked them out of police lineups. Despite the brutality of the bias-motivated crime, the accused men were released on bail. Although both Khalsa and Singh were assaulted, court documents listed Khalsa as the sole victim. According to the *New York Times*, Singh expressed surprise that his name was not included because he was also physically attacked.[184]

Although the drunken restaurant patrons were charged with assault, investigators apparently never considered whether DUI charges might also be warranted, since the attackers drove off while intoxicated. During the trial, Khalsa was able to identify the men who attacked him. Witnesses corroborated the Sikhs' version of events. According to the *New York Post*, Alison Pfluger, one of the party guests, testified that Ryan Meehan taunted the Sikh men and ridiculed their turbans, asking them why they stole the sheets from his house.[185] She also described how the restaurant customers beat Khalsa while he was collapsed on the ground.

The five attackers were eventually convicted in a non-jury trial. Despite the guilty verdict, South Asians and Sikhs were disgusted that Queens Superior Justice Seymour Rotker acquitted the men of the most serious charges, allowing them to dodge hate-crime convictions. The judge concluded that the assault was not a hate crime because the attackers began beating the Sikhs because of their decision to involve the police by calling 911. Khalsa expressed his shock at the judge's failure to recognize that the assault was a hate crime, telling the *New York Post* that the beating was clearly bias-motivated, triggered by his South Asian appearance and religiously-mandated turban.[186]

Because the judge did not convict the batters of hate crimes, he was able to give the assailants light sentences for their roles in the vicious hate-motivated beating. Rotker sentenced Victor Consentino, 58, to only five days in jail and a $250 fine.[187] The judge also convicted Ryan Meeham, 24, and Terrance Lyon, 53, of aggravated harassment, a misdemeanor offense.[188] Rotker failed to give these assailants the maximum penalty for the misdemeanor, sentencing Meeham to a mere 60 days in jail and three years probation. Meeham was also ordered to do 150 hours of community service and take sensitivity training, anger management, and drug counseling. Nicholas Macelli was sentenced to only six months in jail and five years of probation. He was also court-mandated to complete 150 hours of community service with the Sikh Coalition and take sensitivity training and anger management courses. Salvatore Macelli received only two years in state prison and two years of parole supervision. Khalsa told the *New York Post* that he found the sentences completely inadequate, and questioned what constituted a hate crime in the U.S. if his assault did not meet the criteria.[189]

The convicted men were also surprised by the verdict, shocked that they would receive jail sentences for harassing and viciously beating the two Sikhs, something they apparently felt entitled to do with impunity. Expressing no remorse about the attack, Salvatore Macelli told the *New York Daily News* that the American justice system sucked, and that the verdict was a crock of shit.[190] Victor Consentino told the newspaper that he was upset that he and his companions were facing jail time for their conduct, explaining that he never thought in a thousand years such a verdict would be rendered in the U.S.A.[191]

A year after the attack, with the backing of the Sikh Coalition, Khalsa filed a civil suit against the five assailants who beat him. Because of the injuries he sustained, he was unable to work for four months. He also had extensive medical bills because he did not have insurance at the time of the assault. He was also suing the restaurant for irresponsibly serving alcohol to patrons already inebriated. Khalsa said that if he won the case, he intended to donate much of the settlement to a charity.

ASSAULTS, 2005

The 9/11 backlash continued throughout 2005. On August 9, an African-American woman wearing a hijab was threatened and attacked in Arlington, Virginia. The 23-year old Muslim, who was eight months pregnant, was taking a morning walk when three white men in a pick-up truck approached her and began calling her a 'terrorist bitch' and a 'nigger bitch,' demanding that she return to her country of origin.[192] The men drove away but soon afterward decided to return. One of the men, wearing military-style clothing, exited the truck and began shoving her, blocking her path, calling her a terrorist, using profanities, and threatening to beat her.[193] The attacker then rejoined his friends and drove away.

Some activists saw a connection between xenophobic hate crimes and Islamophobic comedies and dramas. A few days after the Arlington bias attack, the film, *Deuce Bigalow: European Gigolo*, was released in American theatres. This movie makes fun of Mahmoud, a dapper Middle Eastern prostitute.[194] Like so many other racist films, it depicts an Arab as a sexual deviant.

As the fourth anniversary of 9/11 approached, minorities in the U.S. continued to feel the effects of the backlash. According to the *New York Community Media Alliance*, Bangladeshi Muslims were targeted by New York bigots in three separate incidents on September 11, 2005.[195] The first attack took place when imam Moulana Muhibbur Rahman was on Roosevelt Avenue in Jackson Heights, en route to a mosque in Woodside, Queens. As he was crossing the street, a Latino teenager assaulted him and then fled the scene.[196] Two community members found Rahman lying in the street and called an ambulance. At Elmhurst Hospital Center, he was treated for injuries to his right elbow and leg.

The same day, two Bangladeshi Performing Arts students were verbally harassed and assaulted by three Latino women on the corner of 36th Avenue and 36th Street.[197] When the Muslim students called the police, responding officers opted against arresting the assailants, who claimed that they were simply participants in a mutual brawl. Some community members wondered if there was a connection between this attack and the assault on the imam.

A third incident took place in Astoria, when a Bangladeshi Muslim was parking his car on 31st Street and Broadway. Moulana Abdul Latif, imam at the Abu Hanifa Mosque, reported that a white woman approached his vehicle and started verbally abusing him.[198] Concerned for his safety, he drove away. Some community members were disappointed that Bangladeshis were still being scapegoated four years after 9/11.

The same month these hate crimes were taking place, television audiences were watching shows depicting American Muslims as terrorists. On September 20, 2005, FOX's hit drama "Bones" first aired "The Man in the SUV." In this disturbing episode, the character Hamid Masruk, the head of the fictitious Arab-American Friendship League, accidentally dies in a botched terrorist bombing. The show's protagonists eventually arrest Masruk's brother Farid shortly before he is able to instigate another attack on American civilians. What makes this episode so alarming is it suggests that the heads of Arab-American organizations are involved in nefarious plots to kill their countrymen. These types of xenophobic shows convey the pernicious message that immigrants and minority community members are in league with America's enemies.

ASSAULTS, 2006

Throughout the country, Sikhs continued to be attacked by bigots who mistook them for al-Qaeda terrorists. On January 21, 2006 in Yuba City, California, several men assaulted Harbans Singh, an 80-year old Sikh. At the time of the incident, Singh was riding his bicycle from Guru Nanak Sikh Temple on Bogue Road to his home in Labor Camp along the Garden highway. According to *India-West*, at about 4:51 p.m., four or five men in an SUV began yelling racial epithets at Singh and hurling rocks at his back.[199] At first, he tried ignoring his attackers. The men in the vehicle then drove ahead of Singh and stopped at a corner, where one man got out and pushed Singh off his bicycle, fracturing his pelvis. At this point, the attackers drove away.

After the attack, a good Samaritan saw the injured Sikh lying on the ground and called an ambulance, assuming that he was the victim of an accident. At a nearby hospital, Singh was treated for his injuries and then released. On January 24, 2006 he was readmitted, still unable to walk because of his broken pelvis.[200]

Singh, who had lived in the U.S. for more than a decade before the attack, told *India-West* that he was deeply troubled by the unprovoked assault, especially since he had changed his style of tying his dastaar after 9/11 to avoid any confusion with the turbans worn by the Taliban.[201] As a Namdhari Sikh, he traditionally tied his religious headwear in the front, but altered this practice so that he would not be mistaken as a terrorist.

Singh was dismayed that his assailants still lumped him with America's enemies.[202] He was also devastated that his pelvic fracture severely limited his mobility and prevented him from biking, one of his favorite activities.

Soon after the attack, Singh gave a detailed account of his assault to the police. He described his assailants as young men, possibly Hispanic, between the ages of 18 and 30. He noted that his attackers were wearing red bandanas and driving a maroon Chevy Tahoe SUV. Although Singh told investigators about the racist and derogatory comments that precipitated the unprovoked attack, the police report omitted mentioning the offensive epithets. Police spokeswoman Shawna Pavy told *India-West* that the assault report did not include any information about racial remarks.[203] Because the report failed to mention the derogatory slurs, police officers were reluctant to view the assault as a hate crime. More than two weeks after assailants taunted Singh and broke his pelvis, police were still debating whether to classify the attack as a bias-motivated assault.[204] Instead of recognizing that police investigators neglected to include vital information in their report, officer Pavy told *India Abroad* that there was nothing to indicate a trend in which people were specifically targeting East Indians as a specific group or individuals.[205] Many members of the Sikh community were dismayed by the police department's reluctance to recognize that Singh's attack was clearly a hate crime. Because Sikh residents comprise 10% of Yuba City's total population, community leaders felt disappointed that the police were ignoring the bias component of the assault, putting area minorities at risk by failing to disseminate details of the crime.

Bias-motivated attacks in the U.S. may have been fueled in part by movies depicting foreigners as murderers. The film, *Munich*, released in the U.S. in January 2006, re-exposed American audiences to the notion that overseas Muslims were civilian-killing terrorists.[206]

While Americans were watching inflammatory movies, bigots were attacking Muslims in various parts of the U.S. *The New York Daily News* reported that on October 29, 2006, shortly before 8:00 p.m., five Orthodox Jewish teens brutally beat a Pakistani immigrant in Brooklyn.[207] On the evening of the attack, the 24-year old victim, Shaid Amber, was eating ice cream outside a Midwood Dunkin' Donuts when the teenagers approached him and asked him if he was Muslim. When Amber replied affirmatively, one of them spat on him and another knocked the ice cream out of his hands. They then jumped him. Amber was terrified by the viciousness of the assault, telling the *New York Daily News* that one of the assailants held his hands while the others repeatedly punched and kicked him.[208] During the beating, the assailants screamed anti-Muslim religious slurs and profanities.[209] They also blamed Amber for the 9/11 attacks, calling him a terrorist, accusing him of harming the U.S., and ordering him out of the country.[210] The victim's father, Umbar Islam, told the *New York Daily News* that his son's assailants showed no mercy, breaking his son's nose, ripping his jacket, and punching him so severely that he began bleeding profusely from his multiple injuries.[211] He was particularly upset that one of the attackers had beaten his son with brass knuckles.

The *New York Daily News* reported that a Jewish girl, horrified by the gang beating, called 911 to report that 10 to 12 youths were pummeling a South Asian man.[212] When the paramedics arrived, Amber was taken to a nearby hospital, where he received fifteen stitches and reconstructive surgery to repair his broken nose. The attack left him with two black eyes and extensive facial injuries.

According to the *New York Daily News*, Yitzi Horowitz, 15, David Brach, 15, Yossi Friedman, 17, Shulomi Bitton, 16, and Benjamin Wasserman, 16, all of Borough Park, were charged with multiple offenses, including assault as a hate crime, gang assault, menacing, harassment, and criminal possession of a weapon.[213] Horowitz and Brach were released on their own recognizance. The other three defendants were ordered to pay a $5,000 cash bond before being released.

Amber, a photo lab technician who had lived in the U.S. since 2000, told the *New York Daily News* that despite the emotionally-traumatizing assault, he continued to believe in interfaith co-existence.[214] The attack also did not alter his admiration of America and its commitment to cultural pluralism.

Many community members hoped that news of the beating would not escalate ethnic tensions in the area. According to the *Forward*, the assault took place in an area of New York with a high concentration of members of the JDL and Kahane Chai or 'Kach,' organizations that call for aggressive confrontation with Muslim opponents of Israel.[215] The area also had a growing Pakistani population, leading to significant intermingling between the two communities. Jewish and Muslim community members were outraged by the attack, and were dismayed when the perpetrators and one public official accused Amber of instigating the beating, despite witness statements and police reports to the contrary.

The same year, Muslims were singled out in other parts of the U.S. On November 14, 2006, a 42-year old North African Muslim was badly beaten in Melbourne, Florida. While the attack was in progress, one of the assailants shouted anti-Arab slurs and profanities.[216] Community members saw the hate crime as a manifestation of area Islamophobia, which had intensified after the terrorist strikes.

ASSAULTS, 2007

Throughout 2007, Muslims continued to be targeted by bigots. On January 21, 2007, white male assailants attacked a 26-year old Yemeni man outside a restaurant in Lackawanna, New York. During the assault, one of the men used profane language and an anti-Arab slur.[217] Another attacker grabbed the victim from behind and threw him on the ground, rendering him unconscious. As a result of the bias-motivated attack, the victim suffered a broken nose and a fracture under one eye. He also required six stitches on his face and staples on the back of his head.

The same week, Arabs were singled out in other states. In Florida, Derar Ahmad, a 30-year old Largo resident of Palestinian descent, was assaulted on January 24, 2007. The *St. Petersburg Times* reported that at the time of the attack, the Arab-American was shopping at Sam's Club in Clearwater, speaking to his wife in Arabic on his cell phone.[218] Hearing the non-English conversation, another customer ran up to Ahmad and began shouting ethnic and religious slurs. According to the *St. Petersburg Times*, Ahmad's assailant used anti-Muslim language and profanities, making derogatory comments about Islam and the prophet Mohammed.[219] The assailant then started jabbing Ahmad in the head with his finger, telling him to go back to his own country. Although there were many witnesses to the attack, no store employee came to Ahmad's assistance. When the security guard approached, he failed to protect Ahmad, simply telling the two men to take their business outside. Deborah Butler, one of the customers who witnessed the racial bullying, called 911. The security guard then warned Ahmad's assailant to leave the store before the police arrived. When the attacker ran to his car to avoid the authorities, Ahmad attempted to follow him to write down his license plate number. The security guard then stopped and detained the victimized Palestinian-American, preventing him from getting the information he needed to bring his attacker to justice. Ahmad was shaken by the assault, telling the *St. Petersburg Times* that the assailant and the security guard made him feel sub-human.[220] Butler was so disturbed by Ahmad's mistreatment and the security guard's conduct that she decided never to shop at Sam's Club again. Instead of assisting Ahmad, Clearwater police Cpl. Robert Fava refused to file a complaint or document the incident.

The same month these attacks were taking place, American audiences were viewing television dramas that demonized Muslims. In January 2007, the show "Shark," starring James Woods, featured an Islamophobic story line. In the episode, "The Wrath of Khan," a villainous South Asian international arms merchant kidnaps Casey Woodland, the show's sympathetic blonde assistant district attorney. Because the terrorist bomber's Muslim surname was repeated dozens of times throughout the program, viewers learn to associate it with danger and attacks on American civilians. In the months that followed, Muslims continued to be targeted in many parts of the country.

In Palmdale, California, a Muslim student was taunted and assaulted after a showing of the movie, *Not Without My Daughter*.[221] This 1991 drama pits a sympathetic white Western wife against her sexist Iranian husband, who kidnaps their daughter and takes her to Iran, in the hopes of raising her in subservient fashion. Muslims in this film appear as sexist, law-defying Neanderthals, who are intolerant of liberated Western women. Activists felt that pernicious cinematic depictions of Muslims contributed to a climate of Islamophobia in the U.S.

Throughout the spring, Florida Muslims were singled out in many parts of the state. The Panama City *News Herald* reported that in May 2007, Thomas Plaisted, a 60-year old school bus driver, cursed and spat at

Muslim children at a Taco Bell in Lynn Haven.[222] The incident happened after Asma Sidani, a 36-year old Lebanese-American who wore the hijab, entered the fast food restaurant with her four children. Sidani went to the counter to order while her kids sat at a nearby table. Plaisted approached the unattended children, cursing them and making threatening gestures. While uttering anti-Muslim comments, Plaisted spit food on Sidani's five-year old son. Sidani told the *News Herald* that she realized that the man was threatening her children when her five year old son ran up, grabbed her leg, and informed her that the stranger wanted to break his neck.[223] She then saw the angry man staring at her children and pounding his fist into his palm. At that point, another customer told her that the stranger had spit on her son. Sidani then took her boy back to the table, told him to remain there, and approached Plaisted, asking him if something was the matter. In response, the man began screaming profanities and making derogatory references to all Muslims, including her two daughters.

As he got up to refill his drink, he shoved Sidani's 11-year old son. Plaisted's behavior became so inappropriate that the restaurant manager, other employees, and customers demanded that he leave. One customer recognized Plaisted by name and wrote down his license plate number.[224] Before Plaisted exited the facility, he stepped toward Sidani as though he was about to hit her, but backed down after the manager came to her defense.

When Sidani called police to report the incident, the responding officer refused to take her complaint or interview witnesses, who had waited at the restaurant to give statements. According to the *News Herald*, the policeman trivialized the assault and told her that cussing was not a crime in the U.S.[225] He refused to document the attack, telling her simply to go home and forget about the incident. Sidani found the officers' response unacceptable, outraged that a bigot could threaten, spit on, and shove her Muslim son without facing any consequences.[226] After the other customers urged her to be persistent, she went to the Bay county sheriff's office to complain. A deputy took her report, and told her he would keep her informed about the status of the investigation.

She and her husband called the police station later to discuss the case. They spoke with Sgt. Jim Smith, the same officer she had met earlier at the Taco Bell. He told the Sidanis that he had no intention of filing charges and hung up on them. Asma Sidanis told the *News Herald* that the officers acted unprofessionally at this time, baiting her husband to act violently by offering to give him Plaisted's address and photo.[227]

The experience left her feeling disgusted. She told the *News Herald* that her family members were American citizens, and they were dismayed to face religious discrimination in their own country.[228] She also felt saddened that her hijab would engender so much hatred in the U.S. in the years after 9/11.

Perhaps in response to local media coverage criticizing the police's handling of the situation, the Sidanis finally succeeded in getting officers to take an incident report. According to Lynn Haven Police Chief David Messer, the department decided to conduct an internal investigation and found that the officers violated departmental policy by failing to investigate the situation. Because of their poor job performance, Sgt. James Smith and Officer Chris Faircloth received official letters of reprimand.[229] Ahmed Bedier of Tampa CAIR was pleased that the two responding officers were held accountable for their failure to protect the public but said that a third-party investigation was necessary to determine whether the officers acted inappropriately out of racial bias.

Following the incident, many members of the community worried that minority students might be at risk if Plaisted continued working as a school bus driver, especially since he had shoved Sidani's son for being Muslim and threatened to break the boy's neck. Bay County School Board Chairwoman Donna Allen said that Plaisted was entitled to due process, and that school superintendent James McCalistwer had to make a recommendation to the board before taking any action.[230] She added that the issue was not on the schedule for the next board meeting. Many community members were outraged that the bigoted bus driver was allowed to continue working with local children. In court, Plaisted pleaded not guilty to two counts of evidencing prejudice while committing an offense.

The *News Herald* reported that the two hate crime charges against Plaisted were eventually dropped because the Sidanis wanted to spare their children the trauma of being deposed by lawyers and testifying in court.[231] Assistant public defender Matt Meredith said that no plea offers were made by the state to resolve the case without a trial. Area Muslims felt that authorities had completely mishandled the situation, and their incompetence endangered the minority children the school district put in Plaisted's daily care.

The same month that Plaisted targeted the Muslim family, American movie audiences were watching films that disseminated negative stereotypes of Middle Easterners. In *Home of the Brave*, Iraqi characters ambush and kill U.S. troops on a humanitarian mission. This movie, released across the U.S. in May 2007, pits fictitious Arab terrorists against the two central protagonists, a sympathetic black man and white woman, played by Samuel L. Jackson and Jessica Biel. Because of the ruthlessness of the Iraqi villains, the U.S. troops appear justified in killing scores of Arabs in retaliation.

In the months that followed, American bigots continued assaulting area minorities, accusing them of being affiliated with the Taliban. On July 14, 2007, 53-year old Joseph Frank Silva and his 9-year old wife, Georgia, attacked three Indian Americans: 38-year old Vishal Wadhwa, his fiancée, and her cousin. The two South Asian-American women were walking along El Dorado beach in Lake Tahoe when one of the Silvas called them 'Indian sluts and whores.'[232] Wadhwa approached the Silvas to ask why they were harassing his wife and her cousin. At that point, the two bigots from Fairfield unleashed a volley of ethnic slurs, calling them 'Indian garbage,' 'terrorists,' and 'relatives of Osama bin Laden.'[233] The Silvas also called Wadhwa an 'Arab asshole,' mistaking him for a Middle Easterner.[234] The three Indian Americans tried fleeing, but the Silvas followed them and continued their verbal harassment. When Wadhwa went to call the police, the Silvas attacked him in the parking lot, knocking him down. While Georgia Silva held Wadhwa on the ground, her husband kicked him and punched him repeatedly in the face.[235] As a result of this assault, emergency medical personnel took him to a local hospital where he was treated for facial contusions, multiple broken bones, and a fractured orbital socket. Wadhwa's injuries were so severe that his physicians predicted he would likely have dizzy spells throughout his life.

Officers responding to a 911 call arrested the Silvas at the scene. Joseph and Georgia Silva were initially charged in the El Dorado County Superior court with felony assault with hate crime enhancements. At their August 22 arraignment, the Silvas pled not guilty to all charges.

Civil rights attorney Harmeet Dhillon viewed the attack as part of the ongoing 9/11 backlash, telling *India-West* that he was dismayed that bias crimes continued to take place so many years after the terrorist strikes. He also felt that anti-Sikh attacks seemed to be accelerating in their frequency.[236]

Members of the Indian community were outraged when local Judge Suzanne Kingsbury dismissed the felony assault charges and ruled the crime a misdemeanor, despite substantial evidence that the brutal attack was motivated by racial bigotry. Wadhwa was also stunned by the court's decision, telling *India-West* that the judge's ruling made him feel as if the whole Tahoe region was dangerous for South Asians and other people of color.[237]

Once the felony charges and hate enhancements were dismissed, the Silvas pled no contest to misdemeanor battery charges. Judge Suzanne Kingsbury sentenced Joseph Silva to six months in El Dorado County Jail. Georgia Silva received a year. The court allowed them to serve their time consecutively, so their child would have a continuous caregiver. Outraged by the lenient sentences, the South Asian community eventually convinced authorities to bring federal hate crimes charges against the Silvas, who were indicted by a grand jury in Sacramento in 2009.[238]

In the summer of 2007, South Asians were also attacked in the Pacific Northwest. On August 5, 2007, three white men assaulted Sikh-American Ranjit Singh outside a convenience store in Oakland, Oregon.[239] During the attack, the men tore off Singh's turban before fleeing the scene in two separate cars. The store's surveillance video camera recorded the men stalking Singh and planning the crime at the truck stop. One of the assailants was a former store employee who allegedly attacked another Sikh in the same manner on a previous occasion.

Although the August 5th assault was recorded on the store's surveillance camera, a grand jury in Douglas County declined to indict Singh's assailants on hate crime charges. Instead of recognizing that the defendants committed a serious bias-motivated attack, the grand jury indicted the three men on the lesser charges of harassment and theft in the third degree. Singh was troubled that the grand jurors failed to comprehend the gravity of what transpired, viewing the dastaar as an inexpensive hat instead of as a priceless symbol of his faith.[240] Singh and other members of the Sikh community were outraged that the monetary value of the turban arose during the proceedings as a means of determining the degree of the theft. According to Amardeep Singh, the executive director of the Sikh Coalition, the grand jury erred by interpreting the theft of the dastaar as a minor incident instead of a shocking post-9/11 hate crime.[241] According to Singh, some Sikhs throughout history have chosen death over removing their turbans since it encapsulates a practitioner's commitment to their faith. Rather than accept the grand jury's decision, the Sikh Coalition expressed its disapproval to the Douglas County District Attorney's office, asking that the senior prosecutor intervene so that the attackers would not able to plea down to misdemeanor charges. The Sikh Coalition also requested the U.S. government file federal hate crime charges against the assailants.

While anti-Sikh hate crimes were taking place, American audiences were watching movies ridiculing people with long hair and beards. In the 2007 comedy, *Knocked Up*, a group of stoners mercilessly harass a friend who decides against cutting his facial hair, making him the subject of a barrage of unfunny jokes. They repeatedly call him a terrorist and refer to him as shoe bomber Richard Reid. They also compare his long facial hair to a vagina, teaching audiences that it is socially acceptable to torment men with unshorn hair and beards. Many activists saw a connection between offensive movies and anti-Sikh attacks.

On occasion, elderly Sikhs were gang-beaten by bigots. On September 15, 2007, a group of Maryland teenagers jumped two septuagenarian Sikhs. On the afternoon of the assault, Bhupinder Nibber, 77, and Darshan Sarang, 75, were taking a walk in a park near their Burtonsville homes. Sarang was a former teacher who had taught in the D.C. public schools since the 1960s. His friend, Nibber, was also a retiree. Suddenly, six teenage males – approximately 14 or 15 years of age - approached the pair and confronted them. According to *India-West*, one of the assailants used a rock to hit one of the Sikhs on the side of his face, causing him to fall to the ground and lose consciousness.[242] When his companion tried to call the police, another assailant snatched his cell phone and began beating him as well. The teens then left the scene without stealing anything.

Local police and the FBI offered a $2,000 reward for anyone with information about the attack, which they were investigating as a hate crime. Rajbir Singh Datta, associate director of SALDEF, told *India-West* that the attack was a backlash hate crime, occurring four days after the sixth anniversary of 9/11.[243] According to Datta, the annual anniversary caused a significant increase in assaults directed against Sikhs, Muslims, Arabs, and South Asians across the U.S.[244] He expressed frustration that law enforcement officials failed to act appropriately when teenagers harassed Sikhs, calling them 'Osama bin Laden' and other derogatory names.[245] He also urged authorities to curtail ethnic harassment before it escalated into violent crimes.

On September 16, 2007, the day after the Sikhs were beaten, Majid Aziz, a Muslim of Afghan descent, was assaulted about a mile away from the first attack.[246] Local police wondered whether the two attacks were linked, since minorities were targeted in both instances and both took place near the anniversary of 9/11. David Bater, the hate crimes coordinator for the Montgomery County police, told *India-West* that bias-motivated attacks were becoming increasingly common as the area diversified, with South Asians, Sikhs, and Muslims representing about 15-18% of county residents.[247]

ASSAULTS, 2008

Muslims and Sikhs continued to be targeted the following year. In Hoboken, New Jersey, Carrie Covello attacked Hansdip Singh in January 2008. According to *India-West*, Covello told the South Asian that she had a problem with 'that stuff' on his head, and then jumped him from behind.[248] While attempting to pull off Singh's turban, Corvello yelled at him to remove it.[249] Singh was able to get free before she could yank it from his head. The prosecutor opted against charging Corvello with assault as a bias crime, apparently accepting her explanation that she was only joking when she verbally abused and assaulted the South Asian man while forcibly trying to remove his dastaar.[250] Sikh Coalition activists told *India-West* that they were deeply troubled by the prosecutor's failure to press hate crime charges and accept Corvello's word that she didn't mean anything by 'touching' the turban.[251] Many South Asian community members viewed the attack in the context of post-9/11 bigotry.

The same month, Sikhs were targeted in other states. On January 14, 2008, 36-year old David Wood brutally assaulted 63-year old Chadha Baljeet Singh in Jamaica, New York. On the day of the attack, Singh parked his car on the street opposite the gurdwara, located at 95th Avenue and 222nd Street in New Hyde Park. Although the elderly South Asian man was in a legal public parking space, Wood became enraged that the Sikh had parked in front of his house. According to *India Abroad*, Wood was upset that the gurdwara was located so close to his residence, and frequently interrupted prayer services by playing loud music through speakers.[252] Because of Wood's long history of belligerent behavior towards Sikhs, gurdwara officials told devotees to park some distance from the temple to avoid getting harassed or assaulted. Sikh leaders also warned parents to keep their children away from Wood's house.

Because Singh was a senior citizen, he decided to park in the open space to avoid a long walk to the gurdwara. Reacting to the South Asian man's physical features and turban, Wood called him an Arab and screamed at him to go back to his country of origin.[253] Wood then approached Singh, berated him for not listening, and punched him in the face.[254] While screaming racial slurs and profanities, Wood continued to beat Singh, knocking him to the sidewalk and breaking his nose and jaw. During the assault, Wood forcibly removed Singh's turban and destroyed his glasses.

Seeing Singh bleeding on the ground, two of Wood's relatives approached the injured man to ask him if he was all right. Singh then went to the gurdwara, where he called 911. Wood and his relatives left before the police arrived.

When Detective Michael Theogene of the Police Community Affairs Department learned of the assault, he contacted Jaspreet Singh, a staff attorney of United Sikhs. Theogene informed Singh about what transpired and asked him to alert the Hate Crimes Task Force.

Wood was eventually arraigned before Judge Gene Lopez at Queens Criminal Court. According to Queens District Attorney Richard Brown, Wood was charged with second-degree assault as a hate crime, second and third degree assault, and second-degree aggravated harassment.

The same month these xenophobic attacks were taking place, Americans were watching television shows depicting foreigners as blood-thirsty terrorists, intent on murdering sympathetic Western civilians. In January 2008, the hit drama "Nip/Tuck" aired the Islamophobic episode, "Rachel Ben Natan." This program featured the ghost of a Palestinian suicide bomber, a freakish monster with a bloody mouth and no teeth, who haunts one of his victims, a sympathetic woman he horribly disfigured, burning off her face. In a particularly gruesome plot twist, the woman discovers that a tooth belonging to her killer had become lodged into her skull at the time of the explosion. This episode fueled nativist fears of Middle Easterners by depicting them as anti-Western killers.

While American audiences were being entertained by xenophobic shows, immigrants were being targeted in different parts of the U.S. On February 28, 2008, a Sikh graduate student at Texas A&M was attacked at a Wal-Mart parking lot. According to *India-West*, the assailant called the South Asian man a 'terrorist,' and made other disparaging remarks before punching him in the face and head.[255] The blows were so powerful that the turban-wearing Sikh was knocked to the ground. Despite the seriousness of the crime, police failed to devote adequate manpower to the investigation. Even though a witness gave investigators a description of the vehicle and a partial license plate, a police spokesperson declared the crime a closed case two weeks later. Due to community pressure, the police later re-opened the case and classified it as a hate crime.

Bias-motivated assaults continued in the summer of 2008. In Cleveland, a group of men harassed a Muslim businessman and his son, who were filling up their car at a gas station. After hearing the father and son speak in their native Uzbek language and say a prayer in Arabic, the onlookers mockingly imitated their foreign speech. Soon thereafter, one of the men shot the elder Muslim in the abdomen, a crime that was captured on a nearby surveillance video.[256]

Many Arabs and South Asians hoped that the election of Barack Obama would improve race relations in the U.S. and curb post-9/11 bigotry. Because the president-elect's father was a Muslim from Kenya, many minority communities hoped that his election was a sign that racism and Islamophobia was abating in the U.S. Unfortunately, anti-Muslim attacks continued after Obama's election. In the midst of a hate crime spree on election night, a group white and Hispanic Staten Islanders, who called themselves the 'Rosebank Krew,' assaulted Ali Kamara, a 17-year old African-American Muslim, beating him with a metal pipe and a collapsible police baton as they shouted the name of the newly-elected president.[257] The attackers then assaulted a second African-American man, knocking him to the ground. Early in the morning of November 5, 2008, they attacked a third victim, 38-year old supermarket manager Ronald Forte, ramming the father of five with a car. During this vehicular assault, Forte was thrown into the hood of the car, smashing the front windshield. The injury inflicted so much head trauma that he ended up in a coma for several days. Investigators eventually learned that the assailants had mistakenly assumed that Forte was African-American because he had been wearing a black hoodie at the time of the attack. While Forte was sprawled out on the street, one of his assailants stole his wallet. The violent teens were eventually apprehended and charged with multiple offenses. While awaiting trial, 21-year old Brian Carranza petitioned the court that he be released from house arrest for more than three hours each day so he could play handball and exercise at the College of Staten Island or Intermediate School 27. Forte's sister Donna Ramos was outraged by Carranza's request, telling the *Daily News* that it was ridiculous that Carranza was concerned about handball when his victim, her brother, was forced to go to physical and speech therapy on a daily basis.[258] One of the assailants, 18-year old Ralph Nicoletti, admitted that the crime spree was bias-motivated. On February 2, 2009, Nicoletti told a judge that he was drunk and angry about Obama's election, and wanted to go after minorities who likely voted for the Democratic candidate.[259] Many community members viewed the attack in the context of post-9/11 bigotry. In federal court, Nicoletti was sentenced to 108 months in jail, and Carranza received 70 months. The other two assailants also received jail sentences: 18-year old Bryan Garaventa got 60 months, and 19-year old Michael Contreras was sentenced to 55 months.

ASSAULTS, 2009

Despite community optimism over Obama's inauguration, minorities continued to be targeted by bigots. In the Bronx, Muslim and West African immigrants were repeatedly attacked during the summer of 2009. In many instances, Muslims were robbed and assaulted coming out of a neighborhood mosque. Mahamadou Soukouma, an immigrant from Mali, told the *Post* that the frequent hate crimes disturbed congregation members, making them afraid to walk to and from the local Islamic prayer center.[260] In response to the bias-motivated attacks, police commissioner Ray Kelly increased area patrols and met with Muslim groups to improve public safety.

The same year, minority women were targeted in bias crimes. On August 20, 2009, a New York driver attempted to run over a Muslim woman and her daughter in Islandia.[261] At the time of the attack, the two Muslim women were in the parking lot of a Hess gas station in Smithtown, in Suffolk county. Disturbed by their Muslim attire, 23-year old Joseph Ballance threatened to kill them, spat on their car, and tried to hit them by driving in reverse towards them.[262] Witnesses were able to write down Ballance's license plate before he drove away from the scene. Detectives arrested Ballance at his home and charged him with second-degree aggravated harassment as a hate crime, a misdemeanor. Community members were dismayed that veiled women were still being singled out so many years after the terrorist strikes.

Muslims were also attacked following the Fort Hood shooting, in which Virginia-born Army Major Nidal Malik Hasan killed 13 of his fellow servicemen. One backlash incident involved an assault on a Muslim woman. On November 7, 2009, Valerie Kenney, a bank teller, began harassing Amal Abusumayah, who was waiting in line at a jewel store in Tinley Park, Illinois. The *Christian Science Monitor* reported that Kenney blamed the veiled woman for the Fort Hood massacre, approaching her and shouting that the gunman responsible for the Texas shooting was from the Middle East.[263] The enraged woman then assaulted the

Muslim customer, pulling at her hijab. Kennedy, who was originally charged with a hate crime, later pled guilty to the lesser charge of misdemeanor battery. Area Muslims were dismayed that Kenney was not convicted of committing a hate crime, and they saw the attack as a manifestation of post-9/11 Islamophobia.

Later the same month, two men beat a Muslim man outside a tavern in Kinsman, southwest of Chicago. According to the *New York Times*, Scott Finch and Luke Harty attacked Fuad Nafie, a 35-year old Muslim farmer and processing plant worker on November 22, 2009. According to Morris County Sheriff Terry Marketti, Finch said he and Harty attacked Nafie because they wanted to defend the nation against terrorists.[264] Community members were disturbed that Muslims were still being scapegoated more than eight years after 9/11.

ASSAULTS, 2010

Despite efforts by the Obama administration to stem xenophobia, bias attacks continued to take place across the U.S. In many parts of the country, Muslim inmates were assaulted by bigots. In Idaho, prison guards allegedly violated the civil rights of a Muslim inmate, who was beaten into a coma in January 2010.[265] A similar prison attack took place in Oregon. In this assault, an assailant used anti-Islamic slurs when beating up a Muslim inmate.[266]

On many occasions, Somalis in Minnesota were targeted by bigots. On May 4, 2010, 64-year old George Thompson approached an 83-year old Somali man and began yelling anti-Muslim slurs at the immigrant, ordering him to go back to Africa. According to the *Minneapolis Star-Tribune*, Thompson chased the senior citizen into the street, threatening to kill him.[267] Following the assault, Minneapolis police arrested an intoxicated Thompson at the Nomad World Pub, and informed concerned community members that he had a permit to carry a weapon.[268] Thompson later pled guilty in federal court to committing a hate crime based on his victim's religion and national origin.

On occasion, minority competitors were racially-harassed in athletic competitions. The *Telegraph-Herald* reported that on May 23, 2010, an 18-year old Iraqi refugee was targeted at a softball game in Cedar Rapids, Iowa.[269] During the sporting event at Tait Cummins Park, opposing team members shouted racial slurs at Saif Al-Safi. They also insulted the Arab player's minority team mates, calling them 'nigger' and 'spic.'[270] After the game ended, 24-year old Donald Schminkey III viciously attacked the Iraqi teenager, breaking his jaw while calling him a 'raghead,' 'terrorist,' and 'camel jockey.'[271] Schminkey also assaulted Al-Safi's mother when she intervened to protect her son.[272]

According to the *Telegraph-Herald*, police responded to 911 calls and found the Iraqi teenager knocked on the ground.[273] His facial injuries were so severe that he required surgery, and his jaw was wired shut for several weeks. Community activists regarded the brutal attack as a post-9/11 hate crime, and were shocked that Schminkey received only four days in jail after pleading guilty to disorderly conduct in a deal in which assault charges were dismissed. Prosecutors also failed to charge him for the assault on Al-Safi's mother. Schminkey told journalists he had no remorse about his actions, and would beat the teen again if given the opportunity.[274]

Bigots also attacked Muslims in other states. In San Diego, a white man in his 50s assaulted a Muslim man. During the June 2010 hate crime, the assailant made racial slurs, used profanity, and demanded that the other man return to his country of origin.[275]

The following month, a Muslim man was beaten in Northern California. At about 1:30 p.m. on July 11, 2010, two young men approached a Muslim man on El Camino Real, a busy street in Sunnyvale, as he was waiting for a ride to a nearby mosque to attend afternoon prayer services. The troublemakers realized that he was not a Christian because he was holding a Quran and wearing a black religious cap. Captain Dave Verbrugge, a spokesman for the Sunnyvale Public Safety Department, told the *Oakland Tribune* that the assailants first asked the victim if he was Jewish.[276] When the pedestrian replied that he was a Muslim, they told him that his religion was even worse, and that his faith made him a terrorist.[277] One of the assailants, a blond youth in his late teens or early 20s, struck the Muslim man three or four times. The victim fell to the ground, suffering facial cuts and bruises. The targeted man, who was in his 40s, told the *Oakland Tribune* that the unprovoked attack left him fearful of his safety, unable to worship freely in the U.S.[278] Because of the religious component of the attack, authorities opted to investigate the assault as a hate crime.

Muslim women were also targeted in 2010, particularly if they wore hijabs. The *Los Angeles Times* reported that on October 16, a woman verbally and physically assaulted two veiled Muslim-Americans at an Arco gas station and minimart in Tukwila, Washington.[279] On the evening of the attack, 37-year old Jennifer Leigh Jennings approached the Somali women at an AM/PM station. Jennings then began yelling at them, calling them terrorists and suicide bombers and ordering them to get out of the U.S. because they didn't know how to pump gas.[280] When one of the Muslims tried to re-enter her vehicle, Jennings slammed the door on her leg and kicked her. Jennings then pushed the other woman while yelling racial and religious epithets. When one of the victims attempted to take a photo of their assailant to give to the police, Jennings attempted to run her over with her car.[281] Jennings also attempted to intimidate the two Somali women, declaring that she would never be prosecuted for her actions because she was an American veteran. The *Seattle Times* reported that when Jennings was booked on two felony charges of malicious harassment, she looked at a dark-skinned police officer and said that he was only taking action against her because he was the same race and religion as the two women.[282]

During the 9/11 backlash, Muslims were occasionally attacked while taking public transportation. In New York, Rod Peterson, a Muslim community leader wearing a traditional prayer cap, was assaulted on the A-train on the morning of December 8, 2010. According to the *New York Daily News*, one of the assailants, Albert Melendez, called the imam a 'camel-jockey' before grabbing him and hitting him in the face.[283] The newspaper also reported that Melendez made anti-Muslim comments during the assault, using profanity and asserting that all followers of Islam were terrorists.[284] Melendez punched Peterson in the face and threw his prayer cap onto the subway tracks, while his friend, Eddie Crespo, grabbed and held him during the attack.[285] The blow left Peterson with a black eye. The *Los Angeles Times* noted that Melendez and Crespo denied beating the Muslim out of bias, claiming that it was a straightforward scuffle over an accidental nudge on a train.[286] A grand jury indicted Melendez on a misdemeanor offense, but failed to bring charges against Crespo, a Metropolitan Transportation officer engaged to Melendez' sister. Area Muslims were skeptical of Crespo's claim that he was simply acting to break up the fight when he physically restrained Peterson while Melendez was attacking him. Many community members viewed the hate crimes in the context of post-9/11 bigotry.

ASSAULTS, 2011

Muslims, immigrants, and other minorities continued to be targeted in 2011. The *Tampa Tribune* reported that on February 4, 2011, Bradley Kent Strott stabbed an Iranian-American at a bar in St. Petersburg, Florida.[287] The attack occurred at Marsha's Wayside Inn. Samad Ebadi, a 57-year old U.S. citizen who had immigrated from Iran in 1975, was sitting at the bar when he saw Strott, a 52 year old man who sometimes shopped at his convenience store. At first, the meeting was cordial, with Strott offering him a slice of pizza and Ebadi buying a round of drinks in response. Later in the evening, Strott asked Ebadi if he was a Muslim. According to the *Tampa Tribune*, Ebadi initially declined to answer the question, telling Strott that he didn't want to talk about religion in a bar.[288] When Strott persisted, Ebadi eventually admitted to being a Muslim, clarifying that like all followers of Islam, he believed in the holiness of Jesus. Upon hearing his companion's religious affiliation, Strott's demeanor abruptly changed. He threatened to kill Ebadi, pushing him on the floor and jumping on top of him.[289] Strott then stabbed Ebadi in the neck with a pocketknife. The *St. Petersburg Times* reported that shortly after the attack, Strott asserted that Muslims were the root of America's problems.[290]

In response to the assault, a female bar patron ran next door to Sam's Market, where the victim's son Ali was working. After learning of the stabbing, Ali Ebadi rushed to the bar and found his father covered in blood, slumped on a stool. Ali Ebadi told the *St. Petersburg Times* that he was upset by witnesses' failure to call 911 or take action to help his father, who was bleeding out from the gash.[291] The elder Ebadi was transported to

Bayfront Medical Center, where physicians stitched up his neck wound. They also treated him for injuries to his throat, neck, and back. Shortly after the attack, local police arrested Strott and charged him with aggravated battery, a hate crime. Authorities reported that Strott was so inebriated that he did not seem to grasp the magnitude of what he had done. Strott was able to post the $15,000 bail bond and was released after spending only one night in jail. Ali Ebadi told the *St. Petersburg Times* that he thought Strott deserved to be charged with attempted murder as a hate crime for stabbing his father in the neck and threatening his life.[292] He also worried that unless more serious charges were filed, Strott might act in a similar manner the next time he encountered a Muslim. Because of the Islamophobic comments Strott made during the attack, many area minorities viewed the assault as part of the ongoing backlash to the terrorist strikes.

Sikhs were also targeted in 2011, particularly in the aftermath of Osama bin Laden's death. In New York, an off-duty Sikh MTA engineer was assaulted on a Brooklyn-bound subway train by an attacker who accused him of being related to the 9/11 mastermind. The *News India-Times* reported that the attack took place on May 30, 2011, after an African-American man in his late 20s approached 59-year old Jiwan Singh and demanded that the Sikh passenger give up his seat.[293] Singh attempted to diffuse the situation by pointing out that there were many unoccupied seats, but the irate man attacked him anyway. According to *India Abroad*, the assailant grabbed Singh by the shirt collar, picked him up, and threw him into one of the other seats.[294] The assailant then punched him twice, knocking out three of his teeth while accusing him of being Osama bin Laden's brother and a member of the Taliban.[295] The attacker fled when the train stopped at the Utica Avenue station.

Because of the slurs used during the attack, Singh was convinced that he was targeted because of his turban and long beard. Singh, a father of five, told *India Abroad* that the subway attack was not his first experience with post-9/11 bigotry.[296] In the years following the terrorist strikes, he and his family members were repeatedly harassed by bigots, who called them Osama bin Laden and accused them of being part of a terrorist network. The most serious incident happened in 2009, when Singh's 23-year old son Jasmir lost an eye after being stabbed by bigots who targeted him because of his turban and beard.[297] According to ABC Action News, Jasmir Singh's assailants shouted racial slurs during this attack, which took place outside of a New York grocery store.[298]

Years after 9/11, Muslim women continued to be scapegoated by xenophobes. The *New York Post* reported that female assailants beat up 56-year old Aissatou Diallo in Harlem.[299] The nativist incident took place on July 6, 2011, two days after Independence Day, when Francesca Johnson began snapping pictures of the burqa-wearing Diallo walking down St. Nicholas Avenue near West 141st Street. Diallo politely asked Johnson, a 28-year old African-American woman, to stop photographing her with her cell phone. In response, Johnson went into a building and reappeared with a 60-year old white woman, Linda Paplow. Diallo told the *Post* that the white woman called her a terrorist and threatened to kill her, punching her in the left eye.[300] Paplow and Johnson then started to run off but then abruptly returned, attacking Diallo from behind, throwing her on the floor, pulling off her burqa, and cursing her. Because of the slurs used by the perpetrators, NYPD hate crime detectives opted to treat the assault as a bias crime.

As the ten-year anniversary of 9/11 approached, minorities in the U.S. continued to feel the effects of the backlash. On September 8, 2011, the *Seattle Post Intelligencer* reported that many American Muslims continued to be harassed or attacked a decade after the terrorist strikes.[301] Because of the ongoing existence of hate crimes, some American Muslims opted to postpone praying in public settings, waiting until they were at home or in a safer location.[302]

CHAPTER FIVE:

BACKLASH ATTACKS AT MOSQUES, GURDWARAS, HINDU TEMPLES, SYNAGOGUES, AND CHURCHES, SEPT. 2001 TO SEPT. 2011

Along with physical assaults against minorities, the 9/11 backlash included attacks on mosques, gurdwaras, and temples. In some instances, synagogues, Coptic churches, and immigrant-friendly houses of worship were also targeted. This chapter explores how American vigilantes scapegoated vulnerable community members for the terrorist strikes by desecrating their prayer centers. These hate crimes began immediately after 9/11 and continued for more than a decade afterwards.

Immediately after the planes hit the World Trade Center, enraged bigots across the U.S. began attacking unfamiliar places of worship. Beginning about 10:00 a.m. on 9/11, before there was definitive information about the background of the hijackers, the president of the Islamic Society of Dayton began receiving phone calls blaming all Muslims for the terrorist strikes. The *Dayton Daily News* reported that callers repeatedly threatened the mosque in the days after 9/11, leaving messages declaring that congregation members must be happy about the civilian deaths, and that Muslims should be forced to leave the country.[1] Also on September 11, 2001, a mosque in Everett, Washington began receiving threats on the center's voice mail.[2]

Mosques in the Southwest were also targeted. In the first two days after 9/11, the Islamic Center of Greater Austin received at least seven menacing messages.[3] Along with racial slurs and physical threats, some callers challenged Muslims' right to remain in the U.S. According to the *Austin American Statesman*, one caller phoned the mosque and told worshippers that they should leave the country because they weren't Americans.[4] A Bangladeshi man who lived next to the house of worship was so frightened by the threats that he spent the evening of September 11th camped out in his car.[5]

In other states, bigots threatened to kill mosque staff members in retaliation for the terrorist strikes. According to the *Providence Journal*, Rhode Island Islamic centers received menacing calls in the immediate aftermath of 9/11, with callers expressing their desire to murder local Muslims.[6] These xenophobes succeeded in making congregation members afraid to enter their houses of worship. One Rhode Island woman from Bangladesh told the *Providence Journal* that she was so disturbed by the death threats left on her mosque's answering machine that she wondered if it was safe to attend services.[7]

Massachusetts Muslims were also frightened. The *Asian Wall St. Journal* reported that shortly after 9/11, bigots called the Islamic Center of New England and threatened to kill Muslims in Quincy.[8] Congregants were deeply saddened that their fellow citizens viewed them with fear and loathing. Zaida Hassan Shaw, the mosque's secretary, felt particularly vulnerable since she worked in the building. She told the *Patriot-Ledger* that she was especially terrified of a September 11, 2001 caller who kept repeating that he wanted Muslims' filthy religion out of his country.[9] Shaw drew upon her faith to deal with the harassment, asking God to forgive the ignorance of others.

According to the *Patriot-Ledger*, Shaw's parents were among the Lebanese immigrants who came to the area to work in the shipyards in the early 1900s.[10] Her six brothers fought in World War II., Korea, and Vietnam. Although many Quincy Muslims were U.S. veterans and the mosque had been in the city since 1964, nativists repeatedly targeted the worship center in the decades it had been operational. Muslims were dismayed that authorities never made an arrest in the 1990 arson attack that did more than $500,000 damage to the mosque's interior.[11] The Islamic Center also faced other forms of community bigotry. On the same day that Muslims were supposed to close a land deal that would enable them to expand the Islamic Center into neighboring Milton, some local businessmen abruptly bought the property. According to the *Asian Wall St. Journal*, the mosque's 800 members – whose ancestors came from approximately 24 countries – felt the threats were a clear indication that they were not welcome in the community.[12]

In many parts of the U.S., vigilantes began acting on their verbal threats to mosques. A Muslim house of worship in Toms River, New Jersey began receiving threatening calls on September 11, 2001 and later had its window broken.[13] Mosques were also desecrated on the West Coast. In San Francisco, a mosque was splattered with blood.[14] This hate crime frightened Bay Area Muslims, who were disappointed they were being blamed for 9/11.

In the South, mosques were also attacked. A vandal targeted a Muslim prayer center in Augusta, Georgia on the evening of September 11, 2001. The *Augusta Chronicle* reported that the mosque graffiti associated local Muslims with Osama bin Laden.[15] Vigilantes also targeted Augusta's Muslims en route to their prayer centers. According to Islamic Society President Shariq Hashmi, one enraged bigot drove up to the mosque's front door and handed religious leaders a copy of a *Miami Herald* editorial describing what journalist Leonard Pitts Jr. would like to do to the terrorists.[16] The man then told congregation members that it was what he and others were planning on doing to them.[17] In response to the threats, mosque leaders hired a Richmond County sheriff's deputy to park outside the facility during Friday prayers. Hashimi said that area Muslims were having difficulty dealing with both the psychological horror of 9/11 and backlash hate crimes.

An Islamic center in Sterling, Virginia was also targeted. On September 12, 2001, Muslims arrived at this mosque to take a bus they had chartered to donate blood at the Red Cross to help World Trade Center victims. At this time, they discovered that their religious center, the All Dulles Area Muslim Society, had been grossly vandalized. According to the *Washington Post*, an intruder spray-painted violent messages on the walls, carpets, and doors of the mosque. Congregants were particularly upset that the vandal wrote Islamophobic death threats in letters over seven feet tall, declaring, "Die Pigs" and "Muslims Burn Forever."[18] The building's director also received a call threatening Muslims.

Mohammed Khan told the *Washington Post* that he was deeply troubled by the bias-motivated vandalism, particularly since Sterling Muslims were American citizens or permanent residents who had nothing to do with 9/11.[19] In response to the graffiti, congregation members repainted the walls and used throw rugs to cover the destruction. Worshippers eventually raised $6,000 for the Red Cross and went forward with their blood drive to help World Trade Center victims.

Vigilantes also targeted mosques in other states. In Texas, Islamic prayer centers were repeatedly attacked by bigots. *The Christian Science Monitor* reported that on September 12, 2001, a gunman fired on a North Texas mosque. During this incident, the shooter pumped dozens of bullets into the house of worship and shattered its front window.[20] Other mosques in the state were also desecrated. In Austin, vandals scrawled anti-Islamic graffiti on the Al-Farooq Masjid shortly after 9/11.[21] In Carrollton, an assailant smashed a window of the Islamic Center.[22]

Texas mosques were firebombed in backlash crimes. In Denton, bigots threw a Molotov cocktail at a mosque on September 13, 2001, causing $2,500 in damage.[23] According to *ADL on the Frontline*, this hate crime constituted the third attack on a North Texas mosque in the first 48 hours after 9/11.[24]

In a couple of states, motorist deliberately crashed into mosques, endangering the lives of worshippers. Shortly after 9/11, a drunk driver rammed his car into the Islamic Center of Evansville, Indiana. According to the *Evansville Courier and Press*, the assailant told police that he acted in relation for the terrorist strikes on the World Trade Center and the Pentagon.[25] This vehicular assault frightened Indiana's Muslim community, especially since the building included a prayer area, classrooms, a community dining area, a kitchen, and a library used by congregants and their families. After the hate crime, officials increased security to ensure the safety of worshippers, keeping doors locked to curtail access to the building. Many Evansville Muslims were determined not to let the attacker intimidate them or undermine their sense of place in the community. Mohammed Hussain, an Evansville pediatrician and Islamic Center president, was grateful for the condolence messages he received in the aftermath of the hate crime.[26]

Islamic houses of worship were also targeted in the Pacific Northwest. Two days after the terrorist strikes, an arsonist in Washington state attacked an area mosque. According to the *Los Angeles Times*, Patrick Michael Cunningham, a 54-year old Snohomish resident, decided to avenge 9/11 by burning down a

Muslim house of worship.[27] On September 13, 2001, he drove 25 miles to the Idriss mosque in Northgate, armed with a loaded revolver and gasoline to use as an accelerant. Two Muslim congregants discovered Cunningham splashing gasoline on cars parked in the mosque's lot in an attempt to set the vehicles on fire and burn down the prayer center. When he realized he had been caught, Cunningham fired his .22 caliber revolver at the worshippers. According to Assistant U.S. Attorney Steve C. Gonzalez, the gun misfired, allowing the Muslim congregants to escape unharmed.[28] Cunningham then fled the scene with the gas can, but was arrested after he crashed his car into a telephone pole, injuring himself. Gonzalez told the *Los Angeles Times* that officials recognized that the mosque attack was a backlash hate crime.[29]

Cunningham was booked in Seattle and charged with four offenses: using a gun in a violent crime, obstructing the free exercise of religion, attempting to damage a building, and attempting to deface religious property.[30] After he was taken to a local hospital, Cunningham admitted to being angry after the terrorist strikes, but denied participating in the mosque arson and shooting, saying only that he had fired a gun at coyotes earlier in the evening.[31]

Seattle resident Issa Qandeel, a mechanical engineer who emigrated from Jordan in 1996, was one of the worshippers targeted by Cunningham. Qandeel told the *Seattle Post-Intelligencer* that he came to the U.S. to better himself, not to hurt other people or be attacked by them.[32] He reported being traumatized by the bias-motivated arson and his assailant's erroneous belief that Muslims were collectively responsible for 9/11.

Cunningham's attorney, Olaf Hansen, argued that his client was shooting at the ground instead of at worshippers. Hansen also claimed that his client's drinking impaired his judgment. In court papers, the defense attorney argued that Cunningham's intoxication should be regarded as a mitigating factor, since he wrongly believed that there was a terrorist cell at the mosque. Hansen explained to the court that Cunningham had family in New York, although none of them had been hurt or killed. Many Washington state Muslims were appalled that Cunningham would use the 9/11 victims as justification of such an un-American hate crime.

Many Muslims were angry that Cunningham failed to take responsibility for his actions after he was arrested. Idriss mosque director Hisham Farajallah told the *Los Angeles Times* that Cunningham's behavior revealed that he had no true knowledge of Islam or Muslims, since he committed the attack out of hatred and ignorance.[33]

Cunningham eventually pled guilty to two federal felony charges of obstructing the free exercise of religion and using a firearm in a crime of violence. In the plea agreement, Cunningham admitted that he failed to differentiate between ordinary Muslims and the 9/11 hijackers.[34] Some Muslims were upset that prosecutors agreed to drop the other two felony charges, instead of making Cunningham responsible for all of his crimes. They were also disappointed that the gun-wielding arsonist was never charged or convicted of attempted murder or drunk driving, especially since he admitted to traveling more than 25 miles while extremely intoxicated before smashing his car into the pole.

At sentencing, Cunningham finally apologized for his actions.[35] U.S. District judge Barbara Rothstein told the defendant that the free exercise of religion was a cornerstone of the Constitution and chastised him for his intolerant conduct.[36] Despite her words, Rothstein sentenced Cunningham to a total of only six and a half years, considerably less than the law permitted or prosecutors demanded for these two felonies. Count one carried a maximum sentence of 20 years and a fine of $250,000. The second count included a minimum sentence of five years and a maximum one of life in prison and a $250,000 fine.

Justice Department attorneys Donald Currie and Malachai Jones were disappointed with the outcome, especially since they had gone on record expressing their hopes that Cunningham would receive at least seven years in prison for his offenses. In their December 2001 sentencing memorandum, they emphasized the seriousness of Cunningham's anti-Muslim crimes, which they characterized as part of a premeditated plan instead of a drunken impulse.[37] Some Muslims were also dismayed that Cunningham got off so lightly for such serious offenses, seeing the minimal sentence as a product of community xenophobia. Other mosque members were more accepting of the outcome.

In court, Qandeel publicly forgave Cunningham for shooting at him, attacking the Islamic prayer center, and pouring gasoline on worshippers' cars.[38] Mosque director Farajallah told the *Post-Intelligencer* that Cunningham's actions were not typical of the community, which was overwhelmingly respectful, tolerant, and supportive.[39]

In the immediate aftermath of 9/11, other Islamic prayer centers were targeted in Washington state. The *Columbian* reported that a Lynnwood mosque was desecrated shortly after the terrorist strikes. In this attack, a vandal defaced the sign in front of the Dar al-Arqam mosque, covering it with tar.[40] Another Washington mosque was set ablaze by bigots. According to the *Seattle Times*, the Omar al-Farooq mosque in Mountainlake Terrace was one of six U.S. houses of worship that was targeted by arsonists at the height of the 9/11 backlash.[41] Police apprehended and charged one local teen with arson, and another with harassment. This premeditated crime further traumatized Washington Muslims, who were already reeling from previous mosque attacks and threatening phone calls.

Mosques were also attacked in Florida. Two days after the terrorist strikes, a gunman fired at the only mosque in Hernando County.[42] Bigots also scapegoated other prayer centers in the state. In Ft. Walton Beach, the city's only mosque was repeatedly targeted. Congregation members were frightened by all the menacing phone calls the house of worship received in the immediate aftermath of 9/11. Fears intensified on September 16, 2001, when a gunman took aim at the building.[43] Police Chief Steve Hogue told the *St. Petersburg Times* that this attack was the city's first reported hate crime in 2001.[44] Some area Muslims wondered if the shooting could have been prevented if community authorities had taken steps to protect the house of worship after the threatening calls.

In response to the hate crimes taking place across the U.S., some mosques cancelled worship services. According to the *Washington Post*, religious leaders decided against conducting Friday prayers at the Dar al-Hijrah Islamic Center in Falls Church after receiving numerous threats targeting the facility.[45] In other parts of the country, Muslims avoided going to mosques. In Washington state, congregants were too frightened to show up for afternoon prayers at the Islamic Center of Spokane at the height of the backlash.[46]

A few days after 9/11, the Colorado Muslim Society Islamic Center in Arapahoe County began receiving menacing phone calls. Shortly thereafter, congregation members were attacked on mosque grounds. According to the *Rocky Mountain News*, Victor Amosov, a 46-year old Russian immigrant, threatened worshippers in the parking lot, telling them that he had an AK47.[47] He was later found guilty of disorderly conduct. Congregation members thought that more serious charges were warranted since he committed a bias crime by threatening the lives of worshippers and interfering with their ability to practice their religion.

Mosques were also targeted in other states. In California, attackers threw fire crackers and paint balls at the Islamic Center of San Diego on September 16, 2001. According to the *Daily Herald*, the onslaught forced worshippers to evacuate.[48] Congregants saw the incident as a post-9/11 crime.

As the days passed, backlash attacks continued. On September 17, 2001, arsonists attempted to burn down a Nation of Islam mosque in East Austin.[49] The incident began when the assailants drove by the Muslim prayer center on 12th and Chicon Street and lobbed two Molotov cocktails at the house of worship, hitting its roof. Minister Cedric Muhammad told the *Austin American Statesman* that that Nation of Islam members were African-Americans, not Arabs, and had nothing to do with 9/11.[50] He added that the firebombing was somewhat expected since the mosque received several threatening phone calls prior to the arson.[51] Many community members speculated that local authorities could have done more to prevent the hate crime, especially since bigots had broadcasted their intention to target the prayer center.

Austin fire spokeswoman Dale Whitaker told the *Houston Chronicle* that the firebombs were thrown from a dark-colored car accompanied by a white van.[52] In her press interview, Whitaker never disclosed that a white van had been involved in previous attacks on American mosques. Instead of drawing attention to the possibility that a hate group was repeatedly targeting Islamic centers and warning Muslims to take appropriate security measures, she downplayed the East Austin arson, saying only that the Molotov cocktails were crudely-made and were likely the work of amateurs.

Austin police chief Stan Knee told the *Austin American Statesman* that apprehending the arsonists was important to ensure public safety.[53] Knee said that immediately after 9/11, his officers began patrolling mosques to deter backlash attacks. Because hate crimes were taking place in spite of the patrols, East Texas Muslims asked local police to provide them with round-the-clock protection. To deter bigots from acting on their Islamophobia, Robert Pitman, U.S. attorney for the Western district of Texas, reminded the public that attacking a mosque was a felony punishable by up to 99 years in state prison.[54]

In response to community intolerance, the Islamic Society of Denton held an interfaith prayer vigil in late September 2001. Mosque spokesman Irfan Ali told the *New York Beacon* that the event was intended to be a peaceful gathering, building bridges across religious lines.[55] According to news reports, the city mayor and more than 15 church groups attended the service to pray for community harmony. Baptists, Catholics, and Presbyterians were among the denominations in attendance. During the event, the student body president of the University of North Texas hand-delivered 50 condolence posters and flowers to mosque officials.

In addition to arsons in Texas, bigots firebombed Islamic prayer centers in other states. In response to the terrorist strikes, a New York man threw a Molotov cocktail at a Bensonhurst mosque, according to a September 18, 2001 article in the *Atlanta Constitution*.[56]

The same week, an arsonist in Florida torched a roadside planter at a mosque. The *Sarasota Herald Tribune* reported that the flames burned shrubs and melted a plastic sign at the Islamic Community of Southwest Florida before firefighters were able to extinguish the blaze.[57] The arson traumatized mosque members, who were still reeling from the fact that their worship center's American flag had been stolen a few days previously.[58] Congregation members were concerned that the thief might have been trying to communicate the message that Muslims had no right to fly the stars and stripes.

Many Muslims felt that the xenophobic attacks were not representative of community sentiment. Ahmed Abdalla, a mechanical engineer and mosque member, told the *Sarasota Herald Tribune* that he was grateful that well-wishers left flowers and fruit baskets on the mosque's doorstep in a gesture of solidarity.[59] He also urged area residents to practice tolerance and respect the county's commitment to religious diversity, expressing his hope that although terrorists might have succeeded in destroying buildings, they should not be permitted to break the fabric of American society.[60]

Local Muslims were angry that investigating officers were reluctant to recognize that the mosque arson was a backlash hate crime. Lt. Pete Sbarbori, who was involved in the sheriff's office investigation of the blaze, told the *Sarasota Herald Tribune* that he hoped the fire was started unintentionally, unable to believe that a bias-motivated arsonist was operating in his community.[61] Area Muslims were frustrated that authorities were unwilling to acknowledge the bias component of the crime.

Bigots in other parts of the country continued to attack American mosques. On September 18, 2001, a driver used his vehicle to damage the Islamic Center of Greater Cleveland. The perpetrator, Eric Richley, drove his Ford mustang approximately 80 miles per hour through the front doors of the mosque, located in Parma, Ohio. According to the *New York Times*, this attack caused between $70,000 and $100,000 in damage to the 13,000 square foot facility, which included a Muslim school and community center.[62] Local police arrested the 29-year old Middlebury resident at the scene, charging him with drunken driving, felony assault, burglary, and vandalism.

Some Cleveland residents felt strongly that the mosque attack was bias-motivated, and were disappointed that Richley was not charged with a hate crime. Cleveland resident Bernice Jackson told the *Oakland Post* that Richley's decision to ram a mosque with his car should be regarded as a backlash incident, particularly since it occurred a week after 9/11, when anti-Muslim tensions were running high.[63] Dismissing the perpetrator's excuse that he was drunk and had just argued with his girlfriend, Jackson noted that Richley chose to target a mosque instead of a drug store or car dealership. He later pled guilty to burglary, ethnic intimidation, and vandalism. Ohio Muslims were dismayed that by accepting a plea bargain, Richley was able to dodge hate crime charges.

American Muslims were also frightened after a mob of between 300 to 700 people tried to storm a mosque in Bridgeview, Illinois, on September 19, 2001. At the demonstration, anti-Muslim bigots carried

Confederate flags, shouted pro-American chants, and made death threats.[64] The content of the mob's hate speech indicated that many Americans were conflating patriotism with nativism in the aftermath of the hijackings. Area Muslims were particularly concerned that mob participants were asserting that Muslim and Arabs ought to be exterminated as a means of purifying the U.S.[65] One demonstrator, 19-year old Colin Zaremba, told the *Daily Herald* that he was proud to be an American, and that he had always hated Arabs.[66] In response to the escalating situation, police pushed back the crowd and made three arrests. Local Muslims thought that more of the Islamophobic protestors should have been taken into custody for threatening the lives of congregants. The same day as the Bridgeview demonstration, an Arab-American community center in the area was firebombed.[67] Arab-Americans were dismayed that the two incidents received little media attention, with journalists downplaying the seriousness of the attacks and the threats directed against local minorities.

Mosques were also targeted in the South. On September 23, 2001, the *New Orleans City Business* reported that a mosque in St. Bernard Parish was attacked.[68] During this assault, an intruder fired a BB gun at the Islamic Association of Arabi's Yaseen mosque, frightening worshippers.

SEPTEMBER 2001 GURDWARA AND HINDU TEMPLE ATTACKS

Along with mosques, gurdwaras in the U.S. were also frequently targeted in post-9/11 hate crimes. In suburban Cleveland, an arsonist tried to set fire to the Guru Gobind Singh Sikh temple on September 12, 2001.[69] The hate crime unnerved worshippers. Gurdwaras were also targeted on the West Coast. According to the *San Francisco Chronicle*, a Northern California man went to a Sacramento Sikh temple on September 13, 2001 and demanded that practitioners remove a religious flag.[70] Although congregants forced him to leave, he returned a little later, blocking the temple gates with a tractor and trailer. He then jumped into the gurdwara's sacred pool, desecrating it.

Gurdwaras throughout the country continued to be targeted in the days following the terrorist strikes. The *Hindustan Times* reported that an arsonist set fire to the Sikh Culture Society – one of the largest Sikh places of worship in New York – barely a week after 9/11.[71] The destruction frightened congregation members, who worried about their safety. Gurdwaras were also attacked in other parts of the city. In Queens, an assailant fired rubber bullets at a Sikh temple in a backlash incident.[72]

Other houses of worship were targeted at the height of the backlash. Shortly after 9/11, a Hindu temple was firebombed in Matawan, New Jersey.[73] Bigots also targeted Indian prayer centers in other parts of the state. In Jersey City, an arsonist hurled a Molotov cocktail at a temple.[74] Although the religious facility was fire-damaged, religious leaders went ahead with their scheduled memorial service for the World Trade Center victims.

SEPTEMBER 2001 CHURCH AND SYNAGOGUE ATTACKS

On occasion, Christian churches in the U.S. were attacked after 9/11, particularly if they were confused with mosques. Across the country, many Coptic churches covered up Arabic signs to prevent hate crimes. Churches were especially likely to be targeted if they had Arab parishioners or participated in interfaith activities with non-Christians. For example, in late September 2001, an arsonist targeted St. John's Church, a house of worship with a diverse congregation and religious mandate to unite Christians, Muslims, Sikhs, and Hindus. The *Chicago Sun-Times* reported that this Christian facility, known as the "Church of the East," sustained smoke and fire damage in what was presumed to be a bigotry-motivated arson.[75] Congregation member Samira Tchiko said that the fire made her concerned about religious intolerance, a vice that the interfaith Church of the East hoped to eradicate.[76]

During the 9/11 backlash, a synagogue was attacked in Washington state. In Tacoma, the town's only Jewish house of worship was repeatedly targeted by bigots. In the aftermath of 9/11, someone vandalized the parking lot of Temple Beth El, writing graffiti blaming Zionism for the terrorist strikes and the deaths of thousands of Americans.[77] The following weekend, on September 23, 2001, two flaming, fire-starting logs were left at the back of the synagogue, including one placed underneath a natural gas line.[78] The hate crime terrified members of the congregation, who were dismayed they were being blamed for the hijackings.

MOSQUE AND TEMPLE ATTACKS CONTINUE IN LATE 2001 AND 2002…

In the weeks and months after 9/11, American mosques continued to be attacked by bigots. The *Telegram & Gazette* reported that the Islamic Society of Greater Worcester experienced three separate hate crimes in the month after the terrorist strikes.[79] On two different occasions, a trespasser threw rocks through the building's windows. In another attack, an intruder vandalized cars parked at the house of worship.

In many parts of the country, bias crimes continued to surge in late 2001. Along with vandalizing religious buildings, intruders sometimes targeted non-Christian clergy members. On October 9, 2001, three assailants beat up a Muslim imam at a mosque in the Bronx. The *New York Times* reported that the intruders entered the Islamic Cultural Center at about 8:00 p.m. and abruptly attacked the 35-year old mullah, striking him on the head.[80] Because the imam was black and the assault happened at a mosque, investigating officers thought it likely that it was a post-9/11 hate crime.

Also in October 2001, a Muslim was attacked coming out of a mosque in Lemon Grove, California. According to police reports, 18-year old Thomas Cervantes and his friends approached a group of men near the Usman mosque and stabbed 22-year old Aweis Addis in the stomach. According to the *San Diego Union-Tribune*, a witness told investigating officers that he heard one of the assailants make a derogatory comment about Muslims, demanding that they leave the country.[81] Addis survived the stab wound, although his injury required him to be hospitalized. Despite the assailant's anti-Muslim remark and the location of the attack outside a mosque, Sheriff's Detective Gilbert Grayson opted to label the assault an ordinary stabbing instead of a hate crime.[82] Rather than attributing the incident to the 9/11 backlash, Grayson viewed it as a simple case of drunks starting a fight.[83]

The same month, mosques were targeted on the West Coast. The *New York Times* reported that on October 17, 2001, a member of the Jewish Defense League informed the FBI of an immanent bomb plot.[84] Danny Gillis told the FBI that two JDL leaders who solicited his participation in a plan to set off pipe bombs at one of Los Angeles' largest mosques, as well as bomb the office of Darrell Issa, a Southern California Congressman. After learning of the terrorist conspiracy, the FBI asked Gillis to act as an informant. He agreed to help foil the plot, after admitting that he once planted a bomb under orders from the JDL in the past.[85] The *Times* reported that he taped conversations in which Irv Rubin, a 56-year old resident of Monrovia, and Earl Kruger, 59, of Reseda, discussed the logistics of their terrorist plans.[86] The call transcripts compiled by the FBI documented the different motives of the JDL plotters: Krugel hoped that the bombing would terrorize the Muslim community by depriving them of one of their filthy mosques.[87] Rubin said that he decided to participate because he wanted to hunt down Palestinians to prove that the JDL was still alive and active.[88]

According to the *Times*, the JDL was an organization founded in 1968 in New York by Rabbi Meir Kahane, with approximately 13,000 members.[89] Because of the group's involvement in attacks and bomb plots in the U.S., the federal government officially designated the JDL a domestic terrorist organization.

Before deciding on which facilities to bomb, Krugel and Rubin considered different targets, including the offices of the Muslim Political Action Committee. They finally decided on the King Fahd mosque, used by 1,000 congregants during Ramadan.[90] By targeting this $8.1 million Islamic Center, they hoped to send a message that Muslims were not welcome in the U.S.

After learning of the plot, FBI agents raided Krugel's home and garage, where they found numerous weapons and explosives, including: a dozen firearms, ammunition, several pounds of explosive powder, pipes, fuses, and other bomb-making equipment.[91] They then arrested Krugel and Rubin, charging them without bond for engaging in a conspiracy and possession of explosives.

Southern California Arabs and Muslims were shocked by the bomb plot. Mosque director Tajuddin Shuaib was particularly disturbed that the JDL terrorists were planning to carry out the attack at the holiest time of the Muslim calendar, when it was used most heavily by congregants. He told reporters that the mosque received no warning of the coming attack, and asserted that the worship center had no animosity towards other religions or ethnic groups.[92]

Area Muslims also found it shocking that the JDL terrorists hoped to kill Congressman Issa, a Christian moderate Republican who had never championed Palestinian rights. Congressman Issa was also surprised to learn of the assassination attempt, stating that he had no insight about why anyone would want to attack his district office and kill him and his staff.[93] Although Issa claimed not to know why he was being targeted, the *New York Times* reported that Issa's Lebanese ethnicity was likely the reason he was singled out.[94]

Arab-Americans and Muslims throughout the U.S. were outraged that Krugel and Rubin were not charged as terrorists for their involvement in JDL plots to bomb a mosque and firebomb the offices of a U.S. Congressman. Many Americans were also upset that Gillis was not prosecuted for his admitted participation in a previous JDL attack on a U.S. mosque.

Krugel and Rubin were eventually indicted in Los Angeles for conspiring to bomb Congressman Issa's district office. Rubin committed suicide before trial but Krugel was held legally responsible for his involvement in the bombing conspiracy. Krugel was later killed by another inmate while in custody.

In the decade before 9/11, the JDL and other militant groups had targeted Arab-American activists who championed civil rights or were critical of Israeli foreign policy. According to the *Boston Globe*, JDL members were suspected in the 1985 killing of American-Arab Anti-Discrimination Committee activist Alex Odeh.[95] In the 1990s, the FBI investigated the JDL and Kahane Chai for threatening to attack American mosques and ethnic organizations in the U.S. According to the May 9, 1996 issue of the *Jewish Telegraphic Agency*, religious extremists allegedly sent death threats to mosques and Islamic organizations, comparing American Muslims to sheep en route to the butcher.[96] Members of the JDL denied sending the menacing letters, suggesting instead that the Muslims probably sent the hate-filled death threats to themselves.[97]

While authorities were investigating the JDL plot to bomb the King Fahd mosques, bigots unaffiliated with hate groups were targeting Islamic prayer centers in other parts of the country. In Washington state, a 36-year old man and two teenage boys attempted to burn down a Seattle mosque on November 2, 2001. The *Columbian* reported that after they were apprehended, they were charged with suspicion of second degree arson and malicious harassment.[98] As a result of the attack, some congregation members wondered whether it was safe to pray outside of their homes.

The same month, arsonists set fire to other houses of worship. One of the most serious hate crimes occurred on November 18, 2001, when intruders vandalized and burned down a Sikh temple in upstate New York. The hate crime took place in Palermo, an almost exclusively-white rural community 30 miles north of Syracuse. Four teenagers were eventually arrested and charged with the attack on the Gobin Sadan house of worship. One of the assailants, 18-year old William Reeves of Parish, New York, told the *Post-Standard* that he and his friends were upset about 9/11 and thought that area Sikhs were Muslim terrorists, mistakenly believing that the temple was called 'Go bin Laden.'[99] The other arsonists were 19-year old Cassie Joan Hart of Parish and 18-year old Joshua Centrone of Mexico, New York. Their companion, Mitcheal Trumble, 19, was involved in the temple destruction but left before the others set the gurdwara on fire.

The *Post-Standard* reported that on the night of the arson, the four young adults were in the process of drinking two 12-packs of beer when they decided to drive to the Gobin Sadan temple to make the turbaned people pay for 9/11.[100] They arrived at the temple a little after 9:00 p.m., desecrating the gurdwara by breaking windows with beer bottles. They drove away, but decided to return a little while later to inflict more damage. At this point, three of the vigilantes resumed their destruction, smashing windows, using racial and religious slurs, and discussing how the temple worshippers were followers of Osama bin Laden.[101]

The vandals then left the temple and drove away, dropping Trumble off at his home. Reeves, Centrone, and Hudson returned 15 minutes later, after deciding to burn the temple down in retaliation for 9/11. The three arsonists used a can of motor oil to start the fire, and then drove away.

Initially, media coverage of the fire offered conflicting perspectives about the blaze. The November 22, 2001 issue of the *New York Times* reported that investigators were almost certain that the fire was a case of arson since it began outside of the building.[102] Ignoring the physical evidence, other New York newspapers erroneously asserted that the blaze was unintentional. A November 24, 2001 *Times Union* article, entitled "No Sign of Arson in Fire at Temple," claimed that there was no evidence that the destruction was deliberate.[103]

Early into the investigation, police officers issued public statements challenging the Sikhs' assertion that the fire was a manifestation of the 9/11 backlash. In an interview with the *Times Union*, Oswego County Undersheriff Robert Lighthall questioned the widely-held belief that the fire was a hate crime, claiming that investigators had not confirmed that the fire was the result of arson and that there was nothing at the scene to suggest that it was bias-motivated.[104]

The November 18th arson was one of three post-9/11 attacks on the Gobin Sadan gurdwara, including an incident on November 12th in which a vandal smashed one of the temple's windows. Gurbachan Singh, a spiritual practitioner at the temple, told the *Post-Standard* that he found it unbelievable that investigators were unable to realize that the arson and the other two incidents of vandalism were almost certainly manifestations of backlash bigotry.[105]

As the investigation proceeded, more evidence began emerging that the destruction was bias-motivated. While collecting evidence after the November 18th fire, investigators found a large rock, approximately the size of a clenched fist, inside the temple's two-car garage. Authorities concluded that this stone was likely the projectile that a vandal used on November 12th to smash the gurdwara's window. Singh told the *Post-Standard* that this discovery indicated that the house of worship was being deliberately targeted, noting that a rock could not fly through the air on its own.[106] Singh was also upset about finding two smashed beer bottles near the meditation center, especially since Sikhism asks practitioners to refrain from using alcohol or drugs. Undersheriff Lighthall finally acknowledged that the fire was intentional, but told the *Post-Standard* that he didn't know if the site itself was a random or deliberate target.[107]

Although most of the rooms of the Gobin Sadan gurdwara were destroyed, the fire spared a room containing a 400-year old copy of the sacred Sikh text, Guru Granth Sahib, and another Sikh holy book, the Dasam Grath.[108] The intact temple room also contained the holy books of several major religions. Congregation members regarded the preservation of these religious manuscripts as a miracle.

Area Sikhs were disturbed that other New Yorkers failed to recognize the peaceful mission of the gurdwara and its history in the area. Sikh spiritual practitioner Baba Virsa Singh Ji dedicated the Gobin Sadan USA temple in 1993, and modeled the facility as a working farm like five similar religious centers in India.[109] The Palermo temple was originally used to grow food and provide outreach to the homeless, hungry, destitute, and addicted. After the farm faltered in the 1990s, the gurdwara continued to be used by approximately 50 to 100 practicing Sikhs, who used the building as a weekend spiritual retreat.

Temple spokesman Ralph Singh told *India-West* that he found it troubling that bigots assumed that turbans were un-American.[110] He explained that Sikhs see their dastaars as the symbol of truth, justice, and ethical principles, similar to the values embodied in the American way of life.

In response to intense national media scrutiny, investigators launched a thorough investigation into the November 18th fire. Local police, ATF investigators, and FBI agents from the state Fire Prevention and Control Office worked more than 12 hours a day, seven days a week on the case. They also used a $15,000 reward to generate dozens of tips and interview scores of people. They eventually arrested the arsonists, who confessed to the crime.

According to the *Post-Standard*, investigating officers compiled reports filled with accounts of the various anti-Arab, anti-Afghan, and anti-Muslim slurs used by the teens during the commission of their crimes.[111] The police used this information to prove that the temple attackers were definitively motivated by post-9/11 bias.

Reeves and Centrone, who used lighters to start the fire, were charged with third-degree arson, and held on $10,000 bail or $20,000 bond. Hudson was charged with fourth-degree conspiracy and released on $5,000 bail. Despite overwhelming evidence that the temple attackers used racial and ethnic slurs, prosecutors initially refused to file bias charges against Reeves, Hudson, or Centrone. Only Trumble was charged with criminal mischief as a hate crime. All were subsequently freed on bail.

Although the teens were chugging beer the night they repeatedly drove to and from the temple, no one was charged with driving while intoxicated.[112] The district attorney also failed to file charges against any adult involved in providing the underage teenagers with the six-packs of beer.

The arsonists' defense attorneys argued that their clients should be found innocent of committing bigotry-motivated offenses. Because they were targeting Muslims from Afghanistan, they reasoned, their clients could not be found guilty of committing hate crimes against South Asian Sikhs. Charles Goldberg, Mitcheal Trumble's defense lawyer, said his client and his companions were innocent of committing a bias attack, telling the *Post-Standard* that the teens merely said some words and broke some windows.[113] Joseph Pagano, Reeves' attorney, agreed that the teens did not commit a hate crime, pointing out that they didn't even understand the difference between Islam and Sikhism.[114]

Rather than act as an advocate for the victimized South Asians, District Attorney Dennis Hawthorne, Sr. was reluctant to charge the vandals with hate crimes because he felt that the teenagers were products of their environment. He told the *Post-Standard* that they were too young to be held fully accountable, and were likely influenced by a racist mentor who spent years planting the seeds of bigotry.[115] Some civil rights activists were disturbed that Hawthorne was making public speculations about the arsonists' non-existent mentor, faulting the district attorney for making excuses for the vigilantes. Community activists pointed out that it was not the prosecutor's job to provide justifications for why the hate-motivated vandals terrorized an innocent religious community in the aftermath of 9/11.

Mark Centrone, Josh Centrone's father, disagreed with Hawthorne's assertion that the teens acted because they were exposed to a racist mentor. In an interview with the *Post-Standard*, the elder Centrone recognized that it was impossible to say anything to justify or mitigate his son's decision to commit arson, and acknowledged that his son had to face the consequences of his mistake.[116]

Josh Centrone eventually pled guilty to two felonies: third degree arson as a hate crime and first-degree reckless endangerment. Sikhs who prayed at the targeted center asked Judge Walter Hafner, Jr. to show mercy when sentencing the vandals who had destroyed their gurdwara. Temple spokesman Ralph Singh told the *Post-Standard* that forgiving the arsonists was in keeping with Sikh religious practices.[117]

On April 19, 2002, Judge Hafner sentenced Trumble to three months in jail, five years probation, 200 hours community service, and $1,000 in restitution. Hudson received a similar punishment. The judge then sentenced Centrone to three to nine years in prison, and ordered him to help pay for the destruction he caused.

Hafner indicated that although Centrone and Reeves had committed similar crimes, he felt that Reeves deserved a more severe punishment since he violated the terms of his pre-trial release and sent a foul letter to his own mother. Reeves eventually accepted a plea bargain and pled guilty to third-degree arson. He was sentenced to four to 12 years in prison for his role in the November 18th fire, and was ordered to contribute to the $127,000 repair costs.[118]

Reflecting on the temple arson, Ralph Singh urged the Sikh community to resist hating the ignorant perpetrators. He told *India-Abroad* that he and other Sikhs were not after vengeance, and shared a love and respect for all people.[119] He also noted that the fire could be seen as an opportunity to teach others about Sikhism and the faith's values of love and tolerance. He felt that the tragedy created an occasion to engage in interfaith dialogue, rebuilding and repairing the community as well as the building.

Many Palermo residents offered condolences and support to temple congregants. One school in the area conducted a fund-raiser to help pay for temple repairs. Baxter Vall, headmaster of the Manlius Pebble Hill School, held a 'dress-down day' fundraiser in which 60 pupils paid $3 each for the privilege of being allowed to wear casual clothes to class instead of the formal outfits mandated by the dress code.[120] Ralph Singh was grateful for all the community support the temple received after the fire, seeing some of the best qualities of humanity emerging out of the ashes of the blaze.

In addition to the Palermo arson, Sikhs across the country were traumatized by other attacks on their temples in November, 2001. The *Washington Post* reported that at least one vigilante yanked off and stole the sign announcing the construction of the 'Sikh Cultural Center of Washington, D.C.'[121] The trespasser also took the gurdwara's American flag, sending the nativist message that Sikhs were not entitled to fly it. In addition, a vandal damaged the trailer on the temple building site, covering it with black curls of graffiti and smearing its window screen with eggs.

South Asians in the area were upset by the vandalism because the building site was to become the capital's first Sikh temple. Without a gurdwara, approximately 10,000 Sikhs in Fairfax and Montgomery counties were compelled to hold prayer services in their homes. Many Sikhs were convinced that the temple vandalism was part of the 9/11 backlash. Sikh congregant Shamsher Singh told the *Washington Post* that in the year and a half prior to the terrorist strikes, the trailer had never been disturbed.[122]

Once the police finished collecting crime scene evidence, a group of nine Sikh volunteers cleaned up the temple destruction. Wearing surgical masks and gloves, the group painted over the black graffiti. Two Alexandria college students also replaced the stolen U.S. flag, putting the stars and stripes above a sign declaring, 'Sikh Americans Join All Americans in Prayer.'[123]

Clean-up crew members spoke with reporters about how some community members vocally opposed their plans to rebuild the temple. Some neighbors objected to the size of the building and the possibility of additional traffic. In response, Sikh leaders reduced the scale of the construction, but speculated that the real source of the opposition was religious intolerance. Tejpal Singh Chawla, a Georgetown attorney, told the *Washington Post* that the recent wave of hate crimes made him worry about the future.[124]

In addition to attacks on gurdwaras, other non-Christian religious centers continued to be targeted throughout the U.S. On December 5, 2001, a gunman with a small-caliber weapon fired on the Northwest Indiana Islamic Center. The attack occurred while worshippers were praying upstairs. The intruder shot into an area frequently used by Muslim children. Ali Khan, a member of the congregation, told the *Post-Tribune* that when he first heard the gunfire, he thought immediately of his two nephews, ages five and seven, who often played in the basement where the gunman blasted the windows.[125] Khan acknowledged that the attack could have been even more tragic if a member of the mosque had been killed. Detective Commander Tim Wardrip reported that local police had been working in conjunction with the FBI to solve the case. In the course of their investigation, crime scene analysts processed the recovered bullets at the Lake County Crime Lab. Many members of Gary's Muslim community remained shaken by the shooting, especially since the mosque had received a threatening phone call on 9/11 and had flags stolen from the center later the same month. Since these previous incidents had been reported to the police, area Muslims felt that authorities could have done more to protect them.

In late 2001, California mosques were occasionally targeted. In Lomita, vandals threw bricks through the window of a mosque, according to the December 21, 2001 issue of the *Daily Breeze*.[126] In Hawthorne, a vigilante used a brick to smash the window of a car parked outside of an Islamic prayer center.[127]

Mosques in the Midwest were also attacked. On December 30, 2001, Columbus Muslims arriving at 7:00 a.m. for morning prayers found their Islamic Center horribly desecrated. According to the *Columbus Dispatch*, intruders broke through the side door and vandalized the building's interior, ripping out carpets, defiling religious books, and destroying the floor.[128] The assailants also pulled the water pipes from the sink and walls in the third floor bathroom.[129] In addition, they clogged up drains and water-saturated the floors and ceilings, causing more than $100,000 in damage.[130]

Siraj Haji told the *Cincinnati Post* that water had soaked the floors and ceilings of the mosque, making it look as though it were raining.[131] Many Muslims were particularly disturbed that the vigilantes had shredded several copies of the Quran and had thrown them into the parking lot. Other religious artifacts were also mishandled.

Columbus Muslims were upset that the hate crime was clearly premeditated. According to police reports, the vandals used drills to maximize the water damage. Asma Mobid-Uddin, vice president of Ohio CAIR, told

Columbus Dispatch that the attack was extremely frightening.[132] She felt that the flooded mosque reflected the intolerance that Muslims were subjected to in the state.[133] She claimed that ignorance about Islam was the root of much of the bigotry, expressing her sadness that many Americans had such a negative view of her faith.[134]

Mohammed Shareef, the President of the Islamic Foundation of Central Ohio, told the *Cincinnati Post* that the mosque attack showed that the 9/11 backlash was still ongoing.[135] He said that although hate crimes had diminished somewhat, the December 30th vandalism indicated that there was a revival of Islamophobia in the area.

Despite the extensive destruction, worshippers were determined to rebuild their facility, which was the oldest center of its kind in central Ohio.[136] While the mosque was being repaired, Muslims used an adjacent facility, also owned by the Islamic center, for daily prayers. Since this site was not big enough to accommodate all the Muslims who attended the mosque's bi-weekly worship services, mosque officials were compelled to search for another building to accommodate all congregants.

Mayor Michael B. Coleman told the *Columbus Dispatch* that he was upset by the mosque attack, which he characterized as being either a burglary or a hate crime.[137] Since no money was taken from the collection boxes near the front entrance, local Muslims wondered why the mayor was willing to speculate publicly that the mosque desecration might have been a robbery. Whereas Coleman expressed uncertainty about the cause of the destruction, congregation members regarded it as a backlash crime, particularly since the house of worship received a threatening letter the week before it had been targeted.

Ignoring evidence suggesting the vandalism was deliberate, Columbus police refused to label the mosque attack a hate crime and did not speculate on an alternative motive. They did, however, assign bias-crime officer Wes Johnson to the case, which was also investigated by burglary detectives and FBI agents.

In early January 2002, about 150 people rallied to condemn the destruction. Bonnie Awana, who ran the Islamic Foundation of Central Ohio, told the *Arab American News* that the actions of the Islamophobes did not represent the majority of the people in the area.[138]

As a result of the mosque destruction, area Muslims needed a new place to pray and study. Congregants expressed gratitude for all the community support they received, particularly from Rabbi Harold Berman of Congregation Tifereth Israel and Reverend Timothy Aherns of First Congregational Church.[139] These religious leaders offered to share their houses of worship with the 500 Muslims and 130 Islamic school students who lost their prayer center.[140] The Rotary Club also volunteered to help the mosque congregants find new accommodations.

During the rebuilding, Islamic school began attending religious classes inside First Congregational church, which was located about 10 blocks away from the destroyed house of worship. Mahmudur Rahman, director of the weekend Islamic school, told the *Arab American News* that his students felt relatively comfortable in their new surroundings because they considered Jesus a prophet.[141] Reverend Aherns agreed the Muslim students were adjusting well to their new accommodations. He reported that the Muslim girls told him they were happy to be in class, and the boys told him they would rather be elsewhere, acting just like the girls and boys at his school.[142]

At a January 26, 2002 meeting at the Ohio State Fawcett Center, Columbus Muslims grilled police about their handling of the mosque attack and their inability to arrest any suspects. Many audience members expressed their outrage that the police took so long to designate that the vandalism was a hate crime. According to the *Columbus Dispatch*, police officer John Rockwell responded by claiming that investigators had no way of knowing the perpetrators' motives.[143] Congregation members felt that detectives should have been more aware of the intensity of Islamophobia in the area.

It took approximately one year to repair the damage to the point that the building was once again useable. Instead of re-opening with fanfare, the Islamic house of worship resumed prayer services discreetly, to avoid attracting the attention of local bigots.

RELIGIOUS ATTACKS, 2002

Months after 9/11, churches serving minority parishioners continued to be attacked. The *San Francisco Chronicle* reported that a Los Altos Hills church with a predominantly Arab-American congregation was burned down by an arsonist on April 7, 2002.[144] According to the Marti McKee, spokeswoman for the Federal Bureau of Alcohol, Tobacco, and Firearms, flammable liquids were used to start the fire inside the Antiochain Orthodox Church of the Redeemer, a 5,000 square-foot house of worship. Because many of its parishioners were from the Middle East, many community members and public officials believed that the arson was a manifestation of the 9/11 backlash. Democratic Congresswoman Anna Eshoo, a co-sponsor of hate crime legislation, donated $5,000 towards a reward fund and urged a full federal investigation of the blaze. Samer Bahou, a church youth counselor, told the Chronicle that adult parishioners hoped to use the arson to teach children about their theological beliefs.[145] Gesturing towards the fiery remains of the wooden alter, he explained that Christianity teaches that the true altar of God lies inside every person.[146]

The same month, a Florida assailant was indicted for committing a mosque attack. On April 17, 2002, Charles D. Franklin was charged with deliberately crashing his pick-up truck into a Tallahassee house of worship.[147] In the aftermath of this hate crime, area Muslims worried that it was unsafe to attend religious services in such a hostile environment.

Islamic buildings were also targeted in other parts of the South. In Herndon, Virginia, intruders repeatedly vandalized the Ahmadiyya Muslim Community Center in May 2002, shattering the glass panes on the center's door on several occasions and urinating on the floor during one of the break-ins.[148] Fairfax police began an investigation after an employee reported the destruction to local authorities.

West Coast mosques were also targeted. In Milpitas, California, a vandal attacked a mosque construction site on June 11, 2002. According to the *San Francisco Chronicle*, responding officers found windows shattered and belongings strewn about a construction trailer and camper belonging to the Al-Hilaal Islamic Charitable Foundation.[149] Some of the graffiti included obscene messages about Arabs and references to the devil. Because of the derogatory ethnic words, police acknowledged the break-in was a hate crime. The destruction worried area Muslims, who noted that an Islamic house of worship in the city had also been vandalized on 9/11.[150]

On occasion, hate groups planned coordinated attacks on American mosques. On August 22, 2002, authorities uncovered what many law enforcement personnel characterized as one of the most serious domestic terrorism plots in U.S. history. According to the *Forward*, podiatrist Robert J. Goldstein and his co-conspirators meticulously mapped out an attack against approximately 50 mosques and Islamic facilities in Florida.[151] The *Forward* described Goldstein as a self-appointed avenger of 9/11 who referred to Muslims as "rags."[152] With the help of his wife, Kristi Goldstein, and his friend Michael Hardee, a local dentist, Goldstein planned to attack and destroy the Islamic Education Center in Penellas and other mosques with enough C4, homemade explosives, guns, and napalm to reduce the buildings to rubble.[153]

The police discovered the terrorist plans by accident, while responding to a domestic violence complaint. Authorities conceded that it was a fortunate fluke that the plot was uncovered.[154] While searching Goldstein's house, ATF agents found his weapons cache, making them realize they had foiled a significant and legitimate terrorist operation.[155] They recovered 15 ready-to-use bombs and the necessary materials to make additional explosive devices. They also retrieved automatic guns, hand grenades, armor-piercing rockets, a 50-caliber sniper rifle, 25,000 rounds of ammunition, and a Kevlar vest.[156]

ATF investigators unearthed detailed records delineating how Goldstein planned to use a tripwire to exterminate fleeing Muslims.[157] They also found evidence that he intended to engage in face-to-face combat with any remaining survivors and kill any cops assisting them.[158] He also expressed his willingness to use knives to stab Muslims who were not killed by other means. Along with his detailed plans targeting the

Islamic Education Center in Pinellas, Goldstein had a list of dozens of other mosques he intended to destroy with the assistance of Hardee, his driver.[159]

Many Americans were outraged when federal authorities decided against leveling terrorism charges against Goldstein and his co-conspirators, allowing them to plead guilty only to civil rights allegations, conspiracy charges, and weapons violations. Muslims and Arabs across the U.S. were outraged, arguing that Goldstein was extremely dangerous and that leveling terrorism charges against him and his accomplices would have protected the public safety by doubling their sentences. Ahmed Bedier of CAIR questioned whether federal prosecutors would have been so lenient if the bomb plotters had been Muslims. He told the *Forward* that Goldstein's actions unquestionably fit the definition of terrorism.[160]

According to Steve Cole of the U.S. Attorney's office in Tampa, Goldstein and his accomplices did not receive special treatment because they were Jewish or because they were American-born.[161] Prosecutors insisted that Goldstein and his co-conspirators were treated the same as anyone else accused of the same crimes. Activists questioned whether this was indeed the case, pointing out that the term "terrorists" should apply to a group of violent bigots who built bombs, hoarded automatic weapons, collected hand-grenades, and amassed napalm in preparation for a deadly assault on dozens of minority-owned houses of worship, in the hopes of exterminating American civilians and wiping out police officers assisting the wounded.

Goldstein was eventually sentenced to only 12.5 years in jail for his plot to attack the Islamic Education Center in Pinellas and approximately 50 other Islamic sites in the state. Florida Muslims felt that Goldstein's punishment did not match the severity of his crimes, and that the light sentence gave the green light to other violent bigots.

Other Florida Islamophobes also targeted area Muslims. On one occasion, an Arab-American Christian targeted a mosque under construction. In September 2002, police caught George Aboujawdeh, a 45-year old Boca Raton man, setting fire to the sign of a partially-built Muslim center at 1400 NW Fourth Ave. This was the fourth attack on the Assalam Center's sign since March 2002.

Because of these earlier attacks, the local police's crime suppression team had the property under surveillance. The *Palm Beach Post* reported that officers saw Aboujawdeh repeatedly pass the sign before he set it on fire on September 4, 2002.[162] The two officers chased Aboujawdeh and apprehended him, finding matches in his hand. They also recovered the bottle of clear liquid he threw on the ground.

According to the *Post*, Aboujawdeh initially told investigators that he started the fire to send a message to Muslims that they were not liked in the community.[163] He later denied making the statement, saying only that he disliked terrorists. Since he was a first-time offender, he was charged with criminal mischief and evidencing prejudice while committing an offense. Because the arson was bias-motivated, it elevated the offense to a first-degree charge. Police Captain Jim Burke said crime investigators hoped to link Aboujawdeh to the three previous sign attacks. Aboujawdeh was incarcerated at Palm Beach County jail while he waited to undergo a judge-ordered mental evaluation.

When the case came to court in February 2003, assistant state attorney Renelda Mack interrogated Aboujawdeh about whether bias against Boca Raton Muslims factored in his decision to burn the sign. The *Palm Beach Post* reported that Aboujawdeh avoided answering the prosecutor's questions directly, attempting to justify his actions by claiming that Muslims at a mosque in Illinois had recently been arrested on suspicion of terrorism.[164] Aboujawdeh then attempted to characterize the arson as an attempt to act against Muslim extremism.

His defense attorney, Bert Winkler, characterized his client's bias-motivated arson as a petty offense and attempted to portray Aboujawdeh, owner of Arz Builders, as a traumatized victim of violence, having spent years fighting Muslim extremists in Lebanon.[165] Winkler explained that Lebanese militants had killed members of Aboujawdeh's family and asked the court for leniency, requesting that Judge Jonathan Gerber sentence his client to probation or house arrest instead of the maximum sentence of one year in jail.[166] The prosecutor responded by characterizing the sign arson as a serious bias-motivated crime that terrorized the

Muslim community in Boca. She asked that Aboujawdeh be jailed, ordered into psychological treatment, and court-mandated to write a letter of apology.

Four members of the Assalam Center attended the hearing, and urged the judge to hold Aboujawdeh accountable for his actions. The *Palm Beach Post* reported that Nazih Ibrahim testified about the crime's effect on the community, asking the judge to treat the matter as seriously as an assault on a church or synagogue.[167] Ibrahim also reminded the court that Muslims were Americans, and deserved the same legal protections as other citizens. Another mosque member, Munzir Zirli, urged the judge to recognize that Aboujawdeh committed a hate crime, suggesting that the mosque arson was a symbolic act like burning the American flag.[168]

Prior to sentencing, Aboujawdeh finally apologized and accepted responsibility for his actions.[169] After he was convicted of a misdemeanor, the judge sentenced him to 21.5 days in jail, allowing the contractor to continue running his business. He was ordered to pay restitution for the destruction of the $900 sign, attend an anger-management course, and watch an anti-discrimination video. Aboujawdeh was also required to perform 100 hours of community service at three religious institutions that practice a faith other than his own.

Throughout the country, mosque personnel continued to receive death threats. The *Los Angeles Times* reported that in the year following 9/11, officials at the Islamic Center of Claremont received several menacing calls targeting area Muslims.[170] One caller blamed the Southern California center for the deaths in New York and D.C., promising to bomb the facility in retaliation for the attack on America.[171]

Hate crimes escalated near the first anniversary of 9/11. The weekend after September 11, 2002, a mosque in Sterling was repeatedly attacked.[172] Because another Islamic center had been vandalized in the town in 2001, Muslims in the area felt under siege once again. According to the *Washington Post*, the September 2002 attackers spray-painted black swastikas and racial profanities on the Sterling mosque's tan walls.[173] The vandals also damaged six cars parked near the prayer center, drawing black lines on the vehicles. Two days after the first incident, the intruders attacked the building again, spray-painting another swastika on the back of the house of worship.

According to the Loudoun County Sheriff's Office, two Sterling teenagers were later arrested and charged with one count of felony hate crime, one count of felony destruction of property, and five counts of misdemeanor destruction of property. To alleviate community fears, Kraig Troxell, a spokesman for the Sheriff's Office, told the *Washington Post* that the crime was committed by a 14-year old and a 16-year old acting on their own.[174] Yasir Syeed, community relations director of the All Dulles Area Muslims Society, expressed his relief that the suspects were apprehended, and were not part of an organized hate group.[175]

Mosque attacks continued in other states. Early in the morning on September 15, 2002, an armed vigilante fired seven bullets at a mosque in Cuyahoga Falls, Ohio. One of the bullets entered the prayer hall after piercing a plate-glass window. Ihsfan Ul Haque, president of the Islam Society of Akron and Kent, told the *Plain Dealer* that the gun attack threatened the safety of worshippers, noting that hundreds of congregants attended religious services and Sunday school at the facility.[176] Haque called on Ohio residents to take a unified stand against xenophobia, so that bigots would know that they were not acting on behalf of the larger community.

Although the gunman chose to shoot up the Islamic center less than four days after the first anniversary of the terrorist strikes, Cuyahoga police did not publicly acknowledge that the mosque attack was a hate crime.[177] Cuyahoga mayor Don Robart conceded that mosque security should be tightened anyway, especially since Ohio Muslims were targeted in the immediate aftermath of 9/11.[178]

Hate crimes directed at American mosques may have been fueled in part by movies featuring nefarious dark-skinned Muslims killing sympathetic white Christians. In the 2002 movie, *Four Feathers*, British soldiers are dispatched to Sudan in the late 19th century after an army of Muslims attacked one of their overseas regiments.[179] The film does not clarify what prompted the Africans to take up arms against the British invaders. Since their actions seem unprovoked, the Sudanese appear as blood-thirsty savages who pray facing Mecca before they torture and murder British soldiers. Film critic Shaheen notes that in one scene, the movie's fair-haired Christian protagonist, Harry Feversham, played by Heath Ledger, puts on Arab garb and kills dozens of his desert-dwelling Muslim enemies.[180] One of the only positive dark-skinned characters in the movie is Abou, played by Djimon Hounsou, who betrays the Muslim Sudanese rebels and helps the white British Christian occupiers against his fellow Africans.

While American theatre audiences were watching Islamophobic movies, attacks on mosques continued. On October 21, 2002, someone left hundreds of anti-Muslim pamphlets outside of Honolulu's Islamic Center, Oahu's only mosque.[181] According to the *Honolulu Star Bulletin*, the suspect or suspects threw the leaflets over the mosque's fenced yard at approximately 8:00 a.m. These jingoistic, pro-American flyers referred to Muslims as curry-eating 'rag-heads,' and proposed that they should be killed for their financial support of terrorist groups.[182] Members of the Muslim community were disturbed by the pamphlet's content. Rashid Abdullah, information officer for the Muslim Association of Hawaii, told the *Star Bulletin* that he was dismayed by the ignorance and bigotry of the author of the leaflet, pointing out that the writer could not even spell correctly.[183] He felt that the hate messages did not reflect the sentiments of most Hawaiians, who were tolerant of religious differences and outraged by the bias attack.

Daniel Dzwilewski, special agent in charge of the FBI's Honolulu division, told the *Honolulu Star Bulletin* that the federal government was investigating the case, in conjunction with local police.[184] According to Dzwilewski, agents were exploring whether the hate pamphlets were an attempt to intimidate Hawaii's Muslim community, which consisted of approximately 3,000 residents. Minority community members were frustrated that federal agents were reluctant to acknowledge that the racist attack was intended to frighten worshippers.

Some area Muslims felt that local Islamophobia was fueled by nationally-televised hate speech. Nihad Awad told the *Honolulu Star Bulletin* that he saw a connection between anti-Muslim crimes and evangelical anti-Muslim sermons given by Franklin Graham, Jerry Falwell, and Pat Robertson.[185]

RELIGIOUS ATTACKS, 2003

Mosques and temples continued to be targeted in 2003. On the same evening, Hindu temples in two mid-Western states were attacked. The *St. Louis Post-Dispatch* reported that in Shawnee, Kansas, a vandal broke the glass front door of the Hindu Temple and Cultural Center of Kansas City, causing about $700 damage.[186] An FBI spokesman in Kansas City said that the incident was not being investigated as a hate crime. Congregants were dismayed that federal authorities were unable to see the likely bias motive of the temple vandalism. On the same evening in Missouri, another Hindu temple was damaged. On this occasion, an arsonist threw a Molotov cocktail against the front door of a Queeny Park Hindu house of worship in West St. Louis.[187] The firebomb charred the temple's door, and prompted religious officials to install a video camera to increase security.

About two weeks later, on the morning of March 8, 2003, the same Missouri Hindu temple was firebombed again. According to police reports, a vandal threw a brick through a window and tossed a flaming container into the building, charring the window frame.[188] This time, the Hindu temple's security camera captured footage of the Molotov cocktail. Unfortunately, the recording device did not capture any pictures of the arsonist. Hindu worshippers wondered whether the perpetrator would have been caught if federal officials had helped protect the temple by adding their own surveillance after the first arson attack.

Many of the 600 Hindu families who prayed at the house of worship were frightened by the hate crimes. Former temple president Jiwan Singla told the *St. Louis Post-Dispatch* that the attacks terrified Hindu congregants, who worried about their safety.[189] Singla also said that the two firebombings undermined his own sense of security. Realizing that they could not rely on local or federal officers to protect the building, Hindu temple officials debated paying out-of-pocket for additional security measures, such as hiring a security guard, installing motion detector lights, building perimeter fencing, and adding additional video cameras.

Investigators admitted having few leads in the attacks. St. Louis police officer Mason Keller reported that the arsonist involved in the second firebombing may have left footprints in the snow, but acknowledged that chasing this trail was not promising.[190]

Local police downplayed the possibility that the repeated firebombings were motivated by post-9/11 xenophobia. St. Louis County police officer Mason Keller told the *Post-Dispatch* that there was no evidence that the two arsons at the Hindu temple were triggered by intolerance.[191] FBI officials were also reluctant to characterize the Molotov cocktail attacks on the Hindu temple as bias crimes. Agent Peter Krusin told the *Post-Dispatch* that the FBI opened an investigation, but concluded that the agency was unable to determine whether the temple firebombings were linked to bigotry.[192] Area Hindus were incredulous, unable to believe that law enforcement officers actually thought that the escalating temple attacks were simply random.

Some community members speculated that the arsonists may have mistakenly assumed that the Hindu temple worshippers were Muslims, especially since their house of worship was located down the road from the Islamic Foundation of Greater St. Louis. Discussing the post-9/11 attacks, Manjit Singh of the Sikh Mediawatch And Resource Task Force told the *Post-Dispatch* that many Hindu and Sikh South Asians in the U.S. were routinely targeted because they were mistakenly thought to be Arab Muslims.[193]

Local investigators eventually apprehended two teenagers and charged them with the firebombings. Newspaper articles about the perpetrators sometimes neglected to acknowledge the seriousness of their actions. The *Tulsa World* downplayed the gravity of the Molotov cocktail attacks by reporting investigators' findings that the arson attacks were pranks committed by bored teenagers.[194] Community activists were shocked by this conclusion, pointing out that most young people do not firebomb religious buildings out of boredom. Many South Asians were dismayed that the *Tulsa World* failed to explore why local police immediately accepted the suspects' self-serving explanation of events, instead of delving deeper into the reasons why they repeatedly targeted this non-Christian house of worship.

Rather than face stiff penalties for their actions, the arsonists were treated leniently by judicial officials. One of the perpetrators received only four months in jail after pleading guilty to charges of arson and weapons possession. Apparently, Missouri prosecutors felt that the firebombing of a Hindu temple did not merit hate crime charges.

The St. Louis prayer center was only one of several temples targeted during the 9/11 backlash. The *Post-Dispatch* reported that since the terrorist strikes, other houses of worship had been vandalized or set ablaze, with arson attacks at temples in Flushing, New York; Hamilton, Ontario; and Warrenville, Illinois.[195]

Because of the ongoing hate crimes, many temples and mosques increased their security protocols. A Manassas mosque in Virginia began using four volunteers to watch for unfamiliar faces in the building in the hopes of preventing future hate crimes. Religious officials hoped these crowd monitors would identify potential assailants before they hurt congregants.[196] Other mosques, including large ones in Detroit, posted volunteer security officers outside during prayer sessions. Because local law enforcement officers were unable to protect non-Christian prayer centers, religious leaders spent considerable amounts of money adding security cameras and paying for private security guards. The *Daily Herald* reported that officials at the Omar Shahin mosque in Tucson added cameras in the hopes of deterring or recording future hate crimes. Religious officials in other states also re-examined their security procedures after worshippers were harassed on mosque grounds. In Fremont, California, mosque officials explored hiring a private security officer after bigots threw eggs at a car outside the worship center and yelled at Muslim women wearing the hijab.[197] Despite these added precautions, mosques and temples continued being targeted.

Religious bigotry continued to be propelled by American movies pitting a white Christian hero fighting dark-skinned Muslim villains. The 2003 film, *Tears of the Sun*, depicts Nigerian Muslims as intolerant religious fanatics who murder Christians.[198] In the movie, the African Muslim characters are shown setting a Christian village on fire, killing women, children, and nuns. Film critic Shaheen observes that in one particularly graphic scene, a villain uses a machete against the defenseless Catholics, and displays a priest's severed head in dramatic fashion.[199] A white Christian Navy SEAL officer, played by Bruce Willis, eventually kills the Nigerian Muslim savages. This movie was released in the U.S. on March 7, 2003, four days before a mosque attack in Illinois.

On March 11, 2003, an assailant fired projectiles at the window of a Villa Park mosque in a Chicago suburb. Cars in the parking lot showed that the house of worship was in use at the time of the attack, suggesting that the assailant intended to intimidate or harm congregants. According to the *Daily Herald*, more than 100 people were inside, finishing their evening prayers, when they heard two loud bangs that sounded like gunfire.[200] Some of the congregation members were praying close to the shattered window and were traumatized by the frightening interruption.

Although the double-paned window on the north side of the mosque had two distinct holes, local police did not find conclusive evidence that the window was broken due to gunfire. Villa Park police officer John Szkolka suggested that an object could have been used to break the glass, and that worshippers might have heard echoes that merely sounded like gunfire.[201]

Even though investigators did not definitely determine what caused the two shattered holes in the mosque's windows, Chicago-area Muslims were concerned about the safety of their families. Many community members saw the attack as a manifestation of post-9/11 bigotry and a response to American militarism overseas. Naim Mansour told the *Daily Herald* he and the other congregants saw a connection between the hate crime and the beginning of the Iraq War.[202] He urged community members of all religious affiliations to come together and stand up against baseless hatred and intolerance.

Despite security concerns, the mosque's school resumed its school classes the day after the attack, hoping that Muslim students would be safe from further violence. Mosque officials also announced plans to hire private security guards to deter future hate crimes, especially since the worship center had been targeted previously and their American flag had been stolen three times in 2002.[203] Local Muslims refused to regard these thefts as simple burglaries, seeing them as a deliberate attempt to convey the bigoted message that non-Christians should not be allowed to fly the stars and stripes. Congregation members were also disturbed that local residents felt comfortable enough to air Islamophobic views openly, without concern that such intolerance would meet with community disapproval. According to the *New York Times*, one disc jockey in the area played an incendiary parody of an Elvis Presley song, with the lyrics, "hunka, hunka burning mosques."[204]

Ignoring widespread anti-Muslim sentiment in the neighborhood and previous attacks on their house of worship, Villa Park police officers told reporters that they were unwilling to describe the destruction of the mosque's windows during prayer services as a bias-motivated assault. In a March 17, 2003 article in the *Daily Herald*, police officials went on record saying that they didn't characterize the incident as a hate crime.[205] Abdul Hameed Dogar, director of the Islamic Foundation, disagreed with this conclusion. He told the *Muslim Journal* that the March 11 incident was clearly bias-motivated, leaving worshippers feeling frightened and vulnerable.[206]

To show support for the Villa Park mosque, the Chicago-based Council for a Parliament of the World's Religions organized an interfaith vigil after the attack. The groups in attendance included Lutherans, Catholics, Zoroastrians, Bahais, and Wiccans.

U.S. tensions with Iraq may have contributed to a new wave of anti-Muslim hate crimes. The *Washington Post* reported that an Islamic center in Glendale Heights, Illinois received a bomb threat the day before the war began.[207] Local FBI agents launched an investigation into the case.

Because mosques were being threatened and attacked with increasing regularity, many Islamic centers across the country began keeping a "safety kit" near their phones, to protect congregation members and collect evidence for police.[208] In the event that a caller claimed to have planted an explosive device, mosque staff members could easily access a list of important questions concerning the location of the bomb, its trigger mechanism, and the culprit's motive. This safety checklist, created by CAIR, reminded mosque officials to keep hate callers on the line as long as safely possible, write a detailed description of their voices, and summarize the nature of the threats.

Despite the increased vigilance and added security precautions, mosques continued to be attacked. The Glendale Heights Islamic Center was burglarized after the Iraq War began.[209] Mosques in other states were also targeted. In San Francisco, a bigot mailed a local mosque a rambling hate letter. Soleiman Ghali, president of the Islamic Society of San Francisco, told the *Chronicle* that the sender made death threats, suggesting that area Muslims needed to be exterminated.[210]

Many of the hate crimes endangered the lives of children. In Fairfax, Virginia, youngsters playing in a mosque playground on April 5, 2003 discovered that their school bus was burning. Before firefighters successfully extinguished the blaze at 10:00 a.m., the fire destroyed the diesel vehicle, which had been parked outside of the Dar al-Hijirah Islamic Center. According to the *Washington Post*, Firefighter Lt. Raul Castillo determined that an arsonist deliberately ignited the bus.[211] Although no one was physically injured by the arson, Fairfax county officials and federal agents launched an investigation into the crime, exploring whether it had been motivated by bias. Many area residents saw the attack as part of the wave of bigotry unleashed by 9/11.

Gurdwaras were also attacked in the spring of 2003. In Washington state, the Spokane Valley Sikh Temple was targeted by vandals. The *Spokesman Review* reported on April 20, 2008, an intruder threw rocks through a window, stole religious artifacts and money, and spray-painted a swastika and other racist graffiti on the house of worship.[212] The trespasser also put large white Xs on both sides of the temple sign, suggesting that the house of worship and its congregants needed to be erased. Gurjeet Singh Aujla discovered the destruction when he went into the gurdwara to meditate. He told the *Spokesman Review* that he was disturbed that bigots had such a poor understanding of the peaceful Sikh faith.[213] Although he was unsure why the temple was attacked, he suspected that the assailants may have intended to target Muslims. Many congregation members saw the vandalism as a manifestation of the ongoing 9/11 backlash.[214] To prevent future hate crimes, Sikh worshippers decided to upgrade the gurdwara's locks to deter assailants and get a security system to record future intrusions.

Xenophobic attacks coincided with the release of American movies depicting Middle Eastern Muslims as hijackers. In what Shaheen characterizes as a shameless exploitation of 9/11 victims, the film *Air Marshall* reinforced anti-Arab stereotypes by depicting Middle Easterners as heartless terrorists, reveling in killing airline passengers.[215] This movie was released in the U.S. on June 23, 2003. According to Shaheen, this film rehashed two 1986 Arab hijacker films: *Hostage* and *Delta Force*.[216] At a time when dark-skinned foreigners were already dealing with Islamophobia, *Air Marshall* transmitted the nativist message that foreigners were plotting to kill Western civilians.

While *Air Marshall* was being shown in American theatres, attacks on U.S. mosques continued. In July, 2003, an arsonist deliberately set a fire to the Islamic Center of New England's mosque, located in Quincy, Massachusetts. According to the September 10, 2003 issue of the *Patriot-Ledger*, local police saw the mosque fire as simple vandalism.[217] This conclusion upset area Muslims, who saw a bias component to the post-9/11 crime. Imam Talal Eid told the *Patriot-Ledger* that the July arson attack terrorized the community, making Muslims fear for their lives.[218] Reflecting on anti-Muslim hate crimes and community bigotry, he told the newspaper that the months after 9/11 had been the most awful period of his life, significantly worse than the Islamophobia he experienced prior to the terrorist strikes.[219]

The same summer, a vandal in California attacked gravesites at the Islamic Youth Organization Cemetery in San Bernardino County. According to sheriff's investigators, five gravesites were damaged and white paint was splashed on a marble grave marker of the remote Mojave Desert burial place. A cemetery manager told the *Press Enterprise* that this was the second or third time the Muslim graves had been desecrated in the past year.[220] In the years prior to 9/11, the north Adelanto Muslim grounds had not been disturbed. Since the burial place was only accessible by dirt roads, the sheriff's office conceded that the desecration of Muslim graves was likely premeditated. Because there were no explicit religious slurs on the tomb stones, investigators decided not to categorize the repeated vandalism of the Islamic cemetery as hate crimes. Community members were outraged that officials failed to recognize that anyone who traveled to a remote location to desecrate Muslim graves was almost certainly committing a bias-motivated attack.

In other parts of the country, Muslims were subjected to even more obvious hate crimes. In the summer of 2003, College Park, Maryland earned the dubious honor of becoming the site of the first cross-burning at a U.S. mosque. Discussing this post-9/11 attack, Nihad Awad told *India Abroad* that the crime constituted an assault on liberty and religious toleration.[221] The mosque's surveillance tape recorded two white men pushing a three-foot, six inch wooden cross on a patch of ground in front of the mosque and setting it on fire. According to county fire department officials and FBI investigators, the wooden cross had been coated with a flammable substance before it was ignited. One witness, who was at the mosque waiting for the custodian, saw the cross burst into flames before the perpetrators fled the scene in a van. Fire department spokesman Ramon Korionoff acknowledged that the cross-burning was motivated by bias.[222] Police asked mosque officials to review the videotape closely, hoping that they might be able to recognize the perpetrators if they did surveillance at the house of worship prior to the arson.

Mosques in Georgia were also attacked. In August 2003, vandals repeatedly targeted the Islamic Center of Savannah. The anti-Muslim hate crimes terrorized the 100 costal families who worshipped at the prayer center. The first incident happened on August 3, when mosque officials found five bullet holes in the garage door. Mosque board members discovered the gunfire damage when they went to attend a monthly board meeting. Masood Ahmed told the *Atlanta Journal-Constitution* that they discovered the bullet holes in the walls, and realized that a gunman had fired the shots through the door.[223] The attack left many worshippers afraid for their safety, particularly since the gunfire took place in a part of the mosque often used by women and children. Ahmed told the newspaper that the mosque had not been a frequent target of bias crimes before 9/11.[224] He added that anti-Muslim sentiment in Savannah had been intensifying as the religious community grew.

Fears escalated in Savannah as the hate crimes continued. On August 18, 2003, an Egyptian Georgia Tech student returned home from prayer services at the mosque and found his nearby apartment ransacked. The burglar stole Mohamed Abd Elhafez' laptop computer, cell phone, check book, social security card, CD player, and cash. According to the *Savannah Morning News*, the thief also left a note threatening the lives of area Muslims, demanding that they leave the city and informing them that they were being watched at all times.[225] This hate letter contained a Nazi swastika, suggesting that the crime may have been committed by a white supremacist. The menacing letter made Elhafez feel so unsafe in his apartment in the Hoover Creek Villas that he decided to stay with friends indefinitely. The mosque shooting and the anti-Muslim home invasion were reported to the local police and the FBI shortly after they occurred.

The most serious of the three anti-Muslim crimes took place later the same month, when an arsonist burned down the Islamic Center. According to the *Savannah Morning News*, the fire began at around 3:00 a.m. and spread quickly until it engulfed the grey brick building, leaving nothing but a blackened skeleton and blown-out windows.[226] The fire also destroyed Islamic holy books, including a rare 200-year old hand-written copy of the Quran.

Because the Islamic Center was housed inside a two-bedroom home in a residential neighborhood, some members of the congregation worried that the arsonists were trying to kill Muslims sleeping inside the building. Because Savannah's Muslim population had recently grown to about 500, mosque officials had hoped that one day they would be able to move the Islamic Center into a larger facility, and convert the Dutchtown Road building into an Islamic library. Because the targeted house of worship was under-insured, Savannah Muslims were unsure about how they could rebuild it. Board member Masood Ahmed told the *Atlanta Journal-Constitution* that the mosque had only a small amount of insurance on the building and nothing on its contents.[227]

Savannah fire investigators confirmed that the blaze was intentionally set, but hesitated to state that it was motivated by bias. Bill Kirkconnell, an FBI agent based in Savannah, reported that his office was investigating whether the deliberate fire was a hate crime. Area Muslims thought that the arson was almost certainly bigotry-motivated. Mosque board member Saad Hammid told the *Savannah Morning News* that he was convinced that the arsonist was motivated by Islamophobic sentiment.[228] Mark Potok of the Southern Poverty Law Center agreed that the mosque arson was likely an anti-Muslim hate crime, noting that authorities were often unwilling to acknowledge bias-motivated attacks. Explaining this reluctance, Potok told the *Savannah Morning News* that many authorities feared that their community would be regarded as hateful if others learned of bias crimes taking place in the area.[229]

ATF agents responding to the arson looked into the possibility that the blaze was started by a hate group based outside of Georgia. According to Steve Pugmire, an agent from the Atlanta Bureau, ATF investigators had jurisdiction in fires or bombings committed by an organization with ties extending outside of the state where the crime occurred.[230]

Following the fire, about 45 Savannah Muslims gathered in a small white tent erected after the arson demolished their house of worship. After this prayer gathering, Mohammed Sammor attempted to dispel Islamophobic misconceptions about mosques, telling the *Savannah Morning News* that they were places to worship God, not practice evil.[231]

In the aftermath of the fire, Rabbi Robert Wolkoff offered Savannah Muslims the use of his synagogue, Congregation Agudath Achim, so they would have an indoor place to pray. He also expressed his condolences for the loss of their house of worship, reminding the *Savannah Morning News* that all people were children of God, and that Jews could empathize with other victims of hate crimes.[232]

Other religious leaders in Savannah expressed more lukewarm sentiments about the arson. Philip J. Hammond, pastor of Temple of Praise Church, told the *Savannah Morning News* that he was sorry the mosque had been set on fire, although he did not agree with the teachings of the Islamic faith.[233] He added that he was dismayed that Muslims were unwilling to accept that Jesus was God, or that He was killed on the cross.[234] Hammond also stated that he did not know the targeted worshippers personally, revealing that he had made no effort to build interfaith bridges with these vulnerable community members.

In many parts of the U.S., mosques were repeatedly targeted by vandals in the summer and autumn of 2003. According to the October 3, 2003 issue of the *Arab American News*, a mosque in Tempe, Arizona was desecrated when two vandals spray-painted a swastika, a "SS" thunderbolt, and other Nazi symbols on the door.[235] Deedra Abboud, director of CAIR in Arizona, noted that the hate crime constituted the fifth incident of vandalism at the Tempe mosque in less than a year.

In other states, vandals also attacked prayer centers that had been targeted on previous occasions. In 2003, for the third straight year, the All Dulles Area Muslim Society was once again desecrated by vandals. On November 11, worshippers discovered that anti-Islamic graffiti had been spray-painted on their center's 15-passenger van. In previous attacks in 2001 and 2002, vandals damaged the mosque itself. Mohamed Magid, executive director of the Sterling-based center, told the *Washington Post* that he was dismayed by the repeated attacks.[236] He also expressed his appreciation of the community support he received from neighbors horrified by the ongoing hate crimes.

RELIGIOUS ATTACKS, 2004: MOSQUES

Mosques continued to be targeted in 2004. In El Paso, Texas, a man was arrested for threatening an Islamic center.[237] Mosques were also attacked in other parts of the state. *San Antonio Express-News* reported that Lubbock vandals ransacked a mosque on March 7, 2004, breaking windows and writing pro-American and anti-Muslim messages on the walls.[238] They also stole mosque equipment and cash. Authorities estimated that the Lubbock attack caused about $12,000 in damages to the Islamic Center of the South Plains.

When the mosque assailants were apprehended days later, the police simply charged them with burglary. Perhaps because the four suspects were underage, police and prosecutors were unwilling to charge the youthful offenders with hate crimes, although they desecrated the mosque with Islamophobic messages. Two months after the Lubbock attack, *San Antonio Express-News* failed to characterize the mosque vandalism as a hate crime, accepting investigators' illogical conclusion that the perpetrators were not acting out of political, personal, or religious bias when they wrote anti-Muslim and pro-American graffiti on the house of worship.[239] The *Augusta Chronicle* also accepted officers' specious assertions that the crime was not committed because of anti-Muslim sentiment. According to this newspaper, assistant police chief Thomas Esparanza publicly stated that the perpetrators did not target the center or its congregants because of their religious affiliation.[240] Rather than question Esparanza's illogical conclusion that desecrating a mosque's walls with anti-Muslim messages is no indication of bias, the newspaper's coverage of the mosque attack downplayed its severity and portrayed the vandals as youthful troublemakers. The *Augusta Chronicle* and the *San Antonio Express-News* also failed to challenge assistant Criminal District Attorney Matt Powell's characterization of the mosque vandals as the least culpable suspects.[241]

Although one of the assailants was incarcerated with the Texas Youth Commission, most of the vandals were awarded lenient sentences, receiving probation and community service for attacking the house of worship. The offenders were also required to contribute to the repair costs. Southern journalists did not question whether probation was a fair punishment for the youths, highlighting instead the views of congregants who reported being satisfied with the vandals' apologies.[242] The *Augusta Chronicle* failed to include viewpoints of those who thought that the intruders were old enough to be punished more appropriately. It is possible that some mosque members may have been concerned that community sentiment might turn even more strongly against them if they demanded harsher punishments for the youths who desecrated their prayer center.

In some instances, Muslims were targeted while on mosque grounds. In the April 12, 2004 issue of the *Capital*, Rawaida Arafa describes how a group of men threw a bottle at her as she was unloading items from her car in the parking lot of a Maryland mosque.[243] Arafa heard the projectile hit the ground beside her shortly after she left the Islamic Society of Annapolis. According to the police reports, Arafa turned around and saw four or five men walking into a nearby office. Her husband, Mohammed Arafa, reported that the bottle came close to hitting her on her shoulder. He wondered if the attackers targeted his wife because she wore a hijab, or because he was the imam of the religious center. Even though the incident took place outside of a mosque and the victim was a veiled Muslim woman, local police concluded that there was no evidence indicating that the attack was a hate crime.

Bigots also targeted Islamic centers under construction. In the spring of 2004, the New Jersey attorney general Peter Harvey launched a bias crime investigation into the repeated vandalism of a mosque being built in Toms River, New Jersey. According to an April 24, 2004 article in the *New York Times*, vandals drew swastikas and racist graffiti on the partially-finished building, including a pro-Hitler statement.[244] They also punched holes in the walls, damaged the framework of the building, and broke windows on a trailer at the site. Mosque officials reported that it was the seventh time that the Islamic Center of Ocean County had been attacked since construction began.[245] On previous occasions, vandals damaged the mosque's plumbing, windows, and walls. They also desecrated a sign and set a trailer ablaze, causing an estimated $10,000 to $15,000 in repair costs. Garden state Governor James McGreevy told the *New York Times* that he was outraged about the mosque attack, finding the crime despicable.[246]

Elsewhere in New Jersey, vandals threw liquor bottles on the grounds of the Islamic Education Center in Union City. Area Muslims believed that the crime was bias-motivated. According to the *Bergen County Record*, worshippers were saddened that the anti-Muslim attack took place while congregants were inside, mourning an Arab-American teen killed in an automobile crash.[247]

In South Florida, three different mosques were targeted in May, 2004, frightening the 200,000 Muslims in the state. The *South Florida Sun-Sentinel* reported that bigots spray-painted a black swastika on the Islamic School of Miami and defaced its sign, covering it with obscenities.[248] Later the same week, intruders broke into the Al-Ihfan mosque in Miami and vandalized the inside of the house of worship. Soon afterwards, officials at the Dar Ul-Uloom mosque received a letter suggesting that all Muslims should be killed and judged by God.[249]

In other parts of the country, mosques continued to be targeted. According to the May 18, 2004 issue of the *Colorado Springs Gazette*, vandals painted an anti-Muslim death threat near a mosque in Greenwood Village, Colorado.[250] The same assailants also painted swastikas and the letters, "KKK," near the same house of worship.

In June 2004, a vandal desecrated the Islamic Foundation of Greater St. Louis, painting a Nazi swastika and the word, "die," on a gymnasium wall under construction.[251] A builder noticed the hate graffiti, but waited a few days before reporting it to his supervisor. The construction supervisor then notified mosque officials, who called the police. The St. Louis county police told the *Post Dispatch* that they had no suspects, even after reviewing the surveillance tape and canvassing the neighborhood for witnesses. [252] The targeted mosque was located near a Hindu temple that had been firebombed twice the previous year.[253] Many neighborhood residents attributed the hate crimes to post-9/11 nativism.

Throughout the summer of 2004, Muslims in Florida were frightened by repeated attacks on their houses of worship. In the Tampa suburb of Charlotte Harbor, vandals desecrated the Islamic Community Center by scrawling "Kill All Muslims" on its walls.[254] Vandals also wrote the same death threat on the Islamic Community Center in the Tampa suburb of Lutz, frightening congregation members.[255] Civil rights advocates were dismayed that their fellow Americans were still confusing local Muslims with the Taliban.

On occasion, bigots attacking mosques attempted to convey the message that the Islamic faith was un-American. On July 4, 2004, an arsonist exploded a bomb inside a mailbox at mosque in Houston.[256] Many area residents felt that the bomber deliberately chose to attack the Muslim house of worship on Independence Day to convey the message that following Islam was unpatriotic.

In December 2004, arsonists targeted mosques in Massachusetts and Arizona. In Springfield, investigators determined that arson was responsible for heavily damaging the Al-Baqi Islamic Center.[257] Seven juveniles eventually admitted to setting the mosque on fire, but denied that they were motivated by bias.[258] Area Muslims were upset that investigating officers took the teens at their word, noting that the arsonists would face stiffer sentences if they admitted to being motivated by anti-Muslim sentiment. Other Arizona mosques were also targeted by bigots. In Glendale, another suspicious fire damaged the As-Sadiq Mosque.[259]

RELIGIOUS ATTACKS, 2004: GURDWARAS

Sikh temples were also frequently targeted throughout 2004. In California, vandals attacked the Gurdwara Sahib temple in central Fresno on March 13, 2004. According to the *Fresno Bee*, the assailants desecrating the shrine entrance by spray-painting racist comments and religious slurs, including: "Rags Go Home," and "It's Not Your Country."[260] On the rear of the temple, another ethnic slur and a four-letter obscenity were scrawled in black on the back door. Local investigators doubted their ability to apprehend the perpetrators. Police Captain Marty West told the *Fresno Bee* that he had no leads in the case.[261] Although Fresno officers met with congregants about the temple assault, the Sikh community was upset by the police department's repeated failure to protect their gurdwara. Less than a year before, vandals targeted the same temple five nights in a row, defacing the house of worship with paint and firecrackers that caused a small fire at the rear of the building.[262] Some community members felt that local police or federal authorities should have installed security cameras or stepped up patrols to protect the gurdwara. In response to the March 13th incident, Lt. Governor Cruz Bustamante spoke out against the attack at a March 17th gathering, telling congregation members that acts of bigotry were unacceptable.[263] Dhaliwal Bharpur, a member of the Sikh Council of Central California, told the *Fresno Bee* that hate crimes were underreported in Fresno and other parts of California because many victims were seasonal workers who were too disempowered to prosecute their attackers.[264] To reduce area xenophobia, Bharpur urged Sikhs and other minorities to reach out to others in the community, so they would not be seen as an alien presence.

In response to the repeated attacks, the Fresno police department decided to train school resource officers and other deputies to improve the city's handling of hate crimes. Police chief Jerry Dyer assigned a deputy chief to act as a liaison to Fresno's Human Resources Commission to educate the community about Sikhs and address their misidentification as members of the Islamic faith. Dyer also publicly urged seasonal workers to report bias attacks, pointing out that officers had no way of solving unreported crimes.[265]

Many local Sikhs saw a connection between the March 13th attack and American nativism, which was fueled by 9/11 and the invasion of Iraq. In an article in the *Fresno Bee*, Balvedx Sangha, the temple vice president of the Sikh Center of the Pacific Coast, attributed the Fresno temple vandalism to post-9/11 Islamophobia, noting that most community members thought that they were Muslims.[266]

Along with religious centers, vandals also targeted signs belonging to non-Christian houses of worship. In May and June 2004, a gunman repeatedly targeted a well-lit sign of the Guru Nanak Sikh Temple in Solano County, California. The first attack took place on May 29th, damaging the light fixtures on the front of the $7,000 sign. According to *India Abroad*, temple founder Paul Randhawa initially dismissed this first incident, hoping it was a prank committed by teenagers.[267] He became more concerned after the second shooting, which took place on June 13, 2004. Suspecting that the sign was not a random target, he reported the destruction to the police. On both occasions, the gunman fired multiple bullets into the plastic and steel sign.[268] In response to these attacks, temple officials installed bullet-proof glass over the gurdwara's sign.

Some members of the Sikh community were concerned that the shootings may have been related to post-9/11 threatening phone calls targeting the temple and area Sikhs. Sheriff Gary R. Stanton, who led the investigation into the shootings, was not convinced that the repeated gun attacks were bias-motivated crimes. He told *India Abroad* that every year in Solano county, hundreds of road signs are knocked down or shot at each year.[269] He declared that he was unwilling to call in the FBI and California's Department of Justice until local police determined that the shootings were motivated by hate.

Rather than challenge Stanton's assertion that the repeated targeting of a Sikh temple sign by a gunman was something other than a hate crime, members of the Sikh community were afraid to draw attention to themselves by vocally advocating for a more rigorous investigation into the attacks. Randhawa told *India Abroad* that he thought it best for the community to keep a low profile and let the police deal with the hate crime, rather than create discord in the community by causing a fuss.[270]

RELIGIOUS ATTACKS, 2005

Hate crimes targeting mosques and temples continued throughout 2005. On May 28, 2005, a Florida vandal threw a large rock through the glass front door of a Miami mosque minutes before evening prayers. According to the *South Florida Sun-Sentinel*, the projectile was approximately the size of two fists, but resulted in no injuries.[271] A little over a week later, the Islamic School of Miami was attacked again in a similar manner, perhaps by the same perpetrator. On June 6, 2005, a vandal broke the gate leading to the mosque and threw rocks at the house of worship, shattering two of the glass doors.[272] Area Muslims were dismayed that local police were unwilling to investigate the repeated attacks as hate crimes, or protect the house of worship from bigots. Because the mosque had been hit six times since 9/11, area Muslims worried about their safety.

Mosques in California were also targeted by bigots. The *Los Angeles Times* reported that on June 3, 2005, a suspicious fire destroyed a prayer center at the Islamic cemetery in Adelanto, California.[273] The fire gutted the United Islamic Youth Organization's house of worship, leaving only two stucco walls standing. The blaze, which inflicted more than $225,000 in damages, also incinerated prayer rugs, Islamic manuscripts, and over 1,000 books, including Qurans.[274] Because the remote desert facility had no electric or gas service, investigators concluded that the fire was intentionally-set. Local police suspected that the arsonist may have been motivated by anti-Muslim bias. The fire terrified Southern California Muslims, who worried about an upswing in Islamophobia in the area. Mosque board member Seyed Mousavi told the *Los Angeles Times* that he was worried that an anti-Muslim bigot found out that it was the only Islamic cemetery in the U.S.[275] At the time of the blaze, more than 600 Shia and Sunni Muslims had been buried there, with each grave facing northeast towards Mecca.

Weeks after the arson, investigators failed to arrest any suspects, but two teenagers were charged in a separate Father's Day attack on the Islamic cemetery. According to the *Inland Valley Daily Bulletin*, the shooters took multiple weapons and fired more than 100 bullets into a washroom of a small building where Muslim bodies were being prepared for religious burials.[276] Dale June, a cemetery caretaker and husband of owner Muslima Fazal, witnessed the shooting. Their 14-year old son then called sheriff's deputies, frightened that the gunmen would turn their weapons on his family members or on bereaved Muslims visiting the graves of loved ones.

On July 17, 2005, an interfaith group gathered to speak out against the mosque destruction and community Islamophobia. The San Bernardino *Sun* reported that some in attendance wondered if the repeated Islamic cemetery attacks were part of the ongoing 9/11 backlash against Muslims, fueled in part by news of terrorist activity in London.[277] Although local police and the ATF were investigating the possible bias motivation of the arson, the FBI was hesitant to view the mosque fire as a hate crime. Community members were frustrated that the FBI was unwilling to or provide surveillance for the remote desert burial grounds, which had been targeted so frequently after 9/11.

The same summer, bigots also attacked Southern California mosques. In July 2005, vandals desecrated an Islamic center in Pomona. The *Los Angeles Times* reported that intruders broke into the Ahlul-Beyt mosque and left pornographic pictures on the mihrab, the prayer niche revealing the direction of Mecca to worshippers.[278] The vandal damaged and destroyed three doors inside the house of worship, and desecrated a white board with graffiti. They also rearranged the furniture, stole a television, and took the donation box. Congregation members, who were mainly Shias from Iraq, told the *Los Angeles Times* that they saw the vandalism as part of the wave of Islamophobia that began after 9/11 and surged after the terrorist strikes in London and Madrid.[279] Despite finding graffiti and pornographic material inside the house of worship, local police were reluctant to label the mosque attack as a hate crime, investigating it primarily as a robbery. Area Muslims were dismayed that local law enforcement officers were unwilling to recognize that the mosque desecration was likely bias-motivated.

The same month, a mosque in Indiana was targeted. The *Chicago Tribune* reported that an arsonist set a fire at the Islamic Center of Bloomington at 2:00 a.m. on July 9, 2005.[280] A community member reported the blaze, which was extinguished after damaging the kitchen area of the building. According to the *Denver Post*, the arsonist also broke a window at the mosque and left a burned Quran outside the house of worship, suggesting that the attack was bias-motivated.[281] Some community members speculated that the incident may have been triggered by the July 7, 2005 bombings in London. Although FBI investigators decided to treat the arson as a hate crime, they failed to make an arrest in the case.

Attacks on religious buildings escalated near the fourth anniversary of 9/11. The *South Florida Sun-Sentinel* reported that a Boca Raton Islamic center was targeted twice in less than a month, with one of the hate crimes taking place on September 12, 2005.[282] On this occasion, a vandal threw basketball-size rocks through two of the mosque's glass doors, and spray-painted one of its walls. According to Boca Raton police investigators, some of the rocks landed as far as 20 feet inside the Assadiq Islamic Education Foundation, spraying glass shards on the prayer rugs. The assailant also desecrated the mosque with graffiti, leaving clear evidence that the house of worship was deliberately targeted. Because this attack happened the day after the fourth anniversary of the terrorist strikes, many area Muslims viewed the vandalism as part of the ongoing 9/11 backlash.

Other American mosques were also singled out the same week. On September 14, 2005, the Islamic House of Worship was vandalized in Dearborn Heights, Michigan. During the attack, the intruder broke the mosque's sign, shattered the glass doors, destroyed the interior lighting, and desecrated the interior walls with paint. Dearborn police officers, alerted by the mosque's security alarms, responded to the scene and arrested 27-year old Nicholas Sterns, charging him with malicious destruction of property. Investigating officers were unwilling to connect the September 14th mosque desecration with the ongoing 9/11 backlash. According to the *Arab American News*, Detective Lt. Jeff Seipenko took the suspect at his word when he claimed that the vandalism had nothing to do with ethnic hate, even though he also admitted that he was angry when he attacked the prayer center.[283] Area Muslims were concerned that the vandalism was not being investigated as a bias crime, even though Sterns targeted a mosque and left other area buildings untouched. Imam Mohamad Ali Elahi told the *Arab American News* that Sterns should face hate crime charges for his actions, arguing that his behavior should not be excused simply because he was inebriated at the time.[284] Rather than view the mosque destruction as a crime of opportunity, Elahi saw it as part of a larger pattern of post-9/11 attacks deliberately targeting Muslims. Because local authorities were unwilling to charge Sterns with a hate crime, FBI agents were exploring whether federal bias charges were warranted. Other mosques, such as the Al-Islah Center in Mamtramck, were also vandalized in the region.[285]

One of the most serious attacks happened in November 2005, in Landsdale, Pennsylvania. According to the *Philadelphia Inquirer*, Robert Blackburn drove up to the Montgomery County Islamic Center and opened fire, shooting over 50 bullets while on mosque property.[286] In the parking lot, investigating officers counted 37 gunshot holes in a 2000 Honda Accord and 15 in a Lincoln Town Car, vehicles owned by Mostafa Hossain, the mosque's imam, and Mohammad Ensad, a Bangladeshi Muslim journalist. Area Muslims were particularly concerned that the intruder fired so close to the mosque's main entrance, putting in danger the lives of the 300-400 congregants who regularly attended Friday prayers. Some Muslims worried that anti-Islamic attacks were becoming increasingly dangerous, noting that on an earlier occasion, a vandal fired a BB gun at the center and broke one of its windows. Escalating hate crimes worried Muslims across the country. According to the *Bergen County Record*, the national office of CAIR reported a 30% jump in civil rights complaints from 2004 to 2005, suggesting that Islamophobia was surging in the U.S.[287]

On many occasions, police officers failed to launch comprehensive investigations of attacks on non-Christian houses of worship. Perhaps the most egregious example of ineptitude was the police inquiry into a December 22, 2005 incident at a Sikh temple in Bakersfield. According to *India-West*, worshippers at the Gurdwara Guru Angad Darbar discovered two freshly-severed pigs' heads, dripping with blood, on the ground outside the temple's dining hall.[288] Although police officers learned the names of the two perpetrators, they decided against charging the men with a hate crime. In a January 3, 2006 interview with *India-West*, Bakersfield police detective Mary DeGeare explained that department officials knew the culprits responsible, but decided against filing serious criminal charges against them.[289] Instead, officers charged the two men with the misdemeanor crime of improperly disposing of animal remains. The 18-year old suspects claimed that one of their mothers had instructed them to dispose of the pigs' heads in plastic bags.[290] While on the way to the disposal site, one of the bags flew out of their car window and broke apart. According to DeGeare, the men said they chose to leave the animal parts behind, because they were too messy to pick up.[291] Manbir Singh, board chairman of the gurdwara, told *India-West* that he found the men's explanation highly unlikely, pointing out that there was no reason for them to be driving on private property.[292] Many Bakersfield Sikhs viewed the incident as part of an ongoing pattern of post-9/11 community harassment, noting that just two weeks previously, someone had pelted elderly Sikhs in the area with eggs.[293] Rather than viewing the "flying pigs' head" story with skepticism, Bakersfield police refused to investigate the matter further, failing to count the incident as a hate crime.

RELIGIOUS ATTACKS, 2006

On occasion, internet footage recorded attacks on non-Christian houses of worship. On MySpace.com, two men posted a video of themselves shooting up a Quran and throwing it at a mosque located on 1410 Cemetery Avenue in Chattanooga, Tennessee. Although the video was apparently filmed the previous summer, it surfaced on the internet on June 17, 2006. According to the *Chattanooga Times Free Press*, the video begins with a man, identified as 'mully88,' holding a paperback copy of the Quran outside of a Barnes & Noble bookstore.[294] In the next scene, the man and an associate appear in a wooded area, shooting at the Islamic holy book with a Colt M-16. The video ends with the man throwing the bullet-ridden Quran at the front of the entrance of the Islamic Center, shouting what appears to be, "Jesus Rocks."[295] The man who posted the video described himself as a 33-year old resident of Chattanooga, and listed as his heroes anyone who had killed a Muslim or ever attempted to kill one.[296] The man's web site contained numerous swastikas and pictures of illegal high-powered firearms, displayed while white supremacist music played in the background. The site also featured racist slurs targeting Latinos and African-Americans. According to CAIR legal director Arsalan Iftikhar, the man's decision to desecrate a Quran and throw it at a mosque constituted an overt act of religious intimidation, exceeding the boundaries of free speech. Iftikhar maintained that the website violated the federal civil rights law that made it a crime to injure, threaten, or intimidate any person in the free exercise or enjoyment of any right or privilege secured by the Constitution or the laws of the U.S.[297] The FBI opened an investigation into the case.

Authorities looking into post-9/11 bias incidents sometimes disagreed about whether particular actions were against the law. For example, police officers expressed uncertainty about whether a perpetrator committed a crime by leaving an anti-Muslim sign on public property next to a South Houston mosque. According to Houston authorities, the large plywood placard, written in black crayon, labeled Muslims as the enemy.[298] It also included an offensive drawing of a bearded character representing Mohammed. Congregation members were offended by this cartoon's hateful message as well as its depiction of the prophet's physical body, which orthodox Muslims regard as a step towards idolatry. In a February 8, 2006 article in the *Houston Chronicle*, Nat McDuell, a spokesman for the Houston police department, said that the sign's placement on public property adjacent to the mosque made it difficult to prove it was intended to intimidate Muslim worshippers.[299] Federal authorities expressed similar sentiments. FBI agent Shauna Dunlap informed the *Houston Chronicle* that the anti-Muslim sign was not left on private property, making it impossible to prove that local Muslims were the intended audience.[300] Other investigators declared that it was difficult to know the motive of the creator of the sign.

Mosque officials found this reasoning absurd, angry that authorities failed to understand that the derogatory sign was an overt attack aimed at intimidating nearby worshippers. Imam Zoubir Bouchikhi told the *Houston Chronicle* that he was disturbed that the police seemed to be waiting for a major crime to take place before taking action to protect members of the congregation.[301] Kaleem Siddiqui, of Houston CAIR, was also troubled by investigating authorities' unwillingness to see that the offensive sign was clearly directed at the adjacent South Houston mosque, arguing that the perpetrator's intention was the same whether the sign was on mosque property or right beside it.[302] He added that he was surprised that the mosque was singled out at all, since Houston was a relatively cosmopolitan and tolerant city.

Around the country, mosque attacks continued. In April 2006, a gunman fired shots at a Maryland Islamic center.[303] In June, an Arizona mosque received a hate message attacking Mohammed and declaring that Muslims worship the devil.[304] The following month, another shooter fired at an Islamic prayer center in Michigan City, Indiana. During the July 2, 2006 attack, the bullets damaged the house of worship, making six holes in the copper dome of the One Michigan City Mosque. According to the police report, the gunman or an accomplice inflicted additional damage to the house of worship, scratching "KKK" on the center's sign.[305] Someone also smashed or vandalized ten windows, two glass doors, and a spotlight belonging to the religious facility.

One of the more egregious mosque attacks occurred in Maine on July 3, 2006, when Brent Matthews rolled a pig's head into the Lewiston-Auburn Islamic Center. The desecration occurred in the middle of evening prayer time, when 40 Somali congregants were at the house of worship. According to witnesses, the pig's head was larger than a basketball and rolled like a bowling ball through the mosque's open door into the crowd of congregants engaged in prayer.[306] No one was hit by the animal remains. Mosque spokesman Imam Nuah told the *Portland Press Herald* that worshippers continued to be frightened by the attack, even though the spot on the carpet where the pig's head came to rest had already been cleaned several times to erase physical evidence of the crime.[307] Abduallah Yousef said that the incident caused many Somali Muslims to wonder if Lewiston was a safe place for members of their faith.[308]

Before the attack, Matthews discussed his criminal plans with police officer Eric Syphers during a chance encounter at the Lewiston Mall. According to the *Press Herald*, officer Syphers claimed that he discouraged Matthews from committing the mosque assault, warning him that leaving the pig's head in a doorway as a practical joke might result in charges of littering or the improper disposal of animal parts.[309] Once Syphers heard that Matthews' proposed crime had actually taken place, he realized he knew the likely culprit. When officers questioned Matthews, he admitted to rolling the frozen pig's head into the mosque as a prank.[310] Maine Attorney General Steven Rowe filed an injunction against Matthews on July 20, 2006, saying that his actions damaged property and threatened congregants. Matthews was later arrested on the misdemeanor charge of desecrating a house of worship. This was not Matthews' first run-in with the law. Prior to the July 3, 2006 mosque attack, he had been charged with assault, operating a vehicle under the influence, and other minor crimes.

Matthews' defense attorney James Howaniec told the *Press Herald* that his client did not intend to target Muslims or their mosque, characterizing the building as a run-down store front with no sign identifying it as a religious institution.[311] Howaniec also argued that Matthews had no idea that pigs and pork products were considered offensive to Muslims, and that officer Syphers had given his client the mistaken impression that committing such a practical joke would not result in serious legal charges.[312] Matthews told the *Press Herald* that police officers laughed about his actions on the night of his arrest and on the day he was booked, with one officer telling him that he wished he had thought of taking such action himself.[313] Consequently, Matthews felt that the incident should not be considered a hate crime if local authorities and the general community found it comical.

Somali Muslim residents of Lewiston did not find Matthews' action amusing or his explanation convincing. Abi Sheikh, a Somali resident and local leader, told the *Boston Globe* that the mosque attack deeply troubled Maine's Muslim community, suggesting that if a pig's head could be thrown with impunity, a bomb might follow.[314]

Lewiston Police Lt. Michael McGonagle argued that Syphers should not be held accountable for giving Matthews incorrect counsel since the police officer was not familiar with civil rights statutes. Local Muslims rejected this reasoning, maintaining that any competent officer should have known that attacking a mosque with a severed pig's head was a serious hate crime. McGonagle also proposed that the officers who made light of the incident may have done so to elicit more cooperation from Matthews, since suspects were more likely to divulge information to policemen who were sympathetic to their views.[315] Many Muslims were skeptical of this explanation, seeing officers' dismissive treatment of the hate crime as an indication that post-9/11 attacks were not being taken seriously by the police.

Some community members suggested that it would be helpful if the police department created a policy requiring investigating officers to email a superior before intentionally making provocative statements during interrogations. That way, minority residents could be shown the time the email was sent and know for sure whether bigoted statements made by police officers were orchestrated or inappropriate. Because there was no such policy in place, many area Somalis assumed that the police officers' offensive comments were indicative of their racism.

Many locals saw the Lewiston mosque attack as a manifestation of escalating racial tensions resulting from increased Somali immigration to the city. At the time of the pig's head incident, there were approximately 2,000 Somali Muslim residents in the city, out of a total population of 36,000. According to Lewiston Town Administrator Jim Bennett, Somali Muslim refugees in Lewiston had unemployment rates in excess of 70% in the summer of 2006, draining community resources.[316] In 2002, Lewiston's mayor Larry Raymond wrote an open letter to the Somali community urging them not to send for their relatives because the town was financially, emotionally, and physically maxed out from the influx of immigrants.[317] In response to this letter, film maker Ziad Hamzeh created a 2003 documentary about the mayor's public appeal to the Muslim residents of Lewiston to keep their relatives and friends from moving to the area.[318] The same year this film was released, the white supremacist group, World Church of the Creator, organized an anti-Somali rally, with 32 attendees. In response to this show of nativist sentiment, a progressive group, Many In One, held a counter-rally, attended by 4,500 people.

A few years later, on July 12, 2006, Maine residents held yet another pro-diversity rally to promote religious tolerance and to protest the Lewiston-Auburn mosque desecration. According to the *Savannah Morning News*, Maine Governor John Baldacci was in attendance, accompanied by Christian, Muslim, and Jewish leaders.[319] They all condemned the hate crime and declared that an attack on any house of worship was a blow against all people of faith.

Perhaps embarrassed by the extensive press coverage of police officers' jovial response to the mosque assault, the district attorney levied additional charges against Matthews. They also publicly stated that they were taking the case seriously, charging Matthews with desecrating a place of worship. The attorney general also charged Matthews with infringing on the civil rights of others. Because Maine categorizes all hate crimes as misdemeanors, state prosecutors were unable to charge Matthews with a felony. U.S. attorney Paula Silsby was exploring the possibility of prosecuting Matthews federally, although the Justice Department was in the habit of pursuing indictments in only about two dozen bias cases a year in the entire country. Defense attorney Howaniec stated publicly that federal hate crime charges were redundant. He also pointed out that a civil rights injunction prohibiting his client from harassing Somali Muslims was unnecessary because Matthews' bail condition already included that provision. Assistant attorney general Thomas Harnett disagreed, telling the *Press Herald* that a civil rights complaint served to protect the entire community, as opposed to one person or entity being targeted.[320]

The same summer, vandals attacked mosques in other states. In La Miranda, California, two shooters with BB-guns fired at a mosque on August 10, 2006. During the attack, the assailants shattered two of the windows of the Muslim Community Services mosque on Imperial Highway.[321] This attack deeply troubled local Muslims, especially since their house of worship had been threatened in the past. According to the *Whittier Daily News*, the mosque had received menacing letters characterizing Islam as a cult and declaring that Mohammed was a terrorist and an outlaw.[322] Another message asserted that Muslims had no future in the U.S.[323]

A few days after the mosque destruction, Muslims arrived at their house of worship on August 14th and realized that vandals had struck again. On this occasion, the assailants had shot up and destroyed a glass door. Mosque president Rezaur Rahman told the *Pasadena Star-News* that this second intrusion further unnerved congregation members, who felt as though someone was trying to scare them out of the area.[324] Rahman believed the mosque was being deliberately targeted in bias-motivated attacks. Local police investigators were unconvinced. Sgt. Angela Shepherd of Norwalk Station told the *Pasadena Star-News* that the mosque may have been a random target since there was no physical evidence suggesting that the shooting was a hate crime.[325] Rahman disagreed with investigators' conclusions, pointing out that the windows and door targeted by the gunmen were adorned with Muslim symbols, such as a crescent, a minaret, and the mosque's logo. He also noted that the gunman shot the two windows right near the Islamic symbols and the word, "Muslim," suggesting that the location of the shots was intentional.[326] Rahman also noted that none of the other storefronts were damaged in the Home Depot shopping center where the mosque was located.

In the course of the investigation, Sgt. Brian Doyle learned that the two perpetrators, Kevin Mortellaro, 25, and Ryan Rivera, 18, hit approximately 40 other locations in a week of vandalism, including shooting at a school bus and injuring a child. As a result of this last incident, the gunmen were being charged with assault with a deadly weapon. Some Muslims felt that if the police had taken the first mosque attack more seriously, the perpetrators would have been apprehended before injuring the student and frightening the other children on the bus. Because other buildings were also attacked, investigators told the *Pasadena Star-News* that the mosque was a randomly-selected target.[327]

Although it is clear that the shooters were on a spree, their choice of targets may have been somewhat deliberate. Some local Muslims pointed out that the gunmen refrained from "randomly" targeting houses of worship linked to their own faiths, although churches were significantly more common than mosques in the area. Of all the buildings in the Home Depot shopping center, the gunmen only shot at the Islamic house of worship. The mosque was also attacked on different days, suggesting that the shooters were particularly interested in damaging it.

At the conclusion of the investigation, Doyle told reporters that police investigators had found that the mosque had not have been deliberately targeted because it was indistinguishable from the other storefronts in the shopping center.[328] Area Muslims once again asserted that this was clearly inaccurate, pointing out that the mosque's numerous visible Islamic symbols – including its logo, minarets, and crescents – were obvious identifying features, unique among the buildings in the mall. Despite evidence to the contrary, Doyle and other local investigators shared their specious conclusions with the FBI, discouraging federal agents from further investigation.

Rahman remained unconvinced that the precise shooting of the Islamic symbols was purely coincidental. He told the *Pasadena Star-News* that the shooting spree may have been orchestrated to hide what might have been the primary target.[329] Other Muslims noted that although many of the vandalized buildings appeared to have been randomly selected, the shooters' decision to shatter the windows of a mosque and attack it more than once seemed more calculated. Regardless of whether the repeated shooting of the mosque was random or deliberate, local Muslims remained deeply troubled by the attacks, and wondered if they were part of the backlash unleashed by 9/11 and the thwarted bombing plot in Britain.[330]

Muslims in other parts of the U.S. also felt under siege. In September 2006, a mosque in Melborne, Florida was struck by gunfire as worshippers prayed inside.[331] This incident further undermined American Muslims' feelings of safety.

At times, Sikh houses of worship and their signs were targeted in the resurgence of xenophobia directed primarily against Arabs and Muslims. In Pennsylvania, World Sikh Syndicate, a central Pennsylvania Sikh group, placed a billboard along interstate 78. The sign, located near a Sikh gurdwara, included a picture of a male Sikh and words about the Sikh faith:

SIKHISM
FREEDOM PEACE EQUALITY
ONE GOD

According to the *Patriot-News*, a vandal defaced the billboard on September 24, 2006, covering it with hate phrases and four-letter profanities directed at Arabs and Allah.[332] Because of the position of the sign, the vandal had to reach a high elevation along a bus highway to deface it, showing an alarming degree of determination. The content of the graffiti showed that many Americans were just as ignorant as they were on 9/11, when they confused Sikhs and Muslims and mistakenly assumed that anyone who wore a turban was a terrorist.

Bigotry-inspired attacks coincided with the release of American movies featuring foreign villains. The movie, *The Marine*, released in the U.S. on October 13, 2006, depicts Iraqis as anti-American terrorists. The opening scene informs audiences that the film takes place at an al-Qaeda terror base in Iraq, 100 miles from Tikrit.[333] According to film critic Shaheen, this movie promotes the damaging misconception that Iraq was linked to 9/11, thereby justifying the American invasion.[334] Throughout the movie, Arabs are portrayed as blood-thirsty savages who beat defenseless American POWs. The film also conflates Islam with violence, with one of the terrorists praying in Arabic before going to behead an American prisoner. In dramatic fashion, American soldiers rescue their imprisoned colleagues, killing Muslim enemies in the process.

While filmgoers were watching Islamophobic movies, American bigots continued to target mosques in late 2006 and early 2007. In Kennewick, Washington, a vandal broke a window of the Islamic Center of the Tri-Cities.[335] Investigators recovered the rock used in the mosque attack.

RELIGIOUS ATTACKS, 2007

Attacks on non-Christian prayer centers continued in 2007. In New Jersey, arsonists occasionally targeted mosques. In Newark, a suspicious fire burned the rear porch and wall of the National Islamic Association in January 2007. Worshippers arriving for 6:00 a.m. weekend prayers discovered the building ablaze. Mosque president Ashraf Latif told the *Arab American News* that investigators determined that the fire appeared to have originated in coils of ropes laced with accelerants and placed on the facility's back deck.[336]

On occasion, New Jersey mosque officials were targeted by area xenophobes. In January 2007, a bigot mailed menacing and derogatory letters to two Muslim leaders and a layperson. The imam of the Muslim Center of Middlesex County in Piscataway reported that the sender declared that all Muslims had to die because they worshipped a devil known as Allah and brought death, destruction, and hatred into the U.S.[337] Because of the indirect reference to the terrorist strikes, congregation members saw the hate mail as a manifestation of the ongoing 9/11 backlash. About the same time, the Muslim center of Middlesex County also received a derogatory phone call making similar threats.[338]

Across the country, Muslims were often dissatisfied with shoddy investigations of mosque attacks, as well as police unwillingness to acknowledge the bias-motivation of the perpetrators. In January 2007, mosque officials arrived at the Islamic Center of the East Bay and discovered that a gunman had shot up their house of worship. According to the *Oakland Tribune*, investigators determined that seven bullets, approximately the size of golf balls, hit the mosque's walls and windows, causing considerable damage and frightening worshippers who regularly prayed near the targeted areas.[339] Mosque President Mohammed Chaudhry worried that future assaults might injure or kill congregation members.[340] Since the gunman shot up a window facing Antioch Middle School, many community members were particularly concerned that future attacks might endanger nearby school children.

This was not the mosque's first hate crime. Although the house of worship had a long history in Antioch, bigots attacked the building on four other occasions in the previous two years.[341] According to the *Oakland Tribune*, Chaudhry blamed the media's derogatory depiction of Muslims for the upswing in violence.[342] He was dismayed that news stories about terrorism often showed unrelated footage of praying Muslims, unfairly associating Islam with acts against humanity.

Despite the repeated attacks on the Islamic Center of the East Bay, local investigators were treating the crime as a case of simple vandalism. Investigating officer Lt. John Vanderklugt told the *Oakland Tribune* that police found no evidence that the destruction was bias-motivated since no hate messages were left at the scene.[343] Mosque officials disagreed with investigators' conclusions, seeing the golf-sized bullet holes in the mosque as an unmistakable hate message. Chaudhry did not view the assault as a random act, noting that the house of worship had been targeted so frequently. The previous year, a vandal hurled a brick through the same front window of the mosque. In September 2006, a threatening caller left derogatory messages on the mosque's answering machine. Congregation member Humera Arshad told the *Oakland Tribune* that the gun attack was by far the most disturbing, threatening the lives and well-being of area Muslims.[344]

In other parts of the U.S., bigots continued to target Islamic centers and their staff. In Michigan, mosque officials were occasionally targeted. In January 2007, an assailant was sentenced to 21 days in jail for taunting an imam with a stick and threatening to deface his mosque, located on the East Side of Detroit.[345] Despite the arrest and sentencing of this perpetrator, other assailants continued attacking mosques in the state.

In Detroit, vandals painted racist graffiti on the Islamic Center of America. The Karbala Islamic Education Center in Dearborn was targeted four times between late 2006 and early 2007. On January 21, 2007, an assailant destroyed several windows. A few months later, in May 2007, a vandal painted derogatory words in Arabic on the building, proclaiming the house of worship to be the "Center of the Party of Satan."[346] According to the *Detroit News*, local Islamic leaders doubted that the incident was perpetrated by other Muslims or native Arabic speakers, since the phrase had been painted with the use of a stencil and included an archaic word not in common usage.[347] The repeated hate crimes frightened congregants, who included Shia Muslims who had emigrated from Iraq in the 1990s.

Bigots also desecrated houses of worship in Michigan. Two mosques located fairly close to one another were vandalized in a similar manner in January 2007.[348] A Christian church with an Arab-American congregation was also targeted in the state.[349] Although local police were still investigating these attacks, many residents were disheartened that no one had been arrested and punished for these crimes.

Along with other prayer centers with large minority congregations, Sikh gurdwaras continued to be attacked in various parts of the country. *India-West* reported that on March 12, 2007, Michel Benjamin Rafferty, a 39-year old man from Redding, California, targeted a Sikh temple under construction in Anderson.[350] Rafferty stole a 25-ton loader from a heavy-loading lot, drove it half a mile, and then rammed it repeatedly into the partially-completed Sikh temple. According to Anderson police officer Tim York, Rafferty confessed that he committed the crime because he was angry that the site was owned by foreigners constructing a non-Christian house of worship. Discussing Rafferty's motivation in his arrest report, York maintained that the perpetrator acted out of ethnic and religious bias, targeting people he thought were non-Christian Arabs.[351] Many congregation members saw the attack as a product of post-9/11 xenophobia. Rafferty was charged with numerous offenses, including: stealing a vehicle, committing felony vandalism as a hate crime, and being under the influence of a controlled substance. In response to the attack on their house of worship, Sikhs in Anderson called on the interfaith community to join them in planting a "Garden of Peace and Hope" at the temple site.

While Sikhs in California were repairing their damaged gurdwara, Muslims in Florida were rebuilding a mosque that had been torched in Tampa. On April 12, 2007, an arsonist set fire to the Islamic Education Center, damaging the building and its contents. Discussing this attack, the *St. Petersburg Times* reported that the blaze scorched prayer rugs and bookcases containing dozens of Qurans.[352] The fire also ruined other religious artifacts, destroyed photos, and burned the mosque's green carpet down to bare concrete. According to Hillsborough Fire Rescue Spokesman Ray Yeakley, the arsonist used gasoline to ignite one of the mosque's windows at around 9:30 a.m. A neighbor in the suburban area noticed the fire and called 911. After 20 minutes, firefighters were finally able to control the blaze.

The mosque attack left congregant Hamid Faraji stunned. He told the *St. Petersburg Times* that he was dismayed that anyone would choose to burn a house of worship, and promised that the attack would not disrupt religious services, even if it meant that worshippers had to pray out of a tent.[353] At the time of the attack, approximately 50 congregants regularly attended services, and about 300 area Muslims prayed at the mosque on holidays. In addition to adult worshippers, children ages six to 14 received religious education at the mosque on Saturdays, and used the center's soccer fields, swing set, and picnic tables on a regular basis.

Community members attributed the mosque attack to post-9/11 Islamophobia. Bruce Tokarski, a Tampa resident who lived next to the center, told the *St. Petersburg Times* that many people in the neighborhood were frightened of the mosque, making the erroneous assumption that Muslim congregants were involved in terrorism.[354] In an interview with the *Tampa Tribune*, Tokarski recalled that when he first moved into his home in 2005, he heard locals make flippant remarks about a terrorist camp on mosque property.[355] His own concerns dissipated as he watched adults and children mingle in the playground and play soccer, realizing there was nothing to fear.

According to the *Tampa Tribune*, the April 2007 arson was the fourth time the mosque had been attacked in the previous two years.[356] In July 2005, arsonists burned religious objects on one of the walls and vandalized the building. No one was arrested. On another occasion, intruders entered the building and shifted objects around. Later the same summer, trespassers once again broke into the Islamic center, disturbing religious artifacts and desecrating carpets by walking on them with shoes.

Although the mosque had been repeatedly targeted, investigators refused to see the gasoline-induced fire and the scorching of the Qurans as a hate crime. FBI spokesman Al Rivera told the *Tampa Tribune* that his agency was investigating the crime as a case of simple arson, and that agents found no evidence that the attack was motivated by bias.[357] Congregants were shocked by this conclusion, viewing the burning of their holy book as clear evidence of religious intolerance.

In other parts of the country, churches were occasionally attacked if they were perceived as being friendly to Muslims. According to a June 27, 2007 article in the *Tampa Tribune*, a Catholic church was targeted for its support of the local Muslim community.[358] The Church's pastor, Bishop Chuck Leigh, arrived at the Christ the Servant Apostolic Catholic Church and discovered framed pictures smashed on the floor and graffiti on the wall declaring that the prayer center's parishioners were traitors who supported terrorists.[359] Leigh believed that the hate crime took place because he backed a failed 2005 proposal to add the Muslim holiday Eid Al-Fitr to the Hillsborough County school district calendar. Leigh also vocally condemned religious intolerance and bias attacks during his tenure as the president of the Florida Council of Churches. Leigh opted to continue his work despite the community intimidation, telling the *Tampa Tribune* that the Gospel compelled him to defend victims of bigotry.[360]

While some priests were being attacked for defending Muslims' religious freedoms, other Christian leaders in the U.S. were launching derogatory attacks on Islam and its followers. According to the May 5, 2007 issue of the *Arab American News*, one American church leader publicly denounced Muslims and their faith, instructing his congregation that Islam was an evil religion that taught its followers to hate other people.[361]

While this inflammatory rhetoric was being circulated, anti-Arab stereotypes were resurfacing in movies shown across the U.S. In the 2007 movie, *The Condemned*, reality show producers release ten convicted killers in a remote island in New Guinea and order them to eliminate one another, with the promise that the sole survivor would win his freedom. Before the contest begins, one of the producers learns that another prisoner has killed the Arab terrorist contestant.[362] The producer then clarifies that he is upset because Arab viewers will be disgusted if they cannot cheer for a child-killing Muslim religious fanatic.[363]

One of the worst cinematic portrayals of Arabs appears in *The Stone Merchant*, released in the U.S. on DVD on June 26, 2007. Film critic Shaheen describes this movie as one of cinema's most odious productions, suggesting it should be studied as film-as-hate propaganda.[364] In this picture, Muslims attack and murder civilians in Somalia. The movie centers on Muslim convert Ludovico Vicedomini, played by Harvey Keitel, who believed that practicing terrorism was an integral part of his new faith. Vicedomini's nemesis is Professor Aleco, played by Jordi Molla. In one scene in the movie, Aleco, a handicapped teacher who lost his legs in a terrorist attack perpetrated by an Arab, lectures his university students that their country has failed to thrive after Middle Eastern Muslims brought their money and their Quran schools to Somalia. Shaheen observes that throughout the film, Aleco makes anti-Muslim slurs, telling his pupils that Islam is at war to conquer the West, and that terrorists were infiltrating the country disguised as ordinary people.[365] In the middle of his anti-Arab diatribe, Professor Aleco shows footage of 9/11 and declares that only a Christian army was capable of repelling the Muslim invasion. Arab-American Oscar winner Farid Murray Abraham plays the ruthless terrorist Shadid, who tells his henchmen that they must exterminate the enemies of Islam.[366] In one scene, a heartless Arab villain cuts off the hand of one of the Somali characters. Arab terrorists also plant a bomb in the bag of one of their unsuspecting wives when she was en route to London.

The release of these anti-Muslim movies coincided with summer 2007 attacks on American mosques. The Islamic Center of the East Bay in Antioch, California, was targeted once again in August 2007. According to the *San Francisco Chronicle*, it took six fire trucks thirty minutes to extinguish the August 12th blaze, which began shortly after midnight.[367] This arson attack caused approximately $200,000 in damage to the religious facility, rendering the building unusable.[368] The arsonist attempted to set fires in four spots of the mosque, eventually igniting the middle of the building using newspapers, carpets, tables, and chairs as kindling. At the time of the arson, approximately 500 congregants belonged to the mosque, with about 150 worshippers regularly attending services.

Although the prayer center had been targeted several times in the recent past, investigators still refused to characterize the arson as a hate crime. Contra Costa fire spokeswoman Emily Hopkins told the *San Francisco Chronicle* that investigators found no evidence that the mosque was burned out of religious bias.[369] Muslim leaders disagreed, characterizing the fire as an act of terror targeting congregants and their faith. Area Muslims pointed out that the mosque had been repeatedly vandalized in the months prior to the destructive fire. The Friday before the arson, an intruder broke into the house of worship. The mosque also had its windows smashed three times the previous year.[370] In 2005, a gunman shot up the windows and walls, and an intruder smashed its windows with a brick.[371] The mosque also received a threatening phone call. Congregants believed that the frequency and maliciousness of these crimes indicated that the attacks were not random. Abdur Rahman told the *Chronicle* that he was dismayed that investigators were unable to recognize that the mosque was being repeatedly targeted by bigots, noting that any attack on a religious organization was a crime against humanity.[372]

Across the country, mosques and their members continued to be particularly at risk near the anniversary of 9/11. Discussing one backlash crime, the September 19, 2007 *Columbus Dispatch* reported that approximately 20 black male teenagers attacked Muslims with rocks when the worshippers were exiting a local mosque after Friday night Ramadan prayers.[373] Along with injuring worshippers, the assailants also broke two windows of the Masjid As-Sahaaba in South Linden. The perpetrators were walking past the mosque on East Hudson Street when they suddenly turned around and started throwing rocks. During the attack, the youths yelled at the Muslims while pelting them with stones.

According to the Columbus police report, the assault appeared to be a hate crime against Muslims leaving their house of worship during Ramadan.[374] Because of the bias component, investigating officers turned the case over to the department's Strategic Response Bureau.

Mosques in other states were targeted the following month. In California, a group of bigots smashed car windows and attacked worshippers at a mosque in Bakersfield. During the October 2007 assault, the perpetrators made derogatory comments, referring to Arabs as terrorists and instructing them to leave the U.S.[375] Because of these obvious manifestations of bias, the Kern County Sheriff's Department investigated the incident as a hate crime.

In many parts of the country, proposals to build Islamic prayer centers triggered community Islamophobia. The *Christian Science Monitor* reported that in 2007, a Texas farmer, angry about plans to construct a mosque next to his farm, held pig races on Friday, the Muslim holy day, to express his disapproval.[376]

RELIGIOUS ATTACKS, 2008

On occasion, bigots assaulted Sikhs near their houses of worship. On January 14, 2008, 36-year old David Wood attacked Baljeet Singh, a 63-year old Sikh, as he was parking his car outside of a gurdwara in New Hyde Park, New York. The *Hindustani Times* reported that during the unprovoked hate crime, Wood screamed racial abuses at Singh, calling him an Arab and telling him to return to his country of origin.[377] Because of the nature of the slurs, area Sikhs saw the assault in the context of the ongoing 9/11 backlash. The beating left Singh with a broken nose and a fractured jaw.[378] His injuries were so severe that required surgery and remained on a liquid diet for two weeks. In response to the attack, Wood was charged with second-degree assault as a hate crime and second-degree aggravated harassment. Before the January 14th incident, Wood had targeted the gurdwara and its Sikh worshippers on at least one previous occasion, turning speakers playing loud music toward the gurdwara during a prayer service.[379] Some Sikhs wondered if Wood would've continued targeting Sikhs and the gurdwara if he had been punished appropriately the first time he interfered with their First Amendment right to worship unmolested.

In subsequent months, religious attacks took place in other parts of the country. In February 2008, authorities apprehended three men in an arson attack on the Islamic Center of Columbia mosque in Tennessee. The perpetrators, Jonathan Stone, 19, Michael Golden, 23, and Eric Baker, 32, were arrested for setting fire to the house of worship and spray-painting Nazi swastikas and white supremacist messages on the walls. According to a Justice Department press release, Baker was eventually sentenced to 183 months in prison for his role in the bias attack, and Golden received 171 months.[380] Stone pled guilty and also received a lengthy sentence for the mosque arson.

In some instances, bigots targeted prayer centers with noxious materials. On September 26, 2008, two white men sprayed a toxic substance through the window of a Dayton mosque, targeting a room where infants and children were waiting for their parents during Ramadan prayers.[381] The hate crime deeply disturbed the three hundred Muslims who regularly attended religious services at the house of worship. *Tennessee Tribune* reporter Erik Ose expressed dismay that the gassing of Dayton's Muslims received little media coverage. In an article about this hate crime, he raised the possibility that the attack may have been triggered in part by local and national newspapers' participation in the September 22, 2008 mass distribution of an Islamophobic DVD to subscribers.[382] Ose argued that newspapers sold off their journalistic integrity by accepting money to distribute *Obsession: Radical Islam's War Against the West*.[383] He also claimed that the video instilled fear and hatred in the U.S., making American families distrustful of their minority neighbors.[384]

The Clairon Fund paid 70 national and local newspapers to distribute the right-wing DVD to 28 million households in a propaganda campaign that coincided with the seventh anniversary of 9/11.[385] The *New York Times*, *Wall St. Journal*, and other national newspapers disseminated the DVDs to their subscribers. Local papers also brought the DVDs to targeted swing state voters in Ohio, Pennsylvania, Michigan, Colorado, Iowa, Florida, Wisconsin, Nevada, New Hampshire, and West Virginia. Only two newspapers refused to distribute the DVDs – the *St. Louis Post Dispatch* in Missouri and the *Greensboro News Record* in North Carolina.

The racist film juxtaposes scenes of Nazis with footage of Muslims, implying a connection between the two groups. The movie also suggests that Muslims recruit children to become suicide bombers. Many progressive groups, including Jews On First, criticized the Clarion Fund for disseminating the hateful DVDs. Muslim subscribers to the *Dayton Daily News* and other participating publications were dismayed to receive copies of the 60-minute film bundled in their newspapers. In the aftermath of the Dayton attack, local newspaper editors defended their decision to distribute the bigoted DVDs, comparing the delivery of the hate film to the dissemination of product samples like cereal or toothpaste.

RELIGIOUS ATTACKS, 2009

Throughout 2009, mosques were targeted throughout the U.S. In Florida, the Islamic School of Miami was repeatedly attacked.[386] At the beginning of the year, a gunman sprayed 51 bullets into the West Kendall mosque, shattering its windows and damaging its golden dome.[387] Six months later, the mosque was targeted by a vandal who smashed two of its windows. These 2009 attacks disturbed Miami Muslims, who were already rattled from previous hate crimes directed against their house of worship: in 2004, the sign of the Islamic School of Miami was defaced with a Nazi swastika, and in 2005, a vandal shattered the mosque's door with a large rock.[388]

Mosques were also attacked in other states. According to the Raleigh *News & Observer*, an Islamic prayer center near the North Carolina Central University campus was repeatedly targeted over a six month period.[389] In the spring of 2009, two men burst through the doors of the Jamaat Ibad Ar-Rahman mosque, hurling rocks and screaming obscenities at Muslims in the middle of a prayer service.[390] Although the attack on the Fayetteville Street house of worship was reported to the police, no arrests were made. In the summer, a vandal destroyed the mosque's windows and doors. The house of worship was targeted again on November 2, 2009 by a vandal who stole computer monitors, knocked over religious supplies, and smashed its windows and doors.

Mosque officials believed that the attacks were triggered by religious or ethnic bias, since the majority of worshippers were recent immigrants from non-European countries. Discussing the crime, maintenance supervisor Iqbal Ahmad reminded the Raleigh *News & Observer* that burglars don't routinely break all the windows and doors of the building they are targeting, suggesting that religious bias was responsible for the maliciousness of the vandalism.[391] Durham police Captain Rick Pendergrass said that officers were taking the crimes seriously.[392] Many congregants were worried that future incidents might endanger Muslim children, since they frequently used the playground in the front of the house of worship and attended Sunday school in classrooms in the back of the building.

Islamic prayer centers were also attacked in other regions of the U.S. In Southern California, an anti-Muslim bigot desecrated a mosque on June 4, 2009. According to the *Los Angeles Times*, at about 4:00 a.m., a patrol officer discovered anti-Muslim graffiti scrawled in still-wet paint on the walls of the Islamic Center of Cypress.[393] The vandal had written death threats and profanities on the house of worship, declaring that community members and the U.S. military were going to kill all Muslims.[394] The graffiti, written in letters more than four feet high, stretched approximately 30 feet horizontally around the house of worship. Some community members suggested that the attack was part of the 9/11 backlash, and speculated that the hate crime might have been triggered by President Obama's attempts to build bridges with Muslims overseas.

Two months later, a gunman shot a Muslim exiting a mosque in Portland, Maine. At the time of the August 2009 incident, the 25-year old Somali man was coming out of the house of worship after finishing Ramadan evening prayers.[395] The attack left him seriously injured. Many Muslims in the state viewed the attack as part of the ongoing 9/11 backlash.

Hate crimes continued taking place in the fall. In Texas, a mosque inside a Turkish cultural center was defaced on October 7, 2009. The *Houston Chronicle* reported that the vandal was caught on video surveillance writing derogatory remarks about Muslims and Islam on the walls of the Turquoise Center in Southwest Houston.[396] The perpetrator also left a business card at the scene, making it easy for responding officers to track him down and arrest him. The center's leaders refused to press charges, arguing that it was up to the vandal to seek forgiveness from God.

RELIGIOUS ATTACKS, 2010

Mosques were also targeted throughout 2010. On New Year's Day, a Muslim attending religious services at Costa Mesa's Islamic Educational Center in Southern California found a burnt Quran in the mosque's parking lot. The *Orange County Register* reported that worshippers broke down in tears at the sight of their torched book.[397] The discovery of the ruined Quran was only one of the disturbing incidents that took place in the area. The same day, an anti-Muslim bigot targeted an interfaith display in Mission Viejo. The vandal used red spray paint to deface the part of the holiday display containing a verse from the Quran. The perpetrator also pinned a sign to the exhibit, comparing mosques to lighthouses and suggesting that they were unwelcome in the U.S.[398] Lt. Mike Gavin, the chief of police for Mission Viejo, understood that the attack was a hate crime, not a case of simple vandalism.

The following month, anti-Muslim sentiment flared in Oostburg, Wisconsin, after area Muslims bought a health food store and made plans to convert it into a mosque. *Time* magazine reported that at a February 8, 2010 town hall meeting, local opponents of the plan suggested that the non-Christian house of worship was an attempt to subvert the Constitution and replace it with Islamic law in the U.S.[399] Instead of pandering to area xenophobes, community officials unanimously approved the building plans, permitting the mosque construction to go forward.

Elsewhere in the country, anti-Muslim attacks continued throughout 2010. Islamic prayer centers were vandalized in the South. In Nashville, a vandal attacked the Al-Farooq mosque, writing derogatory messages and demanding that Muslims return to their homelands.[400] Crosses were also painted on the exterior of the religious center, suggesting that Islam was not welcome in the area.

In Jacksonville, the Islamic Center of Northeast Florida was repeatedly targeted. The *Florida Times Union* reported that on April 4, 2010, a man entered the mosque, disrupted prayer services, and accused worshippers of blaspheming against God.[401] As congregants chased him away, the man yelled that he would return.

The following month, the same house of worship was firebombed. At approximately 9:30 p.m. on May 10, 2010, an arsonist used a crude pipe bomb to attack the Jacksonville mosque. According to FBI agent Jim Casey, investigators recovered shrapnel a hundred yards away from the blast, which took place when 60 Muslims were inside. Casey told the *Florida Times Union* that if worshippers had been closer to the epicenter of the blast, they would have been killed.[402] Despite the dangers posed by the bomb, it caused only $500 in physical damage to the property. Investigators speculated that the post-9/11 attack was motivated by religious bias and the controversial appointment of Parvez Ahmed to the Jacksonville Human Rights Commission, since the high-profile public official regularly worshipped at the targeted prayer center.

Many area Muslims were deeply disturbed by the firebombing of their house of worship. The day after the arson, Ashrad Shaikh, the mosque's vice chairman, told the *Florida Times Union* that the hate crime was the worst experience he had in the 36 years he lived in the city, undermining his hope that most community members were learning to co-exist with area Muslims.[403]

In their investigation of the explosion and fire, the FBI agents reviewed the mosque's surveillance footage showing a male suspect with a gas can. Based on their analysis of the video, investigators did not believe that the arsonist was the same man who interrupted religious services the month before the fire. Area Muslims wondered if the arson could have been prevented if police or federal agents had taken steps to protect the building after the April 2010 attack. Attorney General Eric Holder spoke out against the Jacksonville mosque bombing and vowed to prosecute hate crimes targeting American Muslims. A year later, FBI officials in Orienta, Oklahoma shot and killed the suspect, 46-year old Sandlin Matthew Smith, who was also implicated in the bombing of an abortion clinic.[404]

The same month as the Jacksonville attack, mosques in other states were targeted. The Islamic Association of Michigan was vandalized on May 9 and May 15, 2010. During these incidents, vandals broke the glass part of an entryway door of the Brownstown house of worship.[405] Mosque officials reported the hate crime to the FBI, and informed investigators that the perpetrators were caught on a surveillance video.

Mosque attacks continued in other parts of the country. According to Deputy Trent Givens of the Rutherford County Sheriff's Office, the Islamic Center in Columbia, Tennessee was vandalized in the summer of 2010. Because this same prayer center had been torched by an arsonist in February 2008, area Muslims once again worried about their safety.

The Columbia attack was one of the many hate crimes taking place while New Yorkers were debating the construction of what pundits pejoratively referred to as the 'Ground Zero mosque.' Like an Islamic YMCA, Park51 was designed to include a fitness center, a swimming pool, a basketball court, a performing arts space, a bookstore, and a food court. This facility was slated to be built two blocks north of the former World Trade Center site, just a few hundred yards closer than an existing neighborhood mosque. Xenophobic Americans opposed the building's construction on the grounds that all Muslims were collectively to blame for 9/11. According to a 2010 CNN poll, 68% of Americans opposed the community center, ignoring federal laws protecting the construction of houses of worship in sites zoned for religious purposes.[406] The poll also showed that opposition to Park51 was consistently high across all age groups.

Journalists, political candidates, and scholars vocally opposed the facility, loudly expressing their Islamophobia. Republican Vice Presidential nominee Sarah Palin characterized the Ground Zero mosque as an unnecessary provocation that struck at the hearts of Americans.[407] Other Republican politicians publicly denounced the project. Minnesota Governor Tim Pawlenty argued that the mosque would be disrespectful to the World Trade Center site. Former House speaker Newt Gingrich argued that there should be no mosque near Ground Zero until there were churches and synagogues in Saudi Arabia.[408] Presidential hopeful Mitt Romney also criticized the construction of the Islamic community center, suggesting that extremists could use the mosque for disseminating anti-American propaganda and recruiting supporters.[409]

Pundits repeatedly characterized the facility as a breeding-ground for terrorists. The *Christian Science Monitor* reported that Mike Adams, a criminology professor at the University of North Carolina, proposed building a large bomb filled with bacon grease and using it against the 'Ground Zero mosque.'[410] According to this newspaper, Adams hoped this theoretical bomb, which he dubbed the 'Mother of All Bacon,' would not harm anyone but would defile the location so the mosque could not be built on the site. Right-wing organizations also denounced the Park51 center. The National Republican Trust Political Action Committee released a video explicitly declaring that the 'Ground Zero mosque' was intended to celebrate the murder of thousands of Americans on 9/11.

Social commentators also denounced the building plans. On May 26, 2010, radio personality Michael Berry, a former Houston City Council member, told his KPRC-950 AM talk-show audience that he wished the Park51 facility would be destroyed, telling an on-air caller, "I'll tell you this – if you do build a mosque, I hope somebody blows it up... I hope the mosque isn't built, and if it is, I hope it's blown up, and I mean that."[411] Progressive listeners were horrified by Berry's comments, wondering why he felt entitled to make repeated terrorist threats targeting a specific American prayer center. Some activists questioned why Homeland Security or the FBI failed to take legal action in response to Berry's shocking declarations, speculating that federal agents would've responded differently if a Muslim Arab publicly threatened to blow up a specific church.

Muslims across America saw a connection between hateful rhetoric directed against the Park51 center and anti-Muslim hate crimes. According to the *New York Daily News*, bigots threatened to kill the imam in charge of the mosque construction project, hoping to terrorize area Muslims into canceling their building plans.[412] Supporters of Park51 pointed out that there were two gentlemen's clubs in a three-block radius of the World Trade Center site – the 'Pussycat Lounge' and the 'New York Dolls,' but Americans were not clamoring to have these 'Ground Zero Strip Clubs' relocated because their presence constituted an affront to 9/11 victims.[413]

Some opponents of Park51 might have inspired terrorist acts against civilians. On July 22, 2011, Norwegian bigot Anders Behring Breivik opened fire and killed 77 of his countrymen, angry about what he perceived to be the Islamification of his country and the rest of the West. According to the *New York Times*, Breivik repeatedly cited the anti-Muslim writings of American bloggers Robert Spencer and Pamela Geller in his 1,500 page manifesto.[414]

The same summer, New Yorkers acted to prevent the construction of other neighborhood mosques. At a Sheepshead Bay protest, neighborhood residents held signs blaming area Muslims for 9/11, and suggested that building an Islamic prayer center on Voorheis Avenue would bring terrorists to the area.[415] Some demonstrators argued that the proposed mosque would result in the establishment of Islamic law in America. To emphasize this point, some protestors held signs containing the word, 'Sharia,' in red ink, with large blood droplets dripping from the letters. *Newsweek* reported that some of the demonstrators associated the Park51 facility with forced child marriages, gang-rapes, and beheadings, and suggested that the construction of the house of worship was as offensive as building a victory monument to Hitler at Auschwitz.[416] Many of the protestors compared American Muslims to Osama bin Laden and accused them of being in league with nefarious foreign interests. One bigot dressed up a mannequin in a kaffiyeh and sat it on a fake bomb containing the inscription, 'Made in the USA.' New York newspapers reported that some of the demonstrators made anti-Muslim threats, promising to bomb the house of worship and kill congregants.[417] According to the *Brooklyn Paper*, a former Israeli soldier and longtime resident of Voorheis Avenue told reporters that he planned to bomb the mosque once construction was completed, so that area Muslims would be unable to stay in the area alive.[418] Demonstrators had no qualms about making such public death threats. Many Park51 supporters were worried that no one was taking their safety seriously, outraged that law enforcement officials failed to arrest protestors who matter-of-factly threatened their lives in area newspapers.

Islamophobes also opposed the construction of other New York mosques. In Staten Island, Midland Beach residents challenged plans to build an Islamic center in the area. In the summer of 2010, the board of St. Margaret Mary R.C. Church bowed to community pressure and decided against selling an empty parish convent to a Muslim organization intent on converting the property into a mosque.[419] The controversy began in May 2010, after Rev. Keith Fennessy entered into an agreement to sell the unused building to the Muslim American Society for $750,000. In response, angry community members organized protest rallies for six consecutive weekends, waving American flags and holding up signs declaring their opposition to the 'No MAS' Mosque. Responding to widespread fear of the proposed Islamic center, Rep. Michael McMahon instigated a federal probe into the MAS' background, and was told by the FBI that the group appeared harmless.[420] Despite this finding, area opposition continued unabated. In June 2010, Rev. Fennessy bowed to community pressure and reneged on the sale, upsetting area Muslims. In response to the controversy, the trustees of the parish voted to uphold Rev. Fennessy's decision to cancel the sale, placating area xenophobes.

While these controversies were raging, anti-Muslim attacks continued in other parts of the country. In the Pacific Northwest, nativists occasionally targeted cars on mosque grounds. In Bellevue, Washington, a bigot damaged a van parked at the Islamic Center of Eastside. During this attack, the assailant smeared dog feces on the vehicle, which had Islamic ads on its exterior.[421] The Muslim owner discovered the vandalism to his van's window, windshield, and side door handle as he was emerging from noon prayers at the mosque on June 24, 2010.

103

The same summer, California xenophobes opposed the construction of a mosque in Temecula, a town Southeast of Los Angeles. To protest the building plans, We the People-Citizens in Action organized demonstrations in late July to express their disapproval. According to the *Los Angeles Times*, the group urged protestors to bring their dogs in what many community members regarded as a blatant attempt to intimidate local Muslims.[422] During these gatherings, some community members suggested that all Muslims shared the blame for the 9/11 attacks.

In the South, bigots also rallied to prevent the construction of Islamic centers. In June and July 2010, anti-Muslim activists actively opposed plans to build a mosque in Rutherford County, Tennessee, even though area officials had already approved the building plans. Capitalizing on public sentiment against the proposal, a Tennessee GOP Congressional candidate issued a statement claiming that the Islamic Center of Murfreesboro threatened the state's moral and political foundation.[423] Other mosque opponents filed a lawsuit to block the building's construction, claiming that the county needed to determine whether Islam was a recognized religion entitled to First Amendment protections. In response to this rather specious lawsuit, federal attorneys filed a brief saying that the center's construction should continue, since Islam had been officially recognized as a religion by all three branches of the U.S. government. According to the Midland *Daily News*, Kathleen Bergin, a professor at South Texas College of Law, characterized the federal support for the Tennessee mosque as part of a larger effort by the Department of Justice to curb the post-9/11 backlash against Islam.[424] Attorneys arguing in support of the mosque also pointed out that the 2000 Religious Land Use Act prohibited local areas in the U.S. from using land regulations to prevent the construction of churches, synagogues, mosques, and other places of worship. While attorneys were arguing about the legal issues involved, community members continued to express hostility to area Muslims and their building plans.

Along with opposing the construction of Islamic centers, Southern xenophobes harassed Muslims attending religious services. In July 2010, North Carolina community members protested outside the Islamic Society of Greater Charlotte during Friday prayers.[425] During the rally, protestors held up signs declaring that Islam was a lie and that Mohammed was a false prophet. The rally was organized by Operation Save America, a group opposed to non-Christian faiths and abortion clinics in the U.S.

On occasion, Muslims were assaulted in front of mosques. In California, a navy reservist was attacked outside of the Islamic Society of Corona-Norco, when the house of worship was conducting its annual Independence Day activities. At the time of the July 4th assault, the victim was staffing an outreach booth containing the sign, "Ask a Muslim," to address community questions about Islam.[426] Two men, walking to nearby Santana Park to enjoy the fireworks show, saw the booth and began cursing. The volunteer responded by telling the hostile men that he would answer any questions they had about his faith. The men then called the Muslim a "raghead," and punched him in the face.[427] Mosque members worried that the timing of the assault was significant, suggesting that Muslims had no right to participate in Fourth of July activities.

In other parts of the country, bigots continued to target non-Christian religious centers. In July 2010, an arsonist set fire to the Dar El-Eman Islamic Center in Arlington, Texas.[428] The following year, 34-year old Henry Clay Glaspell pled guilty to setting the mosque playground equipment on fire and committing other acts directed against Arabs and Middle Eastern Muslims who worshipped at the religious center. He also told Judge Terry Means that he stole and damaged mosque property, threw used cat litter at the building's main entrance, and shouted ethnic slurs at Arab and Middle Eastern worshippers on several occasions.[429] At the conclusion of the proceedings, FBI officials announced that this was the 50th federal prosecution of post-9/11 attacks against Arabs and Muslims, and that Gaspell's arrest and conviction ensured that religious minorities in the U.S. would be able to worship free from violence, fear, and intimidation. Area Muslims wondered why federal officials were so proud of the 50 prosecutions, pointing out that this was a pathetically-small percentage of the thousands of documented 9/11 backlash attacks.

Despite this successful prosecution of the Arlington arsonist, bigots continued to attack American mosques. In many parts of the country, protestors staged demonstrations or interrupted prayer services at Islamic centers. On August 6, 2010, a mob harassed Muslims outside a Bridgeport mosque. The *Connecticut*

Post reported that while worshippers were arriving for Ramadan prayer services at the Masjid An-Noor, hecklers shouted offensive comments, telling congregants that Islam was a false faith and that Jesus hated Muslims.[430] The protestors also shoved anti-Muslim signs at worshippers, who worried for their safety.

Islamophobes also targeted Muslims attending prayer services in other states. In New York, teenagers repeatedly disrupted Ramadan religious services at a mosque in Carlton. According to the Midland *Daily News*, five teenagers from Holley yelled obscenities and honked their car horns outside of the World Sufi Foundation mosque.[431] On August 30, 17-year old Mark Vendetti fired a shotgun twice into the ground outside the mosque, alarming worshippers inside.[432] Another teen, 18-year old Dylan Phillips, was driving away from the scene when he sideswiped congregation member David Bell, who had come out of the mosque to ascertain why the youths were interrupting Muslims in the middle of prayers.[433]

The perpetrators were charged with harassment and disrupting a religious service, two misdemeanor offenses. Two of the teens also faced more serious charges: Vendetti with criminal possession of a weapon, and Phillips with vehicular assault. Since area Muslims asked that the teen assailants be treated with leniency, Orleans County district attorney Joseph Cardone held off filing hate crime enhancements.

Also in August 2010, Islamophobes targeted mosques in other parts of the country. In a particularly disturbing attack, a bigot used a brick to vandalize the Madera Islamic Center. The intruder also left signs at the house of worship, declaring, "American National Brotherhood," "Wake up America, the Enemy is here," "ANB," and "No Temple for the God of terrorism at Ground Zero."[434] Area Muslims were especially upset that the harassment took place during Ramadan. Because one of the signs referenced 9/11, community activists saw the vandalism as part of the ongoing backlash to the terrorist attacks. Seven months later, authorities arrested Donny Eugene Mower in connection with the mosque vandalism, noting that he was also a suspect in the September 2, 2010 attempted firebombing of a Planned Parenthood clinic in the city.[435]

The same summer, Gainesville pastor Terry Jones frightened American Muslims with his plan to burn stacks of Qurans on the ninth anniversary of 9/11 as a protest against the construction of the 'Ground Zero Mosque.' President Obama spoke out against the proposed book burning, maintaining it would inflame radical Muslims overseas and endanger the lives of U.S. servicemen fighting in the Middle East. At a White House celebration of Ramadan, a tradition started by President Thomas Jefferson, Obama preached tolerance and defended the construction of the Park51 facility. At this August 13, 2010 event, Obama stated that Muslims, like all Americans, were entitled to First Amendment protections and had the right to build community centers and houses of worship on private property, in accordance with local ordinances.[436] Mosque opponents and news commentators suggested that Obama's support for the community center stemmed from the fact that he was actually a Muslim. While this controversy was raging, the *Christian Science Monitor* published the results of a August 24, 2010 Pew poll that found that 20% of Americans believed President Obama was a Muslim, and that the vast majority of respondents had an unfavorable view of Islam.[437]

Although Jones eventually aborted his Quran-burning plans, other bigots followed up on the Gainesville pastor's suggestion and torched Islamic holy books outside of mosques. On September 11, 2010, a Michigan man set fire to a Quran outside of the Islamic Center of East Lansing. According to the *Detroit News*, Ingham County prosecutor Stuart Dunnings III. said that although the perpetrator confessed, he could not be charged with a hate crime because no Michigan law had been broken.[438]

In Illinois, another bigot left a burned Quran outside of the Muslim Community Center, located on the Northwest side of Chicago. Because the incident happened in mid-September, congregants wondered if the perpetrator sought to punish area Muslims for 9/11. The *Chicago Tribune* reported that local police were investigating the incident, exploring whether it ought to be considered a hate crime.[439] Area Muslims were dismayed at investigators' reluctance to realize that the torched Quran was an overt attempt to intimidate them.

Americans from many faiths spoke out against the malicious destruction of Qurans in the U.S. Rabbi Nancy Meyers told the *Orange County Register* that she was disturbed by this new trend, comparing the situation to the burning of Torahs in Nazi Germany.[440]

Despite the efforts of interfaith groups to curb Islamophobia, hate crimes continued taking place throughout the country. On occasion, bigots used pork to attack American Islamic centers. In September 2010, near the ninth anniversary of 9/11, the U.S. Postal Inspection Service discovered that a sender in Denver had mailed four American mosques packages containing bacon and hate letters.[441] On other occasions, vandals referenced pigs and ham in attempts to intimidate American Muslims. In California, a bigot left a plastic pig with anti-Islamic graffiti in the mailbox of a Madera mosque. The disturbing messages on the animal proclaimed, "Remember 9-11," ""MO HAM MED the pig," and "No Mosque in NYC," referencing the Park51 controversy.[442]

Bigots in other states committed equally disturbing attacks. In Florence, South Carolina, a house of worship was desecrated with pork. The *Christian Science Monitor* reported that on the weekend of October 9, 2010, an assailant used strips of bacon to spell out the words, "PIG" and "CHUMP" at the entrance to the mosque.[443] When congregation member Mushtaq Hussain first saw the words, he thought they had been written by neighborhood children as a prank. Once he realized that the culprit had used bacon, he understood that it was a deliberate attempt to frighten worshippers. Discussing this incident, the *Christian Science Monitor* characterized it as one of many post-9/11 crimes that used pork products to express contempt for American Muslims.[444]

On occasion, certain mosques were targeted repeatedly in 2010. In Huntington, New York, an Islamic center was vandalized four times in the span of a few months.[445] One of the more serious incidents occurred on October 25, 2010, when an assailant threw a jar of nails near the entrance of the Masjid Noor. The container broke, scattering the nails around the driveway. Since the incident took place while 30 Muslims were attending religious classes at the facility, Suffolk County police chose to investigate the incident as a hate crime. Because this was the fourth time the building had been attacked since August 2010, congregants asked local police to increase patrols near the facility. Many area Muslims felt that law enforcement officials could have prevented the hate crime if they had done more to protect the repeatedly-targeted building.

An Islamic center was also targeted in Oklahoma. According to the *Tulsa World*, Jesse Guinn Harrison, a 33-year old man, sent a strange package to the Islamic Peace Academy in Tulsa in October, 2010.[446] This mailing included Harrison's résumé, a letter addressed to the people of Islam, and a disturbing DVD. The video began by showing Harrison rubbing pork chops over a Quran and a picture of an Islamic religious figure. The footage then showed Harrison grilling the meat, feeding it to his dog, and engaging at target practice. Harrison also sent the Islamic Peace Academy his personal information and his Facebook aliases, which included the name, 'Michele Heindenberger,' an American Airlines flight attendant who died on 9/11 when her plane crashed into the Pentagon.

After launching an investigation, authorities discovered that Harrison also wrote anti-Muslim messages on his Facebook account on December 31, 2010, voicing his intention to march against the Tulsa mosque and tell Muslims that their leaders were pathetic weaklings.[447] In response to his overt acts of bigotry, Harrison was charged with violating the state's hate-crime ordinance. At a January 2011 hearing to determine whether he should be involuntarily committed to a mental health facility, Harrison told a local jury that he planned to impart his message on the tenth anniversary of 9/11. Disregarding psychiatrist Sunita Mall's testimony that Harrison suffered from a delusional disorder, the jury voted against having him committed, concluding that he needed no treatment because he made no direct threats.[448] This decision disturbed Mohammed al-Ghobashy, the imam at the Islamic Society of Tulsa, who received Harrison's DVD and frequently saw him walking his dog in front of the mosque.

Along with these kinds of troubling incidents, Muslims across the U.S. continued to be alarmed by news of mosques being firebombed. In Oregon, an Islamic center was attacked by an arsonist in late 2010.[449] The FBI offered a reward for information about the fire, which involved the use of a liquid accelerant. In response to arson attacks, CAIR launched a "Learn, Not Burn" educational initiative, giving out Qurans to teach Americans about Islam.

Mosques were also targeted out in Wisconsin, Arizona, Louisiana, Kentucky, and Texas.[450] These incidents made American Muslims feel unwelcome in their own country.

RELIGIOUS ATTACKS, 2011

In 2011, mosque attacks continued. In Ohio, a vandal wrote hate graffiti on the Islamic Center of Springfield on the evening of January 7th or the morning of January 8th. The FBI was investigating the vandalism, which included obscenities, a Star of David, and a warning to area Muslims, threatening to retaliate against them for anti-American violence in Pakistan.[451]

In the months that followed, mosques across the U.S. continued to be singled out by bigots. On April 23, 2011, an arsonist set fire to a mosque in Stockton, California.[452] Congregants worried about their security, and hoped that authorities would investigate the blaze as a bias crime.

The same month, a Missouri mosque was targeted. The Islamic Center of Springfield received a death threat in the mail on April 10, 2011. Local police viewed the menacing letter as a hate crime since it called for the extermination of Islam and declared that Muslims stained the earth.[453] The letter also included a disturbing drawing of a severed ram's head. On the day the letter was received, a congregation member discovered the charred remains of three Qurans left at the mosque's entrance.[454] Local police and the FBI were investigating these incidents as overt attempts to intimidate Muslim worshippers in Springfield.

Other Southern mosques were attacked in the spring of 2011. In Louisiana, a bigot used pork to desecrate an Islamic house of worship.[455] The attack frightened area Muslims, who worried about an escalation of community Islamophobia. In Georgia, vandals targeted the Islamic Center of Cartersville on two separate occasions.[456] During each of these attacks, the xenophobes used rocks to shatter the doors and windows of the house of worship. One of the rocks was painted with the words, "Muslim murderers," suggesting that the attackers blamed congregation members for 9/11.[457]

Islamic centers in Texas were also targeted in early 2011. The *Houston Chronicle* reported that in one week, two deliberately-set fires occurred at the Clear Lake Jama Masjid Education Center.[458] Although the Houston Fire Department and the FBI found no evidence that the blazes were bias-motivated, many area Muslims suspected that the attacks were hate crimes.

In California, an arsonist burned down a Stockton Islamic center on April 23, 2011. The blaze destroyed the Al-Emaan Mosque located on 4212 N. Pershing Ave. Security footage showed a perpetrator, wearing a bag over his head, committing the crime at approximately 3:00 a.m. The deliberate fire also damaged adjacent buildings, including the Reliance Real Estate Office and the Living Well Ministries and Christian Center. According to ATF spokeswoman Helen Dunken, the arson resulted in approximately $400,000 damage.[459] Despite the deliberate destruction of the Muslim house of worship, Dunken maintained that the ATF had found no evidence that the mosque arson was a bias attack, although investigators were still considering that as a possibility. Area Muslims were disappointed that investigators failed to realize that the torching of a mosque was almost certainly a hate crime.

In many parts of the country, Americans commemorated Osama bin Laden's death by attacking Islamic religious centers. In Maine, a mosque was covered with anti-Muslim graffiti a few hours after community members learned about the death of the 9/11 mastermind. According to the *Star Tribune* and the *Portland Press Herald*, the vandal spray-painted anti-Muslim threats and political messages on the Portland house of worship, writing: "Osama Today, Islam Tomorrow," "Go Home," "Long Live the West," and "Free Cyprus."[460]

In the aftermath of this mosque attack, American Sikhs expressed concern that widely-disseminated media images of the turbaned Osama bin Laden would prompt bigots to lash out once again at innocent South Asians. Rajwant Singh, chairman of the Sikh Council On Religion and Education, told the *Press Trust of India* that he worried that extensive media coverage of bin Laden's death would trigger a backlash resurgence.[461]

Unfortunately, Singh's fears came true. American bigots continued to target local minority groups in the aftermath of the al-Qaeda compound raid. In Brooklyn, the construction site of a mosque was vandalized by Americans celebrating Osama bin Laden's death. Referencing the killing of the al-Qaeda leader, the vandal wrote "He is dead" on the fence of the Sheepshead property, suggesting that local Muslims needed a special reminder of the elimination of the 9/11 mastermind.[462]

Mosques were also singled out in other parts of New York. In East Amherst, Michael Heick, a homeowner who lived next to a mosque, openly displayed a large lawn sign declaring, "Bomb Making Next Driveway."[463] Members of the Jaffarya Center, a new 11,600 square foot Islamic worship site, were troubled by the unfounded accusation, as well as law enforcement's unwillingness to take the matter seriously. Mubarak Abidi told the *Buffalo News* that he contacted the Amherst police about the sign but was told that it was not illegal since it did not specify which driveway.[464] Mosque congregation members disagreed with the police's conclusion, maintaining that all worshippers were being collectively accused of terrorism in an effort to dissuade them from praying at the religious center.

Bigots continued to target Islamic centers in the South. In Louisiana, bigots attacked Shreveport's Bossier Mosque shortly after Osama bin Laden's death. According to Shreveport's KSLA News 12, a white male in a blue truck desecrated the house of worship by leaving pork on its door handles.[465] Mosque members opted against pressing charges, but reported it to police so the incident would be documented. Authorities viewed the vandalism as a likely hate crime, intended to frighten area Muslims. Christian and Jewish groups spoke out against the bias-motivated incident, which happened in early May, 2011.

Mosques were also attacked in other Southern states. In Texas, two young men parked outside the Madrasah Islamiah in Southwest Houston and set fire to the building at 3:30 a.m. on May 14, 2011. According to the Houston Fire Department, the arsonists broke a window, poured gasoline on the mosque's interior carpet, and set it ablaze. Surveillance videos captured images of the perpetrators, who covered their faces to avoid detection. Despite a likely bias motive for the attack, the FBI and the ATF opted against becoming actively involved in the case.

In Tennessee, vandals destroyed property associated with the Islamic Center of Murfreesboro, which was in the process of constructing a house of worship. WSMV TV reported that on May 25, 2011, vandals defaced the religious group's 'Adopt a Highway' sign 48-hours after the road marker had been unveiled, spraying black paint on the word, 'Islamic.'[466] ATF agents became involved in the investigation since the crime was a bias-motivated attack. Area Muslims had been awarded the sign after agreeing to pick up trash along a designated stretch of the Bradyville Pike. According to WSMV TV, this was not the first hate crime directed against the Islamic Center of Murfreesboro: another sign had been vandalized, and an arsonist had burned equipment at the mosque's building site in 2010.[467] The station also reported that the mosque construction was a hot topic for bloggers, who openly suggested that the prayer center should be burned down if it was ever completed.

While these hate crimes were taking place, the legal battle over the Murfreesboro mosque construction continued to be waged in court. After reviewing both sides of the case, Chancellor Robert Corlew affirmed the Islamic group's First Amendment right of freedom of religion, but acknowledged the plaintiffs' statutory right to sue the government and hold a trial about whether the county violated open meeting laws by failing to provide public notice before approving the building plans.[468] As a result of Corlew's ruling, local Islamophobes continued to have a legal basis to challenge the construction.

Mosques were also targeted in Massachusetts. At approximately 10:30 p.m. on May 31, 2011, a neighbor called the police and reported that a man was trying to set fire to the Islamic Society of Greater Worcester. Before the arsonist had a chance to do serious damage to the mosque, responding officer Sean Sullivan used his boots to stomp out the two-foot high blaze, which was traveling up the handicap access ramp to the main part of the house of worship.[469] Relying on the witness's description of the perpetrator, the police arrested 33-year old Joseph Brignola, charging him with burning a building and inflicting injury to a church or synagogue. The suspect had previous run-ins with the law, with convictions for assault on his record. Because the arsonist did not write anti-Muslim graffiti at the crime scene, the local newspaper, the *Telegram & Gazette*, published an article on the attack, entitled, "Arson Attempt Not Seen as a Hate Crime."[470] Civil rights advocates took issue with this headline, suggesting that the arsonist was likely acting out of anti-Muslim bias when he set fire to the house of worship, particularly since the mosque had been vandalized three separate times in the month following 9/11. Other activists were dismayed by the FBI's lackluster response to the mosque arson, noting that agents were aware of the attack but were not launching their own investigation of the crime scene or aggressively investigating the perpetrator's background to determine whether anti-Muslim bias played a role in the case. Despite these concerns, area Muslims were grateful of the support they received from other members of the community, particularly from Christian and Jewish community leaders who expressed public outrage at the hate-motivated arson.

A decade after 9/11, American nativists continued to fear mosques under construction in the U.S. According to the *Tennessean*, contractors in Murfreesboro were reluctant to bid on a contract to build the Islamic center.[471] Some contractors backed out of talks and didn't return calls to mosque staff members. The *Tennessean* reported that although the economy was slow and work was scarce, many builders were afraid of losing business and facing social ostracism if they accepted the controversial project, noting that local pastors frequently criticized the mosque in their weekly sermons.[472] Other contractors cited safety concerns, noting that in August 2010, an arsonist used a flammable liquid to set fire to four pieces of construction gear at the mosque construction site.[473] The *Tennessean* also reported that in mid-September 2011, around the time of the tenth anniversary of 9/11, a staff member of the Islamic Center of Murfreesboro received a bomb threat, scaring area Muslims and making local contractors even more reluctant to pursue the building job.[474]

The ten-year anniversary of 9/11 triggered additional hate crimes at non-Christian prayer centers. On September 10, 2011, an area bigot hand-delivered a burnt Quran and a threatening drawing to a mosque in the Bronx. According to WABC News 7, Issa Yaya, the African imam of Masjid Hefaz, was shocked by the destruction of the holy book and the offensive picture, which expressed the sender's hatred toward Muslims.[475] The incident was not the first bias crime that took place at the mosque, which was located on East 198th St. The local news reported that in late August 2011, at the end of Ramadan, an intruder broke into the house of worship and flooded it.[476]

Hate crimes also took place in other parts of the state. On September 11, 2011, a truck driver traveling at high speeds deliberately rammed the sign of a mosque in Buffalo. According to WIVB Channel 4 News, witness Dorothy Chandler reported that the assailant appeared to be traveling in excess of 80 miles per hour before he deliberately swerved onto the sidewalk in front of the Islamic center, crashing into the sign and driving destructively over the lawn.[477] As a result of the intentional impact, the mosque's sign, which was written in English and Arabic, was smashed to pieces. Area residents were shocked at the hate crime. In response to the bias attack, Buffalo police chaplain Bilal Abdullah told the local news that he assumed that the vehicular assault was part of the ongoing 9/11 backlash, and called on community members to come together instead of scapegoating local Muslims.[478]

CHAPTER SIX:

BACKLASH HATE CRIMES AT SCHOOLS AND UNIVERSITIES, SEPT. 2001 TO SEPT. 2011

Along with assaults and attacks on prayer centers, the 9/11 backlash also took place on academic campuses. The wave of xenophobia unleashed by the terrorist strikes affected students and educators across the U.S. Although religious and ethnic minorities experienced harassment and discrimination in classrooms throughout the 20th century, the events of 9/11 triggered a dramatic upswing in reports of bias-motivated threats and assaults at schools. Almost immediately after the terrorist strikes, newspapers began publishing stories about minority students targeted in the backlash. These attacks continued throughout the decade that followed.

ISLAMOPHOBIA IN PRE-9/11 CHILDREN'S MOVIES

The virulence of the backlash can best be understood in its cultural context. Prior to 9/11, many young Americans were exposed to movies containing harmful stereotypes of Middle Eastern Muslims. Anti-Arab movies released in the 1970s, 80s, and 90s were widely available on video and DVD prior to 9/11, exposing impressionable children to harmful ethnic and religious stereotypes. In his book, Reel Bad Arabs, Jack Shaheen draws attention to many racist and Islamophobic children's movies.[1] What follows is a summary of some of these anti-Arab films, since they play an important role in disseminating the kinds of racial stereotypes that enabled the 9/11 backlash to flourish at American schools.

Francis Ford Coppola's 1979 movie, *The Black Stallion*, features a heartless Arab who whips and abuses his Arabian horse. This nameless villain also threatens the child protagonist and steals a sugar cube intended for the stallion. According to Shaheen, this nefarious Muslim does not appear in Walter Farley's book, which features instead a generous sheikh who befriends the child protagonist.[2] It is alarming that such disturbing racist stereotypes are deliberately incorporated in films intended for children. Young viewers may have been psychologically traumatized by scenes showing this cruel character mistreating animals. Shaheen notes that in one of the most disturbing parts of the movie, the Arab abuses the young white hero aboard a sinking ship.[3] The selfish Arab sees the boy wearing a life preserver and pulls a knife to take it for himself, even though this action will cost the youngster his life. The young hero is saved when his father appears and knocks out the evil Arab, saving the boy's life.

Black Stallion sequels also include evil Arab characters. In the 1983 film, *The Black Stallion Returns*, an Arab villain sets fire to a horse stable, putting the animals' lives in jeopardy. According to Shaheen, this racist scene was not in Walter Farley's book.[4] The film's young protagonist rescues the stallion from burning to death in the fire, and follows the horse to Morocco. Shaheen maintains that the scriptwriter drove home the message that Arabs are unworthy of the stallion when the horse boots off any rider except the Caucasian boy.[5] At the end of the movie, the white protagonist publicly bests all the Arab riders in a dramatic horse race, demonstrating his superiority to American movie viewers.

Throughout the 1980s, films aimed at teen audiences propagated harmful stereotypes of Middle Easterners. In the 1981 hit movie, *Raiders of the Lost Ark*, Indiana Jones encounters a turbaned-clad Arab, dressed in black and wielding a large scimitar. Rather than engage in swordplay with the formidable foe, the heroic white protagonist shoots the swarthy Semite, to the delight of American movie audiences. These types of scenes turn the killing of Arabs into a comical event. In the 1989 sequel, *Indiana Jones and the Last Crusade*, Harrison Ford's character triumphs over Nazis and a pro-Nazi Arab sheikh, who epitomizes harmful stereotypes of Middle Easterners.

Arab villains also appear in teen movies that have little connection with the rest of the plot. In the 1985 movie, *Back to the Future*, Marty McFly and Dr. Brown steal plutonium from a Libyan terrorist group who were planning to use in a nuclear device. Afraid for his life, one of the protagonists uses derogatory language in reference to the Arab shooter. As Shaheen acutely observes, the incorporation of Arab terrorists in this time-traveling comedy seems somewhat gratuitous.[6] Shaheen recalled going over to an Arab-American friend's house, where his host's young daughter was watching the movie. Disturbed by the violence, she told her father that she was too alarmed to watch anymore, frightened by the Libyan villains.[7]

In some coming-of-age movies, killing Arabs becomes a right-of-passage. In the 1986 movie, *Iron Eagle*, a fighter pilot is shot down by evil Arabs, prompting the captive's teenage son Doug to launch a rescue. Chappy, a retired Air Force colonel played by Lou Gossett, Jr., assists the boy in rescuing his father from the menacing Muslim captives. The common use of white and black protagonists in many anti-Arab movies suggests that African-Americans and Caucasians can achieve racial reconciliation by teaming up against a common Middle Eastern enemy. In the climax of the movie, the young protagonist finally becomes a man when he succeeds in destroying Il Kharem's air base, sending the Arab soldiers to a fiery death. Shaheen compares audiences' enthusiastic responses to this racist film with American moviegoers' disturbing reaction to the 1944 movie, *None Shall Escape*, in which viewers demonstrated their xenophobia by cheering Jews getting shot.[8]

In the 1988 sequel, *Iron Eagle II*, American and Russian pilots find common ground warring against the Arab menace. They join forces to take out missiles before the heartless Middle Eastern villains have a chance to use the weapons against innocent civilians. These films teach young viewers to hate Muslim foreigners.

Libyan villains are featured in the 1988 movie, *Terror Squad*. In one scene in the film, anti-Western demonstrators at Arab universities hold up signs calling for the death of Americans, who are referred to as dogs.[9] In this improbable suspense film, Libyan terrorists invade Kokomo, Indiana and take high school students hostage. The three Arab thugs – Mohamed, Yassir, and Gemal – kill the school's black janitor and terrorize the students. Shaheen provides his readers with an in-depth discussion of the movie's overt xenophobia and racist language.[10] The movie employs ethnic and religious slurs in reference to the three Muslim villains, calling them "camel jockeys" and other derogatory names.[11] The movie depicts the Arab terrorists as sexual perverts. When one blonde female student asks to use the bathroom, Yassir tells her that Gemal would accompany her. Afraid of getting sexually assaulted or having to urinate in front of her abductor, she decides to remain seated. In another scene, a female student shoots one of the Muslim terrorists when he grabs her leg. The movie also shows another student shooting one of the Arabs with a bow and arrow. This movie, aimed at young American audiences, suggests to adolescent viewers that Middle Easterners and Muslims are enemies who need to be eradicated.

Muslims are depicted as dangerous killers in the 1991 movie, *American Ninja 4: The Annihilation*. In this film, Ali Maksoud, an Islamic sheikh obsessed with using nuclear weapons against civilians, threatens a U.S. schoolteacher and sympathetic African villagers.[12] Maksoud captures and tortures four Americans, holding them hostage and demanding a $50 million ransom. Delta Force commandos eventually defeat this Muslim villain, his Arab cohorts, and their Ninja guards. These movies teach young viewers that it is sometimes advisable to exterminate Arabs and Muslims, who are out to destroy the West.

Disney movies released during this period often featured racist stereotypes of Middle Easterners and Muslims, causing many thoughtful viewers to question president Michael Eisner's claim that his company creates wonderful family-appropriate entertainment. For example, the 1992 movie, *Aladdin*, portrays Arab characters as hook-nosed villains and Semitic buffoons. The opening song in the film informs children that Aladdin is from a barbaric Middle Eastern land where its inhabitants cut off strangers' ears if they don't like their faces.[13]

Other film studios also created movies for young audiences depicting Arabs and Muslims as cruel misogynists. In the 1993 comedy, *Son of the Pink Panther*, a belly dancer expresses her fear of Omar, a swarthy, knife-wielding Arab who terrorizes her. Shaheen takes issue with the film's Islamophobic dialogue, particularly a scene in which the belly dancer tells Inspector Clouseau that she must finish her dance or Omar will cut off her nipples.[14] In another scene, General Jaffar kidnaps Princess Yasmine, who is half-American. Clouseau, the French protagonist, eventually rescues her from her unscrupulous Semitic captor.

In the mid-90s, Disney produced other children's movies containing evil Arab characters. According to Shaheen, the 1994 *Aladdin* sequel, *Return of Jafar*, features buck-toothed Middle Eastern goons and thieves who attempt to murder Aladdin and knife his parrot companion.[15] Another 1994 Disney-company movie,

In the Army Now, shows Middle Easterners as desert-dwelling terrorists who attempt to use chemical weapons against the troops. The 1996 Disney movie, *Kazaam*, also contains racist Arab characters. Discussing this film, Shaheen maintains that Arab-Americans appear as swarthy gangsters who brutalize an American teenager and other innocent characters.[16]

Anti-Arab messages also appear in the 1999 cartoon comedy, *South Park: Bigger, Longer, and Uncut*. In this movie, the protagonist Kenny is killed and finds himself in hell because he once threw a rock at a bird. In the netherworld, the boy encounters Satan, a frightening demonic creature. American audiences eventually learn that Satan is not the underworld's most sinister character; even the devil himself is cowed by the presence of Saddam Hussein, who arrived in hell after being killed by wild boars. In this comedy, Saddam Hussein has entered into a gay relationship with Satan, bossing around the prince of darkness. Discussing this movie, film critic Tim Jon Semmerling argues that the film ridicules the American belief that Saddam and the Arabs have displaced the devil himself as the personification of evil in the world.[17] Another cartoon protagonist, Cartman, uses profanity to overpower Saddam, proving to audiences that the act of destroying the evil Arab will usher in world peace and happiness.[18] All of these anti-Arab movies, widely available on DVD both before and after 9/11, teach young audiences lessons in intolerance, giving them permission to hate their ethnic classmates.

THE 9/11 BACKLASH ON AMERICAN CAMPUSES

Sept. 2001 Bullying at Kindergartens and Elementary Schools

In the aftermath of the terrorist attacks, Arab-American, Muslim, and Sikh students reported being harassed and attacked at public and private schools across the U.S. Even kindergarteners and elementary school children were targeted. In San Francisco, Eureka Valley grocery store owner Saif Ataya told the *Chronicle* that his five-year old daughter was called a 'terrorist' at her school after 9/11.[19] The kindergartener asked her father about the meaning of the derogatory term and then expressed shock that her classmates would call her such a horrible name.[20]

In other parts of the Bay Area, Sikh kindergarteners were bullied by their peers. In Oakland, California, Jaspreet Singh, a five-year old Sikh boy, was singled out and harassed by other children after 9/11. According to the publication *Colorlines*, the young boy's peers teased him about his uncut hair and told him he shouldn't come to class.[21]

Elementary school pupils were also singled out by their classmates. Muslim students were frequently harassed by other children in Massachusetts. Imam Eid told the *Patriot-Ledger* that his nine-year old son was particularly unnerved by the backlash, becoming wary of disclosing his ethnicity to his classmates.[22] The boy told his father that he planned on telling other students that he was Irish so they wouldn't beat him up.[23]

Minority students were also bullied in other parts of the state. In Duxbury, a fourth grader told his father, Syrian-American political candidate Aboud Al-Zaim, not to address his class about Islam, since the other children were blaming Muslim students for the terrorist strikes. According to the *Patriot-Ledger*, Al-Zaim was deeply troubled that his son was being bullied by his peers, who failed to realize that the boy was as American as apple pie.[24]

Students with Arabic or Muslim names were harassed at school in the days and weeks following 9/11. The *ADC Times* reported that students with Arab names were singled out by bullies, noting that a boy named "Ghassan" was called "Ghassama bin Laden" by his classmates, and a girl named "Khatib" began being called "Q-tip."[25]

On occasion, elementary school children were physically affected by the intense psychological bullying they experienced. Shortly after 9/11, nine-year old Zuhdi Abdelkarim told the *Los Angeles Times* that the harassment was so awful that he became unwell.[26] At his Southern California primary school, one student told Abdelkarim that 9/11 was his fault because he was an Arab. Another student glared at him when he sang patriotic songs, and proclaimed that Arabs and Muslims attacked the U.S. because they were jealous of it.[27]

Zuhdi's father, Dr. Riad Abdelkarim, said that the racial targeting of his son was not the first time that his family experienced bigotry in America. Although he was a Santa Monica native, Riad Abdelkarim and his family members had been frequently targeted by bigots because they were of Palestinian descent. The *Los Angeles Times* reported that in the past, bigots vandalized their car, drove vehicles over their lawn, and poured gasoline over their grass.[28] The most harrowing incident occurred in his own childhood, immediately after the local paper announced that he won the local spelling bee. A bigot, upset at his academic success, telephoned his home and terrorized his mother with a false claim that he had been kidnapped.[29] For Riad Abdelkarim, the harassment his nine-year old son was experiencing at school after 9/11 was a painful reminder of the persistence of intolerance in the U.S.

Sept. 2001 Bullying at Junior High Schools

Although non-white children in kindergarten to fifth grade experienced some post-9/11 harassment, most reported backlash incidents involved students at middle schools or high schools.[30] Many pupils felt particularly vulnerable in districts where they were stood out as visible minorities. The September 13, 2001 issue of the *Austin American Statesman* describes how one Eanes Middle School student was singled out after 9/11 and harassed by his classmates.[31] The victim's father, Ali Khataw, reported that the other children taunted his son and challenged his family's nationality, although the boy and his relatives were American citizens.

In many instances, backlash harassment turned physical. In Northern Virginia, one minority middle school boy reported being violently shoved in the playground on three separate occasions in one week.[32] Concerned parents wondered if the school's inadequate response to the first assault allowed the post-9/11 attacks to continue, giving the bullies a sense of entitlement.[33]

In school districts across the U.S., middle school students received death threats from their peers. In Fort Worth, Texas, two 13-year olds and one 14-year old from Forest Oak Middle school were taken into custody on September 14, 2001 after making death threats against a classmate from India. According to *India-West,* the South Asian victim told authorities that the bullies repeatedly taunted him and threatened to shoot him to death in the wake of 9/11.[34] The *Dallas Morning News* reported that the three bullies were suspended and charged with making a terrorist threat, a misdemeanor, but local law enforcement were considering asking the Fort Worth District Attorney's office to elevate the charge to a hate crime.[35] In response to bias attacks taking place in his district, Ft. Worth school superintendent Dr. Thomas Tocco sent letters home to parents on September 17, 2001, urging them to promote tolerance towards ethnic students and their families.

Junior high school students were also signaled out in other parts of the country. In the wake of 9/11, Maryam Ahmed told the Syracuse *Post-Standard* that she was called an Arab terrorist by another classmate.[36] In addition to being singled out by her peers, she was also harassed by a school employee. When she and other Muslim girls were climbing aboard the school bus, the driver made a wisecrack about terrorists.[37] Her father, Amin Ahmed, complained, and the driver was dismissed.

Other minority students were attacked while commuting to and from school. The *Washington Post* reported that an assailant in Fairfax threw rocks at a minority student walking home from campus in retaliation for the terrorist strikes.[38] In other parts of the country, Arab and South Asian students were hassled at bus stops by classmates who wanted them to stay home. Shortly after 9/11, the Portland *Oregonian* reported that Washington County authorities were taking action against students who assaulted an 11-year old Iraqi boy in a racially-motivated attack at a school bus stop.[39] In California, a Sikh boy was also bullied by his classmates, who prevented him from boarding the school bus.[40]

Sept. 2001 Bullying and Attacks at High Schools

Along with younger pupils, teenagers were also harassed or assaulted during the backlash. Bias-motivated fights broke out at two high schools in Fremont, California. In these post-9/11 attacks, Afghan students were singled out and assaulted by their peers.[41]

Minority high school pupils were also targeted in other states. In Northern Virginia, an Arab-American teenager was physically attacked at school during the 9/11 backlash.[42] In Missouri, the *St. Louis Post-Dispatch* reported cases of backlash bullying, including an incident on September 11, 2001 in which students at Parkway West High School harassed sophomore Atif Sial, demanding that he tell other Muslims to stop bombing the country.[43]

In Ohio, minority students in Cleveland were racially bullied by their peers at Westlake High School.[44] In response to this harassment, Arab-American and Muslim parents expressed their outrage that their children were being blamed for 9/11. Freddie Assad, a parent of two of the targeted students, told the *Plain Dealer* that his family was just as American as anyone else's, noting that he had been in the U.S. since 1967.[45]

In Utah, a predominantly-Mormon state with relatively few Muslims, high school students occasionally singled out their non-Christian peers. According to the *Deseret Morning News*, 15-year old Shahbaz Ahmad was called a terrorist at Bingham High School shortly after 9/11.[46] Although he was born in the U.S., his Utah classmates bullied him because his parents were originally from Pakistan.

During the 9/11 backlash, minority students were often harassed in areas of schools where there was minimal adult supervision. The *Detroit Free Press* reported that Muslim and Arab-American students in Michigan were subjected to death threats in the hallways.[47] In some incidents, peers compared Arab students to camels, and suggested that they should all be exterminated.[48]

High school students in Florida were also targeted in-between classes. After 9/11, Komal Mirza, a ninth grader at Nova High School in Davie, Florida, told the *Seattle Times* that she was occasionally stopped and bullied in the hallways.[49] She was particularly upset when she received death threats from students she used to consider friends. According to the *Seattle Times*, Mirza was shocked when a boy she had known since the fourth grade told her that he hoped she would die because she was a Muslim.[50] After her parents and the principal intervened, the boy apologized for his bigoted remarks.

Latina Muslims were also singled out in Florida schools during the 9/11 backlash. Sussan Salazar, an 18-year old Colombian immigrant who converted to Islam, told the *South Florida Sentinel* that she was bothered by classmates' comments that Muslims were deranged and homicidal.[51] When she challenged their views in her American history class, her peers refused to take her seriously, dismissing her as a girl from Colombia who could not speak authoritatively about her adopted faith.

Muslim students who wore hijabs were frequently harassed on American high school campuses. In Los Angeles, bullies accused veiled girls of being involved in the terrorist attacks, and demanded that they leave the country.[52] Even in U.S. school districts that were heavily Arab-American, veiled Muslim students were sometimes attacked. The *Boston Globe* estimated that in 2001, approximately 60% of Dearborn's high school students were ethnically Arab.[53] Despite having a large number of Muslim classmates, one Dearborn teenager, wearing the hijab, was viciously beaten on campus in a post-9/11 hate crime. Describing this backlash incident, the *Boston Globe* reported that the Muslim student was slammed into a locker, kicked, bruised, and verbally taunted by a male peer.[54] According to the *Boston Globe*, the perpetrator also physically attacked a second Arab-American girl on another occasion, kicking her, using profanities, and telling her to leave because she was a terrorist.[55] Parents wondered if the attacks could have been prevented if administrators had done more to protect vulnerable students.

Bigots also attacked veiled Muslim teenagers in other Michigan cities. In Detroit, assailants targeted two veiled girls walking home from school, threatening them and pelting them with stones.[56] The attack made them fearful of attending classes.

Along with their Muslim peers, Sikh high school students were frequently targeted in the aftermath of the terrorist strikes. In upstate New York, a bigot screamed a death threat at Prabhdeep Singh, a 17-year old Sikh, soon after 9/11. The victimized senior told the Albany *Times Union* that he was just standing in front of the Albany Academy when someone called him a terrorist and yelled that he should be killed.[57] Although Singh was born in the U.S. and lived in Loudonville, he realized that uneducated Americans were assuming he was affiliated with the hijackers simply because he wore a turban.[58] To prevent further taunts and attacks, he began driving around with an American flag on his car.

Other Sikh high school students experienced similar mistreatment. Shortly after 9/11, Romi Singh, a 15-year old pupil from West Los Angeles, felt compelled to cut his hair because of the widespread harassment he experienced during the backlash. He told the *Los Angeles Times* that he was frequently called 'Osama bin Laden,' and had peers and strangers spit on his clothes.[59]

Along with being targeted by their classmates, minority students were sometimes threatened or assaulted by adults on school grounds. The *Pittsburgh Post-Gazette* reported that an Arab-American high school student in Meadville, Pennsylvania was attacked in his school's parking lot on September 19, 2001 by a man from Crawford County.[60] The assault made minority children fearful of their safety at the height of the backlash.

In many school districts, teachers compounded the harassment by blaming their own students for 9/11. In Connecticut, one teacher lashed out against Arabs and Muslims and forced her own Arab-American pupils to leave the classroom.[61] Similar scapegoating took place in other parts of the country. In Florida, a volunteer school speaker made repeated disparaging remarks about Muslims, telling the students that Middle Easterners hated Americans, and that Arabs wanted Westerners to die and be sent to Mohammed.[62] The xenophobic diatribe caused one minority student to hide her face from her classmates, making her feel ashamed of being Arab and Muslim.[63]

Some schools in Louisiana cancelled classes in response to the widespread harassment of minority pupils. Because children in Jefferson Parish were taunting and threatening students of Arab origin, Superintendent Elton Lagasse cancelled classes the day after 9/11.[64] In the September 14, 2001 issue of the *Times-Picayune*, Lagasse acknowledged that Arab-American students were being harassed in his district.[65] Because tensions were high and the students needed a cooling-off period, he decided to close the schools until the shock of the terrorist strikes abated.

In many parts of the country, concerned parents kept minority children at home, causing absenteeism to skyrocket. The *Village Voice* reported that in Palmdale, California, minority students stopped attending class in mid-September 2001 when they found out that their names had been written on a hit list, promising to avenge 9/11 with a massacre.[66]

In response to the widespread harassment, volunteers across America began accompanying Muslim students to and from school. In New York alone, an Arab-American family support center screened and trained 500 escorts, who were from different ethnic and religious backgrounds. In other U.S. cities, volunteers also acted to protect at-risk children. In San Francisco, Sonya Kaleel, a marketing consultant, learned of the plight of Muslim students through a hate crimes hot line. Kaleel, a Christian woman originally from Illinois, offered to help a local Iraqi-born Muslim girl, Hiba Al-Gizawi, get safely to and from Balboa High School in the weeks following 9/11, particularly after someone spit on the girl's mother two days after the terrorist strikes.[67] To protect Al-Gizawi from bias-motivated harassment, Kaleel repeatedly drove her to school, and waited to make sure that she got safely behind school gates. Al-Gizawi told the *Charleston Daily Mail* that the backlash changed her life, preventing her from going shopping and having fun in public.[68] In the weeks following 9/11, she stayed indoors with her parents and her two brothers, watching Arabic television and calling friends.

While some Arab-American high school students relied on escorts to commute safely, others took different precautions. One Chaldean Christian girl began wearing a cross so that her classmates and neighbors would not mistake her for a Muslim and attack her.[69]

Sept. 2001 Attacks at Islamic Schools and Predominantly-Arab Campuses

Students at Islamic schools felt particularly vulnerable and afraid in the aftermath of 9/11. The *Daily Herald* reported that hours after the Twin Towers fell, a bigoted caller phoned the Islamic Institute of New York and threatened to paint the streets with Muslim students' blood.[70]

In response to the backlash, some Islamic schools in the U.S. closed temporarily out of concern that their facilities might be targeted by bigots. The *Los Angeles Times* reported that the 274 students at the Islamic New Horizon School in Pasadena were sent home at noon on September 12, 2001 out of fear that students might be attacked by angry nativists.[71] Panicked parents rushed to pick up their children, worried that the campus might not be safe. In Fremont, California, a local Islamic school was closed for two days following assaults on Afghan students in other parts of the city.[72] In Birmingham, Alabama, a Muslim academy cancelled classes in response to the 9/11 backlash.[73]

An Islamic school in West St. Louis also closed of fear for students' safety. On September 13, 2001, the *St. Louis Post-Dispatch* reported that the Daar ul-Islam Mosque school cancelled classes for a couple of days after receiving menacing phone calls threatening to retaliate against the campus for 9/11.[74] Imam Muhammad Nur Abdullah told the newspaper that he was concerned about re-opening the school while tensions were so high in the area.[75]

On occasion, schools were firebombed or attacked if they had a predominantly-minority student body. The *Chicago Defender* reported that on 9/11, an arsonist lobbed a Molotov cocktail onto the steps of the Arab-American Educational School.[76] The hate crime frightened students and parents, who worried about an escalation in violence. In Detroit, a school with a large number of Muslim students received a bomb threat in mid-September, according to the *St. Louis Post-Dispatch*.[77]

Throughout the South, bigots frequently targeted Muslim-run campuses. The *Times-Picayune* reported that shortly after 9/11, a 15-year old youth and a 20-year old man from Chalmette fired a pellet gun into an Islamic school in Louisiana.[78] Xenophobes also attacked Muslim students in other Southern states. Bigots threatened to kill students at the Islamic Academy of Florida. Principal Abdulmajid Biuk told the *St. Petersburg Times* that he considered closing the campus the day after 9/11, after fielding so many menacing calls from angry Americans calling themselves patriots.[79] After much deliberation, he and the other administrators decided to keep the 300-pupil academy open, after arranging for a sheriff's deputy to check cars at the school entrance and using parents to stand guard at the facility after work. Biuk also told the *St. Petersburg Times* that they decided to remove the word "Islamic" from the side of the school bus after other drivers began intentionally swerving at the vehicle in order to frighten Muslim children.[80]

Religious schools were also targeted on the West Coast. After the Twin Towers fell, a bigot with pepper spray was caught trespassing at an Islamic school in Henderson, Nevada, attempting to attack students in retaliation for 9/11. As the intruder was escorted off school grounds, he vowed to return to the Omar Haikal Islamic Academy and reclaim the neighborhood, according to a September 18, 2001 article in the *Las Vegas Review-Journal*.[81] Worried about student safety, academy founder Osama Haikal said that the school hired 24-hour security to protect students from hate crimes.

Even when Arab-American and Islamic schools resumed classes, many fearful parents kept their children at home. In Beavercreek, Ohio, many students at the Bright Horizon Islamic School missed classes in the days following 9/11. Principal Heather O'Bannon told the *Dayton Daily News* that absenteeism had more than quadrupled.[82] She also reported that many of the students were afraid to go out in public, particularly if they wore Muslim attire.

Sept. 2001 College Attacks

Minority college students were also harassed or attacked during the 9/11 backlash. According to the Arlington Heights *Daily Herald*, there were at least 250 cases of anti-Arab and anti-Muslim hate crimes on American college campuses in the two weeks after the terrorist strikes. At many American universities, international students were physically assaulted by their peers. On September 16, 2001, two college-age assailants attacked 19-year old Mazen Ahmad El Kassaa at the University of North Carolina at Greensboro.[83] While beating up the Lebanese student, the perpetrators screamed racial epithets, calling him a terrorist and demanding that he return to his homeland.[84] They also broke his glasses and inflicted physical injuries serious enough to necessitate medical treatment at a nearby hospital. As a result of the assault, he decided to drop out of school and return to Beirut, but had difficulty returning to Lebanon because of increased airport security.

Many UNC students and faculty members were upset that the school did not promptly inform members of the college community about the hate crime. An email sent to students and faculty two days after the attack urged tolerance and sensitivity towards minority students, but did not directly mention the bias-motivated beating. Some students felt that administrators had been reluctant to publicize news of hate crimes because they were concerned about negative publicity. One of Kassaa's roommates, Hassan Abdul Wahab Hamze, told the *Greensboro News Record* that he had also been harassed on campus, first by about eight people on 9/11, and again near the same place where Kassaa was attacked.[85] Minority students wondered if El Kassaa's beating could have been prevented if campus security had been more proactive. In response to this criticism, the school decided to re-evaluate how it informed students and faculty of bias-motivated assaults. Helen Dennison, assistant vice chancellor for university relations, stated publicly that the school would be more diligent about reporting future attacks on the campus crime alert web site.

In response to Kassaa's beating, Amnesty International organized a 'teach-in' on the campus. Bella Siddick, the vice-president of the Muslim Students' Association, told the *Greensboro News Record* that the attack deeply troubled members of his organization, who felt they were being scapegoated for the terrorist strikes.[86] Colleen Kriger, a history professor at the college, hoped that the teach-in would create a more tolerant campus environment.[87]

Muslim women were also targeted on college grounds, particularly if they wore hijabs. At Indiana University, an Afghan-American student was singled out on the morning of 9/11, as she was leaving a campus lecture hall. The *Denver Post* reported that a classmate accused the Muslim girl of being responsible for the hijackings.[88] She was outraged that so many people were quick to blame their fellow citizens. Veiled college students were also bullied in Texas. Nora Ashour, president of the Arab-American Students Association, told the *Houston Chronicle* that male students at the University of Houston verbally harassed their hijab-wearing peers, calling them Osama bin Laden.[89]

In some instances, the verbal attacks turned physical. According to the *Irish Times*, two young Muslim women were attacked and beaten at Moraine Valley College in Palos Hills, Illinois, shortly after 9/11.[90] This hate crime garnered considerable overseas attention, damaging America's international reputation as a tolerant country.

Veiled students were also attacked in California. The Los Angeles *Daily News* reported that in the first three days after 9/11, Muslim students at USC had their hijabs pulled off by assailants, and anti-Arab signs were put up on the campus.[91] Many international students questioned their safety at the school in the aftermath of the hate crimes, which they attributed to post-9/11 nativism.

Similar bias assaults took place in Northern California. At U.C. Berkeley, two Muslim students were attacked and had their hijabs yanked off in the aftermath of the terror strikes.[92] Other backlash hate crimes took place on the campus. The Muslim Student Association reported that it received over 200 hate letters after 9/11. Someone also removed one of their banners from Sproul plaza. *Asianweek* reported that when students notified campus security about the excessive hate mail and the loss of their sign, one U.C. police officer told them to grow a thicker skin.[93] Many Muslim students were dissatisfied with campus police's slow response to reports of racially and religiously-motivated harassment. When Waheeda Samady, a college senior and MSA member, was verbally attacked on her evening walk home from class, the campus police refused to take the incident seriously, accusing her of being overly dramatic.[94] Campus police finally arrested the man responsible after the bigoted bully harassed two other students.[95] Muslim students were dismayed that it took authorities so long to take action, wondering if the bullying could have been prevented by a more timely response. To protect themselves, MSA members organized their own escort service, concerned that university security was inadequate. Some students felt that the school could be doing more to stem campus xenophobia. After the college newspaper, the *Daily Californian*, ran a cartoon depicting Muslims as terrorists in hell, one hundred people attended a demonstration to protest the drawing and the surge in anti-Islamic bigotry.[96]

Minority college students were particularly at risk on campuses that failed to take adequate steps to protect their security. At Arizona State University at Tempe, there were three reported incidents of 9/11 backlash hate crimes, the first of which proved to be false. On September 13, 2001, Ahmed Saad Nasim, a Muslim-American ASU student, claimed to have been assaulted with eggs in a backlash hate crime. On September 28, he confessed that he had fabricated the incident to increase campus security of vulnerable minority students.[97]

Although the attack on Nasim was a fabrication, other ASU students were targeted by bigots. Shortly after 1:00 a.m. on September 25, 2001, a 19-year old student of Indian origin was assaulted on the way home from his campus job. The student asked the police to keep his name confidential, because he was concerned about further reprisals. *India-West* reported that the victim was approached from behind and pushed to the ground by three assailants, who then punched and kicked him while making remarks about his national origin.[98] The student later complained of soreness to his head but declined medical attention.

A few days later, shortly before midnight on September 27, 2001, a 31-year old male ASU student was walking on the eastern edge of the campus on Terrance Road when the driver of a black pickup truck threw an egg at him, perhaps inspired by publicity surrounding Nasim's fabricated September 13th attack.[99] While driving away, the occupants of the vehicle made ethno-racial slurs directed at the victim. Following an investigation, police arrested and charged four male teenagers: 18-year old Justin Medhi Falsafi, an ASU student, 18-year old Kevin Michael Gabriel of Phoenix, and two minors.[100] According to ASU police spokesman Keith Jennings, Falsafi was charged and released, and Gabriel was booked at the jail. The minors were referred to juvenile authorities in Maricopa County.

In many parts of the country, Iranian-American college students received death threats. At Pierce College in Woodland Hills, California, two bigots were arrested after writing a death threat on a booth operated by the school's Persian Club.[101] In other states, minority college students were harassed or attacked en route to class. In one instance, passengers shouting anti-Arab threats pushed an Indian-American student en route to the University of Maryland out of a metro train.[102]

Across the country, Sikh college students were frequently singled out because of their turbans. A few days after 9/11, Cleveland State University student Navtej Singh told the *Plain Dealer* that he was surprised at the verbal harassment he encountered in the aftermath of the World Trade Center and Pentagon attacks.[103] Strangers gave him the finger and treated him as a terrorist, instead of realizing that he was a Cleveland-born American and one of the biggest Browns fan in the city.[104]

In response to the surge in post-9/11 hate crimes, U.S. Secretary of Education Rod Paige sent out a "Dear Colleague" letter to school administrators and college presidents across the country. In this communication, he pointed out that many students were being unfairly targeted, and reminded educators that all institutions receiving federal funding were bound by the Civil Rights Act, which mandated that instructors and school officials provide an educational environment free from discrimination.[105] Paige also acknowledged the fears and concerns of Arab-American parents, who were worried for their children's safety.

Because of the intensity of the backlash, some college students were too frightened to appear on campus. At Loyola University, Dr. Ann Kalayil reported that her South Asian students were paralyzed with anxiety, making them too nervous to venture outside of their homes.[106] In Massachusetts, minority students also missed school. Usman Khan, a member of Tufts' Muslim Students' Association, told the *Boston Herald* that many minority students stopped going to class after being harassed by peers, who accused them of being pleased by 9/11.[107] Other Massachusetts college students experienced similar discrimination. Numan Waheed, a member of MIT's Muslim Students Association, reported that minority students at his school had received threats, interfering with their ability to concentrate on their studies.[108]

Bias-motivated crimes also took place on Colorado campuses. On September 18, 2001, four men threatened a minority student at the University of Colorado-Boulder.[109] The following day, hate graffiti directed against Arabs and Afghanis was discovered in the library. In response to these incidents, Saudi students took refuge in the school's religion department, where they spoke with Islamic Studies professor Frederick Denny about their fears of campus intolerance.[110] Denny and other educators organized a special meeting to address the 9/11 backlash and racial scapegoating.

In other parts of the state, minority college students experienced off-campus harassment. Larry Bell, director of the office of international students at Colorado University-Denver, told the *Denver Post* that four minority students were racially-targeted near the school, including one bias-motivated assault.[111]

College students were occasionally attacked while returning to campus after vacations. One of the worst incidents occurred in September 2001, when a Pakistani international student was detained in Alabama for carrying an expired visa. He was then taken to a Mississippi prison, where he was severely beaten by inmates who blamed him for the terrorist strikes.

According to the *Houston Chronicle*, Hasnain Javed, a 20-year old New York community college student, was visiting his aunt in Houston on 9/11.[112] The anti-Muslim backlash left him afraid to fly back to New York, where he was enrolled in classes. Instead of taking an airplane, the South Asian student decided to return to New York via bus, leaving from Houston on the night of September 18, 2001. The following morning, Javed arrived in Mobile, Alabama, where he was detained by border patrol officers who discovered his visa had expired. Although Javed legally came to the U.S. to attend high school, he had not renewed his paperwork.

Border patrol officials told Javed and a few Latino detainees that they would be transported to an INS regional office in New Orleans. En route to Louisiana, the government officials decided to hold Javed and the other detainees overnight at the Stone County Correctional Facility in Wiggins, Mississippi.

Javed was housed in a large dorm room with six Mississippi prison inmates. He told the *Houston Chronicle* that the convicts singled him out immediately, looking at him strangely as soon as he entered the dormitory.[113] Another prisoner approached him and threatened him, pushing him in the face and breaking his tooth.[114] Two inmates then started to beat him, referring to him as Osama bin Laden.[115] The other later inmates joined in the assault, stripping the South Asian student naked and beating him severely.[116] Javed told the *Houston Chronicle* that although he pushed the alarm bell, the guards just waited in the doorway for about 20 to 25 minutes before the attack stopped.[117] The assault left Javed with multiple injuries, including fractured ribs and a ruptured eardrum. After the beating, he was taken to a prison nurse, but was not allowed to see a doctor.

His aunt traveled to Mississippi as soon as she learned of her nephew's plight, but she was denied access to him. She asked prison administrators why Javed was being held in a correctional facility for criminals, but they refused to answer her question. According to INS spokeswoman Karen Kraushaar, the agency had a rule against housing non-criminal detainees alongside convicted felons, but this only applied to illegal immigrants held for more than 72 hours.[118]

Two days after his arrest, Javed was taken to INS headquarters in New Orleans and released after his relatives posted a $5,000 bond. He returned to Houston, where he stayed with his aunt awaiting an INS hearing on his expired visa. His aunt viewed Javed's attack as a hate crime, since his assailants knew he was Muslim and blamed him for 9/11.[119] She speculated about whether the prison guards colluded with the inmates who attacked Javed, and questioned the INS' practice of occasionally housing non-criminal detainees alongside hardcore convicts. The Jackson FBI office eventually agreed to look into the case.

Javed was not the only incarcerated Muslim singled out after the terrorist strikes. The *Washington Post* reported that immediately after 9/11, Muslim prisoners were subjected to religious slurs and attacked by other inmates in Washington state.[120]

While Javed was trying to get back to school, other international students were attempting to return to their countries of origin. At the University of Colorado at Denver, 42 of 250 Middle Eastern students withdrew in the immediate aftermath of 9/11. Mohamed Al-Suwaidi told the *Denver Post* that the racial backlash prompted his decision to leave the college and return to the United Arab Emirates, since his parents worried about his safety in the U.S.[121]

Other Colorado students also left school to return to the Middle East. At the University of Denver, Chris Johnson, director of international student and scholar services, said that many students from Kuwait, Qatar, Saudi Arabia, and the United Arab Emirates dropped out of school as a result of the backlash.[122] Middle Eastern students also withdrew from Colorado State and Colorado University at Boulder.

Faculty members sometimes targeted Muslim college students. The *St. Petersburg Times* reported that soon after 9/11, a professor at the University of South Florida wrote a letter to the student newspaper comparing Muslims to dogs.[123] Other faculty members were outraged, and the religious studies department issued a statement in support of the school's Muslim population.

Sept. 2001 Attacks Targeting Teachers

On occasion, American students targeted their own teachers in the days following 9/11. At Deady Middle School in Houston, two students assaulted an instructor of Middle Eastern descent on September 19, 2001, according to the *Houston Chronicle*.[124] During the attack, the students made death threats and promised to kill the teacher's family. In response to the assault, the young perpetrators were arrested, issued citations, and suspended from school for several days. Some community members wondered whether the punishment was adequate, particularly since the victimized instructor would have to interact with the students once they resumed classes.

Some teachers and school volunteers worried that their Muslim attire would attract the attention of xenophobes. According to the September 20, 2001 issue of Missouri's *Kansas City Star*, a bigot made violent threats against Muslim-American educator Marie Hasan.[125] Born in Piper, Kansas to a Catholic family, Hasan converted to Islam and married a Pakistani man she met at the University of Kansas. Prior to 9/11, she worked as a volunteer for the Missouri Department of Conservation, conducting educational nature hikes to school children in the wooded acreage behind a school in South Kansas City. After Hasan received the threats, she became concerned about the safety of students accompanying her on the secluded trails. She felt dismayed that the simple act of wearing a Muslim headscarf in public might endanger school children in her presence.

Other Muslim educators faced similar harassment. In Tennessee, a teacher said that she was harassed by community members who blamed her for 9/11, according to the *Knoxville News Sentinel*. Maha Ayesh, an educator at a private school affiliated with the Knoxville Anoor Mosque, said that bigots noticed her hijab and ordered her to leave the country and return to Afghanistan.[126]

University instructors were also targeted during the backlash. Mohammad Mohammad, an Arabic professor at the University of Texas, told the *Denver Post* that he stopped wearing his Arab headdress after someone spat on him in the aftermath of 9/11.[127] Educators in other states were also singled out. According to the September 28, 2001 issue of *India-West*, an Indian-American faculty member at New Mexico State University was attacked by xenophobes. As he was walking to the parking lot, three white men in their 20s struck him with a water balloon and then jumped him.[128] While one of the assailants held him down, another attacker beat him on the stomach and head. The victim told police that his attackers saw his dark skin and beard and mistook him for an Arab.

Persian instructors also felt the wrath of bigots. The *Capital Times* reported that an Iranian professor at the University of Wisconsin was repeatedly targeted in the aftermath of the terrorist strikes.[129] Majid Sarmadi, an instructor at the School of Human Ecology, was shocked to learn that a vandal thrashed his office in misplaced retaliation for 9/11.[130] Soon afterwards, he began receiving threatening phone calls at his home in the middle of the night. When the young man who trashed Sarmadi's office was apprehended, the Iranian instructor asked prosecutors to treat him with leniency, in the hopes that community service would make him rethink his xenophobic views. Local authorities were surprised by the surge in xenophobia in the area. According to detective Alix Olson, there were no reported anti-Muslim hate crimes in Madison in the five years prior to 9/11, but more than 20 in the aftermath of the terrorist strikes.[131]

CAMPUS ATTACKS, FALL 2001

Despite the efforts of educators and administrators to stem intolerance, attacks against minority students continued in the weeks and months following 9/11. On October 13, 2001, Muslims at the University of Colorado at Boulder received a threatening email and two menacing phone calls. The *Denver Post* reported that these messages promised to kill followers of Islam enrolled at the school.[132] History student Amina Nawaz discovered one of these threats on the Muslim Student Association's answering machine.[133] The caller used derogatory language to refer to Muslim students, promising to murder them unless they dropped out of school and moved out of the U.S. by Christmas.

In response to these messages, Boulder police sent an email to all Colorado University students asking them to listen to the calls posted on the campus security office's web site in the hopes that someone might be able to identify the voice of the perpetrator. Officials offered a $1000 reward to elicit information about the crime. Acting on a tip generated through the Crime Stoppers program, campus police eventually arrested Glenn Dale Ewell, a 48-year old local cafeteria worker.[134] Ewell was charged with harassment and criminal extortion, but the district attorney later dropped the charges for lack of evidence.

Because of the threats and the failure of the district attorney to prosecute the suspected perpetrator, Nawaz told the *Rocky Mountain News* that her Pakistani family became afraid for her safety.[135] Muslim students on campus began carrying pepper spray and walking everywhere in pairs or groups.

In other parts of the country, minority students continued to feel under attack in the weeks and months following 9/11. Amelia Derr, the education director of Hate Free Zone, reported that many teachers and administrators in Washington state refused to address racial bullying at schools in the fall of 2001. On occasion, the teachers themselves participated in the harassment. Derr told *Asianweek* that one boy's teacher told him that he was going to hell because he was a Muslim.[136] In other states, bigoted instructors discriminated against minority students. Ibrahim Dremali, an Egyptian parent living in Boca Raton, told the *St. Petersburg Times* that his son's sixth grade teacher demanded that the boy be removed from her class because he was an Arab.[137]

On occasion, minority school children received inappropriate academic assignments during the backlash. According to the October 25, 2001 issue of the *Dayton Daily News*, a local elementary student was asked to write an essay critical of the veiling of Muslim women.[138] Since the nine-year old boy's grandmother wore the veil, he refused to criticize this practice and received a low grade. Discussing the incident in the *Dayton Daily News*, the boy's grandfather, Dayton mosque president Aminullah Ahmad pointed out that religious discrimination made Muslim-American students feel unwelcome in their own schools.[139]

Other Muslim students were inappropriately singled out by teachers, administrators, coaches, and sports referees. On occasion, teachers accused Arab and Muslim students of knowing something about the attacks on the Pentagon and World Trade Center. One Palestinian-American student reported that her teacher made racist comments in class, telling her students that all Muslims were terrorists.[140] When the teacher was required to apologize, she did so in perfunctory fashion, then quipped caustically that she hoped that the Muslim student was now happy.[141] As a result of this mistreatment, some minority students made the drastic decision to change schools to escape campus-based racial bigotry and religious persecution.

Contributing to a climate of intolerance, movies sometimes portrayed Arab students in the U.S. as merciless killers. In the 2001 movie, *Full Disclosure*, Algerians in California recruit two Palestinian students to murder a peace activist.[142] Their nefarious plans are foiled by a pretty blonde who kills the Arab assassins. These damaging cinematographic depictions of Arabs reinforced nativists' worldviews, and undermined the safety of international students enrolled in American schools.

Some Arab and Muslim students reported that school administrators blamed them for 9/11. The *ADC Times* reported that a minority pupil was sent to the principal's office after commenting in class that the terrorist strikes might be connected to U.S. foreign policy.[143] The school vice principal then grilled the student, asking about the family's origins and whether he knew someone named Osama.[144] As a result of these types of occurrences, many Arab and Muslim students became too frightened to speak freely in class, worried that a comment might be misconstrued as being unpatriotic or seditious. Some parents wondered if the silencing of their children's voices caused other students to remain unaware of Middle Eastern viewpoints on foreign policy issues. In many parts of the country, American students and teachers simplistically attributed anti-American sentiment abroad to "freedom-envy," instead of having a more sophisticated understanding of Middle Eastern history, American foreign policy, and religious opposition to military bases in Saudi Arabia. Many Muslim students and teachers were fearful that others might mistakenly think that they were defending the 9/11 mass murderers if they raised some of these issues in class.

Coaches and referees also discriminated against minority students. In Ferndale, Michigan, administrators fired a high school athletic coach and teacher who made racial slurs and refused to instruct a Muslim girl.[145] Minority athletes also felt the 9/11 backlash. An Arab-American high school football player was subjected to racism on the field when a member of the opposing team made death threats against him, accusing him of being an Arab terrorist who bombed the U.S.[146] When the referee was informed about what had been said, he refused to take action and turned his back to the Arab-American player who had made the complaint.

On occasion, minority students got into fights with bullies after school officials failed to protect them. In New York state, school officials neglected to take action when a classmate used anti-Arab and anti-Afghan ethnic slurs against a minority student. During a field trip, the bully hurled rocks and dirt at him.[147] No action was taken when the boy reported the abuse. When tensions escalated further, both students were suspended.

School bullies attacking Muslims and Sikhs came from a wide range of ethno-racial backgrounds. According to the *Atlanta Inquirer*, African-American students in New England harassed a Kurdish classmate for wearing her hijab.[148] This attack saddened civil rights activists, who had hoped that community bigotry would bring minority groups together.

As 2001 drew to a close, Muslim and Arab students continued to be assaulted near their schools. At the University of Illinois, a Tunisian-American student was brutally attacked in mid-December, 2001. Saleem Mahjub, his brother Ghazy, and some friends were walking at the intersection of 5th and John St. on Sunday morning when they were beaten by a group of at least six men. According to the Champaign *News Gazette*, the assailants held back Ghazy and his friends while they pummeled Saleem with their fists and with a blunt object.[149] According to the police report, at least one of the attackers made racial slurs while beating Saleem, a senior majoring in mechanical engineering. The 24-year old victim was then taken by ambulance to Carle Foundation Hospital, where he received numerous stitches and medical treatment for a broken nose. While recovering at his parents' home in the Chicago suburb of Barrington, Saleem told the *News Gazette* that the assailants attacked him and his friends simply because they were Muslim Arabs, not realizing that they were 100% American.[150]

Saleem's brother Ghazy told Champaign police about the racially-charged remarks he heard during the assault.[151] He also identified one of the attackers and gave the assailant's name to police. Along with pressing criminal charges, the victims contacted an attorney to explore a civil suit against the assailants. According to assistant police chief John Murphy, investigators initially treated the attack as an aggravated battery, not a hate crime, because they were unaware that ethnic slurs were used during the beating.[152]

William Riley, Dean of Students at the University of Illinois, told the *News Gazette* that school administrators were waiting for a copy of the police report before beginning their own formal investigation of the hate-motivated attack, adding that any student convicted of assault should expect a stern response, with expulsion a possibility.[153] By delaying investigation into the attack and by stating that expulsion was a mere "possibility" for convicted batterers, Riley failed to convey the seriousness of the hate-motivated aggravated assault, making other minority students worried about their safety on campus.

As a result of these types of bias-motivated attacks, foreign college students continued to leave the U.S. in the months following 9/11. The *New York Times* reported that scores of international students withdrew from American college campuses in late 2001, at the urging of their families.[154]

In response to backlash school crimes, the Saudi government offered to pick up the travel tabs of returning nationals and put their scholarships on hold, just as it had done during the Gulf War. Saudi embassy officials also explained to frightened students that they could not guarantee that American universities would hold their spots if they opted to resume their studies once the backlash had abated.

CAMPUS ATTACKS, 2002

In 2002, minority students continued being targeted by their peers. In early February, a gang of youths jumped two Muslim students outside of Brooklyn's Lafayette High School, pummeling an Egyptian and a Pakistani student with chains. The victims sustained multiple injuries, including wounds to their heads and knees. Although police and school officials claim that the boys were victims of a random attack, parents were unconvinced, seeing the assaults as a manifestation of post-9/11 intolerance. Sajjad Khan, whose son Ali was also assaulted by chain-wielding youths on a separate occasion, told the *New York Post* that Muslim and Arab students were being targeted in backlash hate crimes.[155] Brooklyn state senator Seymour Lachman, a former Lafayette teacher, reported being shocked by the vicious assaults, which he characterized as unacceptable.[156] NYPD inspector Charles Scholl told the *Post* that one of the suspects was a former student who had been suspended from school as a result of chronic absences.[157] As a result of the bias-motivated beatings, minority students became fearful, questioning their security at the school.

Because of frequent threats directed against Muslim students, Islamic schools across the U.S. remained on high alert. Principal Abdulmajid Biuk told the *St. Petersburg Times* that he continued to take elaborate security precautions throughout 2002 to protect the K through 12th graders at the Islamic Academy, particularly after learning of Robert Goldstein's plot to blow up Muslim-run buildings in the state.[158] Every school day, Biuk would arrive at 6:00 a.m. to search the bushes surrounding the 15-acre campus. He also checked doors to ensure that they had remained locked, and recorded information on suspicious vehicles in the vicinity. According to the *St. Petersburg Times*, Biuk came to the U.S. in 1981, after being put on Mommar Gadhafi's liquidation list in Libya.[159] He was granted political asylum, and commenced his Ph.D in electrical engineering in California. Biuk felt that the racial profiling of Arabs and South Asians was disappointing in a country as tolerant and diverse as the U.S.

RESPONDING TO BULLYING

On occasion, bullied students got into fights at school. In February 2002, a Sikh honor student at a middle school in Auburn, Washington slapped a classmate who had repeatedly harassed him, fracturing the other boy's skull.[160] According to the publication, *Asianweek*, the judge overlooked the unrelenting harassment that the Indian boy experienced before he finally snapped and fought back.[161]

According to *Asianweek*, the bullying started several years earlier, when Parteek was only eight years old.[162] Even before 9/11, he was repeatedly singled out and physically assaulted by bigoted classmates, who called him "diaperhead" and "raghead."[163] Parteek reported that every year, the emotional and physical abuse escalated, and he was repeatedly taunted and punched by his classmates.[164] Parteek's father, Satwinder Singh, told *Asianweek* that his family fled India in 1984, after 20,000 Sikhs were killed in clashes with the army over the Golden Temple.[165] Once in the U.S., the family moved seven times to escape the extreme harassment that Parteek and his younger brother Shami continued to experience at their American schools. According to *Asianweek*, the racial torment intensified after 9/11, with students from Rainier Middle School and Auburn High school repeatedly calling him derogatory names in halls, classrooms, and gym class, referring to him as "Osama bin Laden," "Osama's son," and 'terrorist."[166] Because of this harassment, Parteek became quieter every year.

Although Shami was only 11 years old, he was also targeted and bullied by his classmates in the aftermath of 9/11.[167] The boys' parents reluctantly broke with their religious faith, cutting their sons' hair in the hopes that it would lessen attacks against them. Parteek's heartbroken mother preserved her sons' shorn hair. The boys' father, Gurmeet, stopped taking his sons to religious services at the gurdwara because he was concerned that other Sikhs would say hurtful things to them in response to the family's controversial decision to cut their sons' hair and allow them to stop wearing the kesh. The boys hoped that they would be able to re-grow their hair in the future, when they were in a more tolerant environment. Shami told *Asianweek* that he was saddened that he had to cut his hair, an exterior symbol of his faith, simply to protect himself while attending school in the U.S.[168]

Despite the Sikh parents' best efforts to protect their children, the racial harassment continued. Finally, in February 2002, Parteek fought back after a classmate repeatedly threw a pencil at him while calling him "towel head" and "diaperhead."[169] The Sikh boy first asked the other boy to stop, but the bullying continued unabated. In response, Parteek struck back at his assailant, slapping him near the temple.[170]

Many of his teachers claimed to be unaware that Parteek was being racially bullied, seeing him simply as a respectful and intelligent student. Other educators in the area claimed that a lack of teacher awareness contributed to Parteek's negative educational experiences. Terri Herrin, the vice president of Auburn high school, told *Asianweek* that many local instructors were ignorant or apathetic about minority students' needs.[171] She recalled that when she asked teachers to prepare activities in honor of black history month, they insensitively suggested that the school designate a white history month.[172] Because Parteek's history of harassment was not documented in school records, Judge Rammerman refused to consider it as a mitigating factor. As a result, he convicted Parteek Singh of third-degree assault, a felony conviction that would become a part of his permanent record.

Bullied students continued to be punished for defending themselves against their attackers. In November 2002, a 14-year old Egyptian student at Boca Raton Middle School claimed that several boys jumped him in the locker room and beat him up while making fun of his religion and ethnicity.[173] During the assault, Abdelrahman Dremali stabbed assailant Joshua Reynoso with scissors in the locker room. Reynoso disputed this version of events, claiming that Dremali spit on him and stabbed him after they briefly argued. According to the *Palm Beach Post*, the physical evidence supported Dremali's account, since the Egyptian middle school student had bruises on the left side of his body and neck, indicating he had been beaten.[174]

This was not Dremali's first encounter with school racism. Prior to the November 2002 fight, he had spoken to the *St. Petersburg Times* about how his sixth-grade teacher ordered him out of class after 9/11 because he was a Muslim.[175] He also had reported being physically attacked at school because of his religion.[176] According to his defense attorney James Eisenberg, the Muslim boy was the true victim, who had been mercilessly teased by bullies who ridiculed his faith and ethnicity.[177]

Although he continued to protest his innocence, Dremali took his lawyer's advice and pled "guilty in his best interest," a legally-distinct plea which is not automatically regarded as an admission of guilt.[178] Under the terms of the February 2003 plea agreement, Dremali would not have a felony on his permanent record if he performed 50 hours of community service, agreed to pay the Reynoso family $1500, and submitted to a psychological evaluation. Many area Muslims saw the case as an unfortunate consequence of administrators' failure to stem backlash bullying.

HARASSMENT CONTINUES AT SCHOOLS AND UNIVERSITIES

In some school districts, teachers acted inappropriately around Muslim students observing Ramadan. In Anaheim, California, first-year high school student Ghazal Alloulo told her gym teacher that her parents did not want her to run a mile while she was fasting. According to the *Orange County Register*, the gym teacher responded by saying that the American military should wipe out Iraqis during the Islamic holy month.[179] Another teacher overheard the remark, and started laughing with the gym instructor.[180] When recounting the incident to her parents, Alloulo began crying, upset at her teacher's callous disregard for Muslim lives and religious practices.

Along with high schoolers, minority university students were also targeted in 2002, causing many of them to miss classes or drop out of school. The *New York Times* reported that on June 20, 2002, a Jordanian Ph.D student en route to a final exam was attacked by an undercover police officer.[181] Basim Alkhateeb, who was studying electrical engineering at Oakland University, was in suburban Waterford when the officer approached him and asked him if he was an Arab. When the graduate student answered affirmatively, the officer pulled out a gun and became physically abusive, pushing him to the ground and beating him on his back and leg. After attacking Alkhateeb, the officer did not arrest the graduate student. Alkhateeb told the *Times* that he found the bias-motivated beating particularly alarming because it happened in the U.S.[182] As a result of the attack, Alkhateeb decided to file a lawsuit and return home to the Middle East, where he felt safer.

College students in other states also faced harassment and discrimination in 2002. At West Virginia University in Morgantown, a drunken football fan made anti-Muslim death threats against a Pakistani engineering student. On August 31, Sohail Chaudhry was delivering the student newspaper outside Mountaineer Field when an inebriated man began harassing and threatening him. Chaudhry told the *Sunday Gazette-Mail* that the man blamed him for the terrorist strikes and threatened his life, telling him to expect reprisals for 9/11.[183] Chaudhry believed he was singled out because of his dark skin, black hair, and beard. He also reported that the Muslims in Morgantown were worried that the anti-Muslim backlash would escalate around the anniversary of 9/11.[184]

While South Asian students were being targeted on American college campuses, movie audiences were laughing at buffoonish portrayals of international students. In the 2002 comedy, *Van Wilder*, Indian-American actor Kal Penn plays the hero's side-kick Taj, an exchange student who longs to have sex with a white American girl. Audiences laugh at his Taj's stupidity when he inadvertently sets himself on fire with massage oil while trying to get a college girl into bed. Reminiscent of other racist movies showing dark-skinned characters lusting after Caucasian women, this 'comedy' popularizes disturbing stereotypes of South Asian men. Some activists saw a connection between xenophobic comedies and a climate of bigotry in the U.S.

On occasion, international students experienced discrimination obtaining housing near their campuses. Wafi Albalawa, a computer science Ph.D student at West Virginia University, told the *Sunday Gazette-Mail* that he encountered Islamophobia when he tried to rent a house for his family near his school.[185] Because Albalawa's apartment was too small to accommodate his wife and four small children, he found a suitable house for rent near the university. After providing the landlord with the necessary rental information, Albalawa casually mentioned that the Saudi government was funding his education. Immediately afterwards, the landlord changed his mind about renting the house to the Arab student.[186] Albalawa had other experiences with post-9/11 bigotry. Because he had a beard and his wife wore the hijab, members of the college community could easily tell they were Muslim. According to the *Sunday Gazette-Mail*, West Virginia University students frequently verbally harassed Albalawa, calling him Osama bin Laden and other derogatory names.[187] He decided against informing campus administrators about the bias-motivated bullying, resigning himself to a certain level of discrimination. Rather than fear for his own safety, Albalawa worried about Muslim women in the area, particularly after hearing that veiled women in Morgantown had been assaulted by local bigots.[188] He said that news of these backlash hate crimes caused many of his friends in Saudi Arabia to abandon their plans to attend school in the U.S. When he went back to the Middle East to visit his family, his relatives urged him to stay home, arguing that America was no longer a safe place to study.

The 9/11 backlash also prevented some Muslim students from obtaining re-entry visas to the U.S. Peter Li, the dean of international students at West Virginia University, told the *Sunday Gazette-Mail* that many Muslim students from the school were stuck overseas after the State Department began conducting background checks on all foreign male students between the ages of 16 and 45.[189] Li estimated that in the 2001-2 academic year, there were about 135 WVU students from the Middle East and Pakistan. There were also many Muslim students from India, Malaysia, Indonesia, Europe, South Africa, and Canada. Because of heightened security concerns, many WVU students were stuck overseas, missing the crucial first few weeks of classes while waiting for security clearances. Some had already been absent from so many classes that they were unable to get academic credit for the semester.

Muslim students and educators in Florida also experienced the 9/11 backlash in 2002. At the University of South Florida, Muslim students were threatened and harassed on and off campus. Undergraduate Amal Kurdi told the *St. Petersburg Times* that she was targeted by a bigot while riding horses with other members of a school organization, the Sisters United Muslim Association.[190] While participating in this college extracurricular activity, she heard a heckler making racial slurs, ordering the Muslim students to ride their camels back to Saudi Arabia. Kurdi also experienced harassment while shopping in town. On one occasion, a man approached her at a mall and began yelling obscenities, telling her to return to Afghanistan.[191] Kurdi, who was born in Gainesville to an American-born convert, was dismayed that she was being treated like an outsider in her own country.

Muslim university students were targeted in other parts of the South. In the fall of 2002, Sean Blevins, a white student from Clinton, told the *Knoxville News Sentinel* that he was singled out at the University of Tennessee.[192] A bigot saw his Islamic attire and harassed him outside of Hodges Library. Belvins felt that domestic hate crimes often escalated in response to overseas conflicts, since many Americans mistakenly assumed that all Muslims were the enemy.

Along with undergraduates, medical students in Florida also experienced racial discrimination. On September 13, 2002, Eunice Stone, a Georgia nurse, reported that she overheard what sounded like three Muslim medical students making vague threats. According to the *St. Petersburg Times*, Stone claimed that the men said that Americans mourned on 9/11, and would do so again on 9/13.[193] Based solely on what Stone thought she might have heard while eavesdropping, authorities arrested the three Muslim medical students, who were on their way to a nine-week clinical rotation at a Miami hospital. The medical students were detained for 17 hours, and a 20-mile section of interstate 75 was closed for most of a day while hundreds of law enforcement officials and dogs searched the area for evidence of an impending attack.[194] Finding nothing, authorities finally ascertained that Stone's allegation was unfounded. Many Muslims in Florida found it disconcerting that it was so easy to subject minority residents to a media spectacle and tarnish their reputations without cause.

As the year drew to a close, minority students continued to be targeted by bigots. On December 2, 2002, three South Asian graduate students were assaulted in a bias crime on the Lowell campus of the University of Massachusetts.[195] According to the *Lowell Sun*, the attack took place while the Indian students were walking to attend a study session.[196] A woman in a van drove up beside them and began screaming racial epithets. At that point, two males got out of the vehicle and began beating the students, yelling "Osama bin Laden" during the attack.[197] Because the victims had only been in the U.S. for a few months, they were shocked by the bias-motivated assault. They reported that they began becoming extremely anxious when walking to class, and had difficulty concentrating on their studies. Some community members were upset that other newspapers failed to cover the crime, which they attributed to the ongoing 9/11 backlash.

CAMPUS ATTACKS, 2003

As tensions with Iraq escalated in early 2003, American bigots continued to target Arab and South Asian pupils. At Lincoln High School in San Francisco, Middle Eastern students were singled out by their classmates. In a March 2, 2003 article in the *San Francisco Chronicle*, Hannah Frank reported that many of her classmates harassed and bullied their Middle Eastern peers, who used profanities in their presence.[198] Frank also suggested that students faced social ostracism if they associated with their Palestinian classmates. Maha el-Genaidi, the executive director of the Islamic Networks Group, told the *Chronicle* that many of the post-9/11 backlash attacks at schools went unreported because they occurred in unsupervised areas, like bathrooms, hallways, and the cafeteria.[199]

Along with post-9/11 attacks taking place inside of school buildings, neighborhood bullies targeted minority students outside of class. In March 2003, the *Los Angeles Times* reported that kids in the playground constantly taunted Gurdev Singh, asking him if he was Osama's son.[200] Sikh girls were also singled out. Sirisat Khalsa told the *Los Angeles Times* that other students in her Santa Monica neighborhood teased her and her family, accusing her father of being a terrorist.[201] Her parents were dismayed that the 9/11 backlash was still affecting minority kids.

Minority high-school students were harassed at school by their teachers and classmates in the months and years following the terrorist strikes. After 9/11, Jana Abdelgawad faced constant discrimination at her high school in Santa Clara, California. In March 2003, she told the *San Francisco Chronicle* that her classmates insulted her repeatedly, and a teacher ordered her to remove her hijab on school grounds.[202] Other community members questioned her American citizenship and ordered her to leave the country. These experiences undermined her sense of belonging, making her feel as though she had to prove her loyalty to the U.S.

The same year, minority students experienced post-9/11 discrimination in Florida. Asil Al-Jamal, a pupil at Miami Southridge high school, told the *Seattle Times* that her classmates began subjecting her to death threats, insults, and attacks after the terrorist strikes.[203] In response to the strikes on the Pentagon and World Trade Center, her peers began harassing her constantly, telling her that they wanted to kill all Arabs. Her house was egged on two different occasions, presumably because her mother was Palestinian and her father was Jordanian. Once the Iraq War began, the racial harassment intensified, turning her life into a living hell. She told the *Seattle Times* that she cried on a daily basis because of the racial bullying, and began sitting at the front of the bus so that she would be unable to hear the negative remarks the other students were saying about her on the ride to and from school.[204]

Asil's mother, Karam Al-Jamal, told the *Seattle Times* that she planned to move her whole family back to Jordan as soon as her daughter finished high school, since her children stopped feeling safe in the U.S. after 9/11.[205] She reported that whenever the family spoke Arabic in public, strangers looked at them with hostility, making them feel unwelcome in the community.

Other Florida students reported that their classmates made racially-inappropriate comments in class. At the onset of the Iraq War, Amna Sultan, a 10th grade honor student at Coral Springs High School, told the *Seattle Times* that her peers proposed nuking the Middle East and killing the region's inhabitants.[206] Because she was of Pakistani descent, she was frequently singled out by ignorant classmates who assumed she was an Arab terrorist, particularly after they heard her last name.[207] Their cultural insensitivity hurt her feelings.

Immigrant students were attacked in other parts of the country. In Erie, Pennsylvania, a 14-year old Iraqi girl was assaulted by one of her classmates in mid-May, 2003.[208] Instead of coming to the aid of the victim, the other students yelled death threats and anti-Muslim comments during the attack, suggesting that she deserved to be beaten because of her religious background.[209] After the bias-motivated assault, the victim reported feeling unsafe in the U.S, fearing her classmates were after her.

Many bullied students began to show signs of severe emotional strain. San Francisco psychologist Jess Ghannam told the *Chronicle* that since the onset of the Iraq War, local Arab and Muslim children began manifesting their stress in different ways, including bed-wetting, having nightmares, and experiencing trouble concentrating, which was affecting their school performance.[210] Several of these students also had heightened anxiety about the war and fears that their American allegiance was being questioned.

Dr. Ingrid Mattson, professor of Christian-Muslim relations at Hartford Seminary in Connecticut, told the *Seattle Times* that she had received numerous reports from across the country about hate crimes targeting Muslim students.[211] She also said that parents began noticing that their children were having psychological, academic, and behavioral problems as international tensions increased. Many pupils were frightened by images of Iraqi casualties on satellite television, including pictures of young victims who resembled their siblings or relatives. Minority-American students were also troubled by racial profiling, fearing that their family members might be detained or deported. Because of the 'War on Terror,' they worried that other Americans had negative views of their ethnic heritage.

On occasion, minority high school students were singled out on school trips. According to the April 27, 2003 issue of the *Kansas City Star*, a U.S.-born Muslim pupil of Indian descent was traveling with her classmates when she was ordered off a flight for an intrusive body search.[212] The girl's mother, Shaheen Ahmed, was angry that her daughter was the only child in the group singled out for extra screening, humiliating the girl by racially-profiling her in front of her peers. At their home in Leawood, Missouri, the South Asian family had other experiences with post-9/11 bigotry. Mrs. Ahmed told the *Kansas City Star* that she was particularly shocked when a firefighter told her son that he wished to see his head squashed on the concrete.[213]

Along with their younger counterparts, Muslim college students continued to be targeted in 2003. In California, anti-Muslim graffiti was discovered on the campus of San Jose State University. According to the *San Francisco Chronicle*, the expletive-ladened messages included a death threat on a bathroom wall, informing the college community that on March 10, 2003, Muslims would be shot on school grounds.[214] Because the death threat included a precise date and place for the massacre of Muslim students, Helal Omeira, the executive director of CAIR-Northern California, requested meetings with the FBI, local police, campus security, and college president Robert Caret. Perhaps to emphasize that SJSU was fundamentally a tolerant place, Caret told the *Arab American News* that he assumed only one perpetrator was involved.[215] Some Muslim students were angry that Caret was willing to state publicly that he found it unlikely that a hate group was responsible when the police investigation was still open and no suspects had been identified. They were also concerned that Caret encouraged the student body to report future incidents to campus security instead of to the police or FBI, jeopardizing the safety of minority students and giving the college community the mistaken impression that hate crime investigations were best handled internally. Many area Arabs and South Asians saw the bias-motivated vandalism as part of the ongoing 9/11 backlash.

Muslim students at the University of Wisconsin-Milwaukee also received death threats. The *Milwaukee Journal Sentinel* reported that during the Iraq War, a bigoted vandal used a permanent marker to write an anti-Muslim death threat next to the office door of the Muslim Students' Association.[216] The message, written on a glass case, instructed campus Muslims to "suicide bomb" themselves.[217] This campus hate crime left many minority students afraid for their safety.

Even though Muslim college students were frequently attacked or harassed, authorities repeatedly dismissed the bias component these assaults, suggesting that the targeted minorities were victims of random violence. At Georgia Tech, a Muslim student from India was attacked by two white males, according to a March 19, 2003 article in the *Atlanta Journal-Constitution*.[218] Because the assailants beat the South Asian student but left his wallet and backpack at the scene, many area Muslims believed that the assault was likely motivated by post-9/11 ethnic or religious bias. Investigating authorities refused to acknowledge that the unprovoked assault was a hate crime, and did not label it as such.

Sometimes, bias attacks were so blatant that it was impossible for authorities to ignore them. On April 19, 2003, the staff at UCLA Medical Center discovered that a vandal had smeared pigs' blood on Muslim prayer rugs at the facility's chapel. UCLA police department spokeswoman Nancy Greenstein told the *Los Angeles Times* that the crime was clearly motivated by Islamophobia, since the attack involved the deliberate desecration of Muslim prayer rugs.[219] At the scene, investigators discovered that a supermarket container, marked "pig's blood," was left next to the prayer mats, which came from a drawer labeled, "Islamic Prayer Rugs."[220] A compass, used by Muslims to determine the direction of prayer, was also missing, suggesting that the intruder hoped to interfere with minority students' ability to worship facing Mecca.

In response to the campus hate crime, staff members held a meeting on April 22, 2003 to discuss campus Islamophobia and explore how to prevent future incidents. Since the chapel was used by worshippers of many faiths, the chapel desecration affected several religious communities. Many UCLA medical students, staff members, and visitors felt victimized by the defiling of the interfaith prayer area. At this gathering, Muslims expressed their concern that more violent bias attacks might follow, particularly

128

when they were prostrating themselves during prayers. In response, officials promised to increase chapel security and devote resources to apprehend the perpetrator responsible for the chapel vandalism.

According to the *Arab American News*, other bias-motivated crimes had taken place at this UCLA prayer room prior to the April 19th vandalism. The Quran had been stolen so many times that authorities decided to remove all religious books from the chapel.[221] Some community members questioned whether administrators should have done more in response to these earlier incidents as a means of preventing an escalation in bias crimes.

Sometimes, minority graduate students were attacked at their residences near campus. In chapter five, I discussed how a Savannah mosque hate crime affected congregation member Mohamed Abdel Hafez. Because he was a Georgia Tech graduate student, it is important to examine the attack in the context of his academic experience, to understand how the 9/11 backlash undermined international students' ability to focus on their studies. On August 18, 2003, Hafez went to pray at a nearby Savannah mosque at 5:30 a.m. When he returned to his apartment on Apache Avenue, he discovered that someone had vandalized his apartment with racist insignias and messages. According to the *Savannah Morning News*, Hafez also found a menacing letter filled with Nazi swastikas, demanding that all Muslims get out of the city.[222] The note also warned Muslims that they were being monitored constantly. Hafez discovered that the racist vandal had also stolen his money, cell phone, CD player, social security card, laptop computer, and checking account book.

When Hafez came to America on January 3, 2003, he knew that the country was still reeling from 9/11. He told the *Atlanta Journal-Constitution* that he had expected some degree of ethnic hostility, and attempted to prepare for it psychologically.[223] Hafez was excited about enrolling in the electrical engineering Ph.D program, seeing the chance to study in America as a great opportunity. Hafez was saddened when he learned that his mosque, located on the suburban South side of Savannah, had been attacked in early August, when a gunman fired bullets at the house of worship, damaging the door to the garage. He became concerned but not frightened when he discovered that his own apartment had been targeted by the Islamophobic vandal.

When his mosque was burned to the ground a few days later, Hafez told the *Atlanta Journal-Constitution* that his view of a tolerant America had been irrevocably shattered.[224] Hafez decided to move out of his apartment because he no longer felt safe there. He opted to stay with a friend temporarily until he could find another place to live. Because of these experiences with American bigotry, Hafez decided to move back to Egypt after finishing school, particularly since he never heard anything positive about Muslims in the U.S.[225] As a result of the racial hostility and hate crimes, he had difficulty devoting his full attention to his academic work.

Other Muslim students in the U.S. were also affected when their houses of worship were attacked, particularly if they attended religious schools located next to targeted mosques. According to the *Washington Post*, students at an Islamic school in College Park, Maryland had difficulty concentrating on their academic work after a cross was burned outside their classrooms in the summer of 2003.[226] This traumatizing hate crime upset students and interrupted their academic routine.

Years after 9/11, Muslim students continued to be unfairly disciplined by racist instructors. The *Seattle Times* reported that a local teacher became alarmed after a Muslim student drew a picture of someone wearing a turban.[227] Believing that the drawing was a manifestation of Islamic radicalism, the teacher punished the student. Muslim activists felt that the school overreacted to the art work, pointing out that turbans are common in many parts of the world and are not a symbol of radicalism or violence. Mubarak Elamin of CAIR Seattle said that the school was unsure about how to deal with the incident, and planned to work on diversity issues to ensure that Muslim students were treated more appropriately in the future.[228]

In the fall of 2003, minority students were bullied in many parts of the country. In Valparaiso, Indiana, a student at Ben Franklin Middle School punched an eighth grade classmate in the face and called him Osama bin Laden. Discussing this backlash incident, principal Robert Rarick told the *Arab American News* that he was saddened that the student was targeted because of his Middle Eastern appearance.[229] Police reported that the victim required stitches to close a cut sustained in the assault, as well as dental care to treat injuries to his teeth.

In other states, minority students continued to be targeted by their peers. In the Bronx, a 14-year old Muslim girl was punched in the face at her Baychester school.[230] The assailant, a 14-year old boy, used an anti-Muslim slur during the attack. Authorities arrested him on charges of assault and aggravated harassment.

On occasion, Muslim students were unjustly suspended for observing their faith. Some parents took legal action against schools that were treating their children unfairly. Memphis *Commercial Appeal* reported that on September 11, 2003, the second anniversary of 9/11, school officials in Oklahoma raised complaints that Nashala Hearn, a Muslim 6th grader, was violating the dress code by wearing a hijab.[231] For several weeks, she had been wearing her head scarf to class, and administrators said they were concerned that other students were becoming frightened by it. Since academic rules prohibited children from wearing hats and other head coverings, they suspended the 11-year old girl twice for wearing her veil on school grounds. Nashala's parents took issue with the suspensions, arguing that their daughter's head scarf was a Constitutionally-protected expression of the family's Islamic faith. In March 2004, the U.S. Justice Department filed suit in the federal district court in Oklahoma, charging the Muskogee Public School District with religious discrimination. In May, 2004, the school and the justice department reached an agreement, valid for six years, in which the school district agreed to allow dress code exceptions for religious reasons. The settlement also put in place a training program to inform school officials about the new dress code and the importance of respecting student diversity. R. Alexander Acosta, Assistant Attorney General for Civil Rights, applauded the court's decision, telling the Memphis *Commercial Appeal* that it was un-American to require students to leave their religious beliefs outside the school door.[232]

Long after 9/11, minority undergraduates continued to confront xenophobia on American college campuses. According to the September 2003 *Sikh Coalition Newsletter*, Tariq Khan, a third-year undergraduate at George Mason University, was verbally and physically assaulted by other students, a university employee, and at least four campus security officers.[233] Khan, an Air Force service member, was attacked after he voiced opposition to U.S. Marine recruitment efforts on campus. In response to the crime, eight civil rights organizations demanded a serious investigation into the incident and sensitivity training on campus to protect other South Asian students. Many community members saw the beating in the context of American xenophobia, which rose dramatically in the aftermath of 9/11.

The same month, minority students were targeted on other college campuses. A September 11, 2003 article in the Madison *Capital Times* reported that a bigot vandalized the Muslim Students' Association room at the University of Wisconsin-Milwaukee.[234] Because the timing of the attack was near the second anniversary of the terrorist strikes, many community members saw it as a manifestation of the ongoing backlash. In response to the incident, minority students urged the administration to take action to promote diversity on campus. Some Middle Eastern students expressed concern that Arabs were not among the four ethnic groups targeted in the University of Wisconsin's diversity plan, which focused on recruiting and retaining African-Americans, Native Americans, Latinos, and Southeast Asians.

Sikh students were also targeted on American campuses in 2003. At Marlboro High School in New Jersey, a Sikh boy was attacked in a brutal bias-motivated assault.[235] Because of the beating, which left him with severe head contusions, his parents decided to take him out of the high school and move him back to Britain. After an investigation of the assault, New Jersey's Division on Civil Rights determined that the school shirked its legal obligations when it failed to protect the boy from racial and religious harassment at the school.

In other parts of the country, Sikh university students were attacked. At U.C. Berkeley, law student Neilinder Ranu was assaulted while walking along Bancroft Way, just outside the campus. According to an article in *India Currents*, Ranu's assailant called him "Osama" and beat him up in broad daylight.[236] Ranu believed he was targeted because he wore the customary Sikh turban and beard.

While these 2003 backlash attacks were taking place on school campuses, young audiences continued watching movies containing racist depictions of Arabs. In his book, Guilty, film critic Shaheen discusses some of the most offensive post-9/11 films intended for children.[237] In the movie, *Secondhand Lions*, the protagonist Walter learns that his uncles routinely killed Middle Easterners while working in the French foreign legion. While fighting villainous Arabs in North Africa, they slice up dozens of swarthy Moroccans. In one particularly offensive scene, a lecherous sheikh makes advances at Yasmine, an unwilling Arab woman. Because of the intervention of the other characters, she does not have to succumb to the Muslim villain's unwelcome advances. This movie was released in the U.S. on September 19, 2003, close to the second anniversary of 9/11. Arab-American activists wondered how any responsible parent could allow a child to watch this xenophobic movie, which shows white Westerners triumphing over a foreign menace.

On occasion, Hollywood costume designers dressed movie villains in Middle Eastern garb, reinforcing the notion that Oriental attire is somehow evil. In the 2003 movie, *Lord of the Rings: Return of the King*, nefarious Bedouin creatures appear in black headscarves before attacking the movies' protagonists.[238] This movie was released in the U.S. on November 5, 2003.

Other children's movies also contained xenophobic messages. The movie, *Young Black Stallion*, uses Arab villains to create tension and suspense.[239] In one scene, a lecherous Arab leers at Neera, the female child protagonist. In another scene, unscrupulous Middle Easterners take financial advantage of a senior citizen, teaching young American audiences that foreigners are not to be trusted. This movie was released in the U.S. on December 25, 2003, to entertain American family audiences at Christmas time. Some activists saw a connection between Islamophobic children's movies and anti-Muslim hate crimes taking place on American school campuses.

CAMPUS ATTACKS, 2004

Minority students continued to be attacked throughout 2004. On April 5, four boys assaulted a 12-year old Muslim girl at Congress Middle School in Boynton Beach, Florida. The *Palm Beach Post* reported that the boys cornered the Pakistani girl in a school hallway, grabbed her hijab, pulled her hair, and hit her across the mouth with a leather belt, injuring her lip.[240] The assailants also made derogatory remarks, calling her "Osama" and warning her that they would beat her up again if she told school officials.[241] The seventh grader was emotionally traumatized by the bias-motivated attack.

Altaf Ali, executive director of CAIR Florida, told the *Palm Beach Post* that he girl's teacher failed to act appropriately after learning of the hate crime, dismissing it as a case of normal rough-housing.[242] School district spokesman Nat Harrington said that the school did not initially investigate the assault because the girl was unable to provide a complete description of her assailants.[243]

Prior to the April 5th attack, the Pakistani girl reported other incidents of discrimination to school officials, but they failed to take action to curb the harassment. Since the girl's father was out of the country and her mother spoke no English, her parents were unable to act as advocates for her.

Perhaps to avoid negative publicity or a lawsuit, school officials told reporters that the attack was just a case of horseplay.[244] School officials pointed out that when the girl was interrogated by police, she failed to confirm that the racially-derogatory comments were made or that she was called "Osama" by the boys.[245] Downplaying the bullying, the administrators claimed that students frequently slapped one another with belts in joking fashion, not intending to cause injury.[246]

When the girl's uncle found out that authorities were not investigating the attack as a hate crime, he contacted Muslim organizations and requested that they intervene on her behalf. CAIR officials said the 12-year old Pakistani girl was scared during the police investigation, and was intimidated into denying that the assault was bigotry-motivated.[247] When she signed the police statement pressing charges against her attackers, she did not understand that it failed to mention the bias aspects of the assault. The girl's parents were alarmed by the handling of their daughter's case, demanding that the hate component of the attack be acknowledged.[248] They were also disappointed that administrators were doing so little to protect minority students, particularly since the school had a previous history of racial tensions. In 2002, parents complained that educators often treated its black students unfairly, causing the school to provide more training for teachers through the "Safe Schools" program. In 2003, a feud between some of the black and white instructors at the school prompted the district to fire two teachers, reassign the principal, and compel all educators to reapply for their jobs.

The same month, older students were being harassed in other parts of the country. In late April 2004, undergraduates at the University of Wisconsin-Milwaukee discovered raw pork stuffed under the office door of the Muslim Student Association. They enlisted the help of non-Muslim students to throw away the pork, and then called the police. Aamer Ahmed, president of the organization, told the *Milwaukee Journal Sentinel* that Muslim students were offended by the bigoted incident, which they regarded as a hate crime.[249] He said the students who discovered the pork disposed of it quickly so that other Muslims would feel comfortable entering the group's Student Union office. Ahmed also reported that someone had stripped a large number of flyers off the bulletin boards outside the group's office, further indicating that Muslim students were being deliberately targeted. Instead of taking the bias crime seriously, UWM police opted to regard the incident as a simple vandalism case. According to Lt. Ernest Meress, UWM police spokesman, there wasn't enough evidence to warrant calling the incident a hate crime.[250] Ahmed was unconvinced, particularly since the group had been targeted by Islamophobic bigots in the past. In 2003, a vandal used a permanent marker on a nearby glass case to write a threat against Muslim students, suggesting that they "suicide bomb" themselves.[251] Area minorities saw the attacks as part of the ongoing 9/11 backlash.

Hate crimes took place on other college campuses. At the University of California, Irvine, a bias-motivated arson fire burned down a peace display erected by Muslim and Arab students in mid-May, 2004. Members of the Muslim Students Union and the Society of Arab Students obtained a campus permit to erect the peace wall in the university's main quad. The monument included quotations and photographs of Nelson Mandela, Malcolm X, and Martin Luther King, Jr. According to the Torrance *Daily Breeze*, the peace monument's central aim was to provoke discussion of the 425-mile stretch of fences and barbed wire Israel was constructing to keep out Palestinians.[252] When the fire began, Falali Farooqi, a 19-year old member of the MSU, told the *Los Angeles Times* that she felt heartbroken after she ran out of the library and watched the exhibit go up in flames.[253] She also worried that the arson would silence minority students' voices, since the point of the display was to provoke thought and communication. Hadi Ghazvini, an international studies major, told the *Los Angeles Times* that he was appalled that such a hate crime would happen on Irvine's campus, pointing out that the views expressed by the monument were protected free speech.[254]

In response to the arson fire, the Society of Arab Students held a rally attended by students, faculty members, and representatives of human rights organizations. UCI police chief Al Brown said that arson investigators were collecting evidence to determine whether the fire was deliberate or opportunistic. Perhaps to minimize negative publicity for the school, UCI spokesman Tom Vasich told the *Daily Breeze* that the peace wall might have been a random target.[255] Vanessa Zuabi told the *Los Angeles Times* that she disagreed with Vasich's assessment, regarding the arson as an attack on minority students' viewpoints and presence on school grounds.[256] Many Muslim and Arab students felt that Vasich appeared more concerned with protecting UCI's reputation than the students themselves, noting that most administrators agreed with their assessment that the arson was a politically-motivated act.

The same year, minority students were targeted at U.C. Berkeley. According to the September 20, 2004 issue of the *Daily Californian*, eight Muslim co-eds were accosted by three white males, who screamed derogatory statements, sprayed them with water, and pelted them with bottles.[257] Students saw the hate crime as a manifestation of post-9/11 bigotry.

While Muslim and Arab students were being harassed on American campuses, Hollywood was releasing movies reinforcing negative stereotypes of Middle Easterners. In the movie, *Around the World in 80 Days*, Hapi, a misogynistic Middle Eastern ruler, openly lusts after white women.[258] When the French heroine realizes that he is a polygamist, he explains that he has seven wives, one for each day of the week. He then begins to pursue her against her will, reinforcing the stereotype that Middle Eastern men are sexually-obsessed with white women. This film, starring Arnold Schwarzenegger, was released in the U.S. on June 16, 2004. Despite its mature themes and racist messages, it was intended for young audiences.

CAMPUS ATTACKS, 2005

Hate crimes on school grounds continued in 2005. In Medford, Massachusetts, an Arab-American student at Tufts University was assaulted in a bias-motivated attack. According to WCVB Channel 5 Boston, Riyad Mohammed, the president of the Arab Students Association, was walking his girlfriend home past the Sigma Phi Epsilon fraternity when three members got into an argument with him after demanding to know his ethnic background.[259] The frat boys first asked Mohammed if he was of Indian descent. When he replied he was an Arab, the other students began calling him an Iraqi terrorist and a supporter of Saddam Hussein.[260] The situation soon escalated into a racially-motivated beating.[261] In response to the hate crime, hundreds of students attended a rally on May 3, 2005, calling for an end to campus bigotry, which escalated considerably after 9/11. Other Arab-American and Muslim community members were outraged that police characterized Mohammed's assault as a university matter instead of filing criminal charges against the assailants. Minority students also felt that the administration was not taking the incident seriously enough. Rather than pressuring authorities into filing criminal charges against the perpetrators, university administrators opted to handle the matter internally, believing suspension or expulsion were adequate punishments.

Some activists saw a connection between post-9/11 prejudice against minority students and the dissemination of anti-Arab racism in popular culture, such as American teen movies containing anti-Muslim slurs. In the 2005 film, *Pretty Persuasion*, Kimberly, a popular white high school student makes bigoted comments in front of Randa, an obsequious and dim-witted Palestinian girl. This movie was released in the U.S. on August 12, 2005. Shaheen takes issue with the film's offensive plot and racist characters.[262] He observes that in one scene, Kimberly makes anti-Arab remarks, telling Randa that she was glad to have been born white instead of Arab, her last choice. Kimberly also tells Randa offensive jokes, suggesting that Arab men use flies to get their wives pregnant. Rather than showing Randa reacting in horror, the script forces the Palestinian character to laugh. Kimberly then reprimands Randa, telling her that finding the joke funny is insulting to her people. In another scene, Woods' character makes anti-Islamic comments about Randa's hijab, suggesting that it is a garment worn by terrorists. Kimberly eventually persuades Randa to fabricate false sexual abuse allegations against an English teacher, and the guilt-ridden Palestinian girl ends up killing herself, lacking the strength of character to stand up to her abusers. Shaheen points out that because Randa is such a weak-willed unsympathetic character, her death is not particularly moving.[263]

In other films, South Asian Muslims are depicted as anti-American terrorists. In the movie, *The War Within*, a Pakistani student, enrolled in the University of Maryland's engineering program, joins a New York terror cell and plots to blow up Grand Central Station.[264] This movie was released in the U.S. on September 30, 2005, disseminating the xenophobic message that international students pose a threat to the country.

While movie audiences were watching Muslim movie villains, minority school children were being attacked on American campuses. According to *USA Today*, a Seattle high school junior was viciously beaten at school in October 2005 because he was an Afghan Muslim.[265] The boy, who emigrated from Afghanistan in 2002, said that his classmates harassed him because of his Middle Eastern appearance and Muslim faith. The verbal harassment turned physical when the boy was brutally assaulted in gym class. As a result of the attack, he suffered a collapsed lung and a hemorrhage behind his eye. Almost a year after the violent beating, the victim remained too traumatized to return to class. Amelia Derr, director of Seattle's Hate Free Zone Washington, told *USA Today* that the boy continued to be haunted by the bias-motivated attack, too frightened to talk to strangers or return to school.[266] Area Muslims saw the beating as a manifestation of post-9/11 nativism.

Muslim college students on Baptist campuses were frequently subjected to verbal mistreatment and physical attacks. In Texas, Baylor University junior Hoda Said told the *Waco Tribune-Herald* that she was repeatedly harassed in 2005 for wearing a hijab to chapel.[267] During campus religious services, bullies pelted her with paper wads. She tried to ignore them, hoping that they would find other ways to amuse themselves. The harassment eventually escalated after a student threw a full bottle of water from the balcony, striking her in the head. The *Waco Tribune-Herald* reported that when the projectile struck her, the girls around her laughed, hurting her feelings and making her concerned about her safety.[268] In response to the incident, Baylor University administrators closed the chapel balcony for several weeks and instructed chapel assistants to be more vigilant. The vice president for student life, Dub Oliver, suggested that Said sit at the rear of the auditorium, where she would be less vulnerable.[269] Some Muslim students felt that campus officials could have done more to find out who was responsible for the harassment so that Said would not have to sit in the back of the room to be safe from bias-motivated attacks.

Perhaps because so little was done to address campus bigotry, Muslim students continued to be targeted at Baylor University. In the fall of 2005, senior Nohaiya Javed was assaulted because she was a South Asian Muslim. She told the *Waco Tribune-Herald* that two men spit in her face and pulled off her hijab, waving it around like a trophy prize.[270] Javed, who was born in Chicago, said that the attack made her feel unsafe in her own country.[271]

In other parts of the country, minority students on university campuses were occasionally subjected to instructors' offensive views on the 'War on Terror.' At a December 1, 2005 debate at the University of Chicago, many Arab and Muslim students were shocked to hear U.C. Berkeley law professor John Yoo defend the legality of torture as an interrogation technique. When University of Notre Dame law professor Douglass Cassel asked Yoo if there was a law that would prevent U.S. interrogators, acting on behalf of the President, from crushing the testicles of a suspect's child as a means of eliciting information, the former Deputy Assistant Attorney General replied that no treaty prevented Americans from the practice.[272] During this debate, Yoo also defended his highly-controversial 2003 81-page legal work justifying torture.[273] Because of his offensive views on the treatment of Middle Eastern and South Asian terror suspects, many Arab and Muslim law students felt uncomfortable in his classes and marginalized on school grounds.

CAMPUS ATTACKS, 2006

In the spring of 2006, minority students and instructors continued feeling the effects of the 9/11 backlash. When I was teaching history at Hebrew Academy in San Francisco, I was shocked by some students' reaction to a lecture I was giving on the internment of Japanese-Americans during World War II. One student defended the U.S. policy, and suggested that the same thing ought to be done to Arabs and Muslims currently living in America. Horrified, I pointed out that I was of Lebanese ancestry, and asked the student if he thought I should be rounded up and put in a concentration camp. He didn't respond. A few minutes later, I heard some students laughing and intercepted a note declaring that "Dr. Karam is a terrorist." When I turned in the racist note to the principal, no disciplinary action was taken against the students, even though they openly admitted to writing and laughing at the offensive words.

Some activists saw a connection between intolerant attitudes and xenophobic children's movies featuring Middle Eastern villains. In some films, adorable animal protagonists combat swarthy foreigners. In *Spymate*, released on January 14, 2006, a super agent Chimp named Minkey dresses in Middle Eastern garb in order to infiltrate and exterminate Arabs at a terrorist camp. Film critic Shaheen notes that in one scene, the chimp overhears the terrorists' nefarious plans, learning that the missile was timed to detonate and interrupt a peace summit attended by world leaders.[274] The chimp then kills the Arab villains by reprogramming the missile to target the desert tents.

American horror movies sometimes used Middle Eastern imagery to scare teen audiences. Discussing *Final Destination 3*, Shaheen observes that Oriental symbols are used throughout the film to foreshadow death and destruction.[275] In one scene at an amusement park, the protagonists see a whirling dervish ride adorned with symbols of bearded Arabs with crossed swords. Later in the movie, a decorative dangling Arab sword in the Sultans' high school gymnasium falls and kills an unsuspecting student. These scenes suggest that anything Middle Eastern is potentially dangerous or lethal. This movie was released in the U.S. on February 10, 2006.

Other demeaning depictions of Arabs appear in American comedies. In *Larry the Cable Guy: Health Inspector*, the protagonist dresses up as an Arab to rescue the heroine after she was caught spying on the mayor and a French chef. This movie was released in the U.S. on March 24, 2006. Shaheen is especially bothered by a scene in which Larry bursts into the room wearing Middle Eastern attire and whisks away the heroine, chastising her for flaunting her body in front of imperialist swine.[276]

The teen comedy, *Scary Movie 4*, also exposed young audiences to anti-Arab stereotypes. In one scene, the swarthy Middle Eastern character Ali straps dynamite to his torso and utters anti-American death threats.[277] When his detonator doesn't work, onlookers attack and pummel the Arab terrorist. According to Shaheen, this scene depicts Arabs as insane, stupid, pathetic, and laughable.[278] The movie also contains other offensive content – the U.S. President punches an Iranian, and Middle Eastern diplomats suddenly appear naked. These bigoted scenes give teen viewers permission to laugh contemptuously at Muslims, who are repeatedly depicted as America's enemies. This movie was released in the U.S. in April 2006.

The same month, a minority student was once again assaulted on the Baylor University campus. When 19-year old Nohayia Javed was walking to her dorm room, a 200-lb. blond man in his 30s jumped her from behind. During the assault, he grabbed her hijab and pulled her to the ground. Javed told the *Waco Tribune-Herald* that her white assailant repeatedly made anti-Muslim slurs and racist remarks in a pronounced Southern accent.[279] He also told her to keep quiet, threatening to kill her if she uttered a sound. Javed reported being stunned into silence by the abruptness and ferocity of the attack, but then started fighting back and screaming once her assailant dug his nails into her chest.[280] In response, her attacker slapped her and kicked her several times in the ribs with his steel-toed cowboy boots before running away.

Immediately after the attack, Javed called her fiancé, Adeel Zeb, who took her for x-rays at Presbyterian Hospital in Greenville, Texas.[281] The medical exam revealed deep bruises to her rib cage and injuries to her rotator cuff. She did not immediately inform campus security about the assault because she thought they would be unresponsive. Her family and friends finally convinced her to report the hate crime, which they saw in the context of post-9/11 xenophobia.

Javed's physician recommended that she remain out of school for two weeks to recover physically from the vicious beating. Her relatives urged her to drop out of Baylor University, since it was unsafe for Muslims. Even her fiancé Zeb, a Baylor graduate himself, advised her against returning to campus after her wounds healed.   Recalling the brutality of the attack and the university's past failures to curb bigotry on campus, Javed told the *Waco Tribune-Herald* that she was doubtful that she would ever go back to that school.[282]

Many Baylor faculty members were saddened by Javed's decision to drop out. Dub Oliver, Baylor's vice president for student life, told the *Waco Tribune-Herald* that the bias-motivated attack diminished the Christian witnesses of the university.[283] Mark Ellis, director of Baylor's Center for Jewish Studies, expressed his hope that the attack would prompt administrators to take diversity concerns more seriously.[284] Baylor spokesman Larry Brumley acknowledged that many of the university's 14,000 students had not developed an appreciation for religious or ethnic differences.[285] He said that the school hoped to encourage interfaith dialogue by encouraging American and international students to interact with each other during cross-cultural events.

The FBI eventually joined the investigation into Javid's bias-motivated assault. Al Siddiq, president of the Islamic Center of Waco, told the *Herald Tribune* that he was pleased that the federal government was interested in the case, particularly since university administrators had not given adequate attention to previous campus hate crimes.[286] Sadiqqi questioned whether Baylor would have been as forgiving of earlier incidents if the victimized student had been a blonde, Caucasian co-ed.

In the aftermath of the April 2006 attack, approximately 250 Baylor students held a candlelight vigil to pray for greater religious tolerance at the school. At this event, Hoda Said told the crowd that she regretted being soft-spoken after own experiences with campus bigotry, suggesting that her silence may have emboldened bullies to act more aggressively.[287] She also read an email from her absent friend Javed, who was recovering from the attack at her family's home in Tulsa.

Along with their Muslim counterparts, Sikh students continued to face religious challenges on American campuses. The *Orange County Register* reported that Valencia High School students repeatedly harassed Angad Chadha for wearing a patka in 2005 and 2006.[288] In the spring semester of 2005, students verbally taunted the Sikh student. The harassment eventually escalated when one of the male students grabbed the Sikh boy's turban and pulled it off.[289] Chadha continued to be singled out through the summer of 2006, when neighborhood children targeted the boy at home. In response to these incidents, Angad's father, Arinder Chadha, met with the principal and the parents of one of the bullies to demand an end to the harassment, which community members saw as a product of post-9/11 xenophobia.

Other Sikh students faced campus bigotry in the summer of 2006. A Sikh student attending Harvard's academic summer program was not permitted to carry his kirpan on school grounds.[290] Rather than understand the religious significance of the small knife, administrators regarded it as a weapon, fearing it might endanger the safety of other students. Civil rights activists were dismayed that such religious ignorance was occurring at an Ivy League university.

Some educators were so troubled by the harassment of South Asian students that they took steps to prevent future attacks. In New Jersey, the commissioner of New Jersey's Department of Education sent a strongly-worded memorandum to all school principals reminding them to create a safe environment for Sikh students. This letter cited post-9/11 bias incidents targeting South Asian pupils in the state.

In other parts of the country, minority students and educators continued to feel the ongoing backlash. In August 2006, Jafumba Asad, a 32-year old graduate student and community college teacher in Tulsa, told *USA Today* that anti-Muslim bigotry caused her to change her appearance and stop wearing her chador and other traditional clothing to class.[291] She said that employers were reluctant to hire Muslim teachers, particularly if they wore full cover.

College instructors continued to encounter anti-Muslim bigotry on school grounds. At the University of Utah, political science teacher Hakan Yavuz said he was disturbed by Islamophobic comments students routinely made in class. According to a September 9, 2006 article in the *Deseret Morning News*, some of his pupils told him that they had enrolled in his course on Islam and politics to learn more about the enemy.[292] Prior to 9/11, he never heard such comments. Yavuz reported that in the years after the terrorist strikes, anti-Muslim bigotry had become progressively worse. He maintained that George W. Bush, government officials, and the American press frequently negated Muslim identity by equating Islam with terrorism. Yavuz told the *Deseret Morning News* that he was upset by a schism taking place between the Muslim community and the government, fueled in part by visa inquiries of male immigrants from the Middle East.[293] He claimed that as a result, American Muslims were adopting a siege mentality, avoiding participation in national politics and community organizations.

Near the five-year anniversary of 9/11, Islamic schools continued to be targeted by bigots. On September 23, 2006, an arsonist set fire to the Abraar School, a Muslim educational institution, causing about $100,000 in damages.[294] No one was apprehended in the attack, which community members attributed to the ongoing backlash.

The same month, a hate crime took place in New York. In late September 2006, a Pace University student found a Quran, covered with feces, tossed in the men's toilet at the downtown campus. In mid-October 2006, a second Quran was discovered in the same toilet. A swastika and bigoted slurs were also written on the bathroom wall of the Manhattan campus. Rakshan Khateeb, a 19-year old student from New Jersey, told the *New York Times* that the Islamophobic hate crimes left her concerned about her safety on campus, particularly since her hijab made her such a visible target.[295]

Pace officials said they did not file a report after the first Quran was discovered in the toilet because they thought it was just an act of vandalism, not a hate crime targeting a particular group of students. Pace's president David Caputo told the *Times* that finding a second Quran desecrated in the toilet prompted the university to contact the police.[296]

Muslim students at Pace were disappointed that administrators took so long to realize that desecration of the first Quran was a bias-motivated crime. Some students suggested that Pace officials did not report the first incident to outside authorities because the school did not want the negative publicity. Nadia Jarkirlic, a 20-year old Bosnian student, was upset by the school's handling of the hate attacks, telling the *Times* that administrators might have acted more promptly if another minority community had been targeted.[297]   She also expressed her hope that the university would hire an interfaith chaplain and mandate a course on world religions to promote campus tolerance.

Working with a surveillance photo showing the perpetrator leaving the library reading room, New York police officers eventually tracked down the perpetrator, Stanislav Shmulevich, a 23-year old Ukrainian immigrant.   According to police reports, Shmulevich admitted to taking the paperback Qurans out of the library and putting them in toilets because he was angry at Muslim students on campus, and wanted to desecrate their holy book.[298]   He was later arraigned on two charges of criminal mischief in the fourth degree as a hate crime.   His defense attorney, Stanley Thorpe, questioned whether his client committed a hate crime or engaged in a protected act of free speech.[299]   Another of Shmulevich's defenders declared that prosecuting him for throwing Qurans in toilets was a step towards implementing Islamic law in America.[300]

While Muslim students were experiencing Islamophobia on campuses, young audiences were lining up to watch the hit xenophobic comedy, *Borat*.   This movie, released in the U.S. on November 3, 2006, employs Islamophobia for cheap laughs.   In Borat's homeland, the Muslim townspeople are depicted as religious bigots, participating in hateful activities like the "running of the Jews."   When a mock Kazakhstan "anthem" is played in the movie, the song makes two references to "Jewtown" and declares that the country has "prostitutes, best in the region," suggesting that the Muslim residents are misogynists.   The film's protagonist also reveals that his family members practice prostitution, incest, and rape.   When Borat and Azimat travel to the U.S., they make derogatory remarks about a kind, elderly Jewish couple.   Like 20th century American movies featuring swarthy Semitic aggressors chasing unwilling blonde women, Borat spends most of his time in America pursuing Pamela Anderson, eventually throwing a sack over her head in an attempt to abduct her and marry her against her will.

Even more demeaning stereotypes of Muslims appear in the movie, *Home of the Brave*.   This film premiered in New York and Los Angeles on December 15, 2006, and was released in other parts of the U.S. on May 11, 2007.   In one scene in the movie, an Arab child with a tootsie pop detonates a bomb. According to film critic Shaheen, the image of the Arab child-as-terrorist surfaced in other movies, including the *Kingdom* and *Rules of Engagement*.[301]   By depicting young Middle Eastern children as amoral assassins, these movies drive home the xenophobic message that killing Muslim kids is sometimes justified.

CAMPUS ATTACKS, 2007

More than five years after the 9/11 attacks, minority students continued to be harassed and assaulted on American campuses.   In January 2007, three football players at Guilford College severely beat up three Palestinian students in a racially-motivated attack in the campus courtyard.[302]   Two of the three victims – Faris Khadar and Osama Sabbah – were enrolled at the school.   The third victim, Raleigh NCSU student Omar Awatani, was visiting his friends when he was brutally assaulted.   Awatani told the *Greensboro News Record* that the unprovoked hate crime was the most horrific experience of his life.[303]   According to court documents, the assailants, who were armed with brass knuckles, viciously punched and kicked the three Arab students.[304]   The perpetrators also made racial slurs during the attack, calling their victims "terrorists" and "sand niggers."[305]   At least 15 football players were present during the beating, which lasted several minutes.

The *Greensboro News Record* reported that the Palestinian students experienced significant injuries as a result of the attack.[306]   Awatani's beating left him with a concussion, causing him to have difficulty walking for several days.   Police arrested the assailants, and charged Michael Bates, 20, of Reidsville, Michael Robert Six, 20, of Greensboro, and Christopher Barnette, 21, of Semora, with ethnic intimidation, assault, and battery.[307]   The football players were released on January 22, 2007 on $2,000 bail.

Guilford College, a school with a Quaker background, issued a statement that said that the student perpetrators had no prior history of conflict and that some were under the influence of alcohol at the time of the incident.   Minority students at the school saw the hate crime as a product of the 9/11 backlash.

Media critic Shaheen observed that the gang beating at Guilford College took place while American television audiences were being entertained by the second season of *24*, in which super agent Jack Bauer defends the country against Arab, Arab-American, and Muslim-American villains, including nuclear terrorists and suicide bombers.[308] In the first four episodes of the season, Kal Penn plays Ahmed Amar, a teen terrorist. Although Penn was troubled by the racist part and considered turning it down, he eventually decided to do the role, frustrated by a dearth of other opportunities for South Asian actors in Hollywood.[309] Many viewers were troubled that Penn accepted the part, worried that harmful stereotypes of immigrant teens would endanger minority students on American campuses.

In the spring of 2007, Muslim students and Islamic schools continued to be targeted. In South Florida, a white powder was found spread around Nur Ul Islam Academy in Cooper City.[310] Although the substance turned out to be non-toxic, community members were still extremely frightened by the attack.

On occasion, faculty members made derogatory comments about Middle Easterners and Muslims in their classes. The *Arab American News* reported that during the spring semester of 2007, a university professor warned his students against talking to Muslims about religion, claiming that they turned into animals.[311] At other schools, Muslim instructors reported being harassed by their colleagues. When a Muslim teacher asked for a day off to observe a religious holiday, a colleague commented that administrators would certainly comply, afraid of being killed if the request was turned down.[312]

Throughout 2007, minority children were repeatedly harassed and attacked on school grounds, causing many of them to feel unsafe in post-9/11 America. One of the most heinous hate crimes occurred at Newton High School in New York, when two boys cut the hair of a Sikh classmate against his will. According to the *New York Post*, problems began on May 23, 2007, when Harpal Vacher insulted the mother of Umair Ahmed, a Pakistani Muslim.[313] Ahmed allegedly responded by telling the 15-year old Sikh that he would beat him up and send him home naked. The attack occurred the next day, when Ahmed approached 15-year old Harpal Vacher in the Newton High School cafeteria and informed him that he planned to cut his hair.[314] Using 15-year old Waqas Ali as a lookout, the 17-year old Ahmed dragged Vacher into the bathroom, removed his turban, and cut his hair from his waist to his shoulders using a pair of scissors.[315] Ahmad then flushed Vacher's hair down the toilet. Sikhs around the country were outraged by the assault. Sikh Coalition executive director Amardeep Singh told the *New York Daily News* that Sikhs consider cutting off their hair a crime akin to losing their heads.[316]

The two Pakistani youths were arrested and charged with unlawful imprisonment, coercion, menacing, and aggravated harassment. Since Ahmed and Vacher exchanged words prior to the bias-motivated haircutting, many South Asians speculated that the assault might have been prevented if school administrators had created a more functional system to address interfaith bullying, which was happening with increased frequency in the years after 9/11.

Vacher testified for about ten hours about the assault and its effect on his family. A Queens jury eventually convicted Ahmed of felony menacing as a hate crime, felony coercion as a hate crime, criminal possession of a weapon, and harassment. District attorney Richard Brown told the *Post* that hate crimes should never be tolerated in New York, the most culturally-diverse region of the U.S.[317] Prosecutor Michael Brovner asked the judge to give Ahmed a prison term of one to three years, and Vacher asked that his assailant receive the maximum sentence.

Area Sikhs were outraged that Ahmed ducked jail time for the assault. The *New York Daily News* reported that acting Queens Supreme Court Justice Joel Blumenfeld sentenced 19-year old Ahmed to just two years of probation and 180 hours of community service.[318] The judge also ordered Ahmed to write an essay about what he learned from the experience. Ahmed, who came to the U.S. at the age of 13, planned to complete his volunteer work at the South Asian Youth Action organization, and undergo tolerance counseling at the Holocaust center. Because of the seriousness of the bias-motivated attack, Sikh activists found the sentence woefully inadequate. Prabhjot Narula of United Sikhs told the *Daily News* that the outcome was a disgrace, a mere slap on the wrist for a traumatic hate crime.[319] Many activists thought that a more appropriate punishment was warranted in order to deter other bigotry-motivated attacks and curb intolerance in post-9/11 America.

Social scientists confirmed that attacks targeting Sikh children were becoming ubiquitous in New York schools in the years following the terrorist strikes. After surveying 200 Sikh students from Richmond Hill and Flushing, Sikh Coalition researchers reported in 2007 that over 40% of turban-wearing youths experienced some physical harassment in the city's public schools[320] They also found that approximately 75% of Sikh boys in Queens had been bullied because of their religion. The survey conductors also discovered that 20% of the Sikh youths had been told that they look like terrorists, suggesting that minority youths were still being scapegoated for 9/11. The study, "Hatred in the Hallways," alarmed Sikhs in the U.S. and India, who read about the researchers' findings in New Delhi's *Hindustan Times*.[321] Many parents wondered why the attacks were occurring with such frequency, and why administrators were so unsuccessful in preventing religiously-motivated bullying.

To help vulnerable kids, Sikh activists and educators created "Khalsa Kids," an interactive website that allowed educators and students to obtain videos, download presentations, and participate in a discussion forum about Sikh harassment in schools. Despite these educational efforts, minority students continued being singled out on American campuses.

In mid-2007, a Muslim teenager experienced discrimination while attending summer school in California. At Seaside high school in the Monterey Peninsula Unified School District, a lunchroom supervisor demanded that the girl remove her hijab.[322] Although she protested that she wore it for religious reasons, the employee insisted that wearing the headscarf was a violation of the school's 'no hat' policy. At the time of the June 19th incident, the 13-year old girl was attending a summer algebra program. Many community members were dismayed that so many years after 9/11, school employees were still mistreating Muslim students. A few months later, the school employee offered the girl a public apology and acknowledged her right to wear the veil.

American movies released the same summer disseminated xenophobic messages to young viewers. In the movie, *Transformers*, an American security specialist investigating an attack makes an ethnic slur, suggesting that Persians were not intelligent enough to have carried out the assault.[323] This action-based film was released in the U.S. on July 3, 2007. In his discussion of this movie, Shaheen voices concern that the Qatari village depicted in the movie looks like a wreck, suggesting that 21st-century Arabs live in anti-modern conditions. The racism in the film contributed to a zeitgeist in which young viewers were given permission to feel superior to their minority classmates and community members.

In some parts of the U.S., Islamophobic students harassed Muslim adults. According to the July 26, 2007 issue of Vermont's *Brattleboro Reformer*, a junior high school pupil threw a piece of leftover Easter ham at Somali Muslims sitting at a table in Auburn.[324] The victims were convinced that they were being singled out because of racial and religious bias. Many area residents saw the incident as a manifestation of post-9/11 nativism.

On occasion, xenophobic adults protested the opening of schools serving minority populations. In Brooklyn, bigots actively opposed the creation of the Kahlil Gibran School because its proposed curriculum included daily instruction in Arabic and a focus on international studies.[325] Although administrators and parents confronted neighborhood opposition to the academy, the school enrolled 44 students in September 2007. Despite community fears that the school would bring an influx of Middle Eastern immigrants to the area, the majority of the sixth graders identified as black and only six were Arabic-speaking.

Attacks on minority students escalated near the sixth anniversary of 9/11. On September 19, 2007, a 12-year old Muslim girl was beaten by a classmate at Carusi Middle School in Cherry Hill, New Jersey. According to the *New York Times*, the boy approached the girl and told her that there was a terrorist on the loose.[326] He then choked her and punched her in the face, leaving her with a bruised and swollen cheek.[327] After the bias-motivated attack, school administrators told her relatives to keep news of the beating quiet, instructing them to refrain from contacting authorities. The Shnewer family called the FBI anyway, where they were told to report the crime to local police. The Cherry Hill police department finally learned of the attack in mid-October. Police Lt. William Kushina told the *Times* that he was alarmed that school officials did not promptly report the crime to local authorities.[328] Although he knew that the school had an obligation to report physical assaults to the police, he was unsure about how quickly they were required to do this. As a result of the beating, the girl, two of her sisters, and her mother relocated to Jordan. Defending his handling of the case, principal Kirk Rickansrud told the *Times* that progress on the case was hampered by the fact that the victim and her mother left the country.[329] Many Muslims and Arabs were dismayed that more than six years after 9/11, children were still being subjected to bias-motivated attacks.

In other parts of the country, Muslim middle school children were targeted by bullies. In late 2007, a Florida sixth grader was harassed and assaulted at Azalea Middle School. According to the *St. Petersburg Times*, students repeatedly taunted Hannah, making fun of her hijab, calling her a terrorist, and asking her if she was hiding bombs.[330] The harassment escalated further when a sixth-grade boy physically assaulted her, punching her in the shoulders and trying to strangle her.[331] On November 7, 2007, the bully ripped off her hijab in their science class.[332] The teacher failed to take appropriate action in response to the attack and refused allow the girl to change seats so she would not have to sit near her assailant. The following day, the boy promised to get a gun and kill her, and threatened to start school rumors that she was a lesbian.[333] Muslims in the area were dismayed that school administrators were downplaying the seriousness of the hate crimes. To escape the mistreatment, the girl contemplated transferring schools.

The same month, Muslim college students were harassed on American campuses. In the fall of 2007, Islamophobic pamphlets were distributed on the grounds of Central Michigan University. According to the *Detroit News*, the leaflets asserted that all Muslims were terrorists.[334] Soon thereafter, four nooses were hung in a classroom lab of the school's Engineering and Technology building. The perpetrator fashioned them from hoses used to deliver compressed gas to lab instruments. To combat campus bigotry, sophomore Shannon Salk got 2,000 students to agree to wear their school colors to defend the university's image and protest crimes targeting minority students. She told the *Detroit News* that she sympathized with African and Muslim students who were frightened by the hate literature and the nooses, and felt that no one should be afraid on campus.[335] In response to the incidents, college President Mike Rao offered a $5,000 reward for information about the perpetrators. Later that week, a CMU student confessed to hanging the nooses as a prank, but denied distributing the leaflets.

CAMPUS ATTACKS, 2008

Bias-motivated attacks at schools continued throughout 2008. In the spring, staff members at the Tarek ibn Ziyad Academy charter school in Minnesota received hateful phone messages and emails. The threats were made soon after Minneapolis *Star Tribune* columnist Katherine Kersten questioned whether the publicly-funded K-8 school promoted the Muslim faith.[336] Addressing community concerns, director Asad Zaman pointed out that the school was non-sectarian, and that the harassment frightened many of the students and their parents, who came from diverse backgrounds.[337] In response to the threats, Chuck Kleckner, Inver Grove Heights police chief, said his department would patrol the school more frequently to deter attackers.[338] Many interfaith leaders and organizations preached tolerance and condemned the post-9/11 scapegoating.

Also in 2008, school bullies continued harassing Sikhs. In Hightstown High School in New Jersey, a South Asian teenager was attacked in an unprovoked assault. On May 5, 2008, students were instructed to go to the courtyard during a fire drill. While a Sikh student was chatting with his friends, another student, Garrett Green, came up behind him and set his patka on fire.[339] Feeling something hot on his head, the Sikh student patted his small turban to put out the flames. The teen's mother, Sukhjot Kaur, reported that her son was emotionally scarred by the bias attack, pointing out that no parent should have to worry about hate crimes on American campuses.[340] Many area South Asians saw the attack as a product of post-9/11 xenophobia.

In response to the incident, Sikh Coalition attorney Harsimran Kaur declared that academic personnel needed to do more to ensure the safety and well-being of minority students.[341] She suggested that

140

administrators and teachers should implement programs to foster cultural sensitivity and increase security on school grounds.

The same year, Sikh students were attacked in New York. In Queens, Jagmohan Singh Premi, a practicing Sikh from India, was bullied for months by his classmates at Richmond Hill High School in Flushing. According to the publication *Colorlines*, the other students mercilessly teased Premi, calling him "terrorist" and "Osama bin Laden" on a daily basis.[342] They would also yell that his patka was a bomb and that everyone should run away from him because he was going to blow them all up. Although Premi and his father repeatedly complained to teachers and school administrators, they failed to end the abuse.

The ringleader was in two of Premi's daily classes. According to *India Abroad*, the bully repeatedly threw paper wads at the Sikh student and tormented him with derogatory comments about his hair.[343] Soon, the harassment escalated. On June 3, 2008, the 15-year old bully assaulted 18-year old Premi during an ESL class, pulling at his patka, yanking on his beard, and punching him in the eye with keys held between his knuckles.[344] Premi's doctors reported that the Sikh student suffered from a facial contusion, a large laceration under his left eye, and an orbital fracture. Although the assault was witnessed by a teacher, school officials still failed to protect Premi, allowing the assailant back in their shared classes following the assault.[345] Initially, the school's assistant principal refused to recognize that a hate crime had taken place on campus, but finally acknowledged the bias component of the attack after Sikh Coalition officials compared the forcible removal of a Sikh patka to the yanking off of a Jewish yarmulke. Worried about Premi's safety, his family transferred their son to another school. Premi was not the only member of his family affected by anti-Sikh sentiment: his father had worked at National Wholesale Liquidators, a New York company found guilty of religious and sexual harassment of its Sikh employees.[346] The company went bankrupt, and Premi's father lost his job.

Premi's assailant was eventually punished for his misconduct. A family court judge in Queens found the bully guilty of aggravated assault, possession of a criminal weapon, and hate crime battery, charges that carry a maximum penalty of 18 months in juvenile detention. Some New Yorkers wondered if the crime could have been prevented if school officials had stemmed the harassment before it escalated into an assault. To improve the way the school district deals with bias-motivated bullying, Premi's family filed a lawsuit against the New York City Department of Education and Richmond Hill High, which was declared a "problem school" in a Sikh Coalition report.[347] Some New Yorkers also maintained that religious and racial bias affected the coverage of hate crimes at school, pointing out that newspapers were unwilling to print the name, racial identity, and religious affiliation of Premi's 15-year old assailant, but had no problem identifying Waqas Ali, Harpal Vacher's 15-year old assailant, or publishing that he was a South Asian Muslim from Pakistan.

Five days after Premi was attacked, another Sikh student was assaulted in New York. At PS 219 in Flushing, a student assailant cut off 12-year old Gurprit Kaur's religiously-mandated long hair and threw it in the garbage.[348] Her brother Talwinder Singh was also harassed by classmates, who called him "potato head" and "turbanator."[349] School bullies also suggested that his patka was a bomb and that he was going to use it to blow them all up. Outraged by the ongoing mistreatment of Sikh students, hundreds of community activists took to the streets in Flushing to demand that the Department of Education end the racial bullying of South Asian and Middle Eastern children. In response, Mayor Michael Bloomberg announced a new protocol to address hate crimes at schools, but activists felt that the measure was insufficient to stop campus intolerance and the widespread use of the epithet, "terrorist," to describe South Asian and Middle Eastern students in the years after 9/11.

Minority students were also bullied in the Southwest. In Texas, a Muslim student at Friendswood Junior High School was assaulted and stuffed head-first in a trash can by a classmate, according to the June 11, 2008 *Houston Chronicle*.[350] In response to the campus attack, principal Robin Lowe agreed to allow CAIR-Houston representatives to give a 40-minute presentation to the mostly-Anglo student body on the basic beliefs of Islam. Rather than appreciate the educational presentation, the community reacted with hostility. The lecture drew considerable protest from many parents, Christian clergymen, and talk radio hosts. Superintendent Trish Hanks told the *Chronicle* that because of the intensity of the controversy, principal Lowe requested and received an academic transfer because she no longer felt able to remain on the campus.[351] At a school board meeting after her resignation, many Friendswood residents defended Lowe's conduct and called for her reinstatement. Other community members disagreed, claiming that CAIR had links to terrorism and arguing that groups with religious affiliations should not be allowed to address public school audiences.

CAMPUS ATTACKS, 2009

In many instances, educators and administrators failed to act as advocates for minority students. In Clute, Texas, school officials refused to enroll fourth-grader Gundeep Singh in the fall of 2009 because he had unshorn hair and wore a patka. According to *India Abroad*, Deputy Superintendent Dennis McNaughten told Singh's parents that their son's appearance violated the Brazosport Independent School District's 'no hats' policy and a mandatory short hair requirement for boys.[352] The fourth grader's parents found this policy an unacceptable violation of the first amendment, noting that their son simply wanted to be able to attend school with his religious identity intact. After involving civil rights attorneys and Sikh organizations in the case, the school district agreed to make an exception for Gundeep Singh, enabling him to attend Gladys Polk Elementary School.

Along with Sikhs, Muslim and Arab students continued to face discrimination on American campuses. The *Orange County Register* reported that in 2009, two bullies threatened to kill a Muslim classmate at a local junior high school.[353] They cornered the boy and threatened to shoot him if he came to class the next day. The attack frightened minority students, who worried that post-9/11 campus bigotry was imperiling their safety.

One of the most egregious hate crimes occurred in Ann Arbor, Michigan, when a group of students attacked a 16-year old Iraqi-American classmate on September 8, 2009, a few days before the eighth anniversary of 9/11. According to the *Detroit News*, the assault happened as the Arab-American victim was returning home after her first day at Skyline High.[354] After she got off the last step of the school bus, approximately five to seven African-American students jumped her. They dragged her to an area near her home in the North Maples Estates where several more attackers – including an adult man and woman – joined in the beating. The assailants made racial slurs during the assault, yelling anti-Arab slurs and calling the Muslim girl a "raghead."[355] When the victim's 15-year old brother attempted to intervene, a group of assailants attacked him as well, kicking him in the back and the jaw.[356] When the victims' 20-year old sister attempted to help her siblings, she was pushed into a white car and had her hijab forcibly removed by the attackers.[357] The hate crime finally ended when the victims' father arrived. Because his younger children were not safe commuting on their own, the father felt compelled to drive his teenage son and daughter to school every day to ensure their safety.

Kelvin Scott, director of the Michigan Department of Civil Rights, reported that racial tensions between Arab and black students were already high prior to the September 8, 2009 assault. Todd Roberts, superintendent of the school district, told the *Detroit News* that four students – two boys and two girls – were disciplined following the incident.[358]

The Washtenaw County Prosecutor's office decided against filing ethnic intimidation charges against the perpetrators involved in the racially-motivated beating. Civil rights activists thought hate crime enhancements were warranted because the assailants tore off the two sisters' hijabs and used racially-derogatory language during the attacks, which left the 16-year old victim with a black eye and facial injuries requiring six stitches.[359] Muslim community members were also upset that only four of the 12 to 15 perpetrators were facing charges for the assault, and that the attackers were being tried in juvenile court. Nabih Ayad, the attorney acting on behalf of the victims, told the *Arab American News* that he was disturbed that the school principal suspended the victimized 16-year old Muslim girl and only one of her attackers, suggesting that the case would have been handled differently if the victim had been of another ethnicity.[360] The principal justified the suspensions on the grounds that both students were arguing on the school bus prior to the attack. Arab and Muslim members of the community felt it was ridiculous that a minority student was getting suspended after being harassed and viciously beaten in a hate crime.

The bias assault was not the Iraqi-American family's first encounter with racism. In August 2009, the father was called a "fucking Arab" by someone in the neighborhood, giving the family the clear message that they were not welcome in the community.[361] As a result of the intolerant atmosphere, Arab parents in the area worried about the safety of their children on school grounds.

Muslim students were also attacked in other states. In New York, an American-born teenager was repeatedly bullied and assaulted by his classmates in Staten Island. Worried about attracting the attention of community bigots, his relatives requested that local and national newspapers refrain from publishing their actual names. According to the *Los Angeles Times*, the harassment began in October 2009, at Edwin Markham Intermediate School, after his peers found out that "Kristian" was Muslim.[362] The boy, whose family emigrated from Trinidad in the 1980s, started losing interest in his studies in response to the constant bullying. When he began his freshman year at Port Richmond High School, the 16-year old Muslim was dismayed to learn that two of the bullies were in one of his classes. The racial and religious harassment escalated until he was being physically assaulted on a regular basis.

CAMPUS ATTACKS, 2010

Kristian's bullying continued into 2010. His father noticed his son was regularly coming home with dirty clothes and missing personal items, and eventually decided to report the bullying.[363] The family filed a police report, and had Kristian examined by a neurologist and a psychologist. The repeated physical abuse left the Muslim student with psychological trauma and bodily injuries so severe that a physician found blood in the boy's urine.[364] The family was considering legal action against the school because teachers saw students hit Kristian in the head with large books but did nothing substantive to end the bias-motivated abuse.[365] Richard Condon, a special commissioner on the New York School Board, investigated the case.

According to AM New York, Kristian's four assailants included one 15-year old African American and three 14-year old Latino students.[366] Over the course of eight months, they jumped the Muslim boy on numerous occasions, using racial and religious slurs while kicking him, spitting on him, and punching him in the groin. On some occasions, they used anti-gay and anti-Muslim slurs, comparing him to the 9/11 attackers and calling him a terrorist.[367] Kristian told WPIX-TV that on one occasion, a bully accused him of coming into the country to blow Americans up.[368] In response to the ongoing torment, prosecutors charged the bullies with assault and aggravated harassment as a hate crime.

While Kristian was being beaten in New York, Muslim students in other states were being bullied by their peers. In Texas, an Arab-American 8th grader was assaulted at Beckendorff Junior High School in Katy, Texas. A school bigot singled out the Muslim student, calling him a terrorist and using Islamophobic slurs.[369] The bully also accused the Muslim boy of plotting to blow up buildings, blaming him for 9/11. Along with the verbal harassment, the bully physically attacked his classmate, injuring him severely. The Muslim boy was hospitalized after undergoing surgery to insert pins and a plate in his jaw, which had been broken in two places. In the weeks prior to his assault, the boy told three school officials that he was being bullied at school, but they did nothing substantive in response.

In Minnesota, Muslim students were also targeted by their peers. According to the *Christian Science Monitor*, two high school bullies shoved bacon in the faces of Muslim classmates in March 2010.[370] Because pork was used in the attack, the victims were convinced that they were being targeted due to post-9/11 religious bias. After this incident, they felt scared on school grounds.

The same month, the Muslim center at Brandeis University was attacked. A vandal turned lamps upside down, unplugged appliances, and scratched the door. The perpetrator also stole imam Talal Eid's Quran, which contained his religious notes and sermons. Brandeis Muslims were upset by the damage done to their prayer space, located in a basement of one of the buildings on campus. Although this was clearly an anti-Muslim attack, Brandeis spokesman Dennis Nealon refused to acknowledge that the vandalism was motivated by bias, telling the *Boston Globe* that he and other administrators did not believe that the ransacking of the Islamic center was a hate crime.[371] Arab and South Asian students disagreed, particularly since a sign clearly identified the space as a gathering site for Muslims. Because Middle Eastern students had experienced harassment and other forms of overt campus bigotry in the past, minority groups felt that the administration needed to do more to promote tolerance at the school.

Brandeis University was not unique in its reluctance to acknowledge campus hate crimes. In his essay, "Higher Education, Inc. in the Age of Branding," James Twitchell argues that administrators often treat their universities like commercial products, and attempt to suppress news that could hurt the brand.[372] For this reason, many administrators are hesitant to acknowledge or publicize campus bias attacks, worried that they might frighten away prospective applicants and compromise booster donations. By downplaying or denying hate crimes, university officials believe that they can protect their school's reputation and maintain their competitive edge, even if this is done at the expense of the minority members of the academic community.

Years after 9/11, minority instructors continued to be targeted by area bigots. In California, Muslim teachers were occasionally singled out by community members. The *Oakland Tribune* reported that on March 31, 2010, a woman verbally harassed and attacked two Muslim instructors who worked at As-Safa Academy in San Jose.[373] Also in Santa Clara County, a Muslim teacher was targeted at Luther Burbank Elementary School. She was called a terrorist, and had her room vandalized in April, 2010.[374]

In some parts of the country, Muslim art students worried about the consequences of displaying politically-themed work. In Illinois, an Islamophobic bigot defaced a student exhibit at the Art Institute of Chicago in mid-May 2010. According to the *Chicago Tribune*, a vandal ruined her art works by drawing offensive caricatures on them and defacing them with a death threat, urging viewers to kill all Arabs.[375] The Muslim graduate student, Anida Yoeu Ali, believed that her creative pieces, known collectively as the "1700% Project," were intentionally damaged because they addressed the spike in U.S. hate crimes in the aftermath of 9/11.[376] Shortly before the vandalism, Ali appeared on NPR to discuss her exhibit as part of the station's series on Islamic identity and reform. Although Ali's art project was the only one defaced at the Sullivan Galleries, Chicago police officers were hesitant to label the incident a hate crime, even though the graffiti included an ethnically-motivated death threat. Instead of admitting that the attack was bias-motivated, they opted to regard it as simple vandalism involving damage to property. Ali told the *Arab American News* that the death threat and the defacement of her work was an assault on all Arabs and Muslims in the U.S.[377]

CAMPUS ATTACKS, 2011

Minority students continued to be singled out on American campuses in 2011. According to the *New York Post*, two Staten Island bullies repeatedly harassed and attacked a 12-year old Muslim girl attending Dreyful Intermediate School 49 in Stapleton.[378] Investigating officers reported that the bullies tormented the Muslim student for at least three months, taunting her and threatening her on at least four separate occasions.[379] In a series of bias-motivated incidents, 11-year old Osman Daramy and 13-year old Krystal Callenger beat up their classmate and tried to rip off her veil, calling her a terrorist and using anti-Muslim slurs. The *New York Daily News* reported that the first attack happened in January, when the honors student was ambushed on her way to pick up her brother at a nearby school.[380] On this occasion, the bullies kicked and punched the girl, leaving her with a bruised lip, facial lacerations, and a tattered hijab. She reported this attack to school officials, but was too scared to identify her assailants by name. After enduring months of abuse, including another assault in late March 2011, the victim finally told her older brother about the bullying. After he called the police, the girl's assailants were arrested.

Callenger and Daramy were remanded to juvenile lockup, charged with assault as a hate crime and attempted robbery.[381] At a hearing about the case, Osman Daramy gave the finger to the court, showing his contempt for authority figures.[382] After spending a few days behind bars, his behavior quickly improved, appearing contrite and frightened at his next court appearance.[383]   Frank Davies was confused by his son's participation in the bias-motivated attack, pointing out that the boy's own mother was Muslim.[384]   Some community members speculated that Daramy had internalized post-9/11 community Islamophobia and was expressing his own anti-Muslim self-loathing. Davies suggested that his son was misbehaving in response to his own experiences with American bigotry and racism, pointing out that the boy had been born in a Sierra Leone refugee camp and had come to the U.S. when he was six months old.[385]   Because of his son's arrest, Davies bought Osman an April 17, 2011 ticket to Sierra Leone, hoping that the boy's behavior would improve by spending time with relatives.   Osman Daramy's participation in the anti-Muslim attack generated considerable media attention overseas.   The *Hindustan Times* and the *Jakarta Post* informed international audiences about the bias-motivated bullying, leaving readers wondering why school officials failed to act in a timely fashion to protect the repeatedly-bullied little girl.[386]

Islamophobia on American campuses surged following the death of Osama bin Laden. At times, anti-Muslim harassment came from minority students' own teachers. The *Houston Chronicle* reported that on May 2, 2011, a math teacher at Clear Brook high school made a derogatory comment to a ninth-grade Muslim student, telling the boy that he must be grieving the death of the terrorist mastermind.[387]   Because the racist and humiliating comment was made in front of the boy's algebra class, the teacher was put on administrative leave without pay, and was asked to resign at the end of the academic year.   Community activists were disturbed by the incident, particularly since the school had gotten negative publicity in 2006 after another instructor distributed articles suggesting that Muslims beat their wives.[388]   Minority students who hoped that the backlash would be over after bin Laden's death were disappointed that they continued to be singled out at school.

A decade after 9/11, minority students continued to feel the effects of the backlash. In September 2011, American schools throughout the U.S. held memorials to honor the victims of the terrorist strikes.[389]   In many parts of the country, Muslim and Sikh parents worried that campus bullies watching graphic 9/11 news clips in class would decide to harass or attack minority children in misplaced retaliation for the hijackings.

On occasion, post-9/11 bigotry intruded into school theatre departments. In mid-September 2011, the Richland School District in Johnstown, Pennsylvania abruptly decided to cancel its February 2012 production of *Kismet*, a 1954 Tony Award-winning musical about a Muslim street poet from ancient Baghdad.[390]   According to Superintendent Thomas Fleming, the decision was made in response to complaints that the production was inappropriate in light of the tenth anniversary of 9/11.[391]   Fleming told reporters that these community concerns were valid since United Airlines Flight 93 crashed in nearby Shanksville, and that putting on a Middle Eastern-themed musical was potentially detrimental to children.[392]   Throughout the country, Arab-Americans and Muslims were outraged by Fleming's decision, alarmed that he saw a connection between a school play and a terrorist hijacking. They noted that the school had previously staged *Kismet* in 1983, indicating that the show had no inappropriate content.   Many civil rights advocates felt that Fleming was pandering to xenophobes and transmitting the alarming message that anything Middle Eastern was inherently suspect. Some Muslim community members pointed out that American school officials never thought twice about performing Shakespeare in the aftermath of the 1995 bombing of the Alfred P. Murrah federal building even though terrorist Timothy McVeigh's ancestors were from Europe, the setting of most of the Bard's plays. Minority school children in Pennsylvania were dismayed that such rampant campus bigotry was continuing more than a decade after the terrorist strikes. Parents continued to worry about their children's safety in schools where academic administrators were validating the nativist fears of racial and religious bigots.

American colleges and universities also felt the ongoing effects of the backlash ten years after 9/11. According to USC education professor Shafiqa Ahmadi, the Patriot Act continued to discourage foreign students from coming to study at American colleges.[393]   Across the country, many admissions officers and administrators were dismayed that ongoing campus hate crimes were compromising the global reputation of American higher education, causing many top international students to attend college outside of the U.S.

CHAPTER SEVEN:

BACKLASH ATTACKS AT WORK,
SEPT. 2001 TO SEPT. 2011

Along with hate crimes at religious centers and schools, the 9/11 backlash included attacks at immigrant-owned or operated businesses. Immediately after the Twin Towers fell, store owners across America began worrying about the safety of their minority employees. Angry with Osama bin Laden, nativists began attacking innocent immigrant employees and minority-run companies, unleashing a wave of work-related hate crimes that continued for over a decade.

At the time of the terrorist strikes, many Middle Easterners and South Asians in the U.S. were employed in sales jobs or service occupations, making them visible targets for bigots. Foreign-looking workers were often targeted, even if they were native-born or naturalized Americans. According to the findings of a 1999 study published in the *Los Angeles Times*, Arab-American entrepreneurs were disproportionately represented in sales, nearly double the rate of non-Arabs.[1] In some urban areas, minority-owned businesses were highly concentrated. By 2001, there were approximately 5,000 to 7,000 Arab-American businesses in Metro Detroit, with around 40% in retail.[2] The same year, Christians of Iraqi descent owned approximately 85% of the 800 San Diego retail outlets belonging to the California Independent Grocers and Convenience Stores Association.[3] In many American cities, Muslims and Sikhs worked as taxi drivers and gas station workers, placing themselves in constant contact with the public. In many regions of the country, South Asians were overrepresented in the motel industry, where they were required to interact with strangers.

Minority service workers were easy targets for xenophobes because their jobs involved extensive interactions with others. Across the country, bigots angry about the terrorist strikes vented their rage at Arab and South Asian convenience store operators, gas station attendants, taxi drivers, and motel employees. These workers bore the brunt of the 9/11 backlash.

On many occasions, vandals targeted stores specializing in Arabic food or Middle Eastern merchandise. In the aftermath of high-profile hate crimes, many customers became afraid to shop at minority-owned stores or eat at ethnic restaurants, causing these businesses to suffer dramatic declines in revenue.

Physicians, attorneys, and other professionals were also scapegoated during the backlash, encountering racism from co-workers and clients. As a result of community xenophobia, minority professionals began questioning the limits of tolerance in America.

PRE-9/11 MOVIES THAT DEMEAN ARAB AND MUSLIM WORKERS

To understand backlash hate crimes targeting minority businesses, it is important to understand the image of Middle Eastern and Muslim merchants in American popular culture. Even before 9/11, Western movies frequently depicted Muslim and Middle Eastern financiers and store owners as hook-nosed money-grubbers, recycling earlier anti-Semitic stereotypes. In many films from the 1970s, Arab businessmen repeatedly appear as anti-Western villains, intent on buying up the U.S. In the 1976 movie, *Network*, a television newsman alarms audiences by announcing that rich Arabs were attempting to purchase the network and infiltrate the country. In the course of a particularly vicious diatribe, anchor Howard Beale accuses banks of selling America to the Arabs, warning his television audience that rich sheikhs and OPEC ministers were trying to take over the station. Beale then asks his viewers to go out on their balconies and scream out their anger. In the documentary film, *Reel Bad Arabs*, based on his book of the same name, Jack Shaheen powerfully juxtaposes this scene with Nazi propaganda footage of Germans on balconies, showing how both xenophobic films teach viewers to fear a lurking Semitic menace.[4]

Films from the 1980s also capitalize on viewers' fears of Arab financiers. In his book, 'Evil' Arabs in American Popular Film, critic Tim Jon Semmerling argues that the 1981 movie, *Rollover*, exploits American fears about the Middle East by suggesting that Arabs are the wrong kind of capitalists, villains who should be hated and feared.[5] In his discussion of how this movie plays upon Americans' economic concerns, Semmerling writes that it depicts Arabs as having acquired wealth they have not earned, subjecting capitalism to their destructive and business-immature whims.[6] The movie suggests that American businessmen are jeopardizing the U.S. economy through their dealings with the sinister Arabs. In one pivotal scene in the film, the Arabs withdraw all of their U.S. investments, causing American and international financial institutions and markets to collapse. The Arab villains are then able to achieve capitalistic control over the U.S. economy.

Other movies contain buffoonish stereotypes of Middle Eastern businessmen. In the racist 1990 comedy, *Hollywood Hot Tubs 2: Educating Crystal*, sexist Arab financiers attempt to seduce a white American Valley Girl and appropriate her hot tub company.[7] One of the misogynist male characters is Nahbib, a swarthy knife-carrying Arab, who views American women with distain. Film critic Shaheen takes issue with the film's blatant anti-Semitism, pointing out that in one scene, Arab villains fight each other while 'Hava Nagila' plays in the background.[8] By using this song in this fashion, the filmmakers transmit the troubling message that all Semites are laughable subjects of ridicule.

Many 20th-century movies reinforce the anti-Semitic stereotype that greedy Arabs use shady means to profit from the misery of others. In *Operation Condor*, a 1991 movie re-released in the U.S. in July 1997, Jackie Chan's character fights money-grubbing Arab villains. In this film, the protagonist defeats Arab buffoons and Bedouin slavers. Middle Eastern characters are also depicted as money-oriented villains, obsessed with searching for gold. Shaheen is troubled by this racist movie, observing that the Arab villains speak fractured English, and are referred to as "pigs" and "vampires."[9] In a particularly offensive scene, Middle Eastern characters auction off two abducted women like chattel, with some Arabs offering to buy them for 150 camels.[10] Shaheen is also disturbed by an unscrupulous Arab character with an Indian accent who takes financial advantage of the movie's protagonists.[11] Movies perpetuating stereotypes of stingy Arab and South Asian businessmen may have fueled xenophobic attacks on minority store owners during the backlash.

Although hate crime statistics are always problematic, there is some evidence that post-9/11 hate crimes occurred particularly frequently when minorities were at work. According to a December 21, 2001 article in the *Daily News*, businesses were the most likely places for hate crimes and bias-motivated incidents in Los Angeles county, with approximately 42% of all the cases occurring at gas stations and convenience stores, 17% at residences, 8% at religious sites, and 6% at schools.[12]

SEPTEMBER 2001 ATTACKS AT WORK: NORTHERN EAST COAST

Soon after the terrorist strikes, minority American workers on the East Coast began getting harassed or assaulted at their places of employment. The *Boston Globe* reported that a consultant for RSA security was viciously beaten on September 11, 2001 in a backlash hate crime.[13] On the day of the assault, Mohammed Atari, a Revere man of Palestinian descent, joined other workers in the cafeteria of a UPS facility, watching television coverage of the attacks on the Pentagon and World Trade Center. Atari left the room after UPS workers began making angry and derogatory comments about people of Arabic descent. A work supervisor assured Atari that he was safe, and urged him to resume his job. Later that day, Atari was severely beaten in the bathroom, presumably by a co-worker. According to the *Boston Globe*, Atari suffered a brain injury and lost wages due to the bias-motivated beating.[14] After the attack, he filed a $270,000 lawsuit against UPS for failing to create a safe work environment.

Elsewhere in Massachusetts, bigots attacked minority-owned businesses. In Somerset, three teenagers firebombed the roof of the Olde Village Convenience store on September 12, 2001. The *Boston Globe* reported that prior to the arson, the young perpetrators confronted 30-year old store owner Ashwin Patel and asked him about his country of origin.[15] Patel, an American citizen of Indian descent, told the teens that his national origin was none of their business. The youths later returned to the shop and threw a Molotov cocktail at the business because they assumed Patel was an Arab Muslim. Patel, a Hindu, was in the building at the time of the firebombing, and saw the three arsonists running from his store into the woods after throwing the incendiary device.[16] Much of the gas spilled instead of exploding, and the store opened as usual the following morning.

Patel told the *Boston Globe* that he and other area South Asians were being targeted in backlash hate crimes because they were being confused with Middle Easterners.[17] He was grateful at the support he received from his customers and neighbors after the arson attack, which caused over $1,000 in damage to his store. Well-wishers brought hydrangeas and chrysanthemums to comfort Patel, and wrote letters-to-the-editor condemning the hate crime. Somerset Hindus were disturbed by the bias-motivated arson. Nimesh Patel, a 25-year old cashier at the targeted business, told the *Globe* that the incident caused him to postpone his plans to bring his wife over from Bombay.[18]

Soon after the attack, police arrested the three assailants: Craig Jennings, 18, of Fall River; Jeffery Lizotte, 17, of Somerset; and a 16-year old from Somerset.[19] According to the *Boston Globe*, two of the teens admitted to investigators that they set fire to the building because they wanted to retaliate against Arabs.[20] The youths were charged with assault with intent to murder, assault to intimidate, possession of an infernal machine, and burning a building. They also became the first Massachusetts residents to be prosecuted for committing a 9/11 backlash hate crime. Along with the criminal and civil charges, State Attorney General Thomas F. Reilly filed legal documents prohibiting the teens from harassing Ashwin Patel while they were awaiting trial. Responding to the climate of xenophobia, Patel reminded the *Boston Globe* that Muslims and Arabs were citizens, and that all Americans should feel obligated to stand up to backlash hate crimes.[21]

Although Reilly responded appropriately to the bias-motivated arson, other Massachusetts officials dismissed the seriousness of the attack. In an interview with the *Globe*, Somerset town administrator John McAulifee described the assailants as the kinds of teenagers who would under normal circumstances be targeting mailboxes with baseball bats.[22] Many of Patel's customers disagreed with McAulifee's sympathetic characterization of the assailants as wayward teenagers, seeing them as dangerous criminals. Wayne Massie told the *Boston Globe* he was glad the perpetrators were apprehended, since they were targeting hard-working immigrants.[23]

Judy Rezendes, the mother of Craig Jennings, told the *Globe* that she and her son were stunned by the severity of the charges.[24] She blamed the media for inciting her son to commit a hate crime, suggesting that the teens had been riled up by the inflammatory news reports of the terrorist strikes. In statements made to police, the teens said that they hoped to join the patriotic feeling by buying American flags for Jennings' car. Instead of following through with the purchase, they decided to find an Arab-owned business and throw rocks at it. This plan eventually turned into the arson attack on Patel's store.

The *Globe* reported that Massachusetts Muslims agreed that the television coverage of 9/11 may have exacerbated emotions, particularly the repetitive airing of footage showing the Twin Towers collapsing.[25] Although they understood why the youths were angry, Muslim community leaders thought that the arsonists should be held accountable for their actions. At a news conference, Tahir Chaudhry of the Islamic Center of Boston told journalists that he was becoming aware of the omnipresent American flag, which reminded him of seeing anti-immigrant community members in Britain flying the Union Jack as a gesture of nativism.[26]

Family-owned convenience stores were particularly vulnerable to post-9/11 attacks if they were built prior to the 1970s, when store entryways were redesigned to protect cashier safety. In response to the surge in hate crimes taking place across the country, security expert Rosemary Erickson recommended that minority-owned "mom-and-pop" stores install slow-entrance surveillance cameras, use fencing, and clearly define property borders to deter bigots and other assailants.[27]

The same evening as the Somerset arson, other Massachusetts businesses were targeted in backlash hate crimes. Shortly before 10:00 p.m. on September 12, 2001, a gunman in Sterling threatened a clerk outside of an In and Out Market, blaming the minority employee for 9/11. Sheriff's officials reported that David

Wayne Murray, a 34-year old resident of Lovettsville, was arrested and charged with brandishing a firearm during the commission of this crime.[28]

On occasion, Bay state arsonists attempted to burn down minority-owned businesses. *Newsday* reported that on September 12, 2001, an arsonist targeted the Mahmanawaz Grocery in Nesconset.[29] This attack alarmed ethnic communities, who worried about an escalation of xenophobia. Elsewhere in Massachusetts, arsonists attacked ethnic restaurants in the days following 9/11. In Plymouth, an Arab-American man discovered his pizzeria had been destroyed by an arsonist on September 15, 2001. According to the *Globe*, local police suspected that the arson was likely a bias-motivated attack since its owner, Salah El-Ehmeada, was a Muslim of Iraqi descent.[30] The fire caused $60,000 in damage to the restaurant.

At the height of the backlash, Massachusetts vandals targeted businesses that sold Arabic and Persian food. In Wollaston, a vandal threw a rock through the window of a Middle Eastern grocery store.[31] Other businesses were attacked in similar fashion. In Quincy, vandals used rocks to smash the window of Almaeedah Market. In the aftermath of this crime, Iranian-American owner Mohammed Saadat told the *Patriot-Ledger* that he was so worried about additional reprisals that he put an American flag in his store window to reassure customers of his patriotism.[32] Saadat told the newspaper that he appreciated neighbors' offers to pay for the store repairs.[33] Despite the hate crime, Saadat still felt grateful to the U.S. for allowing him to immigrate in 1984 to obtain medical care for his son, who had cystic fibrosis.[34]

Along with damaging their property, vigilantes openly threatened minority business owners. According to the *Patriot-Ledger*, bigots repeatedly harassed Quincy road construction businessman Robert Derbes, a U.S.-born senior citizen whose father had emigrated from Lebanon. Derbes told the *Patriot-Ledger* he received three menacing phone calls and seven hate letters after 9/11.[35] He also said that the backlash was un-American, undermining the country's commitment to pluralism.[36] Because bias crimes were becoming increasingly frequent, Massachusetts police officers advised ethnic minorities to change their routes and travel in groups whenever possible.

Bigots sometimes targeted Bay State businesses mistakenly associated with the Middle East. The Araban Coffee Company, located in Hingham, received several menacing calls after 9/11 questioning whether the business was Arab-owned. A few days later, on September 18, 2001, a vandal threw a rock at one of the company-owned trucks, shattering the window. The *Patriot-Ledger* reported that company owner Joseph Leary was not Middle Eastern, and had chosen the Oriental-sounding business name because it was close to "arabica," which refers to high-quality coffee beans.[37]

On occasion, angry Americans attacked immigrant-owned coffee shops. In Everett, a vandal used softballs to shatter the window of a Mediterranean café. According to the *Boston Globe*, the perpetrator wrote pro-American slogans on the projectiles.[38] Owner Niko Vramis, an American of Greek and Italian ethnicity, speculated that the assailant was aiming for a nearby Middle Eastern café, and hit the wrong business.[39] Other members of the community wondered if all ethnic businesses were becoming potential targets of angry nativists.

Muslim-owned food stores were singled out in other parts of Massachusetts. The *Patriot-Ledger* reported that in the days following 9/11, a vandal attacked Tedeschi's Food Shop in North Quincy, writing "support boycott" on the store windows.[40] Investigators assumed that the perpetrator mistakenly associated the Pakistani-American store owner with the 9/11 terrorists, and was acting to damage business revenues.

Massachusetts bigots also hurt minority-run businesses by spreading malicious rumors about their owners' political views. In Worcester, xenophobes circulated an email falsely claiming that when Farid Aoude first heard about the terrorist strikes at his Middle Eastern restaurant, he began celebrating, causing patrons to leave in disgust. The email urged community members to punish Aoude by boycotting his business. The false rumor became so ubiquitous that Dianne Williamson, a journalist for the *Telegram and Gazette*, devoted her September 16th and September 18th columns to clearing Aoude's name, informing her readers that Aoude was attending a wedding in Ireland at the time he was supposedly celebrating the hijackings in Massachusetts.[41] Because of Williamson's intervention, many community residents began eating at Aoude's restaurant, The Sahara, as a show of support against racial scapegoating.

Minority workers were also singled out in other states. In New York, bigots frequently targeted minority employees in the aftermath of the terrorist attacks. Since so many area residents were traumatized by 9/11, many locals vented their rage on innocent Middle Eastern and South Asian service workers. Street merchants and outdoor food vendors were harassed if they looked Middle Eastern or wore Islamic attire. Because of their constant exposure to the public, these workers had difficulty protecting themselves from unwelcome attention. At times, verbal harassment escalated into physical confrontations. According to the *New York Times*, immigrant news stand workers were occasionally punched in post-9/11 assaults.[42]

Other minority employees were also targeted in the city. On September 12, 2001, a Palestinian-American answering phones at NYC's Arab-American Family Service Center received death threats, with one caller informing staff members that they should all die for what they did to the U.S.[43] Workers found it difficult to concentrate on their jobs in such a hostile environment.

South Asian businesses owners were also attacked in New York. In East Harlem, a Pakistani candy store owner was beaten by five teenagers in a bias assault, according to the September 14, 2001 issue of the *Boston Globe*.[44] The victim believed he was singled out because of his religion and national origin. Elsewhere in New York City, Yemeni delis were vandalized, frightening Muslim employees.[45]

The 9/11 backlash also affected minority business owners in the area. In Westchester, an Arab-American store owner was assaulted with pepper spray in mid-September, 2001.[46] The attack alarmed area residents, who worried about escalating xenophobia.

In Suffolk county, an arsonist poured a flammable substance on the rear door of Nehman Nawarz's grocery store and set it ablaze.[47] According to the *New York Post*, the perpetrator likely targeted the business because its owner was a Pakistani Muslim.[48]

Minority-owned businesses in Collingswood, New Jersey were also targeted during the 9/11 backlash. Bigots vandalized two Indian businesses in mid-September 2001, writing menacing graffiti warning the owners to leave town.[49] These bias-motivated attacks reminded some Garden State residents of the "Dot-buster" attacks of the 1980s.

Minority journalists were sometimes harassed or assaulted while researching news stories about the 9/11 backlash. In mid-September, 2001, Suman Mazumar, journalist for *India Abroad*, was struck by a man in Jersey City while investigating hate crimes.[50] Because bias incidents were occurring in areas where race relations were inflamed, Mazumar and other minority reporters often put themselves in perilous situations while chronicling American hate crimes for domestic or foreign news agencies. Prior to his bias-motivated attack, Mazumar had interviewed community members in intolerant neighborhoods, and visited a Jersey temple that had been damaged with a Molotov cocktail shortly after the terrorist strikes.[51]

While bigots saw 9/11 as an opportunity to vent their racism, other Americans were outraged that their fellow citizens would blame innocent minorities for the strikes on the Pentagon and World Trade Center. Many community members took it upon themselves to reassure backlash victims that they were integral parts of the American fabric. In Rhode Island, residents of Pawtucket intervened collectively after bigots wrote anti-Arab graffiti in town and smashed the front windows of Basra's Market on September 15, 2001.[52]

Business owner Khalil Elmasri was shocked by the attack on his store. When the alarm company called at 3:00 a.m. and alerted him that his business had been attacked, he drove to the crime scene and surveyed the broken glass covering the floor. He then called 911. Pawtucket police chief George Kelley II. told the *Providence Journal* he was dismayed that such an ugly act of intolerance took place in his district.[53] Elmasri, a Lebanese-American Muslim, was so disturbed by the incident that he took a week off of work, staying home with his American-born wife and two children in Rehoboth. He told the *Providence Journal* that the attack made him afraid for his life, reminding him of the dangers he experienced in the Middle East.[54]

Elmasri's faith in his adopted country was restored when Pawtucket residents came to his assistance. According to the *Providence Journal*, T-shirt printing shop owner Rick Roth was so disheartened by what happened to Elmasri that he organized a community fund-raising drive to cover the costs of repairing the damage.[55] Roth collected $1,086 from area businesses and schools, limiting each donation to a maximum of

$10 so that the entire community could contribute to the repairs.[56] Roth also delivered messages from many of the donors, handing Elmasri letters from children and adults expressing their outrage about what happened to his store. Students from Samuel Slater Junior High in Pawtucket also sent Elmasri a letter, telling him they contributed $80 because they wanted to take a stand against intolerance.

A year after his store was targeted, Elmasri told the *Providence Journal* that he felt more welcome than ever in Pawtucket.[57] He reported that many new customers came in to reassure him that the community was a tolerant place. To honor his American and Lebanese heritage, Elmasri hung 10 American flags on the store's awning and put up a sign containing an Arabic blessing.[58] He acknowledged that many of his customers enjoyed the bi-cultural flavor of his store, appreciating its Arabic music and prominent Red Socks banner.

To thank Roth for organizing the fund-raising drive, community residents allowed him to paint the first of approximately 11,000 tiles on the Wall of Hope, Providence's permanent monument to 9/11. According to the *Providence Journal,* Roth took the opportunity to inscribe Edmund Burke's famous proverb, "All that is necessary for the triumph of evil is that good people do nothing."[59]

Despite the laudable efforts of activists, hate crimes continued taking place throughout the East Coast. In the immediate aftermath of 9/11, minority-owned businesses were targeted in Connecticut. In Bristol, a bigot walked into a sandwich shop owned by a man of Middle Eastern descent and threatened to blow up the eatery.[60] Police arrested the perpetrator for making the death threat. In Torrington, a bigot attacked a Muslim-operated convenience store, breaking the window with a rock bearing the message that the businesses' minority employees should return to their own countries.[61] In Bethel, a vandal threw a 60-pound rock through the window of a Pakistani-owned shop. In response to this attack, owner Hamid Raza told *Asianweek* that he was dismayed to have been victimized during the 9/11 backlash, particularly since his Discount Dollar store sold American flags and other patriotic merchandise.[62]

In Pennsylvania, Arab-owned businesses were scapegoated shortly after the terrorist strikes, perhaps in part because one of the hijacked planes crashed in the state. In mid-September 2001, intruders ransacked two Philadelphia grocery stores owned by Arab-Americans, taking merchandise in retaliation for 9/11.[63] Many community activists were dismayed that ethnic groups were being scapegoated in a city that had a reputation for liberty and tolerance.

SEPTEMBER 2001 ATTACKS AT WORK: DC, VIRGINIA, AND MARYLAND

Minorities working near the Pentagon were particularly vulnerable during the backlash. A few hours after the hijackings, a bigot attacked a Muslim book store in Alexandria, Virginia, frightening store manager Hazim Barakat, a 44-year old Palestinian immigrant. According to the *Washington Post*, the vandal shattered the store's windows with two bricks, which were inscribed with obscenities and racist remarks.[64] One contained anti-Arab slurs and explicit death threats, comparing Barakat to the 9/11 hijackers. Barakat, who ran the Old Town Islamic Bookstore for the American Muslim Foundation, told the *Post* that he was not surprised by the hate crime, noting that on many occasions, American news programs unfairly associated Islam with terrorism.[65]

In the aftermath of the bias attack, Barakat said that many people from Alexandria sent condolence cards and flowers. Other members of the community, outraged by the bigotry-motivated vandalism, offered to repair the broken windows. These acts of kindness made Barakat feel more accepted in the U.S.

Other minority-owned businesses were targeted in Alexandria. On September 23, 2001, a vandal threw a rock through a convenience store owned by Mohammed Waheed, a Pakistani-American. He told the *Times-Picayune* that he had trouble understanding why he was being blamed for 9/11, particularly since he was a naturalized citizen and his children had been born in the U.S.[66]

Backlash hate crimes also took place in the nation's capital. High-profile employees of Arab-American organizations were particularly at risk. James Zogby, the director of the Arab-American Institute, received a menacing voice mail message at 7:30 a.m. on September 12, 2001 at his D.C. office. According to the *Boston Globe*, the caller referred to Zogby as a "towel head," and threatened to slit the throats of all Arabs, including the civil rights leader's children.[67] Since the Arab-American Institute's office had been firebombed in 1980 and ADC activist Alex Odeh had been murdered in a bias crime, Zogby took the threat seriously and reported it to governmental authorities. The death threat was traced back to Hanover resident Zachary Rolnik, a 40-year old academic publishing executive with a master's degree from the Kennedy School of Government. Rolnik eventually pled guilty to the offense and was sentenced to two months of community confinement and a $5,000 fine. Federal attorney Ralph Boyd, Jr. told the *Globe* that the sentence was appropriate, since the caller threatened a national figure who championed the rights of a vulnerable minority group.[68]

Along with targeting civil rights organizations, bigots attacked ethnic restaurants in D.C. In Georgetown, employees at the Afghan Kabob restaurant began receiving anonymous death threats shortly after 9/11. Owner Sameera Sayed contacted police after the first few calls, but authorities told her that they were unable to take action.[69] Sayed, who had fled Afghanistan in the 1980s, was dismayed that police officers were unwilling to take steps to protect her business. The verbal harassment eventually escalated into a serious hate crime. On September 14, 2001, assailants trashed the restaurant, breaking the front window and overturning flower pots.[70] The vandals also left death threats at the scene, writing graffiti on the store front associating the owners with the 9/11 terrorists.

Although Sayed was disheartened by the attack, she was comforted by the compassionate community response to the hate crime.[71] Despite the verbal sympathy she was given, Sayed suffered financially as a result of the vandalism. Although many customers expressed their condolences, many regular patrons began eating elsewhere because they were afraid the assailant might attack again. Sayed reported that wedding reception reservations were down, although the restaurant was used to having the ballroom fully booked three months in advance.[72]

In Maryland, bigots targeted businesses owned by South Asians. According to the *Washington Post*, an arsonist firebombed a Sikh-owned restaurant in Baltimore shortly after 9/11.[73] In the aftermath of the attack, residents wondered if it was safe to eat at ethnic eateries, since so many of them were being torched by nativists.

SEPTEMBER 2001 ATTACKS AT WORK: SOUTH

At the height of the 9/11 backlash, minority-owned businesses were targeted by angry nativists in the South. The *St. Petersburg Times* reported that on September 13, 2001, an arsonist in Hernando County, Florida tried to burn down a wall of a commercial building after spray-painting it with ethnic slurs about Arabs and Hispanics.[74] Latino community members were dismayed that they were being targeted by bigots and worried that post-9/11 nativism would affect their employment prospects.

Florida Muslims frequently experienced post-9/11 job discrimination and workplace harassment, particularly if they also happened to be Middle Eastern, Asian, black, or Latino. In chapter six, I discussed how Sussan Salazar, a Muslim convert from Columbia, encountered 9/11 bigotry at her American school. The 18-year old also dealt with employment discrimination in South Florida during the backlash. When she wore a short head scarf to work, she was immediately fired from her snack stand job after her employer realized she was Muslim.[75] She interviewed bareheaded for another job at a different stand at the same mall, and was hired by a manager who said her religious background was not a problem. When she began this position, the owner informed her that she was not permitted to wear her head scarf at work. Salazar told the *Florida Sun Sentinel* that she was surprised by the mistreatment, particularly because the store predominantly displayed a sign saying that the business would not tolerate discrimination on the basis of race or religion.[76]

Backlash racism also affected minority workers in Louisiana. In New Orleans, a restaurant chain that served Middle Eastern food was targeted a few days after 9/11. According to the *Times-Picayune*, the restaurant received bomb threats in mid-September 2001 in misplaced retaliation for the terrorist attacks.[77] Elsewhere in the city, Arab service workers were threatened by area nativists. Mahmoud Sarmini, a spokesman for the Islamic Center of New Orleans, reported that Muslim businessmen in the area began receiving menacing calls immediately after the terrorist strikes.[78] In New Orleans, two Arab store owners were threatened by an angry bigot. Discussing this incident in the New Orleans City Business, Palestinian merchants Atef and Odeh Nassar reported that a man came into their store and told them that someone ought to blow them up.[79] Rather than contact the authorities, they decided to take no legal action against the stranger who threatened their lives, realizing that his conduct was likely a grief response to the hijackings. Although the Arab brothers could empathize with the man's horror about 9/11, the incident made them take additional security precautions. Like so many other minorities, Odeh Nassar began curtailing his evening activities, going straight home after working from 7:00 a.m. to 8:00 p.m.[80]

Other minority-owned businesses were targeted in the state. In Chalmette, a vandal damaged the window of a convenience store in mid-September, 2001.[81] Since the shop owner was a Muslim, the *New Orleans City Business* speculated that it was likely a post-9/11 bias attack.[82]

Elsewhere in Louisiana, bigots slandered minority employees by claiming they supported terrorism. In Denham Springs, local residents spread false rumors that Middle-Eastern workers at the Cactus Café celebrated when learning about the attacks on the Pentagon and World Trade Center.[83] Shortly thereafter, on September 23, 2001, a vandal shattered the window of the restaurant.

According to the Baton Rouge *Advocate*, the attack was apparently a post-9/11 nativist hate crime targeting Iranian owner Jerome Saleh and Palestinian manager Samir Tanib, even though the two men had lived in the U.S. for decades.[84] Police chief Jeff Wesley launched an investigation, exploring whether the vandalism was linked to the malicious gossip about the business. Tanib told the *Advocate* that he and the American-born employees were horrified by the hijackings, and would never celebrate such a tragedy.[85] Mayor Jim DeLaune, an occasional patron of the restaurant, said that prior to the rock-throwing attack, he assumed that community members were savvy enough to realize that the rumors were untrue.[86] Since the local investigation produced no suspects, authorities contacted the FBI, hoping that federal agents could make progress in the case.

On occasion, Louisiana bigots attempted to organize community boycotts of minority-owned stores in retaliation for the terrorist strikes in New York and Washington. According to the *Times-Picayune*, a September 2001 flyer listed 51 Muslim-owned businesses in the state and urged the public to boycott all of them.[87] The leaflet also cautioned restraint when targeting Muslim-owned businesses, so that American employees would not be hurt inadvertently.[88] The author of the flyer apparently never considered that the minority store owners might also be Americans. Damin Horieh, a Pineville store owner targeted by the boycott, told the *Times-Picayune* that he felt angry and hurt when concerned customers showed him copies of the leaflet.[89] Despite the boycott, he told the newspaper that minority businesses were not going anywhere, and that most Americans were above this kind of scapegoating.

SEPTEMBER 2001 ATTACKS AT WORK: MIDWEST

During the backlash, minority-owned businesses were targeted throughout the Midwest. In Missouri, a man threatened a Palestinian-American store owner on September 12, 2001. According to the *St. Louis Post Dispatch*, the attacker told the Arab-American merchant that he was at war with him.[90] Rather than escalate the situation, the businessman calmly replied that he was also an American, deserving the same rights and protections as any other citizen.[91]

Many hate crimes took place in Ohio, a state with a large number of Arab-Americans. The *Plain Dealer* reported that in the first week after 9/11, there were 34 bias-motivated attacks in Cleveland, particularly in a retail neighborhood known as "Little Arabia."[92] In one of the more serious incidents, three assailants threw bleach in the eyes of an Arab-American shopkeeper.[93] Following the assault, the perpetrators ran off into the night.

Some Cleveland businesses were repeatedly attacked. Holy Land Imports, a grocery store specializing in Middle Eastern food, was targeted several times in the first three days after 9/11. On two separate occasions, vandals threw a bottle through the store's front window. Bigots also heckled minority customers from cars, singling them out for shopping there. Arab-American owner Mohammad Mohammad told the *Plain Dealer* that the attacks and harassment scared away shoppers, causing a steep decline in revenue.[94]

Stores in Dayton were also targeted. On the evening of September 11th or the morning of the 12th, an assailant shattered the window of the Food Mart on Linden Avenue.[95] The Middle Eastern owner told police that immediately before the attack, he had received calls threatening to burn down his building. On occasion, vigilantes in the area looted minority-owned businesses in misplaced retaliation for the terrorist strikes. According to the *Dayton Daily News*, police responded to a burglar alarm call at Go Wireless at 1:20 a.m. on September 12th' and found the display cases shattered and the contents ransacked.[96] While investigating the burglary, authorities discovered anti-Arab graffiti on the walls of the store. The perpetrator also defaced the store owner's car with anti-Arab, pro-U.S. messages.[97] Community activists were dismayed that the perpetrators were conflating American patriotism with xenophobia. Minority-owned stores were also targeted in other parts of the city, including a break-in at Food City.[98]

The backlash was also felt in Illinois, particularly in cities with prominent Arab-American business districts. In Chicago, a mob shattered the windows of 18 Arab-owned stores on Harlem Avenue.[99] Because most of the 180,000 Arabs in that metropolitan area lived within a 14-mile corridor from 63rd and Kedzie to 180th and Lagrange Road, these ethnic shops were easy targets for angry bigots.

Sikh professionals were also singled out in the city. In many instances, they were viewed with suspicion while performing their regular work activities. According to the September 28, 2001 issue of *India Abroad*, Harpal Singh, a Caucasian Sikh, was visiting a client in Chicago when someone called the police about him, assuming he was a terrorist because of his turban and beard.[100] Minority employees who worked in the vicinity of landmark buildings were especially likely to be treated with open hostility.

In other parts of the Midwest, nativists targeted ethnic restaurants. A few days after 9/11, a bigot vandalized Samira's Restaurant, an Afghan eatery in Bloomington, Indiana. While surveying the destruction, owner Anwar Naderpoor discovered that the vandal had smashed a window and covered a wall with bias-motivated obscenities. Naderpoor told the *Denver Post* that the destruction made him fear for his personal safety, particularly since the culprit had not been apprehended.[101] Although Naderpoor had come to the U.S. from Afghanistan more than two decades prior to 9/11, he was dismayed that the perpetrator blamed him for the strikes on the Pentagon and World Trade Center. Naderpoor's worries about backlash bigotry abated somewhat when his customers brought him flowers as a show of support.

Elsewhere in the state, Arab businesses were attacked in the aftermath of the terrorist strikes. In South Bend, an arsonist doused the exterior of grocery store with flammable liquids and set it on fire on September 29, 2001. The *South Bend Tribune* reported that a concerned citizen called the fire department after noticing the 11:15 p.m. fire at John's Friendly Super on East Calvert Street.[102] Although firefighters got the blaze under control within ten minutes, it caused $3,000 in structural damage and an additional $5,000 in lost merchandise. The arson attack also damaged the store's cooling system. Although the building was owned by Bruce Tassell, investigators suspected that the deliberately-set fire was a bias crime targeting Marwan Farhan, an Israeli Arab Muslim who leased space in the building for his grocery store.

The *Tribune* reported that Farhan was deeply troubled by the arson, believing that he was being singled out because of his religious background and ethnicity.[103] He noted that the grocery store was important to his family's financial survival, since he and his wife had nine children. Abdal Farhan, the victim's 17-year old son, told the *Tribune* that he was upset by the hate crime and the post-9/11 hostility he experienced while working at his father's cash register, noting that customers had began telling him to leave the country and go back to where he belonged.[104] The teenager explained that the bigotry was misplaced because his family supported America and participated in fundraising efforts to help the families of the World Trade Center victims, collecting $500 for the Red Cross.[105] Although the Farhan family handed out American flags to children, some members of the community began treating them like outsiders.

In response to the surge in hate crimes, minority workers in Indiana became concerned about their safety, particularly since the state had the dual distinctions of having been a KKK stronghold in the early 20th century and having the fifth-largest concentration of Muslims in the U.S. in 2001.

In other parts of the Midwest, minority professionals and business owners received threats at the height of the backlash. In Wisconsin, Thomas Iverson called an Arab-owned liquor store on September 29, 2001 and frightened the Jordanian-American owner with a bomb threat. According to the *Madison Capital Times*, Iverson later pled guilty to the crime and was sentenced to 27 months incarceration on April 12, 2002.[106] Other Wisconsin bigots were also convicted of bias-motivated crimes. In the aftermath of the terrorist attacks, Wesley Fritts sent an anthrax hoax to an Arab-American restaurant in the state.[107] He admitted his culpability, and was sentenced in Madison to 21 months in jail on May 13, 2002.

SEPTEMBER 2001 ATTACKS AT WORK: CENTRAL STATES

The 9/11 backlash also reached into the heartland of America. Just as innocent ethnic and religious minorities were attacked in the region in the aftermath of the Oklahoma City bombing, immigrant groups in the Central States were scapegoated after 9/11. In Oklahoma, South Asian employees were targeted in the wake of the terrorist strikes. The *Tulsa World* reported that a knife-wielding assailant terrorized an Indian convenience store worker in Broken Arrow shortly after 9/11.[108] Later that same week, the victim's brother, Subneet Sahjal, was attacked at his apartment, presumably by assailants who followed him home from his convenience store job.[109] At the same Quik Stop where Subneet Sahjal worked, customer Naveed Alam was assaulted in yet another bias-motivated attack.[110] In the aftermath of these hate crimes, Quik Stop owner Aris Saboor told the *Tulsa World* that his other South Asian store employees had become terrified that they might also be assaulted during their shifts.[111] Because so many South Asians in Oklahoma were being targeted at their service jobs, many employees became reluctant to go to work.

Hate crimes also took place in nearby states. In the introduction, I briefly mentioned that a Utah bigot set fire to a restaurant owned by a Pakistani-American family at the height of the 9/11 backlash. On September 13, 2001, James Herrick, a 31-year old resident of Salt Lake City, poured two jars of gasoline on the Curry-in-a-Hurry restaurant, igniting the eatery while it was full of diners. Customers helped douse the blaze, which charred a wall. Mona Nisar, one of the owners, told the *Los Angeles Times* that she was grateful that the damage was contained, thanks to the heroic actions of the restaurant patrons, who came from diverse racial and religious backgrounds.[112] She also expressed her dismay that she knew the assailant, who sometimes ate there.

The Nisars said they were shocked by the arson attack, especially since they were American citizens who had lived in Salt Lake City since 1984. Yassir Nisar told the *Deseret Morning News* that his family was stunned that such a reprehensible bias crime could occur in the U.S.[113] The family was grateful for the community support they received after the arson, noting that customers and neighbors came by with flowers and condolence cards.[114]

Prosecutors acted promptly to bring Herrick to justice, issuing a statement condemning backlash hate crimes as an assault on the values embodied in the U.S. Constitution. Defense attorney Tom Rasmussen advised Herrick to take a plea on the federal charges so his sentence would be reduced from 10 years to four, even though accepting the agreement meant that he still faced an aggravated arson charge in state court. On October 24, 2001, Herrick pled guilty to a federal hate crime, admitting to U.S. Magistrate Ronald Boyce that he committed the arson in response to 9/11 and the hatred he felt for Arabs and Muslims.[115] He also confessed that he targeted members of the Nisar family because he thought they were of Middle Eastern heritage.[116] He expressed remorse for his actions, telling the court that what he did was very stupid.[117] The Nisars accepted his apology, and hugged Herrick's fiancée.

On January 7, 2002, Herrick was sentenced to 51 months incarceration for the bias-motivated offense. He eventually served concurrent sentences on state charges of first-degree felony aggravated arson and a federal civil rights violation. He told the *Deseret Morning News* that he had difficulty understanding why he tried to burn down the Pakistani-Americans' business, since he frequented the restaurant prior to the arson and thought the owners were nice.[118]

SEPTEMBER 2001 ATTACKS AT WORK: SOUTHWEST

Minority merchants were also targeted in the Southwest. According to the *Arizona Daily Star*, a local Hindu shopkeeper, Jayanti Patel, was harassed during the 9/11 backlash.[119] Customers entered his convenience store and accused him of being Muslim, yelling that he and other members of his faith needed to get out of the U.S.

Sometimes, customers reacted poorly when they saw minority-owned businesses flying the American flag. The *Arizona Daily Star* reported that a local shopper demanded that an Arab-American convenience store owner take down the stars and stripes he had displayed in his front window.[120] Civil rights activists were disturbed that ultra-nationalists were undermining the true meaning of the flag by using it as a symbol of exclusion.

On occasion, dark-skinned physicians experienced post-9/11 discrimination in Arizona. In Tempe, a drunken emergency room patient attacked a South Asian doctor who was trying to treat him at St. Luke's Medical Center. According to *Asianweek*, police and hospital staff reported that the 39-year old patient choked the Pakistani-American physician and yelled derogatory remarks at him, blaming him for the terrorist strikes.[121]

The 9/11 backlash also affected minority employees in New Mexico. In Santa Fe, a vandal painted a racial slur on a Middle Eastern man's business in mid-September, 2001. Deputy police chief Beverly Lennen told the *Albuquerque Journal* that other minority-owned stores in Santa Fe were also attacked by vandals, who scratched the buildings and pelted them with eggs.[122] The city council condemned these bias-motivated attacks, urging U.S. citizens to treat one another with respect and ensure that no one was singled out because of religious or ethnic differences.[123]

Minority business owners and workers were also harassed in other parts of the Southwest. Reacting to the heavy losses the NYPD suffered when the Twin Towers fell, police officers in Texas occasionally vented their rage on area Muslims. The *Austin American Statesman* reported that on the evening of 9/11, an off-duty police officer put a gun to the head of a local Pakistani store owner.[124] In the aftermath of this incident, community organizations expressed concern that police departments were doing so little to protect vulnerable immigrant groups from attacks perpetrated by bigots and law enforcement officials.

Throughout Texas, nativists frequently targeted Middle Eastern restaurants in the aftermath of the terrorist strikes. In some instances, bigots made threatening calls and vandalized minority-owned eateries. The *San Antonio Express-News* reported that assailants smashed the glass door and two windows of Shiraz Fine Persian Cuisine in Olmos Park on September 13, 2001.[125] Although owner Rashin Mazaheri was upset by the attack, she was also appreciative of the interfaith community support she received after the hate crime. At a San Antonio community meeting about the bias-motivated vandalism, approximately 70 members of Tri-faith Dialogue, a group uniting Christians, Muslims, and Jews, sent messages decrying the destruction and offering condolences.[126] Area Sikhs also gave Mazaheri their support, acknowledging that ethnic minorities were part of the fabric of the U.S. and affirming that all citizens were entitled to equal protection under the law. Mazaheri was deeply thankful that so many community members vocally condemned the hate crime. She was also appreciative of the fact that her business improved after the vandalism since many area residents showed their support by eating at her restaurant. Many customers were saddened that Mazaheri was being unfairly associated with the 9/11 hijackers since she had done her part to help 9/11 victims. On October 20, 2001, she hosted a benefit brunch to help the families of the terrorist attacks, demonstrating her willingness to help others in a time of national crisis.

Although many Americans worked to curb hate crimes in their communities, minority businesses continued to be targeted. In Southwest Houston, a Goodyear tire store was burned down in a deliberately-set fire in mid-September 2001.[127] Although officials were reluctant to declare it was a bias-motivated arson, many news publications asserted that the attack was clearly hate-motivated. The *Houston Chronicle* reported that the Pakistani-owned business was set on fire after several customers made threats and racial slurs against the owner and his son.[128] According to this newspaper, the three arsonists flew into a violent rage when they noticed the tire store owner had a Muslim name.[129]

Muslim service workers were occasionally assaulted in Texas. According to the *Houston Chronicle*, Bangladeshi convenience store owner Rafiq Punjwani was attacked at work in a backlash hate crime.[130] A man claiming to have a knife entered Punjwani's store in Southwest Houston on September 14, 2001, and threatened to burn the business down. During the incident, Punjwani pushed an emergency call button alerting the police that a crime was in progress. They responded to the distress signal, and promptly arrested the perpetrator. Although his assailant was apprehended, Punjwani was shaken by the backlash attack, realizing his neighborhood business and standing in the community was irrevocably altered by the terrorist strikes.

Backlash attacks took place in other Texas cities. In Hewitt, Joe Montez made threatening phone calls targeting two Muslim clerks at a truck stop on September 17, 2001. According to the *Los Angeles Times*, Montez first asked the clerks if they were Iranians, and then told them that there was a bomb in the building, right where they were standing.[131] Months after the phone threat, Montez apologized for his actions. On January 30, 2002, he was sentenced to two years of probation and a $500 fine.

In Northwest Austin, an arsonist set a Muslim-owned carpet store on fire on September 23, 2001. Jerusalem-born Marwan Janlani told the *Austin American Statesman* that he discovered the blaze when he opened the door of Capital Carpet and discovered hot smoke engulfing his face.[132] By following a trail of fuel, investigators discovered that someone used flammable liquid to start the fire, which resulted in approximately $150,000 in smoke and water damage to the building and its contents. The fire and sprinklers also caused minor damage to nearby businesses, including a Chinese restaurant, a smoothie shop, and a furniture store. The day after the destruction, Capital Carpet's "Grand Opening" banner still remained above the store's entrance.[133] Janlani told the *Austin American Statesman* of his determination to re-open his store, noting that his loss was nothing compared to the tragedy of 9/11 victims.[134]

During the backlash, many Arab-Americans were upset that their fellow citizens were attacking their businesses and questioning their patriotism. Nicole Betters told the *San Antonio Express-News* that she was outraged that her countrymen refused to acknowledge that ethnic minority workers could be loyal Americans, pointing out that her Arab-American great grandfather was a decorated World War II. paratrooper who dropped on D-Day and spent time in a German prison camp.[135]

SEPTEMBER 2001 ATTACKS AT WORK: WEST COAST

On the West Coast, minority employees were frequently targeted during the 9/11 backlash, particularly in service industries where they were highly concentrated. Throughout California, minority store owners and clerks were often harassed or attacked by customers and other members of the public. Because of their extensive contact with strangers, minority personnel had difficulty shielding themselves from the anger of nativists.

In Southern California, Muslim health care workers were occasionally scapegoated during the backlash. The *Los Angeles Times* reported that on the day of the terrorist strikes, a female client grilled physical therapist Salwa Abdel-Aal about her religious background and demanded to be treated by a caregiver of another faith.[136] Abdel-Aal told the newspaper that she was an American, and was outraged that her fellow citizens would act so shamefully. Because of the intensity of the post-9/11 xenophobia, she worried that minority children would become emotionally scarred by community intolerance.[137]

Arab merchants were frequently scapegoated in the region. In Riverside, Abdullah Abdullah, a 35-year old Arab shop owner on University Avenue, was repeatedly harassed. He told the *Press-Enterprise* that he began receiving between 10 and 15 menacing phone calls a day at his shop in the weeks after 9/11.[138] Since his business catered to Arab-Americans, he experienced a dramatic decline in revenue during the backlash, since so many of his customers were staying home instead of venturing outside.[139] To protect himself against hate crimes, Abdullah began start closing his store early, instead of keeping it open until 10:00 or 11:00 p.m. on week nights.

Bigots also targeted Arab businesses in other parts of Southern California. On September 29, 2001, the *Los Angeles Times* reported that a gunman shot at an Antelope Valley convenience store owned by a Syrian-American.[140] Although community members were relieved that no one was injured, they worried that ethnic-looking locals might be less fortunate in the future.

On occasion, anti-Arab backlash attacks turned deadly. In Reedley, a Yemeni store owner was shot in an apparent post-9/11 hate crime. On September 29, 2001, shopkeeper Abdo Ali Ahmed, a father of eight, was killed after receiving a death threat and a hate note attacking his ethnicity. The gunmen, who were not apprehended, drove away as Ahmed bled to death on the floor of his store. A more comprehensive discussion of this crime will appear in chapter ten.

At the height of the backlash, Afghan-owned businesses were also singled out throughout the state. The *Los Angeles Times* reported that an Afghan restaurant was destroyed in Encino.[141] This apparent hate crime frightened employees and customers, who feared for their lives.

Afghan workers were particularly vulnerable in Northern California, where they were highly concentrated.[142] On occasion, Afghan managers and employees living in the Bay Area received menacing messages. Wahid Andesha, the owner of the Salang Pass restaurant in Fremont, told the *Boston Globe* that he received a death threat at work on 9/11.[143] Although a customer offered to let Andesha's family stay at his house for safety purposes, the Afghan restaurant owner dismissed the disturbing phone call as the work of a lone idiot. Other Afghan-owned eateries in the city were also targeted. The *Boston Globe* reported that Fremont vandals hurled a bottle and a rock at Pamir Food Market shortly after 9/11 in what authorities presumed was a bias-motivated crime.[144]

Afghan-owned businesses were also targeted in other parts of the Bay Area. In Palo Alto, three teenagers made an obscene gesture at the owner of a pizza parlor shortly after the terrorist strikes. The *Riverside Press-Enterprise* reported that the Afghan-American businessman was initially puzzled by the youths' hostility, and decided to venture outside to ask them why they were angry with him.[145] Before he could speak, they attacked him and shoved him to the ground. They then told him that they blamed him for 9/11 because of his ethnicity. He was shocked by the experience, particularly since he had owned the California pizzeria for 12 years and considered himself an integrated member of the community. After learning of the hate crime, customers and friends sent flowers and condolence cards, expressing their support.

Ethnic eateries were also attacked in San Francisco and other nearby cities. According to *ADL on the Frontline,* Bay Area Afghan and Iranian restaurants were targeted by vandals in the fall of 2001.[146] Some of these businesses were defaced, and others were hit by bottles and rocks. Many diners began eating elsewhere, worrying about their safety.

At the height of the 9/11 backlash, Persian-owned coffee shops were occasionally singled out by Bay Area bigots. Nick Heydarian told the *Chronicle* that he received threatening calls after 9/11 at City Blend Café.[147] He was also harassed in person. In one incident, two women yelled "Palestinian bastard" at him through the open doors of his store, which was located in San Francisco's Mission District.[148] Heydarian was confused about why others were mistaking him for an Arab, explaining that he was a non-practicing Muslim who had emigrated from Iran after spending two years and six months in solitary confinement for writing political poetry and lyrics.[149] He became an American citizen and opened up the café in early 1997, while working as a singer specializing in Farsi love poetry.

Armenian service workers were also harassed in California. In San Diego, Hani Ilaian, owner of a Middle Eastern restaurant on El Cajon Boulevard, told the *San Diego Union Tribune* that he received several death threats in the aftermath of the terrorist strikes.[150] One caller expressed his wish that the ethnic eatery sold rat poison so he could kill Ilaian with it. Another caller said he wished that all Muslims were dead, including members of Ilaian's family. Despite the vicious threats, Ilaian told the *Union Tribune* that he had no choice but to continue running his business, pointing out that he was a naturalized American who had lived in the U.S. for 25 years.[151]

Because of their visibility, South Asian restaurants were frequently attacked during the backlash, endangering minority employees and customers. In Anaheim, bigots repeatedly targeted the Islamic Halal Tandoori Pakistani and Indian Cuisine Restaurant, which was especially popular with local Pakistanis and foreign tourists visiting nearby Disneyland. Even before 9/11, xenophobic teenagers sometimes harassed diners, banging on the glass and then running away.[152] After 9/11, owner Akbar Ali considered changing his restaurant's name so that the eatery would not become a backlash target.[153] Before he had a chance to do so, the harassment escalated.

According to the *Orange County Register*, a group of men pulled up to the restaurant a few days after the terrorist strikes, honking their car horns and yelling at diners and staff.[154] About two weeks later, on September 27, 2001, an arsonist attacked the eatery, causing approximately $150,000 in damages to the 2,400 square foot building.[155] Standing in the charred and smoky remains of his business, Ali told the *Los Angeles Times* that the arson devastated him financially and professionally, leaving him unable to fill eight catering orders for more than 100 people.[156] According to the *Orange County Register*, the 47-year old Pakistani-American was unsure about how he would be able to support his wife and two young children because the demolished restaurant was his sole source of income.[157]

Restaurant employees were also emotionally crushed by the arson. Mohammed Yaqoob, Ali's nephew, lost his job as a cook. He told the *Los Angeles Times* that he was shocked by the hate crime, particularly since his family had worked so hard to give customers a positive dining experience.[158]

Many of Ali's regular clients were also deeply disturbed by the attack. Reacting to the surge in area xenophobia, restaurant patron Ahne Alb said that he wanted to return to his native Yemen after living in the U.S. for 20 years.[159] His wife was also shaken, afraid to leave the house wearing her hijab.[160] Because of the intensity of the backlash, she felt as if she didn't belong in America anymore.

Rather than reach out to Ali and other ethnic community members under attack, some locals expressed their opinion that the South Asian restaurant owner got what he deserved for being Muslim. Tim Lotman, wearing an 'Osama bin Laden, Wanted Dead or Alive' t-shirt, told the *Los Angeles Times* that since the U.S. was at war, Americans needed to round up Muslims and ship them out of the country.[161] When someone informed Lotman that the arson victim was an American, he responded by declaring that the restaurant owner's citizenship should be revoked since he was a Muslim, and that members of his faith needed to get used to being subjected to hate crimes if they chose to continue living in the U.S.[162]

After the arson attack, Ali was forced to spend six months rebuilding his business, exhausting $100,000 of his savings and accumulating another $40,000 in credit card debt.[163] Even after receiving an $80,000 insurance settlement, the fire still ended up costing him tens of thousands of dollars in rebuilding expenses and lost income.

Officials were unwilling to rule the arson attack a hate crime, maintaining that it was possible that the perpetrator randomly-selected the building. South Asians in the area disagreed, suggesting that an arson attack on a Muslim Pakistani restaurant less than two weeks after 9/11 was almost certainly bias-motivated. According to the *Los Angeles Times*, Ali and his clients believed that the fire was triggered by misdirected anger over 9/11.[164] Ali told the *Orange County Register* that he was angry and frustrated that the deliberate fire was never ruled a hate crime, particularly since there was no other explanation for the attack.[165] He was also distressed that he and other innocent minorities were being targeted in backlash hate crimes, pointing out that he and other Muslims were U.S. citizens.[166]

Rather than rebuild his restaurant in the same location, he re-opened it in Diamond Bar, California, in the hopes that the move would deter the arsonist from attacking him again. According to the *Los Angeles Times*, he planned on altering the restaurant's name so that it would no longer be such a conspicuous target for religious and racial bigots.[167] He told the *Register* that relocating to a new venue placed a tremendous emotional and financial burden on his family.[168]

Other South Asian service workers were also harassed by California bigots angry about 9/11. The *Orange County Register* reported that two Sikh ice cream vendors were attacked in Fullerton on September 14, 2001 in a backlash hate crime.[169] While working their regular route, Gucharan and Banso Singh were chased by a bat-wielding bigot in Buena Park. The assailant, 31-year old Jason Fulkerson, was apprehended by police shortly after targeting the married Indian couple. Fulkerson eventually pled guilty to two hate crimes: a felony count of brandishing a dangerous weapon with a hate crime enhancement and a misdemeanor count of violating the civil rights of his victims. Prior to his sentencing, he apologized to his victims on the radio. Superior Judge Roger Robbins ordered Fulkerson to serve 45 days in jail.

Because of their visibility, Sikh managers and clerks were occasionally harassed and beaten by nativists who unfairly associated all turbans with terrorism. In late September 2001, two men attacked and severely injured a South Asian shopkeeper in Northridge, Los Angeles. The *San Francisco Chronicle* reported that the assailants pummeled the Sikh while repeatedly asking him if he was Osama bin Laden.[170]

Along with worrying about hate crimes, Indian merchants were troubled by the financial repercussions of the backlash. The Northern California store, Kumar Jewelers, suffered a precipitous drop in business in the weeks immediately after the terrorist attacks. Discussing this revenue decline in *India-West*, owner Rakesh Verma pointed out that many of his regular customers were worried that they would be targeted if they were seen holding bags from South Asian shops.[171]

SEPTEMBER 2001 ATTACKS AT WORK: PACIFIC NORTHWEST

While American television stations were airing footage of the 9/11 attacks, angry viewers were scapegoating foreign-born workers in the Pacific Northwest. In Washington state, bigots blamed area minorities for the terrorist strikes. The *Tacoma News Tribune* reported that an Indian Hindu employee was harassed and threatened at a Puyallup minimart shortly after 9/11, traumatizing him so severely that he began crying.[172] Elsewhere in the state, nativists targeted ethnic restaurants and their employees. According to the *Yakima Herald*, someone vandalized the Olympic View Deli in Edmonds on September 16, 2001.[173] Although the restaurant owner was a longtime area resident, police suspected that the Iranian business owner was attacked out of bias.

To protect minority workers, sympathetic managers sometimes reassigned vulnerable employees to jobs away from public view. Because fast-food franchise owner Jasmel Sangha was of Indian descent, he worried about backlash hate crimes in Washington state. To prevent bias attacks, he told the *Tacoma News Tribune* that he decided to alter job assignments so that employees who looked Middle Eastern or South Asian had minimal contact with customers.[174] Activists were dismayed that xenophobia had become so prevalent in the U.S. that dark-skinned service workers needed to hide from strangers.

Minority workers in Oregon also felt the effects of the 9/11 backlash. On September 14, 2001, two customers threatened an Iraqi convenience store clerk in Portland. When the Arab merchant asked the men to show their IDs before purchasing beer, the men responded by telling him they planned to blow up Iraq and the store where he was working.[175] In other parts of Oregon, South Asian workers received death threats. In Eugene, Joseph Mungara, a 35-year old Indian-American owner of a Dunkin' Donuts franchise, told *Asianweek* that he had received more than a dozen menacing phone calls blaming him for the terrorist strikes.[176] Vandals also painted graffiti on his store windows.

SEPTEMBER 2001 ATTACKS AT GAS STATIONS

Throughout the U.S., minority service station attendants were frequently targeted during the 9/11 backlash. In some instances, Arab and South Asian workers received death threats. Shortly after the terrorist strikes, an irate man in New Jersey entered a gas station in Monmouth County and asked the clerk about his country of origin.[177] When the employee replied that he was Indian, the bigot took out a knife and said that he would have killed him if he had been Pakistani or Afghani.[178]

Service station workers were also scapegoated in Illinois. In Palos Heights, a Moroccan gas station attendant and convenience store employee was assaulted on September 12, 2001. During this incident, a bigot tried to stab the Arab worker with the blunt end of a machete in retaliation for 9/11.[179] Bias-motivated incidents took place in other parts of the state. In Naperville, gas station owners were falsely accused of being terrorist sympathizers. Irshad and Jafar Khan reported that their service station and grocery store business fell by a third after bigots spread malicious rumors on the internet claiming that the South Asians proudly displayed a portrait of Osama bin Laden.[180] In response, the Khans filed an anti-defamation lawsuit against the community members responsible. Customers who had boycotted the gas station eventually returned once they learned that the service station owners denied the rumor and were taking legal action to challenge it.

In Louisiana, bigots spread racist gossip about minority gas station employees. The owner of Ahmad's Shell station told the *New Orleans City Business* that community members called his establishment and accused his workers of throwing a party after the terrorist strikes.[181] Ahmad felt there was little he could do to shield his employees from xenophobic customers, who frequently gave his service station workers dirty looks. Although Ahmad had received threatening phone calls throughout the 49 years he worked in the U.S., he said the post-9/11 threats were particularly vicious.[182] Instead of protecting Ahmad and his employees from the wrath of area bigots, the FBI opted to investigate Ahmad on suspicion of terrorism because a customer claimed to have overheard a mechanic making a comment about explosive devices.[183] FBI spokeswoman Sheila Thorne defended her agency's investigation of Ahmed, telling the *New Orleans City Business* that the federal government had an obligation to look into all leads regarding future terrorist actions.[184] Some community members questioned why terrorist threats against minority businesses were being discounted by federal authorities.

Gas station employees were also targeted in other states. In Long Island, an irate man singled out a South Asian service station worker, blaming him for the terrorist strikes. Discussing this hate crime, *Newsday* reported that on September 12, 2001, Brian Harris was arrested in Ronkonkoma after waving a pellet gun and screaming anti-Arab obscenities at the Citgo employee.[185]

Bigots in Massachusetts also attacked minority gas station workers. In Weymouth, two arsonists targeted Global Gas at 11:00 p.m. on September 12, 2001. The *Boston Globe* reported that during this attack, a man and a woman doused a pump with gasoline and set it on fire, presumably because the owner was from Lebanon.[186] Firefighters were able to contain the blaze before there were any fatalities.

Arson attacks on service station workers took place in other parts of the Bay State. On September 13, 2001, bigots targeted minority employees at a Mobil gas station across the river from Somerset. Imam Shah, a Pakistani-American, told the *Globe* that a car drove by in the dark, yelled at workers, and threw a chlorine-containing plastic bottle at a pump.[187] Although chlorine is highly flammable when mixed with gasoline, the bottle did not explode because the perpetrator neglected to put oil inside of it. Shah said it was the first time he had ever been a victim of a hate crime in the U.S., noting that he had lived in the country unmolested for 18 years prior to 9/11.[188]

Arsonists also struck in other parts of the country. On September 15, 2001, a Muslim-owned gas station was firebombed in Austin.[189] The attack frightened area minorities, particularly those who worked with the public.

In Oklahoma, community members threatened minority-owned service stations. The *Tulsa World* reported that in the first few days after 9/11, a local Conoco service station received hundreds of menacing calls from enraged residents blaming the Pakistani owner for the terrorist strikes.[190] Gas station worker Lynelle Englehardt answered many of the calls, and was shocked by their viciousness.[191]

On occasion, angry gunmen shot at minority service station attendants. In Indiana, an armed bigot attacked an Arab-owned gas station on September 19, 2001.[192] On this occasion, the gunman opened fire at two Middle Eastern employees in Gary. According to the *Post-Tribune*, the crime took place at Marathon gas station, located at 15th Avenue and Chase St.[193] Although the gunman used an automatic rifle to fire 31 bullets at one of the attendants, the bullet-proof glass protected the targeted service station employee, who was of Iranian descent. The other employee frightened by the gunfire was a Yemeni-American. Because the assailant wore a ski mask and all-black clothing, the victims were unable to give police a helpful description of their attacker.

A week later, another Indiana gunman attacked a Marathon station employee working near Interstate 65.[194] The *Post-Tribune* reported that the victim, who was of Indian descent, was ambushed from outside the building by automatic rifle fire.[195] According to Merrillville FBI agent Charles Porucznik, Lake County crime lab workers performed forensic analysis of the spent shell casings and determined that the bullets from the two attacks were fired from different guns.[196]

In many parts of the country, bigoted customers and community members yelled threats at minority gas station attendants. The September 20, 2001 issue of the *Milwaukee Journal Sentinel* reported that Ashraf Khaled, a Jordanian-American owner of Grafton Citgo, was harassed by a racist woman screaming at him outside his gas station.[197] During this bigoted rant, she told Khaled to return to his own country and informed him that she was sending over her children to beat him up.[198] This was not Khaled's only experience with backlash bigotry. Shortly after the attacks on the World Trade Center and Pentagon, customers asked him and other gas station employees if they were pleased by the terrorist strikes.[199]

In the Los Angeles area, Middle-Eastern service workers were often singled out in the aftermath of 9/11. In Bellflower, James Scott Yungkans targeted a gas station attendant on September 21, 2001. According to the *Los Angeles Times*, Yungkans became enraged when he learned that the employee was from Jerusalem, vowing to blow him up and bomb Israel.[200] Yungkans eventually left the service station, only to return later holding an ammunition canister with the words, "mortar shells," written on its side.[201] The attendant and customers fled in terror, fearing for their lives. Yungkans was eventually apprehended and charged with making a criminal threat.

Attacks on family-run gas stations endangered children as well as adults. In September 2001, a gunman in San Diego sprayed bullets at Mohsen's Oil, destroying the front window and shooting up a patriotic sign in the window. According to the *San Diego Union Tribune*, the hate crime affected every member of the Arabshahi family, who relied on the business for their financial survival.[202] The gas station was owned by Mohsen Arabshahi, an Iranian Muslim who had lived in America for decades, and his wife, Susana Arabshai, a Mexican citizen with permanent U.S. residency. The Arabshahis fell in love at the University of Arizona, and married in 1982. They decided to live in San Diego because they both enjoyed the city's climate. After their second child Nadia was born, Mohsen dropped out of his civil engineering program at SDSU. To support his family, he worked as a real estate broker in the 1980s, but stopped when the recession hit and the market dried up.[203] Mohsen then bought a gas station, and began working from 5:00 a.m. to 11:00 p.m. Many customers came to value Mohsen's friendliness and his interest in learning their names; they also appreciated that during a spring 2001 spike in gas prices, he opted to sell fuel 40 cents cheaper than other area service stations out of concern for working families.[204]

At the time of the hate crime, the Arabshahis' three children were ages 9, 10, and 13. Their youngest child, Nacer, told the *Union Tribune* that he was disturbed to find bullet holes near the cash register where he sometimes worked.[205] The boy also said he was glad his parents hadn't been shot, because that would've ruined his life. Mohsen Arabashahi told the newspaper that the attack made him constantly vigilant, and left him feeling vulnerable.[206] At the same time, he was heartened by customers who sent flowers and offered to replace his window. Rather than cash donations, he told well-wishers that he just wanted to see cars at every pump.[207] The family especially appreciated customers who drove miles out of their way to fill up at the station to show their support.

Hate crimes took place at service stations in the Southwest. In Arizona, Coxco's Green Valley Exxon Super Center received the first bomb threat in its history a little over a week after the terrorist attacks. According to the *Arizona Daily Star*, the bomb threat forced dozens of employees from the building so that police could sweep the store for explosives.[208] In response to this incident, the Coxco Corporation, based in Tucson, put up American flags at seven locations. They also gave workers American flag pins to wear and flag decals to display on cash registers, so that customers would know that their employees were good patriots. To ensure worker safety, President Cheryl Cox sent gas station managers and convenience store workers a list of talking points to use when dealing with hostile customers.[209]

Other companies took similar precautions. Worried about backlash intolerance, executives at the Tempe-based Phillips 66 Company took steps to shield minority employees from angry bigots. They recommended that franchise owners use American flags to allay customers' fears and protect immigrant workers from racist attacks. Phillips 66 spokeswoman Julie Igo told the *Arizona Daily Star* that her company was planning to use American flags and patriotic decals to deflect customers' hostility after 9/11.[210] She hoped that these American symbols might help protect her company's workers at Circle K, Exxon, and 76 gas stations across the country.

FALL 2001 BACKLASH ATTACKS AT 7-ELEVENS

The 9/11 backlash disproportionately affected minority workers at chain stores. Across the U.S., employees at 7-Eleven stores were often harassed, threatened, and attacked. Company spokeswoman Margaret Chabris told the *Arizona Daily Star* that there were more than 100 bias-motivated incidents at 7-Eleven stores in the three weeks following 9/11, ranging from bomb threats to serious assaults.[211] For example, in mid-September, 2001, an arsonist torched a Sikh-owned 7-Eleven in New York.[212]

Sikhs were also targeted at 7-Elevens in California. At a Fremont press conference on September 19, 2001, Jasjit Kaur described how her Sikh husband was working at a local 7-Eleven when a group of youths surrounded him and threatened him, expressing their desire to get rid of him and other "ragheads."[213] According to *India Abroad*, Kaur told California Lt. Governor Cruz Bustamante and journalists in attendance that her husband refused to change his appearance to protect himself from this type of post-9/11 bigotry, since the Sikh turban was a sign of sovereignty.[214]

Many minority-run 7-Eleven stores received bomb threats. The September 28, 2001 issue of *India-West* reported that a teenager from Farmingville, New York was arrested for threatening to blow up an Indian-owned 7-Eleven.[215] In response to the frequency of the attacks, the Dallas-based company circulated a safety plan for workers to deal with the backlash. They also disseminated corporate-issued posters expressing sadness and outrage in response to 9/11.[216] Tucson 7-Eleven store owner Suresh Thathi told the *Arizona Daily Star* that he appreciated having the company-issued posters, particularly after one of his clerks received a death threat.[217]

Despite these anti-racism efforts, bigots continued to target minority franchise owners and clerks. Many 7-Eleven employees were dismayed to learn of a fake photo circulating around the country showing Osama bin Laden in a 7-Eleven uniform. In an October 14, 2001 article in the *San Diego Union Tribune*, Richard Louv urged Americans to disregard the photo-shopped picture and the danger it represented to ethnic employees pumping gas or working behind the counter at each of the 119,750 convenience stores across the U.S.[218]

To help service workers deal with post-9/11 racial and religious hostility, the Alexandria-based National Association of Convenience Stores sent its members a list of suggestions to disseminate to employees: 1) display a donations canister that customers and employees can use to contribute to relief efforts; 2) produce a flyer for front counters about what the company is doing to help the 9/11 families; 3) give employees and customers patriotic stickers or buttons; and 4) display the American flag outside the store.[219]

Although these measures might have had some beneficial effect, 7-Eleven managers and sales associates continued to be harassed or attacked in the months following the terrorist strikes. For example, the December 21, 2001 issue of the Torrance *Daily Breeze* reported that a 7-Eleven employee in Gardenia received an anonymous call from someone threatening to blow up his store in retaliation for 9/11.[220]

FALL 2001 BACKLASH ATTACKS AFFECTING TAXI DRIVERS

Along with 7-Eleven employees, minority taxi drivers confronted post-9/11 bigotry on a regular basis. Because tempers were running particularly high near the World Trade Center site, New York cabbies faced some of the worst harassment during the backlash. According to the *New York Times*, approximately 60% to 75% of the city's licensed cab drivers were of Arab, South Asian, or North African descent in September 2001.[221] In the first two weeks after 9/11, the Taxi Workers' Alliance reported that drivers had been physically assaulted and their vehicles had been deliberately damaged.[222] In Manhattan, two minority cabbies were attacked.[223] In the Bronx, two taxis operated by Muslims were set on fire.[224] In Bensonhurst, nine livery cars and taxis were vandalized.[225] Although Arab-American drivers told the *Times* that these attacks were likely bias-motivated crimes, local authorities professed to be unaware that they were taking place.[226] In a September 24, 2001 article in the *Times*, NYPD spokeswoman Carmen Melendez said that she knew of no hate crimes against taxi drivers in the city.[227] Bhairavi Desai, chief organizer for the Taxi Workers' Alliance, responded that this was almost certainly because victimized drivers were not reporting the attacks to police.[228]

Because taxi operators are required to display their vehicle licenses, drivers with Muslim or Middle Eastern names were frequently harassed by bigoted passengers. Mohammed Qadery, a cab driver from Bangladesh, told the *New York Times* that he decided to stop posting his hack license so that passengers could not read his name and discern that he was Muslim.[229] Even though he knew he could be fined by the Taxi and Limo Commission for failing to display his photo ID, Qadery thought that the safety benefits were worth the risk of getting a ticket. He also noticed that tips improved when he kept his religious affiliation a secret. He told the *Times* that he became concerned for his physical well-being after teenagers in Queens threw rocks at his taxi on September 12, 2001.[230] He didn't report the backlash attack to the police because he did not think they would care enough to investigate the incident.

On occasion, bigots tried to kill taxi drivers. Because many cabbies were undocumented, they sometimes failed to inform police about attempts on their lives. *India-West* reported that on September 30, 2001, a nearby motorist fired a bullet at the head of an undocumented Sikh taxi driver in New York City.[231] Even before the attempted murder, the driver had been concerned about the 9/11 backlash, worried that Americans were confusing Sikhs with the terrorists.[232] To spread awareness about his faith, the cabbie gave passengers copies of a flyer explaining that Sikhs love America and that South Asians had nothing to do with the terrorist strikes. The taxi driver even laminated a copy of the flyer and posted it on the back seat, facing passengers. Unfortunately, this proactive work did not prevent him from being targeted. After picking up a fare on September 30, 2001, he stopped at a traffic light. When his passenger asked him a question, the cabbie turned around suddenly to respond. At that moment, a bullet passed close to his left ear, leaving a hole in the window.[233] The shooter drove away quickly, and Singh pulled over. The passenger ran out of the cab, worried about another gunshot. According to *India-West*, the Sikh cab driver never informed the police about the attempt on his life, afraid that they might alert immigration officials of his undocumented status.[234] Because the crime was never reported, the gunman was never apprehended or held accountable.

Since the *India-West* story did not disclose the full name of the crime victim, it is unclear whether the undocumented driver was the same cabbie as the one mentioned in a October 10, 2001 *New York Times* story about a gunman shooting at a Sikh-operated taxi.[235] This confusion underscores the difficulty of investigating bias-motivated felonies when undocumented workers are too fearful of deportation to come forward. In response to these types of incidents, some activists have argued that in the interest of public safety, Congress should pass legislation prohibiting U.S. immigration officials from being contacted when undocumented community members report bias attacks to local or federal officials.

Some Sikh taxi drivers were so traumatized by hate crimes that they took the drastic step of cutting their hair and wearing it uncovered. According to the *New York Times*, Sikh cabbie Parwinder Singh was attacked by a gang of thugs in East New York in a 9/11 backlash hate crime.[236] During the incident, the assailants used beer bottles to break three windows of Singh's cab while screaming that he was Osama bin Laden.[237] Afterwards, Singh's mother made him quit work, and the 20-year old South Asian cab driver stayed home, worried and despondent. Finally, in a moment of desperation, Singh decided to cut his hair so that area residents would not kill him. Because this action was a violation of his faith, Singh told the *Times* that his whole family sat in the living room, crying, when they discovered his shorn hair.[238] Balaka Singh, the young man's uncle and the vice president of Sikh Youth of America, felt that his nephew disgraced the family, particularly since he and other Sikh elders instructed younger family members to keep their hair uncut.[239] To minimize his family's social shame, the victimized cabbie began praying at the gurdwara on Saturdays, when it was less crowded. Although his mother implored him to resume wearing his turban, he remained too fearful to do so in public.

164

Taxi drivers were also targeted in other East Coast cities. The *Patriot-News* reported that Philadelphia cabbies were pulled from their cars and beaten during the 9/11 backlash.[240] Because of these attacks, many Pennsylvania taxi drivers feared going to work, viewing picking up fares like playing Russian roulette.

Along with coping with community xenophobia, taxi companies had to absorb the costs of bias-motivated vandalism. According to the *Madison Capital Times*, a Sikh cabbie in Wisconsin was dismayed to discover his tires were slashed in the aftermath of the terrorist strikes.[241] Bigots who damaged taxis put an additional financial burden on minority drivers, who were often required to pay out-of-pocket to repair their vehicles.

Taxi drivers in the Pacific Northwest also experienced backlash bigotry. One of the most serious attacks occurred in Seattle, Washington. According to the *Post-Intelligencer*, Raymond Isais Jr. punched and choked a Sikh cabbie in Sea Tac on September 13, 2001.[242] During the assault, Isais knocked off Kulwinder Singh's turban and pulled out tufts of his beard while demanding to know if he was a terrorist.[243] Singh, an East Asian Sikh, tried to explain that he was not affiliated with the 9/11 hijackers, but his assailant was too intent on attacking the Farwest Cab driver to listen. Isais was later arrested and held on $25,000 bail, facing charges of committing malicious harassment as a hate crime. Some Sikhs felt that the charges were inadequate, since they carried a penalty of only three to nine months in jail.

In the South, minority taxi drivers were also scapegoated by nativists. In Alexandria, Virginia, a white man assaulted a Middle Eastern cabbie. According to police Lt. John Crawford, local police were investigating the attack as a post-9/11 hate crime.[244] On occasion, immigrant and ethnic-looking cabbies were cornered by other drivers, who objected to their presence on American roads. The *Atlanta Constitution* reported that shortly after 9/11, Park Slope motorist targeted a taxi because he thought its driver was an Arab-American.[245] During this incident, the assailant blocked the cab's path, got out his vehicle, and pounded on the taxi while yelling anti-Muslim death threats.

Arab-American and Muslim cabbies in the Midwest were also harassed in the aftermath of the terrorist strikes. Since taxi operators are required to display their licensing information to passengers, drivers with Middle Eastern names often experienced bigotry at work. *The Los Angeles Times* reported that men assaulted cab driver and college student Mustafa Zemkour in the Chicago suburb of Evanston.[246] In the course of the mid-September 2001 attack, the assailants called him a mass-murderer and told him he deserved the beating they were administering.

Many cabbies took individual action to ease post-9/11 religious bigotry. To educate the public about his faith, a Sikh taxi driver in Chicago taped an educational flyer on the glass partition separating him from the passengers. Discussing this posting with the *New York Times*, Inderjit Singh expressed his hope that the leaflet would correct the widespread misperception that Sikhism was an offshoot of Hinduism or Islam, since many passengers failed to realize his faith was a separate religion.[247]

Despite individual attempts to spread awareness about non-Christian faiths, South Asian taxi drivers continued to face discrimination in Midwestern cities. Harjit Dhillon, a Sikh co-owner of the United Cab Company of Cleveland, told the *Plain Dealer* that he experienced post-9/11 discrimination when youths harassed him and gave him the finger, failing to understand that he was also an American citizen.[248]

Out of concern for their safety, many drivers decided to turn in their vehicles and take time off from work. According to the *Plain Dealer*, 60% of Arab-American taxi drivers in the region opted to stop working for more than a week after 9/11.[249] Many Sikh and Pakistani cabbies also turned in their vehicles. Minority taxi operators who continued showing up reported that customers hailing cabs often rejected rides from South Asian or Middle Eastern drivers.

Because so many cabbies were taking safety sabbaticals, taxi companies suffered financial losses. Devo Bavishi, owner of Ace Taxi service in Cleveland, told the *Plain Dealer* that his business was down 50% in the week after the terrorist strikes, due in part to frightened cabbies refusing to drive.[250] The decline in taxi revenue was not limited to large metropolitan areas. Alfred La Gasse, spokesman for a cab association representing for-hire vehicle companies in 50 states, told the *New York Times* that nationally, his business was down 67%, compared to mid-September revenues from 2000.[251]   According to La Gasse, many cabbies were not working and business was slow because Americans were canceling business conferences and vacations.

MUSICIANS AFFECTED BY THE BACKLASH, SEPTEMBER 2001

Along with taxi drivers and service-industry workers, Middle Eastern musicians were frequently harassed or attacked during the 9/11 backlash. In some instances, performers cancelled concerts because of safety concerns. Prior to 9/11, Egyptian pop star Hakim and rai singer Khaled had been contracted to perform in the Desert Roses and Arabian Rhythms Festival, touring ten American cities, including New York and Washington, D.C. In the weeks before the terrorist strikes, the tour had been enjoying good ticket sales as a result of Sting's and Cheb Mami's 1999 hit song, "Desert Rose," which brought rai music to American audiences. After 9/11, the musicians decided to discontinue the tour. In the September 21, 2001 issue of the *Los Angeles Times*, music promoter Dawn Elder explained that the 34 participating Middle Eastern musicians felt compelled to cancel upcoming concerts because the high-profile tour could easily attract the attention of bigots who might target group members while they were boarding a plane or performing on stage.[252]

HOTEL AND MOTEL ATTACKS, FALL 2001

Along with other minority workers who had extensive contact with the public, ethnic motel and hotel employees were dramatically affected by the backlash. In many parts of the U.S., South Asian professionals were disproportionately represented in the hotel and motel industries, putting them in frequent contact with strangers.   In the South, minority-owned hotels and motels were sometimes targeted by area rednecks. According to the September 16, 2001 issue of the *Augusta Chronicle*, a local bigot threatened to bomb a hotel on 15th St. because he thought its Indian owners were Muslim.[253]

Motel employees were also harassed or assaulted in other Southern states. In Knoxville, Tennessee, brothers Jason and Travis Kitts attacked an Indian-American manager of a motel restaurant on September 24, 2001.[254] They later told authorities that they selected the South Asian man because they thought he was of Arab descent. The victim suffered numerous injuries, including a broken sinus bone, a fractured cheek bone, and a concussion. The brothers eventually pled guilty to federal hate crime charges.

South Asian motel workers were also attacked in the Pacific Northwest. One of the most vicious bias-motivated crimes happened at a motel in Washington state. A week after 9/11, John Bethel began harassing 49-year old Karnail Singh, the owner of a SeaTac motel. The *Post-Intelligencer* reported that Bethel blamed the South Asian man for the terrorist strikes, although Singh's appearance conformed to Western cultural norms.[255] Originally from India, Singh was a clean-shaven Sikh poet who wore his hair short and uncovered. In mid-September, Bethel, a Renton resident, entered the SeaTac motel and ordered Singh to return to his homeland.[256]

Weeks later, Bethel returned and once again confronted Singh. Instead of cooling off in the weeks after 9/11, Bethel had become progressively more hostile. In mid-October, 2001, he went into the motel lobby and clubbed Singh unconscious with a metal cane.[257] During the attack, Bethel beat Singh on the head while screaming that he should get out of the U.S. and return to Allah. According to the *Post-Intelligencer*, Bethel was incensed that the South Asian had opted to remain in the U.S., ignoring his demands to leave the country.[258] As a result of the brutal caning, Singh was hospitalized and treated for bruises on his scalp. He also received ten stitches to close the bloody head gash that caused him constant and severe headaches.

The *Post Intelligencer* reported that Bethel was arrested and sentenced to two years in prison for assault with a deadly weapon, a charge that carried a stiffer penalty than malicious harassment, the only hate crime Washington state had on its books.[259] Like many other members of the Sikh community, Singh thought Bethel's sentence did not reflect the gravity of the vicious assault.

After the attack, Singh told the *Post Intelligencer* that he took down the Sikh calendar on the motel wall, concerned that the photos of bearded, turbaned South Asians would make him vulnerable to other area nativists.[260] Singh occasionally had flashbacks of the beating, particularly when he heard about other bias-motivated assaults in the area. Singh hoped that over time, his traumatic memories would become less vivid. Although he took more safety precautions at work, he continued to display an ethnic bumper-sticker on his car, proclaiming that he was proud to be a Sikh.[261]

ATTACKS AT WORK, FALL 2001

In the months following the terrorist strikes, hate crimes targeting minority workers continued to take place throughout the country. Many minority-owned businesses were attacked in California. Some Bay Area business owners were targeted on more than one occasion. In the weeks and months following 9/11, corner store owner Ahmad Namrouti was repeatedly harassed by San Francisco bigots. The *Chronicle* reported that a few days after 9/11, a customer in his 20s stopped into the store, asked Namrouti if he was an Arab, and cursed the Islamic faith.[262] The man then threatened to return the following day and fight him. On another occasion at around 4:00 a.m., an assailant threw a 15-pound brick through the store window. Because Namrouti was sleeping in the closet-sized back room, this attack frightened him considerably.[263] He noted that the brick landed near his usual chair next to the counter, and would have likely hit him in the head if it had been thrown during business hours.

According to S.F. police spokesman Dewayne Tully, the investigation into the brick attack was limited because there were no leads or witnesses. Because the perpetrator was never apprehended, Namrouti became increasingly fearful about his safety. Since he didn't have the money to pay $1,500 to replace the window, he was forced to cover the large hole with a board. In December 2001, Namrouti told the *Chronicle* that he decided to sell his convenience store and return to Jordan because it had become too difficult to be an Arab and live in the U.S.[264] As a father, he knew his children depended on him emotionally and financially, and he was no longer willing to endanger his family's security by working in such a hostile environment. Because he was so anxious to leave, he decided to sell the store for $10,000 less than what he paid for it. Joann LaGrone, a regular customer of Namrouti's, told the *Chronicle* that she was sickened to see such a nice man emigrating because of post-9/11 xenophobia.[265]

Other Arab merchants were also targeted in the city. A vandal attacked an Iraqi-owned grocery store, scrawling, "Terrorist go home" in black marker on the front of the building.[266] In the Mission District, a Middle Eastern store owner covered over an Arabic peace mural adorning the side of his store, worried that the painting's content might make his shop a target for vandals.

Elsewhere in the state, minority politicians were targeted during the backlash. In chapter five, I discussed how members of the JDL targeted the offices of Congressman Darryl Issa in October 2001, endangering the lives of the Lebanese-American elected representative and his employees.[267] This attack worried other high-profile Arab-American public officials, who feared that they might also be singled out by bigots at their places of employment.

Minority taxi drivers in California remained particularly vulnerable. In San Diego, a physician visiting the state from Oklahoma attacked an Afghan cab driver outside the Marriott hotel on October 20, 2001. According to the *Tulsa World*, Dr. Stanley Grogg and two companions got into an argument with the driver, accusing him of being in the U.S. to blow it up.[268] Police noted that several witnesses outside the hotel saw Grogg put a hand on Tamim Keshawarz's neck and hit him repeatedly in the head. *The San Diego Union Tribune* reported that during the assault, Grogg's female friend screamed at onlookers that the driver was from Afghanistan, trying to arouse others to support Grogg in the bias-motivated beating.[269] At the time of the incident, the Oklahoma State University professor and his two colleagues were in town attending a week-long medical convention. State prosecutors decided that Grogg had committed no felonious conduct when he assaulted the Afghan driver, and opted to charge him with two misdemeanors in connection with the post-9/11 attack. Area Muslims were outraged that Grogg dodged felony hate crime charges even though the attack took place in front of witnesses.

In Southern California, minority journalists were frequently targeted by bigots. Throughout the fall of 2001, the *Arab World Newspaper*'s Anaheim office received racist phone calls and emails. According to the *Orange County Register*, some of the messages contained explicit death threats, expressing the hope that all Arabs would be killed.[270] Samir Abdalla, the Egyptian-American editor-in-chief of the ethnic paper, told the *Register* that his office received the most calls immediately after 9/11 and fewer threats as time passed.[271]

On occasion, Muslims in Los Angeles sold their businesses at a loss in order to protect themselves from Islamophobic community members. In November 2001, two gunmen burst into a minority-owned store and threatened owner Mujibur Raman Baval, a Bangladeshi immigrant. Baval told the *Los Angeles Times* that one of the intruders shoved a gun into his gut and threatened to kill him, calling him an Arab Muslim.[272] Because of the bias attack, Baval sold his business for less than it was worth in order to escape misplaced American hostility.

The same month, Horatio Plascencia attacked a Middle Eastern service station clerk with a screwdriver in San Diego. According to the *New York Times*, the 30-year old assailant was sentenced to three years after he pled guilty to battery during a hate crime.[273] Because Plascencia had a previous conviction for robbery, his sentence for the November 18th assault was doubled under state law.

A particularly serious backlash crime occurred at a Northridge liquor store, outside of Los Angeles, on December 3, 2001. On the evening of the attack, Sikh store owner Surinder Singh Sidhu was wearing a star-spangled turban given to him by his 14-year old son Jugjeet. Sidu told *India Abroad* that he loved America, and enjoyed customers' reactions to his patriotic head wrap.[274] Despite his red, white, and blue dastaar, two men walked into the Liquor Mart store at 11:00 p.m. and began harassing him, calling him Osama bin Laden.[275] *India Abroad* reported that Sidhu tried to diffuse the situation by explaining that he was a Sikh and that the 9/11 mastermind did not live in America.[276] Instead of following his reasoning, the men told him that they would kill bin Laden that day. At first, Sidhu thought they were updating him on U.S. military forces' attempts to catch the terrorist leader, and replied that it was possible that the troops would finally get him. The men repeated their words, making Sidhu realize that something was wrong and that he was in danger. The two men then took out large metal poles, approximately four ft. in length, and began beating him with them.

According to *India Abroad*, Sidhu's assailants struck him repeatedly all over his body, including on his head and arms.[277] During the attack, Sidhu began fighting frantically, throwing store merchandise at the two men. The assailants jumped over the counter and started beating him on the back. Terrified that they would make good on their death threat, Sidhu fought even harder and pushed a five-foot candy rack on his attackers.[278] He then ran out of the store, where he encountered a familiar customer who called 911 on his behalf. Before the police arrived, Sidhu's assailants fled the scene.

Since he had been struck about two dozen times with the metal poles, Sidhu was taken to a local hospital, where he was treated for his injuries. He told *India-West* that he credited his turban for cushioning his head against more serious physical damage.[279] Sidhu said the attack left him feeling shaken, particularly since he was a naturalized American citizen who had lived in the U.S. for decades.

Captain Joe Curreri told the Los Angeles *Daily News* that the attack was likely pre-meditated because the perpetrators brought the metal poles with them.[280] Although the incident was initially labeled an assault with a deadly weapon, it was later categorized as a bias-motivated assault. Investigating authorities determined that no money or merchandise had been taken. Sidhu was able to give investigating officers a good description of his attackers, who were in their early 20s. One was about 5 ft. 6 inches, and 190 pounds. The other was approximately 5 ft. 9 inches, and 160 pounds. One of the assailants was black and the other was Hispanic or white. Despite the physical evidence left at the scene and Sidhu's description of the perpetrators, LAPD detectives were unable to apprehend the men responsible.

Elsewhere in California, gunmen targeted minority merchants in the months following the terrorist strikes. In San Joaquin Valley, an Arab shop worker was shot through the glass of a grocery store on December 5, 2001. At approximately 9:40 p.m., the gunman opened fire on 49-year old Fadhl Albusaisa while he was locking the front door of the S-mart store in Lindsay, California. Wesam Masam, Albusaisa's co-worker, told the *San Francisco Chronicle* that he was helping close the store before dinner when he heard his wounded friend crying for help.[281] Albusaisa required hospitalization to treat his shoulder wound and stem his extensive bleeding.

Several years prior to 9/11, Albusaisa had emigrated from Yemen to the U.S. After arriving in California, he worked at a store in Poplar before finding employment in Lindsay in mid-2001. Although his wife still lived in Yemen, Albusaisa's 12-year old son came from North Africa in late August 2001 to join him in America. S-mart store owner Ahmed Shaibi told the *Chronicle* that he postponed telling the young boy that his father had been shot.[282] Rather than traumatize the youth with the truth, Shaibi told the youngster that Albusaisa had gone to Fresno for immigration papers. While Albusaisa was being treated for his wounds, his friends took care of the boy, who spoke little English. Shaibi told the *Chronicle* that he assumed Albusaisa's unprovoked shooting was a 9/11 backlash crime, since the victim had no personal or financial problems that would give anyone motive to shoot him.[283] Because Albusaisa was targeted only 50 miles away from where another Yemeni shopkeeper, Abdo Ali Ahmed, was shot to death in his store, authorities wondered if the two post-9/11 crimes were connected.

In Southern California, Muslims were occasionally physically assaulted at work. According to the *Los Angeles Times*, a security guard in Orange County was severely beaten in December 2001.[284] While guarding an apartment complex in Costa Mesa, victim Mohamed Slam was brutally attacked by two assailants, who punched and kicked him repeatedly until he lost consciousness. Slam was injured so badly that he spent five days in a coma. Because of his extensive injuries, he had no memory of the attack. Consequently, authorities were unable to establish an anti-Muslim motive when they arrested the two suspects, who were charged with attempted murder. Slam's wife, Nuha Jaludi, told the *Los Angeles Times* that she was convinced her husband was the victim of a hate crime, particularly since the assailants didn't touch his watch, credit cards, or gold bracelet.[285]

The 9/11 backlash continued to affect workers in other states. In Texas, Persian employees were targeted in the weeks after the terrorist strikes. In October 2001, the *Houston Chronicle* reported that a caller threatened to come to an Iranian man's workplace and shoot him.[286] Because of the ubiquitousness of guns in the state, the victim took the call seriously, worrying about his safety during business hours.

In other parts of Texas, community members picketed minority-run businesses, spreading rumors that owners and employees were unpatriotic enemies of America. The *Houston Chronicle* reported that a few weeks after 9/11, the Ku Klux Klan organized a pro-America protest at a Pakistani-owned convenience store in the Montgomery county of Splendora.[287] This community action was instigated by a false rumor claiming that minority employees had ripped down American flags. In response to the gathering, the owner met with protest organizers and clarified that local teenagers removed the store's flags when they weren't permitted to buy cigarettes.

In another post-9/11 incident in Montgomery County, vandals shot up an Indian-owned convenience store, spraying the building with bullets. The *Houston Chronicle* estimated the store lost $16,000 in business as a result of the shooting, in addition to approximately $3,500 in physical damage.[288] Authorities were unable to determine the perpetrators' identities or motives, but some residents viewed the attack as a backlash hate crime.

South Asian and Muslim convenience store employees were targeted in other parts of Texas. A Pakistani proprietor of a Pearland convenience store told the *Houston Chronicle* that his tires were slashed on ten different occasions in the months following 9/11.[289] Because of the frequency of the attacks, he thought that they were motivated by his South Asian ethnicity and Muslim faith.

On occasion, minority physicians in Texas experienced the 9/11 backlash. In addition to being harassed by patients, they were occasionally singled out by their co-workers. The *Houston Chronicle* reported that at Methodist Hospital, a Palestinian anesthesiologist was expelled from an operating room during heart surgery because of post-9/11 tensions with another doctor.[290]

As 2001 came to a close, minority business owners and employees continued to make financial sacrifices to protect themselves from backlash bigotry. The December 14, 2001 issue of the *Houston Chronicle* reported that Pakistani immigrant Syed Kamal became too terrified to operate his dry cleaning store after he received a letter containing threats to burn down his store and kill him because he was a Muslim.[291] Kamal said that he felt like a sitting duck in the business he had opened a few months prior to 9/11.

ATTACKS AT WORK, 2002

In early 2002, work-related hate crimes continued to take place throughout the country. In San Francisco, MUNI bus drivers were harassed if they looked Middle Eastern or South Asian. In a January 2002 interview with the *Chronicle*, Nuwafq Shiekh, a driver with more than a decade of experience prior to 9/11, reported that he had been constantly harassed in the months following the terrorist attacks.[292] On multiple occasions, passengers suggested that he was affiliated with the hijackers. They called him a terrorist, compared him to Osama bin Laden, and asked him if he planned to crash the bus into a building.[293]

Bay Area workers also received death threats at Muslim-run facilities. Amatullah Almarwani answered a menacing call while working at the Islamic Center of San Francisco. In mid-January 2002, Almarwani told the *Chronicle* that the caller stated his intent to shoot him in the head and do the same to his child.[294] Because Muslim and Arab organizations received so many threats, employees began fearing for their lives whenever they came to work.

Minority-owned stores in San Francisco were also attacked in early 2002. During this period, the *Chronicle* reported that a vandal targeted Saif Ataya's Eureka Valley neighborhood store, defacing the building with bigoted graffiti.[295] This attack frightened Ataya's minority customers and angered members of the community.

While minority store owners were being harassed and attacked throughout the U.S., American audiences were watching movies depicting Middle Eastern and Muslim merchants as unscrupulous Semites. A particularly offense film was *Two Degrees*, which was released on DVD in late 2002. Instead of portraying Arab-American store owners as victims of backlash bigotry, the film depicts them as morally-bankrupt misogynists. Shaheen is especially disturbed by a scene in which the two Arab shopkeepers tell Angela, a poor African-American drug addict, that they will not give her anything to eat unless she has sex with them.[296] Offended by their lechery, her boyfriend arrives and shoots them dead in a jealous rage. Because the Middle Eastern store owners are so unsympathetic, film audiences are not disturbed when they are murdered. At a time when so many Middle Eastern and Muslim shopkeepers were being harassed and attacked throughout the country, Shaheen finds it unfortunate that Hollywood portrayals of Arab businessmen were reinforcing pernicious stereotypes.

Along with immigrant shopkeepers, minority construction workers were harassed during the 9/11 backlash. In Gaithersburg, members of a construction crew repeatedly insulted a 44-year old co-worker who was of Middle Eastern descent.[297] Along with verbal taunts, they threatened to beat him with a metal pipe. When the man complained, his supervisor did nothing in response, telling him that they had the right to be angry.[298] The victim eventually filed an employment discrimination complaint, although he was told by a supervisor that making such a claim would be detrimental to his career.

South Asian employees were sometimes attacked by Islamophobic co-workers during the backlash. On August 30, 2002, an employee at a Palo Alto drug store raped another clerk in the bathroom. The 15-year old Muslim victim was treated at Santa Clara Valley Medical Center before being released the next day. Physical evidence substantiated the girl's rape report. According to the *San Francisco Chronicle*, the police initially charged Sanjay Nair, a South Asian Hindu originally from Fiji, with a hate crime because he made anti-Muslim statements during the sexual assault.[299] Responding to news of this bias-motivated crime, Manzoor Ghori, chairman of the Indian Muslim Relief Committee, told the *Chronicle* that he hoped that overseas Muslim-Hindu tensions would not take root in the U.S.[300] Some area Muslims wondered if the rape was triggered by the ongoing 9/11 backlash and long-standing animosity between different South Asian religious communities.[301]

In its coverage of the crime, the *Chronicle* ran a series of articles exploring whether Nair committed a 'hate rape' motivated by religious prejudice or if he was just a sexual predator with an incidental bias towards

Muslims.[302]   According to *India Abroad*, the police investigation determined that religious bias was an important factor in the assault, even though detectives also uncovered that Nair sexually harassed other women at work.[303]   Initially, Nair's bail was set at $150,000, but was lowered to $20,000 when prosecutors opted against charging him with a hate crime after deciding that the anti-Muslim comments made during the rape were not central to the attack.[304]   *India Abroad* reported that many members of the Muslim community were deeply disappointed that Nair would not face hate crime charges, arguing that the assailant's antipathy to the victim's religious background played an essential role in why he chose to rape her.[305]

Because of widespread Islamophobia, some minority employees felt compelled to change jobs during the 9/11 backlash.   Attorney Zareefa Kahn told the *South Florida Sentinel* that the office harassment she experienced in the 12 months following the terrorist attacks prompted her to look for work elsewhere.[306]   Khan was dismayed that her colleagues at the Palm Beach County State Attorney's Office began acting inappropriately towards her in the aftermath of 9/11. Although some of her co-workers had dined at her house in the past, they began making anti-Muslim comments in front of her and treating her like an unwelcome foreigner, even though she had been born in Brooklyn. Along with the bias-motivated harassment she was experiencing at work, she also dealt with bigotry outside of the office. She was frequently singled out because of her South Asian ancestry. On one particularly memorable occasion, she had the unpleasant experience of having a store clerk throw a credit card back at her after looking at her name and discerning that she was Muslim.[307]   To escape work-related harassment and to help other Muslims in the U.S., she quit her prosecutor's job and found employment at a private immigration law practice.

ATTACKS AT WORK, 2003

About a year after 9/11, some minority-owned businesses hoped that the worst of the backlash was behind them. Unfortunately, a new surge of hate crimes began as tensions with Iraq worsened in the first few months of 2003. Discussing this resurgence in xenophobia, Fasal Khan told the *Atlanta Journal-Constitution* that community residents sometimes threw bottles at his truck, which advertised his name and his company. [308] On other occasions, bigots threatened him directly. While visiting a subdivision under construction, he heard a white man in a pickup truck call him by name and threaten him, telling him to leave the area and never return.[309] Khan realized that the stranger had gotten his name from the writing on his company vehicle. Because of escalating Middle Eastern tensions and concerns about recent hate crimes, Khan decided to cancel a Muslim voter registration drive and picnic he had been planning at Lake Lanier.

In some instances, minority business owners were unsure about whether store vandalism was motivated by racial or religious bias. The *Washington Post* reported that on March 4, 2003, while the U.S. was preparing for war against Iraq, a vandal smashed the window of Mateen Chida's Halal Meat Market in Falls Church.[310] Chida wondered if the assailant targeted his store because it served a predominantly-Muslim clientele.[311]

During the 9/11 backlash, Muslim, Middle Eastern, and South Asian workers were sometimes detained by government officials, who closed down their immigrant-owned businesses without evidence of wrongdoing. In the Oakland publication, *Colorlines*, journalist Silja Talvi argued that government officials contributed to an atmosphere of xenophobia by targeting innocent minority businesses in the first year and a half after the terrorist strikes. [312] Talvi criticized the federal government for the baseless ransacking of minority-owned grocery stores, the detention of innocent employees, and the raids carried out by the U.S. Treasury, INS, FBI, and USDA.[313]

These governmental intrusions established a nativistic atmosphere in which xenophobia was increasingly tolerated throughout the country. In the Southwest, Arab and Muslim businesses continued to be plagued by bias-motivated crimes. According to the March 9, 2003 issue of the *San Antonio Express-News*, Arab-Americans in Texas were frightened when a bigot drove a truck through the front of Sahara Mediterranean Groceries.[314] This hate crime made many customers fearful of patronizing ethnic businesses.

As tensions in the Middle East intensified, angry nativists continued to vent their frustrations on innocent minorities. According to the *Modesto Bee*, local bigots repeatedly targeted businesses owned by Christian Arab-Americans in 2003.[315] In March, arsonists burned down the French Cleaners in Modesto.[316] The owners were Assyrian Christians originally from Lebanon, and had no ties to the French government. Authorities suspected that the crime may have been motivated by the owners' ethnicity as well as opposition to France's refusal to support the U.S. invasion of Iraq. Assailants also vandalized the French Cleaners' store in Turlock with graffiti and shot pellets at the Ceres store, shattering the windows.[317] In other parts of the U.S., attacks targeting Middle Eastern workers were even more violent.

One of the most serious incidents occurred at an Afghan restaurant in Indianapolis. On March 24, 2003, two assailants burst into the kitchen and set the Afghani-American owner on fire. According to the *New York Times*, Abdullah Naderi, the 37-year old Muslim victim, suffered severe burns over 60% of his body.[318] Investigators speculated that Naderi's ethnicity and Muslim faith may have triggered the assault at the Middle Eastern restaurant.

In San Francisco, community centers were attacked if they were perceived as pro-peace or pro-Arab. On several occasions, vandals defaced the muraled walls of the San Francisco Women's Building, covering the facility with hateful messages targeting Arab-Americans, Muslims, and African-Americans.[319] In response, center employees organized an all-night vigil to protest the $15,000 in damage done to the facility and the threats to minority workers and clients. In an April 2003 interview with *Asianweek*, Jovida Ross said that repairing the damage took time that she and other center employees could've used pursuing other projects.[320]

Throughout the country, minority truck drivers were often harassed or assaulted at the beginning of the Iraq War. On May 19, 2003, Avtar Singh Chiera was shot three times in Phoenix. *India-West* reported that on the evening of the attack, Chiera had finished work and was waiting in his 18-wheeler tractor trailer for his 23-year old son Hardeep, an ASU undergraduate, to pick him up at Ninth St. and Bell Road.[321] Although Chiera had lived in the U.S. for 18 years and worked as a truck driver for 14 years, he sometimes drew stares because of his beard and turban. At about 9:30 p.m., two white men in a small red pick-up truck approached him while he was stepping out of his vehicle, waiting for his son's arrival. One of the strangers then shot Chiera, and told him to go back to where he belonged.[322]

According to Phoenix police detective Becky Bulkley, the gunman was in the back of the red pickup, not sitting beside the driver.[323] The first bullet penetrated Chiera's thigh and then exited. The second shot hit Chiera in the stomach and passed through his body. The third bullet became lodged in Chiera's lower abdomen. Feeling the stabbing pain in his groin, Chiera dialed 911 and called home.

Chiera's wife Surindar told *India-West* that when the family learned of the shooting, their worst post-9/11 fears were realized.[324] The victim's son rushed to the scene, and found his father lying in a pool of blood. Hardeep Chiera wanted to drive his father to the hospital, but the injured man realized that he needed the ambulance's life-saving treatment or he would likely die. He survived the shooting, but ended up spending 10 days at Lincoln hospital. He was unable to work for three months, incurring more than $100,000 in medical expenses and $3,000 in additional debt from the attack.[325] To cover his house and truck payments, he was given some financial support from the Valley Sikh community.[326]

Phoenix police investigators told *India Abroad* that the crime was likely motivated by the shooter's antipathy towards the Sikh's beard and turban, and their mistaken belief he was an Arab Muslim.[327] Since nothing was taken from the truck, police ruled out robbery as the motive. Despite a $20,000 reward and Congressional attention to the case, the Phoenix police and FBI were unable to apprehend the shooter, causing the family to fear that the case would remain unsolved. To reduce the likelihood of other bias-motivated attacks, the Sikh family moved into a gated community. Because of all the bigotry, one of Chiera's sons opted to cut his hair, while another remained adamant about retaining it.[328]

Along with truckers, other minority drivers were singled out in the aftermath of 9/11. Because of their frequent contact with the public, immigrants working delivery jobs were especially at risk. One of the most horrific hate crimes occurred in North Bedford, Massachusetts, when five men abducted and tortured Saurabh Bhalerao, an Indian pizza delivery man, because they thought he was from Iraq. News of this terrifying attack spread quickly around the world, disseminated by European, Latin American, Middle Eastern, and South Asian news sources.[329]

On June 22, 2003, Bhalerao was delivering pizzas for Sarducci's Subs and Pizzas, an Egyptian-owned business that was open until 2:00 a.m.[330] At the time of the attack, Bhalerao was a 24-year old textile engineering student at the University of Massachusetts at Dartmouth, working at the $6-an-hour delivery job to help pay for school. It was his second day on the job. He was delivering a $10 pizza to an apartment in Fairhaven when the tenant and his four friends began harassing him. After Bhalerao knocked on the door, one of the occupants opened the door, handed the delivery man $10, and obnoxiously told him to keep the change. Bhalero told *India Abroad* that the men then attempted to rob him, hoping to get free pizza and his cash, but the crime soon turned into a bias-motivated assault.[331] Judging Bhalerao by his physical appearance, they assumed he was a Middle Eastern Muslim. Incensed by his perceived ethnicity, they shoved him into their apartment, where they began kicking him and beating him up. According to *Noticias Financieras*, Bhalerao's attackers screamed at him to go back to Iraq as they pummeled him and kicked him in the face, breaking his jaw in three places.[332] They also made anti-Muslim comments, even though Bhalerao told them that he was Hindu from Indore, India. Bhalerao told the *Birmingham Post* that his attackers didn't know the difference between India and Iraq, and looked at him with hatred because they thought he was from the Middle East.[333] Bhalero's attackers bound his body with a rope and stuffed dirty socks in his mouth to muffle his screams. They also burned his face with cigarettes, using the back of his neck and the skin near his ear like an ashtray.

The assailants then threw Bhalerao into the trunk of his own car, a Honda Civic. Bhalerao told *India Abroad* he became terrified that his life was about to end, worrying they were taking him to the sea to dump him.[334] To calm himself, he began repeatedly chanting the mantra, "Shri Ram Jai Ram Ram Jai Jai Ram."[335] Groping around the trunk, he found a hammer. One of the attackers opened the trunk with the intention of freeing Bhalerao. In mortal terror, Bhalerao hit him with the hammer and tried to grab him by the collar, hoping to lock him in the trunk and call the police.[336] The assailant kept screaming at Bhalerao to release him, reminding him that he had sprung him from the trunk.[337] While Bhalerao was hitting him, the assailant pulled out a knife and stabbed the delivery man in the stomach, causing severe bleeding.

According to *India Abroad*, Bhalerao started yelling for help when he saw an approaching car.[338] At first, he worried that his attackers were returning. He was relieved to see the car was full of four teenage girls and one teenage boy. These good Samaritans stopped to help him, summoning the police and an ambulance on his behalf.

Bhalerao's housemate, Rohit Kale, told *India Abroad* that when he arrived at the hospital, he could not recognize his friend because of the extensive injuries to his face and jaw, which had to be wired shut.[339] Initially, Bhalerao decided against informing his parents of the attack, but was forced to do so when news of the hate crime was disseminated in so many Indian newspapers.

In response to the bias-motivated abduction, community members organized a "No Place for Hate" rally, speaking out against area xenophobia. Hundreds of well-wishers attended the event, including local politicians, the police chief, a Christian minister, a rabbi, and hundreds of students and faculty members from Bhalerao's school.[340]

Police eventually apprehended Bhalerao's four assailants: Chris Pereira, 20; Ryan March, 19; Chris Hansen, 17; and Tyrell Tavarez, 17.[341] According to the *Birmingham Post*, the men were charged with numerous offenses, including attempted murder, kidnapping, aggravated assault, robbery, and committing a hate crime.[342] Heath Antonio, Assistant District Attorney for Bristol County, told *India Abroad* that leniency was not appropriate because the crime was so horrific.[343] Bhalerao's attackers eventually went to prison. Although the bias-motivated attack left Bhalerao with a lacerated liver and severe injuries to his jaw, he told *India Abroad* that he no longer felt animosity towards his assailants and was grateful at all the community support he received from Muslims, Jews, Christians, and other Hindus.[344]

To raise awareness about ongoing hate crimes taking place around the U.S., many victims participated in educational conferences. Mujibur Raman Baval, the Bangladeshi immigrant who had been threatened at gunpoint in Los Angeles, shared his experiences with other participants in a 2003 forum exploring how Southern California immigrants were affected by the 9/11 backlash.[345] At this conference, moderator Robin Toma of the Human Rights Commission expressed his hope that Americans' concern for national security would not translate into increased discrimination against racial and religious minorities. Many of the 150 participants were dismayed that invited law enforcement officials did not attend the conference, and felt that police officers were not making hate crimes a top departmental priority.

Despite the best efforts of community organizers, crimes targeting minority workers continued to take place across the country. According to the October 3, 2003 issue of *India Abroad*, a Sikh convenience store owner in Mesa, Arizona was beaten unconscious by three assailants.[346] While furiously pummeling 45-year old Didar Singh, the three men broke his nose and scarred his face.[347] Because of the intense rage the assailants displayed during the assault, Singh believed that they were primarily motivated by ethnic and religious bigotry, even though they also stole from the store. Didar Singh reported that he had been robbed on two other occasions, including an incident involving men with handguns.[348] Because there was a rise in neo-Nazi graffiti in Mesa, Singh speculated that he was being repeatedly targeted because of his South Asian heritage and Sikh faith. Community activists also questioned whether Singh's beating was linked to the 9/11 backlash, since so many area bigots mistakenly associated Sikhs with al-Qaeda.

The same month, a Sikh taxi driver was attacked in Seattle. On October 18, 2003, a group of five to six men surrounded Harjit Singh and began screaming racial and religious epithets at him.[349] During the attack, the men called him Osama bin Laden, threatened to kill him, and told him to get out of the country.[350] To escape the mob, Singh drove off in his cab. The men followed him and attacked his taxi, shattering the passenger side window and removing a side mirror. Despite the clear bias motivation of the attackers, responding officers failed to include the ethnic slurs in the police report, and did not level bias charges against the perpetrators.[351] Years after the attack, the *Northwest Asian Weekly* reported that Singh's assailants were never prosecuted for committing a hate crime.[352]

Sikh cabbies were also targeted in other states. In Santa Clara, California, a passenger assaulted a 44-year old Sikh taxi driver on December 21, 2003. According to the *News India-Times*, there were seven people in the large cab at the time of the attack.[353] When the assailant struck the South Asian man in the face, five of the six passengers exited the vehicle. The attacker remained behind, making derogatory comments while continuing the assault on the driver.[354] After the beating was over, the driver contacted the police. A month later, Mountain View police arrested the 16-year old responsible.

ATTACKS AT WORK, 2004

Years after 9/11, minority workers continued feeling the effects of the backlash. The March 1, 2004 issue of the *Tampa Tribune* reported that 38-year old Sikh business owner Rajwant Lamda was constantly confronting community bigotry, which escalated considerably after the Twin Towers fell.[355] In the first two weeks after 9/11, the harassment was so severe that mall security guards had to protect him at work.[356] On many occasions, Americans mistook him as an Arab or Muslim and yelled that he was Osama bin Laden. People also spat on him. His business revenue declined 80% when customers stopped buying from his three kiosks at Tampa malls, forcing him to close down these businesses.[357] More than two and a half years after the terrorist strikes, area nativists taunted him and subjected him to obscene gestures on a near-daily basis, in response to his appearance and the mistaken assumption that he was in league with al-Qaeda.[358]

Muslims were also targeted at work in 2004. The owner of a Florida jewelry store kiosk was hassled and attacked at the West Shore Plaza on April 6, 2004. According to the *St. Petersburg Times*, three shoppers from Spain – a couple in their early 50s and a younger woman in her 20s, possibly their daughter – harassed and assaulted a Muslim businesswoman working at her store at the mall.[359] On the day of the attack, the three Spaniards told the Muslim convert to get out of America, and described Islam as a hateful and violent faith. One of them also grabbed her by the throat and tried to yank off her hijab.[360] Although the victim was of European descent, her attacker used an anti-Arab slur during the assault.

In other states, xenophobic arsonists continued to torch minority-owned businesses. On April 9, 2004, Texas bigot Thomas Carroll was apprehended in the act of burning down a Conoco store.[361] He had been under police surveillance because of his involvement in other early-morning fires targeting businesses owned and operated by South Asians. Because investigators worried he might strike again, officers from San Antonio's Repeat Offender Unit did a stakeout of his home. A little after 2:00 a.m. on April 9, 2004, Carroll slipped out of the garage and drove his Toyota SUV land cruiser to the 143000 block of Nacogdoches.[362] Police caught Carroll in the act of igniting the building.

The *Express-News* reported that when the two officers arrived, one approached the crime scene on foot while the other patrolled the area in the police cruiser.[363] The driver suddenly heard an explosion nearby. Worried that his partner had been killed, he looked in the direction of the blast and was startled to see the suspect driving an SUV directly at him before swerving away at the last minute. The officer in the squad car fired at the other driver, who fled the scene. The other cop emerged unhurt from the explosion. Police vehicles pursued the arson suspect and apprehended 35-year old Carroll on Loop 1604 on US 281. At the time of his arrest, Carroll was wearing a black jacket with orange flames.

According to the *Express-News*, the April 9th blaze was the fourth arson attack in a 16-day period targeting area stores owned or managed by South Asians.[364] Investigators believed that Carroll set fire to the Conoco store because its owners were of Pakistani origin. Kabiruddin and Mumtaz Ishmail told reporters that they were dismayed that a stranger decided to burn down their business, treating them as unwelcome foreigners even though they had lived in the U.S. for decades.[365] The arson hurt the Muslim family emotionally and financially. Surveying the store's shattered windows, melted doors, and twisted metal roof lying in the parking lot, Shehzad Ishmail told the *Express-News* that he was outraged by the attack on his parents' business.[366] Many South Asian community members wondered how Carroll was able to burn down the Conoco store since he was under police surveillance at the time of the attack.

The *San Antonio Express-News* reported that at the time of the April 9th arson, Carroll was facing charges for ramming his Toyota Land Cruiser into a Shell station on November 24, 2002.[367] Discussing this attack, Zahid Malik, supervisor of the targeted service station, reported that Carroll's vehicle stopped deep in the store, demolishing its glass doors.[368] Rather than admitting that the destruction was bias-motivated, Carroll claimed that the crash was accidental, occurring while he was teaching his girlfriend how to drive.[369] Carroll was arrested for this crime and charged with driving under the influence, but was released on bail.

Carroll also attacked minority-owned businesses in 2003. According to the *Corpus Christi Caller-Times*, a police officer and two other witnesses saw Carroll burning down a Muslim-owned Texaco convenience store, splashing gasoline on electrical wires and setting them on fire on May 25, 2003.[370] In response to this crime, Carroll was arrested and released on $20,000 bail. According to the *Express-News*, Carroll had a troubled past, marred by a legal problems, a volatile divorce, and business losses.[371] At the time of his 2004 hate crime rampage, he was also facing a cocaine possession charge. Many local minorities speculated that at least two Muslim businesses could have been spared if concerned authorities had locked up Carroll after the first criminal incident.

To punish Carroll for the attack on the Ismails' store, prosecutors charged him with arson, a second-degree felony, but soon added bias enhancements, raising the maximum penalty to 99 years in prison. Although Texas enacted hate crime legislation in 1993, state prosecutors infrequently included these additional charges against criminals, even when bigotry was suspected. The Bexar district attorney's office was responsible for half of the eight times Texas prosecutors filed hate crime charges in the period 1998 to 2004. Since Carroll had been out on $20,000 bail at the time he committed the April 9th arson, the court raised his bond to more than $1,000,000 to ensure that he would be unable to get out and attack any more minority businesses while awaiting trial.

Despite Carroll's bias-motivated reign of terror, U.S. prosecutors decided against levying charges against him. Area Muslims were dismayed that Carroll was not being charged federally for committing hate crimes. U.S. prosecutors defended their decision, pointing out that he was already being charged by the state and they could not prove that he violated federal law.

Carroll's 2004 arrest prompted local journalists to inform the public that hate crimes were political acts instead of crimes of passion. In the June 14, 2004 issue of the *San Antonio Express-News*, Arthea Williams wrote that the recent arsons were intended to disempower minority communities, eroding their sense of safety and undermining their financial base by attacking their businesses.[372] Many community members saw Carroll's racist crime spree in the context of post-9/11 xenophobia.

Carroll eventually pled guilty to committing three bias-motivated arsons, in exchange for a 30-year sentence. Assistant district attorney Cliff Herberg told the *San Antonio Express-News* that he was pleased with the result, showing that backlash bias crimes would not be tolerated in the area.[373]

In the years after the terrorist strikes, American businesses were sometimes attacked if their owners voiced opposition to the Iraq War or acknowledged the human rights of Arabs and Muslims overseas. *The San Francisco Chronicle* reported that Lori Haigh, owner of the Capobianco art gallery, was repeatedly threatened and assaulted for displaying paintings addressing the Abu Ghraib controversy.[374] At the time her North Beach gallery was being targeted, American newspapers and television shows were reporting on Abu Ghraib abuses, which included sodomizing detainees with batons, tying them up, urinating on them, pouring phosphoric acid on their bodies, pounding on their wounded limbs, and dragging them varying distances.[375] Since Haigh's gallery sometimes featured controversial art, she displayed artist Guy Colwell's work responding to revelations about Abu Ghraib, including a black and white painting showing American soldiers subjecting three naked hooded Iraqis to electric shock torture. Haigh was singled out by bigots after Colwell's paintings went up in her gallery. According to the *San Francisco Chronicle*, Haigh found broken glass, trash, and eggs littering the front of her business on May 18, 2004, two days after Colwell's artwork went on display.[376] She then started receiving the first of dozens of angry voice mails, emails, and death threats.[377] The *Chicago Sun-Times* reported that on the weekend of May 22, 2004, one angry gallery visitor spat on her; five days later, another punched her, giving her a concussion and breaking her nose.[378] She was so terrified by these attacks that she ended Colwell's month-long exhibit two weeks after it began and permanently closed her gallery.[379] When other community members learned of the politically-motivated harassment, Haigh's supporters urged her to continue her work. Daniel Macchiarini, another North Beach gallery owner, told the *Chronicle* that he found it outrageous that free speech was being curtailed in San Francisco.[380] City supervisors passed a resolution condemning the attacks on Haigh's gallery and called for one of the politically-themed paintings, "The Abuse," to be exhibited at City Hall. Despite the public support she received, Haigh reported being too fearful to re-open her business. Many San Francisco residents felt that the hate crime perpetrators were sending local Muslims and Arabs the message that they were sub-human, unworthy of Geneva protections. Many community members saw the closing of the Capobianco gallery as a manifestation of the ongoing 9/11 backlash. Rather than expressing sympathy, some political conservatives suggested that Haigh deserved the abuse for naively hanging such provocative art.[381] Citing unnamed sources, they also questioned the veracity of the hate crimes she reported, challenging her credibility on the grounds that she had been sued by a former boss for some business improprieties and had made abuse allegations against a Catholic priest who had confessed to sexually-molesting young girls.[382]

Bias crimes continued. In the summer of 2004, minority-owned businesses were targeted by Rhode Island bigots. In Providence, a convenience store was attacked in July 2004. According to the *Providence Journal*, a vandal spray-painted slurs on the building, which was owned by an Egyptian American.[383]

Muslim cab drivers continued to be attacked throughout the country. In August 2004, a pedestrian punched a Bangladeshi taxi driver in the face near Ground Zero.[384] Prior to striking the driver, the assailant made an anti-Muslim remark. The assailant was charged with two misdemeanors: harassment and third-degree assault. Because of the location of the attack and the religious slur used by the assailant, activists viewed the assault as a 9/11 backlash crime, and felt that bias enhancements were warranted. Community members were dismayed that minority taxi drivers were still being scapegoated so many years after the terrorist strikes and that their assailants were not being charged with hate crimes.

Sikh truck drivers were also harassed in 2004. On the third anniversary of 9/11, the *Fresno Bee* reported that Sikh truck drivers in the San Joaquin Valley had been repeatedly and recklessly cut off by other motorists, presumably because other drivers associated their beards and turbans with Taliban terrorists.[385] The bias incidents frightened area minorities, who wished that authorities would launch additional educational campaigns to stem intolerance.

In the fall of 2004, bigots continued to target businesses owned by South Asians. On November 24, 2004, a Sikh-owned Chevron gas station in Richmond, Virginia was vandalized and set on fire. According to *India Abroad*, the gas station's dumpsters were covered with hateful messages, including: "Go back to bin Laden Bitch," "Never Again Indian Monkey Nigger," and "Fuck Arab Gas."[386] Owners Sarabjit and Sukhjinder Singh were devastated by the attack, especially since they had recently spent $100,000 in renovations, installing a Sub Express and improving the food department.[387] The *Richmond Times–Dispatch* reported that firefighters took 90 minutes to extinguish the blaze.[388] The fire damaged the facility beyond repair, causing the roof to collapse. Although the gas station was insured, the owners reported that the money would not cover the totality of the damages and the lost revenue. Because the business was their sole source of income, the cousins were concerned that they had no way of supporting their two families and feeding their children.[389] Sarabjit and Sukhjinder Singh were also upset that the graffiti compared them to the 9/11 mastermind, suggesting that they were in league with al-Qaeda.

In spite of the hate messages at the crime scene, some local police were unwilling to admit that the arson was bias-motivated. Investigators speculated that the vandalism and arson may have been committed by two different perpetrators, occurring at the same location in temporal proximity. Community activists found this possibility unlikely, and were concerned that authorities were unwilling to recognize that arsonists were continuing to lash out at minority-owned businesses years after 9/11.

ATTACKS AT WORK, 2005

As the war in Iraq dragged on, bigots continued to scapegoat minority professionals in the U.S. The *Orange County Register* reported that in 2005, Dr. Arinder Chadha discovered that a vandal had defaced his San Bernardino clinic with anti-Iraqi and anti-Muslim death threats, although he was neither an Arab nor a Muslim.[390] Chadha saw this bias-motivated vandalism as part of an ongoing wave of intolerance that began on 9/11. Discussing some of his previous encounters with American xenophobia, he told the *Orange County Register* that when he was completing his medical training about an hour's drive from Ground Zero in the aftermath of the terrorist strikes, he noticed that his hospital colleagues suddenly began treating him strangely.[391] He feared they were unfairly associating him with the 9/11 hijackers, not realizing that he was a Sikh from Hemmadebad, India. To ease co-workers' fears, he began wearing a pin declaring that he was a Sikh and inviting people to ask him about his religion.[392]

On occasion, movies that attempted to explore American racism actually ended up reinforcing negative stereotypes. Many critics lauded the 2005 Oscar-winning movie, *Crash*, for its treatment of ethnic tensions. Despite the film's favorable reviews and warm reception at the box office, some minority viewers took issue with the character Farhad, an unlikable Iranian shopkeeper who acts like a stereotypical hot-blooded Middle Easterner. Film critic Shaheen was disturbed by the movie's inclusion of such an irrational and disrespectful racist caricature.[393] In one scene, the nefarious businessman unjustly accuses a competent, polite Latino locksmith of being a cheater, yelling at him and using profanities. Later in the movie, when the Muslim discovers that vandals have attacked his store, he jumps to the inaccurate conclusion that the Latino locksmith was responsible. Farhad then fires a gun at the Latino man and his young daughter, almost killing them. Since the movie pits a Muslim villain against a sympathetic Hispanic family, it transmits the message that Middle Easterners are violence-prone individuals, not to be trusted. Since millions of Americans watched this movie, it is possible that some of the perpetrators of anti-Muslim hate crimes may have been influenced by the film's disturbing portrayal of an Iranian store owner who treats Latinos with contempt.

Negative stereotypes of Middle Eastern businessmen also appear in the film, *The Deal*, which was released in the U.S. on June 17, 2005. Shaheen notes that in this dystopian movie, Arab financiers are portrayed as having ruined the American economy.[394] Because of an ongoing war between the U.S. and the Corporation of Arab States, gas prices have soared to $6.50 a gallon. By pitting the Orient against the Occident, the movie reinforces the notion that evil Semitic money-men are America's political and economic enemies. These racist films fueled a climate of xenophobia, allowing hate crimes to flourish.

ATTACKS AT WORK, 2006

Customers were sometimes endangered by bias-crimes directed at minority-owned businesses. On February 23, 2006, a diner was shot during a racially-motivated assault on a Middle Eastern restaurant in Alabama. The *Birmingham News* reported that 23-year old Jason Michael Gardner urinated on the Arab-owned business, used racial profanities, and slapped one of the customers.[395] Gardner eventually left the Quick Grill, located near the University of Alabama campus, but returned a short time later, alone in his truck. He then fired a .22-caliber rifle at a van parked in the rear of the restaurant, injuring 27-year old Nabil Chagri, a Moroccan-born man who was waiting in his vehicle with his family to place a take-out order.[396] Restaurant owner Jassim Madan, a native of Bahrain, came to Chagri's aid, and used napkins to stem the blood pouring out of his customer's head and back as a result of the gunshot wounds. At the time of the shooting, Chagri's wife, young daughter, and newborn baby were also in the van. John Tyra, a Marine reservist who witnessed the attack, reported that Chagri's relatives were traumatized by the shooting, and that blood had gotten on the infant's blanket.[397] Gardner was eventually charged with attempted murder and firing into an occupied vehicle. Muslim community members were dismayed that Gardner was not charged with a hate crime, noting that he used racial slurs on the evening of the shooting, targeted a minority-owned ethnic restaurant, and shot at an Arab customer waiting to be served. Many local residents viewed Gardener's bias crimes in the context of post-9/11 Islamophobia.

Activists saw a connection between anti-Muslim assaults and bigoted movies. As the Iraq War dragged on, American audiences continued to be entertained by pernicious cinematic stereotypes of foreigners. The 2006 movie, *Looking for Comedy in the Muslim World*, perpetuates negative images of South Asian workers. When the film's Western protagonist travels to India and tries to hire a typist, he is unable to find a suitable applicant. Movie critic Shaheen takes issue with the comedy for suggesting that Muslim job candidates are not worth hiring because they are either incompetent or Jew-haters.[398] The comedy also suggests that prospective Muslim employees have no sense of humor.

Whereas some American comedies ridiculed South Asian employees, others poked fun at Middle Eastern businessmen. In the movie, *Click*, the protagonist makes fun of an Arab bar owner, Prince Habeeboo, referring to him as Ali Poo Poo. The Arab is portrayed as a tasteless pervert, making plans to tear up the atrium of his establishment in order to create a space for wet t-shirt contests.[399] This movie, released in the U.S. on June 23, 2006, reminded American viewers that Semitic foreigners were irresponsible property owners who exploit women for financial gain.

While American audiences were laughing at buffoonish portrayals of Middle Easterners, minority workers continued to be attacked by bigots throughout the U.S. The *Tampa Tribune* suggested a connection between the five-year anniversary of 9/11 and a mid-September 2006 hate crime targeting a Lebanese-American club manager in Ybor City.[400] According to the *Tribune*, Joseph Azzi was at work at Club Fuel, speaking in Arabic to a relative, when two men started harassing him. They hurled racial slurs at Azzi, making bigoted comments and referring to him as a "rag head."[401]   Although Azzi replied that he was an American citizen, the men continued abusing him, and began throwing beer bottles at him. When one of the assailants told Azzi he was going to get a gun and kill him, the club manager ran away and summoned the police.[402]   Responding officers apprehended the two Polk Country assailants: James Butts, 28, of Lakeland, and Lee Hill, 28, of Auburndale. According to police spokeswoman Laura McElroy, the men were charged with aggravated assault and committing a hate crime, which made the attack a second-degree felony.

In other parts of the country, female professionals were scapegoated for 9/11 more than five years after the terrorist strikes, showing the longevity of the backlash in the U.S. On October 2, 2006, an Arab-American manager at a Sheraton Suites Hotel in Philadelphia received a death threat at her place of employment. According to the *Philadelphia Tribune*, the menacing note contained direct references to 9/11 and the suggestion that the woman and her two young children should be tied to a fence and killed.[403]   Worried about her family's safety, the 36-year old mother contacted the FBI. After a six-month investigation, federal agents determined that the hate letter was constructed by cutting words out of the hotel's brochures and publications. Another hotel employee, Kia Reid, was arrested in March 2007 for threatening her supervisor while the victim was performing her federally-protected job.[404]   Reid was eventually convicted on a federal civil rights charge and sentenced to eight months 'confinement in a community corrections center and two years of supervised probation.

Other minority businesswomen were targeted in the U.S. In the fall of 2006 and the summer of 2007, a bigot in Massachusetts sent death threats to an Iranian-American restaurant owner who ran two of Beacon Hill's most popular ethnic eateries. According to the *Boston Globe*, the hate mail, which began in November 2006, consisted of racist messages and photos of gun-carrying men, including a picture of Dustin Hoffman from the 1976 movie, *Marathon Man*.[405]   In June 2007, another letter arrived as the Persian-American restaurateur was preparing to present food at a festival at the Taj Boston Hotel. The *Boston Globe* reported that the envelope included a photo of a soldier brandishing a machine gun, with an attached note promising to find the Iranian-American restaurant owner at the Taj.[406]   The implicit death threat was even more frightening because its sender knew the businesswoman's work schedule.

The FBI eventually arrested Earl McBride, Jr., a 65-year old real estate broker who lived close to the restaurants. Since McBride was suspected of committing a bias crime, he was charged with a federal indictment for mailing a series of threatening communications to the restaurant owner. Boston FBI agent Warren T. Bamford told the *Globe* that the death threats were an indication that even affluent parts of society were infested with bigotry.[407]

While Middle Eastern business owners and employees were being harassed in the U.S., American audiences were watching movies that depicted Muslim workers as terrorists, intent on killing civilians. In his book, Guilty, Shaheen discusses several post-9/11 films that malign minority taxi drivers. In the 2006 movie, *Fatwa*, a villainous Libyan cabbie murders Americans.[408]   In one scene, the taxi driver tries to construct a radioactive bomb with ammonium nitrate. Along with being homicidal, the Middle Eastern cabbie is portrayed as a misogynist who has no moral qualms about targeting women. He tries to assassinate Minnesota senator Maggie Davidson, prompting this female protagonist to compare the Muslim cab driver to the 9/11 terrorists. He later kills the senator's daughter and friend. At the conclusion of the picture, the villainous Muslim dies a fiery death, to the great relief of moviegoers.

In the movie, *Crank*, Arab cab drivers in America are depicted as unsympathetic, avaricious, and ungrateful. This movie was released in the U.S. on September 1, 2006, near the five-year anniversary of 9/11. Shaheen is bothered by the film's repeated associations of Middle Easterners with terrorism.[409]   In a particularly disturbing plot sequence, an unlikable taxi driver refuses to let the protagonist Chev get into the cab with wet clothes, even though he paid him $200 to wait three minutes for him at a stop. To get back at the driver, Chev loudly and repeatedly accuses him of being an al-Qaeda terrorist. This prompts another man and two women to beat up the Arab driver. While the unsympathetic cabbie is being assaulted, Chev steals his vehicle. In another scene in the movie, an image of a gun-toting Arab terrorist appears on a slot machine, reinforcing the message that Middle Easterners are an unwelcome menace.

The movie, *Jackass Number Two*, features a disturbing prank dubbed "terror taxi." Describing this offensive scene, film critic Shaheen notes that one of the actors dresses as a suicide bomber and takes a taxi to the airport.[410] While en route, the faux passenger insinuates that he is planning on blowing up the plane, making disturbing comments about how he doesn't need any luggage where he is going. Unbeknownst to the actor, the Indian cabbie is in on the "prank." The South Asian taxi driver eventually pulls over and points a gun at the pretend terrorist. The terrified actor is finally told that he is the real victim of the practical joke, and that the Muslim beard he is wearing was fashioned out of the crew members' pubic hair.[411] Many viewers were offended by the program's inclusion of a gun-toting South Asian driving around a fake Middle Eastern terrorist wearing a faux beard made of actual pubic hair, especially since Muslim men opt to wear beards as a sign of piety. This offensive comedy was released in the U.S. on September 22, 2006. These types of movies give American audiences permission to look down on minority community members.

While viewers were laughing at offensive caricatures of foreign cabbies and passengers, bigots continued to target real minority drivers more than five years after 9/11. On October 11, 2006, Yankees pitcher Cory Lidle died when a small plane crashed into the upper East Side. This accident reminded many locals of the Twin Tower attacks. According to *India-West*, Lidle's plane crash and the mistaken belief that terrorists were back in town likely triggered Anthony Bryant's decision to target a Sikh-operated cab later that same day.[412] At the time of the hate crime, driver Avtar Singh Dhanjal was 60 years old, and Bryant was 36. After abusing the bearded Sikh with racial slurs and comments about his turban, Bryant started kicking the taxi, breaking the vehicle's mirrors.[413] He then snatched Dhanjal's trip sheet out of the driver's hands and ran off with it. Initially, Bryant was only charged with criminal mischief. After United Sikhs intervened, the charges were upgraded to one count of grand larceny in the fourth degree, aggravated harassment, and criminal mischief as a hate crime, with a maximum penalty of seven years in jail.

ATTACKS AT WORK, 2007

Throughout 2007, hate crimes continued to affect minority workers in the U.S. On February 18, 2007, two white males targeted an immigrant merchant in Omaha, Nebraska. During the attack, the assailants used duct tape to bind Kassahun Geshime's mouth, hands, and waist, and then set the business on fire with the Ethiopian owner tied up inside.[414] Geshime was rescued by firefighters after concerned community members noticed the blaze. He suffered minor burns as a result of the arson attack, which caused so much damage to the building that it had to be demolished. According to KETV 7 News, investigators were treating the assault, robbery, and fire as bias-motivated crimes, noting that the immigrant businessman had been repeatedly targeted by nativist community members in the past.[415] In the two weeks leading up to the arson, Geshime discovered racist slurs on his home and on the walls of his store, Bob's Food Mart, located near 16th and Fort Street. On another occasion, someone threw a brick containing a menacing note through his store window. The NAACP spoke out against the escalating violence, and urged federal agents to get involved with the case.[416] Many area minorities saw the hate crimes as part of the wave of xenophobia unleashed by 9/11. To protect himself and his family, Geshime decided to relocate to Atlanta.[417]

In many parts of the country, attacks escalated near the sixth anniversary of 9/11. In August 2007, a Locus Valley nail salon in Nassau County began receiving threatening calls, accusing Iranian-American businesswoman Zahreh Assemi of being a terrorist and demanding that she close her shop. On September 15, 2007, two men entered the Givan Nail and Skin Center at approximately 6:30 a.m., threatening Assemi with a gun and writing anti-Islamic graffiti on the property.[418] *Newsday* reported that the assailants stabbed her with a box cutter and a knife on her face, neck, back, and chest.[419] They also bashed her head on a counter, shoved a towel in her mouth, and repeatedly smashed her hand with a hammer. During the assault, they used slurs, showing that the crime was bias-motivated. They also threatened to kill her if she called the police or failed to move her business out of the plaza. Assemi, a naturalized U.S. citizen, was treated at North Shore University Hospital in Manhasset for cuts zigzagging across her face and arms. Assemi was upset that she was being targeted because of her religion and national origin. She fled Iranian tyranny in 1982, settling in America with her five-year old daughter and husband. After her spouse passed away in 1993, she relied on the nail salon as her primary means of supporting her family. Nassau Lt. John May told *Newsday* that Assemi's assailants wrote anti-Muslim graffiti on a mirror, stole jewelry, and left with $2,000 in cash.[420] Investigating officers were unsure about whether the assailants were also responsible for making the menacing calls that preceded the attack. Many community members saw the mid-September hate crime in the context of the ongoing 9/11 backlash and the escalation of Islamic sentiment in the U.S.

In 2007, community bigots continued to scapegoat minority cab drivers for the terrorist strikes. One of the most serious hate crimes took place in Washington state on Thanksgiving weekend. On November 24, 2007, Luis Arturo Vazquez and his friend, an Iraq War veteran, went to Husky stadium to attend the Apple Cup football game. After Vazquez was denied entrance for being intoxicated, Seattle police summoned a taxi to take Vazquez home. According to *India-West*, cab driver Sukhvir Singh, a father of two from Kent, had just stopped at a Montlake grocery store when police saw his taxi and asked him to transport Vazquez.[421] The drunken passenger assumed the turbaned driver was an Arab Muslim murderer, not realizing he was actually a South Asian Sikh and a U.S. permanent resident. According to *India-West*, Vazquez called the Sikh driver an "Iraqi terrorist" and attacked him from behind while the cab was going 60 miles per hour on Interstate 5.[422] During the assault, the intoxicated construction worker threatened to kill the driver and repeatedly used racial and religious epithets. As soon as he could, Singh stopped the vehicle and ran out of the taxi. Vazquez then pursued Singh on foot. According to *India-West*, Vazquez followed the South Asian driver before pushing him on the pavement, pulling off his turban and ripping out a chunk of his scalp and hair.[423] Vazquez beat Singh repeatedly and stopped only when a Metro bus pulled up and the drunken assailant tried to board it. Soon thereafter, Washington state police responded to the scene and arrested Vazquez. Singh was treated for his injuries at Harborview Medical Center and released on November 25, 2007. He was re-admitted when he began repeatedly vomiting because his kidneys and lungs worsened. According to the *Northwest Asian Weekly*, Singh was hospitalized for five days and treated for internal organ failure and bodily pain from his numerous injuries.[424] The *Seattle Post-Intelligencer* reported that Singh also had a concussion, lacerations on his face, and bite marks on his scalp.[425]

Although Vazquez used ethnic slurs during the beating, Kent police officers publicly stated that they did not view the attack as a hate crime. Outraged that authorities were dismissing the significance of Vazquez's bigoted comments, the Sikh community pressured the police into re-categorizing the attack as a bias-motivated assault. The Sikh Coalition was particularly instrumental in getting the FBI to file federal hate crime charges in the case. Area residents viewed the attack as a manifestation of post-9/11 bigotry.

Local South Asians attended the legal proceedings, hoping that their vigilance would ensure that the court took the case seriously. In March 2008, Vazquez pled guilty to second-degree assault, reckless endangerment, and committing a hate crime. The *Seattle Times* reported that at sentencing, Vazquez apologized to Singh and the Sikh community, expressing his regret that he had made them hyper-vigilant when interacting with strangers.[426] According to the *Post-Intelligencer*, Vazquez told the packed courtroom that he was sorry for subjecting his Sikh victim to the kind of attack he would not wish on his family members.[427]

Deputy prosecutor Mike Hogan told the *Post-Intelligencer* that Vazquez deserved a stiff sentence because the crime endangered Singh's life and jeopardized the other motorists on the road.[428] Once Singh learned that his attacker was apologetic and had no prior criminal offenses, he asked the judge to show leniency to Vazquez, who claimed to be unable to remember what happened. The *Seattle Post-Intelligencer* reported that Judge Monica Benton sentenced the 21-year old to nine months in work release and 24 hours community service, telling him that it was unfortunate he did not remember the assault since his victim would never forget it.[429]

ATTACKS AT WORK, 2008

American bigots continued to target minority-run businesses in 2008. In Minnesota, arsonists fire-bombed a Muslim-owned convenience store on January 27, 2008. According to the *Star Tribune*, the three perpetrators walked into Blaine Dairy, carrying glass bottles and a paper bag.[430] They then lit the bottles on fire and threw them inside the store. Blaine police officers reported that the owner suffered minor burns and cuts on his arm, and that an anti-Arab slur was found spray-painted on the building's west wall. Police captain Kerry Fenner said the fire caused so much structural damage that the store would need to be torn down.[431] Local residents were so outraged by the hate crime that they held a town forum to promote tolerance and speak out against the attack on a well-respected minority-run business that had sold dairy products and household items since the 1960s.

The same year, Muslim workers were targeted in Kansas. In the spring of 2008, KCTV Channel 5 reported that a man walked into a gas station in Lenexa and asked the attendant if he was Muslim.[432] When the employee affirmed that he was, the customer began harassing him. Shortly after the irate man left, a Molotov cocktail was thrown through the business' front window.[433] A similar attack occurred at another area business.[434] Police later arrested a 26-year old man and charged him with one count of criminal damage and two counts related to the use of explosives.

Minority employees were also singled out in other states. In Pennsylvania, immigrant workers at a Crown Bolt plant in North Middleton Township were disturbed to find xenophobic death threats repeatedly written on the men's room wall in late July, 2008. According to the *Patriot-News*, the graffiti made offensive references to Allah and included death threats against Iraqis, Muslims, and Mexicans.[435] Because company officials failed to respond appropriately to the ongoing hate crimes, 17 Muslim, Arab, and African immigrant workers walked out on the job. Many employees saw the bigoted messages as an example of post-9/11 intolerance.

ATTACKS AT WORK, 2009

In 2009, unknown assailants in the U.S. continued to attack immigrant-run businesses. The *Commercial Appeal* reported that on January 30, 2009, 19-year old Yemeni clerk Mohammed al Hadi was murdered in a store robbery in Memphis.[436] Discussing this attack, My Eyewitness News reported that the unknown shooter calmly took aim and fired, as if he had some kind of vendetta.[437] Hadi's dreams of college ended after he staggered out to an alley and collapsed next to his shop. The same evening, another Yemeni store owner, 47-year old Sam Nagi, was also shot to death in the same city. Reporters questioned whether there was a bias component to these killings, causing some area residents to fear a resurgence of post-9/11 Islamophobia.[438] According to the *Commercial Appeal*, anti-Arab sentiment was on the rise in Memphis. The same month that Hadi and Nagi were killed, unknown perpetrators set fire to a Middle Eastern clerk's car and called for a boycott of all Arab-owned businesses in the neighborhood.[439]

The same year, bias incidents took place in other states. In Feltonville, Pennsylvania, vandals wrote anti-Iranian graffiti outside of Premium Seafood, a Palestinian-owned store. The *Philadelphia Inquirer* reported that during the August 20, 2009 attack, the vandals broke glass windows and doors, shattered display cases, overturned counters, scattered food, and threw merchandise around the shop.[440] Despite the existence of racist and derogatory writings at the crime scene, detectives characterized the crime as a simple burglary.[441] The Middle Eastern community in Philadelphia urged investigators to treat the Islamophobic vandalism as a bias-motivated attack, comparing it to hate crimes that took place in the city in the immediate aftermath of 9/11.

Throughout 2009, Sikh cab drivers were targeted by bigoted passengers who accused them of being in league with Osama bin Laden. In late August, two passengers in Pleasanton, California assaulted 38-year old cab driver Jaswinder Bangar of Livermore. On the night of the attack, Bangar picked up 33-year old Michael Goldstein of Danville and 27-year old Jacob Billingsley of Alamo. The *Oakland Tribune* reported that Goldstein and Billingsley punched the Sikh driver in the head while making racial slurs.[442] Bangar told *India-West* that his assailants repeatedly called him a Taliban terrorist, and told him that they knew he was in the U.S. to kill them.[443] When Bangar tried to call the police, the assailants broke his cell phone. Desperate for help, the targeted cabbie attempted to drive to a nearby 7-Eleven, where he knew the owner. Once Bangar exited his vehicle, Goldstein and Billingsley resumed their assault, savagely beating him until he fell to the ground. Bangar, a former Punjabi farmer who emigrated to the U.S. in 1997, told *India-West* that he feared for his life during the brutal attack.[444] After the assailants fled the scene, a delivery driver saw the injured cabbie and called 911.

The beating left the Sikh with bruises, a broken tooth, and facial injuries that required stitches. Bangar, the father of two preschool-age children, was uninsured at the time of the crime, and accumulated more than $16,000 in medical bills.[445] Unable to work for weeks, he was forced to depend on his wife's inadequate income as a Subway sandwich maker to cover their mounting expenses.

Following the arrest of the two assailants on August 27, 2009, the Alameda County District Attorney's office charged Goldstein with felony battery and Billingsley with misdemeanor battery. Despite the assailants' extensive use of ethnic and racial slurs during the beating, prosecutors declined to add hate crime enhancements because the assault began after Bangar refused to allow the passengers to pay by credit card. Pleasanton police Lt. Darrin Davis told *India-West* that although the assailants made inappropriate comments, the primary motivation for the crime was the payment dispute.[446] Officials also pointed out that in California, an attack is only considered a hate crime if it was bias-motivated from its inception. Civil rights activists were outraged that the assault was not being treated as a hate crime, arguing that the assailants' use of racial slurs showed that ethnic hatred was the primary motive for the vicious and prolonged beating.

Hate crimes continued to affect employed Muslims in 2009. On occasion, anti-Islamic drawings were put outside of Muslim-owned businesses in Minnesota. In December 2009, a vandal in St. Cloud posted sexually-graphic and derogatory pictures in front of Somali stores. The offensive drawings included images of the Prophet Mohammed and a swastika. Deko Farah, manager of Mandeeq Shop, told the *St. Cloud Times* that she was disturbed that a bigoted community member posted five pages of Islamophobic cartoons outside of her business.[447] In response to the incident, she began closing early, afraid for her safety.

ATTACKS AT WORK, 2010

Attacks on minority workers continued throughout 2010. In San Diego, California, a Muslim taxi driver was assaulted on May 12, 2010. The Afghan-American cabbie was completing his evening prayers at a park near Mission Bay when a white man in his 50s began screaming at him, using profanities and telling him to return to his homeland.[448] After the Muslim driver got back to his taxi and put on his seat belt, the assailant grabbed his shirt and punched him in the right eye and left shoulder. While beating the driver, the bigoted assailant made racist slurs. Community members were dismayed that religious minorities were still being singled out so many years after 9/11.

The same month, a Muslim construction worker was assaulted in Brooklyn, New York. According to the *New York Daily News*, Kamal Uddin, a 57-year old man from Bangladesh, was on his lunch break when four men approached him and asked him if he was Muslim.[449] The men then jumped him but refrained from robbing him. At the time of the attack, Uddin was wearing a traditional Muslim prayer cap. The May 22, 2010 beating was so severe that Uddin became disoriented, thinking it was August. He was taken to Bookdale University Hospital, where he told family members that his assailants targeted him because of his religion.[450] He also reported that his attackers spouted hate speech during the beating. The NYPD Hate Crimes Task Force investigated the assault, but did not classify it as a hate crime because witnesses were unable to confirm that ethnic slurs accompanied the beating. Community activists argued that authorities did not need independent corroboration to know that the Bangladeshi Muslim was the victim of a hate crime, pointing out that Uddin heard the slurs and that his attackers could have not have missed his South Asian appearance and Islamic prayer cap.

In the summer of 2010, Islamophobes targeted Muslim-owned businesses in many parts of the country. In Minnesota, a vandal attacked a Somali-owned hair salon in St. Cloud, using paint to deface the windows and the front of the store. Jibril and Linda Wander, who owned Sheer Dynamics for more than 15 years, viewed the vandalism in the context of other post-9/11 attacks in the city.[451]

In other parts of the U.S., anti-Muslim hate crimes were considerably more vicious. One of the most serious bias attacks occurred on August 24, 2010, when a 21-year old film student slashed the throat of a Muslim cab driver in Midtown, New York. After hailing the cab, Michael Enright engaged in small talk with the Bangladeshi driver, 44-year old Ahmed Sharif. According to the *Wall St. Journal*, the passenger asked the driver how long he had been in the country, if he was a Muslim, and if he was fasting for Ramadan.[452] Enright then commenced a diatribe against Islam, telling the driver that he intended to bring him down.[453] The *New York Times* reported that Enright was in the middle of his bigoted rant when he reached across the plastic barrier and attacked the Muslim cabbie, slashing his throat and stabbing him in the face, arms, and hands.[454] The injuries were so severe that Sharif required two dozen stitches to close his wounds.

Following the attack, mayor Michael Bloomberg linked Sharif's stabbing to post-9/11 bigotry and the furor over the "Ground Zero" mosque.[455] The *New York Post* reported that Sharif also speculated that anti-Muslim outrage over the construction project may have contributed to Enright's decision to stab him.[456] When asked about his own thoughts on the Park51 Islamic center, Sharif claimed that he was opposed to building the house of worship on the designated site.[457] Some New York Muslims wondered if Sharif was genuinely against building the controversial mosque in its intended location or if he felt compelled to speak out against the project to protect himself from additional hate crimes.

Because of Enright's use of anti-Muslim statements during the attack, prosecutors charged him with second-degree attempted murder and assault as a hate crime. Enright was initially taken to Belleview Hospital Center for a psychiatric evaluation before being moved to Rikers Island. He was released from custody after his mother posted $500,000 bail. At a hearing, Enright's attorney claimed that his client suffered from alcoholism and PTSD, a condition he developed while filming Marines in Afghanistan. Some of Enright's acquaintances were surprised by the attack, noting that the film student had volunteered for Intersections International, a progressive organization that supported the construction of the Park51 Islamic center.

New York Muslims were disturbed that some community members failed to appreciate the severity of the bias-motivated stabbing. The *Wall St. Journal* reported that one of Enright's professors, Reeves Lehmann, went on record saying that he would welcome the film student back to class upon his release from custody.[458] It is unlikely that Enright's minority classmates would have been as enthusiastic about having a violent anti-Muslim bigot and attempted murderer back on campus.

The same year, minority taxi drivers were targeted in bias attacks in California, showing that xenophobia was still strong nine years after the terrorist strikes. On November 28, 2010, Harbhajan Singh, a Sikh driver, was assaulted after picking up four passengers – two men and their wives – at Harlow's bar in West Sacramento. The *Sacramento Bee* reported that 41-year old Pedro Ramirez and 33-year old Johnny Morales uttered anti-Muslim slurs while beating the bearded Sikh driver, who wore a turban.[459] Responding to the derogatory remarks, Singh tried explaining that he was from India and was not Muslim. Because he thought he was being robbed, Singh tossed $40 at his assailants. They threw the money back at him, and continued the assault. According to *India-West*, Ramirez and Morales threatened to kill Singh during the attack, yelling anti-Arab slurs, accusing him of being a Muslim, and calling him Osama bin Laden.[460] Ramirez punched Singh in the head about ten times and tried to pull him from the cab, but was unable to do so because the driver was wearing a seat belt.[461] Horrified by what she was seeing, Ramirez's wife interrupted the beating by throwing her body between Singh and her husband. Once the passengers exited the cab, Singh escaped and contacted authorities. At first, police Lt. Tod Sockman viewed the attack as a simple alcohol-induced robbery, but later appreciated the bias component of the crime. Because the assailants compared Singh to the al-Qaeda ringleader, community activists viewed the beating in the context of the 9/11 backlash.

The Sacramento Bee reported that a few days after the attack, Ramirez and Morales were booked at Yolo County Jail after being arrested for felony assault with a deadly weapon and commission of a hate crime.[462] FBI investigators were also looking into Singh's vicious beating, which left the father of four with a spinal fracture, a broken nose, rib cage bruising, knee problems, damage to his eye, and head injuries that required seven stitches. Singh told *India Abroad* that he was surprised by the sudden assault, since he was a peaceful vegetarian who had never been attacked before.[463]

In response to the Pleasanton hate crime and other assaults involving black and Hispanic perpetrators, cabbies in Sacramento began racially-profiling potential passengers. Kazman Zaidi, vice president of the Sacramento Taxi Cab Association, told KTXL-TV that many drivers felt so frightened that they were unwilling to pick up some male fares.[464]

Singh's assailants eventually pled guilty to felony assault. According to the *News India-Times*, Ramirez admitted to punching Singh in the face repeatedly and yelling racial epithets during the attack.[465] He was sentenced to 13 years in jail. Morales was sentenced to felony probation after admitting that he struck Singh from behind.[466]

Along with minority taxi drivers, immigrant convenience store workers continued being assaulted in the fall of 2010. On election night, November 2, 2010, a man and a group of teenage boys attacked Turkish employees at the OK gas station in Levittown, Long Island. Tensions began after 37-year old clerk Yuksel Cebeci refused to sell a package of cigarettes to one of the teens. The *New York Post* reported that at that point, the youths attacked Cebeci and fled.[467] Twenty minutes later, when responding officers were interviewing Cebeci at the station, the assailants returned, joined by Richard Vitale, the father of two of the youths and a retired NYPD officer. According to the *Post*, Vitale began screaming at Cebeci and manager Yavuz Erdogan, calling them "aliens" and yelling for them to get out of his country.[468] In front of witnesses, the former cop began clubbing 38-year old Erdogan, a Turkish-American, in the face and chest with a pole attached to the U.S. flag.[469] Nassau police officers on the scene stopped the xenophobic attack and arrested Vitale, his sons Gregory and Richard Jr., and their friends, 19-year old Christopher Makhmaltchi and 17-year old Nicholas Lazarus. Although Vitale screamed an anti-immigrant remark when he bludgeoned Erdogan, he was not charged with a hate crime on the grounds that the beating began after Cebeci refused to sell cigarettes to Lazarus. Community activists were horrified that the assailants were able to dodge bias-crime enhancements.

The following month, a Sikh delivery man was attacked by bigots. In mid-December 2010, a South Asian in West Texas was assaulted by four men who referred to him as Osama bin Laden.[470] *The Hindustan Times* reported that when the Sikh brought a food order into a customer's home, the occupants took the pizzas, started eating them without paying, and began screaming racial epithets.[471] They then threw the South Asian delivery man into a swimming pool, and surrounded it to prevent him from escaping. While he swam for his life for 20 minutes, the four men repeatedly kicked him in the head and body, striking him whenever he got in range or tried to get out of the water. During the assault, they kicked off his dastaar and told him told him to return to Afghanistan.[472] They also made other derogatory statements, telling him that they would beat him up in Afghanistan, Iraq, and the U.S.[473] Because of the brutality of the assault, the Sikh victim told *India-West* he was afraid his assailants were going to kill him.[474] The drowning delivery man eventually fought his way free, and contacted the police.

According to the *Hindustan Times*, the assailants were charged with a misdemeanor, a crime that had no mandatory jail time.[475] In the months following the racially-motivated attempted drowning, the Sikh victim told *India-West* that he received several death threats from his attackers, who remained free.[476] Area South Asians felt that the perpetrators deserved to be incarcerated pending trial because they posed a danger to minority members of the community. Worried for his safety, the hate crime victim moved out of the area, deciding to continue his graduate education at a different school. Community activists were horrified by the bias-motivated attack, angry that innocent Sikhs and Muslims continued to be compared to Osama bin Laden and scapegoated for 9/11 more than nine years after the terrorist strikes.

ATTACKS AT WORK, 2011

Crimes against minority businesses continued in 2011. On April 17, 2011, a Louisiana vandal targeted a store owned by a father and son of Middle Eastern ancestry. During the attack, 52-year old William Blackford kicked in the glass door at Son's Stop & Shop, and then called the Houma police to tell them that he committed the attack because of the store owners' ethnicity. The local newspaper, the *Courier*, reported that Blackford told officers that he wanted to kill all Middle Easterners or drive them out of the country.[477] Apparently, Blackford was not aware that the Muslim store owners, Omar and Adel Mohamed, were American citizens, born and raised in the U.S. Blackford was charged with simple criminal damage to property, a charge that carried a maximum sentence of two years in prison. Because Blackford admitted that he acted out of bias, he was also faced an additional five years in jail for committing a hate crime. According to the *Courier*, this was the fifth time the store's front door had been smashed. Adel Mohamed, the owner's 19-year old son, was troubled by the most recent attack on his family's business, telling reporters that he found the anti-Muslim hate crime particularly disturbing because he and his relatives did not display their faith in public.[478]

During the 'War on Terror,' bigots frequently vented their rage on minority workers. In Clearwater, Florida, a man attacked an African-American city employee in a vicious hate crime. The *St. Petersburg Times* reported that on April 28, 2011, 35-year old Gerald Christopher Prebe ran down 53-year old road worker Terry Butler with his vehicle.[479] Police reported that the white assailant yelled a racial slur before deliberately hitting him with his Nissan pick-up truck. The hit-and-run attack fractured Butler's neck and caused internal bleeding, requiring the black man to be hospitalized. Prebe told investigators that he intended to kill Butler because he thought the man was a terrorist, possibly of Middle Eastern descent.[480] Prebe was charged with attempted murder, and held on a $100,000 bond. Community activists hoped that prosecutors would add hate crime enhancements to the charges, particularly since Prebe admitted to be motivated by ethno-racial bias.

After Osama bin Laden had been killed, minority business owners and employees hoped that the 9/11 backlash would finally end. Unfortunately, news coverage of the death of the terrorist mastermind corresponded with a new surge of bias crimes singling out minority service workers. On May 8, 2011, two assailants from Eureka, California targeted a gas station attendant of East Indian heritage.[481] During the assault, they claimed that the South Asian clerk was angry that Osama bin Laden had been killed by American troops. They also used racial slurs and called the service worker a jihadist.

Hate crimes targeting Sikh and Arab businesses escalated near the tenth anniversary of 9/11. On September 7, 2011, a bigotry-motivated arsonist threw a Molotov cocktail through the front door of a Sikh-owned grocery store in Clay County, North Carolina, near the Georgia border. In addition to fire-bombing the State Line Grocery, the assailant also wrote "9/11 go home," suggesting that it was a backlash attack.[482] The hate crime traumatized members of the South Asian family who owned the business. According to Sheriff's Deputy Todd Wingate, an accelerant was used to start the blaze, indicating a desire to inflict serious damage to the minority-operated establishment.[483] Officials at the State Bureau of Investigation were looking into the arson, but were not handling the possible bias aspect of the crime. In the immediate aftermath of the fire, federal agents at the North Carolina office of the FBI were unsure about whether they should get involved in the case. The Sikh Coalition was monitoring the matter and encouraging the FBI to join the investigation.

A week later, an arsonist set fire to an Arab-owned business in California. At 4:00 a.m. on September 14, 2011, the fire department arrived at Star Cleaners, located in an Orangevale strip mall on Madison Avenue, and discovered smoke pouring out of a broken window. On a wall next to the entrance, the perpetrator spray-painted a swastika, a profanity, and the word, "Arab."[484]

According to KCRA Channel 3 News, the fire damaged a wall and melted plastic wrappers covering customers' clothes, which were dripping with soot and water.[485] The owners, Joe Kurt and his sister Mona, were Christian Palestinians who had emigrated to the U.S. in the 1970s. They purchased the business a year ago from a Jordanian who bought it from a Korean who took it over from a Syrian owner. Community members believed that the most recent store owners had been targeted in a backlash hate crime because of their Arabic accents and their sale of camel bags and other Middle Eastern paraphernalia at the business.[486] They also displayed pictures of the Virgin Mary and a cross in honor of their Antiochian Orthodox faith. In remembrance of the victims of the terrorist attacks, they hung an American flag at the store on the tenth anniversary of 9/11.

Crime scene investigators determined that the assailant broke into the plate-glass window with a crowbar, poured a flammable liquid from a plastic container onto a Molotov cocktail, and threw the incendiary device onto a wall. Sacramento Metropolitan Fire District investigators told the *Sacramento Bee* that 29 firefighters helped extinguish the blaze, which caused approximately $60,000 worth of damage.[487] According to assistant fire department chief Scott Cockrum, the dry cleaners' sprinkler system saved the building from more extensive destruction, noting that the fire could have easily gotten out of control and engulfed the other businesses at the mall.[488]

Despite the existence of the racist graffiti, an FBI agent was initially reluctant to characterize the arson attack as a bias crime. In an interview with KCRA Channel 3 News, FBI spokesman Steve Dupre characterized the blaze as "a mystery," noting that investigators had no leads in the case and were therefore unwilling to label the fire a bigotry-motivated arson.[489]

Arab-Americans in the area were shocked that the federal investigator was unable to make the rather obvious connection between the firebombing of the Arab-owned business, the racist graffiti, and the timing of the attack near the tenth anniversary of 9/11. They also noted that the same strip mall was targeted on July 4, 2011 by an intruder who wrote "Crip Killer" and anti-Asian graffiti on the facility.[490] Because this vandalism occurred on Independence Day, some area residents suspected that it was inspired by nativist sentiment. Stan Lee, the co-owner of the mall, characterized both the July 4th and September 14th attacks as unbelievable and unacceptable.[491] Some community members speculated that the fire might have been prevented if investigators had taken the earlier hate crime more seriously.

The FBI eventually determined that the Orangeville firebombing was bias-motivated, characterizing it as the nation's "only confirmed federal hate crime" triggered by the tenth anniversary of the terrorist strikes.[492] Community activists were upset that federal agents were discounting other 9/11-related bias crimes, pointing out that the North Carolina arson attack and the vehicular assault on a Buffalo mosque also deserved to be acknowledged.[493] Across the country, minority workers were frustrated that they continued to be targeted in backlash crimes more than ten years after 9/11.

Years after the terrorist strikes, minority workers in America continued to feel the effects of the backlash. In September 2011, the *Seattle Post-Intelligencer* reported that Muslims were often bothered at work, and experienced the stress of finding a place to pray that wouldn't anger or irrationally frighten their colleagues.[494]

CHAPTER EIGHT:

BACKLASH HATE CRIMES AT HOMES AND RESIDENCES, SEPT. 2001 TO SEPT. 2011

Along with hate crimes targeting prayer centers, schools, and businesses, the 9/11 backlash included attacks on minority-owned homes and apartments. In many towns across the country, patriotism took on a nativist flavor. Community members began looking at their ethnic neighbors with heightened distrust and suspicion. In the aftermath of the terrorist strikes, bigots repeatedly vandalized American homes owned by Arabs, Muslims, and South Asians. The harassment began soon after the Twin Towers fell and continued throughout the decade that followed. To understand why American bigots so readily attacked minority residents, it is important to view these hate crimes in the context of pernicious cinematic portrayals of Middle Eastern homeowners and community members in the years prior to 9/11. In his book, <u>Reel Bad Arabs</u>, film critic Jack Shaheen discusses how these late-20th century movies propagated harmful stereotypes of Arabs and fostered anti-immigrant sentiment in the U.S. [1]

In the 1995 Disney comedy, *Father of the Bride II*, an Arab-American home buyer is depicted as a misogynistic money-grabbing opportunist who takes advantage of George Banks, a sympathetic family man, played by Steve Martin. [2] After buying the white protagonist's beloved residence, Mr. Habib decides to demolish it. The regretful Banks then decides to repurchase his house to save it from destruction. Although Habib has only owned Banks' home for one day, he demands $100,000 over his purchase price before agreeing to the sale. Once again, American audiences are "entertained" by the anti-Semitic message that Arab-Americans are not the sort of people who deserve to live in American neighborhoods.

Other pre-9/11 movies feature Arabs or Muslims living in America and plotting to kill American civilians. The 1998 movie, *The Siege*, features a white female CIA agent, played by Annette Benning, and a black FBI investigator, played by Denzel Washington, working together against Arab terrorists scheming to murder American civilians. After a terrorist incident, federal officials round up Arabs and Arab-Americans and place them in U.S. concentration camps. Community activists were upset by the movie, since it leaves viewers with the impression that Arabs and Muslims living in the U.S. pose a danger to the country and should be regarded with suspicion. Film critic Roger Ebert compared this racist movie to anti-Semitic pictures of the 1930s. [3] The ethnic and religious stereotypes in *The Siege* contributed to a zeitgeist in which Arab-Americans and Muslims were seen as a menacing presence in U.S. neighborhoods. These types of Islamophobic films may have contributed to the intensity of the 9/11 backlash.

HOME ATTACKS, SEPTEMBER 2001

As news of the terrorist strikes spread across the U.S., bigots began looking up immigrant surnames in phone books and on-line directories, and using the information to target Middle Eastern and South Asian homeowners and tenants. At 6:15 a.m. on September 12, 2001, Sarah Mohamed, a 34-year old accountant from Garden Grove, started getting menacing calls blaming her for the terrorist strikes. According to the *Los Angeles Times*, one caller threatened to go over to her house and show her what needed to be done to her people. [4]

In some instances, backlash hate calls escalated into attacks on minority-owned residences. Throughout the U.S., bigots targeted Muslim-owned dwellings in the aftermath of 9/11. The September 14, 2001 issue of the *Boston Globe* reported that in East Lansing, Michigan, a gunman fired into the residence of a Muslim family soon after the terrorist strikes. [5] Muslim households were also singled out in other parts of the country. The *Columbian* reported that in Everett, Washington, a vandal attacked a Muslim family's house on September 15, 2001. [6] The bigot spray-painted a death threat on the driveway, suggesting that the family should be killed in retaliation for the strikes on the World Trade Center and Pentagon. The hate crime frightened community activists, who worried about ethnic scapegoating and the rise in nativist sentiment across the country.

Muslim-owned homes were also targeted in the South. On occasion, arsonists destroyed minority family residences. The *Roanoke Times and World News* reported that in mid-September 2001, a newly-renovated home in Roanoke was gutted right before an Iraqi family was scheduled to move in.[7] Arab-American groups speculated that the fire was a backlash hate crime, instigated to keep Middle Eastern immigrants out of the neighborhood.

Muslim homeowners living in rural areas were often scapegoated during the 9/11 backlash. According to the *Seattle Times*, a Pakistani-American family in Sheridan, Wyoming received repeated threatening calls in the immediate aftermath of the terrorist strikes.[8] Because the Khans were the only Muslim family living in the town, they were easy targets for xenophobes. On one occasion, bigots called Zarif Khan, Jr. at home and asked him if he had Osama bin Laden's email address or cell phone number, apparently unaware of the fact that the Pakistani-American's family had been in the U.S. since 1908.[9] Since gay activist Matthew Shepherd had been killed in a Wyoming hate crime a few years previously, Khan was nervous that an enraged community member might try to attack his family, his home, or one of the 13 Motel Six businesses he owned in the area. Along with the menacing calls, the Khans witnessed other signs of increasing community intolerance. They were particularly disturbed to see a neighborhood pickup truck with a home-made sign declaring that all "diaper heads" should be nuked.[10]

Although such overt displays of racism made the Khans worried for their safety, they were grateful for the outpouring of support they received from neighbors and friends upset that they were being scapegoated. They particularly appreciated receiving a sympathetic call from the local high school principal, who reassured the family that administrators and teachers would go out of their way to ensure that the family's teenage sons were safe on school grounds.[11]

Minority homeowners sometimes received hate mail from white supremacist groups that blamed non-Christians for 9/11. The *Boston Herald* reported that Stoughton residents found KKK literature on their lawns in late September, 2001.[12] The pamphlets claimed that the recent hijackings proved that Christianity was under attack from Muslims and Jews. Minority community members were dismayed that they were being scapegoated for the terrorist strikes, and were frustrated by the escalation of Islamophobia and anti-Semitism in the area.

Afghan immigrants also experienced post-9/11 harassment in their neighborhoods. The *Times-Union* reported that a family in Albany, originally from Afghanistan, was selecting items to purchase at a neighborhood garage sale in mid-September 2001 when the homeowner suddenly refused to sell them the merchandise.[13] The slighted community members were saddened that they were being unfairly associated with the terrorist hijackers.

Sikh homes and apartments were occasionally attacked in the immediate aftermath of 9/11. The *Washington Post* reported that a on the night of September 12, 2001, a vandal threw a brick through the window of a Sikh's home in Centreville.[14] The attack alarmed area South Asians, who were disturbed by the rise of nativism in the U.S.

Bigots in Colorado also targeted Sikh homeowners. According to the *Colorado Springs Gazette*, Buggie and Pinky Bajwa woke up on September 13, 2001 and discovered that a vandal had attacked their home while they were sleeping.[15] Blaming the couple for the strikes on the World Trade Center and Pentagon, the intruder spray-painted the word "terrorist" in red on their driveway, and wrote "terrorist on board" on their white van.[16]

In the aftermath of 9/11, arsonists occasionally targeted minority-owned homes. In San Mateo, California, an assailant threw an unlit Molotov cocktail into a Sikh family's living room in mid-September 2001. According to the *San Mateo County Times*, investigators recovered a bottle contained a piece of cloth with a faint odor of lamp oil on it.[17] They speculated that the arsonist may have attempted to light the Molotov cocktail before throwing it. The homemade incendiary device did not explode, but hit the family's three-year old son on the head.[18] Although the boy's father was out when the attack occurred, eight relatives were present, including elderly family members visiting from India. One witness saw a six-foot tall brown-haired man run out of the driveway, but was unable to ascertain if the suspect fled in a vehicle. The Sikh homeowner, who worked as a taxi driver, told *India-West* that he refused to allow fear to keep him from wearing a turban in America, his home since 1992.[19]

South Asians were also attacked at their residences in other parts of the country. According to the *Tulsa World*, three local bigots jumped Indian immigrant Subneet Sahjal as he left his apartment at 11:00 p.m. on September 14, 2001.[20] After knocking him down and hitting him, the attackers indirectly referred to the terrorist attacks, threatening to cut Sahjal for what he did to their people.[21] While the three assailants were repeatedly striking him on the mouth and eyes, he asked them why he was being targeted, maintaining that he had done nothing wrong.[22] His assailants ignored his words, and continued beating him. Paramedics transported the injured Sahjal to St. Francis Hospital, where he was treated for multiple lacerations. Since Sahjal worked at the Quik Stop where Naveed Alam had been assaulted by three men, Tulsa police speculated that the two bias attacks may have been instigated by the same three perpetrators.

During the 9/11 backlash, gun-wielding assailants sometimes attacked minorities outside their residences. In Texas, a local Iraqi immigrant was shot by a bigot in a backlash crime. According to the *Houston Chronicle*, the 30-year old Iraqi refugee Hassan Al-Asfar was attacked on September 21, 2001, after finishing his late-night shift as a parking valet.[23] When he arrived at his apartment in the Gulfton area, a young black man greeted him in Arabic. Al-Asfar politely responded. The man then asked Al-Asfar for a cigarette. The Iraqi immigrant complied, offering the stranger a light. Suddenly, Al-Asfar saw the man pointing a gun pointed at his head, and began begging his attacker to take his money without killing him.[24] The gunman replied that he wasn't interested in the money, and was seeking retribution because Middle Easterners killed Americans.[25] The men began wrestling over the weapon, and the gunman shot Al-Asfar in the thigh. The assailant fled with some of Al-Asfar's money but not all of his earnings, suggesting that robbery was not the main reason for the shooting. Al-Asfar was taken to Ben Taub hospital, where responding physicians removed the bullet and treated him for severe blood loss.

Speaking with the aid of an interpreter, Al-Asfar told the *Houston Chronicle* that the attack left him afraid to venture outside his apartment by himself or endanger his friends by standing near them in public.[26] Because he fought against the government of Saddam Hussein and fled Iraq as a dissident, he was dismayed that uninformed Americans saw him as a threat. According to police spokesman Alvin Wright, investigators were regarding Al-Asfar's attack as an aggravated robbery instead of a hate crime.[27] Al-Asfar told the *Houston Chronicle* that he was convinced his shooting was motivated by ethnic and religious bias.[28] Civil rights groups were disappointed that detectives were unwilling to recognize that the shooting was bias-motivated.

On occasion, bigots vandalized cars parked outside of Persian-American homes. According to the September 22, 2001 issue of the *Los Angeles Times*, a young assailant attacked a car belonging to an Iranian-American childcare worker, who had parked her vehicle in her own driveway in Tarzana.[29] The vandal used a baseball bat and hammer to smash the car, presumably targeting the property because its owner was of Middle Eastern ancestry. Condemning the backlash hate crime, the *Los Angeles Times* pointed out that the scapegoated immigrant woman devoted her life to caring for American children and spent the last 20 years of her life in the U.S., after fleeing oppression in Iran.[30]

HOME ATTACKS, FALL 2001

Similar attacks occurred in other states. On October 8, 2001, a vandal damaged two cars parked outside of Mahmoud and Mahra Jawhar's house in East Pennsboro, Pennsylvania. The *Harrisburg Patriot-News* reported that the perpetrator shattered the vehicle's windshield and windows.[31] Although East Pennsboro police could not conclusively determine that religious bias was the main motive of the attack, Mahmoud Jawhar told the *Patriot-News* that he believed his residence and property were targeted because of his Islamic beard and his wife and daughter's hijabs.[32] Jawhar saw the vandalism as a manifestation of the 9/11 backlash, noting that he and his family members had no problems in the neighborhood in the 13 years prior to the terrorist strikes. According to Laura Treaster, communications director of the Human Relations

Commission, there were 47 reported 9/11 backlash hate crimes in Pennsylvania from September 11 to October 5, 2001, including several at minority-owned residences.[33]

In response to the growing 9/11 backlash, many Muslim homeowners tried to educate their American neighbors about Islam, to counter misinformation and answer questions about their faith. A few weeks after 9/11, Ibrahim Dremali, a geology and oceanography instructor at Broward Community College, was scheduled to speak about his religion at one of the churches in Boca Raton, Florida. According to the *St. Petersburg Times*, two gunmen appeared at Dremali's house the evening before the lecture, telling the Egyptian immigrant that they would kill him if he appeared at the church.[34] Terrified, he cancelled the speaking engagement.

To protect their four children, Dremali and his wife, Safaa Eissa, stopped allowing them to play outside of their house. The parents also began limiting their own movements, particularly after several unpleasant encounters with bigots. Essa told the *St. Petersburg Times* that she was repeatedly harassed and threatened when she went shopping wearing her niqab.[35] On one occasion, another customer became enraged that she was wearing a veil, shouting that it was an indication that she was going to bomb the store.[36]

Other members of the family also experienced overt bigotry. Dremali's sixth-grade son was singled out at school, and his teacher asked that the boy be transferred from her class. The family was also harassed at the local mosque where Ibrahim was the imam. The *St. Petersburg Times* reported that local bigots routinely honked their horns and waved their middle fingers at area Muslims, including the Dremalis, outside the Islamic Center of Boca Raton.[37]

The Dremalis also faced discrimination at Miami International Airport after traveling abroad to Saudi Arabia and Egypt. On this occasion, the INS detained and questioned Ibrahim and his son for three hours. Dremali told the *St. Petersburg Times* that the airport interrogator treated them like terrorists, threatening to jail them when they asked about why they were being interrogated.[38]

The persecution the Dremalis encountered in America was particularly alarming because the family immigrated to the U.S. in search of religious freedom. After being threatened by Florida gunmen and repeatedly harassed because of their faith, the Dremalis decided to look for religious liberty in another country, since America was not the tolerant haven they expected it to be.[39] They just didn't know what country to relocate to next.

On occasion, bigots vandalized apartment buildings in the aftermath of 9/11, frightening minority tenants. In Houston, Texas, renters were shocked to discover hate messages and death threats on the walls of their apartment building. According to the October 7, 2001 *Houston Chronicle*, the graffiti suggested that Arabs should be exterminated and Islam should be wiped out.[40] The backlash hate crime terrified Muslim residents, who worried that the vandal might try to kill them.

Although much of the harassment went unpunished, federal authorities occasionally pressed charges against bigots who threatened minority homeowners. On October 10, 2001, Justin Scott-Priestly Bolen left a threatening message on the home answering machine of a Pakistani-American family living in Fenton, Michigan. On February 6, 2002, he pled guilty to interfering with the housing rights of the South-Asian family, and was sentenced to 21 months incarceration.[41]

Rather than receiving support from their neighbors during the 9/11 backlash, some Muslims and Arabs experienced overt bigotry within their homeowners' associations. In Warren, Michigan, residents held a secret meeting before informing Laila Abro that she was no longer welcome on her condominium board, although she had been an active participant for the previous eight years and had done nothing wrong. In the October 19, 2001 issue of the *Boston Globe*, Abro reported that her neighbors treated her with open contempt, telling her that they didn't want her living in the area.[42]

On occasion, Arab-Americans experienced the 9/11 backlash in U.S. housing projects. After the Twin Towers fell, bigots repeatedly targeted the Gazawis, an Iraqi-American family residing in San Francisco's Alice Griffith housing project. According to the *San Francisco Chronicle*, the married couple and their four children endured three separate attacks in the fall of 2001.[43] On October 3rd, a vandal smashed one of the family's front windows with a rock.[44] Less than two weeks later, on October 14th, another front window was once again shattered by a hurled stone.[45] One of the only apartment windows left unbroken contained an American flag, testifying to the national symbol's protective powers. The third attack on the Iraqi residence took place on October 22nd, when an assailant used a pellet gun to shoot a hole in the bedroom window.[46]

More than three months after the October 2001 attacks, the Gazawi family told the *Chronicle* that the Housing Authority had taken months to repair two of the broken windows, and had not yet fixed the third.[47] Because the windows were not replaced promptly, the family was subjected to cold air streaming in their apartment at night and water pouring in whenever it rained.

Many activists were disturbed by the bigotry confronting Iraqi families living in the U.S. Several Bay Area legal groups were disappointed that the Housing Authority did not respond more rapidly to the Gazawi family's plight. Asian Law Caucus attorney Gen Fujioka was concerned that the city government was not acting on a 1999 court order mandating that the Alice Griffith protect Arab and Asian residents from on-site hate crimes. Recalling how previous Arab-American residents were harassed by black tenants in the late 1990s, Fujioka told the *Chronicle* that the Gazawi case was practically identical to previous cases of discrimination, suggesting that the agency had not done enough to protect at-risk minorities.[48] George Williams, the court monitor of the consent decree, agreed that the Housing Authority needed to establish a policy to protect vulnerable tenants from racial harassment and hate crimes.[49] Williams pointed out that the Housing Authority did not have staff guidelines for dealing with on-site hate crimes, and had failed to adopt a zero tolerance policy ensuring that any tenant would be evicted for violating another resident's civil rights.

In addition to the hate crimes targeting the Gazawis at their residence, the Arab-American family experienced racial harassment and attacks while walking in the neighborhood. On one occasion, a bigot spit on the 52-year old Iraqi welder and on his six-year old son. In another hate crime, an assailant pulled on Mrs. Gazawi's hijab in an unprovoked assault.[50] Because of the ongoing harassment, the Gazawis decided to move to San Jose as soon as they received a Section 8 rental subsidy. Despite the repeated bias assaults they experienced while living in San Francisco, they still felt grateful for the freedoms and opportunities they had in America, the country that granted them sanctuary after they fled Iraq in the 1990s.

The Gazawis were one of many Middle Eastern families who were harassed at their residences on the West Coast. In Southern California, minority families were also attacked in the weeks after the terrorist strikes. According to the *Press-Enterprise*, a vandal threw eggs at the home of a Middle Eastern man in Riverside, California on October 20, 2001.[51] The victim contacted police in response to the 3:00 a.m. incident. The backlash hate crime upset Arab-American and South Asian homeowners in the neighborhood.

In the Pacific Northwest, some minority-owned family homes were bombed during the 9/11 backlash. The *Columbian* reported that in Tacoma, Washington, an assailant detonated an explosive device outside the home of a family of Middle Eastern descent on November 2, 2001.[52] The attack stunned area residents.

While Arab families were being terrorized in the fall of 2001, American audiences were viewing movies depicting Middle Easterners as homicidal villains. In the movie, *Time Lapse*, Iraqi terrorists attempt to obtain a nuclear suitcase to use against unsuspecting civilians.[53] Two U.S. agents eventually open fire on the evil Arabs, killing the villain Faisal and his Iraqi henchmen. This movie reinforced the message that Middle Easterners and Muslims were a dangerous threat to the West. Some activists saw a connection between these types of foreign movie villains and post-9/11 hate crimes.

HOME ATTACKS, 2002

Months after the terrorist attacks, minority homeowners continued to be targeted by bigots. On occasion, Sikh-owned homes were attacked multiple times by the same assailant. In a January 2002 issue of *Asianweek*, San Jose Sgt. Tony Ciaburro reported that the same perpetrator who vandalized or firebombed a Sikh residence on five previous occasions – twice before and three times after 9/11 – recently attempted another arson attack on a second Sikh home.[54] Many Bay Area residents wondered why the police had been unable to apprehend the man responsible so the hate crime spree could end.

In response to the ongoing 9/11 backlash, Homeland Security officers held meetings around the country, encouraging minority residents to report hate crimes. The credibility of some of these federal employees was undermined by their previous dealings with ethnic communities. On June 2, 2002, Nadirah Farid was disappointed to learn that William Whitcomb was moderating a Homeland Security forum held at Dar sul-Islam mosque in West St. Louis County, Missouri. Farid told the *St. Louis Post-Dispatch* that Williams had been completely unhelpful ten years before, when she informed him that she was being repeatedly harassed by community members in St. Peters on account of her Muslim faith.[55] In numerous occasions prior to 9/11, Farid's Islamophobic neighbors blocked her driveway or intimidated her with their dogs so that she would be unable to get in and out of her house.[56] When she brought her complaints to Williams, a mediator with the Justice Department, he met with her once but did nothing to end the bias-motivated harassment. Arab-Americans and South Asians were reluctant to report hate crimes to federal officials who had a track record of being unwilling to help Muslim homeowners under duress.

Throughout 2002, minority families continued to be harassed and attacked at their residences by neighbors who suspected them of being terrorists. The September 8, 2002 issue of the *Houston Chronicle* describes the trials that a Pakistani Muslim-American family endured after 9/11 in Katy, Texas.[57] Before 9/11, Mohammed and Zareena Khan and their two sons lived peacefully in their suburban community, feeling accepted by other residents. In the aftermath of the terrorist strikes, their Anglo-Christian neighbors started treating them with open hostility and contempt. One former friend began yelling profanities and making obscene gestures whenever she saw them. When Zareena tried to reason with her, the woman threatened to call the police. Their house was then repeatedly attacked. In one assault, a vandal spread garbage across their lawn and pelted their house with rotten eggs.[58]

Because the federal government was urging Americans to search for terrorists in their backyards, some community residents began spying on their Muslim acquaintances. The *Houston Chronicle* reported that one radio listener called a local station and revealed that she spent sleepless nights worrying that her Muslim neighbors were terrorists because they had visitors and three satellite dishes.[59]

Like so many other Muslim families across America, the Khans were subjected to intense scrutiny by their former friends. Although they flew the American flag in front of their house and put memorial candles for the 9/11 victims on their lawn, they were still regarded with suspicion because they were Muslim. According to the *Houston Chronicle*, a neighbor reported the Khans to the FBI after observing that Mohammed was repeatedly leaving the house late at night and returning early in the morning.[60] When the FBI questioned him, he explained that he was working the late-night shift at the International House of Pancakes. Despite being cleared of terrorist activity, the Khans continued to be verbally harassed by their neighbors.

Bigots in other states also targeted Pakistani homeowners. Syed Gilani and his family woke on veteran's day 2002 to find 150 American flags on their lawn in Bloomington, Illinois. The Muslim-American told the *Pantagraph* that he found the incident unsettling because it suggested that his family needed to be taught a lesson in patriotism, even though he had lived in the U.S. for more than 30 years and his two children were native-born citizens.[61] Minority community members viewed the attack in the context of the ongoing 9/11 backlash.

On occasion, Christian Arab-Americans were harassed at their residences. According to the December 11, 2002 *Richmond Times-Dispatch*, a Christian Palestinian woman received several death threats on her home's answering machine.[62] The Richmond woman refused to report the threats to the police or FBI, concerned about the repercussions of drawing attention to her family.

HOME ATTACKS, 2003

More than a year after 9/11, neighborhood bigots continued to target minority homeowners and tenants, blaming them for the terrorist strikes. Hate crime victims included some undocumented immigrants, who felt unable to report assaults to police. The *Village Voice* and the *New York Daily News* reported the story of Zakir H., a 20-year old Pakistani youth who was stabbed at his Brooklyn home in January 2003.[63] This bias-crime victim had been a resident of New York since the age of 14, but was unable to contact authorities about the attack because his paperwork had expired. According to the *Village Voice*, he came to New York on a visitor's visa seven years ago, joining his parents in Midwood, Brooklyn. After his father passed away, the young man and his brother became responsible for supporting their mother financially, and sending money to their five sisters back home in Karachi. When the young man was coming back from his job stacking groceries, three assailants jumped him in the foyer of his building. According to the *New York Daily News*, the attack was unmistakably a hate crime, prompted by the assailants' anger with the victim's Middle Eastern appearance.[64] Recounting the assault in the *Village Voice*, Zakir H. described how the three assailants chased him into his building, punched him, and stabbed him with a knife.[65] When the ambulance arrived and paramedics attended to his wound, he realized he could not explain what happened without involving the police and risk being sent back to Karachi, where gang violence was rampant.[66] Worried about deportation, he decided against telling the paramedics what actually happened, claiming instead that he stabbed himself.[67] At the hospital, emergency-room physicians sutured the hole in his stomach, administering 40 stitches to close the wound. The *Village Voice* published a photo of the victim's injuries, showing viewers his unsightly scar, which was eight inches long and three inches deep.[68] Months after the stabbing, he still experienced panic attacks and feared leaving the building. Because of injuries to his internal organs, he was unable to continue his job, which involved lifting heavy grocery boxes. He found another position working at the counter of a dessert shop. The crime was never reported to the police, and the perpetrators were never brought to justice.

Some public official used Zakir H.'s attack as an opportunity to urge government officials to renew former mayor Edward Koch's 1989 executive order prohibiting city employees from disclosing crime victims' immigration status to federal officials. Although Koch's order had expired, city councilmember Hiram Monserrate made efforts to renew it, introducing a provision ensuring the confidentiality of undocumented crime victims. Monserrate obtained more than 30 co-sponsors for the proposal, and hoped that news of uninvestigated attacks on undocumented workers would generate further support.[69]

South Asians in New Jersey also reported hate crimes at their residences in early 2003. In some instances, uncooperative local authorities discouraged victims from pressing charges. In the January 10, 2003 issue of *India Abroad*, Suleman Din described finding his car "keyed" whenever he parked it in front of his in-laws' house in Central Jersey.[70] After discovering more than 20 scratches and dents on his vehicle, Din enlisted his father-in-law to keep watch over the car in order to catch the culprit in the act. They eventually discovered the neighbor's teenage son and his friend vandalizing the vehicle. When they confronted the boy's father, the irate man yelled racist remarks and slammed the door in their faces.[71]

India Abroad reported that when Din's wife called the police, the responding officer did not file any charges. Instead, he told the South Asian family to avoid their neighbors, because confronting them would just give them an opportunity to say that the vandalism was justified because of 9/11.[72] Din was incredulous, asking his wife what the terrorist attacks had to do with a young punk vandalizing his car.[73] Din's wife urged him to accept that the system had failed them and that the police would not protect them because they were Muslim. Writing about his experience in *India-Abroad*, Din explained that he found it debilitating to wake up each morning and see a chiseled reminder of post-9/11 bigotry, knowing that local police officers had refused to arrest the white perpetrator responsible.[74]

Hate crimes also occurred at residences in the Southwest. A post-9/11 attack occurred on February 14, 2003, at an apartment near the University of Arizona. Tucson police detective Tim Rupel told the *Arizona Daily Star* that two young men walked into the building and began yelling racial slurs at a tenant, referencing his Middle Eastern appearance.[75] The bigots then assaulted the Arab-looking man.[76] Community groups were dismayed that police were unable to apprehend the two assailants in the weeks after the bias-motivated beating.

On occasion, Muslims were jumped in the common areas of their apartment buildings. On February 28, 2003, a tenant wearing Islamic attire was attacked while she was washing her clothes in the laundry room of her Santa Clara apartment.[77] The assailant punched her in the face, cutting her lip and causing facial lacerations. Investigators determined the attack was likely bias-motivated because the assailant also tore up the victim's laundry and stabbed articles of her ethnic clothing with a sharp object.

On occasion, bigots used explosives to damage minority-owned homes and property. On March 21, 2003, a bias-motivated arsonist put a bomb into a van belonging to a Palestinian family living in Burbank.[78] The explosion causing the vehicle's door blow off, punching a hole in the floor and shattering glass over 30 feet.[79] According to the *New York Times*, police arrested 24-year old Eric Nix and charged him with arson, criminal damage, and committing a hate crime.[80]

Although Nix had already served a 30-day sentence for throwing a brick through a Muslim-owned Chicago-area furniture store two days after 9/11, the 5th District Court of Cook County sentenced the arsonist to just two years of probation and anger management classes. Civil rights activists were outraged by the inappropriate sentence, and demanded that Nix face federal terrorism charges. CAIR national chairman Omar Ahmad told the *Arab American News* that he found it unfathomable that the perpetrator of two anti-Muslim hate crimes, including a terrorist bombing, would be given a mere slap on the wrist.[81] He suggested that if a Muslim or Arab perpetrator committed a similar type of crime, the court would not have been as lenient. Ahmad demanded that federal charges be levied against the perpetrator so minority communities could know that the Justice Department was serious about combating anti-Muslim attacks.[82]

Arsonists also targeted Arab-American homeowners in the Southwest. The *Atlanta Journal-Constitution* reported that on March 26, 2003, an assailant threw bottles of explosives made from dry ice into the backyard of an Iraqi-American family living in Phoenix.[83] The attack unsettled minority residents in Arizona, who were already unnerved by other post-9/11 hate crimes.

Arab-American homeowners who visibly displayed their ethnicity were particularly likely to have their property vandalized. The April 9, 2003 issue of *Asianweek* noted that one San Francisco residence in the Mission district was repeatedly attacked for flying a Palestinian flag.[84] In six separate incidents, bigots hit the home with rotten food and human feces. Because of the frequency of the destruction, community groups were convinced the ongoing attacks were triggered by the 9/11 backlash and racist sentiment in the U.S.

While Arabs and South Asians were being targeted in their homes, movie audiences were watching films featuring Muslim terrorists living in American neighborhoods. On occasion, American movies cast South Asians as Arabs, reinforcing the widespread misconception that the two ethnicities were interchangeable. In the movie, *Malibu's Most Wanted*, released in the U.S. on April 18, 2003, South Asian actor Kal Penn plays Hadji, an Arab-American character nicknamed "the beast from the Middle East."[85] Film critic Shaheen notes that in one scene in the movie, American audiences learn that Haji's uncle Ahmet had given him a rocket-propelled grenade launcher for Christmas.[86] Although Haji is depicted as a basically sympathetic character, his uncle's access to prohibited weapons suggests that they are in contact with terrorists. Once again, American audiences are exposed to the notion that their Arab, Muslim, and South Asian neighbors might in fact be dangerous.

Just as movies conflated Arab and South Asian ethnicities, American bigots continued to associate South Asian homeowners with 9/11 terrorists. According to the *New York Times*, a Sikh-American family was attacked outside of their Queens apartment on August 3, 2003 by a bigot who compared them to members of the Taliban.[87] Prior to the bias-motivated beating, the family spent the day house-hunting on Long Island. Exhausted from looking at real estate, Surinder Singh Gill, his wife, two children, and brother Lakhvir Singh Gill stopped to get curry chicken take-out at the Taj restaurant in Jackson Heights. When they got home, Surinder Gill sent his children inside while he and his brother parked the car. Soon thereafter, they noticed a man urinating in front of the apartment while his two companions waited inside a white livery cab. As the South Asians got out of the vehicle, the three drunks noticed Surinder Singh Gill's turquoise turban and long beard. According to *India Abroad*, the men then began taunting him, calling him Osama bin Laden and instructing him to leave the country.[88] The targeted man told them he was not a member of the Taliban, and pretended to call the police. The men continued comparing him to the 9/11 mastermind, telling him that they would kill him unless he left the U.S.[89] At that point, the intoxicated men got out of the cab and approached the two Sikh men, who were trying to explain that they were Sikh Punjabis from India and had no relation to Arab terrorists. Mrs. Gill saw one of the men spit on her husband and push him on the ground. Worried about an escalation in violence, she instructed her two children, ages 8 and 10, to run and call for help.

The men began punching Surinder Gill in the face. When his brother Lakhvir tried to intervene, the three drunks began pummeling him as well. Lakhvir Gill told *India Abroad* that one of the assailants held him in a headlock, while choking him and punching his face and back.[90] The men then shoved him to the ground, kicking him repeatedly as he assumed the fetal position to protect his head. Because of the attack, he suffered a swollen lip, a cut elbow, and numerous bruises all over his body.

Unable to stand by and watch her male relatives get beaten up, Singh's wife repeatedly implored the attackers to stop. She eventually intervened physically, trying to protect her husband. The assailants then turned their rage on her, hitting her on her head and back.[91]

Acquaintances heard the commotion and came to the Sikhs' assistance. The *New York Times* reported that George Hodge, a passing pizza delivery man who knew the family, saw the fight and tried to break it up.[92] Other community members also helped the Sikhs. James Fasano witnessed the attack from his window and summoned the police, while another neighbor got a baseball bat and frightened off the three drunks. The police arrived ten minutes later, and conducted an unsuccessful aerial search for the assailants. According to *India-West*, the perpetrators were not strangers to the neighborhood, and had visited a nearby resident in the past.[93]

The South Asian victims decided against going to the hospital, preferring to recuperate at home. Although Singh missed several days of work because of his injuries, he refused to shave his beard or give up wearing his turban. Mrs. Gill, a special education teacher, told the *New York Times* that she was outraged by the bias-motivated attacks, pointing out that her husband and other Sikh-American men should not have to cut their hair or abandon their dastaars to feel safe in their own country.[94]

Although the family had resided in the area for nine years, the experience left them shaken. Mrs. Gill became frightened whenever she went outside, and often chose to stay indoors. She also worried about her husband's safety. Their children were traumatized by the attacks. The *New York Post* reported that Gill's eight-year old daughter was troubled that strangers had beaten up her father and compared him to Osama bin Laden.[95] The South Asian brothers were also unsettled by the beatings. Since both men worked at New York cabbies, they had become accustomed to encountering bigotry at work. They found it disheartening that they also had to deal with the 9/11 backlash in their own neighborhoods, unable to view their homes as sanctuaries.

The hate crimes shocked members of the community. Fasano told *India Abroad* that he found it hard to believe that such heinous assaults took place in his integrated neighborhood, where Koreans, Spaniards, Indians, and Greeks had co-existed harmoniously for decades prior to 9/11.[96]

In the years following the terrorist strikes, victimized Sikh homeowners were repeatedly troubled by poor police response time. In September 2003, a Sikh family in a D.C. suburb called 911 after receiving two death threats in the mail. Officers took almost three hours to respond to the distress call. Singh, chairman of the SMART board of directors, told *India Abroad* that he found the long wait unacceptable, sending minority homeowners the disturbing message that bias attacks on minority-owned homes were not a top priority for the police department.[97] Since the menacing letters were sent close to the second anniversary of the terrorist strikes, community groups speculated that they were manifestations of the ongoing backlash.

The same fall, Sikhs in the Atlanta area were harassed by their neighbors. On October 26, 2003, Jatinder Singh was leaving his Windsor home, en route to a nearby gurdwara, when a neighbor began threatening him and screaming ethnic slurs at him, calling him Osama bin Laden and Saddam Hussein.[98] Police responding to the scene warned the abusive neighbor to stay away from Singh and his family.

These anti-Sikh attacks took place the same year that Miramax released its 2003 comedy, *DysFunKtional Family*. In the movie, Eddie Griffin's character points to an elderly Sikh man and calls him bin Laden, shouting that he knew the 9/11 mastermind was hiding in the area.[99] Civil rights activists were horrified by the scene, arguing that in reinforced the notion that turban-wearing South Asians were affiliated with the Taliban. The offensive film also refers to Sikhs as "towel heads" and suggests that airline passengers should gang up and assault a man wearing a dastaar. *India-West* reported that a preview audience in San Francisco laughed at the offensive material, prompting Sikh Mediawatch and Resource Taskforce to urge Miramax to edit the film or run PSAs in theatres. Despite widespread criticism, *DysFunKtional Family* was released on April 4, 2003. The movie played in 602 American theatres and grossed 1.1 million, reaching the number 11 spot.[100]

Other films contained even more harmful characters. The movie, *Belly of the Beast*, released on video in the U.S. on December 30, 2003, rehashes anti-Arab stereotypes. In one scene, Zadir, an Algerian criminal, procures weapons for a Muslim terrorist group.[101] In another scene, members of a Thai Islamic terrorist group abduct and imprison two American women. Once again, Muslims are shown as lecherous Semites who treat Western women like chattel.

Other American films depicted Arab sheikhs as sexual perverts, commodifying American women. The movie, *Call Me: the Rise and Fall of Heidi Fleiss*, included swarthy Arabs who lust after white women. One character in the movie is Prince Hassan, a lecherous Arab who hires Heidi for her sexual services. This film premiered on March 29, 2004. According to Shaheen, the movie's dialogue implies that Arabs are wealthy misogynists and that Palestinians are Jew-hating terrorists.[102] Activists saw a connection between these types of xenophobic movies and hate crimes targeting minority residences.

HOME ATTACKS, 2004-2005

Neighborhood xenophobes continued to single out minority homeowners throughout 2004. The *Patriot-News* reported that Muslim family members in Seattle discovered a five-foot cross burning outside their home on July 8, 2004.[103] Because the hate crime took place so close to Independence Day, area Muslims wondered if the arsonist was trying to communicate the nativist message that followers of Islam were un-American.

In other parts of the country, Middle Eastern and South Asian homeowners were also harassed by bigots seeking vengeance for the terrorist strikes. Although some of the minority victims had been singled out prior to 9/11, the frequency of the hate crimes escalated in the years that followed. In Fremont, vandals targeted the home of a Semergit and Upinder Gupta numerous times between 1998 and 2004.[104] During this period, their son was also harassed at school for wearing a turban. Although the Guptas did not report the first several incidents, opting instead to talk to the culprits directly, they finally went public about how neighborhood juveniles were victimizing them.

According to the *Oakland Tribune*, vandals hit the Gupta's house three times in a 25-day period in August 2004.[105] In one attack, neighborhood bigots threw paint balls at their home and scratched their two cars. On another occasion, the Guptas discovered that their house had been egged. Despite the frequency of the occurrences, the Fremont police were unwilling to categorize the attacks as hate crimes, arguing that they were unable to prove that the assailants were motivated by bias. Upinder Gupta told the *Oakland Tribune* that the young bigots who attacked her house boasted in front of her that they were targeting her family for being Arab terrorists responsible for 9/11.[106] During this conversation, the perpetrators also made racial slurs. Upinder Gupta reported this information to the police chief and commissioner, and argued that the attacks should be reclassified as hate crimes. She also told the *Oakland Tribune* that some of the neighborhood children told her that they were picking on the family because they were Afghans, not realizing that they were actually South Asians.[107] Although she reported the vandals' bigoted comments to the police chief, authorities continued to regard the bias-motivated attacks as simple vandalism. Unable to rely on the police for protection, the Guptas installed a video surveillance camera to record future incidents.

As the third anniversary of the terrorist strikes approached, Sikh homeowners were once again targeted in backlash attacks. *Little India* reported that in September 2004, delivery truck driver Gurcharanjeet Singh

Anand discovered that an arsonist torched his home.[108] Area South Asians believed the deliberately-set fire was a hate crime linked to post-9/11 bigotry.

The same month, Muslim property owners were targeted in backlash incidents. According to U.S. attorney Michael J. Sullivan, vandals repeatedly attacked vehicles parked in front of a duplex shared by two Muslim families in Revere, Massachusetts.[109] On September 19, 2004, shortly after the third anniversary of the terrorist strikes, Adam Bonito, Christopher Gianquito, and others vandalized a Muslim-owned Nissan van, damaging its body and breaking its windshield and windows. According to police reports, the perpetrators singled out the vehicle because it belonged to a Middle Easterner. The following year, in January and March 2005, Bonito and an accomplice targeted the same Muslim property owner, vandalizing a Dodge van parked outside the duplex. The *Boston Globe* reported that Bonito and Gianquito were eventually charged with carrying out a criminal conspiracy and interfering with the fair housing rights of the two Muslim families.[110]

Islamophobic attacks also took place in other states. In Nebraska, a vandal wrote anti-Taliban messages and obscenities on a car parked at the home of an Indian Sikh family on August 7, 2005. Narinder Bajwa told the *Lincoln-Star Journal* that the car belonged to their son, Manjiv, a soldier in the U.S. army who was about to be deployed to Iraq.[111] The Lincoln Interfaith Council denounced the hate crime, characterizing the post-9/11 incident as repulsive.

While Sikhs were being targeted at their residences, American audiences were watching films depicting South Asians as anti-American terrorists. In the movie, *The War Within*, a Pakistani youth travels to New Jersey to live with a Muslim family. The immigrant then joins a terrorist network and plots to kill dozens of innocent Americans. This movie was released in the U.S. on September 30, 2005, transmitting the disturbing message that minority neighbors might be harboring terrorists.

Other movies also perpetuated offensive stereotypes, contributing to an atmosphere of intolerance in the U.S. While filming the 2005 comedy, *Son of the Mask*, the director instructed actor Kal Penn to speak with a thick Indian accent, even though the role of Jorge wasn't even written for a South Asian.[112] After reviewing the film footage, the director decided that the character's voice needed to sound even more comically-ethnic, and made Penn re-do the scenes.[113] Civil rights advocates saw a connection between this type of racist popular culture and backlash attacks targeting minority homeowners.

HOME ATTACKS, 2006

Several years after 9/11, minority homeowners continued to be attacked by community members who associated them with members of al-Qaeda. On April 8, 2006, arsonists targeted a Muslim family in Douglasville, Georgia. The assailants torched the homeowner's van and spray-painted a hate message on the wall of the house, comparing the occupants to the 9/11 killers and insisting that they leave the country.[114] The family expressed disappointment in the police's handling of the attack, upset that local authorities were slow to investigate the bias-motivated crime.

While these minority residences were being targeted, American audiences were watching Islamophobic movies. Middle Eastern villains appear in the 2006 comedy, *American Dreamz*. In this film, Omar, an Arab terrorist, is sent on a mission to become a finalist on an American Idol-style show in order to blow up the U.S. president, who is a guest judge.[115] This comedy was released in the U.S. on April 21, 2006. Like other xenophobic films, this American comedy relied on pernicious ethnic stereotypes to amuse audiences.

Harmful images of Middle Easterners also appear in *District B13*. This French film was released in the U.S. on June 2, 2006. In this movie, two million criminals are walled off in a section of Paris in 2010. According to film critic Jack Shaheen, the leader of this underworld is the Arab villain Taha Bin Mahmoud, who runs a heroin smuggling ring and acts like a violent thug.[116] In one scene, he drugs the heroine Lola, chains her to a leash, and drags her around like a captive slave. Bin Mahmoud and his Arab cronies threaten to bomb Paris unless officials pay them 20 million euros. Their nefarious plans are foiled by the film's heroes, who save Lola and prevent the bomb launch. The stereotypes in this movie transmit the message that Arabs and Muslims are dangerous, since they cannot co-exist peacefully with others in Western residential areas.

Frequently, American hate crimes against minority homeowners made the international news. New Delhi's *Hindustan Times* informed its readers about a May 27, 2006 bias attack targeting the Wayne, New Jersey home of an Indian-American family.[117] The vandals spray-painted anti-Hindu profanities on the back of the two-story house, and covered the front and rear patio with hate messages. Using black, orange, and neon green graffiti, the vandals scrawled anti-Indian death threats, promising to set fire to the house and informing the homeowners that they were watching their kids.[118] A neighbor caught a glimpse of the intruders and called the police, describing the perpetrators as dark-haired males in their late teens or early 20s.

The vandalized home was owned by a 42-year old South Asian businessman, originally from Tanzania but raised in Passaic, and his wife, who was from Mumbai. The Hindu father of three told the *Hindustan Times* that his daughter, age 13, and two sons, ages 11 and 16, had trouble understanding why they were targeted, particularly because they were born in the U.S. and were just as American as their neighbors.[119] The bias attack reminded some community members of the Dot-buster crimes of the 1980s, targeting immigrants in the state. Many South Asians in the area viewed the vandalism in the context of post-9/11 nativism.

South Asian homeowners may have been particularly likely to be singled out if their children wore distinctive clothing. In Southern California, a Sikh physician discovered that his home had been vandalized in June 2006, when he opened the front porch to retrieve the newspaper. He was shocked to see a pornographic picture on his driveway, depicting his son's religious headwear in derogatory fashion. According to the *Orange County Register*, the illustration, done in white chalk or washable paint, was labeled "3 testis."[120] Chadha took photos of the bias-motivated graffiti and then washed it off with a hose.

The victimized homeowner told the *Register* that the drawing was more than a prank, attacking the family's faith and wounding them psychologically.[121] He believed that the obscene picture referred to the knot on the small turban that his 15-year old son wore for religious reasons. In the past, Chadha's son had been teased by his classmates at Valencia High School because of his patka. The boy's parents were upset by the bullying and by the mistreatment of other minority students in the years after the terrorist strikes.

In a July follow-up story on the hate crime, the *Orange County Register* reported that detective Brian Perry and other members of the Placentia police department decided against calling the driveway vandalism a criminal act because it caused no permanent damage and the drawing was easily removed with water.[122] Displeased with this conclusion, Sikh community members pointed out that any explicit or implicit threat written on a minority residence should be considered a hate crime. In response to the vandalism, Chadha's wife distributed educational pamphlets around the neighborhood, so Sikh community members wouldn't be regarded as foreign terrorists.

As the five-year anniversary of 9/11 approached, Sikh homeowners and their family members continued to be targeted. The *San Francisco Chronicle* reported that in August 2006, a 65-year old Sikh man was stabbed by an assailant who expressed his desire to avenge the terrorist strikes by killing a member of the Taliban.[123] At the time of the attack, Iqbal Singh was standing with his grand-daughter at the carport of his family's San Jose apartment, waiting to go to a Sikh gurdwara with family members who had not yet come downstairs. Singh was originally from Khushalpur, and had been living with his son Satinder Singh for the previous year. Seeing the turbaned, bearded Sikh, Everett Thompson, a 25-year old African-American man from Santa Clara, approached the South Asian grandfather and lunged at him with the steak knife, cutting him in the neck.[124] Singh told the *Hindustan Times* that after this terrifying blow, he was able to elude his attacker and run back to the apartment.[125] Hearing the commotion, Singh's son and daughter-in-law rushed downstairs. At this point, Thompson fled the scene.

Singh viewed the attack as a bias crime, telling the *Hindustan Times* that he did nothing to provoke his assailant except show up in public wearing a turban.[126] Police and prosecutors agreed that the attack was bias-motivated, instigated because Thompson thought that the Sikhs were affiliated with al-Qaeda.[127] Thompson was arrested after the attack, and held without bail on attempted murder and hate crime charges.

The injured Sikh was treated for his injuries at Santa Clara's Valley Medical Center. Back in Khushal Pur, Singh's wife Raj Kaur prayed for her husband's welfare, and urged him to return home to India. Raj Kaur told the *Times of India* that her husband would be better off outside of the U.S., even if it meant living in poverty.[128] Singh's son Iqbaql was also troubled by the bias-motivated stabbing, telling the *Times of India* that he blamed the American media for fostering xenophobia.[129]

In late 2006, minorities continued to be attacked at their residences. According to the *Arab American News*, an Egyptian-American was assaulted by ten white assailants in front of his Detroit house on November 27, 2006.[130] During this vicious ten-minute beating, Shafik Shoaib's wife and four children watched in horror from their house, listening to him scream in pain on their porch as the men brutally beat him with bottles. Although they called 911 five times during the prolonged and bloody assault, police failed to arrive while the crime was in progress.

Shoaib's son used his MP3 player to record the attack, which began when one assailant started pummeling the Egyptian-American homeowner and dragging him away from the house.[131] Shortly thereafter, other men joined in the beating. The brutal crime finally ended after an ambulance arrived to take Shoaib to the hospital. Relying heavily on the MP3 recording, police arrested 19-year old Earnest Domenech, charging him with two counts of assault, first degree home invasion, and intent to do great bodily harm.[132]

At a press conference at his house, Shoaib showed camera crews and journalists his extensive injuries, including ugly bruises on his nose, eyes, torso, and legs.[133] He also pointed out the broken bottles used in the attack and the blood-soaked porch where he was brutalized.

Shoaib asserted that some of his neighbors were involved in the assault, and had bothered him on previous occasions. The *Arab American News* reported that in February 2006, Shoaib's Anglo neighbors had begun harassing him and putting garbage on his property.[134] Tensions escalated further on the day of the beating. According to neighbor Kellie DuVall, Shoaib approached her and told her that he didn't appreciate her staring at him.[135] Prompted by this exchange, Domenech, who was dating DuVall's daughter, came outside and had words with Shoaib. Assailants then attacked the Egyptian-American. Domenech denied that he was one of Shoaib's attackers, suggesting that the MP3 image was not really him and declaring he was with friends at the time of the crime. Shoaib challenged the impartiality of one of the alibi witnesses, claiming that one of Domenech's friends, Mark Foy, took part in the beating. Like Domenech, Foy denied participating, and claimed that only one person was involved. Since Shoaib was a relatively large man – 5'10" and 270 lbs. – investigators were skeptical that a single assailant could have pummeled the Egyptian-American so thoroughly.

Linda Parker, director of the Michigan Department of Civil Rights, issued a statement condemning the beating. She publicly acknowledged that the assailants shouted anti-Muslim and anti-Arab slurs, challenging the victim's American citizenship and demanding that he return abroad.[136] She also noted that bias-motivated attacks had a chilling effect on all members of the community.

Despite the attackers' use of racist language and the homeowner's past harassment in the neighborhood, Wayne County Prosecutor Kym Worthy told the *Detroit News* that the attack was a regular dispute, not a hate crime, arguing that slurs were not serious enough to warrant a charge of ethnic intimidation.[137] Arab-American and Muslim activists were outraged that only one of the assailants, Domenech, had been arrested, and no bias charges had been filed against him. At the time of the beating, the only hate crime charge available to Michigan prosecutors was ethnic intimidation, a misdemeanor carrying a two-year maximum sentence. Dawud Walid, the executive director of Michigan CAIR, expressed his disapproval that Shoaib's attackers were not charged with bias offenses, telling the *Arab American News* that there was no reason for the Arab-American father to be beaten like a dog in front of his children.[138] Walid demanded that local and federal officials investigate the assault as a hate crime. Activists saw the beating in the context of post-9/11 Islamophobia.

While bigots were pummeling neighborhood Arab-Americans, television viewers were watching nativist suspense dramas. In his discussion of the program, "24," critic Jack Shaheen argues that the racist characters and plot sequences fueled community xenophobia. According to Shaheen, the show's anti-Western villains contributed to an intolerant America in which nearly 50% of 2006 Gallup poll respondents acknowledged that they perceived Islam as a violent and repressive religion and would be reluctant to have Arab-American or Muslim-American neighbors.[139]

HOME ATTACKS, 2007

On occasion, American bigots targeted Muslim homeowners from Bosnia. On July 6, 2007, an arsonist torched the Sarasota home of 43-year old Hasib Sejfovic, his wife, and their three children.[140] The fire severely damaged the residence, charring the furniture and destroying the kitchen the family recently spent $15,000 remodeling.[141] Local television stations reported that accelerants had been used in ten separate places inside the home. When the blaze began, some neighbors reported hearing what sounded like a bomb going off inside the building.

According to the *Sarasota Herald Tribune*, the arson was clearly a bias crime, since the assailant spray-painted anti-Muslim slurs and anti-Arab death threats on the floor and walls.[142] Because of the graffiti, sheriff's detectives and the state Fire Marshall's office opted to investigate the vandalism and arson as a hate crime. Some community members speculated that the attack was related to 9/11 and Americans' fear of Arab Muslims. CAIR activist Ahmed Bedier told the *Tribune* that the victims were Europeans, not Arabs, indicating that the arsonist was ignorant of the actual ethnic background of the targeted family.[143] Bedier was upset that public officials paid scant attention to the bias-motivated arson in the week following the attack.[144] Because the hate crime happened shortly after Independence Day, some community members wondered if American nativists deliberately timed the bias-motivated fire to send the message that Muslim immigrants were not welcome in the country.

Sejfovic and his family had immigrated to the U.S. to escape war-torn Bosnia, receiving assistance and sponsorship from the Unitarian Universalist Church of Sarasota. Members of this congregation told the *Tribune* that they were upset to learn that the Sejfovics had been attacked, especially because the family had fled Europe to escape religious persecution.[145]

Prior to the 2007 arson, Sejfovic lived peacefully in the neighborhood for three years, learning English and working in lawn maintenance. He speculated that the arsonist may have seen his name on the box and ascertained that he and his family members were Muslim immigrants. Despite the attack, he still had positive feelings about Florida and the U.S., telling the *Tribune* that the arson had no place in the America that he knew.[146]

In many instances, Muslim families were subjected to escalating hate crimes. In San Antonio, an Egyptian-American family's residence was repeatedly targeted by community members in mid-2007. Although Said and Amel Motawea and their four American-born children had lived peacefully in the neighborhood for eight years, their domestic bliss was interrupted in early July 2007 when someone threw beer bottles and eggs at their home and cars.[147] A second attack occurred a few days later, when the Motaweas discovered that a bigot had vandalized their vehicles, writing bigoted graffiti ordering the Muslim family to leave the area. Discussing this July 13, 2007 attack, the *San Antonio Express-News* reported that the vandal had used a permanent marker to write a profane word on their mini-van, in addition to a threat telling them to move out of the neighborhood.[148] The perpetrator also scratched up another vehicle and wrote graffiti on its rear. Police spokeswoman Sandy Gutierrez confirmed that the vandalism was being classified as a hate crime. The Motaweas' neighbor, Leslie Gonzalez, told the *Express-News* that she was upset that the Arab-American family had been targeted, viewing the bias-motivated attack as a manifestation of community ignorance and the ongoing 9/11 backlash.[149]

The same summer, Muslims living in U.S. apartment buildings were harassed by other tenants. According to the *Brattleboro Reformer*, bigots in Auburn, Maine threatened a Yemeni woman and her husband shortly after they moved into the area in July 2007. Instead of welcoming their new neighbors, several of the residents in the apartment building threatened Raihanah Alsameai and her spouse, Kenneth Ost, a Muslim convert. The *Brattleboro Reformer* reported that the neighborhood harassment escalated into a confrontation involving dogs, taunts, and baseball bats.[150] Because the Muslim couple was in danger, the Auburn police escorted them from the apartment building, put them up in an area hotel, and served protection orders barring three of the tenants from interacting with them.[151] To protect the Muslim couple, the apartment building's management company took action to evict the four residents for their criminal conduct. Police chief Phil Crowell told the *Brattleboro Reformer* that his department did not file charges against the perpetrators but submitted investigative reports to the state attorney general's office for review.[152] Civil rights activists wondered why police officers were unwilling to take action against the bigots, who openly threatened the Muslim couple with bodily harm.

Throughout the country, Arab and South Asian homeowners were frequently dismayed by local authorities' unwillingness to protect them. On occasion, victims used the media to draw attention to hate crimes and pressure civil authorities to take action. The *Washington Post* reported that on the sixth anniversary of 9/11, bigots vandalized the residence of a Palestinian-American family in Gaithersburg.[153] When Samira Hussein was getting her daughter ready for school, a neighborhood child informed them that the family's car had flat tires. Hussein went outside her house to investigate and discovered that someone had slashed six tires on the family's Astrovan and Lincoln Continental.[154] She called the police, but officers failed to come to the residence to investigate. Because the vandalism occurred on September 11, 2007, many community members believed that the vandalism was linked to the sixth anniversary of the terrorist strikes.

Prior to the 2007 vandalism, Samira and Mohammed Hussein's house and cars had been repeatedly attacked in bias-motivated crimes. In the 1990s, the family had been terrorized by neighborhood bigots. According to articles in the *Washington Post*, the harassment began in August 1990, after Saddam Hussein seized Kuwait.[155] One threatening caller told the Palestinian-American family that they had only 24 hours to leave the U.S.[156] Shortly thereafter, the Arab-American family discovered that the tires of their car had been slashed, eggs had been thrown at the patio door, and trash had been tossed in their yard.[157] In May 1994, a vandal carved a swastika on her Chevy Impala, flattened a tire, and glued the car's door handles, hubcaps and locks so the vehicle could not be opened.[158] Samira Hussein's children also were harassed at school, with one of the sons being asked by a classmate if Saddam Hussein was his father. To promote tolerance, Samira Hussein began volunteering in the Montgomery county schools to increase awareness about Islam and the Middle East. She also lobbied the school board to recognize Ramadan as a holiday as a way of increasing appreciation and acceptance of non-Christian faiths. In a 1994 interview with the *Washington Post*, Samira Hussein explained that constant harassment profoundly affected the family's sense of security, interfering with their sleep and making them feel like strangers in their own country.[159]

Instead of abating, the hate-based harassment continued for years. The *Washington Post* updated readers on additional hate crimes directed against Samira Hussein's family.[160] In May 1995, a vandal shattered their storm door. In July 1997, a vandal once again scratched up Mohammed Hussein's car. Two months later, on the evening of September 4, 1997, the family woke to discover that their vehicles had been vandalized. The perpetrator severely damaged the family's Chevy, slashing the leather seats and puncturing two of the car's tires. The assailant scratched a swastika and the word, "pig," on the hood, and defaced the rear of the vehicle, writing that the family should return to their homeland.[161] The other car, a 1981 Pontiac LeMans, was damaged as well – the vandal carved derogatory ethnic slurs on the vehicle and punctured three tires, sending a message that Palestinian-Americans were not welcome in the community.

The *Post* also reported that the Husseins had been targeted on several other occasions: they found dead birds near their home, and notes with ethnic slurs taped to their door.[162] Garbage and beer cans had been thrown over their back fence. Their glass door had been smashed, and their children had been taunted and beaten up.

Samira Hussein was furious that authorities had not done more to stop the ongoing harassment.[163] The September 1997 vandalism was particularly troubling to the family's 12-year old child, who wondered why their neighbors hated the family so much.[164]

Authorities finally apprehended the vandal, 18-year old David Leonard Rikon, in 1998. After being convicted of the vandalism, Rikon was sentenced to only five days in jail and two years of probation. Samira

Hussein told the *Post* that she was shocked that the man who had terrorized her family for years was not punished in a more appropriate manner.[165] Arab-Americans and Muslims were also outraged that Rikon received such a light sentence for repeatedly lashing out at the Hussein family.

Samira Hussein told reporters that the repeated attacks, which took place from August 1990 to September 2007, caused her children to distrust the police and feel that they had no homeland security.[166]

HOME ATTACKS, 2008

Minority homeowners were occasionally targeted in 2008. In South Plainfield, New Jersey, a family of Indian descent found a charred cross in front of their house.[167] The hate crime took place in November, shortly after Obama was elected president. The South Asian family, who had supported the Democratic candidate, found their homemade sign celebrating the presidential victory draped over the torched cross, which had fallen down on their front lawn. Area minorities condemned the attack, claiming it was an attempt to deter minority citizens from participating in the political process in the years after 9/11.

Some political activists saw a connection between attacks on minority residences and the fanning of xenophobia during the 2008 presidential campaign. In chapter five, I discussed how the Clarion Fund paid 70 American newspapers to deliver the terror-scare DVD, *Obsession: Radical Islam's War Against the West*, to 28 million American households, in a campaign coinciding with the seventh anniversary of 9/11. Many minority homeowners were dismayed to find this hate DVD delivered to their doorstep, and some cancelled their newspaper subscriptions in response.

HOME ATTACKS, 2009

Muslim homeowners continued to experience hate crimes the following year. On April 13, 2009, a 53-year old mother of four discovered that her home had been egged in Greensboro, North Carolina.[168] This was one of several attacks she experienced after moving into the neighborhood in 2005. The victim believed that her Muslim attire prompted bigoted vandals to single out her home. Minority residents saw the hate crime as part of the ongoing 9/11 backlash.

On occasion, American Muslims were attacked at their residences by their co-workers. In East Texas, Muslim convert James Berry was assaulted in his Gilmer home on June 6, 2009. The *Longview News-Journal* reported that two of Berry's former co-workers used religious slurs while they punched, choked, and kicked him.[169] The assailants also pressed a gun to his head, threatening to return and hurt him again if he spoke to law enforcement.[170] Because the intruders used anti-Muslim slurs during the beating, the assault was investigated by the Upshur county Sheriff's office and the FBI as a possible bias crime. The attack was particularly troubling to the 2,000 to 3,000 Muslim residents of East Texas, who worried about an upsurge of Islamophobia in the area.

In some instances, community bigots targeted Muslim political candidates at their residences. The *Oakland Tribune* reported that in mid-October, 2009, Nadja Adolf, a hijab-wearing candidate for Newark City council, discovered her residence had been egged.[171] Minority homeowners assumed that the assault was bias-motivated since her candidacy upset local bigots and a picture of her wearing a veil appeared in a local paper a few days prior to the attack.[172] Some community members saw the vandalism as a manifestation of the 9/11 backlash.

HOME ATTACKS, 2010

Minority homeowners were also harassed in their neighborhoods in 2010. In June, someone mailed a letter containing a suspicious white powder to a Muslim man in Jacksonville, Florida.[173] The recipient worried that the substance was anthrax, and went to the hospital for treatment. Authorities tested the powder, which turned out to be non-toxic. Since the homeowner worshipped at the same Jacksonville mosque that had been bombed in May 2010, he became concerned about his safety. He assumed that local bigots were targeting him for engaging in religious debates with other community members after he converted to Islam.

The same month, bigots put up anti-Muslim lawn signs in Edmond, Oklahoma after a South Asian family moved into the neighborhood.[174] The Islamophobic messages were placed facing the Indian family's residence, broadcasting that minority homeowners were not welcome in the area. Activists saw the incident as a product of post-9/11 nativism.

HOME ATTACKS, 2011

Minority homeowners continued to be singled out in 2011. Shortly after Osama bin Laden's death, a vandal wrote offensive graffiti on the home of a Somali family living in Rochester. According to the *Saint Paul Pioneer Press*, the intruders spray-painted "KKK" and a swastika on the Muslim residence on May 4, 2011.[175] The menacing graffiti frightened members of the Iowle family, who left Somalia in 1996 and moved to Rochester in 2004. Neighbors were outraged by the bias attack, and helped the family paint over the menacing messages. Because of the racist content of the graffiti, the Minnesota chapter of CAIR asked the FBI investigate the vandalism as a possible hate crime. Although the attack made the news, federal agents failed to take immediate action, telling inquisitive journalists that they were waiting for advocacy groups to contact them with details about the case. Civil rights activists wondered why the FBI was waiting to obtain information groups like CAIR instead of immediately launching their own investigation. Somalis in Minnesota were also dismayed by the FBI's slow response, wondering whether the ethnicity of the victims played a factor in the agency's hesitancy.

According to the *Saint Paul Pioneer Press*, the same family had been targeted on other occasions: someone attacked their house with a paintball gun, made knife marks inside their mailbox, and broke their car window.[176] Because of the frequency of these attacks, the Iowles assumed that the ongoing harassment was backlash-motivated.

Muslim tenants were also assaulted in New York. In Brooklyn, a Turkish couple was attacked by their neighbor. According to the *New York Daily News*, the conflict began at approximately 7:00 p.m. on June 25, 2011, when Simochon Schwartz began harassing Selda Turan on E. 70th St., the block where they both lived.[177] The inebriated Schwartz then poured a can of beer over her head, grabbed her by the arm, and pushed her against her car, leaving her with scratches and bruises.[178] During the attack, he screamed profanities and slurs at her, calling her an Arab terrorist.[179] When her husband Mustafa came to her assistance, Schwartz punched him in the face, leaving him with a gash in his nose that required stitches.[180] Schwartz also keyed the Turans' car.[181] After the Turkish couple called 911, responding officers arrested Schwartz at Chabad House in Mill Basin, smelling of alcohol. Schwartz resisted arrest, struggling with officers and kicking out the window of a police cruiser.[182]

While Schwartz was in jail, his wife Esther made a veiled threat to the Turans, telling them that it was a majority-Jewish neighborhood, and they should expect retaliation from the community.[183] She then circulated a petition, signed by approximately 20 neighbors, demanding that the Turans' landlords, Rusden and Saadet Dolan, evict the Turkish couple from the neighborhood.[184] The Dolans refused to comply with this request, seeing it as an odious manifestation of religious bigotry. Turkish community members were disturbed by the attack on the Turans and by the rise in anti-Muslim sentiment in the area, which had surged in the years after 9/11.

Civil rights groups were outraged by the hate crime. Kaya Boztepe of the Federation of Turkish American Associations compared the attack to the type of scapegoating the community experienced immediately after the terrorist strikes. The Anti-Defamation League also issued a statement condemning the anti-Turkish attack in the strongest possible terms.

Despite physical evidence to the contrary, Schwartz' attorney maintained that his client was the true victim, targeted because of Mustafa Turan's anti-Semitism. Schwartz' daughter also defended her father, saying that he was unable to call police and report the attack because it was the Shabbas. Many New Yorkers were outraged that Schwartz had failed to take responsibility for his actions, comparing his legal strategy to "blame the victim" tactics used to discredit rape victims. Members of the Jewish community were upset that Schwartz was trying to evade responsibility by claiming to be a religiously-minded bias-crime victim, pointing out that it was prohibited to get drunk, injure neighbors, resist arrest, and damage police property on the Shabbas.

Schwartz was charged with felony assault as a hate crime, and was released without bail. Since the Turans lived next door to their assailant, the Turkish couple worried for their safety. The court ordered Schwartz to stay away from his Muslim neighbors, who began limiting their movements following the attack.

In other parts of the country, minority residents were also victimized by strangers. On September 11, 2011, two men targeted a South Asian family in Fremont, California. The intruders entered the residence, held the Indians at gunpoint, and stole their gold jewelry. According to KCBS News, the homeowner, Rakesh Verma of Kumar Jewelers, believed his family was targeted because Indian women had a cultural tradition of wearing expensive bracelets as a sign of affluence.[185] Because the crime took place on the tenth anniversary of the terrorist strikes, some community members wondered if the timing of the home invasion was deliberate, especially since other South Asians were being victimized by bias attacks in the area. Police investigating the break-in viewed the crime as a straightforward robbery, ignoring any connection to the 9/11 backlash.

A decade after the terrorist strikes, many minority homeowners continued to worry about their safety in American neighborhoods, particularly if they had been targeted in the past. Many felt that xenophobia had not abated. A Pew Research Center Study released shortly before the tenth anniversary of 9/11 determined that the majority of Muslim respondents felt that life remained more difficult than it had been in the years prior to the attacks on the World Trade Center and Pentagon.[186] The same survey determined that only 30% of Americans had a favorable view of Islam, down from 59% in 2001.[187]

CHAPTER NINE:

BACKLASH VERBAL ATTACKS AND
DEATH THREATS, SEPT. 2001 to SEPT. 2011

Throughout the 9/11 backlash, bigots repeatedly threatened Middle Easterners and South Asians in the U.S. Although the true scope of these verbal attacks is difficult to determine, large numbers of minority Americans reported these threats to community groups, government agencies, and local news outlets. Other victims remained silent, doubting that authorities would take action and worrying that attracting attention would be unwise. This chapter includes a representative sampling of some of the death threats, verbal attacks, and menacing gestures that frightened minority Americans and immigrants in the immediate aftermath of 9/11 and continued in the ten years that followed.

Movies released prior to 9/11 frequently used anti-Arab derogatory language, normalizing the use of these racist and religious slurs. According to film critic Jack Shaheen, hundreds of 20th century movies feature Western characters spewing out dozens of demeaning epithets, referring to Arabs as: "'assholes,' 'bastards,' 'camel-dicks,' 'pigs,' 'devil-worshippers,' 'jackals,' 'rats,' 'rag-heads,' 'towel-heads,' 'scum-buckets,' 'sons-of-dogs,' 'buzzards of the jungle,' 'sons-of-whores,' 'sons-of-unnamed goats,' and 'sons-of-she-camels.'"[1]

Many of these movies conveyed the message that Arabs and Muslims deserved the verbal abuse because they were terrorists, intent on destroying the West.[2] The 1998 movie, *Freedom Strike*, features Arab villains plotting to murder Americans. In this film, an announcer informs viewers that terrorists in Damascus were in the process of finalizing their nuclear weapons system.[3] In one scene, Arab assassins attempt to kill the U.S. president, but they prove too inept to carry out their mission. Eventually, a UN military unit, dubbed operation "Freedom Strike," kills more than a dozen of the nefarious Syrians, saving Americans from nuclear destruction. While researching the Islamophobic movie, film critic Jack Shaheen interviewed one of the Arab actors, who relayed that he was directed to spit every time he said the word, "America."[4] Along with being troubled by the racist plot, Shaheen was upset with the Department of Defense, the Department of the Navy, and the Marine Corps for their willing participation in this offensive movie, noting that all three organizations were acknowledged in the movie's credits.[5] The active involvement of the U.S. military in the film conveys the message that certain ethnic and religious groups are dangerous and un-American. By fueling nativist sentiments, racist movies contributed to a zeitgeist where hate crimes were able to flourish in the aftermath of the attacks on the Pentagon and World Trade Center.

American xenophobes absorbed anti-Arab messages and verbally lashed out at innocent minorities in the aftermath of 9/11. Middle Easterners and South Asians in the U.S. began receiving death threats right after the Twin Towers fell, and continued to experience backlash harassment in the years that followed. American bigots stalked ethnic and religious minorities, made obscene gestures, and threatened their physical safety.

VERBAL ATTACKS ON MINORITY ORGANIZATIONS, SEPTEMBER 2001

In the first two weeks after the terrorist strikes, Arab and Muslim organizations were frequently targeted by angry callers. Members of the Gay and Lesbian Arab Society were singled out immediately after 9/11. Ramzi Zakharia told the *Advocate* that his organization received death threats and letters containing racial slurs, referring to the group's members as 'sand-niggers' and 'camel jockeys.'[6] Bigots also made homophobic comments. Zakharia, a Lebanese-American marketing executive from New York, was surprised by the volume of the hate mail, making him feel like an outsider in his own country.[7]

Americans enraged by 9/11 also took their anger out on local Muslim groups. In Oregon, Christopher Paul Younce, a 33-year old man, made a threatening call to the Islamic Cultural Center of Eugene. The *Register Guard* reported that when Tammam Adi answered the phone, Younce declared that all Muslims should be erased.[8] Under threat of prosecution, Younce eventually apologized and agreed to perform community service, blaming his actions on his reaction to the inflammatory television coverage of the crumbling World Trade Center.

In Nevada, irate callers threatened local Muslims. At the Islamic Cultural Center in Las Vegas, officials received more than a dozen menacing calls in the first week after the terrorist attacks. The *Las Vegas Review-Journal* reported that one man blamed the Nevada Muslims for 9/11, thanking them for killing his sister.[9] Another caller promised retribution, insisting that local worshippers needed to pay for the murders in New York and Washington.[10]

Muslim organizations in Northern California also received death threats. Maha El Genaldl, the executive director of the Islamic Network Group in San Jose, received several menacing calls and emails, including death threats.[11] Some callers blamed her for 9/11, telling her that Muslims should be killed for ruining the U.S.

In Southern California, Frank Stacy Abbotts made at least four threatening calls to the Islamic Development Center in Moreno Valley and to a local radio station that featured ethnic programming. According to the *Riverside Press-Enterprise*, Abbotts, a 49-year old man from Perris, blamed local Muslims for 9/11 and threatened station KHPY for airing an Islamic show.[12] Authorities took the calls seriously because they made specific threats of violence against area Muslims, promising to kill all worshippers at the local mosque.[13] It was unclear whether Abbots knew that members of this Islamic center were predominantly African-American, not Middle Eastern, when he made the menacing calls.

When investigators searched Abbotts' home, they found rifles, handguns, ammunition, and white supremacist materials. Abbotts denied that the incriminating evidence belonged to him. Prosecutor John Davis filed one felony and one misdemeanor charge against Abbotts for making terrorist threats, telling the *Press-Enterprise* that the hate literature and weaponry indicated that the danger was real.[14] Abbots pled not guilty, and was held on $20,000 bail. Despite the rise in anti-Muslim sentiment in the community, station KHPY continued its regular Sunday broadcast of the Islamic program.

Abbots reluctantly accepted a plea bargain, admitting guilt to only one of the felony terrorist threat charges. He was sentenced to 120 days in custody and ordered to serve three years of probation. He was also prohibited from owning guns at his residence or contacting the Islamic center or the radio station.

Abbotts eventually apologized for his actions and met briefly with Ron El-Amin, the director of the Islamic center, at Riverside County Superior court. In an interview with the *Press-Enterprise*, El-Amin expressed his hope that the convicted felon would turn his life around, putting his considerable energy to good use.[15] Abbotts was also given the option of having his felony count reduced to a misdemeanor if he completed his probation successfully. Some community members wondered if the court was being overly-lenient on the white supremacist, doubting that an Arab Muslim would escape a felony conviction after admitting to stockpiling weapons and promising to kill Americans at a specific house of worship.

DEATH THREATS TARGETING PEDESTRIANS, SEPTEMBER 2001

Along with threats aimed at ethnic and religious organizations, minority pedestrians were occasionally targeted during the 9/11 backlash. Sikhs were often verbally attacked by bigots in many parts of the country. Mikhta Kaur, a Sikh housewife, was singled out at a Dunwoody supermarket on September 16, 2001. According to the *Atlanta Constitution*, the bigoted man threatened her life, telling her that vermin like her should be exterminated.[16] News of this hate crime frightened area South Asians, who began curtailing their movements.

Caucasian Sikhs were also verbally targeted during the 9/11 backlash. The September 19, 2001 issue of the *Oregonian* reported that a group of men in downtown Portland shouted a death threat at a Sikh man with brown hair and blue eyes.[17] Hari Nam Singh Khalsa, who had a long beard and always wore a turban in public, said that the men threatened his life, called him an Arab, and yelled obscenities. Khalsa, a Portland resident, told the *Oregonian* that this was not his first experience with area Islamophobia: he was called the Ayatollah Khomeni in the 1970s, Saddam Hussein in the 1990s, and Osama bin Laden immediately after the terrorist strikes.[18]

Although many threats went unpunished, some local authorities took action when bigots verbally attacked ethnic and religious minorities in the aftermath of 9/11. The Vancouver *Columbian* reported that in Redmond, Washington, 48-year old Richard F. Howell was charged with malicious harassment after shouting racial epithets on September 17, 2001 at a man who appeared to be Middle Eastern.[19] In other parts of Washington state, South Asians were subjected to abusive language. In Colfax, Washington, 21-year old Tyson Druffel was charged with a hate crime after screaming death threats and racial slurs at two men of Indian descent shortly after 9/11.[20]

Sometimes, strangers became nervous when they saw minorities inside landmark skyscrapers, and treated them like potential terrorists. Shortly after 9/11, a Sikh man in Chicago was riding in the elevator to the Sears Tower when fellow passengers pressed the alarm and summoned security personnel, worried that the turbaned man was a Muslim suicide bomber.[21] Sikhs were also under attack in the nation's capital. The September 28, 2001 issue of *India-West* reported that four white males chased Rippy Singh in D.C., calling him a terrorist and threatening to bomb him.[22]

Along with Sikhs and South Asians, Middle Easterners occasionally received death threats while walking on American streets. In California, an Iranian couple was targeted in a backlash attack. The Riverside *Press-Enterprise* reported that on September 24, 2001, 44-year old Steven James McManus was arrested in Huntington Beach, after he threatened to kill an elderly Persian couple, ages 77 and 74.[23] According to the *Los Angeles Times*, the 6 ft. 5 inch McManus saw the pair walking down the street and made a U-turn, demanding to know where they were from and promising to kill them unless they walked directly into traffic.[24] The frightened couple began crossing the busy street against their will, stopping only when a neighbor saw them and offered to give them a safe ride home. The *Orange County Register* reported that McManus also threatened to murder his former landlord for talking to prosecutors about the case.[25] As a result of his criminal conduct, McManus was charged with two felonies, four misdemeanors, and one count of obstructing a police officer, facing up to eight years in jail. He was eventually sentenced to only 180 days in prison for intimidating a prosecution witness and committing a hate crime. Some community members were surprised by McManus' behavior, noting he was a retired Marine who had been publicly lauded for helping the homeless in Costa Mesa.

MINORITY PEDESTRIANS THREATENED BY MOTORISTS, SEPTEMBER 2001

Minority pedestrians were sometimes threatened by bigoted motorists during the 9/11 backlash. The *Austin American Statesman* reported that on September 11, 2001, Mohammed Khan was harassed in Austin while he and a friend were walking in their Brushy Creek neighborhood.[26] Shortly after the terrorist strikes, a man in a pickup truck drove up to Khan and gestured for him to approach the vehicle. Thinking the stranger needed directions, the South Asian pedestrian walked over to see what the other driver wanted. The stranger suddenly began screaming at him, asking him repeatedly if he was responsible for the bombing. Khan answered that he wasn't, and the other man drove away.

Minority pedestrians were also harassed in New York. After 9/11, a *New York Post* journalist reported seeing two men driving a car with an anti-Palestinian death threat taped to the window.[27] The sign unsettled area Arab-Americans, who questioned whether it was safe to take walks in such a xenophobic climate.

Elsewhere in the state, hostile drivers confronted minority community members. While sweeping the sidewalk in front of his family's Staten Island deli, a woman pulled over and threatened Abdul Mohammed, demanding that he return to his homeland.[28] Discussing this harassment, Mohammed told the *New York Daily News* that he was upset that he and his Yemeni family members were unable to feel safe and accepted in their adopted country, particularly after fleeing war in the Middle East.[29]

Black pedestrians were also singled out by angry motorists at the height of the backlash. An East African man was targeted on September 18, 2001 while pushing a shopping cart at the Home Depot in South Seattle. According to the *Yakima Herald*, two white men drove up to the immigrant and threatened his life, promising to shoot him.[30] The victim said that he felt the death threat was bias-motivated, although the strangers did not directly refer to his race or religion.

MINORITY MOTORISTS THREATENED BY DRIVERS, SEPTEMBER 2001

Along with pedestrians, minority motorists were harassed by bigoted drivers in the aftermath of 9/11. In many instances, xenophobes made non-verbal threats. According to the *Augusta Chronicle*, a Pakistani-American woman in Georgia was targeted while driving to pick up her four-year old son from day care on September 14, 2001.[31] On that day, Naeema Kaleem, a 29-year old mother from Martinez, saw two teenagers tailing her in their jeep. She attempted to let them pass, but they pulled in front of her and blocked her path. She tried backing up and leaving, but they kept pursuing her. They then used their hands to make gun gestures, pretending to shoot her. The teens also began insulting her verbally, telling her to return to her country of origin. Kaleen told the *Augusta Chronicle* that the most harrowing part of her ordeal was that she had her eight-month son in the car with her.[32] Although the teenagers eventually left her alone, she said that the experience left her shaken. She believed that the hate crime was triggered by the fact that her hijab identified her as a Muslim. She told journalists that she was just as American as her attackers, and that her hijab did not make her any less of a citizen.[33]

In addition to South Asian Muslims, Arab-Americans were verbally threatened by other drivers during the 9/11 backlash. According to the *Denver Post*, a motorist began screaming insults at another driver, a hijab-wearing Palestinian-American who had stopped her car at a crosswalk.[34] The 32-year old Muslim victim was so frightened by the bigot's menacing conduct that she got out of her vehicle in terror. She was particularly upset that she was being threatened in her own country, pointing out that she had been born in the U.S. and that her ancestors had immigrated to America in 1905.[35]

On occasion, enraged motorists tried to ram South Asian drivers after issuing them non-verbal threats. The September 16, 2001 *Augusta Chronicle* reported that an enraged motorist began tailing Madanjit Singh, a Sikh immigrant who had lived in the U.S. for decades. According to Singh, the driver followed him from Evans to Locks Road, then accelerated as though he intended to crash into his car.[36] At the last moment, the angry driver braked, after making the South Asian man afraid for his life. Singh believed that his turban triggered the backlash incident.

Iranian drivers were also threatened by angry motorists. The September 29, 2001 issue of the *Los Angeles Times* reported that during the 9/11 backlash, Nikolai Delevante was driving on Wilshire Boulevard when he began shouting racial slurs at two Iranian men in another vehicle.[37] Delevante then threatened them and waved a gun at them. According to the *Los Angeles Times*, the 25-year old assailant was taken into custody and charged with three counts: making a criminal threat, exhibiting a firearm, and violating civil rights, carrying a combined maximum sentence of six years and 10 months in state prison.[38] Katherine Voyer, head of the hate crime unit of the LA County Sheriff's department, told the *Los Angeles Times* that her office was investigating over 30 other hate crimes in the city related to the 9/11 backlash, and that authorities were hoping to deter future attacks by taking swift action against vigilantes.[39]

VERBAL ATTACKS AND DEATH THREATS, FALL 2001 THROUGH 2002

In the months following 9/11, minorities continued to be verbally threatened across the U.S. On occasion, gang members scapegoated immigrant groups for 9/11. The *Daily Herald* reported that in Elgin, Illinois, a gang-member, acting on behalf of his crew, called the police department and said that he planned on murdering local Arabs and Muslims in retaliation for the Puerto Ricans killed in the terrorist strikes.[40] Although the caller used a payphone and identified himself only as "Glock," authorities obtained a timed security videotape of the downtown convenience store where the call was made. From this tape, they identified 27-year old Jose A. Ares-Torres as the perpetrator who called 911 at 7:52 p.m. on October 30,

2001.[41] Torres was arrested and charged with committing a hate crime and disorderly conduct. He was held at Kane County jail on a $15,000 bond.

On occasion, South Asians were threatened when parking their vehicles. According to the October 10, 2001 issue of the *New York Times*, a white man threatened and insulted an Indian-American driver attempting to park in a residential area of New Jersey.[42] Frightened for his safety, the South Asian motorist restarted his car and drove away.

As the 9/11 backlash continued in 2002, minority groups continued to receive death threats and menacing messages. Reflecting on the heightened xenophobia he experienced in the months after the terrorist strikes, Harshi Singh Bains, a Sikh resident of Wilmette, Illinois, told the *Daily Herald* that he was particularly saddened when teenagers harassed him out of a misplaced sense of patriotism, not realizing he was also mourning the death of his countrymen.[43]

Like their Sikh counterparts, Muslim immigrants continued to be verbally harassed by strangers in the months after the attacks on the World Trade Center and Pentagon. According to the *South Florida Sentinel*, Palestinian-American businessman Nafez Sammour and his wife Amal were repeatedly threatened by bigoted motorists in the first year after 9/11.[44] Xenophobic drivers swerved their vehicles at them, gave them the finger, and pointed imaginary guns at them.[45] The Sammours believed they were being singled out because of their Middle Eastern appearance – his beard and her hijab made them visible targets. They considered reporting the bias-based harassment, but decided against doing so when other hate crime victims told them that local police were not bothering to investigate backlash complaints.

In one incident, a man threatened Amal Sammour when she was driving her three-year old son to the doctor. She told the *Sentinel* that in the parking lot, a middle-aged man with blue eyes and white hair began banging on her window, calling her a terrorist and demanding that she remove her religious head scarf.[46] She called 911 to report the attack. As she waited for the police, the assailant ran into a nearby building. When an officer arrived on the scene, he simply told her to go home. He informed her that he would try to talk to the man, but was unable to make an arrest because the man's conduct was not criminal. Amal Sammour told the *Sentinel* that the man made her fear for her life, hitting her car and looking at her with obvious hatred.[47] As a result of the constant harassment, the Sammours decided to take their four American-born children out of school and move the family to the West Bank, where they felt it was safer.

In addition to being targeted by strangers, Muslim converts were sometimes harassed by members of their own families. In chapters six and seven, I discussed how Sussan Salazar, a Muslim convert from Colombia, was singled out at school and at work. Salazar was also verbally harassed during the 9/11 backlash. Salazar told the *South Florida Sun Sentinel* that immediately after the terrorist strikes, American strangers cursed her on the street and whispered about her hijab.[48] Even members of her own family in Florida mistreated her. An aunt compared her to the devil, and instructed her never to touch her cousins. The same relative brought a church group to Salazar to warn her about the evil nature of Islam. In response to this mistreatment, Salazar left the U.S. and returned temporarily to Colombia, where strangers threw food at her and attempted to pull off her veil.[49]

Upon her return to the U.S., Salazar was detained by Miami immigration officials, who questioned her for hours about her hijab and her activities.[50] When her interrogators learned that she had entered into a religious engagement at a mosque, they decided that the ceremony counted as a de facto marriage that voided her visa. Governmental officials began deportation proceedings against her. When Salazar requested that she not be forced back to Colombia, where anti-Muslim sentiment was rampant, they began asylum proceedings and sent her to Turner Guilford Knight Correctional Center, where she was finger-printed and told to remove her veil for her identification photo.[51] When she insisted it was her religious right to wear her veil, a corrections officer forced her to comply, saying that the right to worship did not exist in the facility. Before her lawyer was able to get her out, Salazar spent two weeks at the corrections center, wrapping her hair in a bed sheet when praying five times a day.

Muslim women were also targeted in the Midwest. Susan Gailani, an Iraqi-born Muslim from Naperville, Illinois, told the *Daily Herald* motorists routinely heckled her for wearing her hijab in the year after 9/11.[52] At times, Gailani was frightened by the harassment, wondering whether the verbal taunts were a prelude to something more sinister.

A year after 9/11, Muslims in Aloha, Oregon said that they were still altering their conduct to protect themselves during the ongoing backlash. Bangladeshi immigrant Mohammed Haque told the *Oregonian* that he had stopped taking his morning walks and refrained from using Arabic words like "inshallah" after hearing that a stranger walked up to another Muslim at a local supermarket and threatened his life with a gun.[53]

Verbal attacks on Muslims and Middle Easterners were taking place while American audiences were watching movies full of anti-Arab stereotypes and offensive racial epithets. In chapter seven, I briefly discussed the December 2002 movie, *Two Degrees*, focusing on its negative depiction of Arab-American store owners. The film is also noteworthy because of its extensive use of ethnic slurs. According to film critic Shaheen, movie's African American characters repeatedly make derogatory comments about Arab-American liquor store owners, referring to them as "towel-head motherfuckers," and "camel-eating asses."[54] The black characters also tell the minority businessmen, "You Ay-rabs ain't shit."[55] This dialogue gives viewers implicit permission to feel superior to ethnic and religious groups in the U.S.

VERBAL ATTACKS AND DEATH THREATS, 2003

Minorities in America also experienced verbal attacks in 2003. In Tennessee, a Muslim woman was harassed for wearing her hijab. Maha Ayesh, an instructor at the Knoxville Anoor Mosque school, told the *News Sentinel* that a group of people noticed her religiously-mandated veil and told her to return home to Afghanistan.[56] In other parts of the South, South Asians received death threats. According to the April 27, 2003 issue of the *Kansas City Star*, Shaheen Ahmed, an India-born resident of Leawood, Missouri, reported that a firefighter told one of her sons that he wished to see the young man's head squashed on the concrete.[57]

As overseas tensions worsened in mid-March 2003, verbal attacks against ethnic and religious minorities in the U.S. proliferated. The *New York Times* reported that on March 16, 2003, three days before the Iraq War began, four Muslim women were harassed and threatened in Venice, California by another café patron who sang about raping them.[58] According to the *San Diego Union Tribune*, 54-year old Murray Gurfein, a white resident of Marina del Rey, was charged with one misdemeanor count of a hate crime after seeing the veiled Muslim patrons and composing a racist song about them on his guitar.[59] Gurfein's song included menacing lyrics: "Those goddamn Muslim terrorists attack our country... They wear ugly robes that are so stinky... and they rape their women all the time.. but since their women like it, they don't need to get it over there, we can give it to them here."[60] When the women reported the incident to the café manager, Gurfein threatened them with bodily harm. According to the City Attorney's Office, Gurfein pleaded no contest to a misdemeanor hate crime charge on March 21, 2003 and was sentenced to six days in county jail and 36 months probation.

Bigots also verbally harassed minorities in Oregon. Eugene police arrested 28-year old Marc Cohen on March 24, 2003, after he threatened a turban-wearing Sikh woman who had stopped at a traffic light. According to police spokeswoman Pam Olshanski, Cohen got out of his vehicle at 24th and Hilyard St., approached the Sikh woman's car, and used his fingers to simulate shooting her.[61] Police chief Thad Buchanan told the *Register-Guard* that the incident terrified the Sikh driver.[62] Cohen was charged with harassment and released, denying the charge and claiming that he was simply making a "what's up" gesture with his hands.[63]

According to the March 27, 2003 issue of the *Oregonian*, Portland radio talk-show host Lars Larson expressed outrage that Cohen was charged with a crime, telling his listeners that it was not illegal to point at another person.[64] Although many call-in listeners agreed with Larson, other community members were not convinced that Cohen simply made an innocuous hand gesture. Human rights activist Greg Rikhoff asked *Register Guard* readers to imagine how they would feel if a member of their family had been singled out in a similar manner.[65] Tammam Adi, spokesman for the Islamic Cultural Center of Eugene, viewed the death threat as a hate crime. He told the *Oregonian* that many area Muslims were shaving their beards or removing their hijabs in the aftermath of 9/11, concealing their identities from other Americans who assumed that they were all terrorists.[66]

At the beginning of the Iraq War, bigots verbally scapegoated American Sikhs. The May 22, 2003 issue of the *Bergen County Record* reported that an elderly female neighbor repeatedly harassed Jaggit Singh, a 26-year old software consultant from Lodi, New Jersey.[67] On one occasion, she angrily asked him if he was on the side of America or the Muslims, and he took the occasion to explain that he was a Sikh. In other instances, she embarrassed him in front of onlookers. This mistreatment was not Singh's only experience with backlash bigotry. Shortly after the terrorist strikes, a car full of teenagers acted menacingly towards him and told him to go back to his own country.[68] He was so disturbed by the incident that he skipped two days of work. He was also singled out in New York City. When he was visiting Times Square six months after 9/11, three young men saw his black turban and began harassing him, warning him not to bomb another building. As a result of these experiences, Singh became worried that religious minorities in the U.S. would face even more discrimination if American troops began dying in large numbers in the Middle East.

VERBAL ATTACKS AND DEATH THREATS, 2004-2005

Middle Easterners and South Asians continued to receive death threats throughout 2004. According to the *Bergen County Record*, a Muslim van passenger was subjected to taunts and death threats in Patterson, New Jersey.[69] In the aftermath of this 2004 incident, minority groups worried about a resurgence of nativism in the area.

In other states, minority student groups were targeted during the Iraq War. At the University of Michigan, a Middle Eastern students group received a menacing email in 2004. According to the *Arab American News*, a bigot sent the campus group a death threat, expressing the hope that Israeli soldiers would put the students six feet underground.[70] University administrators worried that the death threat would silence minority voices on the campus.

Anti-Arab movies fueled Iraq War xenophobia in the U.S. In the horror film, *Dawn of the Dead*, American GIs were shown fighting Iraqi zombies.[71] This movie, which was released in the U.S. in March 2004, portrays Arabs as the undead, making it easy for the film's heroes to shoot them.

One of the worst depictions of Arabs appears in the movie, *Spartan*, which was released on March 12, 2004. In this movie, Arab villains in Dubai run a white slavery ring, abduct blonde American girls, and sell them to other Middle Easterners. One of the young prisoners is the president's daughter. The movie's central villain is Tariq Asani, a Lebanese sex slaver with a prison record. Asani is depicted as a misogynistic thug who preys upon young girls. In his discussion of the movie, film critic Shaheen notes that in one particularly racist scene, the Arab monster tells another character that he planned on presenting him with underage blonde girls.[72] Asani is eventually killed for his participation in such dastardly schemes, to the relief of movie audiences. Many activists felt that these disturbing films fueled racial animosity in the U.S.

Muslims and Middle Easterners were also harassed and threatened by American bigots in 2005. On August 5, 2005, a man from Illinois was arrested after he threatened to bomb the D.C. offices of CAIR.[73] The hate crime frightened American Muslims, who relied on the group to champion their civil rights.

The following month, film makers released the *Promised Land*, which presented Middle Easterners as misogynists who engage in white slavery. In a particularly offensive scene, Bedouin villains abduct Estonian women and forcibly transport them in a camel caravan across the Sinai desert. Along with trafficking women, Arabs are also seen auctioning off female captives and raping them. In a review of the film, Shaheen takes issue with scenes featuring inexplicable and gratuitous terrorist attacks, including one that takes place when the women are off-loaded outside a brothel.[74] This movie was released in the U.S. on September 24, 2005, shortly after the fourth anniversary of 9/11. Other movies released the same year also contained anti-

Arab scenes. For example, the 2005 science fiction film, *Manitore*, features U.S. soldiers shooting at Iraqis, who are referred to as "lowlifes."[75] These types of racist films contributed to an atmosphere of xenophobia in the U.S.

Throughout the fall of 2005, Middle Easterners and South Asians were repeatedly harassed by American nativists. In November, the *Philadelphia Inquirer* reported that a minority woman from Blue Bell was singled out by a bigoted motorist on Route 202.[76] During the incident, the other driver threatened her and yelled derogatory comments about Arabs.

VERBAL ATTACKS AND DEATH THREATS, 2006

As the five-year anniversary of 9/11 approached, many newspapers across the country interviewed Muslims about how their lives were affected by the backlash, documenting the death threats and bias-motivated harassment they continued to receive years after the terrorist strikes. In the August 10, 2006 issue of *USA Today*, 32-year old Tulsa community college teacher Jafumba Asad reported that she developed ulcers a few months after 9/11, and continued to be affected by anti-Muslim sentiment on an ongoing basis.[77] Asad claimed that the worst incident happened when two men cornered her in a Wal-Mart parking lot, using profanities and yelling that Muslims should all be locked up.[78] She tried backing up to escape the men, but realized that she was trapped by cars parked directly behind her. Because she was pregnant at the time, she worried that her intense fear could trigger a miscarriage.[79] Although the men eventually walked away without physically assaulting her, the incident left her feeling afraid. On each anniversary of 9/11, she became concerned that bigots might target one of her five daughters or other members of the Muslim community.[80]

In other parts of the country, Muslims were harassed in the same summer. The *Tampa Tribune* reported that a hijab-wearing grandmother was verbally attacked on August 11, 2006 while she was picking up her 15-year old granddaughter at King High School.[81] During this incident, two men in a truck activated a siren on top of their vehicle and began threatening the Muslim woman. Dhuha Hannah, a native New Yorker who lived in Tampa for more than 17 years, told the *Tribune* that the men assumed she was a terrorist, yelling that she was about to drop a bomb.[82] Afraid of escalating the situation, Hannah lowered her eyes, making it impossible for her to get their license plate number. She told the *Tribune* that it was ludicrous for someone to imply that she had possession of an explosive device simply because she wore a hijab.[83] Minority community members viewed the incident as a part of the ongoing 9/11 backlash.

Other Muslims in the city also reported being verbally harassed the same month. In August 2006, Mohsin Teladia, a Tampa imam, was singled out by other shoppers at the Wal-Mart on East Fletcher Avenue. Several people stared at him, and one called him Osama.[84] He told the *Tribune* that the bias-motivated incident frightened him and his relatives, prompting them to leave the store.[85]

While American bigots were verbally harassing area Muslims, moviegoers were watching films containing anti-Arab slurs. In his discussion of the 2006 film, *Inside Man*, film critic Shaheen points out that one of the characters refers to a Sikh bank employee as "a fuckin' Arab."[86] The movie also contains a gratuitous reference to Arab terrorists, who are called "ragheads."[87] The inclusion of this offensive dialogue normalizes derogatory language.

Other 2006 films fueled anti-Muslim sentiment in the U.S. The drama, *United 93*, dramatically re-enacts what could have transpired on one of the planes hijacked on 9/11. By viewing this film, Americans were able to re-experience the horrors of that day. In his book, Guilty, Shaheen argues that the movie exacerbated Islamophobia and anti-Arab bigotry in the U.S. He noted that in Phoenix, Arizona, two Arab Muslim women were threatened and verbally harassed by movie-goers who had just finished watching the film.[88]

Along with threatening phone calls, menacing letters, and hostile confrontations, Middle Easterners and South Asians were sometimes frightened by hate messages posted on the internet. In December 2006, Tampa residents were alarmed to discover that a local man owned and operated a web site that urged readers to murder all Muslim children.[89] It suggested that committing religious genocide was a necessary public safety precaution since Muslims were raising their "rug rats" to strap on bombs and kill Americans.[90]

On occasion, bigots followed up their threats with acts of violence. A serious bias-motivated incident occurred on December 5, 2006, when a veiled woman in Ohio was threatened by a bigot who attempted to run over her with his car.[91] The Muslim woman, a U.S. permanent resident who had been born overseas, was using her Saudi passport to cash a check at a Lakewood Walgreens when another customer began making obscene gestures and shouting at her, telling her to leave the country. Although there were many customers and employees who witnessed to the incident, no one in the store came to the shopper's assistance. When she exited the store and tried to write down the abusive man's license plate number, he tried to hit her with his vehicle while backing up in the parking lot.

VERBAL ATTACKS AND DEATH THREATS, 2007

As the wars in Iraq and Afghanistan stretched on, Muslims and Sikhs continued to be targeted across the U.S. On March 6, 2007, Victor Lambot, a 53-year old city sanitation worker from Queens, was arrested for vandalizing a Muslim woman's car. The *New York Daily News* reported that soon after Arfa Yaqub parked near Kissena Park, Lambot smashed her vehicle's mirror with his fist.[92] At the time of the incident, Yaqub was wearing a hijab. Lambot yelled at the woman for being Muslim, the religion of the 9/11 hijackers.[93] Detectives from the NYPD hate crime task force reported that when they interviewed Lambot at his home on the day of the attack, he went on a drunken tirade attacking Muslims, Hindus, African-Americans, and Latinos.[94]

American nativists continued targeting Sikhs, accusing them of being members of the Taliban. The Los Angeles *Daily News* reported that in April 2007, bigots insulted Sikhs celebrating the holiday of Baisakhi at the Los Angeles convention center.[95] At this event, two onlookers made loud racist comments about the 10,000 event participants and their colorful floats, comparing the gathering to an al-Qaeda convention.

While minorities were being victimized, American comedies released in mid-2007 used derogatory language to entertain American audiences, suggesting that racial minorities were objects of ridicule. The American comedy, *Delta Farce*, employs anti-Arab and anti-Latino stereotypes to make viewers laugh. In this movie, Larry the Cable Guy is mistakenly taken to Mexico instead of being shipped to Fallujah, Iraq. Along with ridiculing Mexicans, the film contains offensive anti-Muslim dialogue. In one scene, the protagonist proclaims that he needs to find out whether the villagers are "terrorists, Turds, or Shit-iites."[96]

Other 2007 movies depict Middle Easterners as misogynistic villains. In the film, *Afghan Knights*, many of the Muslim characters abuse women. Shaheen was particularly horrified by a scene in which an Afghan warlord rapes his young wife from behind while referring to her as filth.[97] This film was released on DVD in the U.S. in July 2007. The movie perpetuates the harmful stereotype that Muslim women are passive creatures too disempowered and timid to defend themselves.

While Hollywood films were depicting female Middle Eastern characters as passive victims of male brutality, real Muslim women were standing up to their American assailants. According to the *Buffalo News*, a young veiled woman took action after a 17-year old male threatened to rape her at the Amherst Metro Rail Station in the summer of 2007.[98] On the day of the attack, the young man began insulting the victim as she entered the station, telling her that she was not allowed to talk to him because she was a Muslim. Afraid for her safety, she tried to get away from him by exiting the station. Instead of leaving her alone, he followed after her, threatening to sexually assault her. When her family members picked her up, they discouraged her from contacting the police, warning her that her reputation might be jeopardized by the incident. The victim told the *Buffalo News* that she contacted the police anyway, refusing to be silent.[99] Officers John Popp and Mike Insalaco investigated the case, and found the victim's claims were corroborated by witness testimony. Although the Muslim woman disclosed her name to police when reporting the verbal attack, she told the media that she wished to keep her identity anonymous to prevent further mistreatment.

VERBAL ATTACKS AND DEATH THREATS, 2008-2010

Years after 9/11, Muslims continued to be threatened in the U.S. Because the harassment was so ubiquitous, it rarely made the news, except when the hate crime victims were high-profile members of the community. On occasion, public officials were threatened by bigots. Todd Gallinger, a Muslim candidate for Irvine City Council, was occasionally targeted for his advocacy work. Some public officials attacked him for championing civil rights in wartime. In the years after the terrorist strikes, he had represented CAIR-LA in two class action lawsuits against the Department of Homeland Security and the FBI regarding delays in processing background checks for naturalization applicants who were Muslim. According to the *Los Angeles Times*, Gallinger's political colleagues sometimes harassed him because of his religious background. At a September 19, 2008 forum, council member Stephen Choi pejoratively referred to him as a "born-again Muslim" and attacked him for his association with CAIR.[100] The *Los Angeles Times* also reported that Gallinger received an anonymous death threat in October 2008.[101] The caller threatened to cut off his head, suggesting that all Muslims deserved such a fate.

Muslims in other states were also singled out by bigots. In Oxford, North Carolina, a Muslim woman was verbally assaulted at a Wal-Mart on Oct. 26, 2010. The victim, a 31-year old African American, reported that an older white male approached her and asked her if she was a Muslim.[102] When she replied that she was, the man became hostile, shouting profanities and telling her to go back to her homeland.[103] He then spit at her and approached her in a threatening manner, making her fear for her safety. Although authorities charged him with ethnic intimidation, the woman continued to be afraid of him, concerned that he might retaliate against her for contacting the police.

The same month, a truck driver in Tennessee nearly ran a Muslim motorist off the road. According to the *New York Times*, the reckless driver saw Ms. Suleyman, a Kurdish woman, wearing a hijab and used his vehicle to threaten her, practically causing her to get into an accident.[104] The attack occurred while community members were heatedly debating the construction of a mosque in Murfreesboro. At the time of the incident, Ms. Suleyman, a lobbyist for the Tennessee Immigrant Refugee Rights Coalition, was driving around registering minority voters.[105]

VERBAL ATTACKS AND DEATH THREATS, 2011

Anti-Muslim harassment continued throughout 2011. In February of that year, California protestors hurled insults at Muslim families attending a charity event in Yorba Linda. Expressing their opposition to the fundraising efforts of area Muslims, demonstrators made death threats and Islamophobic slurs, calling the participants terrorists and wife-beaters.[106] Community activists were dismayed that Villa Park Councilwoman Deborah Pauly made bigoted comments at the protest rally, characterizing the nearby Muslims as enemies of America, seeking to destroy the country.[107]

On occasion, Muslim community members were targeted while shopping. In early March, 2011, an Egyptian-American grandmother was carrying her groceries to her car in Anaheim when she discovered that her vehicles had been vandalized in a bias-motivated attack. The assailant had keyed her car, sprayed foam on the driver's side of the vehicle, and taped a torn page of the Quran on her car with the words, "Fuck it," written in red.[108] The vandalism frightened the 68-year old victim, who was angry that the vandal damaged her vehicle simply because she wore a religiously-proscribed head scarf.

Other Muslims experienced similar property crimes. On May 12, 2011, a Muslim of Indian heritage discovered that a bigot had scratched the words, "fucking sand nigger," into his car, which had a mosque parking sticker on the window.[109] At the time of the incident, the vehicle was parked at a public area in Portage, Michigan. Because of the racist content of the graffiti, the bearded vehicle owner was certain the attack was triggered by his ethnicity and religion.

Muslims in the news were often targeted by bigots. In the summer of 2011, Umme-Hani Khan received death threats after filing a lawsuit against Abercrombie & Fitch. According to the *San Francisco Chronicle*, Khan was fired from her job on February 22, 2010 after being told that her religious headwear interfered with the company's wholesome, all-American image.[110] Khan was surprised that she was terminated, since she had worn the hijab when she was hired at the Hillsdale Hollister store in San Mateo County, California, and consistently complied with the store manager's request that she wear her headscarf in the company colors. Although she worked without incident for several months, a district manager conducting an inspection took issue with her hijab, and made her contact the corporate office. During this call, Abercrombie & Fitch administrators fired Khan over the phone for wearing her religious headscarf on the job, even though she worked in the storeroom and had no contact with the public.[111]

By challenging the constitutionality of Abercrombie & Fitch's policy, Khan attracted the unwanted attention of Islamophobes who threatened her life. According to CNN, some of the menacing letters, sent to the offices of CAIR, threatened to cut off Khan's head, wrap it in pig's skin, and bury it.[112] Internet bloggers discussing the lawsuit also made overt threats against Khan, calling her offensive names and suggesting that she ought to leave the country for being Muslim.

Muslim women were also threatened in other states. According to WXYZ Action News in Ann Arbor, a blond man in a black pick-up truck targeted a 21-year old motorist wearing a hijab.[113] While honking his horn and swerving his car into her lane, he called her terrorist, ordered her to leave the country, and declared that her people deserved to die. When she attempted to call the police on her cell phone, he pulled out a gun and pointed it at her, threatening to kill her.[114] The attack took place at the intersection of S. State Street and Eisenhower early Sunday morning, August 7, 2011. Although the victim reported his license plate to investigating officers, they told the news that they were having difficulty locating the suspect.[115] Muslim community activists were shocked that authorities were having trouble apprehending the suspect even though they had his license plate number and DMV information on file. They urged the police to make his arrest a top departmental priority.

On occasion, even bearded white men were targeted by bigots during the ongoing 9/11 backlash. According to a 2010 article in the *San Francisco Examiner*, Tahoe resident Phil Olsen, the star of a television show on competitive facial hair growers, reported that bigots sometimes saw his beard and shouted "Taliban" at him.[116]

A decade after 9/11, Muslims continued to be threatened by community members angry about the terrorist strikes. On September 11, 2011, a bigot threatened a Muslim family attending an air show in California.[117] The incident upset area Muslims, who worried about their safety on the ten-year anniversary of the attacks on the Pentagon and World Trade Center.

The same day, a Muslim in Texas received a threatening note at the Petrol Station, a Houston sports bar. Immediately before the incident, Tarek Ghalayani was having beers with a friend, watching the Jets-Cowboys game, when he decided to order a burger to go. The *New York Daily News* reported that when a restaurant employee handed Ghalayani the take-out container, it had a drawing of a plane crashing into the Twin Towers with the message, "Happy September 11th."[118] Ghalayani was offended by the note's implication that he and other Muslims were celebrating the terrorist strikes. When Ghalayani complained to the restaurant staff, he and his companion were insulted and called offensive names by the bartender. As Ghalayani was leaving the establishment, he heard the employee yell the words, "Allahu Akbar."[119] When bar owner Ben Fullelove learned about Ghalayani's negative experience on YELP, he promptly fired the bigoted bartender. Because no staff member took responsibility for writing the menacing note on the take-out container, it is likely that the perpetrator continued working at the sports bar after the bias-motivated incident. Activists were dismayed that ethnic and religious minorities continued to be scapegoated and harassed so many years after 9/11.

CHAPTER TEN:

POST-9/11 KILLINGS OF MUSLIMS, SIKHS, ARABS, AND SOUTH ASIANS

During the 9/11 backlash, some American immigrants and minority residents were murdered by strangers. In some instances, authorities questioned whether the killings were bias-motivated or opportunistic attacks. To understand the true significance of these crimes, it is important to view them in the xenophobic environment in which they were taking place.

Some activists thought that racist movies released before 9/11 created an intolerant cultural environment conducive to bias-motivated murders. One of the most damaging films was *Rules of Engagement*, released on March 31, 2000, less than a year and a half before the terrorist strikes. Critic Jack Shaheen was offended by this Islamophobic movie, filmed with the cooperation of the Department of Defense.[1] In one scene, Marine colonel Childers, played by Samuel L. Jackson, is shown rescuing the American flag from armed Yemenis, who are using it for target practice. In another scene, Childers commands his troops to fire on a group of Yemeni women and children, telling his men to "Waste the Motherfuckers!"[2] Colonel Hodges, played by Tommy Lee Jones, launches an investigation in what initially appears to be a massacre of 83 Yemeni civilians at the hands of U.S. forces. Examining the victims, Hodges sees a little Arab girl with one leg, and initially concludes that her shooting could not be justified. Later, he learns that all the Yemenis, including the one-legged little girl, were terrorists out to murder Americans. He finds and translates a tape declaring that the Yemenis have declared a holy war against the U.S., calling upon all Muslims to kill Americans and their allies.[3]

Critic Tim Jon Semmerling also took issue with the movie's xenophobic messages. In his book, 'Evil' Arabs in American Popular Film, he argues that the derogatory scenes involving Yemenis are used to justify the massacre of Arab civilians. He writes that the Arab men, women, and children seem to be getting what they deserved when American soldiers shoot at them, inspect the carnage, and declare their mission a success.[4]

Semmerling argues that Arab villains became even more prominent in American dramas and documentaries after the terrorist attacks, when multicultural America was replaced by a world strongly bifurcated between good and evil.[5] These Islamophobic films contributed to a zeitgeist in which Americans envisioned themselves in a struggle with an evil Arab menace, out to destroy the U.S. During the backlash, bigots acted on their xenophobic impulses, occasionally murdering immigrants and ethnic-looking Americans.

POST-9/11 KILLINGS

Many Americans read about the killing of Balbir Singh Sodhi in Arizona, who was shot to death in Mesa, Arizona on September 15, 2001. Because the murder happened so soon after 9/11 and because killer Frank Roque publicly and vocally trumpeted his bias-motivated intentions, the media treated the shooting as a high-profile backlash crime.

Sodhi's brother Rana spoke with *Little India* about the family's experiences in America before and after the terrorist strikes.[6] Prior to 9/11, Rana Sodhi said his relatives always felt safe in the U.S., seeing it as a welcoming and tolerant country. On the morning of September 11, 2001, Rana Sodhi spoke with his brothers Balbir and Harjeet about the strikes on the Pentagon and World Trade Center, which had been attacked earlier that day. Since Rana Sodhi worked in an urban area, his brothers urged him to stay at home, worried about backlash hate crimes.[7] Rana Sodhi reassured them that he would be fine, predicting that nothing would happen to him. Since Balbir Sodhi worked in a low crime area in the suburbs, family members were less concerned about his well-being. During this conversation, Rana and Balbir Sodhi discussed the racism they were both encountering, noting that strangers had begun to give them the finger and stare at their turbans in a menacing manner.[8] Harjeet Sodhi noted he heard profane language while working at his gas station, and cautioned his brothers and other minority workers to stay inside as much as possible.

According to the *San Diego Union-Tribune,* Balbir Sodhi called his worried parents after 9/11 to reassure them that he was safe, living and working far from New York.[9] Despite his hope that the backlash would not extend to Arizona, he was targeted in a hate crime just hours after the terrorist strikes. The *New York Daily News* reported that on September 11, 2001, three men in a pickup truck pulled into Balbir Sodhi's Chevron station and fired three shots at him.[10]

Concerned about this bias attack and the media's misrepresentation of Sikhs as terrorists, Balbir Sodhi and his brothers decided to set up a meeting on September 16, 2001 to educate journalists and the public about Sikhism. They also took steps to help the victims of the terrorist strikes. In addition to putting out a donations jar in his store, Balbir Sodhi contributed to it personally, emptying his pockets and contributing $74 to help with the relief efforts. Because racial tensions were escalating, Balbir Sodhi's son Sukhwinder spoke with his father on September 15, 2001, begging him not to go to work.[11] Sodhi refused, telling his son not to worry because it was a nice neighborhood. Two hours later, Balbir Sodhi was dead.

On the day of the murder, Roque drove his truck to a Mesa Chevron station and aimed his gun at Sodhi, a 49-year old turbaned Sikh with a beard. Landscapers had just finished work in the parking lot of the newly-opened gas station and Sodhi, the owner, was outside inspecting their work. In misplaced retaliation for the terrorist attacks, Roque shot Sodhi in the back several times, killing him and endangering nearby landscapers, including Luis Ledesma.[12]

After killing Sodhi, Roque embarked on a 30-minute hate-motivated shooting spree, driving his black Chevy S10 pickup truck from target to target. He next attacked an Arab-run Mobil gas station, owned by brothers Ali Saad and Saad Saad.[13] At this business, Roque shot at Harry Sleiman, an Arab-American clerk, who had olive skin and was dressed in a Mobil uniform.

Roque then targeted a modest brick house he sold to an Afghan family four years before 9/11, firing several bullets at its occupants. During this attack, the 42-year old gunman shot at Zia Sahak, the Afghan-American homeowner, who was coming out of his residence.[14] Roque also targeted family members inside the home. Hearing the gunfire, Sahak's brother threw his wife to the ground and used his body to shield hers.

Mesa police told the *Boston Globe* that Roque shouted racial remarks when he was arrested: "I'm a patriot. I'm an American. I'm a damned American all the way... Arrest me and let the terrorists run wild."[15] Roque's words are particularly disturbing because they show he thought he was acting patriotically by shooting at innocent South Asians, Arab-Americans, and Afghans, collectively blaming them for 9/11. Following his arrest, Roque was held on a $1,000,000 bond.

Arizona Attorney General Janet Napolitano told the *Houston Chronicle* that she was outraged by Roque's conduct, finding it shocking that anyone would try to use patriotism to justify such a heinous crime.[16] Napolitano said that Sodhi's name belonged alongside other 9/11 victims, and asserted that she was taking Roque's crime spree with the gravity it deserved. To send a message that backlash hate crimes would not be tolerated, Arizona prosecutors charged Roque with first degree murder, four counts of attempted murder, and three counts of committing a drive-by shooting.

Balbir Sodhi's wife, three sons, and two daughters were deeply traumatized by the bias-motivated murder. His brother Rana Sodhi was also distraught, telling *Little India* that he was particularly upset that Roque planned his attack in advance, informing co-workers of his plans to kill "those rag-head people and their children."[17] According to the *Washington Post,* Roque also spoke about his retaliation ideas at a bar, expressing his intention to slay the "ragheads" responsible for the terrorist strikes.[18] Rana Sodhi was dismayed that none of Roque's acquaintances were concerned enough to inform authorities of the bigot's openly-aired plans to murder area minorities.

Some area South Asians felt that if authorities had done more to protect Balbir Singh after he was shot at by bigots on September 11, 2001, his murder might have been prevented.

Many of Balbir Sodhi's friends remembered him as a hard-working, friendly, and devout man. Guru Roop Kaur Khalsa, a Sikh cleric in Phoenix, told the *Arab American News* that Balbir Sodhi was a quiet man who hosted weekly dinners for members of his faith.[19] After Sodhi left India in 1989, he worked as a taxi driver in San Francisco before joining his brother in Phoenix. He purchased the Chevron station more than a year before 9/11, after earning a perfect score on Chevron's qualifying test for prospective station owners. According to the *San Diego Union Tribune*, Balbir Sodhi's customers recalled that he was a generous man who liked to hand out bottles of water to local children on hot days.[20] They also said that Sodhi frequently gave candy to kids and allowed skateboarding teens to hang out at the station. As a surprise for his wife on their 25th wedding anniversary, he had planned to return to India in November 2001, to live with her and their youngest son. He was killed two months before his intended departure.

Roque's surviving victims were shaken up by the shootings. Saad Saad was caught off guard by the attack on his Mobil gas station. In an interview with the *Arab American News,* he recalled that although customers harassed his station employees shortly after 9/11, he did not take the threats seriously.[21] Saad's employees were more wary. Hussein "Harry" Sleiman told the *Boston Globe* that he was not surprised by the bias-motivated gunfire or the wave of hate crimes sweeping the country.[22] Despite his fears about additional reprisals, the Lebanese-American service station attendant was back at work the day after the shooting, replacing a glass window that had been shattered by one of Roque's bullets.[23] He also repaired a glass refrigerator case that had been damaged by gunfire, and the gas station's service counter, which had a bullet hole.

Zia Sahak was shocked by Roque's cultural illiteracy. Zia Sahak told the *Boston Globe* that the gunman was an ignorant man, unable to tell the difference between a Hindu, a Sikh, and a Muslim Pakistani.[24] Sahak, who had lived in the U.S. since 1988, questioned Roque's understanding of patriotism, suggesting that true Americans were the ones willing to stand up to bigotry.

After the hate crime, Sahak took safety precautions to protect his family members from future attacks.[25] He moved his bed from the living room to a safer place in the house. He also arranged for his mother and father to stay with another brother, and forbade his nieces and nephews from visiting the house or playing on the lawn, which they usually did on Saturday afternoons. Despite the climate of xenophobia, Sahak had no plans to move. He told the *Globe* that his mother enjoyed trading recipes with the neighbors, who liked trying Middle Eastern food.[26] He didn't want the 9/11 backlash to take away his home and isolate his family members.

Most community members were outraged by the shootings and the rise of nativism in the area. Mesa resident Sheryl Van Vooren told the *Globe* that the shooter was no different than the terrorists who hijacked the planes.[27] To show their disapproval of backlash hate crimes, approximately 3,000 people attended Balbir Sodhi's funeral, which was held on September 22, 2001. According to the *Houston Chronicle*, the victim's son, Sukhwinder Sodhi, told the crowd that he was comforted by the love and support he received from the community.[28] Sukhwinder Sodhi also spoke out against the 9/11 backlash, telling the crowd that the family didn't want any other innocent people hurt.[29]

Balbir Sodhi's killing received considerable international attention, particularly in South Asia. One of Sodhi's brothers, Latwinder Singh Sodhi, was interviewed on Indian television, where he discussed the anti-immigrant backlash taking place in Arizona.[30] News of Balbir Sodhi's murder and other post-9/11 attacks triggered protests in other countries. In response to overseas concerns, President Bush called India's prime minister, Atal Behari Vajpayee, to reassure him that the U.S. was acting to protect South Asians and other minority immigrants from hate crimes.

Balbir Sodhi's family was profoundly affected by his murder. Following his funeral, widow Harjinder Kaur received her husband's ashes in India. When she tried to come to the U.S. for Roque's trial, her visa application was denied three times. According to *India Abroad*, she was finally allowed into the country after the U.S. Attorney's office made a special request to the INS.[31] Although she was given permission to enter the country, the short-term visa she had been issued expired in August 2003, before the conclusion of Roque's murder trial. She had difficulty getting a visa extension to allow her to remain in the U.S. for the duration of the legal proceedings. After considerable bureaucratic hassle, she was eventually granted permission to stay until the conclusion of the murder case. Because her husband was no longer alive, she was unable to qualify for a permanent resident visa in the U.S., where her children and grandchildren were living.

According to *India Abroad*, Roque's defense attorney, Dan Patterson, argued that his client was an insane person who was pushed to the breaking point by 9/11.[32]   Prosecutor Vince Imbordino was unconvinced by Patterson's characterization of Roque as a mentally-ill individual who deserved sympathy, suggesting instead that he was a lifelong racist who had been expelled from school for harassing an African-American student. The district attorney's office also pointed out that Roque's shooting spree was not his first offense – in 1983, he had been convicted of attempted armed robbery in California.

Attending the trial was emotionally stressful on Balbir Sodhi's family. *India-West* reported that widow Harjinder Kaur fainted twice during the proceedings.[33] Family members observed that her husband's death left her unable to sleep without medication, and elevated her already-high blood pressure. Balbir Sodhi's children were also deeply troubled by their father's murder and by Roque's attempts to justify his crime spree. Balbir's son, Sukhvinder Singh, told *India Abroad* that he was not convinced by attorney Dan Patterson's 'guilty but insane' defense of Roque, pointing out that the gunman deliberately shot his father five times in the back without hitting the other people standing outside the gas station.[34] Sukhvinder Singh was so troubled by his father's murder and the 9/11 backlash that he stopped driving a taxi.

India Abroad reported that during the legal proceedings, Roque appeared unaffected by his crimes.[35] Rather than show remorse, the 44-year old machinist sat in the court room stone-faced, on Zyprexa, an anti-psychotic medication used to treat bipolar disorder and schizophrenia.[36] At the conclusion of the trial, the jury found Roque guilty of his September 15th shooting spree.

During the sentencing phase of the trial, Judge Mark Aceto asked Roque if he regretted his actions. He replied that he was just sorry that it happened. After a day of death penalty deliberations, the jury found only one aggravating factor for execution – that he endangered the life of landscaper Luis Ledesma when he murdered Sodhi. The jury did not find Roque's attempted shooting of Lebanese-American gas station clerk Harry Sleiman or the attempted murder of an Afghan family to be aggravating factors in the case. The court also sentenced Roque to an additional 36 years in prison in the event the death penalty was overturned on appeal.

Roque's sentence was eventually commuted to life in prison, after the Supreme Court took as mitigating evidence Roque's mental condition and low intelligence. Sodhi's brother Harjit told *India Abroad* that he was disappointed that Roque got away with pleading mental illness, pointing out that his brother's killer had worked for the Boeing company for 17 years without incident and had no record of seeking medical help for psychological problems.[37]

After Balbir Sodhi was murdered, his parents asked their sons – five of eight brothers living in the U.S. – to move back to India. According to *India Abroad*, Lakwinder Singh told his mother and father that he was unwilling to emigrate since his children were born in the U.S., reminding them that not all Americans were bad.[38]

Although Balbir Sodhi's killing was undeniably a bias-motivated murder, authorities in other states were reluctant to characterize other post-9/11 killings as hate crimes because of the difficulty of proving that bigotry was the sole motivating factors behind the attacks. Unlike Roque, most of the killers did not broadcast their bias-based motivations for murdering minorities after 9/11. Consequently, district attorneys sometimes failed to prosecute these intentional deaths as hate crimes, concerned that their inability to prove bias might result in overturned convictions.

Many Arab-American, Sikh, and Muslim activists were outraged by authorities' repeated unwillingness to recognize that many of these killings were likely motivated by bigotry. In the September 16, 2006 issue of the *Arab American News*, Ray Hanania argues that police officers were failing minority communities by refusing to treat backlash killings as hate crimes. Hanania reported that although there were about a dozen post-9/11 murders, most investigating officers claimed that another motive – like greed or jealousy – factored into each crime.[39]

The previous chapters have explored the 9/11 backlash on U.S. streets, religious facilities, school campuses, business settings, and residential neighborhoods. The evidence presented in these sections shows that the backlash was real, prolonged, and extensive. By examining post-9/11 killings in this context, it is apparent that many of them should be considered bias-related murders.

On the same day that Balbir Sodhi was shot to death, racial minorities in other parts of the country were killed by strangers. In Southern California, Adel Karas, an Egyptian Coptic Christian storeowner and father of three, was gunned down on September 15, 2001 while working at his San Gabriel store, the International Market.[40] After being shot, he managed to get out of his shop before collapsing on the sidewalk. Despite the efforts of paramedics, the 48-year old Arab died at Huntington Memorial Hospital in Pasadena. Karas' cash register remained full after he was killed, suggesting that theft was not the shooter's central motive. Local police opted to investigate Karas' murder as a robbery, even though the Latino culprits left money and store merchandise behind.

Many of Karas' family members believed he was killed in a backlash hate crime, and urged the police to explore this avenue of inquiry. Shortly after the murder, family friend Sara Eltantawi told the *New York Times* that it was premature for the police to state definitively that the crime was a robbery since the killers left cash at the scene, suggesting that stealing money was not their primary objective.[41]

Whereas local investigators were treating the killing as a robbery-gone-bad, the FBI chose to investigate Abdel Karas' shooting as a hate crime. Karas' nephew, Basem Wasef, told the *Los Angeles Times* that family members were grateful that federal agents decided to treat the crime as a bias-motivated attack.[42] According to the *Los Angeles Times*, FBI agents speculated that the shooter may have mistakenly believed Karas was a Muslim because he was an Egyptian-born Arab. Karas' friends and members of the Arabic community also viewed his murder as a hate crime, pointing out that he had no enemies and he never experienced a violent incident at his store prior to 9/11.

According to the *Los Angeles Times*, Karas' murder had a profound effect on his family, including his three sons, ages 9, 10, and 11.[43] At the time Karas was killed, he was in the process of organizing a celebratory barbeque party to honor his wife Randa, who had just passed her board certification to become an anesthesiologist.[44] Karas' older sister Eva Wasef told the *Los Angeles Times* that her brother loved his wife deeply, telling others how proud he was of her accomplishments.[45]

In articles about Karas' murder, the *Los Angeles Times* repeatedly referenced his Christian background, highlighting the fact that many 9/11 backlash victims were not Muslim.[46] The newspaper reported that Karas was a Coptic Christian who had worked as an agricultural engineer in Cairo.[47] He fled Egypt because fundamentalists were killing Copts, vandalizing churches, and halting the career advancement of Christian professionals. Karas lived in London from 1973 to 1979 before immigrating to America. *The Los Angeles Times* described Karas as a religious man who never missed mass.[48] The newspaper also mentioned that his funeral was scheduled at St. Mary's Coptic Orthodox church in Los Angeles, once again reminding readers that the shooting victim was a Christian.

According to the *Los Angeles Times*, Karas worked 12 hours a day, six days a week at his San Gabriel store, where he sold American, Mexican, and African food items and consumer goods.[49] He often greeted customers in English, Spanish, and Arabic, and had customers and friends of many faiths and ethnicities.

Some community members wondered if Karas may have been killed because of his close association with Muslim customers. On Fridays, area Muslims would visit Karas and purchase merchandise after attending Friday prayers at a nearby mosque.[50] Some area residents speculated that Karas' killers may have mistakenly assumed that the Arab shopkeeper was Muslim, and murdered him in retaliation for the terrorist strikes. After Karas was shot to death four days after 9/11, the head of the Islamic center in Los Angeles visited the grieving family to express sorrow and outrage over the apparent hate crime.[51] Other members of the San Gabriel community brought flowers, candles, and sympathy cards to the store to express their condolences.

A decade after the attack, Karas' killers still have not been indicted for the crime. According to police detective Richard Ramirez, investigators identified the three Latino gang members as suspects in the murder: two who were involved in the shooting, and a third who drove the get-away car, a copper-colored older model Honda.[52] Police officers described the possible perpetrators as clean-cut Latinos with dark complexions in their mid-20s, approximately 5'10" to 5'11" tall.[53] Despite information corroborating their involvement, the three suspects were never charged with the killing.[54]

Although Ramirez took the case to the District Attorney's office a few years after the shooting, prosecutors declined to file charges on the grounds that there was insufficient evidence to proceed. Nine years after Karas' murder, one of the suspects involved was in custody for an unrelated crime, the shooting of a deputy.[55] Detectives investigating Karas' killing were still pursuing a financial motive for the crime, suggesting that he could have been a victim of extortion. Many community members were skeptical of this explanation, pointing out that an extortionist would have had a financial disincentive for killing the target.

Years after the attack, Karas' relatives continued to believe that the murder was bias-motivated. Alvina Karas, Adel's mother, told the *Whittier Daily News* she believed her son was killed in a post-9/11 hate crime, especially because the perpetrators shot him dead without stealing anything.[56] Karas' family members were upset that police failed to update them on developments in the case, such as the identification of three suspects involved in the murder. Karas' wife sold the International Market after the shooting, hoping to distance herself from the place where her husband was gunned down.

In other parts of the country, other innocent minorities were killed in the days following 9/11. Along with Sodhi and Karas, Waqar Hasan was murdered on September 15, 2001. Hasan, a 46-year old businessman originally from Pakistan, was shot to death at his store in Southeast Dallas, leaving behind a wife and four daughters, ages 10 to 16.[57] Hasan and his family members immigrated to the U.S. in the early 1990s, and considered America their home. Shortly before he was killed, Hasan had moved from New Jersey to Texas to start his own business. At the time of his death, his wife and family were still in Milltown, New Jersey, waiting for Hasan to get financially settled in Texas before reuniting with him. Two months before he was murdered, he had purchased Mom's Grocery, realizing his dream of becoming a self-employed businessman. He was at his store, cooking hamburgers, when a gunman approached him and shot him in the face.[58]

Initially, American newspapers and investigators were reluctant to call Hasan's murder a hate crime. According to the *New York Times*, police officers thought that the shooting could have been a robbery, even though the killer left without taking money from the cash register.[59] Although local authorities were reluctant to speculate that a bias crime had taken place in their jurisdiction, Sgt. Gary Kirkpatrick told the *Times* that members of his department did not rule out the possibility that Hasan's murder was a 9/11 revenge killing.[60]

Members of Hasan's family were convinced from the start that the shooting was a backlash attack. Hasan's brother-in-law Zahid Ghani, a Pakistani journalist, told the *Boston Globe* that he was 100% sure that anti-Muslim bias was the motive for the murder.[61] Ghani called attention to the fact that the perpetrators did not touch the money in the cash register or the merchandise on the store's shelves. According to Ghani, the police told the family that Hasan's killing might have been hate-motivated.[62] Ghani had trouble understanding why the police de-emphasized the possible bias-motivation of the crime when they talked to reporters and public officials about the shooting.

Compounding their grief, some of Hasan's family members were themselves singled out during the 9/11 backlash. The *Los Angeles Times* reported that in North Brunswick, New Jersey, Hasan's brother, Choudhry, was stopped by police after he and his friends left a Burger King.[63] The officers told the South Asian group that they had received reports that a suspicious package was left at the fast food restaurant, and told the men that they looked like terrorists. After being detained for a few minutes, the officers let them leave. Responding to news of the ethnically-motivated harassment, North Brunswick Mayor David Spaudling told the *Newark Star-Ledger* that the racial profiling of the South Asians was somewhat understandable because people of their religion killed thousands of Americans the week before.[64] These insensitive remarks put further emotional strain on Choudhry Hasan, who was already coping with the trauma of 9/11, the rise in nativist sentiment, and the murder of his brother Waqar.

Waqar Hasan's death was later proven to be a hate-motivated killing, triggered by gunman Mark Anthony Stroman's misplaced desire to avenge the victims of 9/11. Hasan's murder was only the first in a

222

series of hate crimes that the white supremacist undertook in Dallas, scapegoating South Asian convenience store clerks for the terrorist strikes.

The *Los Angeles Times* reported that on September 21, 2001, Stroman targeted his next victim, an immigrant from Bangladesh working at a Dallas gas station.[65] Assuming the bandana-wearing bandit was committing an ordinary robbery, Rais Bhuiyan opened the cash register and begged the intruder not to harm him.[66] Stroman asked the clerk where he was from, and then shot him in the face. Bhuiyan put both hands on his head to stem the bleeding, worried that his brains were spilling out on the floor.[67] Thinking about his family and his fiancé, Bhuiyan cowered in terror on the ground, pretending to be dead. The gunshot blinded Bhuiyan in the right eye, and nearly cost him the use of his left one. When his parents in Bangladesh were informed about the shooting, they spent several days worrying about their son's fate, unable to get medical updates. His father was so overwrought with worry that he had a stroke, further traumatizing the family.[68] Bhuiyan's gunshot wound was so debilitating that he required multiple surgeries over several years to repair most of the damage. Despite the extensive medical work, Bhuiyan was left with 35 bullet fragments in his face, causing the right side to bulge.[69]

A few days after shooting Bhuiyan, Stroman committed his third 9/11-inspired hate crime. On October 4, 2001, Stroman murdered Vasudev Patel, a South Asian immigrant who had become a U.S. citizen 12 years prior to his shooting. According to the *Washington Post*, Patel had moved to Dallas from India in 1982.[70] In 1987, he married Alka Patel, who joined him in the U.S. after their wedding. They opened up a Shell station in the suburban town of Mesquite, where they worked together behind the counter. Vasudev Patel usually woke up before Alka, taking the early morning shift at the station. He usually called her at 6:30 a.m., waking her up so she could get their two children to school before joining him at work.[71] At 7:00 a.m. on October 4th, when Alka was still at home with their son and daughter, Vasudev Patel was alone at the station. Stroman approached him and said, "God bless America."[72] He then shot Patel in the chest with a .44, and left him there to bleed to death.[73]

After murdering Patel, Stroman refrained from taking cash or merchandise from the station, indicating that robbery was not his motive. He later told the *Post* that he shot the clerk because he wanted to retaliate against local Arab-Americans for 9/11.[74] Apparently, Stroman was ignorant of the fact that Patel was Indian, not Middle Eastern.

Patel's family members, friends, and customers were profoundly affected by his death. Many community members described Patel as a good-hearted and empathetic person. Warren Acrey told the *Post* that his friend Patel was the kind of man who would give another person the shirt off of his back.[75] Many of Patel's customers fondly recalled his generosity. Martin Andrews, a longtime gas station patron, told the *Post* that if he had no money, Patel would give him a full tank of gas on credit.[76]

After his arrest, Stroman expressed no remorse for shooting and blinding the Bangladeshi clerk, or killing Hasan and Patel, seeing his actions as justifiable payback for 9/11. He told the *Los Angeles Times* that on the day of his arrest, he was planning to attack a local mosque and exterminate Arab Muslim congregants in the middle of prayer services.[77]

Stroman's trial lasted less than a week. The jury deliberated for under a hour before convicting him of murder and sentencing him to death by lethal injection. The *Jewish News* reported that Stroman waved an American flag at sentencing, declaring that he killed Hasan and Patel to punish those who attacked the U.S.[78] He remained unrepentant when he arrived on Texas' death row on April 5, 2002.

In a July 6, 2002 jailhouse interview with the *Los Angeles Times*, Stroman explained that he uttered the same patriotic phrase, "God Bless America," before shooting each of his victims to show that he was acting out of love for the U.S.[79] While speaking to reporters, the convicted killer defended his decision to kill Hasan, a man he believed to be an Arab, to avenge the victims of the terrorist strikes.[80] While pounding his fist out of anger, Stroman told the *Los Angeles Times* that he felt terrible about the victims of 9/11, particularly those who fell head-first from the towers, and considered one of the rescue workers to be his hero.[81]   Stroman kept photos of the burning towers in his cell, and got a jailhouse tattoo on his neck honoring the Americans killed by al-Qaeda.

Prosecutor Greg Davis characterized Stroman as a white supremacist affiliated with neo-Nazi groups. In an interview with the *Los Angeles Times,* Davis explained that although Stroman was a longtime racist, the terrorist strikes gave him an opportunity to murder minorities.[82]

According to the *Washington Post,* Stroman claimed that he did what every other American wanted to do after 9/11 but lacked the nerve to carry out.[83]   Stroman, a father of four, told the *Los Angeles Times* that he did not fear death by lethal injection, a fate considerably easier than the horrific deaths that so many Americans suffered on September 11, 2001.[84]

Some activists wondered if one or two of Stroman's victims could have been spared if police had assumed that the first murder was a hate crime and acted accordingly.   Community members faulted the authorities for their failure to urge area minorities to take protective measures when the killer was still at large, like taking time off of work, arming themselves, and installing security cameras to deter backlash attacks.

The families of the murdered men had difficulty handling their grief and adjusting to their new lives. Patel's wife, son, and daughter were still deeply traumatized by the shooting months after his death.   According to the *Washington Post,* Alka Patel was financially compelled to continue working at the same Shell station where her husband was killed, selling gas, lottery tickets, cigarettes, and gum.[85]   On many evenings in 2002, her 13-year old son kept her company, doing his homework on the floor behind the counter.[86]   Her 11-year old daughter usually stayed at home with her elderly grandparents.   Suddenly becoming a single parent, Alka Patel had difficulty juggling her various responsibilities – raising her fatherless children, putting in 16-hour days to support her family, and caring for her elderly parents, who often needed to be taken to medical appointments. Alka told the *Post* that her daughter felt neglected, unable to understand why her mother was so busy working and running errands.[87]   Patel's son told the *Post* that he found life much harder without his father, wishing that there was a reset button to erase the events of 9/11 and its aftermath.[88]

According to the *Post,* the Patels felt overlooked during observances of the first anniversary of the terrorist strikes.   Alka Patel pointed out that her husband would still be alive if 9/11 had not taken place, suggesting that her family should be treated like those of other victims.[89]   In the months following the shooting, the Patels did not receive any offers of free counseling or financial assistance to help with the children's school expenses.   The *Post* reported that Alka Patel was worried about how she could afford to send her children to college without the extra income her husband would have been able to provide.[90]   Anya Cordell, a writer from Evanston, told the *Post* that the 9/11 charities should have offered financial assistance to the Patels and other families like them, instead of giving excuses about why backlash murder victims were exempt from getting assistance.[91]

The Hasans also had difficulty adjusting to life without Waqar, the man Stroman murdered on September 15, 2001.   Because Hasan was the primary breadwinner of the family, his wife and four daughters were financially devastated by his murder.   To support her children, widow Duri Hasan worked long hours in a Styrofoam cup factory, and her eldest daughter, Nida, took on a part-time job while attending Rutgers University.[92]   Two of Duri Hasan's other daughters, Asna and Anum, obtained after-school jobs while attending high school.

Before Waqar Hasan was killed, he had applied for permanent residency status for his wife and children, who were between the ages of 11 and 17 at the time of his death.   As a result of the murder, his 35-year old wife Duri Hasan and his daughters no longer had a basis for a green card application, and faced deportation.   At first, the family hoped that they would be included in legislation allowing foreign nationals to remain in the country if they lost immediate family members in the World Trade Center and Pentagon attacks.   Because their father was not killed in this manner, immigration authorities told the Hasans that they were not covered by the legislation.

At Hasan's funeral, his widow Duri approached Congressman Rush Holt and asked him about how such a terrible hate crime could take place in the U.S.   Holt, a Democrat from New Jersey, became interested in the family's well-being, and introduced HR 867, a Congressional bill allowing Duri Hasan and her daughters to obtain permanent residency status. This legislative measure pertained only to Hasan's family, and did not apply to other family members of murdered hate crime victims. Holt obtained a one-year stay and work permits for the family to prevent them from being deported to Pakistan. To support the Hasans, the National Council of Pakistani Americans (NCPA) sent out an action alert urging members to back Holt's legislation. In the *News India-Times*, Holt affirmed his commitment to helping Duri Hasan and her daughters, explaining that Waqar Hasan, a hardworking immigrant, lost his life simply because he was a Muslim with a Middle Eastern-looking face.[93]

Two years after the shooting, approximately 200 community members in Middlesex stood out in the pouring rain to show support for the Hasan family. On this occasion, Holt urged the community to support HR867 so the family's grief was not compounded by deportation.[94]

Although it seems inconceivable that the humanitarian legislation could face opposition, Holt's communication director, Jim Kapsis, reported that some members of Congress were concerned that the bill could set a precedent, allowing families in similar situations to gain legal status in this manner. Holt's office responded by arguing that the Hasans' situation was exceptional, and that helping them was the moral course of action.

Hasan and her daughters appreciated the support they received from religious and community organizations, including the American-Arab Anti-Discrimination Committee, the American Jewish Committee, the Anti-Defamation League, the Arab American Institute, the Coalition for Peace Action, the Hebrew Immigrant Aid Society, the Lutheran Office of Governmental Ministry, and the New Jersey Council of Churches.

Nadia Hasan expressed her gratitude to the groups attending the vigil, explaining that the outpouring of support made them feel welcome in the U.S.[95] Gerrie Bamira, director of the Jewish Federation of Greater Middlesex County, declared that helping the Hasans was an ethical imperative, pointing out that Jews had a moral responsibility to act on behalf of bias crime victims.[96] Atiya Aftab of the Islamic Society of Central New Jersey also spoke at the gathering, telling the crowd that the 9/11 terrorists had nothing to do with the values of Islam.[97]

Once Stroman was on death row, his one surviving victim, Rais Bhuiyan, turned to his faith and decided to forgive his assailant. Bhuiyan began working with Amnesty International to save Stroman's life, actively campaigning in the press that Stroman be spared the death penalty. Bhuiyan also created a website, 'World Without Hate,' to educate others about hate crimes and xenophobia. Despite Bhuiyan's advocacy work, Stroman was eventually executed on July 20, 2011.

While Stroman's victims were clearly killed in retaliation for 9/11, other South Asians died in suspicious circumstances in the immediate aftermath of the terrorist attacks, prompting some community members to view their deaths as products of the ongoing backlash. In Ceres, California, Surjit Singh Samra left for his daily walk on Sunday, September 16, 2001. While strolling along the Turlock Irrigation Canal near highway 99, the 69-year old Sikh man disappeared. According to *Asianweek*, Samra's body was found underwater on September 18, 2001, snagged on a shopping cart.[98] Because of the timing and circumstances of his death, Samra's family believe he was a victim of a post-9/11 hate crime. At his September 19, 2001 autopsy, pathologists found no concrete evidence of foul play and no signs of a recent stroke, making it difficult to determine the proximate cause of his odd drowning. To answer questions about Samra's death, the Stanislaus sheriff's office opened an investigation about whether the suspicious death was linked to post-9/11 xenophobia. Years later, Sikh activists continue to regard Samra's death as a possible bias-motivated killing.

Minorities also died in other parts of the country soon after the terrorist strikes. On September 19, 2001, Brent Seever killed 45-year old Ali Almansoop in Lincoln Park, Michigan, in what the *New York Times* described as one of a dozen murders nationwide attributed to anti-Muslim sentiment after 9/11.[99] Almansoop, an American citizen originally from Yemen, had lived in the U.S. for 32 years before he was murdered. In Seever's police confession, he admitted to dragging the sleeping man out of bed and telling him he was killing him because of the attacks in New York and D.C.[100] Witnesses say that Almansoop pleaded for his life as he ran in terror from Seever. While Almansoop was frantically trying to explain that he had nothing to do with 9/11, Seever shot him 12 times in the back.

According to the *New York Times*, Seever admitted to police that he shot Almansoop because of the recent terrorist activity, providing them with clear evidence that the killing was a backlash murder.[101] Although the strikes on the World Trade Center and the Pentagon triggered him to kill Almansoop, Seever also said that he was upset that the Muslim Arab had begun dating his former girlfriend. Since Seever was motivated by a combination of racism, religious bigotry, and romantic jealousy, some authorities questioned whether Almansoop's murder, eight days after 9/11, should be categorized as a hate crime. Almansoop's 25-year old son, Saleh Almansoop, told the *New York Times* that he had no doubt that the terrorist attacks played a direct role in his father's shooting, comparing Seever to the 9/11 hijackers.[102]

Maricopa County Attorney Rick Romley told the *Arab American News* that authorities were taking Almansoop's murder seriously, noting that 9/11 should not be used as an excuse to gun down an unarmed American immigrant in cold blood.[103] Seever was eventually convicted of the killing in June, 2002.

A year after his father's death, Saleh Almansoop continued to have difficulties balancing his grief and his extensive family responsibilities. According to the *New York Times*, he was working as a restaurant dishwasher and busboy, trying to pay his bills and support his mother and three younger siblings, who had recently arrived from Yemen.[104] Because of his father's murder, Saleh Almansoop had become responsible for the family's $1500 mortgage, a $420 monthly car lease, and other household expenses.[105] Although his father was excluded from memorials to the victims of 9/11, Saleh Almansoop honored his father by putting his picture on the living room mantel.

Another bias-motivated murder took place on September 29, 2001. At 4:15 p.m., 18 days after 9/11, 51-year old Abdo Ali Ahmed was shot to death behind the counter of his store in Reedley, California, a central valley farm town 20 miles Southeast of Fresno. A naturalized American citizen originally from Yemen, Ahmed left behind a wife and eight children, six of whom were born in America and under age 13.

The *San Jose Mercury News* reported that Ahmed's wife Fatima heard the shots, ran to the store, and held her husband while he bled to death from three bullet wounds.[106] While cradling his bloody torso, she pleaded with Ahmed to describe the shooter; unable to speak, Ahmed simply squeezed her hand twice before dying.[107]

After Ahmed's death, his wife and children continued living behind the store where the crime took place. The *San Jose Mercury News* reported that the couple's one year old son Dean had the black curly hair and brown eyes of his absent father.[108] Fatima Ahmed said that her husband's shooter killed her spirit when he murdered her spouse.[109]

According to the *San Jose Mercury News*, Ahmed immigrated to New York as a teenager with his father and his Indonesian step-mother.[110] After he became a naturalized American citizen, he worked for the U.S. Merchant Marines in the Bronx. In the mid-1970s, he moved to Reedley, where he and other Yemenis were working in the grape fields with the United Farm workers. Ahmed found this farm town a good place to start a family. In the early 1990s, he opened Ahmed's East Reedley Store, selling groceries to local residents. Since Reedly was a low crime area with only one murder in the four years prior to 9/11, Ahmed never locked his door or varied his daily routine.

During Ahmed's 16-hour shifts, he would make short but frequent visits to his wife and children, who lived next to the store. Throughout the day, Fatima would often give their children gifts to give to their father – a fig wrapped in a napkin, or an ice cream bar.[111] She would help her husband at the store while the children were at school. She told the *San Jose Mercury News* that her husband appreciated the company, telling her that it made him happy just looking at her.[112]

A few days before he was murdered, Ahmed found a death threat on the windshield of his car when he went to buy chicken breasts at the local Save Mart. According to the *San Diego Union-Tribune*, the profane note threatened the lives of Ahmed and his family, promising to retaliate for 9/11 by killing all Arabs.[113] Ahmed crumpled up the note and threw it away, telling his 12-year old daughter Diana not to call the police. He told her that God would take care of them, and reassured her that there was nothing to fear because they were American citizens. Showing his patriotism, Ahmed displayed a large American flag in the window of his store. This, however, did not protect him from being murdered at the height of the 9/11 backlash. According to police reports, Ahmed was shot to death while he stood behind a barrel of pickled pig's feet.

Local Arabs and Muslims were convinced that Ahmed was killed in retaliation for 9/11. Yemeni diplomats were outraged by the shooting, which they saw as a bias-motivated hate crime. Mansoor Ismael, consul for the Republic of Yemen in San Francisco, told the *New York Times* that the murder was clearly a backlash attack, not a robbery.[114] Ismael pointed out that no money was taken from Ahmed's store even though the cash register was full, a bag of money was directly behind the counter, the store safe was open, and Ahmed was alone and defenseless.[115]

The *San Francisco Chronicle* reported that patrons sitting in the bar next to Ahmed's store saw two Latino teenage boys fleeing the scene of the shooting.[116] The assailants took nothing as they ran away, leaving behind cash in two registers and open safe full of rolled coins.[117] They then jumped into a white sedan and drove off with two young male passengers in the back seat. According to eyewitnesses, one of the boys sitting in the car during the murder looked as young as 13.[118] Fresno County Sheriff's Sergeant Toby Rein told the *Chronicle* that he was disappointed that the rear passengers did not come forward and turn in the perpetrators.[119] Rein suggested that it was unpatriotic to withhold information about the murder of an American citizen in cold blood.

After the shooting, well-wishers hung a black wreath on the East Reedly store. Hundreds of community members attended Ahmed's funeral, which was held on Tuesday, October 2, 2001. Because so many area residents came to the Fresno mosque to offer support to Ahmed's family, the large crowd was unable to fit inside the house of worship. Commenting on the sizable gathering, family friend Madram Shuabi told the *Chronicle* that it was wonderful for Ahmed's children to see how many Americans were outraged by his murder.[120] The *San Diego Union Tribune* reported that at the memorial service, imam Alauddin Bakri preached against hate and vengeance, and spoke about Ahmed's humble character.[121] The mourners included people from different ethnicities and faiths. According to the *New York Times*, Carol Martin, an African-American Fresno resident, came to the funeral to show support for Ahmed's family, noting that hard-working, loyal Americans came in every skin color.[122] Al-Jazeera television covered the funeral, showing international viewers that Muslim immigrants were being killed in the U.S. and that many Americans were outraged by the attacks.

Both the Fresno County Sheriff's Department and the FBI chose to investigate Ahmed's shooting as a hate crime. Governor Gray Davis drew attention to the case by offering a $50,000 reward for information leading to the arrest of Ahmed's killers.

Despite the sizeable bounty, some community members felt that investigators could have done more to apprehend the perpetrators. Some local Muslims felt that authorities were conducting a shoddy investigation into Ahmed's murder, pointing out that the police and the media did not have to release the fact that Ahmed threw away the note containing the death threat. They believed that investigators should have told the newspapers that they had the letter in their possession, and publicly advised its sender to surrender before finger-print analysis was complete, in exchange for more lenient treatment. Activists also faulted authorities for releasing information that could hamper the investigation, such as publishing the fact that witnesses did not get the full license plate of the get-away car and provided only a partial description of the shooters. By publicly claiming to have more detailed eye-witness information, investigators might have frightened one of the four youths into turning himself in to police as a means of obtaining a reduced sentence. Alaeddin Elbakri, a worshipper at the Badr Islamic Center in Fresno, told the *San Jose Mercury News* that bigots become more prone to commit other acts of violence when a hate crime is not handled well by authorities.[123]

A few months after Ahmed's death, Reedly's mayor, Joe Rhodes, told the *San Jose Mercury News* that he was unfamiliar with the term, "hate crime," and that he was uncomfortable viewing Ahmed's killing as a bias-motivated murder.[124] In response to Rhodes' insensitive remarks, minority community members expressed concern that local politicians were not doing enough to curb the 9/11 backlash sweeping their communities. At the time Ahmed was shot, approximately 6,000 Yemenis lived in the 100-mile area between Fresno and Bakersfield. Despite this high concentration of Arab-Americans, many local politicians seemed oblivious to the harassment minority citizens were experiencing in the aftermath of the terrorist strikes.

Because Fatima Ahmed spoke little English and could not raise her eight children on her own after her husband was murdered, Ahmed's brother-in-law, Ahmed Nagi, moved from Louisiana to help out with the store. According to the *San Francisco Chronicle*, Nagi was concerned about his family and about other hate crimes in the area, noting that another Yemeni store owner, Mr. Albusaisa, was shot through protective glass at his store, which was located 50 miles away. [125] Despite these crimes targeting Arab and Muslim businessmen, Nagi reported that the family had no choice but to endure life's hardships, financially unable to close the store simply because they were scared.[126]

Months after the shooting, Fatima Ahmed continued to be distraught over the death of her husband, saddened that her spouse was not around to see their children reach adulthood. She told the *San Jose Mercury News* that she and her husband had planned to go on a *hajj* once their children were grown, and was disappointed that she would now have to experience that pilgrimage on her own.[127]

Arab merchants were also killed in other parts of California. According to the *Orange County Register*, Abdullah Nimer was murdered on October 4, 2001 while selling clothes door-to-door to customers in South Los Angeles.[128] While Nimer was on the 400 block of E. 74th St., he was confronted by assailants who demanded his car keys. One of the men then abruptly shot him in the abdomen, perhaps when they realized Nimer was an Arab. The shooters then fled in a brown late-model Lincoln without taking Nimer's keys, his van, his merchandise, or his wallet, which was full of money.[129] Nimer left behind a wife and six children. The *Orange County Register* reported that the 200 Muslims attending his funeral all believed that Nimer was killed in a 9/11 backlash hate crime, noting that his assailants did not rob him.[130] Prior to his shooting, Nimer had never been threatened, robbed, or assaulted while working in the area. His relatives told the *Orange County Register* that Nimer had been well-liked in the neighborhood, and had no enemies.[131]

Nimer was born in Turmos Ayya, a village near Ramallah in the West Bank. He left the Middle East in 1986, living in Spain before immigrating to the U.S. Nimer hoped that America would provide him with better economic prospects and good schools for his children, as well as a respite from the chronic violence in his homeland.[132] Nimer sold clothes, bedspreads, curtains, and other household goods to his Southern California customers. Because he had so many loyal buyers, he did not need to seek out new clients. Over the years, his customers became his friends, and he would often stop and chat with families after selling them merchandise. Since many patrons paid in installments, Nimer got to know them well on his frequent visits.

Nimer's customers were distraught that their long-time friend had been so senselessly murdered in what they perceived was misplaced retaliation for the tragedy in New York. Linda Hernandez, who had been a client of Nimer's for 14 years, told the *Los Angeles Times* that he was a wonderful man who had nothing to do with 9/11.[133] She also stated that it was important for angry Americans to look for the real perpetrators instead of scapegoating hard-working immigrants. Nimer's six children appreciated the support they received at their father's funeral. Nimer's son, Islam, told the *Los Angeles Times* that his father's customers and neighbors came from diverse ethnic backgrounds, and many were crying as hard as actual relatives.[134]

Nimer's murder deeply affected members of his family, who saw the killing as a part of the 9/11 backlash. Recalling his father's response to the terrorist attacks, Islam Nimer told the *Los Angeles Times* that his father was saddened that the substantial progress the Arab-American community had made in the decades prior to 9/11 had been wiped out in a few minutes.[135] Islam Nimer said his father was disgusted by the hijackings and declared that any true Muslim, like any real Christian, was incapable of committing mass murder. [136]

In the days after the terrorist strikes, Nimer and his relatives repeatedly experienced racial discrimination and religious bigotry. Nimer's widow, Siham Nimer, reported that her husband had been harassed after 9/11. She told the *Los Angeles Times* that Latinos in the neighborhood had insulted and threatened him, and tried to convince his loyal customers to take their business elsewhere.[137] Out of necessity, Nimer continued his work, going about his business with a mixture of trepidation and determination in the days before he was murdered.[138]

According to the *Los Angeles Sentinel*, Nimer's children expressed their hope that the 9/11 backlash would abate and that other minority families would be spared the horror of having a relative senselessly murdered in a hate crime.[139] Islam Nimer told the *Los Angeles Times* that he and his five siblings had hoped to take care of their father in his old age, so he could rest after so many years of hard work.[140] Unfortunately, they would never get that chance. To help solve the case, authorities offered a $10,000 reward for information leading to the arrest and conviction of Nimer's killer.

In December 2001, the Human Rights Commission listed Nimer's killing as a bias murder in its annual report. Nimer's killing was later declassified as a hate crime following the arrest of three gang members, who denied shooting him out of ethnic or religious animosity.[141] It is important to consider that on October 3, 2001, anti-Arab and anti-Muslim sentiment was extremely high. Since hate crime enhancements lengthen jail sentences, Nimer's killers would have had a reason to deny acting out of bias, even if this was not actually the case. Prosecutors also had an incentive to drop hate crime enhancements, which are often difficult to prove in court and often anger local politicians, who are concerned about their city's reputation.

Other Arabs were also killed in Southern California in possible backlash attacks. According to the Los Angeles *Daily News*, authorities in Sylmar were investigating the October 17, 2001 slaying of Ramez Younan, a Syrian-born liquor store owner, exploring whether the murder was linked to 9/11.[142] News of this killing worried immigrant shop keepers, who wondered if they would be similarly targeted while nativism was surging throughout the U.S.

Other minority groups also worried about hate-motivated attacks in the aftermath of the terrorist strikes. The September 26, 2001 *Oakland Post* reported that a Native American girl was murdered in Oklahoma in a 9/11 backlash crime.[143] On September 14, 2001, Kimberly Lowe, a 21-year old full-blooded Creek Native American, was killed in Tulsa when she and several of her Native friends were followed and harassed by another driver and his passenger.[144] At some point, the cars got into a collision. The *Native American Times* reported that when Lowe stopped and got out of her car to check the damage and confront the men, the enraged driver accelerated towards her and ran her over.[145] According to the *Tulsa World*, Gibson Runningbear, a witness to the killing, initially told police that the men pejoratively called Lowe and her friends "Arabs," but later recanted this statement under pressure from detectives.[146] On September 17, 2001 at the All Tribes Community Church in Tulsa, Runningbear publicly apologized for falsely claiming that an anti-Arab slur was used by the irate driver who killed his companion.[147] According to police reports, all four passengers in the car with Lowe had been drinking heavily on the day of her death.

The *Tulsa World* reported that district judge Linda Morrissey sentenced 23-year old Edwin Charles Doctor to a year in jail for negligent homicide, a misdemeanor, and another year for leaving the scene of an accident, a felony.[148] Doctor was initially charged with first-degree manslaughter because of an allegation that he was under the influence of alcohol when he killed Lowe, but assistant district attorney David Iski said that he did not have evidence that this was the case. Local police pointed out that the perpetrator was also of Native American ancestry, making it unlikely that the killing was racially-motivated. Some community members observed that Americans with Indian ancestry were still capable of committing bias-motivated attacks, and speculated that the criminally-negligent driver may not have decided to hit Lowe and leave her on the side of the road if she had been a white male or another prominent member of the city.

Years after Lowe's murder, some Sikh activists continued to raise questions about Lowe's killing and its possible connection to post-9/11 rage.[149] Rejecting the conclusions of the police investigation, they speculated that misplaced anger over the terrorist strikes might partially explain why a sober but enraged driver crushed to death a Native American woman a few days after 9/11. Many civil rights activists were outraged that the perpetrator responsible for crushing Lowe to death with his car received a total of just two years in jail in what detectives characterized as a case of road rage. Since tensions were running high after 9/11, Lowe's death three days after the terrorist attacks might have been linked to the anger many Americans were venting after the hijackings. Regardless of the precise trigger of Lowe's vehicular death, the media's initial coverage of the case fueled backlash fears across the U.S.

In other parts of the country, minorities continued to be killed in the aftermath of the terrorist attacks. In Minnesota, a Somali immigrant died at the height of the 9/11 backlash. On October 14, 2001, 66-year old Ali W. Ali prayed at a mosque on Lake Street in Minneapolis, and then lunched with Somali friends at an area restaurant. The same day, the Minneapolis *Star Tribune* published an article suggesting that local Somalis contributed money to a charity that supported Osama bin Laden.[150] According to eyewitness accounts, Ali was standing at a bus stop when an angry white man approached him and punched him in the face.[151] As a result of the blow, Ali fell down and hit his head on the sidewalk. A metro bus driver stopped at the corner of E. 17th St. and Chicago Ave. to help the injured Somali, and an anonymous person called 911 to alert police and medical personnel. Ten days later, Ali died in the hospital from his injuries.

The day after Ali was assaulted, members of the Somali, Muslim, and Arab communities blamed the *Star Tribune* for triggering the attack, arguing that its irresponsible publication of an article falsely connecting area minorities to Osama bin Laden fostered a climate of ethnic hatred that lead to the shocking hate crime.[152] Activists also took issue with the newspaper's inaccurate coverage of Ali's attack and its failure to expose the police's botched investigation of the case.

Perhaps to avoid a lawsuit, the *Star Tribune* created considerable doubt as to what happened to Ali, downplaying the possibility that the newspaper's specious article enflamed racial tensions and cost an elderly Somali Muslim his life. For example, in an October 25, 2001 news story, the *Star Tribune* failed to acknowledge that Ali was murdered, reporting instead that he "died Wednesday apparently of natural causes after he was assaulted at a bus stop on October 14."[153] The article's wording is problematic. Since Ali was knocked unconscious and died a few days later, it is apparent that the assault unmistakably led to his death, although pre-existing medical conditions may have precipitated his demise. Because Ali's life-ending coma was a direct result of the blow, it is difficult to escape the obvious conclusion that he was killed. Disregarding the facts of the case, the title of an October 27, 2001 *Star Tribune* article confused readers about the cause of Ali's death: "Somali Man Told Detective He Was Injured by a Car; Police Haven't Found Any Evidence that a Minnesota Man was a Hate-Crime Victim."[154] In this news story, *Star Tribune* reporter David Chanen deflects attention from the possibility that Ali was murdered in a bias crime in response to the newspaper's inaccurate and inflammatory reporting that local Somalis were funding terrorism.

Although *Star Tribune* reporters acknowledged that local police were having trouble solving the crime, they failed to write an exposé of the shoddy investigation. Instead, they reinforced officers' specious conclusion that Ali died of natural causes. By failing to identify several of the responding officers, translators, and witnesses by name, the *Star Tribune* left many questions about the case unanswered. In one news story about the attack, journalists David Chanen and Joy Powell interviewed Sgt. Erika Christensen, who reported that "at the scene, a man in a group across the street from Ali shouted that Ali was hit in the face by a white man."[155] The article also mentioned that "the man who said Ali was punched also told police that the man first took a swing at the group."[156] Discussing the attack, the reporters acknowledged that "an officer had difficulty communicating with the group because most spoke Spanish and little English, but someone helped translate."[157] The newspaper does not identify the main eyewitnesses to the attack, or explore why investigators were so quick to dismiss the possibility that Ali's assault was a hate crime, especially since Ali's white assailant struck him and tried to hit nearby Latinos. The reporters also do not identify the translator who assisted at the crime scene or explore whether the volunteer was competent to do the task without bias or error. Consequently, it is difficult to ascertain whether translation problems were responsible for some of the discrepancies in documenting what took place.

In the same article, Sgt. Erika Christensen is quoted as saying that "nobody saw whether the man hit Ali and nobody could give police a better description of the man."[158] Obviously, this news story contained contradictory information, with Christensen reporting that a man on the scene saw Ali being punched in the face by a white assailant, and then later claiming that no one saw Ali getting assaulted. Since the *Star*

Tribune reported that the other people at the scene were unable to give police a "better" description of the white assailant, it is logical that some of them witnessed the attack. Since non-English speakers and undocumented immigrant workers might be hesitant about getting involved in a homicide investigation, it is possible that some of them might have withheld important information about the crime. The *Star Tribune* did not adequately explore the extent to which ethnic and linguistic barriers were affecting the investigation, which was taking place in a racially-charged atmosphere.

At the hospital, the Minneapolis police once again botched the investigation of what happened to Ali. Although an unnamed investigator brought a professional translator to talk to the injured Somali Muslim, the interrogation was marred by gross incompetence. Discussing attempts to interview Ali at the hospital, the *Star Tribune* reported that the injured man "couldn't stay awake long and the investigator wasn't sure if he was on medication."[159] At one point, the semi-conscious, possibly drugged elderly Somali victim claimed that he was hit by a car, although there was no witness testimony or physical evidence of this at the scene. It is inexcusable that the investigating officer did not ascertain whether Ali was on medication before beginning the hospital interrogation. A competent detective would have checked with Ali's physicians to determine the medications he had been administered, and the effects they might have had on his ability to respond to questions about what transpired at the bus stop.

On October 25, 2001, Sgt. Medaria Arradondo told the *Star Tribune* that "on October 14, officers didn't receive any indication from medical personnel that Mr. Ali's condition was as grave as it was Tuesday."[160] The reporter who wrote this article clearly did not call attention to the fact that it was the officers' responsibility to obtain this vital information from medical personnel, so they could determine whether they were investigating a simple assault, an attempted murder, or a crime that would likely become a homicide.

Two days later, before ascertaining all the facts or properly re-interviewing witnesses at the scene, Sgt. Christensen told the *Star Tribute* that she doubted that Ali was injured in a bias crime, commenting that "if this was a hate crime, [the evidence is] just not there."[161] In the same interview, she admitted that she was unsure about what happened, stating, "I don't know if he was assaulted, hit by a car, or an existing medical condition made him dizzy and he lost his balance."[162] It is troubling that at this early stage of the investigation, Christensen felt comfortable telling the press that there was no evidence Ali was killed in a hate crime even though there was eyewitness testimony to the contrary. Christensen should not have openly speculated about the case when the investigation was incomplete and she had so little idea about what actually transpired.

In the same *Star Tribune* article, Sgt. Christensen prematurely made assumptions about Ali's cause of death, telling reporters that "it appears that Ali died of heart disease."[163] At the time she made this statement, the *Star Tribune* reported that the Hennepin County medical examiner's office was "awaiting more tests before making a final ruling" on Ali's cause of death.[164] It was irresponsible for Christensen to have made statements about why Ali died before the coroner's investigation was completed.

Ali's relatives were devastated when they learned that he had been injured. According to the *Star Tribune*, Ali's son, Abdi Warsame, was extremely upset when members of the Somali community informed him about the assault.[165] Ali's widow, Farah Ali, was also traumatized, telling the *Tribune* that the experience of burying her husband was a profound shock.[166] According to his family members, Ali immigrated to the U.S. in 1995, and considered America his new home.

Members of the Somali community publicly blamed the media for Ali's death, arguing that the *Star Tribune* inflamed community tensions by making false claims that local Muslims were funding the work of Osama bin Laden. Approximately 500 Somalis gathered in response to Ali's killing, waving American flags and chanting pro-Somali slogans.[167] At the demonstration, Zabat Awed spoke about how the 9/11 backlash was affecting local Somalis, characterizing Ali's death as a hate crime committed by an irate bigot.[168] Awed also reported that during the backlash, Somali women had been harassed in the area, and minority children had received death threats.[169] Refuting the *Star Tribune*'s claim that Minnesota Somalis financially supported al-Qaeda, some of the demonstrators made signs declaring that they sent money to their parents, not to terrorists.[170] Protestors also expressed their disappointment with police investigators' unwillingness to characterize Ali's death as a 9/11 backlash homicide.

At the gathering, police and prosecutors addressed the crowd, reassuring concerned community members that local authorities were taking their concerns seriously. According to the *Star Tribune*, U.S. Attorney Tom Heffelfinger spoke out against hate crimes, which he characterized as un-American.[171] Minnesota precinct commander Sharon Libinski told the group that she was working to ensure that the Somali community felt safe and happy in Minnesota.[172] She also urged anyone experiencing post-9/11 harassment to report problems to authorities.

Months after the demonstration, Garry Peterson, the chief medical examiner of Heenpin County, finally ruled Ali's death a homicide. Peterson told the *Star Tribune* that the investigation determined that there was a clear connection between Ali's head injury and his death.[173]

In a January 2002 follow-up article about the crime, the *Star Tribune* reported that additional witnesses had come forward and confirmed that Ali had been murdered.[174] Larry Wesley, a 43-year old pastor, told police that he had been working as an assistant at the homeless shelter across from the bus stop when he saw a white man approach Ali and punch him once in the jaw.[175] Wesley also reported seeing Ali's assailant brashly stand over the elderly Somali man after he fell on the sidewalk. Members of the Somali community felt that the discovery of these additional witnesses was proof that the responding officers failed to canvass the neighborhood thoroughly in the aftermath of the fatal attack, since they missed getting the crucial testimony of eyewitnesses who were directly across the street. As a result of this shoddy investigative work, members of the Somali community began questioning whether the post-9/11 bias killing was a departmental priority. In November 2001, another previously-unknown witness came forward, corroborating that a white man hit the elderly Somali Muslim in an unprovoked assault.[176] In light of the additional information, the FBI began its own investigation into Ali's murder, exploring whether it was indeed a 9/11 backlash homicide.

Many of Ali's family members and friends felt vindicated that the attack was finally being investigated as a bias-motivated murder. Jamie Wellik told the *Star Tribune* that the medical examiner's conclusion came as no surprise, like being told that humans have two feet.[177]

Ali's family members expressed concern that Minneapolis police were not aggressively investigating the case. Despite the appearance of additional eyewitnesses, Christensen declared that the case had gone cold. Ali's relatives eventually refused to speak with Christensen without their lawyer present, apparently upset at her ineptitude and her repeated willingness to circulate the statement that Ali made when he was in a medicated semi-conscious state at the hospital, suggesting that he might have been hit by a car.

In other parts of the country, Somalis were also murdered in suspicious circumstances in the weeks after 9/11. The October 26, 2001 *Everett Herald* reported that 21-year old Somali Mohamed Salah Hassan died after being beaten and left under the Snohomish County bridge in Washington state.[178] It is impossible to know the extent to which post- 9/11 bigotry, Hassan's Muslim faith, and his Somali background contributed to the savagery with which he had been pummeled to death.

These hate crimes and attacks were taking place while Americans were reading best-sellers pitting Christian Americans against Muslim Somali villains. Mark Bowden's 1999 popular book, <u>Black Hawk Down</u>, tells the story of how merciless Somali militants hunt down and kill heroic American servicemen assisting injured comrades in a downed military helicopter.[179] Although this book was based on an actual 1993 U.S. military mission, it conveyed the message that Muslim Somalis were America's enemies.

The film version of the book contained even more pernicious images of Muslims. This movie premiered in New York and Los Angeles in December 2001, and was released in theatres across the country on January 18, 2002. Film critic Shaheen takes issue with the script for depicting Somali Muslims as creepy and savage skinny blacks.[180] The African Muslims appear as anti-American villains, unappreciative of soldiers' efforts to help famine victims. South Asian Muslims are also portrayed unfavorably. In one scene, Pakistani forces in Somalia delay rescuing American troops, and refuse to allow them to ride in their vehicles.

Shaheen maintains that in reality, the pinned down U.S. troops had no contact with the Pakistani commander, and that American troops were never forbidden from riding in Pakistani convoys.[181]

BIGOTRY AND KILLINGS, 2002

While Americans were being entertained by racist movies maligning Muslim Africans and South Asians, Sikhs continued to be murdered across the U.S. Ten months after Balbir Singh Sodhi was gunned down in Mesa, his brother was killed in San Francisco's predominantly-Latino Mission District. Sukhpal Singh Sodhi had just finished his shift as a United Cab driver and was going home when he was shot to death. At approximately 3:50 a.m. on August 4, 2002, the mortally-injured Sikh crashed his taxi into a parked vehicle and struck a utility pole, snapping both high and low voltage wires and cutting off power to 3,600 customers.[182] Sodhi's out-of-control vehicle then struck a parking meter and burst into flames. According to the *San Francisco Chronicle*, firefighters responding to the blaze extracted Sukhpal Sodhi's burnt body from the wreckage and pronounced him dead at the scene.[183] Although no witnesses saw the early-morning shooting, the *Chronicle* reported that a homeless woman named Toni was sleeping nearby when she was awaked by a big boom.[184] Along with breaking wires, the fire destroyed a red sedan and melted the paint on other nearby cars. Police dogs were unsuccessfully used in an attempt to track the gunman, who fled the scene. More than eight hours after the utility pole had been damaged, more than 3,400 nearby households remained without electrical power.

San Francisco residents speculated that Sukhpal Sodhi's death was racially-motivated. His family members thought that the shooting was a hate crime, triggered by the widespread notion that Sikhs were Arab terrorists. Rana Sodhi told *Little India* that his brother's death was not a robbery, pointing out that all of his belongings and $300 in cash in his pockets were left at the scene.[185] Brother Lakwinder Sodhi, a Phoenix gas station owner, told *India Abroad* that he was certain the murder was a hate crime.[186] Sukhpal Sodhi's death devastated his family members, who were particularly heartbroken that he was murdered on his 50th birthday. Lakwinder Sodhi reported that his brother had invited some friends to celebrate with him later in the day, once he had finished work.[187] According to *India Abroad*, Lakwinder Sodhi felt particularly bad about his brother Sukhpal's murder since he had reassured his parents that America was a safe country after his other brother Balbir had been killed in the post-9/11 hate crime in Arizona.[188]

Sukhpal Sodhi's murder was especially difficult on his wife and children – a son, and two daughters - who were living in India at the time of his killing. The targeted taxi driver, a native of India who had emigrated to the U.S. in 1990, was working to send money to his family in Punjab's Passiwal village. *India Abroad* reported that at the time Sukhpal Sodhi was murdered, he was busy looking to find marriage-minded suitors for his daughters, who were in their 20s.[189] Guru Roop Kaur Khalsa, a religious advisor to the Sodhi family, told *India Abroad* that Sukhpal's killing was particularly devastating because relatives were still mourning Balbir's death, which had taken place only 11 months previously.[190] Sukhpal Sodhi's brother Harjit was in shock over the two post-9/11 murders, telling the *New Delhi Statesman* that he prayed for his brothers, who were killed after coming to the U.S. to live virtuous lives.[191] Other relatives were also shaken by the Bay Area shooting. Dave Singh told the *San Francisco Chronicle* that his cousin Sukhpal was an easy-going man who never had problems with anybody.[192]

Family members and Sikh activists were concerned that the SFPD quickly dismissed the possibility that Sukhpal Sodhi's shooting was bias-motivated. Shortly after the Sodhi's death, a police officer admitted to the *Chronicle* that the SFPD had already decided that the shooting of the Sikh cab driver was not a hate crime, even though their investigation had just begun.[193] Manjit Singh, a spokesman for Sikh Mediawatch and Resource Task Force, told *India Abroad* that the SFPD was premature in their conclusion that the murder of Sukhpal Sodhi was a random killing.[194] Sukhpal's brother Lakwinder Singh expressed concern that the SFPD was not well-informed about the prevalence of anti-Sikh hate crimes, noting that South Asians routinely faced harassment and abusive language in the aftermath of the terrorist attacks.[195] Bay Area minority groups saw the shooting as a manifestation of anti-immigrant sentiment and the widespread misconception that Sikhs were affiliated with the Taliban.

Other minorities were also killed in apparent bias-motivated crimes. Mizanur Rahman, a renown Muslim photojournalist from Bangladesh, was beaten to death in Brooklyn on August 11, 2002. According to the *News India-Times*, Rahman was working as a waiter at a Battery Park Restaurant on the night he was targeted.[196] At around 11:50 p.m., he was walking home from the subway station, about half a block from his apartment in Cypress Hills, when he was stopped by four or five men on the corner of Liberty Ave. and Forbell St., who began arguing with him. The men then attacked the 37-year old South Asian Muslim. As many as 20 men joined in the fatal beating, pummeling Rahman with baseball bats, hockey sticks, iron rods, and bamboo sticks.[197] One of the assailants struck Rahman over the head with a thick club, causing him to fall to the pavement. He was declared dead shortly after.

The day before the murder, racial tensions between Latinos and South Asians had escalated considerably in the area. NYPD officer John Solomon told the *News India-Times* that the day before Rahman was beaten to death, a Hispanic man took a bicycle from an Indian immigrant. Another man from India retrieved the stolen bike from the Latino thief, heightening animosity between the two ethnic communities. According to the *News India-Times*, Rahman may have been attacked because the Latino mob might have thought that he was one of the Indian immigrants involved in the bicycle incident.[198] Apparently, Rahman's assailants were unable to differentiate between people from India and Bangladesh, lumping all South Asians together. Some local residents speculated that post-9/11 xenophobia contributed to the brutality of the racially-motivated assault.

Rahman's funeral was held on August 13, 2002 at the Muslim center in Ozone Park, and his body was flown to Bhaka later the same day. At the memorial ceremony, area Muslims expressed dismay that innocent South Asians continued to be beaten by strangers in New York 11 months after 9/11.

Rafael Santos of Brooklyn and Hardy Marston of Queens were arrested and charged with murdering Rahman. According to Brooklyn police detective Michael Gabriel, prosecutors were undecided whether to file state hate crime charges against Santos and Marston for their participation in Rahman's killing.[199] Muslim and South Asian community members hoped that all of Rahman's assailants would be convicted of homicide, adding that they doubted that Rahman would have been attacked and beaten to death by a mob if he had been white or Latino.

BIGOTRY AND KILLINGS, 2003

New York immigrants were also killed in bias-motivated homicides in 2003. In what the *New York Daily News* described as one of the worst series of hate crimes in recent history, a Brooklyn man, overcome by anger over 9/11, murdered four men in a six-week killing spree.[200] Larme Price was arrested on March 28, 2003 after killing four immigrants in Queens and Brooklyn. The *Village Voice* reported that Price confessed to the four bias-motivated homicides and said that he acted out of a desire to punish people of Middle Eastern descent after 9/11.[201] According to the *Daily News*, Price did not express remorse for his actions, referring to himself as a patriot.[202]

Larme Price's mother, Leatha, told the *New York Post* that her son began acting strangely after 9/11, when he began proclaiming that he was going to join the war.[203] She maintained that although he had a history of mental instability, the terrorist strikes unseated him psychologically. Investigators agreed that the attacks on the World Trade Center and the Pentagon triggered Price's killing spree. Deputy Inspector Vito Spano told the *Cincinnati Post* that the hijackings were the proximate cause of Price's murderous rampage.[204] After 9/11, he became overwhelmed with the urge to get in his Lexus and drive around looking for immigrants to kill.

On the morning of February 8, 2003, Price, a 30-year old unemployed ex-con, murdered his first two victims. Price entered the Ozone Park market in Queens and shot 43-year old John Freddy in the head with a .40-caliber semiautomatic weapon. According to the *New York Daily News*, Price told police that he heard and felt bad Arab vibes, prompting him to shoot the seated convenience store worker.[205] After killing Freddy, a Guyanese immigrant of Indian descent, Price shot at another worker, but missed him.[206]

Price then went to the Mill Basin minimart in Brooklyn, where he saw another immigrant he presumed was an Arab. Price originally intended to ask the man for some Doublemint gum, but decided to shoot him instead.[207] The gunfire killed 50-year old Sukhjit "Sammy" Khajala, an Indian immigrant.[208]

Because Price was seen acting strangely at a party, his mother took him to Woodhull Mental Health Center on March 9, 2003, where he was treated and released without being admitted. The following day, Price murdered a third immigrant, 32-year old Albert Kotlyar, who was sitting inside a laundromat in Bedford-Stuyvesant. According to police reports, Price walked into the Laundry King Superstore and abruptly decided to shoot the ethnic-looking man in the head in retaliation for 9/11.[209] After killing Kotlyar, who was from the Ukraine, Price sold his gun because he ran out of bullets for it.

Later the same month, Price continued his killing spree, shooting immigrants with a 9 mm gun. The *New York Daily News* reported that on March 20, 2003, Price walked into a food market in Crown Heights and asked the clerk for coffee, cigarettes, and a pack of matches.[210] Suddenly, Price shot and killed the clerk, 54-year old Mohammed Abdo Nasser Ali. After murdering the Yemeni worker, Price fired five bullets at one of Ali's co-workers, who was in the middle of helping a female customer. The first bullet missed Yakoob Aldailaim, but the next four bullets hit the 20-year old Yemeni immigrant. Despite the seriousness of his stomach and leg wounds, Aldailaim survived the attack after being treated at Brookdale Hospital. According to the *New York Daily News*, Price shot the two Yemenis in retaliation for 9/11 and because he couldn't understand what the men were saying to one other in Arabic.[211]

On March 28, 2003, Price walked into a precinct station and told officers that he was in contact with "Dog," the man responsible for killing the four immigrants.[212] Price later admitted to the shootings, informing police that he shot the men to avenge the World Trade Center attacks. Police searched Price's Lexus and discovered a black jacket and cap with the letter, "B," identical to the one seen on the shooter. During his April 3, 2003 confession, Price told police he cried for days after 9/11, and referred to himself as "an American good guy."[213] Price was initially a suspect in the murders of other New York Arab merchants, but he denied responsibility for the February 1, 2003 shooting death of 38-year old Mohammed Alamgir, a Bangladeshi grocery store owner in Queens, as well as the March 1, 2003 killing of Yemeni immigrant Marc Zanichelli in an auto parts store.

Some New Yorkers were concerned about the sympathetic media coverage Price received, depicting him as a mentally-ill man instead of as a cold-blooded killer who murdered four immigrants out of bias. Some activists pointed out that Price had a criminal record, dating back to 1989, for assault, robbery, burglary, and criminal possession of a weapon. After admitting to the murders, Price was sentenced to 150 years in prison without the possibility of parole. Patrick Young, chairman of the New York Immigration Coalition, told the *New York Daily News* that he viewed Price's murders in the context of the post-9/11 climate of hatred against Arabs and Muslims, proclaiming it a mistake to see the killings as the work of a single deranged lunatic.[214] In response to Price's crime spree, activists expressed their hope that the NYPD and other city agencies would adopt a confidentiality policy so undocumented immigrants who were victims or witnesses of bias attacks could feel safe talking to authorities without fear of deportation.

The families of Price's victims were traumatized by the killings. Yaganon Das, one of John Freddy's relatives, told the *Daily News* that some family members were having nightmares while others were plagued by uncontrollable crying.[215] Mohammed Ali's 12 children and other relatives were also distraught by Price's shootings. Amin Ali, Mohammed Ali's nephew, told the *New York Post* that he felt conflicted about whether Price should get the death penalty, noting that only God had the authority to punish the mentally ill.[216]

Because of all the hate crimes taking place across the country, some minority activists began assuming that bias was involved whenever a Muslim, Arab, or South Asian was inexplicably killed by a stranger. On April 16, 2003, 21-year old Gary Allard murdered a 60-year old Muslim taxi driver on Chicago's North

Side. [217] The Pakistani homicide victim, Mohammed Rafiq Haroon, was a married man with four children. Some community members viewed this post-9/11 killing as a backlash attack.

According to the *Daily Herald*, Haroon picked up Allard near Belmont Ave. and Halstead St. [218] When the cab reached the corner of Albany Ave. and Addison St., the passenger pulled a knife on the Muslim driver and demanded money. According to prosecutors, Haroon grabbed Allard's hand, and the passenger responded by slitting the driver's throat. The mortally-injured Haroon then tossed his assailant $100, and the killer fled the scene. After Allard told friends about the crime, he was arrested and charged with murder and armed robbery. Although Chicago police claimed that religious bias was not a factor in the killing, Illinois Muslims felt otherwise. According to the *Chicago Sun-Times*, Muslim activists demanded that police treat Haroon's murder as a hate crime, instigated because of the South Asian driver's appearance, Islamic hat, and distinctive beard. [219] Because he looked different from non-Muslim cabbies, Allard might have decided to target him instead of a driver of another faith. Mohammed Bawany, Haroon's younger brother who also worked as a cabbie, told the *Sun-Times* that more than a year and a half after 9/11, Muslim drivers continued taking steps to conceal their religious beliefs from passengers because of ongoing harassment. [220] According to Bawany, Haroon was unwilling to hide his Muslim faith, even if doing so jeopardized his safety.

Nahid Haroon was devastated by the death of her husband. She told the *Daily Herald* that her health deteriorated after Allard slit her spouse's throat, causing her to experience acute anxiety and insomnia. [221] Mohammed Haroon's death also constituted a substantial financial blow to his family. Although Nahid Haroon worked part-time, the loss of her husband's income made life much harder for her and her four children. Haroon had spent more than 20 years driving a taxi before he was killed on the job.

Immigrant taxi drivers were also murdered in other parts of the country, especially in the Bay Area. On July 2, 2003, 23-year old Gurpreet Singh was killed in Richmond, California, in what Sikhs across the U.S. believe to be a hate crime. According to *India Abroad*, Singh was dispatched by a Sikh-owned taxi company, Greyline Cab and Super Cab, to pick up a late-night fare. [222] On the night of the shooting, Singh had been working long hours to save up money for his October 2003 wedding in India. When he arrived at the approximate location, he discovered that the address he had been given was fictitious, and that no one was outside waiting for the ride. Singh was about to leave the area when the caller who requested the taxi contacted the dispatcher again and requested that the cabbie remain at the cul-de-sac, which was located in a predominantly African-American neighborhood. [223] At about 1:00 a.m., at the dead end corner near 21st St. and Carlson Blvd., Singh was shot to death in the driver's seat of his Yellow Cab no. 148. Although his taxi had a bulletproof shield to protect a driver from behind, Singh was shot through the front of his vehicle. Police responded to a 911 call about shots being fired in the area, and discovered Singh in mortal distress from a wound to his upper torso. Police Captain Lori Ritter told *India Abroad* that although officers and paramedics administered first aid, Singh died at the scene. [224] Police reported that the gunman did not take Singh's laptop in the front seat of the vehicle, or the gold bracelet and chain he was wearing, indicating that robbery was not a factor in the fatal shooting. [225]

Singh's family members were devastated when they heard that he was murdered. In his hometown in Punjab, Singh's fiancée, Amardeep Kaur, committed suicide upon hearing news that he had been killed. [226] Temple president Harpret Sandhu told *India Abroad* about Kaur's preparations to take her own life, noting that she took her morning bath, recited her morning prayers, and asked her parents-in-law if there was anything they wanted to tell Gurpreet. [227]

Three days after Singh was murdered, another Sikh cab driver was also shot in Richmond after being sent to another fictitious address at another cul-de-sac. *India Abroad* reported that on July 5, 2003, Inderjit Singh, a South Asian Sikh who did not wear a turban, was dispatched to a non-existent address at Roosevelt Avenue and 13th St. [228] Two men accosted him and shot him in the jaw through the window, but the South Asian driver managed to turn his car and drive away. Indirjit Singh's brother, Gurwant, told *India Abroad* that he saw the shooting as a bias-motivated attack since his assailants did not ask for money. [229] Richmond police did not register either Gurpreet Singh's homicide or Indirjit Singh's murder attempt as hate crimes, despite similarities in the two shootings.[230]

In the early morning hours of September 13, 2003, a little over a day after the second anniversary of 9/11, another Bay Area Sikh cab driver was murdered in Redwood City. Lousa Mataele, a 31-year old construction worker from Menlo Park, killed 21-year old Davinder Singh, who had a beard and wore a turban. Another passenger, Mataele's friend, witnessed the shooting.

India Abroad reported that on the night of the attack, Mataele had been drinking at a bar for a few hours before calling a taxi at approximately 3:00 a.m.[231] According to a passenger eyewitness, Mataele instructed Singh to take him and his friend to another bar. Abruptly, less than three minutes into the ride, Mataele took out a gun and demanded money. Before Singh could reply or stop the moving vehicle, Mataele fired two shots through Singh's orange turban into his head.[232] The cab carrying the incapacitated driver rolled forward and hit the bumper of a Ford Tempo. Mataele also shot the other passenger, who survived the wound in his upper body. Mataele then fled from the scene, and was later apprehended by police. Discussing the crime with reporters, Redwood City Police Captain Ron Mutuszake told the *Chronicle* that Mataele murdered the driver before he had a chance to comply with the request for money, suggesting that robbery was not a primary motive for the murder.[233]

Davinder Singh's family members were horrified by the killing and disturbed by the way they were informed of the crime. Although Singh died at approximately 3:30 a.m., his brother did not hear about the murder until 7:00 a.m., after frantically searching for his missing sibling for several hours. Police later told *India-West* that the coroner was responsible for notifying next-of-kin. [234] The coroner told the newspaper that another investigator had properly notified the victim's mother. The victim's brother, Rajeet Singh, denied this took place, pointing out that it was impossible since she didn't speak English.[235]

Davinder Singh's killing further frightened Bay Area cabbies, who were already reeling from the recent murder of Gurpreet Singh and the attempted murder of Inderjit Singh. Sikh drivers reported that they tended to be harassed more regularly if they wore turbans. Redwood city taxi driver Gurmit Singh told the *Chronicle* that after 9/11, he had been singled out on a near-daily basis by passengers who associated him with Taliban terrorists.[236] Just the week before, in early September 2003, someone threw a bottle at his parked taxi.[237] Bikram Jeet Singh, owner of Yellow Cab Peninsula, reported that passengers frequently called South Asian drivers 'Osama bin Laden,' and banged on their vehicles in menacing fashion.[238]

Taxi drivers from across the Bay Area attended Davinder Singh's funeral. According to the *Oakland Tribune*, cabbies in yellow, white, and orange vehicles gathered near San Carlos Airport, holding homemade signs in their vehicles protesting 9/11 backlash hate crimes targeting South Asian cabbies and other area minorities.[239] Members of the Islamic Networks Group joined Sikh drivers on Airport Way. After religious and community leaders spoke about Davinder Singh's murder, the cabbies drove out of the area in a single file line to the Oak Hill Funeral Home in San Jose. At the funeral, Singh's mother, uncle, and brothers sobbed uncontrollably as they walked behind the casket.[240] Hundreds of Sikh taxi drivers, wearing turbans of different colors, stood on tiptoe and watched as the casket traveled slowly along a path shaded by trees.[241] When Davinder Singh's body entered the crematory, his family began wailing in grief and anguish.

His uncle, Gurdev Singh Teer, saw a connection between his nephew's murder, which took place near the second anniversary of 9/11, and the ongoing harassment of other Sikh taxi drivers in the U.S.[242] Teer told the *Tribune* that people sometimes spat on South Asian cabbies or threw money at them while calling them 'Osama bin Laden.'[243]

Davinder Singh's murder attracted considerable international attention. Simranjit Singh Maan, a member of India's Parliament, attended the funeral. Addressing the large crowd standing outside the funeral home, Maan reported that there had been at least 260 anti-Sikh hate crimes in the U.S. after 9/11. [244] According to the *Tribune*, Maan said that he and other public officials urged the Indian government to advertise in the American media that Sikhs were different from Iraqis or Taliban terrorists.[245]

South Asian taxi drivers in the Bay Area saw Davinder Singh's murder as a bias-motivated shooting. San Jose cabbie Raginder Thakur told the *Tribune* that most South Asian drivers were fearful of future attacks, especially since some Americans associated their facial hair with Saddam Hussein's moustache.[246] Bikram Singh, owner of Peninsula Yellow Cab, pointed out that traditional Sikh attire was different from that worn by Taliban terrorists, noting that the 9/11 hijackers were dressed in Western clothing.[247]

Many of the mourners in attendance were outraged that Redwood City police investigators were claiming that Davinder Singh was killed in a robbery, not a bias-motivated crime. Sikh activists found it significant that Mataele executed the driver less than two days after the second anniversary of 9/11, and fled without taking the driver's money or belongings.

In April 2005, a San Mateo County judge ruled that Mataele was incompetent to stand trial. He was subsequently ordered to be treated for mental illness at Napa State Hospital. Three years later, Mataele was declared competent, and criminal proceedings against him resumed in February 2009.[248] Many South Asian community members were dismayed that it was taking so long to bring Davinder Singh's killer to justice.

In response to hate crimes against Sikh and other minority taxi drivers, the San Francisco police department installed cameras in all cabs. Officials reported that the crime prevention measure seemed to be deterring attacks since there were no assaults against minority drivers in the city in the first few months after the cameras were activated. To prevent hate crimes in other urban areas, Sikh activists called for the installation of cameras and bullet-proof glass in taxis across the U.S. They also recommended the recording of phone calls to cab companies to prevent bigots from being able to dispatch and murder cabbies with impunity.

Ten days after Davinder Singh was shot in Redwood City, California, a South Asian convenience store clerk was killed in Tempe, Arizona. On September 23, 2003, Bruce Philip Reed abruptly murdered Sukhvir Singh. According to *India Abroad*, Reed stabbed Singh in the head and walked out the back door, leaving the mortally injured man in a pool of his own blood.[249] At about 6:30 p.m., customers entering the store discovered Singh's body on the floor.

After the murder, Reed fled the city and was arrested in the neighboring town of Mesa. Tempe police described Reed as a 43-year old African-American transient.[250] Singh had known Reed briefly in the past, offering him food and money in exchange for odd jobs, like cleaning the yard and taking out the trash. Despite these acts of charity, Reed decided to kill the South Asian convenience store owner in an unprovoked attack. Police reported that there was no indication that Singh's murder was connected to a robbery.[251] Reed made no attempt to steal any money or merchandise from Singh's business, indicating that the post-9/11 killing might have been a bias crime.

Sukhvir Singh's friends and family members were shocked by his death. Although he had immigrated to the U.S. in 1997, he had a fiancée in India. She was devastated by the murder, ruining their plans to get married later that year. Singh's parents were also distraught, remembering their youngest child as a dutiful son who worked hard to send them money every month. Singh was also close to his elder siblings, who were saddened by his senseless end.

Arizona Sikhs were also upset by Sukhvir Singh's murder, which they saw as part of a backlash that included the September 15, 2001 killing of Balbir Sodhi in Mesa and the May 2003 shooting of trucker Avtar Singh in Phoenix. They were also concerned about an attack on Mesa convenience store worker Didar Singh, a Sikh who had been beaten unconscious by three men who broke his nose and scarred his face.[252] Arizona South Asians noted that prior to this vicious beating, Didar Singh had his store robbed on two other occasions, including an incident involving men with handguns.[253] Many area Sikhs thought that Didar Singh was being repeatedly targeted because of his South Asian appearance and local bigots' misconception that Sikhs supported the Taliban.

Prior to Sukhvir Singh's stabbing, there had been a rise in neo-Nazi graffiti in the area. *India Abroad* reported that a nearby Islamic Community Center was vandalized in late September 2003, and a local mosque was desecrated with swastikas and hate messages.[254] Since Sikhs were sometimes mistaken as Middle Eastern terrorists, crimes targeting local Muslims were seen as an indication that area nativism was on the rise. Onkar Singh told *India Abroad* that he and other South Asians wondered whether they should continue living in a community where so many bias crimes were taking place.[255]

Because of the frequency of attacks targeting Sikhs and Muslims, many South Asians assumed that Sukhvir Singh's murder was bias-motivated. Harjit Sodhi, one of Balbir Sodhi's brothers, told *India Abroad* that Sukvir Singh was likely targeted because of his religion and ethnicity.[256] Afraid that bias attacks would continue, Harjit Sodhi contemplated selling his own convenience store and moving his immediate family back to India.[257] He was particularly disturbed that Sukhvir Singh was murdered even though he had cut his hair, shaved his beard, and took off his religiously-mandated turban in order to blend into American society.[258]

Lakhwinder Sodhi, another one of Balbir's brothers, concurred that Sukhvir Singh's killer was likely motivated by bias since the crime was otherwise inexplicable.[259] Lakhwinder Sodhi told *India Abroad* that he was having difficulty coping with Sukhvir Singh's death, particularly since he considered the murdered convenience store owner a close friend.[260] Like so many other area Sikhs, Sodhi was unnerved by all the attacks against South Asians in the U.S., especially the deaths of two of his brothers at the hands of strangers.[261]

BIGOTRY AND KILLINGS, 2004-5

While minority groups were mourning backlash murders, American audiences were laughing at demeaning caricatures of Middle Easterners. The satire, *Team America: World Police*, featured animated puppets perpetuating stereotypes of homicidal Arabs. This comedy was released in the U.S. on October 15, 2004. At one point of the film, American audiences are told that terrorists spend every minute of their lives exploring new ways to kill Western civilians. In a particularly disturbing scene lampooning the anti-Semitic undertones of the 'War on Terror,' a puppet protagonist obtains plastic surgery to go undercover, replacing his handsome Anglo features with an oversized hooked nose in order to blend in with the foreign killers. Although the movie was intended as a political satire challenging the nationalistic chauvinism of American freedom fighters, unsophisticated viewers took it seriously. Commenting on this film, Shaheen notes that its racist messages inspired Iraq veteran Corporeal Joshua Belile to write and perform a demeaning, Arab-bashing video viewed by thousands.[262]

While moviegoers were laughing at xenophobic films, South Asians were being killed in the South. In Miami, Gurdeep Singh Saluja, a 43-year old gas station worker, was murdered on February 21, 2005. *India Abroad* reported that on the evening of the attack, two gunmen entered the Marathon Gas Station about 15 minutes before Saluja was going to close up for the night.[263] A surveillance camera, installed by Pakistani-American owner Omar Zayeri, recorded the crime. Saluja did not resist the two masked gunmen, and tried to open the cash register, assuming he was being robbed. The video footage showed the two killers were not interested in money – they shot the Indian clerk, ransacked the business, and left without taking any cash or valuables. They also left Saluja's wallet at the scene. Discussing the security tape, Zayeri told *India Abroad* that killers operated in a calm and calculated manner, shooting the compliant and defenseless Saluja and glaring at his fallen body in a menacing way.[264] Since the gunmen did not rob the store, South Asian community members viewed the killing as a post-9/11 hate crime targeting the Indian clerk and the Pakistani Muslim station owner.[265]

Gurdeep Singh Saluja's family members were devastated by the crime. According to *India Abroad*, Sukhbir Saluja became concerned when her husband failed to return home after work.[266] She asked a cousin to check on her missing spouse, and this relative discovered Gurdeep Saluja's bloody body at the station. Gurdeep Saluja's relatives in India were also crushed by his killing. He had not visited them for eight years, but had made plans to return to his homeland in June 2005. His relatives had trouble understanding why anyone would kill such a kind and hard-working immigrant. In addition to his evening job at the gas station, Gurdeep Saluja worked as a warehouse manager during the day to support his dependents. Because Sukhbir Saluja was not employed, the murder was both an emotional and financial catastrophe for the family.

South Asians were also killed in New York. About a week after gunmen murdered Gurdeep Saluja in Miami, an assailant killed a Guyanese immigrant of Indian ethnicity in the Richmond Hill neighborhood of New York. According to the *News India-Times*, Antonio Roque, an 18-year old youth, beat to death 52-year old Jagat Ram Balram near the victim's house.[267] In response to the killing, South Asian community members staged a protest to voice their opposition to Balram's murder and other attacks targeting immigrants. Dilip Nath told the *News India-Times* that Balram's murder was linked to a series of post-9/11 unprovoked assaults targeting Indians, Bangladeshis, and Guyanese in the area.[268] Many concerned South Asians expressed their hope that organizations such as the New American Coalition Against Hate Crimes would help combat these kinds of bias-motivated attacks, which were seen as manifestations of the ongoing backlash.

Despite the anti-racism efforts of community groups, strangers continued killing South Asians. Sikh taxi drivers continued to be murdered in Richmond, California. *India-West* reported that Gurpartap Singh, a 58-year old Punjabi American, was shot in the neck on Christmas day 2005, at about 11:30 a.m.[269] Singh immigrated to the U.S. eight years prior to his killing, and had been a naturalized citizen for more than five years. The South Asian driver wore a trimmed beard, and only donned his turban for special occasions. Because of all the hate crimes taking place across the U.S., minority cabbies viewed Singh's killing as a possible post-9/11 bias attack.

BIGOTRY AND KILLINGS, 2006

While minorities were being killed across the U.S., American audiences were being entertained by movies featuring foreign villains. In the movie *Cavite*, a ruthless Muslim killer in the Philippines tells the Filipino-American protagonist that he must blow up a church full of innocent people or terrorists would murder his mother and sister.[270] The lead character reluctantly complies, killing worshippers to save his relatives. This movie was released in the U.S. on May 26, 2006, exposing American audiences to the xenophobic message that Asian Muslims are diabolical killers.

While American audiences were enjoying Islamophobic movies, Muslims were being killed on the West Coast. An Afghan woman was murdered in California in what many consider to be a post-9/11 bias-motivated attack. On October 19, 2006, Alia Ansari, a 37-year old Afghan mother, was gunned down about a block from her Bay Area home. According to the *San Francisco Chronicle*, the assailant saw Ansari, jumped out of his car, shot the veiled woman once in the head, and drove off.[271] At the time of the shooting, Ansari was walking to Glenmoor Elementary School to pick up two of her children. Since her three-year old daughter Latifa was holding her hand and accompanying her on the walk, the little girl witnessed her mother's shocking murder.

Within an hour of the killing, police arrested 30-year old Manuel Urango on a parole violation, after witnesses provided investigators with a description of the gunman's car. According to the *Chronicle*, three-year old Latifa Ansari identified Urango, a Latino with a long record of criminal convictions, as her mother's killer.[272]

Approximately 400 community members attended a memorial service for Ansari. Congressman Pete Stark of Fremont, Mayor Bob Waserman, and Police Chief Craig Steckler paid their respects to the family and offered support to Afghans and Muslims in the area, who were unsettled by the senseless killing. Widower Ahmadullah Ansari was too distraught to speak to reporters about the case, telling them simply that he had no strength to comment on his wife's murder.[273] After the California memorial, he made the decision to take Alia's body to her native Afghanistan and bury it in Mazar-e-Sharif village, where she lived before immigrating to the U.S. in 1986.

Alia Ansari's family believed that the shooting was an anti-Muslim and anti-Afghan hate crime, triggered by her hijab and post-9/11 nativism. Bay Area community members agreed. Concord resident Nazira Mojadidi told the *Chronicle* that she saw Ansari's murder as a direct attack on all Muslim women.[274]

Four months after the shooting, police charged Urango with murder after tests proved that there was gunpowder residue on his hands the day Ansari was killed. Local Muslims were relieved that the case against Urango was moving forward, since he was such a danger to society.

In February 2008, Latifa Ansari testified in court against her mother's killer. During the trial, defense attorney William Caruthers argued that the young girl's initial identification of his client was flawed because police showed her a picture of Urango surrounded by police officers, with his hands cuffed behind his back. According to the *Chronicle*, the frightened little five-year old girl had difficulty answering questions, repeatedly telling an interpreter in Farsi that she wanted to go home.[275] She told the court that the man who hurt her mother had a gun, but she was unable to state with certainty that Urango was the shooter.[276] Alameda County Superior Court Judge Reginald Saunders instructed the jury and attorneys to be patient with the traumatized witness, who was testifying for the first time in a front of a room full of strangers in the presence of the man who murdered her mother.

On March 10, 2008, Urango was convicted of killing Ansari. Before he was sentenced, community leaders spoke about how Ansari's death affected local Afghan and Muslim residents. They characterized the homicide as a hate crime, arguing that Urango targeted Ansari, a stay-at-home mother, because of her ethnicity and religiously-prescribed head scarf.[277] Because Urango did not know Ansari personally, her Muslim attire seemed to be the only motive for the attack. Many community members viewed the shooting as an example of post-9/11 Islamophobia.

Since widower Ahmadullah Ansari was in Afghanistan during the sentencing phase of the trial, he was unable to testify about how Alia's murder devastated his life and traumatized their six children. Although he did not appear in person, he submitted a letter that was entered into the court record on his behalf. In this written statement, Ahmadullah Ansari communicated to the judge that he missed his wife tremendously, and that nothing would bring her back.[278] He also wrote that more than anything else, he wanted to hear Urango's explanation of why he killed Alia. Because of the heinousness of Urango's crime and his long criminal history, Judge Saunders sentenced him to 50 years to life in prison.

BIGOTRY AND KILLINGS, 2007-8

Post-9/11 intolerance was undoubtedly fueled by negative cinematic portrayals of Muslims. Islamic terrorists appear in the movie, *Red Mercury*, a British film released in the U.S. on DVD in June 2007. In one scene, Muslim villains attack London and take civilian hostages at the Olympus Grill restaurant.[279] The protagonists eventually kill the swarthy terrorists and rescue the Western hostages.

While Americans were watching xenophobic movies, immigrants in California were being murdered in bias crimes. On July 1, 2007, Satendar Singh, a 26-year old Sikh man of Indian descent, was attacked and killed in Folsom. Singh and his friends, who were also South Asians, were picnicking at Lake Natoma Park when a group of Russians began harassing them. According to *India Abroad*, the Russians screamed racist, anti-religious, and homophobic slurs at Satendar Singh and his friends, in what the Sacramento county sheriff's office characterized as a day-long verbal exchange.[280] After harassing Singh, Andrey Vusik punched him in the face, smashed his head on the ground, and knocked him unconscious. Singh's attackers then escaped in two vehicles – a dark green four-door sedan and a red Mitsubishi with a red DMV sticker #7 on its window.[281] As a result of his massive head trauma, Singh fell into a coma and was put on life support in the intensive care unit of Mercy San Juan Medical Center. He never regained consciousness, dying four days later after his aunt and uncle gave physicians permission to remove their brain-dead nephew from life support machines.

Seven years before he was murdered, Singh had immigrated to the U.S. from Fiji, his country of origin, after winning an immigrant visa lottery. Since his parents were thousands of miles away, he lived with his aunt and uncle while working at an AT&T call center. Singh's friends described him as a very jovial person, and claimed that he was beaten up because he was the only man at the picnic without a female companion.[282] Singh was not wearing a turban at the time of the attack.

Activists declared that the assault was unmistakably a hate crime, intended to create fear in the Fijian, South Asian, Arab, Muslim, Sikh, and LGBT communities. Because of the nature of the anti-Arab and anti-Muslim slurs used against the picnicking South Asians, some community members regarded Singh's death as a 9/11 backlash crime. Neilinder Singh, an attorney for SALDEF, told *India Abroad* that the xenophobic July 1st attack was an affront to the freedoms that Americans celebrate on Independence Day.[283] Because Singh's assailant made bigoted comments during the attack, SALDEF and CAIR issued a statement declaring that Singh was targeted because of the color of his skin, his national origin, and his perceived sexual orientation.[284] In response to Singh's killing, the American River Parkway Safety Coalition offered a $1000 reward for information leading to the arrest and conviction of those responsible for his death. Police investigators charged Singh's murderer, Andrey Vusik, with involuntary manslaughter. Rather than answer for his actions, Vusik fled the jurisdiction and was believed to be hiding out in Russia, his country of origin.

Area Sikhs were disturbed that the Sacramento county sheriff's office described the bias-motivated attack as a "fight."[285] They also expressed concern that Vusik had only been charged with involuntary manslaughter instead of murder with a hate crime enhancement, since bias played such an unequivocal role in the fatal attack witnessed by Singh's friends and Vusik's companions.

Newspaper accounts of the murder focused on different reasons why Singh was targeted. Ethnic publications like *India Abroad* and *India-West* called attention to Singh's religion, ethnicity, and national origin, describing him as a "Sikh man," a "South Asian man," and a "Fijian of Indian descent."[286] Although they acknowledged that homophobic statements were made during the assault, these newspapers did not specifically identify Singh as a gay man. In fact, *India Abroad* and the *Sacramento Bee* reported that Singh's friends claimed that he was not gay and was merely singled out because he was picnicking without a female companion.[287] Newspapers and magazines with a GLBT readership identified Singh as openly gay and interpreted the assault primarily as a homophobic hate crime. The December 4, 2007 *Advocate* discussed the murder in the context of tensions between Sacramento-area gays and Slavic evangelical Christians.[288] According to the *Advocate*, Singh's attackers made anti-gay slurs, referring to him as a 'sodomite.'[289]

The *Advocate* described Singh as a gay rights activist who dressed up his dog for local pride celebrations.[290] Singh's friends reported that he had a good sense of humor, and sometimes joked that his dog resembled Paris Hilton. Clayton Pettus told the *Advocate* that he and Singh would sometimes people-watch at the Badlands, a Sacramento gay bar, remembering that his Sikh companion never had a negative thing to say about other people.[291]

LGBT activists claimed that shortly before Singh's murder, Sacramento evangelical church leaders increased anti-gay rhetoric in their sermons. Perhaps inspired by religious intolerance for same-sex couples, immigrants from the former Soviet republics appeared at gay events, spitting on participants and threatening them. In 2006, the year before Singh was killed, hundreds of Sacramento-area Slavic evangelicals appeared at Queer Youth Advocacy Day, harassing LGBT students who were lobbying state legislators.[292] Because ethnic newspapers ignored Singh's sexual orientation and LGBT publications downplayed his ethnicity, different minority communities arrived at contradictory conclusions about whether the bias-motivated attack was triggered primarily by homophobia, xenophobia, or religious bigotry.

Many American newspapers viewed Singh's death in the context of the ongoing backlash. In a September 2007 article about the murder, the *Sacramento Bee* reported that a total of seven Sikh Americans had been killed in post-9/11 hate crimes after being misidentified as Muslims.[293] Instead of abating, the killings continued, while Americans enjoyed racist movies featuring diabolical Muslim characters.

In the movie, *The Kingdom*, Arab terrorists kill hundreds of American civilians, including women and children. In response, four FBI agents go to Saudi Arabia and kill Arab enemies, including the attack's mastermind, Abu Hamsa. This movie, released in the U.S. on September 28, 2007, suggests that Muslims are violence-prone, and that Middle Eastern children and Arab-American organizations support terrorism. *Los Angeles Times* reviewer Kenneth Turan compared the film's malevolent Arab characters to jingoistic World War II films about the 'yellow peril.'[294] Other critics were also disturbed by *The Kingdom*. In his book, <u>Guilty</u>,

Shaheen reported that American teen audiences cheered when scores of Arabs were shot dead in this movie, absorbing the harmful message that Muslims are enemies of America who need to be exterminated.[295]

While film audiences were celebrating the deaths of Muslims, immigrants continued being killed in the U.S. The *San Francisco Chronicle* reported that on the evening of December 27, 2007, two Sikh brothers were shot to death while they were closing up their restaurant in Richmond, California.[296] Based on surveillance footage of the crime, police ascertained that two assailants, who looked Latino or Asian, entered the Sahib Indian Restaurant and gunned down 30-year old Ravinder Kalsi. They then chased his brother, 42-year old Paramjit Kalsi, into the rear of the restaurant and murdered him as well. The gunmen did not rob the store after killing the two Sikh owners.

According to the *Chronicle*, Ravinder and Paramjit Kalsi were from the town of Patiala in the Punjab, located about 150 miles north of New Deli.[297] In 1997, they immigrated to the U.S. penniless, doing construction work in Berkeley. Trained as carpenters in India, the Kalsi brothers bought and renovated Bay Area homes, eventually earning enough money to buy their Indian restaurant in 2002. Their friends described them as hard-working and conscientious, noting that they regularly sent money to family members still in India. One of the brothers was engaged to be married to a woman in India. A few weeks before they were killed, the brothers began making plans to sell the restaurant and return to their homeland for the wedding, which was scheduled to take place at the end of January 2008.

Richmond police officers reported being baffled by the crime, particularly since the gunmen did not steal anything after shooting the South Asian brothers. Lt. Mark Gagan, who regularly frequented the Indian restaurant, told the *Chronicle* that homicide detectives – including veteran investigators – were all puzzled by the double murder, particularly in light of the brothers' innocuous lifestyle and the cold-blooded way in which they were killed.[298] Richmond police offered a $10,000 reward for information leading to the arrest and conviction of the gunmen. An anonymous benefactor offered an additional $10,000 to encourage community members to report any knowledge of the crime to authorities. Surveillance camera footage of the killers gunning down the restaurant owners generated many tips and calls, but produced no definitive leads.

According to the *Hindustan Times*, authorities solicited FBI involvement to explore whether the double murder was bias-motivated.[299] Area Sikhs were convinced that the Kalsi brothers were killed in a post-9/11 hate crime, noting that the gunmen did not steal anything and other Bay Area South Asians had been shot by strangers in equally bizarre circumstances. Some community members wondered if the same perpetrators were involved in the Richmond shootings that killed Gurpreet Singh and wounded Inderjit Singh.

J.P. Singh, former president of the El Sobrante Sikh temple and a personal friend of Ravinder and Paramjit Kalsi, told the *Chronicle* that he was troubled by the double murder and the killing of other South Asian Sikhs in Richmond.[300] Friends and restaurant patrons held a vigil at the restaurant on Friday, January 4, 2008, followed by a prayer service at the Sikh temple two days later.

In other parts of the country, Sikhs continued to be killed under strange circumstances. In New York, a South Asian man was found murdered on August 8, 2008 outside of a Sikh temple on 97th Avenue near 118th St. According to the *New York Times*, the Sikh man was discovered bludgeoned to death near the Sikh Cultural Society, a community center with a prayer hall used by the large South Asian community in the area.[301] Because of the nature of the victim's massive head wounds, investigators speculated that a stone and a stick recovered at the crime scene may have been the murder weapons. The Sikh victim, who had a wife and children in India, prayed in the gurdwara twice a day before he was killed in the post-9/11 beating.[302] Because investigators were not looking at robbery as a motive, many area Sikhs wondered why the South Asian man was beaten to death outside of their house of worship. Since the deceased man was often seen on Lefferts Boulevard, where two Sikhs had been viciously beaten in a hate crime outside the Villa Russo restaurant in 2004, some community members speculated that post-9/11 bigotry might have played a role in the mysterious and brutal attack.

In Arizona, minorities continued dealing with the ongoing murder of South Asians. On August 15, 2008, *India-West* reported that a 27-year old man in Phoenix, accompanied by his two-year old and six-year old sons, walked into a 7-Eleven store and shot to death 62-year old Inder Jit Jassal, the store clerk.[303] According to Phoenix detective Stacie Derge, the surveillance video established that the African-American suspect, Jermaine Canada, did not have an argument with the victim, and had no discernible motive for the unprovoked murder.

Following the killing, the Sikh American Legal Defense and Education Fund reported that the Phoenix Sikh community was in a state of shock. The victim's brother, Tilakraj Jassal, was particularly upset by the senseless shooting. Many area Sikhs speculated that the attack may have been a hate crime linked to the 9/11 backlash. SALDEF Western regional director Kavneet Singh told *India-West* that the shooting was a tragedy, compounding the tremendous hardship that the Phoenix Sikh community experienced in the seven years after the terrorist strikes.[304] Canada was apprehended by the police and arrested after a cooperating citizen recognized him from a television description of the killer. Although Canada may have been mentally ill at the time of the shooting, his choice of victims may have been directly or indirectly influenced by post-9/11 bias against foreigners.

BIGOTRY AND KILLINGS, 2009

On one occasion, an Arab was killed by a police officer in the years after 9/11. In Miami, Florida, a vacationing Palestinian-American Muslim from Woodbridge, Virginia was shot to death on June 14, 2009. At the time of the shooting, officer Adam Tavss was responding to a 911 call about a Hispanic male carrying a gun. A surveillance video showed that Tavss killed 29-year old Husein Shehada a mere 1.8 seconds after encountering him speaking Arabic to his brother.[305] The footage also showed that officer Tavss shot Shehada three times, although both brothers were complying with an officer's request that the two men raise their hands and turn towards the eight responding officers at the scene.[306] After gunning down Shehada, Tavss asked witnesses to go on record to corroborate that the Palestinian-American men were speaking Arabic, as though that fact somehow justified the killing of an unarmed civilian.[307] ADC legal advisor Abed Ayoub suggested that inadequate training and racial tensions led to Shehada's death, speculating that a more culturally-aware officer might have been less inclined to shoot a tourist simply because he was speaking a foreign language.[308] Outraged by the killing, thousands of people around the world demanded an investigation about why an officer felt the need to shoot a vacationing Arab Muslim who was fully cooperating with the police. Many community members saw Shehada's death as a product of post-9/11 xenophobia.

Husein Shehada was not the only Arab killed in the U.S. that month. In Yermo, California, a Jordanian immigrant was murdered in his home on the evening of June 27, 2009. Shortly before his death, Ali Abdelhadi Mohd and his family had been targeted by anti-Muslim vandals. The *Los Angeles Times* reported that at the time of the fatal arson attack, Mohd was in the process of painting over white supremacist graffiti he had recently discovered on the interior walls of his home.[309] The hate messages included: "Fuck you Arab," "KKK," "sand nigger," and "go home Arab," as well as drawings of a Nazi swastika and the American flag.[310] Neighbors reported hearing an explosion that sounded like a sonic boom shortly before flames engulfed the family's house. Firefighters recovered Mohd's charred body at the scene. Some area Muslims saw Mohd's death as part of the wave of xenophobia unleashed by 9/11.

Prior to his death, Mohd, his wife, and his seven children had been repeatedly singled out by bigots. In 2007, arsonists torched a mosque he had built on his Yermo property.[311] In response to this attack, deputies arrested 18-year old Loren Jesse Clark and 16-year old Brian Martin, but did not charge them with hate crimes.[312] The 2007 fire, coupled with anti-Muslim threats and harassment, undermined the Mohd family's sense of security. Along with feeling unsafe in their neighborhood, the Mohd's children were bullied at school. The *Los Angeles Times* reported that the couple's 14-year old son, Ahmad, was repeatedly harassed by his classmates, who challenged him to fights and made anti-Arab slurs, demanding that he leave the U.S.[313] Although a few of the students were suspended, the bullying continued unabated. Mohd's 18-year old daughter Asmaa was also targeted by racist youths, who used ethnic slurs in her presence and tried to tear off her hijab.[314]

One individual responsible for harassing the family was sent to jail in 2008, but the Mohds continued to be targeted by other people in the neighborhood. In response to community Islamophobia and attacks on his children, Mohd moved his family out of the Yermo house, hoping to rent it and relocate permanently to Victorville, a more diverse town. The last time Mohd's children saw their father, he was leaving to buy paint at the Home Depot to cover up the racist slurs he had discovered on the newly-vacated Yermo property.[315] Because he had become accustomed to community intolerance and hate crimes, Mohd hadn't bothered to call the police to report the white supremacist graffiti, which he had photographed for his own records.

FBI spokeswoman Laura Eimiller told the *Los Angeles Times* that agents were investigating Mohd's death as a bias crime since he was a Muslim community leader who had been frequently targeted by bigots.[316] The autopsy showed that there was soot and burning in his esophagus, indicating that he had been alive when the fatal fire began.

Mohd's death angered area Muslims, who remembered him as a civic-minded individual who started mosques in Riverside, Indio, and San Diego after immigrating to the U.S. in the 1970s. Hadie Mohammed, one of the victim's sons, told the *Arab American News* that his father was a caring man who hoped to bring unity among residents of the High Desert.[317]

While bigots were targeting local Muslims, American film audiences were watching violent movies that heightened community xenophobia. The thriller, *Five Fingers*, spreads the disturbing message that torture is effective tool against anti-American terrorists.[318] This film was released on DVD on July 7, 2009. At the beginning of the story, Dutch jazz musician Martijn flies to Morocco where swarthy kidnappers abduct him, drug him, and hold him hostage. After killing his friend Gavin, Martijn's Arab-looking abductors begin to torture him. Aicha, the film's central villain, cuts off the Dutch pianist's pinky finger. The heartless interrogator then severs Martijn's thumb and another finger, ending his musical career. Eventually, the prisoner confesses that he belongs to a Dutch terror cell. At this point, his interrogators reveal that they are actually U.S. intelligence agents conducting the torture session in New York City. The movie justifies the federal agents' harsh interrogation techniques, including the cutting off of digits, as a means of investigating potential terrorists.

In this climate of intolerance, white supremacists continued targeting Middle Eastern immigrants. The *Houston Chronicle* reported that police were investigating the murder of 51-year old Naushad Virani, an Iranian convenience store owner, as a possible hate crime.[319] On December 25, 2009, 31-year old Stevie "Bubba" Walder, an Aryan Brotherhood member with a shaved head and white power tattoos, shot and killed Virani, an unarmed store owner. On the day of the shooting, the Persian businessman was working on the Christmas holiday so his employees could spend time with their families. He left behind a wife and a three-year old daughter. Tyler County sheriff David Hennigan reported that Walder used a racial slur when he confessed to the killing, and told the arresting officers that he opted against fighting them because they were white. Despite evidence suggesting that Walder acted out of bias when he shot the Iranian merchant, police officers thought it unlikely that the white supremacist killer would be charged with a hate crime. Police spokesman Hugh Bishop told the *Houston Chronicle* that collecting evidence to establish racist intent was not a top priority for Texas investigators since Walder was already facing a death sentence for the murder.[320] Some area minorities viewed the shooting in the context of the ongoing 9/11 backlash, and thought that investigators should have made more of an effort to explore whether bias charges were warranted.

BIGOTRY AND KILLINGS, 2010

In 2010, minority community members continued to be attacked and killed by bigots in the U.S. In the summer of that year, an Indian-American was murdered near his home in Old Bridge, New Jersey. According to India Abroad, Dr. Divyendu Sinha, a 49-year old professor, was walking with his family on June 25, 2010 when a group of teens jumped him in a senseless and unprovoked attack.[321] Sinha's five assailants punched and kicked him severely, even after he fell down on the sidewalk. Sinha's sons, Aashish and Ravi, suffered minor injuries trying to end the beating. Sinha's wife Alka was also present during the assault, and watched in horror as her husband was viciously pummeled.[322] Two days later, Sinha died of his injuries at a nearby hospital. Sinha's family members identified the perpetrators, who were arrested and charged with murder and aggravated assault.

In response to Sinha's death, hundreds of mourners attended a July 18, 2010 candlelight vigil at Old Bridge High School. Many South Asians saw Sinha's killing as a hate crime. Since Sinha died as a result of blunt force trauma to the head, many community residents compared his murder to the death of Dot-buster victim Navroze Mody. Other community members saw Sinha's murder as a product of post-9/11 xenophobia.

BIGOTRY AND KILLINGS, 2011

South Asians continued to be murdered in the U.S. in 2011. One of the most shocking attacks occurred in the Sacramento suburb of Elk Grove. On March 4, 2010, 78-year old Gurmej Atwal and 65-year old Surinder Singh were killed on their afternoon walk. The shooting took place near a bright green bus shelter overlooking highway 99, where the elderly Sikhs often stopped to rest on their daily stroll. At the time of the double homicide, the South Asian men were wearing turbans over their uncut hair, making them visible targets for area bigots. According to the *Los Angeles Times*, the wife of a family friend came across the victims' bloodied bodies on the sidewalk at approximately 4:30 p.m.[323] Singh died at the scene, and Atwal was hospitalized in critical condition and put on a breathing tube, after sustaining two bullet wounds to his chest and damage to his lungs, pancreas, liver, and intestines.[324]

The shooting victims were popular members of the community. Surinder Singh was a Punjabi farmer and truck driver who immigrated to the U.S. in 2005 to enjoy his retirement surrounded by his son's family. His companion, Gurmej Atwal, was a retired Punjabi civil servant who walked seven or eight miles a day to keep himself in shape. When Atwal came to the U.S. in 2001, his wife remained in India, unable to travel easily.

The victims' families were devastated by the attack. Gurmej Atwal's son, Kamaljit, told *India Abroad* that he rushed to the crime scene as soon as he learned of the crime, and was traumatized to see his injured father being loaded into an ambulance.[325] Atwal told the *Los Angeles Times* that he believed the shooter was likely motivated by ethnic and religious bigotry, since no other explanation made sense.[326] Atwal's grandchildren, Navjit and Bhagat, were also shaken by the double shootings, wishing that they could return to the morning of March 4th and tell the crime victims to stay home. Surinder Singh's son and other family members were sickened by the violence, horrified that someone would choose to target two elderly Sikh men taking an afternoon stroll.

News of the double shooting quickly spread outside of California, upsetting television viewers across America and news audiences overseas. Floyd Mori, national director of the Japanese American Citizens League, flew out from D.C. to attend Singh's funeral, speaking out against the crime and comparing the 9/11 backlash to the experiences of Japanese-Americans after Pearl Harbor.[327]

On April 6, 2011 – American Sikh Day –- elected officials in Sacramento discussed the shooting in the context of other post-9/11 assaults targeting minority citizens. State senator Darryl Steinberg told the *Los Angeles Times* that such acts of violence would not be tolerated in the state of California.[328] Steinberg also donned a turban and urged others to do the same as a show of interfaith solidarity, telling the media that his action was inspired by the past heroism of the King of Denmark, who urged all his countrymen to wear the Star of David so that Jews could not be singled out during the Nazi period.[329]

Atwal eventually succumbed to his injuries on April 15, 2001, after experiencing multiple organ failure. The killing devastated Atwal's wife, who was paralyzed from a stroke she suffered three years previously. Atwal also left behind three sons, a daughter, and ten grandchildren. Family members were particularly distraught that Atwal died before recovering the ability to speak, unable to say goodbye or provide information about the shooting.[330] According to the *Sacramento Bee*, Kamaljit Atwal told the the that he remembered his father as a loving family man, a bookworm, and a Obama supporter who enjoyed political discussions.[331]

Local law enforcement officers investigated the double homicide as a possible hate crime, linked to the wave of xenophobia unleashed by 9/11. Since approximately 3,000 Sikhs lived in Elk Grove at the time of the attack, police decided to increase patrols in areas frequented by South Asians to prevent other assaults. To help solve the case, Muslim, Jewish, Hindu, and Japanese-American groups offered a $50,000 reward to encourage community members to cooperate with authorities, since the attack may have been visible to passing motorists. Crime Alert Sacramento contributed an additional $10,000 to the reward fund for information proving that the shooting was motivated by ethnic or religious bias. According to Elk grove department spokesman Christopher Trim, investigating officers asked community members to be on the lookout for a tan or light brown 1999 to 2003 Fort F-150 pickup truck, since this vehicle was seen in the vicinity of the crime scene.[332] Because of the high-profile nature of the case, the FBI chose to assist in the investigation. Since the shooter was still at large, Northern California Sikhs remained concerned for their safety. Ten years after 9/11, elderly Sikh men in Elk Grove reported being so afraid of another bias-motivated fatal shooting that they stopped socializing in public settings.[333]

CHAPTER ELEVEN:

75 REASONS WHY BACKLASH HATE CRIMES ARE UNDERCOUNTED

The previous chapters explored some of the manifestations of the 9/11 backlash. The crimes discussed constitute just the tip of the iceberg. In a 2002 study for the Human Rights Watch, Amardeep Singh and Johnathan Horowitz estimated that approximately 6,000 9/11 backlash hate crimes went unreported in the months following the terror strikes.[1] These researchers were disturbed that bias-crime tracking was voluntary for some states, making it difficult to get accurate national numbers.[2] After investigating hate crime reporting in six states, Singh and Horowitz determined that New York did the worst job tabulating bias-motivated attacks. Their report highlights the importance of getting local, state, and federal agencies to work together to improve tracking, so that national statistics accurately reflect the numbers of hate crimes.

In the years following 9/11, there was a large discrepancy between anti-Sikh attacks logged by researchers and those recorded by federal agencies. The *Los Angeles Times* reported the results of a November 2010 survey finding that 10% of Sikhs in nine Bay Area counties had been victims of hate crimes, with the majority involving physical attacks motivated by bias.[3] If the 10% figure is somewhat representative of the actual percentage of Sikhs being victimized across the U.S., it suggests that there could be as many as 30,000 to 100,000 anti-Sikh hate crimes occurring nationally, out of a total population of 300,000 to 1,000,000 religious practitioners. Even if these estimates are off by a factor of 10, with only one in a hundred U.S. Sikhs being attacked out of bias, they still suggest that anti-Sikh hate crimes number in the thousands, considerably higher than official governmental records indicate. In many instances, anti-Sikh attacks were triggered by anti-Muslim sentiment, making it difficult to segregate these bias crimes into discrete categories.

Some writers have looked at low federal tallies of hate crimes and concluded that some minority groups face relatively little discrimination in the U.S. In my introduction, I briefly discussed Jeff Jacoby's December 8, 2010 *Boston Globe* article, "The 'Islamophobia' Myth."[4] In this opinion piece, Jacoby argues that Muslims experienced comparatively few hate crimes in America. He calls attention to 2009 federal statistics, claiming that 14,000 U.S. law enforcement agencies logged a total of only 128 religious crimes against Muslims.[5] Jacoby also points out that in 2001, the FBI reported only 481 anti-Muslim crimes.[6] From this data, he concludes that the 9/11 backlash was highly exaggerated, that Muslims are rarely victimized by bias crimes, and that American Islamophobia is essentially a fabrication. Jacoby fails to consider the discrepancy between actual and reported crimes, or the various factors that cause disempowered minority communities to underreport bias-motivated attacks to governmental officials.

Activists and researchers alike recognize the difficulties involved in accurately counting hate crimes. In an interview with the *Los Angeles Times*, FBI agent Chris Davis acknowledged that law enforcement officers did not have an accurate picture of the scope of bias attacks, and that hate crime statistics were often unreliable.[7]

Civil rights attorneys were even more wary of official counts of bias-motivated crimes. Mark Potok of the Southern Poverty Law Center told the *Los Angeles Times* that hate crime statistics were so fouled up that accurate figures are practically impossible to ascertain.[8] Despite these problems, Potok recognized the importance of trying to determine how many hate crimes were occurring so that policymakers and police officers could take appropriate action.[9]

There are dozens of reasons why local, state, and national post-9/11 hate crime statistics are unreliable. The actual magnitude of the 9/11 backlash and the extent of xenophobia in America cannot be properly grasped without understanding the various impediments to the reporting and recording of U.S. bias attacks against Muslims, Christian Arabs, Sikhs, and Hindus. This chapter challenges 9/11 backlash deniers and Islamophobia minimizers by exploring 75 factors contributing to the undercounting of hate crimes targeting Middle Eastern and South Asian groups in the U.S.

1) Arab, Muslim, and South Asian bias-crime victims are reluctant to report hate crimes to local police in areas where departments are perceived as racist.

Historically, American police departments have had strained relationships with minority communities, especially black Muslims. Because of their mistrust of local law enforcement agencies, dark-skinned orthodox Muslims in the U.S. and members of the Nation of Islam are often hesitant to report hate crimes to police officers. Throughout the 1990s, The *New York Amsterdam News* published dozens of news stories about conflicts between Nation of Islam members and area cops. In these articles, the Nation of Islam is depicted sympathetically and law enforcement personnel are characterized as bigoted thugs. For example, a January 15, 1994 article claimed that police officers from the 25th precinct violated department policy by entering Muhammad's Mosque 7 with guns drawn in response to a bogus 911 call about a robbery in progress.[10] Angry about the intrusion, 1500 people attended a rally demanding the police apologize to worshippers for interrupting prayer services.[11]

Police officers sometimes harassed Nation of Islam members when they were praying in their homes. The *New York Amsterdam News* claimed that approximately 30 Newark police officers invaded the home of Malik and Adilah Karriem on February 17, 1996, interrupting 40 worshippers attending Ramadan celebrations.[12] This publication reported that the officers entered the house without a warrant and maced women and children with pepper spray, compelling Adilah Karriem, her daughter-in-law, and fifteen other women to go to the hospital for treatment.[13] When the residents pointed out that the intrusion was particularly unwelcome during Ramadan, one officer allegedly used profanity, declaring that "he didn't give a fuck" what month it was.[14] The police eventually realized that they were at the wrong address, accidentally storming into 48 Georgia Village instead of 66 Georgia King Village.

The *New York Amsterdam News* also took issue with a police officer's controversial shooting of a Nation of Islam teenager. On January 11, 2004, a New York City police officer gunned down 17-year old Shuaid Abdul Latif. The officer involved claimed self-defense, although there were eight other armed policemen and a German shepherd police dog present at the time.[15] According to the *New York Amsterdam News*, no gun was found on the mortally-injured black teenager, who was only 5'4" and 125 lbs.[16] A female witness claimed that Latif was trying to surrender when he was shot in the basement, and his autopsy revealed that he was not on drugs at the time of his death.[17]

Whereas the *New York Amsterdam News* almost always portrayed Nation of Islam worshippers as innocent victims of police harassment, other newspapers favored the police officers' version of events. These conflicting accounts highlight tensions between the Nation of Islam and the NYPD, and reveal why black Muslims often avoid contacting law enforcement officers in response to bias crimes.

In addition to problems with the Nation of Islam, some police departments have had strained relations with orthodox Muslim groups. In chapter five, I discuss how Muslims in Illinois were disappointed by what they saw as the local police's racist response to a June 6, 1995 arson that gutted the Islamic Society of Greater Springfield Center Masjid. Rather than investigate the deliberately-set fire as a hate crime, the local police speculated that worshippers may have had something to do with the blaze. Instead of interviewing members of local hate groups, the responding officers asked worshippers to take polygraph tests to determine whether they were responsible for the arson. Adil Rahman, a member of the mosque's board of directors, told the *State Journal Register* that he was shocked that the police would focus their attention on the victimized Muslims, particularly since there was no evidence implicating them in the burning of their prayer center and the destruction of their sacred books.[18]

After 9/11, relations between police and "suspect" minorities worsened. Since many NYPD officers were killed in the Twin Towers, some police officers around the country might have consciously or unconsciously vented their anger at local Muslims. In the aftermath of 9/11, Muslim problems with police officers skyrocketed. A September 18, 2001 article in the *Denver Post* reported that Arab-Americans and Muslims filed dozens of complaints against police officers in the days following the terrorist strikes.[19] Greg

Slade, director of Florida's Police Abuse Center, received a record number of complaints in the aftermath of 9/11, averaging ten a day in the first week.[20] Across the country, officers were mourning the loss of the 9/11 victims, who included 23 NYPD officers as well as 37 Port Authority and New Jersey officers and EMTs. On occasion, law enforcement personnel blamed U.S. Muslims for the terrorist strikes, and treated them like possible collaborators. Because of strained relations, minority victims were often reluctant to contact local law enforcement agencies to report hate crimes, worried that doing so might mean inviting trouble.

The police even harassed an Arab-American boy scout troop shortly after 9/11. According to an October 19, 2001 article in the *Boston Globe*, the incident began when Dearborn scoutmaster Khalil Baydoun was accompanying scouts Mustafa, Kaseem, and Jihad on a leadership retreat in northern Michigan.[21] When the scoutmaster and the boys were returning to their campground by ferry, the boat operator called 911 and reported that there were suspicious-looking Arabs on board. The police intercepted the disembarking scouts, held them, and interrogated them for 90 minutes. Baydoun, a Lebanese-American, was told that he needed to produce his passport for the FBI or face detention.[22] Baydoun argued that as a U.S. citizen, he never carried his passport with him. Although troop members were eventually allowed to leave, the experience left them feeling violated. Baydoun told the *Boston Globe* that the racial profiling deeply troubled him, making him feel like a cockroach in his own country.[23] Baydoun discussed the humiliating ordeal with his scouts, hoping it would give them a better understanding of the discrimination that African-Americans and other more visible minority groups routinely experienced in the U.S.[24]

Police harassment took a psychological toll on Arab-Americans and South Asians. Almost a year after 9/11, 60-year old Zubair Haq told the *Houston Chronicle* that he developed a phobia of police officers.[25] He started becoming frightened whenever he saw law enforcement personnel in uniform, even though he was the son of a police officer and was not involved in any criminal activity. On one occasion, he became unreasonably alarmed when he saw two beat cops enter the library, irrationally frightened that they would ask to see his green card and take him into custody if they thought he looked suspicious.[26]

Police officers' willingness to put Muslim and Sikh cab drivers in dangerous situations fostered the perception that cops were not interested in "serving and protecting" minority groups. On some occasions, officers took liberties with minority cabbies' safety by arranging for them to drive home violent drunks. In chapter seven, I discussed how Seattle police endangered cabdriver Sukhvir Singh when they asked him to drive home Luis Vazquez, a severely-intoxicated man who had been kicked out of a football game in 2007. While transporting the inebriated passenger, Vazquez bit, choked, and threatened to kill Singh, calling the South Asian driver an "Iraqi terrorist." [27] Instead of worrying about the well-being of cabbies, state patrolman Jeff Merrill defended the police policy, explaining that its objective was to provide safe transport for intoxicated people.[28] This type of police insensitivity made some Muslims and Sikhs question whether their safety was a top law enforcement priority.

Relations between local police and ethnic groups worsened in parts of the country where officers routinely racially-profiled minority civilians. In chapter ten, I discussed how Miami officer Adam Tavss shot and killed Husein Shehada, a vacationing Palestinian-American Muslim, on June 14, 2009, while responding to a 911 call about a Hispanic male carrying a gun. Shehada's shooting outraged Arabs and Muslims around the world, further undermining minority communities' faith in American law enforcement.

2) Many Middle Easterners and South Asians in the U.S. are reluctant to report hate crimes to local authorities because many of these immigrants come from countries where police officers are viewed as capricious and violent thugs.

In some parts of the Middle East and South Asia, police officers occasionally torture innocent people during crime investigations. Amnesty International has documented numerous examples of police brutality in these regions. On occasion, victims reporting unrelated crimes were beaten to illicit false confessions to close other cases. For example, in the spring of 2002, Amnesty International investigated the case of an Arab man who was physically mistreated at a police station in Alexandria, Egypt after he went to report that his 12-year old daughter had run away from home following an argument with her step-mother.[29] Simply because his child was missing, police officers made the concerned father the central suspect in the murder of a nine-year old girl in the area, and beat the innocent man to compel him to confess to the killing. The man's runaway daughter was later discovered alive and well at a neighborhood orphanage, where she had been taken by a good Samaritan after she was found sitting unattended in a park. Even after his daughter had been recovered, police continued to keep the father in jail as a murder suspect in the other case, although there was no evidence whatsoever linking him to any crime. When his ex-wife brought the repentant runaway girl to the police station to prove that the imprisoned father never harmed her, officers seized both of them, accusing them of lying. They also threatened to assault the man's ex-wife in front of him unless he finally admitted to killing the nine-year old girl. Immigrants coming from countries where this type of police misconduct is rampant might be reluctant to enter U.S. police stations to report hate crimes.

3) Hate crimes are sometimes undercounted when U.S. police officers or their relatives commit bias crimes.

Arresting officers are sometimes reluctant to add bias enhancements when investigating physical assaults committed by cops or their accused relatives, undermining minority victims' faith in the criminal justice system. In chapter seven, I described how retired cop Richard Vitale, his sons, and their friends ducked hate crime charges in Long Island after they harassed two Turkish gas station workers and attacked them while screaming that the aliens should get out of the country. In the aftermath of this incident, outraged internet bloggers speculated that the perpetrators were able to dodge bias enhancements because of Vitale's police connections.[30] It is difficult for minority community members to trust law enforcement officials when they hear stories about a retired cop, his sons, and their friends dodging hate crime charges even though they screamed nativist comments while attacking immigrants with an American flag and pole on election day 2010 in front of active-duty officers and other witnesses.

4) Arab-Americans, South Asians, and Muslims are underrepresented on the police force, making difficult for officers to investigate hate crimes in these minority communities.

Many American immigrants from the Middle East and South Asia view "police officer" as a relatively low-status occupation. For this reason, they do not encourage relatives in the U.S. to join the force, hoping instead that their sons or daughters will become doctors, engineers, or professors. Muslims and Sikhs who became law-enforcement personnel sometimes face discrimination by their peers and superiors, making it difficult to rise in the ranks. With so few Muslims and Sikhs on the job, many minority groups do not have access to sympathetic officers who can navigate linguistic and cultural barriers. Consequently, many hate crimes are not properly investigated or documented.

5) Police officers are sometimes poorly-trained or incompetent, undermining victims' confidence in the utility of reporting bias crimes to authorities.

Because minorities in America are unwilling to report hate crimes to police departments, many attacks go unrecorded. In some parts of the country, local authorities have a bad track record closing bias cases. According to the *New York Daily News*, the Richmond Hill 102nd Precinct received reports of at least 10 bigotry-motivated attacks after 9/11, but none of the perpetrators had been prosecuted as of June 2004.[31]

Inept police officers lose credibility in minority communities, particularly when investigators have difficulty recognizing obvious hate crimes. In chapter four, I discussed how two San Diego men attacked Swaran Kaur Bhullar, a turban-wearing Sikh woman sitting in her convertible on September 30, 2001. While stabbing Bhullar in the neck, her assailants screamed, "This is what you get for what you've done to us! I'm going to slash your throat."[32] Rather than viewing the attack in the context of the 9/11 backlash, Detective Sharlene Ramirez failed to find any motive in the unprovoked assault. In a December 2001 interview with the *San*

Diego Union Tribune, Ramirez claimed that she had exhausted all leads in her investigation, and concluded that the attack was likely the product of road rage.[33] Minority crime victims might hesitate to report hate crimes to such ignorant investigators. In the same chapter, I discussed how police detectives in Lemon Grove, California were unable to recognize the bias motivation that precipitated an attack on a Muslim man outside of a mosque in October, 2001. Although a witness heard one of the assailants shout anti-Muslim slurs, responding officers characterized the incident as just an ordinary stabbing.[34]

Years after the terrorist strikes, police investigators continued to downplay or dismiss community hate crimes out of ignorance or apathy. In chapter four, I discussed a January 2006 bias-motivated assault on an 80-year old Sikh in Yuba City, California. Although the assailants yelled racial epithets while attacking the victim, the responding officer was unwilling to acknowledge or investigate the possible bias motivation of the perpetrators.

Some Arabs, Muslims, and South Asians were shocked at the lengths that investigating authorities were willing to go to deny that minority-owned businesses were being attacked in hate crimes. In chapter seven, I described a November 24, 2004 arson attack on a Sikh-owned Chevron gas station in which vandals covered nearby dumpsters with bigoted graffiti, including "Go back to bin Laden Bitch," "Never Again Indian Monkey Nigger," and "F—k Arab Gas."[35] Despite these obvious indications that the Richmond, Virginia attack was bias-motivated, some investigators speculated that the vandalism and the fire may have been separate crimes, committed by different perpetrators, coincidentally taking place in temporal proximity.

Police also lost credibility by failing to treat attacks on religious sites as hate crimes. In chapter five, I discussed six different hate crimes targeting the Islamic Center of the East Bay between 2005 and 2007. Although one incident involved a gunman firing seven bullets into the house of worship, police Lt. John Vanderklugt refused to believe that the escalating mosque attacks were bias-motivated.[36] Hate crimes go uncounted when clueless investigating authorities discount them.

Lazy police officers also alienated minority citizens by neglecting to protect repeatedly-targeted houses of worship. In chapter five, I described how vandals attacked the same Fresno Sikh temple five nights in succession in 2003. A more astute or responsive police force might have been able to recognize the daily attack pattern and apprehend the suspects. In many instances, incompetent or overworked police officers refused to put at-risk buildings under surveillance and failed to investigate hate crimes until they were pressured into doing so by advocacy groups, poisoning community relations.

Police officers also lost credibility by showing an unwillingness to take proactive steps to prevent hate crimes. Also in chapter five, I discussed how police officer Eric Syphers failed to deter Brent Matthews after learning of his immanent plans to roll a pig's head into a Lewiston mosque in 2008. Local Muslims were infuriated by Syphers' inability to prevent the attack, as well as the discovery that other officers laughed at Matthews' ingenuity when learning of the hate crime. These types of incidents erode minority communities' confidence in the police, reducing the likelihood that victims will report future bias-motivated attacks to local authorities.

6) Poor police response time erodes minorities' faith in authorities, undermining their willingness to report hate crimes.

On several occasions, police officers did not respond quickly when minorities were being brutally assaulted by gangs of bigots. In chapter four, I described how two South Asian Sikhs were savagely beaten while waiting more than 30 minutes for police to respond to repeated 911 calls for help. Because the July 11, 2004 attack continued without interruption for half an hour, Rajinder Singh Khalsa suffered multiple contusions, abrasions, swelling, orbital fractures, vision damage, and other facial injuries. Khalsa told *India Abroad* that he was outraged that the police took so long to arrive at the scene of the crime, indicating that officers did not consider it a top priority.[37]

Police also took their time answering distress calls made by Arabs and Muslims. In chapter eight, I discussed how the Detroit police failed to respond to five urgent 911 calls about ten white assailants viciously assaulting an Arab-American homeowner in the winter of 2006. After gang-beating him for more than ten

minutes, the assailants finally fled when the ambulance arrived. Poor response time dampens community relations and makes minority victims less likely to inform police of bias-motivated attacks.

7) Hate crimes are often undocumented when police investigators are often more focused on arresting suspects than proving intent.

Overworked detectives sometimes concentrate their efforts on apprehending criminals instead of documenting what prompted their crimes. Many police investigators believe that "catching the bad guys and locking them up" is their job, not exploring or proving what factors motivated an assault. Many officers become so preoccupied with "closing the case" that they neglect to get supplemental witness testimony documenting a perpetrator's hate-based motivation. This ends up creating a disparity between the numbers of hate crimes taking place and the number of cases where bias is proven in a court of law, depressing hate crime statistics. Although detectives are evaluated on their ability to solve crimes, they have no extra professional incentive to establish that an incident was triggered by bias. Many detectives fail to collect and log evidence that could be used to prove bigotry factored into an attack, particularly if other physical evidence at a crime scene clearly establishes a perpetrator's guilt.

8) Hate crimes are undercounted when police and prosecutors fail to charge young offenders with bias-motivated attacks.

Both before and after 9/11, authorities often allowed youths to commit hate crimes with impunity. In chapter two, I described how police responded inappropriately when teen mobs repeatedly stoned and injured congregants outside of a mosque in 1992. Rather than appreciate the serious nature of the bias-motivated assault, police and prosecutors refused to acknowledge that the youthful offenders were committing a hate crime when they threw projectiles at Muslims during Ramadan.

After 9/11, police officers across the country continued to allow young offenders to commit bias crimes without facing serious consequences. In chapter five, I discussed how St. Louis police officers easily accepted the specious explanation that the local teens who firebombed a Hindu temple did so simply because they were bored. When teenagers have nothing to do, they normally listen to music, text their friends, or spend hours on the internet; they don't find a weapon, travel to a nearby Hindu temple, and firebomb it. Because Hindu prayer centers are uncommon in Missouri, it is highly improbable that the arsonists' choice of a non-Christian religious site was simply random. Investigating officers illogically concluded that bored criminals were somehow incapable of committing hate crimes, viewing boredom and bigotry as mutually-exclusive categories.

On many occasions, police officers were more concerned about the welfare of young offenders than their minority victims. In chapter five, I discussed how San Antonio police officers and prosecutors were unwilling to charge four young assailants with a hate crime after they ransacked a mosque in March 2004 and wrote anti-Muslim slogans and pro-American messages on the walls. Lubbock police publicly speculated that hate crime convictions might ruin the futures of the young offenders. Ignoring the nativist and Islamophobic graffiti, investigators absurdly concluded that the mosque vandalism was not committed because of personal, political, or religious bias against Muslims.[38] Prosecutors also gave the young perpetrators a pass. Matt Powell, the assistant district attorney of Lubbock county, was unwilling to press hate crime charges against the 14 and 15 year old teens who vandalized the Islamic Center of South Plains. Rather than hold these offenders accountable, Powell referred to them as the "least culpable suspects."[39] Although the mosque attack caused approximately $12,000 in damage, two of the teen perpetrators received probation. In areas where police and prosecutors have a poor track record of holding young criminals accountable, minority communities might be less willing to report hate crimes to unsympathetic officers.

9) Police officers often fail to take hate crimes seriously, discouraging victims from filing charges.

In many cases, authorities refused to investigate obvious bias-motivated attacks. In chapter four, I described how Derar Ahmad, a Palestinian Floridian, was threatened and assaulted by a fellow shopper at Sam's Club in Clearwater.[40] Although witnesses heard the religious slurs that precipitated the 2007 assault, Cpl. Robert Fava did not file a complaint or document the incident. Even after the *Petersburg Times* drew attention to the way the police mishandled the situation, the department refused to initiate an internal review. Police spokesman Wayne Shelor maintained that if Ahmad was unhappy, it was his responsibility to follow up on the matter.

Other victimized minorities found local authorities equally unresponsive. Also in chapter four, I described how police officers discouraged Asma Sidani, a Muslim woman, from pressing charges after an irate man made religious slurs, spat at her children, and threatened her family at a Taco Bell restaurant in May 2007.[41] Although witnesses waited for the police to arrive, the responding officer refused to take their statements or file a report. These types of incidents illustrate how local authorities often fail to appreciate the severity of bias-motivated crimes, eroding minority victims' willingness to report attacks.

Police officers have also dissuaded Sikhs from filing hate crime reports, trivializing bias-motivated crimes that do little property damage. In chapter eight, I explored how Orange County police acted dismissively after Arinder Chadha found an anti-Sikh pornographic drawing on his driveway. Instead of understanding the threatening nature of the graffiti, investigators failed to appreciate the significance of the disturbing picture because it did not permanently damage the homeowner's property. These types of news stories make minority community members reluctant to turn to the police for protection.

10) Hate crimes are undercounted when parents shield victimized children from upsetting legal proceedings.

When children are attacked by bigots, their parents sometimes refuse to allow them to go to police stations to identify their attackers or face their assailants in court. To save their offspring from a defense attorney's ruthless cross-examination and the trauma of reliving a bias crime, parents sometimes withdraw their children from legal proceedings. In chapter four, I discussed how 60-year old school bus driver Thomas Plaisted shoved and spat on Muslim youngsters at a Taco Bell restaurant.[42] The victims' parents decided not to subject their children to the unpleasant experience of testifying against Plaisted in court. When young witnesses are withdrawn from legal proceedings, prosecutors are unable to procure convictions, resulting in lower hate crime statistics.

11) Minorities may also be reluctant to press hate crime charges in areas where district attorneys fail to take bias-motivated crimes to court.

In the immediate aftermath of 9/11, prosecutors in Chicago were unwilling to file hate crime charges in response to backlash attacks. Arab-American attorneys in the city logged 43 hate crimes in the first two weeks after 9/11; months later, the district attorney had not prosecuted any of them, even though some of the attacks were serious offenses.[43] In chapter seven, I discussed how vandals attacked an Arab-American community center and rampaged down Harlem Ave., shattering windows of 18 Arab-owned stores.[44] Because prosecutors were unwilling to file hate crime charges in the months following the backlash, most of these crimes were not included in official statistics, leaving many of the city's 180,000 Arabs feeling unsafe and unprotected.[45] Hate-crime perpetrators in Bridgeview, Illinois also escaped punishment. In chapter five, I discussed a particularly troubling incident involving a mob waving Confederate flags in front of the Bridgeview Mosque, chanting "Death to Arabs!"[46] The vast majority of perpetrators were not held accountable for threatening the lives of Muslim worshippers.

Because intention is difficult to prove in court, many prosecutors are reluctant to file hate crime charges, worried that convictions might get reversed on appeal. In an October 11, 2001 article in the *Los Angeles Times*,

Michael Gennaco, former head of the city's hate crime unit, explained that many state prosecutors were unwilling to file hate enhancements because they were legally complex, making it hard to procure convictions.[47]

12) Plea bargains reduce the numbers of documented hate crimes against Muslims, Arabs, and Sikhs.

District attorneys sometimes drop hate crime enhancements as an incentive to get defendants to plead guilty to lesser charges, saving the time and expense of taking a case to trial. Although this allows prosecutors to keep their conviction rates high, it results in the undercounting of bias attacks. In chapter nine, I discussed how two felony hate crime charges were dropped after Frank Stacy Abbotts agreed to plead guilty to repeatedly phoning the Islamic Development Center in Moreno Valley and threatening to kill worshippers.[48] The plea bargain also stipulated that if Abbotts completed his probation, the one remaining felony count would be reduced to a misdemeanor, even though a police search uncovered handguns, rifles, ammunition, and white supremacist materials at his home.[49] These types of legal arrangements result in fewer bias crime convictions.

13) Hate crime statistics are also compromised because many minority victims are afraid to report assaults to federal law enforcement agencies, which they view with suspicion.

Many Arab-Americans and Muslims are distrustful of the FBI, believing that the agency routinely spies on mosques, wiretaps phones, photographs peace activists, and detains immigrants without due process. Because the FBI has put activist organizations under surveillance in the past, many minority citizens worry that they will get on a government watch list or be racially profiled at airports if they self-identify as Arab or Muslim while reporting a hate crime. The FBI's willingness to single out "suspect" ethnic or religious communities undermines its credibility as an investigative agency combating U.S. hate crimes, since minorities are unwilling to contact an organization that has racially profiled them in the past.

Even before 9/11, many Arab-Americans and Muslims regarded the FBI with distrust. According to the *Arab American News*, the FBI spent the last few decades of the 20th century violating the rights of Arab-Americans instead of protecting them.[50] Under the Nixon administration, federal investigators instigated Operation Boulder, a three-year program targeting hundreds of Arab-American leaders and activists.[51] In the 1970s and 80s, the FBI continued its extensive surveillance of Arab-Americans and Arab residents, uncovering no illegal activities and undermining minority communities' faith in the federal agency.[52]

In the immediate aftermath of 9/11, the FBI interviewed more than 5,000 Middle Easterners in the U.S., causing many Arabs and Muslims to fear federal investigators.[53] In a November 23, 2001 *New York Times* article, Haitham Bundakji, a Jordanian-born Muslim chaplain who lived in the U.S. for 33 years, reported that the FBI interviews reminded him of the undemocratic police states of the Middle East.[54]

After the passage of the Patriot Act, Arab-Americans and Muslims became even more distrustful of the FBI, regarding it as a domestic spying agency that was eroding their civil liberties. Many minorities felt that FBI surveillance undermined their constitutionally-protected rights, turning the U.S. into an intolerant place, reminiscent of the Soviet Union of the 1970s.[55]

Rajbir Singh Datta, associate director of SALDEF, told *India-West* that many poor South Asian and Arab communities in America were particularly alarmed by the FBI raids, which involved the arrest of thousands of non-violent immigrants.[56] In the winter 2002/2003 issue of Oakland's *Colorlines*, Samer Hamouni recounted how his Syrian family was traumatized by an FBI raid in February 2002.[57] Although Hamouni and his family had been living in the U.S. since receiving asylum in 1992, they attracted the attention of the FBI because Hamouni's father had been a pilot in Syria. Because the 9/11 hijackers flew planes into buildings, federal investigators decided to investigate airline personnel from the Middle East. FBI agents stormed into Hamouni's home at 5:00 a.m., detaining both of his elderly parents and his 20-year old sister.[58] Seven months after the FBI raid, his mother, father, and sister remained in detention. Hamouni was particularly alarmed about the health of his mother, who had Crohn's disease and had recently discovered a lump in her breast. Because of the stress of the detention, her health was rapidly failing. Hamouni expressed his anger at the FBI and INS at a September 21, 2002 'Justice for All' conference, condemning the organizations for the unlawful arrest and detention of his family.[59]

Some Arab-Americans and Muslims were alarmed that the FBI's counter-terrorism team occasionally searched their homes and offices without disclosing the grounds for the warrants, which were under federal seal. In March 2002, the FBI searched 14 residences and businesses in Virginia and Georgia, but did not uncover any incriminating information leading to an arrest.[60] Laura Jaghlit, a high school English teacher from Fairfax station, told the *Charleston Gazette* that during a raid on her home, the FBI combed through photos of her children, threw the content of draws on furniture, and seized her family's computer, credit cards, passports, and bank account information.[61] She characterized the FBI raid as un-American. These types of encounters undermine minority communities' faith in the FBI, and lead to an underreporting of hate crimes to this agency.

Many Arab-Americans and Muslims were also troubled by FBI harassment at airports. In a June 23, 2002 article in the *San Diego Union-Tribune*, Arab-American journalist Bina Ahmad described the humiliation she felt after she was told that an FBI agent wished to speak to her after she went through security screening at San Francisco international airport.[62] Afraid that she would be put in detention for refusing, she answered the agent's questions about her ethnicity, educational background, occupation, and organizational affiliations. The racial profiling left her feeling like a second-class citizen.

Minority communities were also wary of how the FBI portrayed them in the press. The July 12, 2002 issue of the *Philadelphia Daily News* published an article with the title, "FBI Searching for al-Qaeda's Hidden U.S. Support Network."[63] These types of stories, full of baseless innuendos, undermine Muslims' confidence in the FBI by suggesting that minority Americans are part of a web of terror spread out across the country.

During the Iraq War, the FBI's reputation in many minority communities worsened. According to the April 1, 2003 issue of the *San Francisco Chronicle*, approximately 11,000 Iraqi immigrants had been interrogated in the national FBI program to ferret out terrorists.[64] Immigration attorney Ban al-Wardi told *India-West* that he was disturbed by many of the questions the FBI asked Iraqis in America, including: 'What are your opinions on the war?' 'Do you support Saddam Hussein?' 'Do you own weapons of mass destruction, like chemical poison or lethal gas?'[65] Al-Wardi maintained that these type of FBI questions sent immigrants the message that their political views were being watched and their religious activities were being monitored. Many activists questioned the utility of these intrusive interrogations, pointing out that it was ridiculous to suppose that a terrorist would stupidly disclose information about a weapon of mass destruction simply by being asked.

According to a January 12, 2006 *New York Times* article, Arabs and Muslims speculated that the FBI was holding hate crime forums as a ruse to conduct secret monitoring of their communities.[66] Some activists expressed concern over the FBI's clandestine program to monitor radiation levels at Muslim-owned buildings around the country, and the inconsistent ways in which the FBI treated 'suspect' minority communities. The *New York Times* reported that each of the FBI's 56 field offices had a separate approach to dealing with Arab-Americans and Muslims in their areas, indicating that the governmental agency had no cohesive program.[67]

Relations with the FBI deteriorated further when Muslim Americans discovered that the agency had been infiltrating mosques and schools, threatening to deport immigrants unless they acted as informants. According to the *Los Angeles Times*, three separate incidents caused friction between Southern California Muslims and the FBI.[68] In 2004, the FBI arrested the popular head on an Anaheim mosque on immigration-related charges and held him for two years before a judge ordered his release.[69] In 2006, an FBI agent told a Newport Beach business group that his agency had put Muslim university students in the area under surveillance.[70] In 2007, an FBI agent assaulted a Muslim UC Irvine student with his car near a campus demonstration.[71] These events further strained relations between area Muslims and the FBI.

In 2009, relations between American Muslims and the FBI grew more tense. The *San Francisco Chronicle* reported that American Muslim groups were upset that the FBI named 300 different individuals and groups as "unindicted co-conspirators" in their investigation into the Holy Land Foundation for Relief and Development.[72] Because they were not officially charged with anything, the individuals and groups mentioned by the federal agency had no opportunity to clear themselves. As a result of ongoing harassment, American Muslim groups circulated a 2009 petition urging their members to limit social outreach with the FBI as long as the agency continued to treat worshippers unfairly.

American Muslims were also disturbed by the FBI's involvement in other forms of intrusive monitoring. In the fall of 2010, a California mechanic discovered a secret tracking device in a car owned by Yasir Afifi, a Santa Clara resident and college student.[73] When Afifi posted pictures of the device online, federal agents demanded that the device be returned to the Bureau.[74] In response, Afifi filed a lawsuit, arguing that his Constitutional rights had been violated. Bay Area Muslims held a press conference in response to the incident, outraged by the warrantless surveillance and the ongoing racial profiling of American Muslims.

Rather than re-thinking its treatment of U.S. Muslims, the FBI continued its offensive tactics. In December 2010, the *Washington Post* reported that Muslims were outraged when they learned that the FBI sent convicted forger Craig Monteilh into the Islamic Center of Irvine to pose as a fundamentalist Muslim and entrap congregation members by making inflammatory statements.[75] Monteilh, who had been working as an informant since 2003, selected the Irvine mosque because it was near his home. FBI agents assigned him the name "Farouk al-Aziz," and paid him tens of thousands of dollars to assume the identity of a French Syrian.[76] Monteilh was also given a microphone and hidden camera to record congregants' conversations. Rather than uncovering a network of domestic terrorists, Monteilh's mission ended in failure. Worshippers were so disturbed by Monteilh's talk of violent jihad that they reported him to the FBI as a terrorist.[77] They also obtained a restraining order preventing him from returning to the mosque and harassing congregants. When they learned that Monteilh was in fact an FBI informant sent there to entrap them, they were outraged that their own government sent a convicted criminal to spy on them and disrespect their houses of worship.

Numerous American civil rights organizations took action against FBI mistreatment of minorities. The Discrimination and National Security Initiative and the Sikh Coalition wrote a Supreme Court amicus brief to support the case of Javaid Iqbal, a Pakistani native who was one of 1,000 New York area Muslims who was held without charges at a special facility in the aftermath of 9/11. *India-West* reported that Iqbal, who was regularly tortured during the two years he was in custody, decided to sue former Attorney General John Ashcroft and FBI Director Robert Mueller III, to discourage the abuse of innocent minorities.[78] These types of cases illustrate why hate crime victims are often reluctant to report attacks to federal investigators, resulting in an undercounting of bias crimes.

14) Disempowered American Muslims and Arabs underreport hate crimes when governmental interrogators are the perpetrators.

A September 19, 2006 article in the *Washington Post* found that 17% of CAIR's 1,972 hate crime complaints for 2005 were in the "due process" category.[79] According to Arsalan Iftikhar, the organization's legal director, many hate crime complaints were in response to overzealous federal interrogators using questionable tactics. A June 15, 2007 article in *India Abroad* claimed that the FBI began using harsh interrogation techniques from late 2002 onward, and that federal agents were present when dogs were used to intimidate prisoners or detainees who had not been formally charged with crimes.[80] An immigrant might be particularly afraid to walk into an FBI office to report a hate crime if the same organization had the power to hold him indefinitely and use coercive interrogation tactics without probable cause.

15) Many of the government's "anti-terrorism" policies undermine minority crime victims' willingness to report attacks to federal agents.

Many Arabs, Afghanis, Iranians, and South Asians were troubled by the U.S. government's passage of the Patriot Act, 'Operation Tarmac,' and the INS/DOJ's 'Alien Absconder Apprehension Initiative,' which involved the interrogation, secret detention, and deportation of Arab and Muslim men in the U.S.[81]

Immigrant communities were also wary of raids conducted by the INS, USDA, and U.S. Treasury Department. According to the winter 2002/2003 issue of Oakland's *Colorlines*, many Somalis in Washington state were traumatized by these intrusions.[82] Community activists in Seattle were particularly alarmed after federal agents dragged Somali men into detention, ransacked minority-owned grocery stores, and closed honest businesses for months on groundless charges of money laundering or food stamp mishandling.[83]

Minorities were also disturbed by the federal government's 'Special Registration' policy mandating that men over the age of 16 to report to local immigration authorities for interrogation and fingerprinting. Many civil rights organizations saw this as an example of governmental racial profiling since the requirement only applied to men from 25 Middle Eastern and South Asian countries.[84] Some unethical immigration lawyers used 'Special Registration' to generate revenue. Community activist Monami Maulik told *India-West* that unscrupulous New York attorneys told their clients to participate in the program so that their firms could charge tens of thousands of dollars in legal fees during the deportation proceedings.[85] Approximately 13,000 of the 83,000 men who complied were deported.[86] Even after community-based organizations like DRUM were successful in getting the 'Special Registration' program discontinued, its legacy undermined minorities' confidence in federal investigators.

Many immigrants were even more distrustful of the U.S. government after learning about abuses at Guantanamo and Abu Ghraib, such as the "waterboarding" of detainees, which sometimes resulted in cracked ribs. American military personnel also upset civil libertarians by threatening naked prisoners with dogs and photographing them in odd sexual groupings. These practices made many immigrant communities less willing to report hate crimes to U.S. government investigators.

16) Another central problem with hate crime statistics is due to the sheer number of advocacy groups taking incident reports, and organizations' failure to share information with one another.

There are hundreds of organizations involved with hate crime issues, including: the American Arab Anti-Discrimination Committee, American Muslim Council, Council on American Islamic Relations, Indian American Center for Political Awareness, National Association for the Advancement of Colored People, Sikh Coalition, Sikh Council On Racial Equality, and South Asian American Leaders of Tomorrow. Victims may not be sure which groups to contact when they are targeted by a racist assailant or religious bigot. Some organizations have higher regional or national profiles than others. Depending on administration priorities and budgetary limitations, these groups also put different emphases on the importance of collecting and tabulating hate crimes.

One of the main problems with hate crime reporting is that most community organizations do not exchange information. Victims might report a hate crime to one group and not another, unaware that most of these groups never pool information. Many victims mistakenly assume that reporting the incident once is enough, wrongly believing that ethnic and religious advocacy groups regularly pass along incident information to one other and to all relevant municipal, state, and federal authorities. Somewhat arbitrarily, an Egyptian-American might report a hate crime to CAIR, the ADC, the NAACP, or the AMC, depending on which organization has done the best outreach work. Consequently, each organization's annual hate crime statistics might include only a fraction of the true total of the specific ethnic or religious demographic group they are supposedly monitoring. Some victims mistakenly believe that the NAACP, the ADC, and CAIR are in constant communication with one another about hate crimes simultaneously affecting blacks, Arabs, and Muslims. In fact, most organizations lack the budgetary resources to allow staff members to dialogue extensively with other groups. Since most ethnic organizations do not have the investigative resources of the local police and the FBI, victims may be unaware that they need to call several agencies and report a hate crime multiple times to different non-profit groups.

In the aftermath of 9/11, hundreds of organizations across the country took hate crime reports, and few shared their information with others. As a result, there are no accurate numbers about how many backlash hate crimes actually took place. Since minority victims are more willing to report hate crimes to community groups than to federal authorities, many ethnic or religious organizations receive information about crimes that have gone unreported elsewhere.

India Abroad published some of the different hate crime statistics collected by community organizations and governmental agencies in the month following 9/11: "The Asian-American Legal Defense and Education Fund in New York has received 100 reports of hate and bias crimes... CAIR reports it has recorded over 750 anti-Muslim incidents since the attacks. The U.S. Commission on Civil Rights hot line has received 310 calls about anti-Arab or anti-Muslim incidents since September 13. A Sikh Web site set up to record hate crimes and harassment has received 274 reports. The FBI is investigating 90 hate crimes across the country..."[87]

At times, the failure of advocacy groups to communicate endangered minority residents. Following the July 11, 2004 beating of two Sikh men in Richmond, New York, ADL-NY spokesman Joel Leavy complimented the police for their fast response to the attack.[88] Leavy was apparently unaware that it took the police more than a half hour to respond to urgent calls pertaining to the prolonged and brutal attack. If advocacy groups communicated more effectively, they could work together to ensure that police responded quickly to all hate crimes.

17) An accurate picture of hate crimes in the U.S. is difficult to obtain because reporting organizations employ different criteria about what constitutes a hate crime.

Some community groups might be more interested in drawing attention to racism or religious bigotry instead of adhering to complicated legal or governmental distinctions between bias-motivated incidents and hate crimes. For example, one ethnic organization might include the public burning of a Quran in its annual hate crimes report; another group might view the incident as protected free speech and omit it from its statistics.

18) Many civil rights groups have become unwilling to forward hate crime reports to federal investigators, resulting in an undercounting of bias attacks.

Because groups like the American-Arab Anti-Discrimination Committee and CAIR have had strained relations with the FBI, staff members are hesitant or unwilling to forward hate crime reports to federal investigators. Arab-American and Muslim civil rights groups have taken issue with the FBI's willingness to wiretap innocent minority citizens and infiltrate mosques. To protect the confidentiality of members who distrust FBI agents, many organizations do not share information about hate crimes with federal investigators. As a result, governmental statistics fail to reflect the totality of bias attacks taking place across the country.

19) Victims of hate crimes sometimes fail to report attacks because they are unsure about which federal agency is the proper one to contact, especially when organizations have overlapping areas of jurisdiction.

Hate crime victims may be uncertain about which governmental organizations to notify following a bias attack, unsure about whether the FBI and the Department of Homeland Security share the task of monitoring domestic terrorist groups like the KKK. Some victims might be unaware that particular government agencies handle different types of hate crimes. For example, the Board of Education oversees hate crimes on campuses. The ATF investigates arsons, including those motivated by bias. The Department of Transportation monitors crimes (including racist or religious attacks) taking place on airplanes, buses, and interstate highways.

In some instances, the heads of particular government agencies determine whether hate crimes falling under their jurisdiction are a central or a peripheral concern. Minority members might be more likely to report hate crimes to governmental departments if their presiding officer is perceived to be minority-friendly. For example, after 9/11, the Japanese-American head of the Department of Transportation issued memorandums reminding employees that racial profiling of Arabs and Muslims was unfair and illegal. Consequently, victims of bias crimes might be particularly likely to report incidents to this agency, since its head was widely perceived as being sympathetic to minority concerns. After 9/11, many Arabs and Muslims in America became concerned that the Department of Homeland Security and the FBI were violating the civil rights of immigrant communities. Consequently, some hate crime victims might have hesitated in reporting bias crimes to employees of these federal agencies.

On occasion, different federal agencies refused to share information on hate crimes. On September 17, 2001, the U.S. Commission on Civil Rights established a hotline for Middle Easterners and Muslims to report ethnic intimidation, hate crimes, and other civil rights infractions. Between September 17 and October 9, 2001, it received over 440 calls, including reports of 137 serious hate crimes.[89] Because of the confidential nature of the hotline, the eight-member Commission refused the Department of Justice's request for tapes, transcripts, or summaries of these calls, opting instead to respect callers' privacy. A few weeks after 9/11, Assistant Attorney General Ralph Boyd Jr. wrote a letter reprimanding U.S. Commission on Civil Rights director Les Jin for failing to share the information the hotline gathered on hate crimes.[90] The Commission defended its decision to keep callers' identities confidential, describing the hate crime victims as "marginal people" who were afraid of the federal government's policies towards Arabs and Muslims in the U.S. According to the *Washington Times*, Justice Department spokesman Dan Nelson said the commission's failure to cooperate would defeat the hotline's purpose, since acts of ethnically-motivated violence were occurring without being investigated.[91] In response, the Commission maintained that the hotline wasn't intended to be a problem solver, even though many callers may have assumed that it was. Since transcripts were never turned over to other agencies, it is unclear whether hate crime victims were aware that phoning the hotline was somewhat pointless since the organization that ran it was unable to file or investigate hate crime complaints.

Many crime victims found out about the hotline after the Commission distributed flyers in New York. When the hotline was first established, a press release mistakenly listed the wrong number, causing callers to phone a dating service that offered them "a chance to meet some exciting new people."[92] Because of this misprint, some hate crime victims might have lost confidence in federal agencies attempting to assist them.

20) Media outlets sometimes confuse the public about how to report bias attacks, resulting in inaccurate hate crime statistics.

Newspapers routinely provide unclear information about whether hate crimes should be reported to community groups, local police, or federal authorities. Some news sources urge victims to call anti-discrimination groups or the local district attorney's victim services unit. Other publications suggest that community members contact local law enforcement or state hate crime hotline numbers. On occasion, newspapers have suggested that hate crime victims call 911, the FBI, or the Department of Justice Community Relations Service. Here is a small sampling of some of the confusing contact information and/or phone numbers that American newspapers have provided Arab, Sikh, and Muslim readers who wished to file hate crime reports:

> 911; Alcohol Tobacco and Firearms hotline – (888) ATF FIRE or (209) 244-6653; American Arab Anti-Discrimination Committee – (202) 244-2990 or 877-282-2288; American Arab Chamber of Commerce – no contact number provided; American Civil Liberties Union hotlines in San Francisco and Los Angeles – no contact number provided; Asian American Legal Defense and Education Fund – (212) 760-9110 or sling@aaldef.org; California Hate Crime Hotline (866) 460-4357/ (866) 460-HELP, specifying that the hotline includes access to Fair Employment and Housing counselors who can inform victims about services and refer calls to local district attorneys; Council on American Islamic Relations – (408) 986-9874; (202) 488-8787 or online at www.cair-net.org/ireport/incident_report.doc; Civil Rights Hotline – 1-877-491-5742; Crime Alert – (916) 443-HELP; Crime Stoppers – 288-STOP; 366-TIPS; (559) 498-7867; Department of Alcohol, Tobacco, and Firearms hotline – (888) ATF-FIRE; Department of Education, Office of Civil

Rights – 800-421-3481; www.ed.gov/office/ocr; Department of Justice Community Relations Service – (713) 718-4861; EEOC, failing to give a contact number but specifying that the organization deals with hate crimes at work; Federal Bureau of Investigation at (713) 693-5000 or (713) 479-6300; www.fbi.gov; Fresno police department hate crime hotline – 621-HATE; Hate Crime Information Line – (888) No2-HATE, specifying that the hotline is staffed by multilingual employees; Hate Free Zone helpline – no contact number provided; Immigration and Naturalization Service – no contact number provided; Indo-American Bar Association of Northern California hotline – 1-888-NO-HATE, specifying that the hotline includes access to multi-lingual psychiatrists and attorneys; Islamic Public Affairs Council of New Jersey hotline – no contact number provided; Law Offices of Mohinder Mann - (408) 287-1600; Omaha hate crimes hotline - 444-HATE; Oswego County Sheriff's Department – 349-3411; San Diego hate crime tip line – (619) 235-TIPS; San Francisco District Attorney's Victim Services unit – (415) 553-9044; San Jose District Attorney's office – (415) 328-1173; San Jose State University police department – (408) 924-2222; Sarasota County Sheriff's Office – 861-4900; Sikh American Legal Defense and Education Fund – (877) 917-4547; Sikh Council On Religion and Education – no contact number provided; Sikh Dharma's website – no contact number; www.sikhnet.com; Sikh Media Watch and Task Force – no contact number provided; South Asian Bar Association's national hate crime hotline 1-888-99-NOHATE; St. Louis Police – (314) 889-2341; U.S. Commission on Civil Rights hotline – 800-552-6843; U.S. Marshalls' Service – no contact number provided; Washington, D.C. police – (301) 330-4471; Washington, D.C. police hate crimes hotline – 800-673-2777.

At the end of hate crimes articles, journalists often provided readers with two or three contact numbers. At times, the selected information is not the most relevant. For example, in the December 8, 2007 issue of *Northwest Asian Weekly*, reporter Eleanor Lee described a violent attack on a Sikh taxi driver from India who was called an Iraqi terrorist.[93] At the conclusion of the article, Lee refers readers to three organizations: the Northwest Coalition Against Malicious Harassment, the Seattle Anti-Defamation League, and the Organization of Chinese Americans - Greater Seattle Chapter. Lee provides no contact information for any local or national Sikh, South Asian, or Arab-American organizations, even though the crime was against an Indian Sikh thought to be an Arab. By offering confusing information to readers, journalists contribute to the undercounting of hate crimes.

21) The use of 'single bias reporting' instead of 'multiple bias reporting' skews hate crime statistics.

Many religious minorities are also racial minorities and "national origin" minorities. For example, when a Pakistani Muslim is assaulted in the U.S., it is often unclear whether the assault was motivated primarily by religious animosity, racial hatred, ethnic bias, or national prejudice. The way in which the FBI tabulates hate crimes is outdated and inaccurate. Their system of dividing crimes into disparate categories (crimes motivated by race, religion, ethnicity, national origin, sexual orientation, and disability) works particularly poorly when trying to tabulate crimes against immigrant communities who are simultaneously targeted because of their race, religion, ethnicity, and national origin.[94]

22) Hate crimes against disabled minorities are sometimes miscategorized as single-category attacks.

Crimes against Sikhs and Muslims are sometimes undercounted when the victims are also disabled. Immigrants who are blind, deaf, mentally-challenged, or physically-handicapped might be targeted for more than one reason. Police officers or FBI agents might categorize an attack as a single-bias crime targeting a person with a disability, overlooking whether the victim's race, religion, or national origin also factored in the assault.

23) Hate crimes against gay minorities are often miscategorized as single-category incidents.

Attacks against GLBT immigrants are sometimes miscategorized as simple gay bashings, causing an underreporting of hate crimes against Muslims, Sikhs, Arabs, and South Asians. In an October 23, 2001 article in the *Advocate*, journalist Chris Bull reported that Arab-Americans were often targeted by homophobic racists during the 9/11 backlash.[95] Bull found it ironic that gay immigrants were being persecuted in the U.S., the country that promised freedoms unavailable in repressive Middle Eastern regimes. Many hate crimes against minority gays are motivated by a combination of factors. For example, in chapter ten, I discussed how Satendar Singh, a Sikh of Indian descent from Fiji, was fatally beaten in Sacramento in 2007 by Slavic immigrants who hurled religious, racial, and anti-gay epithets at him.[96]

In some instances, even the victims themselves may have difficulty assessing all the reasons why they were attacked by bigots, particularly if the attack involved an interfaith or interracial gay couple. When I was co-organizing an antiwar "Blood for Oil Blood Drive" in San Francisco in June 2002, my friend Julie and I set a press release to the *Bay Area Reporter*, a newspaper serving the GLBT community.[97] Our friend Zak Szymanski was a staff writer, and promised to do a story on our unorthodox blood drive, in which all donors would receive a quart of motor oil from an anti-war protestor dressed up as Uncle Sam. In the middle of the night, a few hours after Julie emailed her press release and her contact information to the *B.A.R.* news room, her phone began to ring. The caller left a rambling hate message on her answering machine in reference to the blood drive. A few minutes later, she showed up on my doorstep in tears, terrified that the caller would make good on his threats and come to her house. I never asked Julie about the precise content of the message because she was too terrified to talk about it. Although I am a heterosexual Arab-American secular Christian with a Muslim-sounding last name and Julie is a Jewish lesbian political activist, the caller might have mistakenly assumed that we were a bi-ethnic, interfaith couple. The caller was likely a staff member of the *Bay Area Reporter*, since no one else had the press release or knew about our scheduled blood drive. I would guess that the caller's hate message was inspired by a twisted combination of racism, religious bigotry, sexism, anti-lesbianism, and political intolerance. We were aware that many white gay men were active in the movement to allow GLBT people to serve openly in the military, and some mistakenly associated racist political chauvinism with wartime patriotism. Because Julie was so frightened of further harassment, we never reported the threatening phone call to anyone, not even our friend Zak. As this incident illustrates, hate crimes are underreported when gay minority victims are unsure about whether the perpetrator was motivated primarily by racism, homophobia, or religious bigotry. Instead of being sensitive to the multiple identities of victims, police officers or FBI agents almost always categorize an attack as a single-bias incident, undercounting crimes against all affected communities.

24) Gay immigrants from homophobic cultures underreport hate crimes.

Because many traditional cultures are intolerant of same-sex relationships, some immigrants are unwilling to report hate crimes if doing so involves "outing" themselves as gays or lesbians. In the Middle East and South Asia, homosexuality is not generally tolerated. For that reason, it is sometimes difficult for gay Arabs, Persians, Indians, and Pakistanis to report hate crimes to police officers in the U.S., if doing so might involve revealing details of their personal lives to others.

25) Straight immigrants mistakenly thought to be gay often fail to report bias-motivated attacks.

Sometimes, straight minorities are mistaken as gay and attacked by violent bigots. In Egypt, it is widely considered taboo for an unmarried heterosexual couple to engage in public displays of affection or dance together on a public boat, but it is commonplace to see two straight men holding hands on the beach or dancing together in front of others. Middle Eastern men who engage in these kinds of cultural practices in the U.S. might be mistaken as gay and attacked by racist homophobes. These hate crime victims might be concerned that others might assume they are homosexual if they report that they were beaten up by gay bashers.   A few years after 9/11, a group of bigots assaulted one of my cousins, a fourth-generation Lebanese-American bartender working near Ashland, Oregon. During the attack, the assailants made racist remarks and homophobic slurs, making the incorrect assumption that he was gay because he wore an earring. He did not report the crime to police.

26) 'Mistaken identity' attacks complicate hate crime statistics.

Hate crime statistics are often reported inaccurately when a member of one ethno-racial group is mistakenly thought to belong to a different one. In chapter seven, I discussed hate crime in which a vandal defaced dumpsters at a Sikh-owned gas station, writing, "Go back to Bin Laden, Bitch," "Never Again Indian Monkey Nigger," and "Fuck Arab Gas."[98] Was this hate crime motivated primarily because of the victim's actual race, religion, ethnicity, or national origin, or because of the races, religions, ethnicities, and national origins that the perpetrator was intending to target? FBI statistics do not take into account that multiple communities are often affected by a single hate crime. Instead of recognizing that many 21st century bias attacks defy simple categorization, the FBI clumsily tries to fit them into an outdated framework. As a result, an attack might be somewhat arbitrarily labeled an anti-Sikh hate crime, ignoring that it is also anti-South Asian, anti-Arab, anti-Muslim, anti-Indian, anti-Afghani, and anti-Saudi.

By choosing only one primary bias factor, local and state authorities dramatically undercount crimes affecting Middle Easterners and South Asians. According to a December 10, 2004 article in *India Abroad*, government agencies almost always classify hate crimes as single-bias incidents, rather than recognize that different aspects of victims' identities were simultaneously under attack.[99]

According to FBI spokesman Paul Bresson, the federal government formulates its hate crime statistics using information collected by police departments across the country. Aimee Baldillo, staff attorney for the National Asian Pacific American Consortium, told *India Abroad* that law enforcement agencies often fail to make accurate distinctions about whether a crime was anti-Muslim, anti-Sikh, or anti-South Asian, particularly since many crime incident report forms don't include these categories.[100] For that reason, many uninformed officers are uncertain about how to categorize the ethnicity of some minority hate crime victims, and may lump them incorrectly into attacks against Asians or Hispanics.

Because Muslims in America come from so many different groups, crimes against them are horribly undercounted because they are often lumped into disparate racial, ethnic, or national origin categories. In the U.S., many police officers and FBI agents are accustomed to viewing hate crimes through the interpretive lens of race. If a Christian Sudanese man is attacked by bigots who mistakenly believe he is an Arab Muslim, the responding officer might ignore the religious, ethnic, and national origin factors relevant to the crime, and categorize the assault as a simple racially-motivated attack based on the victim's skin color.

27) Hate crimes against bi-racial or multi-racial people are also capriciously categorized in the U.S.

If a hate crime victim is of mixed Sikh and Mexican ancestry, the investigating officer might fail to tabulate the incident as simultaneously an anti-South Asian, anti-Sikh, and anti-Latino attack. Many second and third generation immigrants – particularly Arab-Americans – are bi-racial or multi-racial, making the tabulation of bias-related crimes against them particularly confusing.

28) The perception that certain local or national media outlets are racist prevents minorities from contacting journalists about bias attacks or using the media as a watchdog.

Rather than rely on newspapers and television stations to draw attention to the undercounting of hate crimes or the failure of authorities to investigate them properly, Muslims and Sikhs often view the media as an adversarial force, spreading harmful stereotypes. In chapter four, I discussed how networks covering 9/11 broadcasted images of a Sher Singh, South Asian Sikh, getting arrested on a train for carrying his religiously-mandated small knife. In an article in the *Bergen County Record*, Singh described the horror he felt when he realized his image was repeatedly televised on a split screen next to Osama bin Laden's face.[101] The media continued to link the two photos for a few days, even after the South Asian man had been released from jail and cleared of all involvement in the terrorist attacks. Sikh leaders across the country were outraged by the way Singh was portrayed, associating South Asians' turbans and beards with those worn by members of the Taliban. Many minority communities attribute anti-Sikh backlash hate crimes to this media story.

American Muslims were also upset when irresponsible news stories linked their faith with violent extremist groups. Viewers watching these programs learned to associate Islam with terrorism. In chapter ten, I discussed how Muslims in Minneapolis saw a direct connection between hate crimes and anti-Islamic reporting, particularly after Ali W. Ali was fatally injured the day after the *Minneapolis Star Tribune* reported that area Somalis were funding bin Laden's work.

During the 9/11 backlash, ignorant journalists occasionally published inaccurate information about minority groups. For example, a week after 9/11, the *Las Vegas Review-Journal* mistakenly reported that Sikhs were members of a Hindu religious sect that originated in Northern India.[102] Even minority journalists sometimes maligned Arabs, Muslims, and South Asians in the U.S., or wrote factually-incorrect information about them. In a March 31, 2002 article in the *Austin American Statesman*, African-American columnist Alberta Philips argued that Muslims "lived white" before 9/11, and were "MIA" on civil rights issues before the terrorist attacks.[103] "Welcome to Black America," she quipped, apparently unaware of the fact that Muslims arrived in the country on slave ships and have been a part of the African-American community for centuries.[104] Ignorant of this history, Philips made the specious claim that prior to 9/11, Muslims in the U.S. did not have to endure what blacks experienced – they never had to learn to "avoid abrupt movements," and were unable to relate to the experiences of "Amadou Diallo, an African immigrant, was shot 41 times in the hallway of his NY apartment for reaching without permission."[105] Philips' article overlooked the fact that Diallo was himself a black Muslim. Her editorial was particularly distressing because it pits minority communities against one another, revealing her lack of awareness of the role that black Muslims played fighting American slavery, segregation, and discrimination. Her words also failed to acknowledge the long history of Muslim-American civil rights advocacy, involving believers from many racial groups.

An April 13, 2007 article in the *Tampa Tribune* also angered minority readers. Journalist Keith Morelli displayed a poor understanding of hate crimes when he wrote the following words about repeated attacks on a Florida mosque that had been desecrated four times in the previous 18 months:

> Local, state, and federal investigators sifted through the ashes of a deliberately-set fire at the Islamic Education center of Florida on Thursday morning and tried to allay fears the arson was a crime of hate… Area Muslims feared the torching of the building, which serves as a mosque and educational center for children, was a hate crime, the next progressive step from a burglary nine months ago in which the culprits set fire to several religious artifacts inside…[106]

It is alarming that Morelli failed to comprehend that the deliberate burning of the mosque's religious artifacts was a hate crime. It is also upsetting that Morelli accepted investigators' specious conclusion that the arson was not bias-motivated, particularly since the same mosque had been struck four times in the previous year and a half. Morelli's problematic article reveals why many ethnic and religious minorities in the U.S. are distrustful of American journalists.

On occasion, minorities were wary of speaking to the press after bigots posed as reporters and called to harass them. According to an April 2004 article in the *San Antonio Express-News*, a man claiming to be a journalist contacted Sarwat Husain of CAIR, and began harassing her about a string of recent arsons targeting Muslim-run convenience stores, suggesting that the perpetrator was "one of her people."[107] Husain responded by agreeing that the arsonist was likely one of her people, an American.[108] In the aftermath of this incident, some minorities became wary of returning reporters' phone calls, since Islamophobes were posing as journalists as a means of intimidating vulnerable communities.

Some journalists alienated minorities by trivializing bias-motivated assaults and attacking the credibility of civil rights organizations attempting to address them. A May 15, 2004 editorial in the *Washington Times* challenged CAIR's hate crime statistics, claiming that the organization's data was phony since it did not distinguish between minor events and true acts of violence.[109] The article questioned whether the Muslim organization inaccurately counted unpleasant experiences as hate crimes, calling attention to an incident in which a man threw a Mr. Potato Head at a Muslim woman shopping in Brooklyn.[110] The opinion piece unfairly discounted the true scope of assaults against Muslims by drawing attention to the least serious one on record. The editorial also failed to acknowledge that targeting a woman because of her religion and hurling an object at her head to intimidate her or inflict bodily harm legally constituted a bias-motivated attack.

In some instances, journalists lost credibility with hate crime victims when they wrote about attacks or arsons from the perpetrators' perspectives. In chapter seven, I discussed a September 13, 2001 hate crime at the Curry in a Hurry restaurant in Utah. Approximately five years after the backlash attack, the *Deseret Morning News* wrote a retrospective piece on the arson, humanizing the bigot who torched the place and endangered the lives of restaurant employees and customers. This article, entitled "Muslims in the U.S. See Little 9/11 Backlash," presented the crime from the perspective of the perpetrator:

> At first, James Michael Herrick didn't believe the 7-Eleven cashier who told him a plane had crashed into the World Trade Center. He thought she was joking. But then after purchasing a cup of coffee and a hot dog on the morning of September 11, 2001, Herrick returned home and turned on the television. 'There it is, the other plane hit. It was for real,' he said. 'I started drinking about that time… I probably like everyone else at that point, was in shock.' Herrick turned to alcohol, and after two days of drinking and watching the non-stop coverage of the turmoil, Herrick, in a drunken daze, attempted to burn down the Curry in a Hurry restaurant on State Street.[111]

Note that the article's focus is on Herrick's feelings and emotions, not on the terror experienced by the Pakistani family he attacked or the customers affected by the fire. The news story refers to Herrick's drinking four times in one paragraph and draws attention to his reaction to 9/11, suggesting to readers that his criminal actions were somehow understandable or excusable. The article later mentions that Herrick characterized his behavior as "embarrassing and idiotic," a rather benign description of his decision to ignite two containers of gasoline and firebomb a Pakistani-American business while the restaurant was full of innocent employees and diners.[112]

Mohammed Chaudhry, president of the Islamic Center of the East Bay, felt that media stereotypes of Muslims as terrorists contributed to an environment conducive to hate crimes. Discussing the January 2007 shooting at the Antioch mosque, Chaudhry told the *Oakland Tribune* that he saw a connection between media racism and hate crimes, especially when news segments about terrorism featured footage of unrelated Muslims at prayer.[113]

Instead of functioning as a watchdog to ensure that hate crime victims are treated fairly by police and prosecutors, newspapers sometimes argued that bias attacks did not warrant special consideration. For example, in a March 23, 2007 article, the editor of the *Honolulu Star Bulletin* criticized the state of Hawaii for passing hate crime legislation six years previously, arguing that it would unfairly punish assailants who, "in the heat of the moment," utter slurs during physical assaults.[114] The editorial also expresses relief that Hawaii prosecutors have declined to add hate crime enhancements when assailants use racial, religious, and anti-gay epithets during beatings, including a case in which soldiers mistook their victims for Arab Muslims.[115]

Newspapers that challenge the need for hate crime laws lose credibility with minority communities, who become unable to rely on the media to ensure that police and prosecutors put bigots behind bars. When local authorities are not monitored by the press, they may be less likely to prosecute and document backlash hate crimes.

Minority victims also lose faith in the media when journalists challenge the legitimacy of bias attacks. In the introduction, I noted that Michelle Malkin took a handful of fabricated hate crimes and used them to discredit the bulk of anti-Muslim incidents logged by CAIR.[116]   Although Malkin acknowledged that newspapers like the *New York Times*, the *Everett Herald*, and the *Los Angeles Times* took the same false bias-crime reports seriously, she never attacked the credibility of these periodicals or accused them of smearing the most tolerant nation on earth, charges she levels against CAIR for being similarly duped.[117]   Just as a four or five fabricated rape cases do not invalidate the vast majority of reported sexual assaults taking place nationally, the existence of a few liars who invent hate crimes should not be used to discredit the thousands of real victims of hate violence or the civil rights organizations working to curtail community bigotry.   Media commentators who deny the existence of bias-motivated attacks do a disservice to minority victims and their families, and make disempowered community members reluctant to report genuine hate crimes to apathetic police and dismissive journalists.

29) Victims may be less likely to report hate crimes when media outlets trivialize them as juvenile pranks.

In chapter two, I discussed the 1997 vandalism of a crescent star sculpture in Washington, D.C. Many of the newspapers covering the Islamophobic attack downplayed the serious nature of the destruction. For example, the *Fort Worth Star Telegram* suggested that the vandal may have been merely pulling a prank when he spray-painted a swastika on the Muslim symbol.[118]   The title of the article emphasizes that the incident may have been intended as a joke:

> *Swastika spray-painted on Islamic Symbol:*
> *Police are investigating whether vandalism to the crescent star sculpture was done as a prank or as a hate crime*

Journalists discourage victims from coming forward when they fail to appreciate the gravity of bias-motivated attacks, using language that trivializes them.

Other news outlets also published insensitive headlines. In chapter six, I discussed a bias assault against a 12-year old Muslim girl at Congress Middle School in Boynton Beach, Florida. On April 14, 2004, the *Knight Ridder Tribune News Service* published an article about the attack, entitled, "Florida Hate Crime May Have Been Horseplay."[119]   This headline minimizes the psychological and physical bullying the girl experienced at school.[120]   The title of the article also ignored the school's history of racism, administrators' dismissive reaction to the assault, and the language barriers that prevented the victim's sole caregiver from acting as her advocate.

Other reporters failed to appreciate the gravity of hate crimes. On January 30, 2007, *Oakland Tribune* journalist Cassandra Braun described five attacks on an East Bay mosque as "pranks," although they included the breaking of the mosque's front window with a brick and a gun assault that left seven golf-size holes in the facility.[121]   Discussing how local Muslims were responding to these incidents, Braun wrote that "the increasing violent nature of the pranks has given them [the Muslims] pause for their safety."[122]   By referring to a gunman attacking a mosque as a "prank," Braun reinforces the Antioch police's contention that the bias-motivated vandalism and shooting were not serious hate crimes.

Newspaper headlines also trivialized crimes against Sikhs. In chapter six, I described how two bullies committed a vicious bias-motivated assault when they cut a Sikh classmate's unshorn hair. On May 28, 2007, the *New York Post* ran a story about this attack with the inappropriate title, "Hair Tomorrow: Shorn Sikh Vows He'll Grow it Back."[123]   Sikhs were disturbed by the *Post*'s use of a pun and humorous tone to introduce an article about a traumatic hate crime at a New York school. These types of news stories undermine minorities' faith that they will be taken seriously if they inform reporters about xenophobic attacks.

30) Hate crimes are likely undercounted in areas with racist judges and court officers.

In chapter two, I discussed an August 2, 1991 mosque attack in Peoria, Illinois. To recover the repair costs and punish the perpetrators, the Muslim Association of Greater Peoria filed a lawsuit against the two men who had vandalized the rural Washington mosque, ransacking the building and writing racist slurs on the walls. The civil suit, filed under hate crime statues, requested that the vandals pay $1,000 to cover the costs of the destruction, plus $2,000 in punitive damages.[124] Prior to the filing of the civil suit, one of the perpetrators, 21-year old Jo Crisp, had been fined $100 and sentenced to one year of court supervision for his role in the hate crime. The other mosque attacker, Richard Nelson, 22, was ordered to pay a $200 fine and undergo a year of probation. The court decreed that the men's records could be expunged if they successfully completed their court supervision. Both men had also been court-ordered to pay restitution for the damages. When they failed to do so, the mosque leaders decided to take civil action.

Although the court had both men's addresses, Tazwell county judge William Young dismissed Crisp from the civil suit on May 7, 1992 because he was in the military and could not be located. The judge then dismissed the civil lawsuit against the other perpetrator, writing a three-paragraph opinion claiming that the hate crime laws applied to individuals seeking damages and not to corporate bodies such as the local Muslim Association.[125] Hate crime victims might think twice about reporting hate crimes when unsympathetic judges ensure that convicted vandals never have to do jail time or pay the costs of repairs.

Sikhs have also been discouraged by unjust court rulings. In chapter four, I described how five men viciously beat two Sikh men after ridiculing their turbans on July 11, 2004. Queens Superior Court Justice Seymour Rotker controversially ruled that the attack was not a hate crime because the drunken men began the assault in response to the Sikhs' decision to report the verbal harassment to the police. Shocked by this decision, Khalsa told the *New York Post* that the attack was obviously motivated by bias, since the assailants threw his turban on the sidewalk.[126] He also told *India Abroad* that the attack was clearly a 9/11 backlash crime, triggered by the mistaken belief that he was a Muslim from the Middle East.[127] The Sikh victims were dismayed that the assailants received relatively light sentences because they were not charged with hate crime enhancements. One of the men involved, Victor Consentino, received only five days in jail and $250 fine for his role in the attack. Minority victims might be less likely to report hate crimes when unsympathetic judges fail to dispense justice.

On occasion, judges have openly discriminated against Sikhs and Muslims in court. In November 2003, the *Sikh Coalition Newsletter* reported that a state judge in northern Illinois demanded that a Sikh defendant comply with the court's 'no hats' policy by removing his turban.[128] In response, the Sikh Coalition provided defense counsel with case law upholding Sikhs' right to wear their dastaars in the courthouse. In other parts of the country, hijab-wearing Muslims experienced similar mistreatment. According to a July 6, 2007 article in the *Oakland Tribune*, a Contra Costa judge presiding for the day in a Sacramento Superior Court denied entry to a Muslim woman who refused to remove her hijab.[129] Judges who openly discriminate against Sikhs and Muslims send the message that some non-Christians are not welcome in courtrooms. When judges discourage minorities from pursuing legal remedies, hate crimes end up under the radar.

Along with judges, court officers have also mistreated religious minorities. According to a September 11, 2003 article in the *Madison Capital Times*, Milwaukee County sheriff's deputies sometimes forced Muslim women to remove their headscarves at the courthouse.[130] Middle Easterners and South Asians are less likely to report hate crimes and testify at a trial if they live in areas where this type of discrimination routinely takes place.

31) Bias crime victims are sometimes unwilling to take their attackers to civil or criminal court because they are wary of unsympathetic juries.

Arabs, Muslims, and Sikhs might think twice about pressing charges when American juries repeatedly refrain from convicting hate crime offenders or compensating minority crime victims for damages. After 9/11, backlash victims worried that the justice system might be unresponsive to their claims. In the October 12, 2001 issue of *India Abroad*, Dallas attorney John Howe reported that after 9/11, Muslims were sometimes treated unfairly by American juries.[131] A month after the terrorist strikes, Howe observed that many attorneys were afraid that jurors would discriminate against Muslim plaintiffs, and sometimes advised their clients to settle hate crime lawsuits or discrimination complaints.[132]

Juries in rural communities or small towns might be particularly inclined to look unfavorably on immigrant plaintiffs who press hate crime charges against native-born citizens. In chapter four, I discussed how three assailants stalked and attacked a Sikh trucker in Douglas county, Oregon, stealing his dastaar. Rather than indict the assailants on hate crime charges, the jury asked about the dollar value of the cloth turban, and decided that the perpetrators should only be charged with misdemeanor harassment and theft in the third degree. Hate crime victims might be reluctant to seek legal remedies if local juries are unable to understand the true significance of bias crimes.

32) Light sentences may discourage victims from reporting subsequent bias crimes.

Many victims are unwilling to file hate crime charges since perpetrators are often given slaps on the wrist for committing bias-motivated attacks. In chapter eight, I discussed how Eric Nix put an explosive device in a Palestinian-American family's van on March 21, 2003, blowing off the vehicle's door, ripping a hole in the floor, and shattering glass over 30 feet. Although Nix had a previous conviction for throwing a brick through a Muslim-owned furniture store two days after 9/11, he received probation for firebombing the Palestinian-American family's van.

Other high-profile hate crimes also resulted in disappointing outcomes. In chapter four, I discussed how an Afghan-American delivery man was severely beaten by Michael Johnson on September 14, 2001.[133] During the 2002 court case, Johnson's attorney, Paul Pepper, argued that his client deserved a modest sentence because the beating was an isolated incident. According to the *Washington Post*, Pepper characterized his client as a tolerant person who simply 'lost it.'[134] Disregarding the fact that Johnson stalked and pummeled another American solely because of his ethnic background, Pepper argued that his client was not a violent man or a bigot.[135] Alexandria's prosecuting attorney, S. Randolph Sengal, wanted Johnson to receive a long sentence to show that the city would not tolerate bias attacks.[136] Sengal argued that the bias-motivation of Johnson's crime injured the entire community and merited additional punishment.[137]

Although Johnson was eventually convicted in a non-jury trial of committing an assault based on his victim's national origins, the judge sentenced him to only 60 days in jail and three years of probation for the vicious hate-motivated beating. The *Washington Post* characterized circuit court judge Alfred Swersky's decision as overly-lenient, far from the maximum five year sentence permitted, pointing out that he failed to discuss hate crimes during sentencing.[138] The judge also allowed the convicted batterer to spend his time in jail incrementally, so he could leave on weekends to care for his elderly mother in their shared Maryland home. Shocked that Johnson received such a light sentence for his hate-motivated attack, the Afghan-American victim questioned whether he and other hate crime victims were being treated fairly as Americans.[139] Months after the hate crime, he continued to be so traumatized by the beating that he stopped gong out at night. Bias victims who hear about unjust legal outcomes might become reluctant to press charges against their assailants, resulting in an underreporting of attacks.

33) Victims' mistrust of prosecutors also leads to an undercounting of hate crimes.

Some minorities believe that district attorneys sometimes place their own professional ambitions ahead of the needs of vulnerable community members. Many Afghans and Muslims in Alexandria were disappointed that the prosecutor Sengal failed to denounce judge Swersky for sentencing Johnson to only two months in prison after he was convicted of a violent hate-motivated beating. Sengal did not criticize the judge's actions in the press, telling the *Washington Post* that the sentence was appropriate.[140] Afghans, Arabs, and Muslims wondered if the prosecutor failed to speak out against a legal outcome that gave an Afghan-American crime victim little justice, afraid of alienating the judge or incurring community disfavor. Since many district attorneys are elected officials, they understand that championing victimized Middle Easterners or Muslims may not sit well with constituents.

34) Misconceptions about hate crime perpetrators cause many attacks to go unpunished, reducing victims' willingness to report bias crimes.

Many Americans believe that hate crimes are committed almost exclusively by white skinheads with swastika tattoos who are members of the Aryan nation and other supremacist groups. Although these hate societies are clearly dangerous, their members are in fact responsible for only a small fraction of all bias-motivated attacks. Social scientists have found that the vast majority of U.S. hate crimes are committed by community members who have no overt "white supremacist" backgrounds or affiliations. As I noted in chapter two, the American Psychological Association reported that only about 5% of hate crimes are committed by members of organized hate groups.[141] Perpetrators of bias crimes also come from a variety of ethnic, racial, religious, and socio-economic communities. Because of widely-held misconceptions, juries and judges are sometimes willing to go easy or give a pass to "normal-looking" assailants who don't fit inaccurate stereotypes of "typical" hate crime perpetrators.

35) Victims often make the mistake of reporting hate crimes to government offices instead of investigative authorities, resulting in an undercounting of bias crimes.

On occasion, hate crime victims report bias attacks to city council members, the mayor's office, state senators, state assemblymen, the governor's office, members of Congress, Senators' offices, and the White House comment line. Interns or receptionists answering phones might simply take down a message, without instructing hate crime victims to contact specific local, state, and federal authorities. This depresses the numbers of hate crimes documented nationally.

36) Hate crimes go undocumented when elected officials and local police sweep disturbing incidents under the rug, perhaps out of concern that they will hurt tourism or damage their area's reputation.

In chapter ten, I discussed Reedley mayor Joe Rhodes' disappointing response to the post-9/11 murder of a Yemeni shopkeeper. Although Abdo Ali Ahmed received a death threat before he was killed, Rhodes claimed that bias-motivated assaults did not occur in his town, and that he was unfamiliar with the term, "hate crime."[142] Public officials might worry that news of a bigotry-motivated attack might brand a town an unsafe place of intolerance. Because mayors exert considerable influence over police departments, they can encourage investigators to interpret possible bias assaults as random attacks. In communities dependent on tourism, public officials realize that the proper documentation of all hate crimes can damage a town's reputation and end up hurting local businesses.

37) Bias-motivated attacks may be undercounted in areas where elected officials fail to act as advocates for the victims.

On occasion, ambitious city officials may be unwilling to expend political capital or community resources investigating and prosecuting hate crimes, worried about the fallout of helping "suspect" minority communities. Muslims in San Diego were outraged that mayor Dick Murphy repeatedly refused to meet with them to discuss anti-Muslim incidents and the September 16, 2001 attack on the Islamic Center of San Diego.[143] Mosque staff member Omara Abdeen told the *San Diego Union Tribune* that the mayor's reluctance to meet with the targeted citizens made local Muslims feel unimportant.[144] When mayors and city officials routinely dismiss bias attacks, they become more likely to take place under the radar.

Islamophobic politicians are unlikely to assist Muslim hate crime victims or make sure that their experiences go on record. Shortly before the Iraq War began, Washington state lawmaker Louis McMahan, a conservative Christian, explained to a reporter that she had left a prayer session conducted by a Muslim leader at the state House of Representatives because the Islamic religion was involved in the attack on America.[145] Her minority constituents might not view her as an ally in improving the handling of anti-Muslim hate crime investigations in the state. Other politicians also expressed Islamophobic views. In the summer of 2003, Massachusetts state senator Guy W. Glodis sent a controversial flyer to his Senate colleagues, suggesting that Muslim terrorists should be executed and buried with pig entrails.[146] In response, community activist Gordon Davis organized a rally and press conference outside Worcester City Hall, denouncing Glodis as a bigot. Hate-crime victims might be hesitant to contact Islamophobic state officials about their experiences with xenophobia.

Federal lawmakers have been just as insensitive to minority concerns. A few months after 9/11, Georgia Congressman Saxby Chambliss said that the World War II. internment of Japanese Americans was justified and that Asian Pacific Americans constituted a threat to national security.[147] Many Arabs and Muslims questioned whether the timing of Chambliss' words was an indication that they deserved similar mistreatment during the 'War on Terror.' Another Congressman, John Cooksey, expressed his endorsement of religious and racial profiling, telling a radio station in Louisiana that law enforcement officials should pull over any driver wearing a diaper on his head.[148] It is unlikely that minority constituents would choose to call on these elected officials to assist 9/11 backlash victims. Because governmental agencies receive funding from these and other Members of Congress, federal prosecutors may have been unwilling to be aggressive in pursuing hate crimes targeting unpopular minority communities.

38) Many hate crimes go undocumented because Arab–Americans and Muslims are unwilling to report incidents to Islamophobic Justice Department officials.

In a November 2001 radio address, Justice Department head John Ashcroft made anti-Islamic comments.[149] In this broadcast, he negatively compared Islam to Christianity, declaring that Islam requires a follower to send his son to die for God instead of the other way around.[150] Ashcroft's words strained relations with Muslim and Arab groups, who wondered if other federal employees shared his views. Not all Americans thought that Ashcroft had spoken inappropriately. *The Washington Post* reported that many Americans rushed to his defense, sending Arab groups death threats and email messages declaring that Ashcroft was 100 percent correct.[151] Muslim bias-crime victims might hesitate to report attacks to the Justice Department if they fear their concerns will be dismissed by bigoted officials.

39) Some bias–motivated incidents are never investigated because authorities are hesitant to arrest and charge high-ranking members of the community.

Detectives and prosecutors might be hesitant to launch investigations against well-connected citizens, resulting in an undercounting of bias crimes. Hate-crime perpetrators who can afford expensive counsel can mount an aggressive defense, telling the court and the press that the attack was actually a fight instigated by the minority victim. Immigrant assault victims might be particularly wary of pressing charges against attackers with significant financial resources or community support.

40) Some hate crimes go undocumented because there is some confusion about which parties are responsible for reporting hate crimes.

Americans who learn of a bias-motivated incident might fail to alert authorities if they were not the ones targeted and have no first-hand knowledge of what transpired. In chapter two, I discussed how a painting of Malcolm X was slashed and covered with cigarettes and trash at Swarthmore College. Although I was an undergraduate at the time, I never took the initiative to call the local police or the FBI. I assumed that school officials had notified the proper authorities about the hate crime. I later learned that Swarthmore administrators failed to report the incident to authorities, knowing that doing so would generate significant negative press for the college. Looking back, I wish I had informed the local police and the FBI about what happened, instead of expecting others to take the initiative.

In America, there is an unspoken assumption that each racial or religious group bears primary responsibility for reporting hate crimes directed against its members. If there is anti-Islamic graffiti in a public area, Americans frequently assume that a Muslim will contact the proper authorities. If there are no Muslim witnesses to the vandalism, the crime might go unreported.

41) Another cause of underreporting is due to victims' confusion about the difference between hate crimes and hate incidents.

On occasion, minorities may be confused about which racially-based encounters constitute hate crimes. Police officers and FBI investigators usually make legal distinctions between hate crimes and bias incidents. Whereas the former involves a criminal act, the latter might be simply an unpleasant experience of bigotry. According to San Jose Sgt. Tony Ciaburro, name-calling is protected by the first amendment and does not constitute a criminal act.[152] If a series of escalating incidents occur at a college or university, the victim might be unsure about which particular episodes of racial harassment are illegal hate crimes or protected free speech.

A few weeks after the Malcolm X portrait was defaced, some Swarthmore frat boys, inspired by Gulf War jingoism, hung sheets outside of their windows, declaring, "By Air, By Land, By Sea, Bye Bye Iraq!" and "Death from Above!" In response, someone set fire to the sheets, and ran away before getting caught. Although the campus grapevine spread rumors that a politically-active Anglo-American senior was responsible for the arson, the frat boys made the racist and inaccurate assumption that the perpetrator was an Arab-American. They then began making repeated threatening calls to Jesse Amar, an apolitical senior who was only one-quarter Moroccan. The frat boys even went so far as to accuse the part-Moroccan student of the arson in front of the entire school, hanging up a large wooden board from their dorm room with the message, "Try burning this, Jesse Amar!" He was terrified that the frat boys would make good on one of their threats or trash his senior art project, since some campus vandals had recently set a student-built peace monument on fire. Because I was Arab-American and a friend of Jesse's, the frat boys also began venting their anger at me, shouting that I must be "happy now" that the sheets had been destroyed.

Since I was unsure about which of the escalating racial incidents constituted hate crimes, I decided to speak with Swarthmore administrators about what was occurring. I assumed that the deans would take the information I was providing them and use it to notify the proper local and federal authorities. A friend also called the American-Arab Anti-Discrimination Committee (ADC) and relayed what was happening on the campus. I later learned that none of Swarthmore's hate crimes were ever reported to the local police or the FBI for inclusion in official reports. To my knowledge, the perpetrators who hung up the board publicly accusing Jesse Amar of arson never faced disciplinary action.

Although the slashing of the Malcolm X portrait and the threatening phone calls targeting minority students were clearly bias-motivated crimes, it is somewhat unclear if the messages on the sheets constituted permissible free speech or death threats targeting Iraqi international students and their overseas relatives. In the U.S., this distinction can be somewhat ambiguous. In the movie, *Borat*, actor Sasha Baron Cohen exposes the xenophobic and blood-thirsty underside of American patriotism when he addresses an American rodeo audience at the beginning of the Iraq War. Crowd members cheer his speech about conquering Iraq, but then grow increasingly hostile as they slowly realize he is mocking them by encouraging to cheer the complete annihilation of every living thing in the area: "May you destroy their country – so that not one single lizard will survive in the desert! May George W. Bush drink the blood of every man, woman, and child in Iraq!"[153] Clearly, Cohen's intentionality makes Borat's comments considerably different from other wartime cries to kill all Iraqis and bomb the country out of existence. One man's death threat might be a comedian's political satire. Because the line between illegal death threats and legitimate political discourse is somewhat unclear,

271

minorities and local police officers might be unsure about whether hate crime charges are warranted. In many cases, this is a judgment call left to the discretion of responding officers. If local authorities have a strained relationship with a particular minority community, they might consider a racist event a "hate incident" instead of a bias crime. If relations are better, the same event might be considered a "hate crime" worthy of follow-up.

42) Hate crime victims are often confused about how to proceed when hate crimes occur on school grounds.

When an incident takes place at schools, targeted students are unsure about whether they should talk to student leaders, schedule a meeting with a dean, call campus security, notify local police, phone the FBI, or contact one of a dozen of advocacy groups. This confusion leads to an undercounting of bias attacks.

43) School administrators often fail to take hate crimes seriously or report them to outside authorities, resulting in an undercounting of bias-motivated attacks.

In many instances, academic administrators discourage victims from talking to police or federal investigators, worried about negative publicity for the school. School officials often attempt to handle violent incidents internally, suggesting that perpetrators belong in college disciplinary hearings instead of prison. In chapter six, I discussed a December 2001 assault on Arab-American student and his brother by six men yelling racial slurs. In response to the attack, William Riley, the Dean of Students at the University of Illinois, commented that any student involved in the bias-motivated beating faced the possibility of academic expulsion. By viewing this as an appropriate punishment for a bias-motivated aggravated assault, Riley transmitted the message that hate crimes are not jail-worthy offenses.

To protect a school's reputation, administrators sometimes make a calculated decision to refrain from reporting hate crimes to local police or federal agents. In chapter six, I discussed how the University of Wisconsin-Milwaukee failed to take appropriate action after the Muslim Student Association was targeted by bigots in 2003 and 2004, when at least one vandal put pork under their office door, tore down posters, ripped down flyers, and wrote graffiti telling the Muslim students to "suicide bomb" themselves.[154] Despite the seriousness of these bias-motivated attacks, the university refused to investigate them as hate crimes. Worried about negative publicity, administrators characterized the assaults as petty offenses involving damaged property. By handling hate crimes internally, school officials contribute to an underreporting of bias crimes to state and federal agencies. The State of California does not consider attacks to be hate crimes if they are triggered by factors other than bias, even if slurs are used once a beating is underway.

44) Hate crimes are also fall under the radar when state criteria is too strict to accommodate the complete spectrum of bias incidents.

Because some states have narrow criteria for defining hate crimes, many reported incidents are never counted. In California, the only hate crimes that are included in state statistics are the ones that local police agencies report to Sacramento. From there, they must meet a narrow set of criteria established by the California Attorney General's office. M. Van Winkle, a California Department of Justice spokesman, told the *San Diego Union Tribune* that threats had to be explicit, and that a brick thrown through a window was insufficient to demonstrate clear evidence of hate.[155] Some minority crime victims might disagree, believing that a projectile thrown at a mosque or temple speaks volumes.

45) Federal criteria may also be too strict to encompass all types of hate crimes.

The U.S. government has traditionally used strict criteria to define federal hate crimes. According to the *San Antonio Express-News*, convicting a defendant under the federal hate crime law involves proving that he or she committed an offense because of the victim's race, color, religion, or national origin, and hampered participation in one of six narrowly-defined federally-protected activities, such as interfering with voting rights.[156] Since federal legislation defines bias crimes so narrowly, many attacks are going unrecorded.

46) The legal definition of hate crimes varies considerably, making the accurate compilation of statistics problematic.

The definition of a hate crime changes from state to state. As of 2007, 45 states have passed their own hate crime laws, some of which are more far-reaching than others. For example, a 1987 California law defines a hate crime as an illegal act motivated by race, religion, sexual orientation, physical disability, or mental impairment.[157] These regional differences make it difficult to compare hate crime statistics across state lines. States also differ on the degree to which bias enhancements lengthen sentences, with some states mandating more prison time for the same offense.

47) There are also significant regional differences in both the reporting and prosecuting of hate crimes, suggesting that attacks in some states may be going undocumented.

It is probable that minorities in more liberal states might be more inclined to file hate crime reports compared to victims from less tolerant regions of the country. According to a November 2002 article in the *Boston Herald*, the FBI reported that Massachusetts had the fourth highest numbers of reported hate crimes for 2001.[158] In that year, the FBI counted 584 hate crimes in the state – including 212 in Boston alone – compared to only 434 in all of Texas. Although these FBI numbers suggest that Massachusetts is less tolerant than Texas, they might simply demonstrate that some states are better than others in recording hate crimes.

California also had a relatively high hate crime rate, perhaps due to its better tracking. The state recorded a huge spike in hate crimes in the four-month period following 9/11, with many of the victims from South Asian and Middle Eastern backgrounds.[159] Relying on statistics from Intergroup Clearinghouse, *Asianweek* reported that there were 76 bias crimes in San Francisco, 338 in the Bay Area, and 610 statewide.[160] Intergroup Clearinghouse also conducted a survey that found that 57% of Muslims and Arabs in San Francisco claimed that they experienced some form of backlash hate crime or discrimination.[161] Since there are thousands of Arab-Americans and Muslims in the city and less than a hundred reported bias incidents, it is possible that many victims felt too disempowered to press charges. Minority victims in more conservative parts of the country might be even more disinclined to report attacks.

48) National hate crime statistics are also unreliable because it is not mandatory for many law enforcement agencies to report crimes to the federal government.

Some police departments collect data on hate crimes; others don't. In an October 2001 article in the *Los Angeles Times*, journalist Beth Shuster acknowledged that federal hate crime statistics are woefully incomplete. She pointed out that local law enforcement agencies were not required to report bias crimes to the federal government, making FBI statistics unreliable.[162] Shuster recognized that this created an inaccurate picture of the true numbers of bias crimes taking place nationally.

49) It is also likely that there is significant underreporting of hate crimes in areas with scant knowledge of advocacy groups.

In rural areas, Muslim and Sikh immigrants may not know of national organizations that could provide them with support services and legal counsel. The *Washington Post* reported that civil rights organizations often received disproportionately more hate crime reports in areas where they were better known to victims.[163] According to the *Post*, CAIR received particularly high numbers of bias complaints in D.C., where the group was headquartered.[164] Hate crimes might be more frequently reported in diverse urban areas, where minority victims have more access to support services.

50) Hate crimes are also undercounted in states that seldom prosecute bias-motivated assaults.

According to a July 2007 article in the *San Antonio Express-News*, Texas prosecuted a total of only eight hate crimes in the six-year period from May 2001 to May 2007.[165] Texas police and district attorneys claimed that hate crimes were difficult to prove because the suspects were rarely identified and establishing bias was often difficult. Some Texas prosecutors thought that hate crime enhancements were seldom necessary since the state already had stiff penalties for serious crimes. Because undocumented immigrant workers in Texas routinely experience racial mistreatment, it is difficult to accept state attorneys' contention that only about one hate crime a year was worthy of prosecution in the entire state.

Along with Texas, other states failed to record or prosecute many hate crimes. Aimee Baldillo, staff attorney for the National Asian Pacific American Consortium, told *India Abroad* that many states dramatically undercount bias incidents, noting that Alabama, Louisiana, Montana, and Mississippi reported ten or fewer hate crimes in 2003.[166] These low numbers suggest that many states do a poor job in documenting attacks motivated by bigotry.

51) Regional differences in sentencing also undermine the reliability of local and national hate crime statistics.

Middle Easterners and South Asians might be unwilling to report bias incidents in areas where these types of threats or attacks do not result in fair sentences. In many states, judges are willing to jail bigots for issuing death threats. In other parts of the country, judges are more inclined to sentence these types of perpetrators to probation. In thirteen states, crimes motivated by gender are considered hate offenses, with enhanced penalties for perpetrators. States also differ on sentencing guidelines for hate crimes, and whether the conviction can be expunged through good behavior. Hate crime victims might hesitate to press charges if they live in a region where bias attacks are not punished appropriately.

52) Victims without clout may be unable to get the federal government to file hate crime charges and document their assaults.

Federal agents and prosecutors are selective about which crimes they choose to pursue; consequently, marginalized victims might be less likely to have their crimes tried in court and included in national reports. During the 9/11 backlash, many Muslims and Sikhs expressed disappointment that federal prosecutors refused to bring charges against the vast majority of hate crime perpetrators. According to a November 26, 2002 article in the *Seattle Times*, in the first 14 months after the terrorist attacks, the Justice Department only prosecuted 11 civil rights cases under its 'Backlash Discrimination Initiative,' even though it investigated an additional 403 complaints.[167] The shocking disparity between reported bias crimes and actual prosecutions makes many victims question whether it is worth the trouble to contact federal agents.

53) Hate crime statistics are also unreliable because traumatized victims often decide against reporting their crimes or filing charges.

Many South Asian and Arab victims do not report assaults because they wish to keep their experiences private. When Sanjay Nair raped a Muslim co-worker in Palo Alto, he made derogatory comments about her faith during the attack.[168] Although this rape survivor made the courageous decision to go public, many other minority women who are sexually assaulted by bigots may be too ashamed to tell others what happened to them. Women from conservative cultures might be particularly wary of reporting bias-motivated rapes or beatings to authorities.

54) Many hate crime victims opt against pressing charges because they are in denial of their own vulnerability.

Sometimes South Asians and Arabs in America fail to report bias incidents because they are unwilling to accept that their neighbors wish them harm. In chapter five, I discussed a May 29, 2004 gun attack on a sign for the Guru Nanak Sikh Temple in Solano County, California. Rather than report the hate crime to authorities, Temple officials initially chose to view the destruction as a random shooting, finding it difficult to believe it was triggered by anti-Sikh bigotry. Minorities unwilling to confront the ugly reality of xenophobia neglect to report attacks, leaving many hate crimes uncounted.

55) Victims also underreport attacks if they fear personal or group retaliation.

Many victims decide against reporting hate crimes because they are worried about social ostracism or further harassment. In chapter seven, I discussed how a food delivery man was practically drowned in West Texas in December 2010 by bigots who called him Osama bin Laden. Before the trial, the Sikh victim received several death threats, encouraging him to drop all charges against his assailants. Victims know that by pressing charges or putting themselves in the public eye, they might face even more serious threats or attacks. News coverage of hate crimes can make bigots aware of a particular ethnic community center or minority-owned business. Since the telephone directory and the internet provide easy access to addresses, many victims are wary of putting their businesses, their customers, and their families in harm's way by standing up to area nativists.

Muslim and Sikh bias crime victims may be particularly unwilling to report attacks in areas that are not racially or religiously diverse. After the federal government urged Americans to participate in a National Neighborhood Watch program, the FBI office in Merrillville, Indiana was inundated with calls about "suspicious" Middle Easterners and South Asians in the area.[169] Minority hate crime victims living in predominantly-white towns might be hesitant to draw attention to their homes or businesses by reporting attacks to authorities.

Minorities who discuss hate crimes with reporters often find themselves targeted by area xenophobes. After publishing an opinion piece in the *South Florida Sun Sentinel* about vandalism at local Islamic centers, Altaf Ali, director of the Florida chapter of CAIR, received a two-page letter threatening his life and referring to him as a walking corpse.[170] The letter also described Islam as the religion of Satan and proclaimed that it should be eradicated.[171] Along with the menacing words, the letter included a cartoon of nuclear bombs raining down on mosques in Medina and Mecca.

Sometimes, appearing anywhere in the news is enough to endanger a Sikh or Muslim. In April 2006, Arinder Chadha, a director of the California Sikh Council, was mentioned in an *Orange County Register* article on International Sikh Turban Day.[172] Two months later, Chadha's home in Orange County was vandalized in an anti-Indian hate crime.[173] When hate crime victims learn of these types of occurrences, they become more reluctant to discuss their experiences in public.

56) Hate crimes are also undercounted when witnesses fear retaliation.

Prosecutors are often reluctant to press charges unless attacks are corroborated by onlookers, who may be too intimidated to come forward. On many occasions, bigots frighten witnesses to prevent them from testifying at hate crime trials. In chapter nine, I discussed how Steven McManus attempted to harm an elderly Iranian couple in Huntington Beach, California, two weeks after 9/11, forcing them to walk into traffic in the hopes that they would be struck by oncoming cars.[174] McManus later threatened to kill his former landlord for talking to prosecutors involved in the case.[175] Because of the possibility of retaliation, witnesses may be reluctant to speak with investigators.

Along with fearing the consequences of testifying in court, some witnesses are afraid of speaking to reporters. In chapter five, I discussed how a group of 20 rock-throwing bigots attacked an Ohio mosque in September 2007. In news accounts of the attack, one of the witnesses was unwilling to give his last name to the *Columbus Dispatch* because he was afraid that the perpetrators might retaliate.[176] Authorities have difficulty documenting hate crimes when witnesses are too frightened to speak openly about what transpired or share their full names with others.

57) Hate crimes are underreported when victims fear the possibility of copycat crimes.

Many South Asians and Middle Easterners in America fail to report bias attacks if they fear that doing so might inspire other bigots to commit similar assaults. In chapter five, I noted that after the Solano Sikh temple was targeted by a gunman, temple founder Paul Randhawa expressed concern that causing a fuss about the shootings would be counterproductive. He told *India Abroad* that he thought it best for the community to keep a low profile and avoid enflaming ethnic tensions in the neighborhood.[177] Other victims might also refrain from calling attention to bias attacks out of concern for other minority members of the community.

58) Hate crime statistics are problematic because multiple threats to the same group are often lumped together as one hate crime.

Sometimes, federal statistics fail to capture the enormity of bias attacks when multiple threats to the same group are combined in a single police report. In chapter nine, I described how the Islamic Cultural Center in Las Vegas received more than a dozen threatening calls in the aftermath of 9/11. Because of the sheer volume of the threats, center officials reported less than half of the calls to police. If the same organization is threatened multiple times in the same week, police might lump the harassment into a single report instead of counting each incident separately. Federal statistics end up low if local authorities lump disparate attacks together in a single report.

Some bias-motivated crimes affected thousands of minority Americans. In a November 15, 2001 article, the *Palm Beach Post* reported that a computer hacker targeted the U.S. Muslim Council, disrupting communication for a week and repeatedly sending derogatory and virus-laden messages to more than 10,000 of its members.[178] Since 2001 federal hate crime statistics counted only 481 anti-Muslim incidents for the year, the thousands of victims directly affected by this bias-motivated computer attack were clearly not counted individually.

At times, even well-trained police detectives might be unsure about how to tally hate crimes, particularly when several people are victimized by more than one perpetrator on the same evening. In chapter eight, I discussed an August 2003 bias attack on a Sikh family outside their Queens residence. During the assault, the perpetrators physically assaulted Surinder Singh Gill, his wife, and his brother. Singh's children were present at the onset of the attack, which concluded after pizza delivery man Greg Hodge physically intervened and stopped the beating. Police officers might have difficulty deciding whether to combine all of these crimes into a single incident report or tally each one separately. If the two Sikh cabdrivers were verbally threatened as well as beaten, are they each victims of more than one hate crime? Were the two children victimized if they experienced the psychological trauma of witnessing their father getting attacked by bigots, even though they were not physically harmed themselves? Should authorities consider Mrs. Gill a victim of a hate assault if she was hit only after she put herself in harm's way to protect her husband and brother-in-law? If the pizza deliveryman was injured while assisting the Sikhs, should he be included as one of the victims of the hate crime? Federal hate crime statistics do not reflect the complexity of these issues, undercounting bias attacks involving multiple victims.

59) Death threats and other hate crimes are sometimes underreported when they become ubiquitous.

Hate crime victims rarely report attacks if they receive them constantly. Sofian Abdelaziz, the director of the Muslim Association of North America, reported that threatening emails had become commonplace in his line of work.[179] Because of time constraints, some Muslim activists might fail to report each new threat to local authorities, causing federal statistics to undercount anti-Muslim hate crimes.

60) Hate crimes are also undercounted when minority business owners fear scaring off customers.

Restaurant managers and store owners are sometimes reluctant to report hate crimes because they know that nervous customers might avoid a place regularly targeted by vandals or arsonists. In some instances, businessmen might be afraid of customer boycotts if they publicize that their establishment is a minority-owned or operated business.

61) Hate crime victims and witnesses are disinclined to report threats or attacks at work if they fear employer retaliation.

In chapter nine, I described how a construction crew in Gaithersburg threatened a 44-year old Arab-American co-worker with a metal pipe, even though he was a U.S. citizen and had worked for the company for more than a decade. When the employee reported the post-9/11 incident, his supervisor responded that they had the right to be angry.[180] Some hate crime victims lose their jobs or get demoted if they call attention to threats at work. According to a February 10, 2002 article in the *Los Angeles Times*, a nurse in New York City was ordered to take time off and given a demotion after she reported that a co-worker threatened to kill Muslims.[181] Victims and witnesses might be less likely to report hate crimes if doing so might result in career impediments or pay reductions.

62) Some hate-crime victims do not press charges because it's not worth the hassle, particularly since most perpetrators are never apprehended or convicted.

On December 18, 2001, the *San Diego Union Tribune* reported that of the 93 hate crimes that took place in the immediate aftermath of 9/11, police were close to solving only two of them.[182] This suggests that only a small percentage of hate crime perpetrators are apprehended in a timely fashion. Along with being discouraged by low arrest and conviction rates, some victims opt against filing reports because they are unwilling to attend time-consuming court sessions and testify to put their assailants in jail. Arab and South Asian tourists in the U.S. might be reluctant to file hate crime charges if doing so requires extending their stay, which may be cost-prohibitive.

63) Hate crimes are also undercounted because many economically-disadvantaged victims or witnesses find it too costly to attend all the necessary legal proceedings.

Many victims are reluctant to press criminal charges if they have to skip work in order to give a statement, identify their assailant in a line-up, or testify about an attack. Since many bosses are not tolerant of frequently-absent employees, many hate crime victims know that they might lose their jobs if they take the time to put their assailants behind bars. In some instances, crime victims have to pay for child care so they can attend sessions. Economically-disadvantaged victims or witnesses without cars sometimes have trouble commuting to court, making them more likely to withdraw from proceedings. Since some hate crime cases can take weeks to prosecute, minority victims might feel disinclined to bring their assailants to justice if doing so jeopardizes their jobs and financial survival.

64) Some victims may be reluctant to report hate crimes if doing so means dealing with callous defense attorneys who attack their credibility and belittle their experiences.

In the course of defending their clients, many attorneys make offensive comments that further traumatize victims of heinous bias crimes. In chapter five, I described how defense lawyer Joseph Pagano made the insensitive and spurious argument that his client William Reeves and his companions did not commit a hate crime when they set a New York Sikh Temple on fire because they thought the prayer center was a Muslim worship site.[183] Pagano argued that the youths could not be convicted of an anti-Sikh attack because they were targeting another faith. Another defense attorney, Charles Goldberg, told the *Post-*

Standard that the defendants simply broke windows and made comments, actions not serious enough to be considered a bias attack.[184] Along with undermining hate crime victims' experiences, top defense attorneys help accused criminals escape punishment by selecting sympathetic jurors and by reminding the court of mitigating factors. Victims might be wary of pressing charges if it means facing callous lawyers in court.

Defense attorneys sometimes put victims on trial as a way of shifting jurors' attention away from the culpability of their clients. Hate crime survivors might be unwilling to put their own lives under this degree of scrutiny, particularly if they work under the table, live with undocumented relatives, or have personal affairs they wish to keep private.

65) Bias-crime victims also underreport hate crimes because they are reluctant to have their experiences undermined by experts for the defense.

Sometimes, professional consultants challenge the credibility of hate crime victims when testifying in favor of the accused. For example, Harvard law professor Randall Kennedy drew upon his academic expertise to undermine the testimony of an African-American man beaten by Nick Minucci, a previously-convicted hate-crime perpetrator. On September 11, 2001, Minucci fired a paint ball at a Sikh man while screaming "Fucking Indians."[185] He was found guilty of this crime. A few years later, on June 29, 2005, Minucci was brought up on new hate crime charges for beating Glenn Moore, an African-American man, with a baseball bat while calling him "nigger."[186] To try to get his client acquitted of this second bias attack, Minucci's defense attorney Albert Gaudelli used Kennedy to testify on Minucci's behalf. During his testimony, Kennedy spoke about the research he did for his book, <u>Nigger: The Strange Career of a Troublesome Word</u>.[187] Gaudelli used Kennedy's expert witness testimony to bolster Minucci's claim that the word "nigger" was not necessarily offensive, since he heard black people use it in songs and music videos. In a June 21, 2006 article for the *Seattle Skanner*, Margaret Kimberly questioned the value of Kennedy's testimony, suggesting that he is likely the only black person in America who would argue that a bias-motivated beating is not taking place when a white man screams "nigger" at an African-American while striking him on the head with a baseball bat.[188] Some hate crime victims might be unwilling to file charges if one of the consequences of doing so is having their experiences undermined by defense experts who use their credentials to discredit them.

66) Hate crimes are sometimes underreported because many minorities with foreign-language proficiency are underrepresented in the legal profession.

In the Middle East, becoming a civil or criminal lawyer is considered a relatively low-status job. Top students in Egypt and other Arab countries are admitted into Arab medical schools or engineering programs. Other successful pupils earn the grades to become computer technicians or business majors. The students who lack the grades to qualify for these more prestigious programs become attorneys. One Egyptian friend went to law school because he didn't have the grades to get into the more competitive literary studies program at Alexandria University. Because Islamic law or "Sharia" is considered infinitely more important than lowly civil law, students with good grades are more likely to study the Quran and Islamic law while mediocre Arab students are more likely to go into the legal profession. Many Arab immigrants in the U.S. share the Middle Eastern view that civil and criminal lawyers lack the prestige of physicians, engineers, and entrepreneurs. One Lebanese friend said her parents would be deeply disappointed if she went to an American law school instead of doing something more prestigious like starting her own business or getting her Ph.D. For this reason, many immigrant students decide against becoming American attorneys. As a result, many Middle Easterners with Arabic language fluency are underrepresented in the American legal profession, making it more difficult for hate crime victims to find a lawyer who understands his or her specific dialect and culture. Although larger numbers of second and third generation Arab-Americans have become attorneys and joined well-respected professional organizations like the Arab-American Bar

Association, many of these lawyers do not speak any of the four major Arabic dialects and are not sufficient in number to accommodate the needs of all hate crime victims.

67) Bias attacks are also undercounted because hate crime enhancements are difficult to prove in court.

District attorneys often find it daunting to prove a perpetrator's bias-motivated intent, and worry that hate crime convictions can be easily reversed on appeal. For this reason, prosecutors sometimes drop hate crime enhancements in order to win cases and reduce their workloads. Since there is no system of tracking how many hate-motivated attacks result in convictions for bias crimes, prosecutors have little incentive to include these enhancements and risk losing a case.

68) Language barriers can stall investigations, resulting in an undercounting of attacks.

On occasion, communication problems prevent police from properly interviewing victims and witnesses. In chapter ten, I discussed how Minneapolis police were unable to interview Spanish-speaking onlookers at a bus stop to find out what happened to a Somali senior citizen who died after being assaulted in October 2001. Hate crimes pass under the radar when investigators are unable to communicate with immigrant community members who have knowledge of bias crimes.

69) Hate crimes are also underreported because many foreign-born victims have difficulty navigating the American legal system.

Some hate crime victims may be unfamiliar with the American justice system, particularly if they were born abroad. In a 2007 study conducted by the South Asian American Leaders of Tomorrow, researchers argued that immigrants unfamiliar with U.S. legal procedures were less likely to report hate crimes.[189] Since the procedure for reporting hate crimes can be confusing, victims might be unsure how to navigate bureaucratic channels and file the appropriate forms.

On occasion, the location of the bias attack may have bearing on how it is supposed to be reported. Victims experiencing hate crimes on school grounds may be unaware that they are required to provide the following information to the Department of Education's Office of Civil Rights:[190]

1. a signed written explanation of what happened;
2. a way to contact the complainant;
3. identification of the person or institution injured by the discrimination;
4. identification of the person or institution alleged to have discriminated;
5. sufficient information about the factual basis for the complainant's belief that discrimination occurred;
6. any objective evidence (written statements, graffiti, mocking imitation of an accent, negative humor, inappropriate references)

Many crime victims might find these reporting requirements burdensome and the legal jargon confusing. If the information is incomplete or if a third party initiates the complaint, the hate crime is never tallied.

70) Hate crimes are also undercounted because undocumented immigrants seldom report hate crimes.

Illegal workers or foreign visitors with expired visas may be wary of the legal consequences of reporting hate crimes or providing witness testimony. Many are unwilling to alert authorities if doing so means risking deportation. Aimee Baldillo, staff attorney for the National Asian Pacific American Consortium, told *India Abroad* that many undocumented immigrants opted against contacting police about bias crimes because they were unwilling to be questioned about their immigration status.[191]

Even if the victim is in the country legally, he or she may be reluctant to report a hate crime if another household member or witness to the attack has visa problems. By targeting the most vulnerable community members, bigots in the U.S. can strike out at certain demographic populations with impunity.

71) Self-reliant victims sometimes fail to report hate crimes to police, preferring to handle problems themselves.

In chapter eight, I discussed how Upinder Gupta did not contact Fremont police the first few times bigoted vandals attacked her home. Instead, she found out which kids in the neighborhood were responsible and talked to them directly. Hate crimes are undercounted when victims choose to confront their attackers directly instead of going through official channels.

72) Budgetary constraints sometimes hamper hate crime investigations, leading to an undercounting of bias-motivated incidents.

Underfunded police departments sometimes lack the manpower to investigate and solve all reported bias crimes. When Upinder Gupta finally went to police in April 2005 to report a series of attacks on her home, authorities were unresponsive. When asked about these bias crimes, Fremont police Chief Craig Steckler told the *Oakland Tribune* that because of budgetary concerns, his force couldn't possibly respond to every case of vandalism.[192] Police departments that lack adequate resources are unable to devote sufficient manpower to clear bias-motivated attacks.

73) Victims who have concerns about the racist and classist criminal justice system might be reluctant to press hate crime charges against underprivileged minority assailants.

Because of the biases of judges and juries, poor minority perpetrators are not given the same considerations as more affluent white Christian offenders. Victims aware of these legal disparities might be less inclined to press hate crime charges against economically-disadvantaged minority assailants, knowing that they might not be treated fairly.

Minority victims who understand and despise the racist prison system might be particularly disinclined to press hate crime charges. Although jailing a violent bigot might prevent other hate crimes from occurring, many victims understand that segregated prisons do little to rehabilitate xenophobes. Journalism articles have called attention to the deleterious roles that U.S. prisons play in reifying ethno-racial differences.[193] Incarcerated felons are subjected to institutionalized racial segregation. White convicts are often pressured into joining neo-Nazi gangs. Black prisoners come together to avoid white supremacist attacks. Mexican-Americans join exclusively-Latino gangs to protect themselves against other inmates. In the exercise yard and dining room, minority groups maintain their rigid self-segregation, learning quickly that non-compliance could mean rape or death. Convicts who are only minimally racist become much more so after living in this type of segregated and violent environment. Hate crime victims might wonder whether it is at all useful to send their assailants to these types of institutions, where violence is commonplace, bigotry is reinforced, and skin color becomes the totality of prisoners' identities. Instead of investigating their time attending court proceedings to send perpetrators to jail, some hate crime victims opt instead to participate in anti-racism efforts at schools or neighborhood centers. This ends up depressing hate crime statistics.

74) Victims feeling pity or empathy may underreport bias-motivated attacks.

Arab-Americans, Muslims, and South Asians were just as horrified by 9/11 as other community members, experiencing the same intense feelings of impotence and rage. Like everyone else, Muslims, Sikhs, and Arab-Americans felt surges of anger as the magnitude of the tragedy sunk in. In the months after the terrorist attacks, Americans seemed to be experiencing a collective post-traumatic stress syndrome. Although hate crimes are never justifiable or excusable, victims who share their assailants' rage at Osama bin Laden might be more capable of empathizing with their assailants' outbursts.

In chapter five, I described how Tajuddin Shuaib, the director of the King Fahad Mosque in Culver City, refused to press charges against a vandal who spray-painted the word "murderers" on the Islamic house of worship in the aftermath of the World Trade Center attacks. According to a September 13, 2001 *Washington Post* article, Shuaib said he empathized with the woman, understanding that she was overcome with emotions after 9/11.[194]

Some emotionally-sensitive Muslims and Sikhs were also reluctant to report non-violent hate crimes because many of their fellow Americans were coping with more profound tragedies. In a September 18, 2001 article in the *Boston Globe*, Meera Kumar, a Ford executive living in Manhattan, noted that many South Asians were hesitant to report bias-motivated attacks while Americans were mourning the deaths of their countrymen.[195]

75) Hate crime victims raised in religious or moral traditions emphasizing forgiveness might opt against pressing hate crime charges.

Instead of wanting their assailants to go to jail, some victims might hope for their attackers' psychological and spiritual rehabilitation through education and counseling. Religious leaders who preach forgiveness and mercy may be especially reluctant to demand hate crime enhancements for vandals. In chapter two, I discussed how Muslims in West Springfield refused to press charges against three teenagers who broke 18 windows in 1985. According to the *Boston Herald*, Muslims "choosing forgiveness" decided against holding the vandals legally responsible.[196]

Sikhs have also been inclined to forgive their attackers instead of pressing for legal remedies. In chapter five, I discussed a November 18, 2001 fire that destroyed the Sikh temple in Oswego. Days after the bias-motivated arson, Ralph Singh, co-founder of the targeted gurdwara, explained to the *Post-Standard* that prayerful forgiveness could serve as a model for how people can overcome their differences.[197] Rather than fixate on filing hate crime reports and bringing the perpetrators to justice, Singh viewed the arson as an opportunity to repair community relations and use compassion as a weapon against hatred.[198] Although mercy is a virtue, hate crimes are undercounted when victims fail to press charges.

CHAPTER TWELVE:

'A KIND OF SOLUTION' –
75 STEPS TO CURB BACKLASH BIGOTRY

At the beginning of this book, I mentioned Constantine Cavafy's narrative poem, "Waiting for the Barbarians," telling the story of a town obsessed with a foreign menace.[1] The poem ends with the community's disorientation when the enemy fails to arrive:

Why the sudden confusion and bewilderment?

(How serious people's faces look.)

Why are the streets and squares rapidly emptying?

Why is everyone returning home, lost in thought?

Because night has come and the barbarians haven't arrived.

Our men at the border say the barbarians have ceased to exist.

What will happen to us without barbarians?

Those people were a kind of solution.

When I first encountered Cavafy's poem in my childhood, I remember being intrigued by its last line. What, exactly, did it mean?

Rediscovering this poem as an adult, I understood that its ending addresses the need for groups to define themselves against a real or imagined enemy, to keep themselves cohesive and purpose-driven. By adopting an 'us vs. them' worldview, a society can decide who deserves to be included in its circle of belonging.

Many Americans responded to 9/11 by treating certain minority communities as outsiders, undeserving of equal protection under the law. An August 2006 *USA Today* poll reported that 39% of Americans believed that Muslims – even U.S. citizens – should be forced to carry special identification as an anti-terrorist measure. These alarming poll results were publicized overseas, in magazines such as India's *Hindustan Times*.[2] Close to a decade after the terrorist attacks, levels of Islamophobia remained high. In June 2011, U.C. Berkeley and CAIR released a study documenting that Americans' favorable rating of Islam was only about 30%, ten points lower than it was in November 2001.[3]

Some Middle Eastern and South Asian immigrants were so traumatized by the backlash that they fled the U.S., uprooting their families and leaving their jobs. Many moved back to their homelands, even if it meant returning to war-torn countries or financially-destitute areas. Some backlash victims immigrated to Canada and Europe, hoping to find a more tolerant environment elsewhere.

Since the backlash transcended national borders, many immigrants found it impossible to escape bigotry and Islamophobia simply by relocating. Even in Canada, a country known for its progressive policies and tolerant attitudes, Muslims continued to be subjected to bias crimes and discrimination years after the attacks on the Pentagon and World Trade Center. In June 2006, vandals broke into the Manitoba Islamic Association mosque in Winnipeg.[4] A few months later, near the five-year anniversary of 9/11, vandals once again desecrated the house of worship. In this September 16, 2006 attack, the culprits spray-painted swastikas and other hate graffiti on the mosque.[5]

Islamic schools were also targeted in many parts of Canada. On January 23, 2007, vandals in Montreal attacked "Les Jeunes Musulmans Canadiens," a school with 500 registered Muslim students, ages six to 16.[6] During this assault, the vandals used bricks and rocks to shatter 17 of the school's windows. The perpetrators also broke open twenty classroom doors and smashed the windows of the school bus. Canadian Muslims regarded the destruction as a bias-crime, and urged detectives to investigate it as such.

Islamophobes also committed despicable acts in Europe. According to the *Christian Science Monitor*, over 7,000 Parisians held a pork and alcohol party in the summer of 2009, protesting the presence of Muslims in France and the perceived Islamification of the country.[7] Nativism also surged in England. In the summer of 2011, the *Nottingham Evening Post* reported that members of the English Defence League put a pig's head sprayed with anti-Muslim sentiments on a pole at the site of a proposed mosque in West Bridgeford.[8] The hate crime traumatized British Muslims, sending them the message that they were not welcome in the area. Anti-Muslim attacks also took place in other parts of Europe. On July 22, 2011, Norwegian bigot Behring Breivik killed scores of his countrymen, angry at his government for allowing Muslim immigrants into the country. Casualties of Breivik's attack included Muslims. Explaining why he opened fire on youngsters attending the Labour Party's annual AUF summer camp, Breivik said that he was angry at the government's pro-immigration policies, and maintained that all Muslims should be deported from Europe. Breivik's bigotry-inspired massacre showed the intensity of Islamophobia in many parts of the West.

Since bias crimes targeting Middle Easterners and South Asians are so prevalent and underreporting is such a problem, it seems daunting to imagine how the situation can be improved. Instead of becoming resigned to the reality of hate crimes, it is important to adopt a multi-pronged approach to address the problem, while keeping in mind the following bit of South Asian folk wisdom: "How do you eat an elephant? – One bite at a time." There are 75 steps that can be taken to curtail backlash bigotry:

1) End Humiliating Screenings and Unfair Detentions at Airports

An important step in curtailing the 9/11 backlash involves treating "suspect" minorities fairly in public settings. Just as African-American motorists are sometimes pulled over for simply "Driving While Black," Arab, Afghan, and South Asian airline passengers traveling through security checkpoints are often treated inappropriately for "Flying While Brown." To curb xenophobia, it is important to end racial profiling of minority travelers at airports, so that other Americans will not grow accustomed to seeing their darker-skinned countrymen being treated like second-class citizens.

In the years after the terrorist strikes, Sikhs faced heightened scrutiny before boarding flights. The TSA specifically instructed screeners to pay careful attention to turban-wearing passengers. According to an October 2002 article in *Asian Weekly*, Hardeep Singh Rekhi, a Seattle-born Sikh attending Tulane Law School, observed that he had been 'randomly-selected' approximately 80% of the time he went through airport security.[9] American Sikhs were particularly disturbed by a short-lived TSA policy requiring airport screeners to pat down passengers' religious headwear. After contacting the TSA and voicing their concerns, Sikhs convinced federal authorities to remove this screener guideline. After 2007, the wording of the policy was altered so that screeners were instructed to conduct additional screening for all passengers wearing bulky clothing, a more broad category that included turbans. Despite this minor policy change, Sikhs continued to be disproportionately targeted by TSA personnel. In early 2010, the TSA told Sikh Americans that the use of full-body scanners would prevent them from being unfairly singled out at security checkpoints.[10] Unfortunately, once the Rapsican equipment was in place at airports across the country, the TSA declared that the new scanners were unable to see through the layers of a standard dastaar.[11] As a result, screeners were compelled to continue using intrusive secondary screening measures, such as testing turbans with chemical screens and probing them with hand-held metal detectors. Sikh travelers were also humiliated by security personnel who overstepped the boundaries of the law. On two separate occasions in November 2010, TSA officers insisted that airline passenger Daljeet Singh Mann remove his dastaar at Bay Area airports.[12] As a result of these degrading experiences, Mann began wearing a hat on airline flights. In response to the widespread mistreatment of Sikhs at airports, many Sikhs began restricting their air travel altogether, using buses to travel across state lines. The problems Sikhs routinely experience at airports highlight the need for the development and universal use of screening devices capable of seeing through passengers' turbans, so South Asian travelers and other minorities can walk through airport security without being intrusively singled out.

As an Arab-American with a Middle-Eastern surname, I have often wondered whether I was being unfairly profiled every time I was 'randomly-selected' at airport security checkpoints. A few years prior to 9/11, when I was flying from Boston to San Francisco, an airport baggage screener put seven prominent orange stickers on my suitcase, writing my last name, "Karam," on a few of them. I was disturbed that my Middle-Eastern surname was being put on a security alert sticker. I voiced my concern to airport personnel, arguing that last names should not be used in such a manner. I later mailed in the seven orange stickers and a description of the incident to the national offices of the American-Arab Anti-Discrimination Committee, hoping that they would take appropriate action with Federal Aviation Administration officials.

A few months after that, when I was on board another flight, I was shocked that an airline passenger next to me had a large pocketknife, which she was using to cut an apple. When I asked her about how she got that cutting utensil on board the aircraft, she informed me that airline regulations allowed knives on flights. I thought this policy was absolutely crazy, since a hijacker could easily use a sharp utensil to take a hostage and gain control of an aircraft. I considered writing a protest letter to the FAA and my elected member of Congress, recommending that this policy be changed. I never wrote the letter, guessing that aviation officials would likely do nothing except possibly put my name on some list that would end up increasing the amount of humiliating screening I would be subjected to every time I traveled. After 9/11, I berated myself for not taking action to change the airline policy allowing sharp objects on board planes. Minority passengers are undoubtedly less likely to report security concerns if they feel they are already being racially-profiled at airports.

In September 2002, I became a flight attendant for Principal Air, a now-defunct charter airline based in Las Vegas. While working for this company, I was shocked to learn that crew members were expected to pass out extremely large knives to passengers who ordered steak. On a few different occasions, I helped hand out about a dozen of these sharp knives to a group of about a dozen steak-eating Saudi passengers who chartered the company's 707 or 727. The FAA's policy of allowing large knives on private aircraft alarmed me, since it would be relatively easy for a group of armed passengers to overpower an unarmed flight crew consisting of a couple of flight attendants and pilots. The double standard was crazy – anyone who flew commercially after 9/11 could not bring even a small nail scissors aboard an aircraft, but any affluent group who chartered a large aircraft could have sharp steak knives hand-delivered to them during the in-flight meal, even if the plane was above densely-populated U.S. cities. I considered writing the FAA and my Congressional representative of the folly of distributing large knives to passengers on private planes. Because I was already being routinely 'randomly-selected' for heightened security at airports, I worried that sending such a letter might cause me to be placed under even more rigorous and time-consuming scrutiny or detained indefinitely under suspicion of having foreknowledge of some upcoming terrorist plot. I was also concerned that challenging the policy of distributing knives to passengers might endanger my flight attendant job and lead to racial profiling of Arabs and Muslims on charter flights, instead of universally-prohibiting the distribution of sharp utensils on all private aircraft.

The point I'm making is simple – by harassing or intimidating innocent citizens, the FBI and Homeland Security Department make innocent Americans reluctant to contact government agents and report something that might actually help prevent a future attack.

Although it is important to conduct thorough screenings, the TSA should not humiliate minorities in public or engage in racial or religious profiling. Many Middle Easterners, South Asians, Muslims, and Sikhs believe they are almost always deliberately-selected for security screenings, even though airline security personnel reassure them that the selection process is random. Muslims and Sikhs believe that by constantly singling them out in public, the TSA is broadcasting the message that minority travelers are inherently dangerous, and should be treated accordingly. According to a poll published in 2007, 77% of Sikh respondents listed air travel concerns as one of the most important issues they faced, second only to hate crimes.[13] When federal screeners treat minorities unfairly at airports, it unwisely normalizes discrimination in the U.S.

2) Allow Security-Screened Minorities On Their Scheduled Flights

Along with ending the racial profiling of minority travelers at security checkpoints, it is important to curb other forms of discrimination at airports. After the terrorist strikes, minority passengers were repeatedly thrown off of airplanes if their religious affiliation and ethnicity made others uncomfortable. On September 17, 2001, Ashraf Khan, a Pakistani-American, was sitting in the first-class cabin of a Delta Airlines plane, about to leave San Antonio for San Francisco, when the pilot instructed him to leave the aircraft. According to *India-West*, the Delta captain told Khan that he would have to get off the flight because the crew felt unsafe having him on board.[14] Completely shocked, Khan asked why his presence compromised the safety of the aircraft. The captain told Khan he didn't have to give him a reason, and informed him that his baggage would be off-loaded. Because Khan was not permitted to fly on Delta Airlines to San Francisco, he was unable to catch his connecting flight to Pakistan and ended up missing his brother's wedding. In response to his mistreatment, Khan filed an FBI complaint against the carrier. On September 21, 2001, Delta responded to Khan's criticism by maintaining that a captain had the discretionary ability to eject passengers.[15] A company spokesman later apologized for the unfair treatment of the South Asian passenger.

At the height of the backlash, Arab-American and Middle Eastern passengers were also singled out and removed from flights. On September 27, 2001, the Arlington Heights *Daily Herald* reported that several commercial carriers, including Delta, Northwest, and United Airlines, denied boarding to some Arabs who made others uncomfortable in the weeks following 9/11.[16] An Egyptian-American and a 15-year old Saudi teenager were among the minority travelers prohibited from boarding their scheduled flights.[17]

Even security-cleared passengers were sometimes singled out. On December 15, 2001, an Arab-American secret service agent traveling from D.C. to Texas to protect President George W. Bush was instructed to de-board an American Airlines flight, apparently because his ethnicity made him a suspicious traveler.[18]

Sikhs were also harassed on flights in the aftermath of 9/11. In November 2002, Hansdip Singh Bindra, an American passenger of South Asian ethnicity, was harassed by a flight attendant who mistook him for a Middle Eastern Muslim. When Bindra attempted to explain that his turban and beard were part of his Sikh faith, the stewardess told him to shut up. She also made references to 9/11, and solicited other passengers to help her in case she needed to subdue him.[19] In September 2003, Bindra filed a lawsuit against Delta Airlines and its regional affiliate, Atlantic Coast Airlines, alleging racial profiling, intimidation, and harassment. Other passengers gave sworn affidavits that the flight attendant lost her composure and that the traveling computer consultant did nothing to provoke her. Bindra eventually reached a confidential settlement with the carrier.

Despite this legal judgment, Delta employees continued to harass minority travelers. On June 22, 2004, the U.S. Department of Transportation filed a lawsuit against the airline. At the conclusion of this case, the air carrier was ordered to provide at least $900,000 worth of civil rights training to its pilots, flight crew, and other airline personnel.[20]

Unfortunately, minority passengers continued to be ejected from American flights years after the terrorist attacks. The *Arab American News* reported that on August 28, 2007, six Michigan men were escorted off an American Airlines flight 590, which was leaving from San Diego.[21] This Chicago-bound plane took off and then abruptly returned to San Diego, where it was rescheduled for the following day. While the airline assisted the other 113 passengers in finding hotel rooms, the six Arab and Muslim men were segregated from the other passengers and detained.[22] No other passengers were held or questioned. During the ordeal, the profiled passengers, who worked as U.S. government consultants to Iraq-bound troops, claimed that they suffered unlawful detainment, interrogation, and public humiliation, causing others to look at them as potential terrorists. The six minority travelers believed they were singled out because of their Arabic names: Talal Cholagh, Ali Alzerej, Hassan Alzerej, Hussein Alsali, Mohammed Al-Saedy, and

David Al-Watan.[23]   In response to this humiliating experience, they filed a civil lawsuit against American Airlines.   Lawrence Garcia, an attorney representing the plaintiffs, told the *Arab American News* that the airline needed to be held accountable for its reprehensible conduct.[24]

The following year, minority air travelers continued to be racially-profiled.   In November 2008, the *Sacramento Bee* reported that a group of Sikh musicians were asked to leave flight 493 from Sacramento to Phoenix because passengers and airline personnel had security concerns about their presence on board the aircraft.[25]

Progressive Americans also lost faith in the TSA following the August 2009 lengthy detention of Pomona college student Nick George for attempting to board a Southwest Airline flight carrying Arabic-English flash cards.[26]   After apprehending George at the Philadelphia airport on his way back to Southern California, federal investigators reminded the back-packing senior that he was studying the language spoken by Osama bin Laden, the 9/11 mastermind.[27]   The incident upset civil libertarians, who pointed out that George was an American from Wyncote, Pennsylvania who had done nothing other than study a foreign language.

On occasion, Muslim religious leaders were forced off of airplanes.   In the spring of 2011, two imams traveling to a conference on Islamophobia were removed from their flight.   The Muslims had successfully passed through TSA screening and had boarded their Atlantic Southeast Airlines flight 5452 from Memphis to Charlotte when the pilot returned the aircraft to the gate and ordered them off the plane, claiming that their presence made other passengers uncomfortable.[28]   When airline officials asked seated travelers if they minded flying with the Muslims, no one expressed any concern.[29]   Despite the accepting attitude of the other passengers, the pilot refused to fly with the imams.   Because of his insistence, the plane took off without them on board.   Civil rights activists were outraged that the Delta-owned airline would employ a pilot who demonstrated such overt bigotry, kicking off security-cleared passengers solely because of their religious affiliation.   Advocates were also upset that airline personnel asked other passengers to raise their hands if they objected to the Muslims, pointing out that it is not appropriate to conduct a popularity poll on a commercial aircraft, making travelers vote on whether they approved of certain racial and religious minorities.

Another imam, Al-Amin Latif, also experienced difficulty traveling to the same Islamophobia conference. When he went to the airport, he discovered that he was prohibited from boarding his American Airlines flight.[30] The native-born U.S. citizen asked why he was not allowed to fly, and airline personnel gave him a number to call.   Latif spoke with different officials who gave him confusing answers about why he was not allowed to board the plane, with some of them speculating that there might be a problem with the birthdate on his driver's license or the way his name was spelled on his ID.[31]   After being barred from the flight, Latif was forced to drive 12 hours from New York to Charlotte to attend the civil rights conference.   Activists were dismayed that Muslims were still experiencing anti-Muslim discrimination at airports more than nine years after 9/11.

A decade after the terrorist strikes, airline passengers continued to face discrimination.   The *Detroit Free Press* reported that on September 11, 2011, Shoshana Hebshi and two South Asian passengers were treated unfairly on their flight from Denver to Detroit.[32]   Because the Indian men used the bathroom on the flight, concerned passengers and flight crew worried that they were involved in terrorist activity.   In response, authorities scrambled F16 jets to follow the Frontier Airline flight, which was ordered to land in a remote area. After the unscheduled stop, a SWAT team boarded the aircraft and hauled away the two men and Hebshi, a half-Jewish, half-Arab stay-at-home mother of six-year old boys.[33]   The Wayne County Airport Police helped detain the three travelers, who were handcuffed, strip-searched, and made to open every orifice for inspection. Hebshi told the London *Guardian* that during her four-hour detention, federal authorities interrogated her about a 2001 trip to Venezuela, her marriage, her life as a homemaker, and her work as a reporter for *J.*, the Jewish newspaper of San Francisco.[34]   The three travelers were eventually released.   Because Hebshi never left her seat during the flight or spoke with the two South Asian men, she felt that she was being profiled because of her Middle Eastern looks and her Saudi ancestry.[35]   Hebshi reported that the agents who questioned her informed her that the re-routing of her flight was just one of 50 other travel-related suspicious incidents that happened that day, making her wonder how widespread the racial profiling was becoming.[36]   Activists were disturbed by the arrest of the two Indian travelers, pointing out that using a bathroom was a normal flight activity and that the assumption that the passengers were terrorists was based exclusively on their ethnic background. Because the detention of Hebashi and the two South Asian travelers took place on the tenth anniversary of the terrorist strikes, civil libertarians saw it as a manifestation of the ongoing backlash.

To combat xenophobia in the U.S., it is important to eliminate this type of mistreatment. Since racial profiling sends the harmful message that some ethnic or religious communities are inherently dangerous, federal officials need to require pilots, flight attendants, security screeners, and baggage handlers to take well-designed culturally-sensitive training programs to ensure that such blatant acts of discrimination stop happening.

3) End Racial Profiling at Border Crossings

Arab-Americans, Muslims, and Sikhs have filed hundreds of complaints in response to the mistreatment they routinely receive at U.S. border crossings. Beginning after 9/11 and continuing for years afterwards, minority travelers reported being harassed, groped, and grilled about their religious beliefs when entering the country. Muslim women were particularly likely to file complaints alleging racial profiling. According to a March 2011 article in the *Detroit News*, more than a dozen Somali women reported that they were searched in invasive and humiliating ways at the Ambassador Bridge and the Blue Water Bridge in Port Huron, characterizing their experiences as a form of sexual harassment.[37] Muslim men also complained of mistreatment at these sites, describing how border guards handcuffed them, searched them intrusively, and asked them inappropriate questions about their religious practices. According to the *Detroit News*, Kheireddine Bouzid, an Ann Arbor teacher of Algerian descent, claimed that he was put in a cell for four hours and questioned about his terrorist affiliations when he re-entered the U.S., although he did nothing wrong and had an American passport.[38]

Other minority travelers were mistreated at airports upon their arrival in the U.S. Imam Ali Suleiman Ali, a native of Ghana living in Michigan, was detained and questioned for three hours at Detroit Metropolitan Airport when he returned home in July 2010.[39] Several months later, when he was coming back from another trip, he was once again harassed by custom agents, who handcuffed him and searched him from head to toe. Minority travelers should complain to their elected representatives to end racial profiling, discriminatory searches, and sexual harassment at border crossings. Constituents should insist that public officials take action on this issue, mandating that border guards take sensitivity classes, comply with regulations, and face sanctions from a specially-designated oversight board for any misconduct.

4) Report Racial Profiling at Train Stations and Bus Terminals

Minority passengers were occasionally profiled at train stations and bus terminals during the 9/11 backlash. In chapter three, I discussed how Sikh passengers were singled out on trains and arrested for carrying their religiously-proscribed kirpans in the immediate aftermath of the terrorist attacks. Media coverage of these high-profile arrests caused many Americans to confuse South Asian Sikhs with members of the Taliban.

Members of "suspect" ethno-racial groups were also singled out and harassed at bus stations. In chapter six, I discussed how Hasnain Javed, a 20-year old Pakistani college student, was racially profiled at a Mobile, Alabama bus terminal on September 18, 2001. He was then taken to a Wiggins jail, where he was beaten by inmates. Racially-profiling minorities at bus stations transmits the intolerant message that certain ethnic groups pose a danger to the community.

Years after 9/11, interstate bus travelers were still being affected by the backlash and the wave of xenophobia it unleashed. According to the March 2006 *Arab American News*, an Iraqi-American man traveling from Chicago to Detroit was forced off his bus as soon as the driver learned of the passenger's national origin, stranding him in the middle of the highway.[40] Rather than apologize, the bus driver continued to maintain that his actions were warranted.

In the same issue, the *Arab American News* reported that another traveler experienced overt discrimination during an interstate bus trip from Detroit to D.C. At a stop in Toledo, Ohio, the bus driver asked the passenger about his national origin. When the traveler replied that he was an Arab-American of Iraqi descent, the driver pushed him out of line, allowed other passengers to board the vehicle, and drove away, leaving the interstate traveler at the station.[41] When the driver was called to task for his actions, he attempted to justify his conduct instead of realizing that his behavior was outrageous.

Ethnic and religious organizations should educate their members about how to report travel-related discrimination, so that other minorities are not similarly targeted. By distributing educational pamphlets and creating web site links, groups could ensure that members of 'suspect' groups know how to make bias complaints to the Department of Transportation.

5) Allow Undocumented Workers To Report Hate Crimes Without Fear of Deportation

Local, state, and federal government need to guarantee that undocumented community members are able to report bias-motivated attacks without fear of deportation. Unless police and federal authorities are prohibited from contacting immigration officials about the residency status of victims and witnesses, they will not be able to collect the information they need to close investigations. By preventing crime victims from being interrogated about their visas, community members would be able to come forward without attracting the attention of border patrol officers.

Without privacy guarantees, undocumented workers often feel unable to report life-threatening hate crimes to authorities. In chapter seven, I recounted how a New York City motorist fired a bullet at the head of a Sikh taxi driver on September 30, 2001. The victim did not inform law enforcement personnel about the attempted murder, worried that investigators would learn of his illegal status and deport him. In chapter three, I discussed how a Pakistani youth was beaten and stabbed in Brooklyn in January 2003. Because his visitor's visa expired, he did not report the vicious attack to police. By allowing undocumented community members to testify about hate crimes without fear of legal consequences, the government could get violent bigots off the streets and ensure that America was a safer place for U.S. citizens, permanent residents, and foreign nationals.

6) Preserve Civil Liberties by Eliminating the Patriot Act

To curb the 9/11 backlash, it is important to preserve civil liberties in wartime. Instead of deterring future attacks, intrusive governmental policies unsettle minority community members by broadcasting the xenophobic message that they might be dangerous. In the March 22, 2003 issue of the *Charleston Gazette*, Kate Long criticizes the Patriot Act, arguing that it expanded the government's ability to detain dissidents, wiretap phones, examine email messages, obtain library records, and search homes without the knowledge or consent of residents.[42] Long also challenges the Patriot Act for allowing the federal employees to use secret evidence to hold immigrants indefinitely, without allowing them to speak to their lawyers, simply by saying that the detainees might pose a threat to national security. Eliminating the Patriot Act would send the message that minority community members should not be singled out unfairly.

In chapter eleven, I discussed how I organized a 2003 anti-war 'Blood for Oil' blood drive at Dolores Park in San Francisco. During this protest, a volunteer dressed up as Uncle Sam gave a quart of motor oil to anyone who donated at the mobile blood bank, drawing attention to the human costs of financing the Iraq War. Because of the novelty of the protest concept, newspapers and television stations covered the event and mentioned me by name, perhaps causing me to come to the attention of overzealous Homeland Security investigators investigating antiwar activists.[43] After the politically-themed blood drive, my friends began asking me about the strange clicking noises they sometimes heard when talking to me on my landline. It was embarrassing to inform them that I may have been one of the thousands of innocent Arab-Americans absurdly placed under phone surveillance after 9/11. On one occasion, my friend Nancy was in the middle of telling me about her dog's hemorrhoids when the phone began clicking. She started laughing hysterically at the thought that this conversation was somehow relevant to the security of the nation. She joked that government agents may have speculated that "taking the dog to the vet for hemorrhoids" might be code for some secret mission. Another friend also heard the clicking noises and found the situation comical. Instead of appreciating the seriousness of the matter, he joked, "Well, I guess we shouldn't talk about that HEROIN SHIPMENT. Ha ha ha." I wondered if I could be placed in indefinite detention if federal agents did not understand his sense of humor. I stopped speaking to this acquaintance, worried that he might make another facetious remark that some phone monitor might take seriously, i.e. "Well, I guess we shouldn't talk about that BOMB PLOT. Ha ha ha." As a result of these experiences, I started avoided using the phone or participating in Bay Area anti-war organizations. Even if the clicks were actually due to some mechanical problem, the awareness that the U.S. government was tapping some phones without probable cause intimidated me to the point that I curtailed my anti-war involvement and became wary of engaging in innocuous phone conversations.

Shortly after 9/11, FBI investigators visited and questioned a progressive peace activist living in my neighborhood. Shocked that she was being interrogated, she told them, "If it's your job to look for Taliban terrorists, it's also your job to know that they're not hanging out with Jewish lesbians in San Francisco." The woman's words highlight the counter-intuitive craziness of some of the governmental approaches to waging the 'War on Terror.' Federal resources are squandered when investigators pursue such remote leads, alienating minority citizens and contributing to a climate of bigotry in the U.S.

7) Eliminate Unfair Immigration Practices, like 'Special Registration'

In chapter eleven, I discussed how the U.S. government decided to require the 'Special Registration' of non-citizen male immigrants from North Korea and two dozen predominantly-Muslim countries. Many Muslims, Middle Easterners, South Asians, and East Asians found this program racist and gender-biased, especially since it mandated that participants be fingerprinted, photographed, and interrogated like criminals.

Suggesting that immigrants from some countries might be higher security risks than others, the INS mandated that men from Iran, Iraq, Syria, Libya, and Sudan comply with its first registration deadline on December 16, 2002. In Southern California, hundreds of male immigrants – ages 16 and over – were arrested at INS offices when they voluntarily reported on the first 'Special Registration' deadline. Many of the detainees were students and professionals. Since the INS had promised that the registration process would only take about 10 to 15 minutes, many relatives of the indefinitely-detained immigrants were shocked that the U.S. government misrepresented 'Special Registration' and took complying immigrants into custody.

Since there were more than 600,000 Persians in California at the time, many Iranian-Americans publicly voiced their disapproval that so many of their relatives and friends were being held by U.S. government officials. Kayham Shakib, president of the Iranian-American Lawyers Association, organized a protest to draw attention to the fact that the INS was inadequately prepared to handle the thousands of people who went to register on the day of the first deadline, causing many of the complying immigrants to be detained unnecessarily. At this demonstration, many protestors carried signs that challenged 'Special Registration,' suggesting that the detentions were paving the road to concentration camps.[44]

'Special Registration' also went poorly in other parts of the country. According to the New York Advisory Committee (NYAC) to the U.S. Commission on Civil Rights, an independent bipartisan agency of the federal government, 'Special Registration' in New York City was characterized by confusion about requirements, long processing time often lasting more than 14 hours, inadequate numbers of translators, and inconsistent application of policies.[45] The NYAC's report concluded that such profiling was an ineffective law enforcement tool that deprived immigrants of the right to counsel during interrogations conducted by the Bureau of Immigration and Customs Enforcement and the Department of Homeland Security.[46] It also faulted these government agencies for failing to inform families of detainees' whereabouts.

A week after the first 'Special Registration' deadline, four national organizations – the American-Arab Anti-Discrimination Committee, the Alliance of Iranian Americans, the Council on American Islamic Relations, and the National Council of Pakistani Americans – filed a class action lawsuit against Attorney General Ashcroft, demanding an injunction against further detentions of immigrants applying for residency. These groups also issued a statement saying that the mass arrests eroded their communities' confidence in the INS and the federal government. A week after the lawsuit was filed, the Justice Department declared that federal courts had no jurisdiction to review decisions carried out by the INS, since the Supreme Court was the only legal body authorized to review immigration policies.

Because the first 'Special Registration' was handled so badly, many immigrants were wary of complying with the second deadline on January 10, 2003, which mandated the participation of men from 13 additional countries: Afghanistan, Algeria, Bahrain, Eritrea, Lebanon, Morocco, North Korea, Oman, Qatar, Somalia, Tunisia, the United Arab Emirates, and Yemen. Because of political pressure from Christian and Armenian-American groups, Armenia was dropped from the list. Some activists questioned why ethnic and religious groups with political clout were able to get the INS to modify which immigrants were forced to comply with 'Special Registration.'

In preparation for the January 10th deadline, the Muslim Public Affairs Council stationed human rights monitors across the U.S. Amnesty International expressed its concern about 'Special Registration,' questioning whether the policy violated United Nations and international treaties signed by the U.S.[47] Many immigrants attempted to flee to Canada rather than comply with this second 'Special Registration' deadline. According to Canadian immigration authorities, when the U.S. was implementing its 'Special Registration' program, approximately 2,000 Pakistanis entered Canada between January and March 2003, a number comparable to all of 2002.[48] Some of these refugees were unable to get Canadian asylum, and ended up stranded in border towns, living out of their cars.

Citing the findings of the NYAC study, *India-West* reported that 'Special Registration' negatively affected about 400,000 undocumented immigrants in New York alone.[49] On April 2, 2003, the *Village Voice* took a stand against the federal policy, arguing that it had a withering effect on some neighborhoods.[50] The newspaper claimed that 'Special Registration' decimated the Midwood part of Brooklyn, causing some community members to be detained on visa infractions and others to flee the U.S.[51]

Immigrants in other parts of the country were also bothered by the governmental program. According to the May 3, 2004 *Los Angeles Times*, more than 82,000 teenage boys and men across the U.S. were eventually registered, of which 16% (13,000) were forced into deportation hearings, frequently on minor visa infractions.[52] By ending 'Special Registration' and other discriminatory policies, politicians could create a more tolerant America and set an example for all citizens to follow.

8) Improve FBI Relations

One important component of stemming the bigotry unleashed by the 9/11 backlash is to ameliorate relations between minority groups and the FBI. Ethnic community members who repeatedly hear about FBI blunders view the government agency with suspicion. The *Houston Chronicle* reported that on September 15, 2001, the FBI arrested two Palestinian-Americans at George Bush Intercontinental Airport in LaBelle, Florida.[53] Fathi Mustapha and his son Nacer were traveling home from a business trip to Mexico when they were charged with passport fraud. The elder American was released on bail, but his son spent more than 67 days in jail after authorities claimed that their passports had been tampered with in a manner similar to the documents of the 9/11 hijackers.[54] The government eventually dropped the baseless charges after lab findings proved that the Mustaphas' passports had not been altered in any way. Although the accused men incurred over $40,000 in legal expenses during this ordeal, a judge rejected their claim that they be reimbursed. The FBI's mishandling of the incident may have alienated many Arab-Americans and Muslims who might have been useful as governmental translators or information-gatherers.

Minority communities' faith in the FBI was also eroded in 2003, when Director Robert Mueller directed each of the organization's 56 field offices to tally mosques and develop a demographic profile of Muslims in their respective jurisdictions.[55] In some parts of the country, FBI field offices refused to comply with the national mosque census. In Oklahoma, FBI employees chose not to follow Mueller's directive, perhaps remembering the unfair scapegoating of Muslims in the aftermath of Timothy McVeigh's April 19, 1995 domestic terrorist plot. Oklahoma FBI agent Gary Johnson told the *Tulsa World* that his field office had no intention of collecting information on mosques, seeing it as unnecessary to its counter-terrorism program and an unfair imposition on civil rights.[56] Sheryl Siddiqui told the *Tulsa World* that she and other area Muslims had a good relationship with the Oklahoma FBI.[57] She noted that even before the Oklahoma City bombing, local FBI agents treated religious practitioners with respect and took steps to establish ties with them.

The relatively positive relationship between Oklahoma FBI agents and local Muslims contrasted sharply with tense FBI-Muslim relations in other states. Omar Dajani, a board member of Central Florida's Arab-American Community Center, told the *Tulsa World* that the FBI's census of mosques in his state angered local Muslims and exacerbated anti-Muslim sentiments in the community.[58] According to Dajani, the survey of Islamic prayer centers gave the public the mistaken impression that mosques were sinister places that needed to be monitored. The National Conference for Community and Justice in New York described the FBI census of Muslims and mosques as a frightening example of religious profiling.[59] In February 2003, Betty Lowery, director of the Orlando chapter of the NCCJ, publicly speculated that the census could be a prelude to the internment of religious and ethnic minorities in the U.S., similar to the treatment of Japanese-Americans after Pearl Harbor.[60] Muslims across the country were outraged by federal investigators' intrusive conduct. Areej Zufari, a fourth-grade teacher at the school of the Islamic Society of Central Florida, told the *Augusta Chronicle* that FBI agents unfairly interrogated mosque officials about how the prayer center spends its money, how it educates congregants' children, and how its members stand on particular issues.[61]

American Muslims were also upset after Mike German, a former FBI agent-turned ACLU whistleblower, reported that the FBI used anti-Muslim instruction materials to train agents. According to the Southern Poverty Law Center and *Wired*, the federal agency used teaching materials claiming that mainstream Muslims were likely to be terrorist sympathizers, that Mohammed was a "cult leader," and that devout Muslims were particularly likely to become violent.[62] The FBI could improve its image and promote a more tolerant cultural environment if it made more of an effort to treat Muslims and other minority groups with consideration and respect.

9) End Racially-Biased Interrogations and Detentions

Since distrustful people are less likely to report hate crimes, it is imperative that the federal government end policies or programs that undermine ethnic communities' trust. In chapter eleven, I discussed the interrogation of Iraqi nationals by FBI agents, and the anger it generated among Arab-Americans and Muslims in the U.S. According to the March 27, 2003 issue of the *Lincoln-Star Journal*, these groups were upset by the FBI's decision to interview thousands of the 90,000 foreign-born Iraqis in the U.S., as well as Americans or non-citizen visitors who had recently traveled to Iraq.[63] Tim Butz, a spokesman for the Nebraska ACLU, told the *Lincoln-Star Journal* that this policy eroded immigrants' faith in a tolerant America.[64] Activists challenged the usefulness of these offensive interrogations, which they felt had little probative value. Some community members thought that the baseless questioning of minority citizens communicated the message that Middle Easterners and South Asians were not to be trusted. Emira Habiby Brown, director of the Arab American Family Support Center, told the *New York Daily News* that the interrogation of minority community members and other discriminatory federal policies created a climate of xenophobia that could lead to an increase in bias crimes.[65]

Civil libertarians also became concerned when the U.S. government began aggressively apprehending Muslims and Middle Easterners for visa violations. According to the Office of the Inspector General of the

Justice Department, the U.S. arrested 738 Muslims and Arabs between September 11, 2001 and August 2002 because their entry visas had expired.[66] This same agency reported that many detainees were held in inhumane conditions, including being incarcerated 23 hours a day.[67] The Justice Department also verified that some detainees were taunted and slammed into walls by detention center officials and other inmates. On May 8, 2004, the *Arab American News* reported that there were 308 incidents of physical abuse by federal prison staff members on the Bureau of Prisons' security tapes.[68] According to this article, none of the abused Middle Eastern and Muslim detainees were found to have any links to terrorism. Other federal security programs, like the airport-focused 'Operation Tarmac' and the INS-DOJ's 'Alien Absconder Apprehension Initiative,' angered American Muslims upset about the interrogation, detention, and deportation of thousands of Middle Easterners and South Asians.[69]

It is difficult to ascertain how many immigrants were indefinitely detained after 9/11, since estimates vary considerably. One periodical reported that there were 1,000 immigrants held in Southern California alone, where the detainees were subjected to harsh treatment and languished for days in crowded, unsanitary conditions.[70] Other newspapers and magazines published different figures. According to the April 16, 2003 issue of the *New York Daily News*, approximately 1,200 male immigrants from predominantly-Muslim countries had been apprehended and held indefinitely throughout the U.S. after 9/11.[71] Regardless of the exact numbers, these detentions undermined many ethnic communities' trust in the U.S. government, and compromised their willingness to report hate crimes to FBI agents.

Many ethnic communities were also disturbed by other federal initiatives, like 'Operation Liberty Shield.' The *New York Daily News* reported that this program compelled the detention of asylum seekers from 33 predominantly Arab and Muslim countries.[72] Because these refugees were fleeing ethnic or religious persecution, some activists found it troubling that the U.S. government was treating these vulnerable immigrants with hostility and suspicion. Civil rights attorneys maintained that 'Operation Liberty Shield' and other discriminatory policies contributed to an atmosphere of intolerance where hate crimes flourished. Reflecting on George W. Bush's 'War on Terror,' Dalia Hashad, an ACLU advocate, told the *Arab American News* that administration policies that criminalize Arabs and South Asians transmit the message that minority communities should be viewed with heightened suspicion.[73]

In response to these unpopular governmental programs, the New York Advisory Committee to the U.S. Commission on Civil Rights made four recommendations to improve the federal government's handling of its security policies.[74] First, the government should end discriminatory policies, like 'Special Registration,' that unfairly profile 'suspect' ethnic and religious groups. Second, Congress should create a fully-independent oversight body, outside the Homeland Security Department, to report and monitor how security measures affect civil rights. Third, the government should implement a viable system to monitor racial profiling and investigate complaints promptly. Fourth, the federal government should organize outreach programs, so that minorities feel that officials are sensitive to their concerns. By instituting these changes, the federal government could improve its relationships with minority communities.

10) Create a Separate Governmental Agency to Investigate Hate Crimes

Many minority communities look upon the FBI unfavorably because of the organization's past history of harassing innocent people in the course of investigations. For this reason, it might be beneficial to create a separate governmental agency devoted exclusively to investigating and deterring hate crimes, instead of asking the FBI to perform these tasks and pursue other law enforcement duties simultaneously.

During the 'War on Terror,' the FBI juggled divergent responsibilities: it conducted interrogations of foreign nationals and attempted to reassure minority communities that it would protect them against domestic hate crimes. *San Francisco Chronicle* journalist Annie Nakao questioned how the FBI could accomplish such conflicting objectives, noting that the first alienates immigrants by treating them as terror suspects and the second attempts to gain their trust by promising to protect them against bigots.[75] By creating a separate agency devoted exclusively to hate crime investigations, the federal government could do a better job protecting vulnerable minority groups in the U.S.

11) Allow Innocent Minorities to Wire Money without Governmental Intrusion

To create a more tolerant environment, the U.S. government should also end other policies that alienate minority communities. The *Star Tribune* reported that in late 2001, many Muslim immigrants were bothered by the federal shut-down of Somali-owned money wiring services in Minnesota.[76] Some activists felt that the disruptive program transmitted the pernicious message that this ethnic community was a threat to the larger society. In other parts of the U.S., native-born Muslims were upset to learn that a federal policy blocked many of them from being able to send money domestically or abroad. On July 9, 2003, the *Washington Post* reported that when Muhammed Ali, an African-American New Yorker, went into a Western Union office in Brooklyn, he discovered he was unable to send $80 to his brother in Connecticut because his name appeared on the U.S. Treasury Department's 103-page list of suspected terrorists.[77] Since 'Muhammed Ali' is a fairly common name, many community members questioned the fairness of punishing everyone sharing the same appellation.

Muslims living outside the U.S. also had trouble sending money through Western Union, an American company. According to the October 3, 2003 issue of the *Arab American News*, Said Ali, a Somali who had immigrated to Canada in 1991, discovered that he was unable to wire $116 to a Dutch citizen in the Netherlands because the Somali recipient's name, Mohammed Ali, was on the Treasury Department's list of suspected terrorists.[78] Rather than have the money returned to him, the Canadian sender discovered that the funds had been frozen by the U.S. government. According to Danielle Jimenez, a spokesperson for Western Union, the Treasury Department required the company to freeze funds when either the sender's or recipient's name appeared on the terrorism suspect list, and stipulated that the money could not be released until the person in question came in and proved that he or she was not the same person identified as a possible terrorist.[79] Jamshed Uppal, a Pakistani-born finance professor at Catholic University, told the *Washington Post* that many Muslims were so unnerved by the Treasury Department's list that they stopped sending money overseas.[80] Discriminatory policies need to be abandoned if they disempower ethnic communities and hurt America's image abroad.

12) Coordinate an International Public Relations Campaign to Respond to U.S. Hate Crimes

The U.S. government also needs to launch a comprehensive program to respond to how American hate crimes are portrayed overseas, since bias-motivated attacks on U.S. mosques and gurdwaras receive considerable international attention. Because satellite television is widespread throughout the Middle East and Southeast Asia, viewers in these regions are repeatedly exposed to stories about American attacks directed against ethnic and religious minorities. Coverage of mosque and gurdwara crimes create disturbing images of the U.S., sending the inaccurate message that Judeo-Christian America is at war with other faiths. This, in turn, can trigger anti-American backlashes overseas. Whenever high-profile cases occur, government investigators and liaisons could make themselves available to foreign journalists and news agencies, so that international audiences can be made aware that hate crimes are being taken seriously. If this does not occur, foreign audiences might be left with the impression that it is "open season" ethnic and religious minorities in the U.S. A reflective governmental response to domestic hate crimes would prevent overseas radical groups from using information about bias attacks to flame anti-American sentiment.

To facilitate intergroup understanding, the Discrimination and National Security Initiative proposed establishing a "brain trust" within the State Department to offer cultural input and evaluate how America was being perceived overseas, particularly in response to military actions in other countries.[81] This would also be a positive step forward.

13) Take Proactive Measures to Prevent Backlash Attacks

To combat hate crimes, it is important that local officials and police respond proactively before a backlash begins. In Dearborn, Michigan, elected representatives and police officers worked together immediately after 9/11 to minimize the possibility of bias-motivated attacks. By 10:30 a.m. on September 11, 2001, the mayor had already spoken about the possibility of a harmful backlash, and by 1:00 p.m., he had instructed police to patrol sensitive neighborhoods to protect the city's 30,000 Arab-American residents.[82] According to *India-Abroad*, the mayor's prompt action and the police's willingness to deter crime may have been factors in why there were only two bias-motivated assaults – one grabbing and one beating by an outsider – in Dearborn in the immediate aftermath of 9/11.[83]

Police departments in other states also worked to prevent hate crimes. In Massachusetts, Bourne police chief John Ford told the *Herald* that his department responded proactively to the terrorist attacks, informing angry citizens that they would be prosecuted if they targeted innocent minority residents.[84] By deterring bigots from acting on their impulses, authorities can curtail community xenophobia and help end "foreign-hate 911."

14) Educate Law Enforcement Officers About Minority Communities

To improve relations between police departments and minority communities, it is important for activists to educate officers about ethnic and religious cultural beliefs and practices. Misunderstandings happen particularly frequently when police officers have poor understanding of other faiths. In the aftermath of 9/11, officers across the country repeatedly arrested Sikhs after mistaking their kirpans as concealed weapons. For example, in July 2002, Gurnam Singh and Surjeet Singh were driving their truck through Montana's Big Horn County when they were stopped and searched by police officers.[85] When they found the Sikhs' kirpans, the officers confiscated one and threw the other in the mud, ignoring the South Asians' attempts to explain their religious significance.[86] The day after their arrest, the Sikhs were heckled and threatened by community members in the courtroom. In April 2004, the Sikh Coalition succeeded in getting the criminal charges dismissed.[87] Integrated police departments may be less likely to practice this kind of unfair profiling. The presence of minority officers might also make hate crime victims more willing to come forward, particularly if these investigators do community outreach before violent incidents occur.

It is also essential to lobby for legislation ensuring that officers receive mandatory diversity training. On June 1, 2009, the California assembly unanimously passed AB-504, a law mandating that the state train officers about the Sikh kirpan.[88] Other states should follow California's lead, so that Sikhs are not needlessly charged with weapons possession if they are found carrying their religiously-mandated small knife.

15) Demand that Police and Federal Investigators Handle Bias Crimes Appropriately

It is important that local, state, and federal agencies improve the ways in which post-9/11 hate crimes are reported. One way of doing this is by encouraging the use of incident intake sheets that include a check box for crimes involving bias.[89] In chapter two, I noted that some police departments began documenting significantly more hate crimes after making this simple paperwork change.

It is also important to mandate that specially-trained officers investigate hate crimes. The *Boston Herald* reported that prior to 9/11, Massachusetts police departments had given special training to officers who handled bias incidents. After the terrorist strikes, the Bay State was able to use these law enforcement personnel when investigating hate crimes. Police departments in other parts of the country were also working to improve their handling of bigotry-motivated attacks. In Phoenix, any cop who suspects that bias is relevant to a crime investigation is required to turn over the case to one of five law enforcement officers specifically trained in handling such matters.[90] Police officers across the country should follow the lead of departments that understand the special nature of bias crimes.

16) Promote the Recruiting and Hiring of Minority Police Officers and Federal Agents

There is also a need to increase the numbers of Arab, Muslim, and South Asian police officers, who may be particularly attentive to the needs of hate crime victims. Officer El-Assis told the *San Diego Union Tribune* that his own experiences with bigotry made him more adept at handling bias crimes.[91] In response to the U.S. embassy seizure in Tehran, nativists repeatedly scapegoated El-Assis, who had recently immigrated to San Diego to escape Lebanon's civil war. Because of his personal encounters with nativism, he became invested in helping other bias crime victims. After 9/11, he worked as a liaison between the police and the area's Arab-American and Muslim communities, coaxing reluctant crime victims to come forward.[92] By navigating cultural and linguistic barriers, minority police officers like El-Assis can assist hate crime victims and collect testimony from nervous witnesses. By routinely seeing Arab, Muslim, and Sikh officers on patrol, community members may become less likely to view certain minority citizens as threats.

Unfortunately, many police departments fail to appreciate the unique contributions of minority officers. In many areas, departmental policies made it difficult for some minority cops to serve on the force. Amric Singh Rathour, a Sikh born and raised in New York, filed suit with the EEOC after his job with the NYPD was terminated on August 27, 2001 because he refused to remove his turban and trim his beard.[93] After Rathour was forced to leave his traffic enforcement job, Sikh Coalition attorneys began working to ensure that he was reinstated, and that police departments across the country allowed Sikhs to protect and serve. While researching the case, civil rights advocates documented that 16 Sikhs were actively serving on London's Metropolitan Police. They also organized a petition asking NYPD commissioner Raymond Kelly to change the discriminatory policy preventing turbaned Sikhs from working as police officers. While the NYPD case was still pending, the Sikh Coalition succeeded in convincing the LAPD and the D.C. Police Force to recruit Sikh applicants and allow active-duty officers to wear their dastaars.[94] Rathour eventually won his case against the NYPD and was reinstated in mid-October 2004, resuming his duties directing traffic near the Manhattan Bridge entrance to Brooklyn. By assisting the public while wearing his turban, Rathour raised awareness about Sikhism and paved the way for other turbaned police officers to maintain their religious beliefs on the job.

Along with more minority police officers, there is also a need for more Arab, Muslim, and South Asian federal investigators. This would improve relations between FBI agents and community groups, since minority residents might be more willing to report incidents to federal agents who had first-hand knowledge of the 9/11 backlash.

17) Promote the Recruiting and Promotion of Minority Employees in the Transportation Industry

Since many hate crimes occur at airports, train stations, and subways, it is important for minority groups to integrate the transportation industry. Travelers who have routine contact with Muslim and Sikh flight attendants, train conductors, or subway operators might be less likely to harass or attack minority passengers. Minority transportation industry employees might also be more likely to intervene appropriately when bias crimes occur in their vicinity. Unfortunately, some transportation agencies fail to recruit Sikhs and Muslims, and occasionally fire them for practicing their religious beliefs. In 2004, Sat Hari Singh experienced discrimination when his superiors at the Metropolitan Transportation Authority removed him from his post as subway conductor because of his refusal to take off his turban at work.[95] With the help of civil rights attorneys, Sat Hari Singh was eventually successful in changing the discriminatory MTA policy, allowing other Sikhs to practice their faith and keep their jobs.

Transportation industry employees might also be more inclined to treat minority travelers fairly if they worked in integrated agencies where they could become familiar with Sikh and Muslim religious practices. In the aftermath of 9/11, Sikhs were repeatedly singled out by airport personnel who were unaware of the theological significance of kirpans. On March 31, 2002, a Sikh traveler was arrested at Philadelphia International Airport and jailed for four hours for wearing his religiously-mandated small knife.[96] Although the South Asian man was released after the police realized he was not a security threat, United Airlines still refused to let him fly home the following morning, citing security concerns.[97] After the Sikh Coalition involved the Department of Transportation in the case, the airline finally allowed the traveler to get on a return flight. If airline employees were more familiar with Sikhism, they might be less likely to view South Asian travelers with suspicion.

In the years following 9/11, Sikh religious practices continued to be misunderstood by uninformed airport personnel. On December 23, 2004, Jagdish Singh, the Bhai Sahib at a gurdwara in San Diego, was arrested at San Diego International Airport after mistakenly carrying his kirpan through a metal detector.[98] The security officer detained Singh for an hour and issued him a criminal citation for carrying a knife, although FAA regulations recommend that screeners in this situation simply direct Sikh travelers to put their kirpans in stowed luggage. If there were more Sikhs working as security screeners, travelers might be less likely to encounter guards who overreact to their religiously-mandated knives.

Airline personnel might become more familiar with other ethnicities and faiths if the TSA hired more minority screeners and treated existing employees fairly. According to the *New York Times*, Ify Okoye, a Muslim convert of Nigerian descent, successfully sued the TSA in 2004 so she could continue wearing her hijab at work.[99] The integration of Muslim and Sikh airline personnel into the TSA can make industry workers and travelers more comfortable around people of other religions and ethnic backgrounds.

Minority TSA officials might be particularly invested in changing policies that unfairly target members of 'suspect' faiths or ethno-racial groups, such as the practice of putting prospective passengers on 'no-fly' lists simply because they happen to have the same name as someone suspected of criminal activities. Since all orthodox Sikh men are "Singhs," the idea of placing common ethnic names on watch lists might seem particularly ill-advised to members of this religious community. Other travelers were also unfairly profiled when their names triggered security alerts. In 2004, U.S. Senator Edward Kennedy was put on a 'no fly' list after his name matched that of a suspected terrorist, causing him to have prolonged waits at airports for weeks until his office was able to get his name removed.[100] Kennedy's experience suggests that screening policies need to be modified so that innocent travelers are not unfairly inconvenienced simply because they have a common ethnic name. By integrating the transportation industries, minorities could help ensure that other travelers could safely and fairly get to their destinations.

18) Ensure that Attorneys and Prosecutors are Sensitive to Minority Concerns

To combat hate crimes, it is important for minority communities to have access to attorneys and prosecutors from diverse backgrounds. Hate crime victims might be more willing to confide in lawyers who have experienced post-9/11 discrimination and prejudice firsthand. In September 2002, Sikh attorney Ravinder Singh Bahalla was denied access to his client at Brooklyn's Metropolitan Detention Center after refusing to comply with security personnel's request that he remove his turban.[101] In January 2003, Bahalla successfully challenged the prison's screening policy in Federal District Court, maintaining that it violated his First Amendment right to practice his religion, and his Fourth Amendment right against unreasonable searches and seizures.[102] He also claimed that the policy violated his client's Sixth Amendment right to counsel with the attorney of his choice. As a result of Bahalla's legal challenge, the prison ended up modifying its policy so that turban-wearing attorneys or visitors did not face additional screening except when there were specific grounds to think that they were engaging in criminal activities. Minority lawyers who are personally acquainted with racial profiling may be particularly qualified to assist hate crime victims because they can relate to the discrimination experiences of others.

Minority attorneys might be especially willing to engage in community outreach efforts to ensure that immigrant communities are aware of their rights. In San Jose, South Asian attorney Mohinder Mann accompanied prosecutor Anastacia Steinberg to local gurdwaras and mosques to reassure congregants that the district attorney's office would protect them using the full weight of the law.[103] This proactive work empowers vulnerable minorities to report bias attacks.

19) Protect Previously-Targeted Buildings to Deter Hate Crimes

It is imperative that local, state, and federal investigators monitor buildings that were attacked by bigots in the past. In many instances, hate-motivated vandals repeatedly targeted the same ethnic centers or minority-run businesses. By putting these vulnerable buildings under police or federal surveillance, it might be possible to apprehend violent criminals before they inflict additional damage on minority-owned properties.

Whenever hate crimes occur, local police need to ensure that victims are protected from follow-up attacks. Authorities should also help vulnerable community members by encouraging them to update their security systems and install equipment to record hate crimes. Even if business owners cannot afford expensive surveillance equipment, motel clerks, convenience store workers, gas station employees, and cab drivers should be urged to display prominent stickers announcing that patrons are being filmed. Additionally, police departments across the U.S. should consider following San Francisco's example and install cameras in all taxis to prevent hate-motivated assaults and other crimes, since minority drivers are particularly vulnerable.

20) Revamp Taxi IDs so Drivers are Identified by Photo and Number, not Name

Since cabbies are required to display their taxi licenses or face fines, drivers with Arabic or Muslim names are put at considerable risk when bigoted passengers are able to ascertain their ethnicity or faith. If taxi licenses were modified so that a photo and identification number was used in place of a name, cabbies would have the option of concealing their Arabic or Muslim identities from certain passengers. Patrons wishing to launch complaints about particular drivers could use the identification numbers to report unsafe driving or other problems to dispatchers.

21) Demand "Homeland Security"

Many minority groups feel that the Department of Homeland Security is more interested in spying on them instead of protecting them from bias attacks. Expressing their contempt for this federal organization, some activists have pejoratively referred to it as the "Department of Homeland Statsi." Vulnerable ethnic and religious groups in the U.S. need to demand protection from federal authorities. To generate community sympathy, civil rights activists might consider referring to violent hate crimes as 'domestic terrorist attacks,' especially when organizations like the Aryan Nation or the KKK are involved. Federal investigators take terrorist strikes incredibly seriously, and their resources could be used to protect racial and religious minorities targeted by white supremacist militias and other hate groups. By framing post-9/11 bias attacks in the context of the 'War on Terror,' minorities can get other Americans to identify with and support their rights in the U.S.

22) Patronize Businesses Affected by Backlash Racism

Some Americans responded to 9/11 by boycotting minority-owned businesses. Arabs, Muslims, and South Asians lost revenue when shoppers refused to patronize their stores. The *New York Times* reported that in August, 2002, a customer in suburban Westland announced to others that she decided not to purchase a Red Wings jersey from the sporting good store because the owner, Mohamed Odetalle, was Muslim.[104] After leaving without making a purchase, she walked across the street to the mall, where bought a jacket identical to the once she had tried on earlier for $10 more. Since Odetalle also owns but never works at the mall store, the bigoted customer failed in her attempt to deprive him of her business. Nevertheless, her action successfully conveyed her belief in Muslim inferiority. According to the *Times*, the manager at the mall store said that customers repeatedly told him that they would rather pay extra than do business with the Muslim foreigner across the street.[105]   To stem xenophobia and support vulnerable businesses, customers should consider shopping at minority-owned stores affected by the 9/11 backlash.

Islamophobic community members also targeted American companies that were perceived as Muslim-friendly. In 2009, Best Buy Inc. was criticized for acknowledging Eid al-Adha in a national advertisement. According to the *San Francisco Chronicle*, the company was flooded with calls, emails, and letters complaining that the company was un-American, even though the ad consisted solely of a small bubble at the bottom of the page in the company's Thanksgiving flyer.[106]   Despite the negative feedback, Best Buy executives stood by their ad, viewing it as part of their campaign to reach out to customers from diverse cultures and faiths. American consumers should patronize companies that acknowledge the diversity of their client base and support minority communities in the U.S.

23) Boycott Racist Businesses

Along with supporting businesses affected by xenophobia, American consumers should boycott companies or restaurants that discriminate against minority customers. *India-West* reported that in mid-September 2001, Ashvani Sood and 10 other members of his family were refused food service at the Mardi Gras Food Court in Las Vegas.[107]   Instead of assisting customers on a first-come, first-serve basis, the counter employee intentionally served white diners who were in line behind the South Asians. After realizing that he and his Indian relatives were being treated unfairly, Sood complained. Rather than reprimand the server, the manager refused to seat the South Asians, telling the stunned family members that he was unwilling to have them in the establishment because he needed to protect the other diners from their presence.[108]   Minority patrons should boycott eateries that practice this kind of blatant bigotry.

Years after 9/11, nativist American workers continued to treat minority customers unfairly. On March 24, 2003, the *Washington Post* reported that a Muslim father and son were harassed at a Meijer gas station in Fraser, Michigan. According to the *Post*, the store's cashier used anti-Arab slurs against the two patrons, refusing to serve them and insisting that they leave the country.[109]   Inspired by the cashier's intolerance, another customer joined in the harassment. The racist incident was captured on the store's surveillance tape. Unless community groups take action against racist businesses, nativism will continue to flourish in the U.S.

Minority customers should also avoid shopping at American companies that pander to bigots. The *Pittsburgh Tribune-Review* reported that in May 2008, Dunkin' Donuts pulled its commercial featuring Rachel Ray wearing a black-and-white scarf because internet bloggers lambasted it as a 'jihad' accessory worn by Muslim terrorists.[110]   Muslim and Sikh patrons should consider buying their desserts elsewhere in light of this company's failure to stand up to post-9/11 xenophobia.

24) Legally Challenge Companies that Discriminate

Minority communities should be encouraged to file civil suits against companies that treat them unfairly. In the decades prior to 9/11, Arab-Americans and Muslims often took action against businesses that practiced ethnic or religious discrimination. For example, in the early 1990s, the Albahris filed a $4,000,000 lawsuit against the Manilow and Silverman mortuary in Los Angeles and its parent company, Service Corporation of Houston, after an employee refused to transport, store, or bury the body of their son, dismissively telling them that the funeral home didn't pick up Muslim children.[111]   The boy's father, Fuad Albahri, told the *Los Angeles Times* that the funeral home's discriminatory policy made him feel confused and physically sick, like he was living in the Dark Ages.[112]   Because of the lawsuit, other mortuaries and businesses were reminded of the financial repercussions of discriminating against minority clients.

During the 9/11 backlash, many activists understood that legal action was an effective means of curtailing unfair practices. In late September 2001, Harpreet Singh, spokesman for United Sikhs in Service for America, told the Vancouver *Columbian* that civil suits acted as a deterrent against discrimination and hate crimes, since they showed the community that bigots would be held accountable for their actions.[113]

298

Many minority groups filed lawsuits against businesses that openly discriminated against them after 9/11. For example, the Midwest Federation of American Syrian-Lebanese Clubs took legal action against the Marriott Corporation for canceling a contract to hold the group's August 2002 conference at the Des Moines Marriott. The *Washington Post* reported that although the Midwest Federation had reserved 60 sleeping rooms and the hotel restaurant for two dinner dances, a hotel employee called the group at 2:30 p.m. on September 11, 2001 and abruptly cancelled the conference contract because of the terrorist attacks.[114] The Midwest Federation, which represented 2,000 Arab-American families in 10 Midwestern states, filed a legal complaint with the Justice Department as well as a civil suit against the Marriott Corporation. The group eventually received a $115,000 settlement, and ended up holding its August 2002 conference at a more tolerant hotel in Troy, Michigan.[115]

On occasion, restaurant patrons have fought xenophobia by mounting legal challenges against eateries that refused to serve minority diners. In Pittsburgh, a Sikh physician and his wife were occasionally turned away from area restaurants. When Harpreet Grewal took his wife out on her birthday in July 2002, Donzi's Restaurant refused to seat them because he was wearing a turban.[116] A year later, on her next birthday, Touch Restaurant turned away the couple for the same reason. Grewal told the *Pittsburgh Post-Gazette* that when he attempted to explain the religious significance of the dastaar, an employee replied that a turban-wearing patron would interfere with the restaurant's upscale image.[117] Grewal was outraged by the eatery's discriminatory dress code, which also prohibited yarmulke-wearing diners from being served. With the help of the Sikh Coalition, SMART, and the ADL, Grewal succeeded in getting the establishment to seat all patrons wearing religious headwear.[118]

Other restaurants also mistreated Sikhs in the years after the terrorist attacks. On October 9, 2003, employees at the Riprocks club and restaurant in Downers Grove, Illinois, ejected Davinder and Ipinder Singh because the two Sikhs refused to remove their turbans.[119] After the Sikh Coalition intervened, the owner apologized and changed the company policy, so that patrons wearing religious head coverings could be served.

In other parts of the country, Sikhs were also unfairly singled out. On February 7, 2004, a patka-wearing Sikh patron was forced to leave a dance club in Decatur, Georgia for violating their 'no hats' policy.[120] After Mandeep Singh paid the admission fee and entered Mama's Primetime Dance Club, a bouncer approached him and demanded that he either take off his headwear or leave the establishment. The Sikh Coalition intervened in the case, demanding that the club owner follow federal law prohibiting businesses from denying entry to patrons on the basis of their religious practice.

Along with Sikhs, Iranians in the U.S. challenged companies that treated them unfairly. In July 2003, Dokhi Fassihian, a policy analyst, openly criticized the Monster online job search engine for asking her to comply with U.S. sanctions against Iran by removing all references to the country on her résumé. She told the *Washington Post* that she found this ludicrous, asking how it was possible to obtain work as an expert on Iran if she was prohibited from making direct references to the country.[121] According to the *Post*, the requirement was intended to dissuade people from job hunting in one of seven countries designated by U.S. authorities as sponsors of terrorism: Iran, Syria, Sudan, Burma, Cuba, Libya, and North Korea. By challenging this questionable policy, Fassihian helped curb a climate of post-9/11 xenophobia.

During the backlash, corporate representatives occasionally placed unfair demands on minority businessmen. In February 2005, a quality-control officer told Harbans Singh, a Subway franchise owner, that he needed to replace his turban with a company baseball cap while working in his own shop.[122] Singh was shocked by this requirement, since he purchased the eatery, underwent training, and passed previous inspections while wearing his dastaar. Enlisting the help of Sikh Coalition attorneys, Singh challenged Subway's anti-turban ban, working to ensure that other franchise owners would be allowed to honor their faith while interacting with the public.

Other Sikh food service workers also faced discrimination on the job. In 2005, a caterer singled out a Sikh employee for wearing his kara, telling him that he could be fired unless he removed it.[123] The Sikh Coalition intervened, explaining the religious significance of the bracelet and urging the employer to re-think the company policy. Challenging unfair business practices is an important step towards creating a more tolerant society.

Abercrombie & Fitch also faced legal action for its discriminatory policies. In chapter nine, I discussed how Umme-Hani Khan received death threats in 2011 after she sued the clothing company for firing her for wearing a hijab on the job.[124] Many American minorities were dismayed by the company's refusal to comply with EEOC guidelines, particularly since it had to pay $40 million in damages in 2004 to African-American, Asian-American, and Latino employees after disproportionately relegating them to stockroom positions where they would have minimal contact with the public. The company attempted to defend itself by maintaining that it did not have to abide by anti-discrimination regulations because the store employees who folded clothes and assisted shoppers were technically in-store models, not clerks. This explanation further angered civil rights activists since it suggested that minorities were ill-suited to be models because they were less attractive than their white counterparts. Even after paying a substantive legal judgment, Abercrombie & Fitch continued to discriminate against minority job applicants. The clothing company was sued in 2008 for its refusal to hire Samath Elauf because she showed up to her Oklahoma job interview in a hijab. She eventually won the civil suit, receiving $20,000 in damages.[125] By mounting legal challenges against racist and Islamophobic companies, minorities can reduce overt bigotry in the U.S.

25) File Civil Suits Against Hate Crime Perpetrators

Along with taking legal action against businesses that discriminate, minorities should file civil lawsuits against hate crime perpetrators. Perhaps some bigots might think twice about targeting minority-owned property if they are forced to pay for the damage they caused. It might be easier for some bias-crime victims to get legal and financial justice by filing civil suits, which require a lower standard of proof than criminal cases. Along with generating neighborhood awareness, lawsuits can deter others from committing similar offenses. Financial judgments can be used to fund charitable work and compensate victims for lost wages. In chapter four, I discussed how Ranjinder Singh Khalsa was viciously attacked at the Il Palazzo di Villa Russo restaurant. In response to this hate crime, Khalsa filed a civil suit against his assailants and the restaurant personnel who served excessive alcohol to the diners who attacked him. When hate crime perpetrators and irresponsible business owners are held accountable for their actions, the community becomes a safer place for minority residents.

26) Take Action Against Racist Police Departments

It is also important to sue racist police departments that overtly discriminate against area minorities. The *Orange County Register* reported that during the 9/11 backlash, some police officers harassed South Asian Sikhs and told them to return to Saudi Arabia.[126] In some parts of the country, law enforcement officials physically mistreated immigrants in the aftermath of the terrorist strikes. Rather than passively accept such mistreatment, targeted individuals should file civil suits against bigoted cops as a means of curtailing intolerance.

If police departments are afraid of lawsuits, officers might be less inclined to behave inappropriately. In chapter five, I discussed how Muslims in Oregon became upset after they learned that local officers laughed and joked with Brent Matthews when they heard that he had rolled a pig's head into a crowded Lewiston mosque. Police administrators might devote more resources to diversity training if embarrassing disclosures result in expensive legal judgments.

On occasion, victimized community members successfully sued racist police departments. The September 16, 2006 issue of the *Arab American News* tells the story of Amna Mustafa, a Palestinian woman who was flying home to be with her dying father. At the airport, she expressed mild astonishment when an airline employee asked her if she wanted "Muslim food," since "halal" is the correct word to describe Islamic "kosher" cuisine.[127] Because of Mustafa's response, she was taken out of line and brought to a designated security station, where all of her belongings were searched, with the exception of her purse. Worried that they had forgotten to check this bag, Mustafa asked the inspectors if they needed to search it for a bomb.[128] Because she referenced an explosive device in an airport, she was arrested and held in jail without bond for three days. Although the FBI declined to prosecute, an irate Chicago police officer refused to release her, blaming her and her people for causing 9/11.[129] Her father passed away and was buried while she was still in custody, and she was fired from her county job because of the arrest. After taking action in response to her mistreatment, Mustafa won a legal judgment against the Chicago Police Department.[130] Civil suits ensure that police treat all community members with respect.

Along with filing legal challenges, victims of police misconduct should organize demonstrations to demand better treatment. In the summer of 2007, over one hundred South Asians gathered in Edison, New Jersey to protest an unprovoked police attack on an Indian during a Navrati celebration.[131] Unless departments are held accountable for their actions, they will continue to abuse minority community members.

27) File Libel and Slander Suits Against Bigots Who Target Minority-Run Businesses

To curb the 9/11 backlash, it is important for business owners to sue anyone who circulates false rumors accusing them of supporting terrorism. According to the *New York Times*, Dean Hachem was shocked when community members disseminated a false email message claiming that employees at his Orchard Lake restaurant were seen celebrating the terrorist attacks at noon on 9/11.[132] Although the business' security tapes definitively showed that this did not happen, Hachem said that the boycott dramatically decreased revenue at the Sheik, the restaurant he opened in 1996. A year after 9/11, he told the *Times* that revenue from this restaurant was down 30%, and the boycott forced him to close a second ethnic restaurant at a nearby mall.[133] Because his Orchard Lake eatery had an Arabic name, community bigots associated it with the terrorist strikes. When backlashes occur, minority business owners should sue community members who slander or libel them.

28) Sue Bigoted Employers and Report Harassment to H.R. Departments

To curb backlash bigotry, Arab, Muslim, and South Asian employees should file civil suits against racist employers. Michigan attorney Shereef Akeel told the Vancouver *Columbian* that he was surprised by the overt discrimination that many work supervisors displayed after 9/11.[134] On many occasions, the bigotry was impossible to miss. The *New York Times* reported that on September 12, 2001, a Muslim welder was sent home by his employer, who began screaming insults about Islam in the aftermath of the terrorist bombings.[135] The victimized Yemeni worker, Ahmed Esa, was shocked by the mistreatment, especially since he had lived in the U.S. since 1976. Esa refused to return to the hostile work environment, getting another job as a security guard. Outraged about the way his employer behaved, he sued the company, IW&S.

Other minorities also filed civil suits in response to blatant cases of employment discrimination. Tarak Devkota, an Arab-American attorney from Kansas City, Missouri, represented several minority workers who were scapegoated during the 9/11 backlash. Discussing these cases in the *Kansas City Star*, Devkota noted that one Islamophobic employer threw a Muslim employee's paycheck on the floor, called him a dog, and ordered him to fetch it.[136] Devkota also reported that other Kansas City employers explicitly prohibited Muslim workers from praying during breaks, speaking Arabic, or accessing websites with Arabic script.[137]

Arab, Muslim, and South Asian employees should be encouraged to file civil lawsuits to remedy employment discrimination. Although many companies have explicit non-discrimination policies, many workers wonder if calling attention to bigotry might jeopardize their future employment prospects. Acknowledging this issue, the *Washington Post* reported in March 2002 that one Arab-American construction worker had been told by a workplace superior that filing a complaint would be detrimental to his career.[138] Activists need to take action when these types of incidents occur.

In the aftermath of 9/11, American businesses frequently tightened security, banning employees from carrying weapons to work. Some employers told Sikh bank tellers and office workers that they were no longer able to bring their religiously-proscribed small knives to their places of employment. In the years following the terrorist strikes, the Sikh Coalition successfully intervened in several cases, communicating with human resources departments to ensure that Sikh practitioners were allowed to continue working with their kirpans.[139]

Since bigotry was so strong in the years after the terrorist attacks, it is imperative that human relations departments proactively address office race relations. In September 2005, the *Oakland Tribune* reported several incidents in which Muslim professionals were harassed by their co-workers. A female employee at a Fremont-based computer company said that her co-workers called her "bin Laden's daughter" and referred to her visiting mother as "bin Laden's wife."[140] Another case involved the repeated bullying of a Muslim engineer, who was called a "terrorist" by his peers and was told to come dressed as a suicide bomber for Halloween.[141]

Muslim employees were also harassed in other states. *USA Today* reported that in July 2006, a Cisco Systems software engineer received an email from a colleague outraged about recent train bombings in India that killed 207 passengers. The email, sent to Motaz El Shafi and other Muslim Cisco employees in North Carolina, began "Dear Terrorist..."[142] Because El Shafi was born and raised in New Jersey, he was outraged that he was being blamed for an attack that took place overseas. Although he did not file a complaint with Cisco's human resources department, he received an apology from the sender after other employees formally reported the harassment. Minority workers should inform human resource departments when bigotry manifests itself at the office, so that all employees have access to a harassment-free work environment.

29) Report Employment Discrimination to the EEOC

It is important that minority job applicants and employees contact government agencies when they suspect that a company is practicing discrimination. The EEOC can launch an investigation and take action if a company fails to comply with federal laws concerning the hiring and treatment of minority employees. On September 19, 2005, the *Oakland Tribune* reported the results of a study on post-9/11 employment discrimination.[143] Researchers found that temp agencies varied their response to identical résumés submitted under different names. When the résumé appeared under the name "Heidi McKenzie," it generated a 37% response rate. The same résumé had only a 23% response rate when it was sent under the name "Abdul-Aziz Mansour," suggesting that Muslim job applicants were still suffering from post-9/11 employment discrimination years after the terrorist strikes. The EEOC could help ensure that all American companies treat minority applicants and employees fairly or face legal sanctions.

30) Take Action Against Administrators and Instructors Who Practice Overt Discrimination

It is important for minority students to take action against administrators or teachers who practice overt discrimination. In March 2003, the *Sikh Coalition Newsletter* reported that admissions officers at the Universal Technical Institute in Phoenix refused to let Prabhost Singh enroll in their school because he refused to remove his dastaar.[144] Administrators told Singh that his decision to wear a turban was a violation of the school's 'no hat' policy. Enlisting the help of civil rights groups, Singh succeeded in getting the school to amend its dress code so that turbaned Sikhs could enroll and attend classes.

Whenever possible, minority students should report school-based discrimination to the appropriate authorities. In September 2005, the *Oakland Tribune* reported that a teacher at a vocational college forbade a Muslim student to wear her hijab, and told her that if she appeared with it on at a job interview, no one would hire her.[145] Minority students need to feel empowered to report such mistreatment to administrators without fear of academic retaliation in the form of lower grades or mediocre letters of recommendation.

31) Expand Affirmative Action and Encourage the Hiring of Minority Instructors and School Administrators

Another important step in curtailing bigotry involves increasing the numbers of minority students on American campuses. In her essay, "Arab-Americans, Affirmative Action, and A Quest for Racial Identity," Christine Tamer argues that students and faculty members of Middle Eastern origin should be included in schools' diversity plans.[146] In chapter six, I discussed how students at the University of Wisconsin-

Milwaukee were upset that Middle Easterners were not among the ethnic groups the admissions office was actively recruiting. As a result, Arabs, Iranians, and Afghanis were not eligible to apply for scholarships and fellowships designed to increase the presence of minority groups at the school.

On many occasions, school employees fail to react appropriately to bias attacks or take proactive steps to stem community intolerance. Many academic departments do not have any Arab-American, Muslim, Middle Eastern, or South Asian instructors. Minority faculty members are also underrepresented in administration posts at schools across the U.S. To create a safe learning environment, it is important that school employees reflect the diversity of the country and are invested in protecting at-risk students.

By focusing on some vulnerable minority groups and not others, some academic departments inadvertently segregate potential faculty hires into two categories: sought-after minorities (African-Americans, Latinos, Native-Americans, and Asians) and less-attractive minorities (Arab-Americans, Middle Eastern Muslims, and non-Asian Sikhs, who are not counted in many schools' minority faculty-hiring statistics). If African-American and Latino students outnumber Arabs and Sikhs at a particular school, department heads might be more inclined to hire a faculty member whose ethnic background coincides with that of the largest minority groups on campus instead of the smallest, particularly if the school tabulates Middle Eastern hires as "whites." As a result, some minority educators have a harder time finding employment than others. To create a safe learning environment for all students, it is important that all ethno-racial and religious communities are represented in academic positions.

32) Ensure that U.S. Census Data is Never Used to Monitor 'Suspect' Groups

During the 'War on Terror,' many targeted communities became afraid of participating in the U.S. Census, particularly after administrators announced their intention to hand over demographic information to the Homeland Security Department. On July 30, 2004, the *New York Times* published journalist Lynette Clemetson's alarming article, "Homeland Security Given Data on Arab Americans."[147] According to this *Times* article, the Census Bureau released information on Arab-Americans in August 2002 and December 2003, in response to a request from the Customs and Border Protection division of the Department of Homeland Security.[148] Along with providing a list of American cities with more than 1,000 Arab-Americans, census employees formulated zip code-level breakdowns of Arab-Americans by their country of origin.[149] After civil libertarians expressed concern, Herman Habermann, deputy director of the Census Bureau, told the *Times* that using information to profile particular ethnicities was standard practice.[150] Civil rights advocates accused the Census Department of being complicit in racial profiling, and pointed out that the U.S. government had used the census in World War II. to assist with the rounding up and internment of Japanese-Americans. Although administrators formally apologized in 2000 for the Census Bureau's role in the Japanese-American internment, many minority groups still worried that voluntarily-provided demographic data could be used to profile them, and might be a preamble to something more sinister.[151]

Upset by the Census Bureau's decision to share voluntarily-provided demographic data, some Arab-Americans began questioning whether they should participate in the federal survey if the ethnic information they disclosed could be used to profile them unfairly.[152] Realizing that community distrust was undermining compliance, census administrators stated that they would no longer allow Homeland Security personnel to access to sensitive demographic records. Despite this development, some activists were still distrustful, wondering if census employees were saying one thing in public while clandestinely doing the opposite. Minority groups become less likely to participate in the census if they face heightened scrutiny for volunteering their ethnicity on federal surveys. If some minority residents are too worried about racial profiling to answer census questions honestly, policy-makers cannot get accurate estimates of the size of particular ethnic communities living in the U.S. The political clout of certain groups is undermined if politicians have no idea about their true size. For this reason, it is important to ensure that minority residents can participate in demographic surveys without fear of reprisals. This would give the government an accurate picture of the numbers of Arabs, Iranians, Afghanis, and South Asians in the U.S., enabling bureaucrats to allocate more community resources to these underserved communities and pay more attention to their domestic political needs.

33) Replace 'Single-Bias' Hate Crime Reporting with More Inclusive Categories

It is crucial that hate crimes that involve more than one ethnic or religious group be recorded in more than one category. In the December 9, 2002 *Columbus Dispatch*, Cleveland police Commander Marvin Cross explained that officers from different cities use their own criteria to categorize hate crimes, noting that Columbus might label an assault anti-Muslim while Cleveland would view it as anti-Arab.[153] Police departments need to understand that the same bias crime may be an attack against Muslims AND Arabs, and record the attack in both categories.

34) Press Charges Against Criminals Who Send Hate Mail or Tamper With the Mail

It is important that hate crime victims contact federal investigators when bigots tamper with their mail. In May 2007, Sofian Abdelaziz, director of the Miami-based Muslim Association of North America, reported that bigots repeatedly interfered with his organization's mailings in the years after 9/11.[154] After staff members mailed Islamic texts to interested parties, the recipients discovered that the Muslim readings had been replaced by Christian materials somewhere en route. Since tampering with the mail is a federal crime, it is important that affected parties report these types of incidents to the FBI and to members of Congress so this type of harassment will end.

35) Mandate Investigations when Religious Signs are Vandalized

Federal law requires that FBI investigators look into arsons at houses of worship in the U.S. Congress should also mandate that federal investigators look into vandal attacks on property associated with churches, mosques, and temples. In chapter five, I discussed how shooters repeatedly targeted a Sikh gurdwara's large sign in May and June 2004. FBI agents or Homeland Security investigators should be required to investigate any attack on private property affiliated with a house of worship, since it might prove a precursor to more serious hate crimes.

36) Report Housing Discrimination and Enforce Zero Tolerance for Hate Crimes in Public Housing

During the 9/11 backlash, many minority renters disclosed that property owners were asking illegal questions about their ethnic backgrounds or national origins. About two years after 9/11, the *Los Angeles Times* reported that Marelene Garza of the Housing Rights Center was initiating legal action against Donald Sterling of Beverly Hills Properties for demanding the birthplace of 13 tenants.[155] One of Garza's clients was a Pakistani evicted a week after 9/11 by a landlord who claimed that the renter was unwelcome because of tensions in the Middle East.[156] Apparently, the building owner was unaware that Pakistan was located in South Asia. Along with private-sector renters, immigrants also experienced discrimination in public housing facilities. In chapter two, I discussed how an Iraqi family in the Alice Griffith projects were repeatedly attacked by their neighbors.

To curb post-9/11 bigotry, prospective renters and current tenants need to report overt cases of housing discrimination to government monitors. Local, state, and federal officials should make sure that there is zero tolerance for hate crimes in public-housing facilities, and that any offending party would get evicted immediately for involvement in a bias-related offense. Housing authority employees should also be required to undergo diversity training, so that they are capable of responding appropriately when hate crimes occur. This would ensure that refugees residing in public housing facilities are able to live without fear of post-9/11 racial or religious harassment.

37) Encourage Elected Officials to Denounce Hate Crimes and Promote Tolerance

Ethnic and religious communities should form political action groups to encourage elected officials to denounce bias crimes and hold hearings on the subject. This would help ensure that apathetic or racist elected officials were voted out of office.

Less than a week after 9/11, President George W. Bush visited the Islamic Center of Washington, telling the country that bias crimes were un-American.[157] This high-profile visit sent an important message that the anti-Muslim backlash would not be tolerated by the U.S. government. Despite this gesture, Bush and his administration were responsible for civil rights violations of Middle Eastern and South Asians in the U.S. during the 'War on Terror.' Minority voters need to pay attention to elected officials' track records to determine which politicians are doing the most to curb post-9/11 xenophobia.

In the years after the terrorist strikes, several members of Congress denounced the 9/11 backlash. On March 28, 2003, *India Abroad* reported that South Carolina Congressman Joe Wilson, Republican Co-Chair of the Congressional Caucus on India and India-Americans, spoke out against the racial and religious harassment of American Sikhs. On the House floor, he told his colleagues that religious minorities should be free from harassment in America and that no child should ever face physical danger inside of a school.[158] Ethnic and religious communities need to give positive feedback to politicians who challenge bigotry and racial scapegoating.

Since Barack Obama's father was Muslim, many minority Americans hoped he would play an active role championing minority concerns. Many activists embraced Obama for defending the construction of the Park51 facility and for speaking up against backlash hate crimes. Despite Obama's outspoken commitment to civil rights, many South Asians were disappointed that he canceled a 2010 visit to the Golden Temple in Amistar. Although a spokesperson maintained that the decision was due to scheduling difficulties, some activists worried that the President opted out of the visit due to pragmatic concerns that right-wing pundits would associate Obama with terrorists if he was photographed wearing a Sikh turban while visiting the holy site.

In many parts of the country, politicians distanced themselves from minority groups that voters unfairly associated with the 9/11 terrorists. Particularly after the November 2010 elections, many public officials began voicing anti-Muslim sentiments as a means of advancing in the polls. In Oklahoma, representative Rex Duncan refused a Quran given to him by a Muslim advisory council, showing his constituents his contempt for Islam.[159] He also proposed legislation prohibiting Muslim women from being allowed to wear hijabs in their driver's license photos. In 2011, U.S. Representative Peter King fanned the flames of Islamophobia by launching a Congressional investigation into domestic Islamic terrorism, perpetuating the pernicious misperception that American Muslims were active members of al-Qaeda.[160]

Other elected officials were outraged that their colleagues were pandering to bigots. Congressman Michael Honda took issue with King's controversial views, comparing the hearings to the wartime round-up of Japanese-Americans and the McCarthy proceedings of the 1950s.[161] Because Honda and his family spent several years living behind barbed wire at Colorado's Camp Amache internment center in the 1940s, he worried that other minority groups might be similarly mistreated during the 'War on Terror.' Richard Durbin also took issue with Congressional Islamophobia, holding hearings on the civil rights of Muslim Americans at the Capitol. Voters need to keep track of the policy positions of elected officials, and act accordingly in the voting booth.

38) Demand Racial and Religious Diversity in Political Appointments

Ethnic and religious community organizations should pressure local, state, and federal elected officials to appoint minorities to important governmental positions. After 9/11, many Arab-American, Muslim, and South Asian groups were delighted that Norm Minetta, a Japanese American, was the Secretary of

Transportation. As a member of an ethnic community unfairly scapegoated after Pearl Harbor, he knew the importance of preserving the civil rights of all minority groups in America, and was able to use his position to advocate on behalf of minority travelers. Under the Obama administration, Arab-American Congressman Ray LaHood was appointed Secretary of Transportation, sending interstate travelers the message that discrimination complaints would be taken seriously. Other minority groups were also pleased with Obama's willingness to choose religious minorities for governmental posts. In the fall of 2010, South Asians commended Obama for appointing a Muslim, a Hindu, and a Sikh to his Advisory Commission on Asian Americans and Pacific Islanders.[162] By fostering diversity in political appointments, Americans can ensure that the U.S. becomes more accepting of diverse faiths.

39) Speed Up Citizenship/Naturalization Applications

Since politicians pay attention to voting constituents, it is important for minority groups to help immigrants become citizens as a means of increasing their political voice. Some naturalization applicants believed that the processing of their forms slowed down considerably during the 9/11 backlash. In June 2007, the *Tampa Tribune* reported that some Middle Eastern immigrants thought the political climate was delaying the review of their applications.[163] Ahmed Sheikh-Khalil, a Syrian-born car salesman in Tampa, was upset that immigration authorities had taken several years to process his naturalization paperwork, although he had passed the qualifying exam in March 2004. When he inquired about the delay, immigration officials refused to give him a legitimate reason why his application had not been approved. Sheikh-Khalil told the *Tampa Tribune* that ethnic bigotry was likely the reason for the extended wait.[164] Because empowered, voting communities can respond more effectively to hate crimes, it is important for Americans to pressure U.S. agencies to expedite the processing of citizenship applications. Sheikh-Khalil may not have been aware that members of Congress frequently expedite citizenship applications for friends or family members of constituents who contact their office and ask that a staff member enlist the help of immigration authorities on their behalf. This is an easy way to combat discrimination in bureaucratic agencies and empower vulnerable ethnic communities by increasing their voting power.

40) End Discrimination against Muslims, Sikhs, and Other Minorities in the U.S. Military

To end the 9/11 backlash, it is important to end discrimination against Muslims and other minorities in the U.S. military. In 2003, the army accused Cpt. James Lee of spying for the Guantanamo Bay prisoners. Yee, one of only 12 Muslim chaplains in the U.S. armed forces, was arrested at the Naval Air Station in Jacksonville, Florida. According to the *Chicago Tribune*, Yee, a Chinese-American West Point graduate who had converted to Islam in the 1990s, was held in solitary confinement for three months, on the grounds that he had mishandled classified documents.[165] These charges were later dismissed, since none of the documents Yee had in his possession were classified. Many Muslim activists questioned the army's motivation in arresting Yee, who was married to a Palestinian from Syria. When he was released from custody on November 25, 2003, he was not allowed to resume his duties as chaplain in Ft. Lewis, Washington. Instead, he was re-arrested and charged with adultery and downloading porn on his computer. Gary Solis, a former Marine Corps judge, said that these new accusations were simply an attempt to discredit Yee, since they had not made the more serious charges stick.[166] The military eventually ruled that a reprimand for these new charges would not go on Yee's permanent record.

Yee's arrest and confinement upset many of the 4,230 Muslim service personnel who were on active duty in the U.S. Armed Forces at the time. Some servicemen and women questioned whether Yee would have been unfairly imprisoned for three months if he had been a Christian. Other Muslims wondered if Yee's baseless arrest indicated that the U.S. government was trying to exclude members of their faith from the military and American public life. Along with Muslims of all races, Arab-Americans have been harassed in the military, bullied by their superiors and called racial epithets like "sand-nigger" and towel head."[167]

The U.S. military has also discriminated against Sikhs. In 1981, the armed forces suddenly prohibited its personnel from wearing turbans, growing beards, keeping unshorn hair, or wearing conspicuous articles of faith, such as the cross, Star of David, Muslim crescent, and Sikh kirpan. This policy change effectively barred Sikhs from the service, with the exception of active duty personnel whose religious observances were grandfathered into the policy. Retired Colonel Arjinderpal Singh Sekhon and Colonel G.B. Singh, who enlisted in the military in the mid-1950s and served in the army with turbans and unshorn hair for over 25 years, spoke out against the 1981 policy, which banned other practicing Sikhs from military service.[168]

Following Obama's election, the Sikh American Legal Defense and Education Fund hoped to get the new administration to overturn the military's policy of excluding Sikhs from military service. Unfortunately, the discrimination continued. According to *India Abroad*, two Sikh-American military recruits were told in April 2009 that they had to remove their turbans, cut their hair, and shave their beards before reporting for active duty in July.[169] Kamaljit Singh Kalsi, a physician, and Tejdeep Singh Rattan, a dentist, had enrolled in the Army's Health Professionals Scholarship Program after a recruiter told them that their dastaars, beards, and unshorn hair would not be a problem. Kalsi had attained the rank of Captain and Rattan had become a Second Lt. before they were told that their outward articles of faith were an unacceptable violation of military regulations. The discrimination that Kalsi and Rattan experienced angered civil rights activists. Singh Datta told *India-West* that military involvement was important since it would allow orthodox Sikhs to demonstrate that they are patriotic Americans.[170] If discrimination is eradicated in the U.S. military, Sikh Americans could serve their country and show their fellow citizens that they are patriotic servicemen and women, undermining nativist fears that non-Christians are a foreign menace.

41) Permit the Construction of Mosques, Temples, and Gurdwaras in the U.S.

An important component of stemming the 9/11 backlash involves supporting the building of minority houses of worship in the U.S. In chapter five, I discussed community opposition to proposals to build mosques in New York, California, Wisconsin, and Tennessee. On many occasions, builders faced community sanctions or had their equipment damaged by accepting these construction projects. When Americans oppose the construction of mosques, temples, and gurdwaras, they violate the spirit of the Constitution. Federal agents and Justice Department officials should ensure that religious minorities' rights are protected and that Muslims and Sikhs can build mosques and gurdwaras without community interference.

42) Strengthen the Wall Between Church and State

Some American citizens and elected officials responded to the 9/11 attacks by attempting to make the U.S. less secular, in clear violation of the First Amendment. In the September 19, 2001 issue of the *Wall Street Journal*, reporter Gerald Seib challenged the willingness of some groups to use 9/11 as a pretext to assault the wall between church and state.[171] Citing elected representatives' official involvement in a national prayer service at a cathedral, Seib expressed his dismay that some American groups were using the terrorist strikes to garner support for the White House Office of Faith-Based and Community Initiatives, which blurred the line between governmental programs and religious organizations. Seib argued that the strikes on the Pentagon and World Trade Center should not be used as a pretext to undermine the Bill of Rights, and took issue with Reverend Jerry Falwell's suggestion that God permitted the terrorist attacks because of the country's tolerance of abortion and homosexuality.[172] Americans should take legal action to ensure that the Constitution does not become a casualty of the 'War on Terror.'

To create a more tolerant America, it is important to support religious freedom, particularly when the beliefs of Muslims and Sikhs clash with governmental policies. According to the *St. Petersburg Times*, some Muslims reported being harassed by employees of the Florida Department of Motor Vehicles in 2002.[173] When Sultaana Freeman and other hijab-wearing women went to have their identification photos taken, DMV officials insisted that the Muslims remove their head coverings. Howard Marks, Freeman's attorney, argued that the Florida

DMV should honor the religious practices of these women, particularly since the state issued more than 5,000 licenses without photographs in the previous few years.[174] By initiating legal challenges to policies that conflict with religious practices, members of minority groups can help build a more inclusive America.

43) End Unwise 'Crusades' Overseas

Another component of ending the ongoing nativist backlash involves curbing American militarism overseas. Ashraf Sabrin, an Arlington EMT who responded to the burning Pentagon on 9/11, told the *Washington Post* that he saw a connection between U.S. foreign policy and the terrorist strikes.[175] By supporting or instigating unpopular wars, the federal government generates anti-American sentiment at home and abroad. Short-sighted foreign policy decisions may increase the likelihood of terrorist attacks and their concomitant backlashes. For that reason, American voters should make sure that military actions have no unforeseen consequences.

When American troops fire on Iraqis, Afghanis, and Pakistanis overseas, unsophisticated bigots occasionally take it upon themselves to target these nationals in the U.S. Since dehumanizing the enemy is an important element of conducting wars, it is important for the U.S. government to launch educational campaigns emphasizing that local minorities have nothing to do with foreign extremists.

American atheists should also consider asking the Supreme Court to decide whether the First Amendment prohibits Congress from engaging in religious crusades overseas or giving foreign aid to countries that practice overt religious discrimination. In some parts of the Middle East, anti-American sentiment is fueled by the notion that the U.S. is engaged in a holy war against Islam. In the introduction, I mentioned that after 9/11, President George W. Bush made the mistake of declaring a "crusade" against America's enemies, not realizing that Arabic-speakers understand this word to mean a Christian holy war to exterminate Muslims. Many overseas Muslims believe – rightly or wrongly – that the U.S. is partial to countries that share its theological roots. In December 2010, *Mother Jones* reported that Christian members of Congress were publicly-funded political junkets overseas to preach Christianity in the Middle East and Africa, trying to convert overseas leaders to their faith.[176] Unless the U.S. embraces an impartial approach to international diplomacy, disparate aid levels and inconsistent foreign policy positions might be construed as a de facto endorsement of some faiths over others. The deranged 9/11 terrorists believed they were fighting a religious war against the anti-Muslim U.S. Eradicating publicly-funded religious missions and disparities in foreign aid to religiously-aligned countries might reduce the likelihood of future terrorist attacks and the backlashes they tend to generate.

44) Conduct Medical Studies on the Physical Effects of Hate Crimes and Ethnic Backlashes

One important component of addressing the 9/11 backlash involves assessing how it affected the physical health of ethnic and religious minorities in the U.S. After studying birth records from 2000 to 2002, University of Chicago epidemiologist Diane Lauderdale reported that in the aftermath of the terrorist strikes, Arab and Muslim women in the U.S. became more likely to give birth to infants with low birth weights. Examining birth records in California, where reported hate crimes tripled after 9/11, Lauderdale analyzed information about more than 15,000 mothers with Arabic surnames. Her results, published in the March 23, 2006 *Washington Post*, showed that minority women who gave birth six months after 9/11 were 34% more likely to have a low birth weight baby, compared to mothers who had children in the same six-month period in the year before 9/11.[177] Lauderdale also determined that the post-9/11 infants were 50% more likely to have been born pre-term, indicating that the backlash had a significant effect on the health prospects of Arab and Muslim newborns.[178] Lauderdale found that women without Arabic surnames who gave birth in the six months after 9/11 did not have higher rates of premature births or low-birth weight babies, suggesting that the racial and religious backlash may account for the differences in the two groups of pregnant women. Lauderdale's research did not determine whether the rise in low-birth weight Arab-

American and Muslim babies was due to high maternal stress levels, missed prenatal appointments, or a decline in exercise because pregnant minority women were too scared to venture out of their houses.

This research suggests that the health care providers might need to re-think the way they provide prenatal services to ethnic or religious communities in times of heightened xenophobia. One possible solution might involve driving a mobile health care unit to mosques or ethnic community events to access underserved populations. Such programs might be considerably cheaper than caring for low birth weight babies. By addressing the health ramifications of racial and religious backlashes, nurses and physicians can ensure that the ill effects are kept to a minimum.

45) Conduct Psychological Research on Hate Crime Perpetrators

It is important to do comprehensive psychological research on hate crime perpetrators, so diversion programs can prevent future attacks. Psychologists need to determine which demographic groups are especially likely to harbor bigoted beliefs, as well as which individuals are particularly prone to act violently toward vulnerable groups. Psychological studies conducted in the years immediately following 9/11 pointed to a connection between strong American patriotic views and anti-Muslim sentiments. Harvard social psychologist Mahzarin Banaji surveyed 89 students and determined that the more they unconsciously favored the U.S., the stronger their bias against Arab-Americans.[179] Other investigators have arrived at similar conclusions. Researchers at Purdue and San Diego State University surveyed 374 students from around the country, and found a strong connection between American patriotism and prejudice against Arab-Americans.[180] These findings bolster the conclusions of other studies. Linda Skitka, a social psychologist at the University of Illinois-Chicago, explored how 9/11 affected Americans' perceptions of different groups. According to the *Village Voice*, Skitka determined that most Americans developed a more favorable opinions of politicians, fire fighters, and most other citizens after the terrorist attacks.[181] They also had more negative impressions of Arab-Americans, recent U.S. immigrants, Palestinians, and residents of Muslim countries.[182]

Virginia psychologist Brian Nosek believed that Americans psychologically justified their government's harsh treatment of Arabs and Muslims in the U.S. by rationalizing that the groups must have done something to deserve the mistreatment. According to Nosek, psychologists call this the "just-world effect."[183] Nosek told the *Village Voice* that this psychological need for justice may help explain why Americans continued to cling to discredited justifications for the war in Iraq, calling attention to 2003 poll results suggesting that more than half of Americans thought that Saddam Hussein was working closely with al-Qaeda, and that 34% of Americans still believed that weapons of mass destruction had been found in the country.[184] Other scholars explored how "conversion bias" (the tendency of people to adopt the views of those around them) promoted anti-Muslim beliefs.

Although many Americans expressed negative views of Muslims, Arabs, and immigrants after 9/11, not all bigots acted violently towards vulnerable communities. More psychological research needs to be done to determine which segments of the population are particularly likely to commit hate crimes. Renown sociologist Lonnie Athens determined that three compounding factors often cause a person to undergo violentization: 1) brutalization, the process in which the individual is physically or psychologically tormented by a bully; 2) horrification, the experience of watching an aggressor attack others; and 3) the intervention of a violence coach, who transforms a victim into an aggressive bully.[185] According to Athens, the violence coach can be an aggressive peer, bullying parent, or military trainer who sanctions brutality. After interviewing hundreds of incarcerated violent offenders, Athens concluded that most men passed through all three stages before committing their first assaults.

Although Athens' research was conducted prior to 9/11, his conclusions shed light on why some Americans lashed out at others in the aftermath of the terrorist strikes. Media coverage of the crumbling Twin Towers caused American viewers to experience "horrification," the psychological damage inflicted by watching helplessly while a more powerful aggressor kills or injures others. Some Americans were also exposed to "violence coaches" in the aftermath of 9/11, since many media personalities, co-workers, relatives, or peers sanctioned violent reprisals against minority communities. Even though many U.S. citizens and immigrant residents underwent exposure to steps two and three, community members who never were brutalized themselves were less likely to complete the process of violentization and attack vulnerable groups. Athens' three-step model helps explain why many violent bigots are themselves members of victimized communities. Because minority hate crime perpetrators look nothing like tattooed white supremacists, juries and judges often make unfair allowances for these "normal-looking" Americans when they commit seemingly-inexplicable acts of bias.

There is also a need for psychological studies on hate crime perpetrators who are themselves racial, ethnic, or religious minorities. According to *India Abroad*, a 2001 FBI report found that 65.5% of known hate crime offenders were white, followed by 20.4% who were black.[186] Conducting research for this book, I was surprised to learn that so many of the 9/11 backlash crimes were committed by minorities, with a large number involving Latinos and African-Americans targeting South Asian Sikhs. Perhaps one way that some minorities channel their own feelings of victimization is by attacking others. By becoming oppressors themselves, they can stop feeling like helpless victims. Many community members inaccurately assume that minorities who have experienced discrimination might be particularly fair-minded. In many instances, the opposite may be true. Just as hostages sometimes experience "Stockholm Syndrome," a psychological condition in which abductees learn to align themselves with their empowered captors, racial or religious minorities might occasionally feel the need to shed their feelings of powerlessness by psychologically-identifying themselves with the dominant cultural group, embracing a nativist worldview and attacking immigrants. Other minorities resist the urge to participate in the marginalization of other vulnerable communities, championing universal human rights instead of adopting an "us vs. them" mentality.

Along with illuminating the root causes of prejudice, psychological studies can shed light on how bigotry can be overcome. David Harris, a racial demographer from the University of Michigan, reported that after the Oklahoma City bombing, Americans did not blame all white males for the attack because they knew from personal experience that not all Caucasians were terrorists.[187] Americans who had minimal daily contact with Arab Muslims or Sikhs were more likely to scapegoat them unfairly. Harris' research suggests that xenophobia can be overcome through extensive interactions with people of other religions and backgrounds.

There is also a need to explore whether hate crimes occur particularly frequently in areas where a large number of residents are suffering from "collective post-traumatic stress disorder." I first heard of this concept when I was taking a history of medicine in America graduate reading seminar at Brandeis University. Aware that many Vietnam Vets suffered from post-war alienation, a history instructor mused that in the 1870s, a large number of former Civil War soldiers may have experienced a group form of PTSD and may have channeled their feelings of rage by brutalizing Native Americans. The concept of "collective PTSD" may shed light on the 9/11 backlash. American television viewers were traumatized by the extensive and repetitive coverage of the Twin Towers collapsing and may not have gotten the psychological help they needed, channeling their feeling of helplessness and rage on minority communities. Some grief counselors speculated that the 9/11 backlash lasted so long because traumatized Americans were incapable of getting closure, especially since the horrific nature of the terrorist strikes and the absence of a remorseful perpetrator made forgiveness practically impossible.[188] The U.S. government should consider funding research on "collective PTSD" and offering free or subsidized psychological help to people who need it before they go off the edge.

In his book, Learned Optimism, Martin Seligman argues that most forms of depression stem from situational-based helplessness.[189] His research establishes that individuals who adopt persistent, universal, and personal explanations for bad life events become considerably more depressed than people who see such setbacks to be temporary, specific, and external. A pioneer in the field of 'positive psychology,' Seligman maintains that by changing patients' explanatory style, he can significantly improve their outlook and eradicate mild forms of depression. It would be interesting for Seligman or other psychological researchers to explore how individuals are affected by racism or religious intolerance, since bias victims often experience "learned helplessness" and begin seeing discrimination as persistent, universal, and personal. Seligman's research may also contribute to a better understanding of assailants who overcame their feelings of post-9/11 impotence by brutalizing others.

46) Conduct Psychological Research on Backlash Victims

There is also a need for more psychological research on hate crime victims. In the aftermath of 9/11, many Muslims, Sikhs, and Hindus in the U.S. began feeling anxious and depressed, particularly after being singled out by bigots. Jafar Siddiqui, a Muslim-American real estate agent in Lynnwood, Washington, told the *New York Times* that the constant harassment was affecting his outlook and well-being, noting that he had been invited to 'go home' at least once a month in the years following the terrorist attacks.[190] Many Arabs and Muslims said that because of the backlash, they had become too afraid to undertake everyday activities in public, like speaking to their children in Arabic, listening to Egyptian music in their cars, or walking to the parking lot without an escort. Aneesah Nadir, a ASU social work teacher, told *USA Today* that the Muslim community was experiencing unprecedented levels of anxiety and stress after 9/11.[191] To address the dearth of psychological research on Arab-Americans and Middle Easterners in the U.S., scholars started the *Journal of Muslim Mental Health* in May 2002 to address how religious bigotry and cultural transitions were affecting minority communities. Ibrahim Kira, a psychologist studying Iraqi-Americans in 2003, determined that members of this ethnic group had much higher rates of PTSD than other Americans: 14% compared to 4%.[192] Kira also found that the more time Iraqi-Americans spent watching television coverage of the war, the worse their mental health became. They also became more likely to suffer from physical ailments related to anxiety, like high blood pressure, headaches, and stomach pains, particularly if they still had family overseas.

Mona Amer, a psychologist at Yale University School of Medicine, studied the mental health of 611 Arab-Americans, and determined that they had significantly worse mental health than other citizens. Her results, summarized in *USA Today* on August 10, 2006, found that about 50% of Arab-Americans had symptoms of clinical depression, compared to about 20% for an average American group.[193] Amer discovered that Arab-Americans who had strong ethnic and neighborhood ties were less depressed than more isolated individuals. Amer also determined that the Muslims in her study had worse mental health than Christians, perhaps because they experienced more religious discrimination and had more difficulty integrating into mainstream American society.[194] Since victims of hate crimes are often afflicted by debilitating bouts of depression, the U.S. government should consider offering free mental health counseling to Americans affected by hate crimes and post-9/11 xenophobia.

Researchers need to investigate the social, political, and economic factors responsible for the high rates of depression among Arab-Americans. Since there were no comprehensive studies on the mental health of this group before the terrorist attacks, it is difficult to determine exactly how much they were emotionally affected by the backlash. It would also be interesting to explore whether certain subgroups of Arab-Americans had a particularly difficult time dealing with post-9/11 bigotry. GLBT Arab-Americans might suffer worse mental health than their heterosexual counterparts, since they have to deal with homophobia as well as ethnic bigotry. Since most Middle Easterners in the U.S. come from religious backgrounds, atheists might suffer comparatively higher rates of unhappiness because they lack the social support of their more devout counterparts.

There is also a strong need for additional psychological studies investigating how Sikh and Muslim students are affected by bullying. In March 2004, the *Sikh Coalition Newsletter* reported that two Sikh boys in Lodi, New Jersey, admitted to cutting off their own hair after falsely claiming to be victims of a hate crime.[195] Many community members attributed the boys' actions to the intolerance Sikh students with unshorn hair were routinely exposed to on American campuses. Because interfaith bullying has become so widespread, it is unfortunate that some persecuted children feel compelled to abandon their religious traditions in order to blend in at school. Child psychologists need to research the short and long-term consequences of ethnically-motivated harassment, to assist children under duress.

Along with studying depression rates and bullying, psychologists should also consider how racial profiling and governmental surveillance is affecting the mental health of "suspect" communities. In March 2006, the *Arab American News* reported that infringements on civil liberties were compromising the mental health of some individuals.[196] After hearing about U.S. surveillance programs, an Arab-American man became extremely paranoid, becoming convinced that he was being watched while driving, eating, and sitting at home.[197] Since many Arab-Americans come from countries that infringe on civil liberties, the U.S. government's security policies might trigger repressed memories in survivors of oppressive overseas regimes. Psychologists should consider evaluating how backlash bigotry and intrusive governmental programs are affecting the mental health of minorities in the U.S.

47) Encourage Muslims and Sikhs to Become Psychologists and Join the APA

Since Arab and Muslim psychologists are under-represented in the American Psychological Association, minority patients might have difficulty finding an emotional healer who understands their cultural heritage and discrimination experiences. Many victims of the 9/11 backlash are unwilling to trust members of the APA because of the organization's past complicity in torture.[198] Although the American Medical Association and the American Psychiatric Association have always banned their members from sitting in on inhumane governmental interrogations, the APA has permitted its members to be present when detainees were water-boarded, a practice that sometimes resulted in near-drownings and broken ribs.[199] Because the U.S. government offered lucrative contracts to psychologists who attended these torture sessions, many of these professionals were hesitant to denounce the brutal interrogation method.[200] Years after 9/11, Steven Reisner and other anti-torture activists within the APA worked to get the organization to ban its members from attending water-boarding sessions on the grounds that torture was an anathema to the group's mission to promote emotional healing.[201] Even though the APA has issued several official statements over the years condemning torture, many of its members continued to act as consultants or observers during government interrogations. Because of all the negative publicity the group received, the APA belatedly began taking action against members who participated in torture sessions.[202] Despite recent attempts to improve the organization's reputation, the past use of psychologists in water-boarding sessions has made many Muslims and Arab-Americans reluctant to turn to these mental health professionals to cope with the stress of hate crimes and discrimination. For this reason, it is important for underrepresented minorities to integrate the field of psychology and instigate research studies that help vulnerable groups.

48) Conduct Social Science Research to Determine Which Demographic Groups are Particularly At-Risk

There is also a need for more research on how hate crimes affect different ethnic and religious communities in the U.S. June Han, a researcher affiliated with the Harvard University Pluralism Project, studied how three different South Asian groups fared during the 9/11 backlash. After analyzing data from 120 respondents, Han concluded that the backlash affected Indian Sikhs and Pakistani Muslims much more than South Asian Hindus. Han's findings, summarized in the September 22, 2006 issue of the *India-Times*, reveal that 24% the Hindu respondents claimed that they were affected by hate crimes or hate incidents after 9/11.[203] Han also determined that 43% of Pakistani Muslims and 83% of Sikhs reported that they or someone they knew personally had experienced a hate crime or bias-motivated incident.[204] Approximately 15% of surveyed Hindus felt afraid for their safety after 9/11, compared to 41% of Pakistani Muslims and 64% of Sikhs. Han also determined that Pakistani Muslims were more likely than other South Asian groups to consider leaving the U.S. after the backlash began. They also expressed more interest in domestic and international politics after 9/11, compared to their Hindu and Sikh counterparts.

Han's results show that the backlash affected South Asian Muslims, Sikhs, and Hindus differently. Han's findings suggest that some American groups might be more at risk than others, and might benefit from different government or community services. Other investigators might wish to expand upon Han's work and explore how Arabs, Persians, and Afghanis fared in America during the backlash, and the extent to which Arab Muslims in the U.S. experienced more discrimination than their Christian counterparts. There is also a need to ascertain how gay minorities and those from particular age groups were affected by post-9/11 bigotry.

The U.S. government should fund research to determine what educational programs or community-based activities are particularly effective in uniting neighborhoods and promoting tolerance. After determining what anti-racism strategies are most helpful, the government could expand the most successful ones.

Social scientists should consider conducting additional research on hate groups in the U.S. In 2003, the Southern Poverty Law Center reported that the numbers of hate web sites rose from 443 in 2002 to 497 in 2003, an increase of 12%. SPLC researchers also documented 751 active racist skinhead group chapters across the country, up 6% from the 708 groups active in 2002.[205] The SPLC found incredible regional disparities in the numbers of hate groups in different parts of the country: Texas had 53 active hate groups, while South Dakota didn't have any.[206] Researchers need to determine why some states have more hate groups than others, and what steps can be taken to prevent the recruitment of vulnerable loners.

49) Compare Hate Crime Prosecution Rates and Conviction Statistics in Different States

Perhaps one reason that Texas has so many active hate groups is because its district attorneys rarely prosecute assaults or murders as hate crimes. The Human Rights Commission reported that the Texas hate crime law had only been used a few times since it was passed in 1993, and that the state did not keep track of hate crime prosecutions before 2001. In chapter eleven, I noted that there were only eight hate crime prosecutions in all of Texas between May 2001 and May 2007.[207] Although federal law requires the FBI to collect hate crime statistics from states that voluntarily report them, no government agency tracks how often state or local district attorneys prosecute defendants for bias-motivated attacks. Rob Kepple, executive director of the Texas District and County Attorneys' Association, told the *Express-News* that prosecutors often decide against seeking a hate crime enhancement because of the difficulty of proving that a crime was motivated by bias, and because the state already had stiff penalties for crimes.[208] Texas law requires county prosecutors to report hate crime enhancements filed under the state law, as well as the outcome of the prosecutions. Dr. Beverly McPail, a researcher who studied Texas' prosecutors reluctance to file bias charges, determined that district attorneys prefer not to file hate crime enhancements because this creates an extra evidentiary burden that may lead to an acquittal.[209] If community organizations or government agencies track of how many hate crime complaints actually result in charges and convictions, district attorneys might have a statistical incentive to include bias enhancements when it is appropriate to do so. The federal government could also offer financial incentives to states to encourage them to prosecute bias attacks.

50) Rewrite State and Federal Hate Crime Laws to Facilitate Prosecutions

It is also important for activists to campaign for better state hate crime laws. In California, an attack is only considered a hate crime if it is racially-motivated from the start. In chapter seven, I discussed how Alameda prosecutors maintained that they were unable to prove that the beating of cab driver Jaswinder Bangar was a hate crime because his assailants did not use racial slurs at the onset of the attack. The wording of California's hate crime law creates a legal loophole for bigoted assailants, who can dodge bias charges if they wait to use ethnic slurs until a beating is already underway.

In other parts of the country, state hate crime laws also create problems for prosecutors. In May 2007, Texas district attorneys told the *San Antonio Express-News* that successful prosecutions are difficult because they involve proving the perpetrators' intent.[210] In many states, hate crime laws fail to include all vulnerable groups, like members of the GLBT community, creating additional challenges for prosecutors.

U.S. attorneys claim that it is particularly difficult to convict an assailant of federal hate crime charges because it involves proving that a perpetrator acted to curtail a minority victim's participation in one of six federally-protected activities, like voting. Congress should expand federal hate crime laws to include attacks on minorities engaging in activities outside of these six designated areas. This would facilitate federal prosecutors' ability to press bias charges against perpetrators, particularly in areas of the country where district attorneys rarely file bias enhancements. Activists have tried to make hate crime legislation more inclusive. In 2009, some members of Congress worked to add members of the GLBT community to the groups protected under federal hate crime laws. When socially-conservative Congressmen opposed this modification on the grounds that it would stifle free speech, comedian Steven Colbert joked that bigots could still insult gays – they just couldn't beat them up while calling them names. By expanding federal hate crime legislation, elected officials could help protect the well-being of minority constituents.

51) Prosecute and Punish Young Offenders and Promote Bias-Free Coverage of Hate Crimes

To curb community xenophobia, it is necessary to punish young offenders when they commit bias crimes. Since many district attorneys know that a hate crime conviction can ruin a young life, many prosecutors give youthful offenders a "pass." This is a mistake, since it sends the message that such crimes are not taken seriously. On September 21, 2007, the *News India-Times* reported that young adults are the main perpetrators of hate crimes in the U.S.[211] For that reason, it is imperative that teenagers understand that committing such an attack is a serious offense, carrying a severe sentence. Youths who are convicted of hate crimes should be sentenced appropriately. When Nicholas Minucci was given probation for firing a paint ball at a Sikh after 9/11, he learned that he could hurt others with virtual impunity. In 2005, he committed another bias crime, beating an African-American man with a baseball bat while screaming, "Nigger!"[212] To keep other youths from re-offending, it is important to punish young offenders appropriately and offer anti-discrimination workshops to incarcerated youths convicted of these types of offenses.

In some instances, assailants from "suspect" racial and religious backgrounds are treated differently from other offenders. In New York, reporters readily printed the name of a 15-year old South Asian Muslim involved in the forced haircut of a Sikh student, but many newspapers withheld the name and religious affiliation of other youths who commit equally serious bias crimes. Discriminatory media coverage of hate crime suspects and disparate legal treatment perpetuate racial inequalities. On June 6, 2007, the *New York Daily News* reported the alarming results of a Sikh Coalition survey. After polling 200 Sikh students from Richmond Hill and Flushing, the researchers ascertained that more than 75% of respondents from Queens had been harassed in school, and 20% had been told they resemble terrorists.[213] The same study also found that 40% of Sikh youths had been physically harassed or assaulted for wearing turbans. If 40% of turban-wearing Sikh students in Queens were being physically assaulted, it is important that teenagers from all backgrounds are publicly reprimanded and punished appropriately for harassing minority peers, not just Muslim South Asian offenders.

52) Offer Rewards To Apprehend Bigotry-Motivated Assailants

To stem the 9/11 backlash, local police and federal investigators should consider offering large rewards to catch hate crime perpetrators. In chapter seven, I discussed how the home of a Palestinian-American family in Gaithersburg was repeatedly targeted by bigots over an eight-year period. Local police finally offered a $2,000 reward for information leading to the arrest and conviction of the perpetrator. Muslim groups added another $4,000 to the reward fund. The *Washington Post* reported that David Leonard Rinkon was apprehended after two of Rinkon's acquaintances turned him in, motivated by the financial offer.[214]

It is upsetting that ethnic groups have to pay out-of-pocket to catch hate crime perpetrators when local, state, and federal investigators are unwilling or unable to do so. Considering that the Department of Homeland Security has such a substantial budget, the agency should offer rewards to catch bigots who terrorize ethnic or religious communities in the U.S.

53) Rank Judges on their Handling of Hate Crimes

To get stiffer penalties for hate crime perpetrators, it may be helpful to grade judges based on their handing of bias cases. Just as some organizations score politicians on a liberal to conservative scale, it might be helpful to rank judges based on their handling of hate crimes. It might be more difficult for judges to attain more prestigious appointments if they have a known record for being overly-lenient on hate crime perpetrators. For example, ethnic organizations could consider giving an "F" to the judge who sentenced David Leonard Rinkon to only five days in jail for his harassment of an Arab-American family. This might prompt judges to issue stiffer sentences to hate crime perpetrators, making criminals more reluctant to re-offend.

54) Extend the Statute of Limitations on Hate Crimes

One particularly important way of curbing hate crimes is by extending the statute of limitations on bias crimes. Sonya Kaleel of ADC-SF reported that victims sometimes wait months or years before reporting hate crimes, too frightened to come forward immediately after a traumatizing event.[215] By giving victims more time to press charges, they can wait until they feel strong enough to confront their assailants.

55) Create Compensation Funds for Hate Crime Victims and Acknowledge Them in Public Monuments

In the months following 9/11, many hate crime victims and their families experienced significant financial hardships after being targeted in bias-motivated attacks. Anya Cordell recognized this problem, and attempted to include backlash hate crime victims in 9/11 victim assistance funds. Through the Campaign for Collateral Compassion, she attempted to assist all the victims of 9/11, including the families of people killed in backlash murders.[216] Americans should pressure the federal government to set aside funds for victims of hate crimes, or create financial incentives to make insurance more affordable for at-risk immigrant groups. If Congress refuses to act on this issue, private citizens should create foundations or charities dedicated to meeting the financial needs of hate crime victims and their families, particularly those with dependent children.

To promote awareness of bias attacks, it is also important to create public monuments or displays that recognize the impact bigotry has on minority families. In Phoenix, Arizona, hate crime victim Balbir Singh Sodhi's name was etched on the state's 9/11 monument, publicly acknowledging him as a victim of terrorism.[217] Civil rights groups should work to ensure that backlash victims and innocent foreign nationals who were killed on 9/11 are included in public memorials so that Americans will stop scapegoating minority groups for terrorist strikes.

56) Target Broadcasters and Corporate Sponsors of "Hate Speech Radio"

To curb a climate conducive to bias crimes, it is important to target the sponsors of "hate speech" radio programs. As Mohatma Gandhi once stated, "Thoughts become words – words become deeds."[218] In April 2004, Boston talk-radio host Jay Severin, the host of WTTK-FM's 'Extreme Games,' told his radio listeners that Muslims should be killed because they were not loyal citizens, functioning as a "fifth column" in the U.S.[219] Rather than fire Severin or issue an apology, the station's general manager Matthew Mills attempted to excuse the hate speech, telling the *Boston Globe* that the radio host was referring to overseas Muslims.[220] Mills' explanation did not satisfy listener Rabiah Ahmed, who told the *Globe* that any on-air death threat is unacceptable, especially if it is directed at a vulnerable religious group.[221] Many activists were outraged that Severin was never reprimanded for his inflammatory comments. In response to Islamophobia on the radio, CAIR began their "Hate Hurts America" campaign, asking listeners to monitor radio content and protest bigotry on the air. Some activists expressed disappointment that the FCC acts immediately when a radio host says a profanity on the air, but responds less quickly when radio commentators like Severin make bigoted comments and death threats that endanger the lives and security of religious minorities in the U.S.

In Rhode Island, listeners were disturbed when radio talk-show hosts demonized Arabs and Muslims at the beginning of the Iraq War, turning the conflict into a battle between America and Islam. Many area Muslims felt that radio coverage of the war exacerbated community xenophobia. Some Muslims saw a connection between anti-Iraqi radio rhetoric and a resurgence of anti-Islamic bigotry in the area. Librarian Maraj Aboudola told the *Providence Journal* that after offensive broadcasts, she observed community members shaking their fists at her when she went out in public wearing a hijab.[222] Muslims pointed out that different demographic and religious populations in Iraq were being affected by wartime conditions. Imam Ansari reminded the *Providence Journal* that 40% of the Iraqi population consisted of children, and that many Iraqi houses of worship – including churches and synagogues – were at risk of being bombed.[223]

Along with Arabs and Muslims, Sikhs were also victims of radio jockeys' bigoted speech in the years after 9/11. After the host of WNEW's "Opie and Anthony Show" referred to Sikh Americans as "diaper heads" and "towel heads," the Indian American Center for Political Awareness pressured the CBS-owned station to run a public service announcement in early 2002 to combat post-9/11 bigotry.[224] Rather than abating, anti-Sikh rhetoric persisted for years. On September 10, 2007, one day before the six-year anniversary of 9/11, Los Angeles radio personality Al Rantel offended Sikhs by making a derogatory reference to their religious headwear. According to the *Hindustan Times*, Rantel said that if his elderly mother had to remove her shoes at airports, a Sikh should be required to remove a hat that resembled a diaper.[225] Sikhs in Los Angeles were outraged by Rantel's comments, and organized protests aimed at his station, KABC 790 AM.

To discourage hate speech on the radio, listeners should write letters to the station expressing their opposition to offensive broadcasting. They could also target program sponsors, threatening to boycott their products unless the company withdraws its support of the station. Since radio stations rely on advertising revenue, contacting corporate sponsors directly can motivate radio station administrators to curb "on-air" hate speech. By taking action in response to hate radio, South Asians and Middle Easterners could foster a more tolerant America.

Radio listeners could also give positive feedback to radio stations that take action against bigoted employees. On October 21, 2010, NPR announced it had fired Juan Williams after he made anti-Muslim remarks on an October 18th appearance on the "O'Reilly Factor." During this program, the African-American guest told the host that he felt worried and nervous when he saw people in Islamic attire on airplanes, since these travelers were identifying themselves first and foremost as Muslims.[226] By giving positive feedback to radio stations that take action against Islamophobic commentators, listeners can ensure that the airways stay free from bigotry.

57) Target Broadcasters and Corporate Sponsors of Offensive Television Broadcasts

Just as listeners should target hate speech radio commentators and sponsors, viewers should express disapproval to television broadcasters and their corporate advertisers if they if they air shows that dehumanize vulnerable ethnic or religious communities. According to cultural critic Jack Shaheen, more than 50 television shows have implied that Middle Easterners and Arab-Americans are hiding in terrorist 'sleeper cells,' waging 'holy wars' against the U.S.[227] In a February 26, 2007 article in the *Augusta Chronicle*, Shaheen took issue with the racist storylines in the show "24," pointing out that the show repeatedly disseminated pernicious racial stereotypes about Arab-Americans and Muslims.[228] Along with civil rights advocates, U.S. military leaders were also upset with the show's inflammatory content. Brig. Gen. Patrick Finnegan, dean of the U.S. Military Academy at West Point, and three top U.S. interrogators recently visited the show's creative team to protest the program's glorification of torture.[229] Finnegan told the *New Yorker* magazine that the show's graphic torture scenes were inspiring U.S. military personnel in Iraq to act illegally, tarnishing America's image abroad.[230]

At times, even American cartoons contained Islamophobic content. In an episode of *South Park*, the show's creators included a drawing of Mohammed, knowing that such an image would be offensive to orthodox Muslim viewers. When television programmers edited this episode to eliminate the controversial picture, a Seattle artist attempted to punish the local Muslim community for the network's action, organizing a religiously-offensive protest, "Everybody Draw Mohammed Day."[231] She eventually cancelled the event in response to widespread Muslim opposition to her idea.

To discourage networks from airing xenophobic shows and movies, activists could create a list of offensive programs and films and inform network executives that irate viewers would contact all commercial sponsors airing ads during the offensive broadcasts. Since television stations depend on advertising revenue, it is likely that Islamophobic television shows and movies would end if corporate sponsors voiced concerns about community boycotts. Targeting racist television shows and movies is different from curtailing free speech – stations would still have the right to film and air such programming, as long as they were willing to stomach the concomitant decline in advertising revenue from the offensive broadcasts.

The U.S. government should also pass laws requiring television shows to furnish viewers with the contact information for each episode's writers and producers. This would allow minority viewers to give feedback whenever they encountered offensive material.

Additionally, television viewers should protest television commentators who make offensive comments on the air. On October 14, 2010, FOX television commentator Bill O'Reilly appeared on the talk show, "The View," and suggested that all Muslims were culpable for the terrorist strikes. Unwilling to stomach his religious bigotry, program hosts Whoopi Goldberg and Joy Behar walked off the set. By voicing community opposition to television commentators who routinely scapegoat Muslims, viewers can ensure that corporations think twice about sponsoring offensive broadcasts.

58) Protest Racist Movies and Support Films that Transmit Messages of Tolerance

To promote tolerance in the U.S., it is imperative for Americans to boycott racist movies that demean vulnerable communities and make them more susceptible to hate crimes. Ethnic organizations need to contact movie reviewers and ask them to pan damaging films so they fare poorly at the box office. Moviegoers can also ask theatre owners to refuse to show offensive films that lead to immigrant scapegoating. Constituents should contact their elected representatives and ask them to voice their disapproval to racist films. In April 2003, U.S. Representative Mike Honda and 12 other members of Congress protested Eddie Griffin's controversial film, *DysFunKtional Family*, for suggesting a connection between American Sikhs and Osama bin Laden.[232] Minority viewers need to protest offensive movies and make sure their elected officials go on record challenging pernicious stereotypes.

One way of promoting tolerance is by paying to watch movies with positive images of Arabs, Muslims, and South Asians. In the 2007 drama, *Rendition*, an Egyptian-born chemical engineer is unfairly abducted and interrogated. U.S. government officials participate in his harsh interrogation, and fail to inform the man's worried American wife or his soccer-playing son about his whereabouts. Because the Arab protagonist is innocent, the torture sessions generate no useful information. Some reviewers saw the movie as an indictment of the U.S.' rendition program, in which federal officials sent suspected wrongdoers to overseas prison camps, where they could be tortured with relative impunity. Other reviewers saw the film as challenge to the unconstitutional use of force at Abu Ghraib and Gitmo, and the need to treat minorities in the U.S. with humanity. By paying to see movies with anti-racism themes, activists can ensure their box-office success.

In chapter four, I briefly discussed the movie, *My Name is Khan*. This 2010 drama explores how an interfaith South Asian family was harmed by the 9/11 backlash. The autistic protagonist's cross-country journey begins after his Hindu step-son was killed by schoolyard bigots alarmed by his

Muslim surname. To fight bigotry in the U.S., Khan embarks on a personal crusade to tell the U.S. president, "My name is Khan, and I am not a terrorist." Unlike movies that demonize Muslims and Hindus, this drama depicts them as loving family members, traumatized by post-9/11 hate crimes. By buying tickets to movies featuring sympathetic minority characters, Americans can ensure that these types of pictures are commercially-viable.

59) Integrate Movie Review Boards

To improve the financial success of movies that promote tolerance and hurt revenues generated by racist movies, it is important for minorities to participate in the film rating process. The 2006 documentary, *This Film Is Not Yet Rated*, takes issue with movie review boards, suggesting that they are biased, undemocratic bodies that display favoritism to studio films. Using a private investigator and hidden camera, Kirby Dick questions the fairness of the movie-rating system, demystifying the process by exposing the inner-workings of movie review committees. Watching this documentary, I was dismayed that no Arab-American, Muslim, Sikh, or South Asian people were shown participating in the movie-rating system. Perhaps movies like *DysFunKtional Family* would receive an "NC-17" or "X" rating if there were a few Sikhs or South Asians on movie review boards, since viewers with these backgrounds would understand the harmful effects of such films on underage audiences. Since many theatres are unwilling to show movies with NC-17 or X ratings, these films would receive a lukewarm reception at the box office, and keep impressionable young audiences from being exposed to racist material. National groups might consider asking local politicians and community leaders to pressure film rating boards to include Arab-American, Muslim, Sikh, and Hindu reviewers. If movie committees failed to integrate, politicians could strong-arm them by threatening to create alternate ways of rating films.

60) Protest Racist Video Games that Demonize Sikhs, Muslims, and Arabs

To curb the 9/11 backlash, it is important to boycott manufacturers of racist or religiously-insensitive video games that demonize Sikhs, Muslims, and Arabs. In 2002, when Eidos released "Hitman 2: Silent Assassin," a coalition of 65 Sikh organizations in the U.S., Canada, and Great Britain, demanded the recall of all games and a corporate apology. According to *India-West*, the Sikh Coalition collected signatures on a petition to Eidos, claiming that the game was offensive since it included pejorative references to Dalits, Sikhs, and gurdwaras.[233] Many Sikhs were particularly disturbed that the video game depicted violence occurring in what is a vaguely-disguised version of the Golden Temple (Harmander Sahib) in Amritsar, incorporating filigree and artwork from this Sikh holy site. The game's critics were also offended by a tunic-wearing Indian character, 'Zip Master,' who leads a gang of murderers and robbers and worships a malevolent goddess of war.[234]

Other video games demonize Arabs and Muslims. In 2006, the Campaign to Defend the Constitution and the Christian Alliance for Progress took action when Wal-Mart began selling "Left Behind: Eternal Forces," since the game rewards players for killing or converting people of other faiths, who are on the side of the Anti-Christ.[235] CAIR Executive Director Nihad Awad also took issue with the game, asking the CEO of Wal-Mart to pull the product from Wal-Mart's shelves.[236] In this protest letter, Awad explained that the game promoted religious intolerance by creating an enemy team full of characters with Muslim names.[237] Responding to this criticism, Left Behind Games' President Jeffrey Frichner told the *San Francisco Chronicle* that Muslims are not believers in Jesus Christ, and therefore cannot be on His side in the game.[238] Awad disagreed with Frichner's reasoning, noting that Muslims revere Jesus Christ as one of God's prophets. By suggesting that Muslims were enemies of Jesus, the game contributes to a climate of Islamophobia. Activists can stem religious chauvinism by taking action against consumer products that promote bigotry.

61) Challenge Hate Web Sites

According to the Simon Wiesenthal Centre 2005 online report, "Digital Hate and Terrorism, 2005," many hate groups in the U.S. use the Internet to spread racism and religious bigotry, demonizing South Asian Hindus and other minority groups.[239] The Hindu American Foundation's February 2007 report, "Hyperlink to Hinduphobia," explores 37 hate websites that depict Hindus as condemned people destined for hell.[240] Many of these websites fuel post-9/11 bigotry by suggesting that Hindus worship demonic beings and embrace bride-burning, female infanticide, and the concept of untouchability. Since internet providers prohibit groups from allowing their sites to be legally used to spread hate speech and ideas, the Hindu American Foundation was working with Internet Service Providers to see if the hate sites could be shut down for violating their contracts. Because these legal challenges needed to be made on a case-by-case basis, the Hindu American Foundation expected that addressing each hate site individually would take considerable time. Although most speech is Constitutionally protected, internet providers are allowed to set rules and regulations about what can be said on their sites, and ensure that no group has the right to threaten members of vulnerable communities with bodily harm. Rather than burden groups like the Hindu American Foundation and the Simon Wiesenthal Centre with the task of monitoring and challenging hate web sites that legally violate their contracts, the federal government should make this a top priority, understanding that bigoted postings undermine the security of vulnerable groups in the U.S.

62) Organize Intimidating-Sounding Organizations

When protesting racist products, policies, or shows, individuals should be encouraged to start their own organizations and sign complaint letters accordingly. In her comedy routine, Kathy Griffin describes her television network's concern after receiving an angry letter from the "Catholic League." Rather than alter the content of her act, she dismissed the criticism by claiming that the group consisted of just one guy with a computer typing away in his parent's basement.[241]

Inspired by this comedy routine, one activist suggested that it might be incredibly effective if individuals or small groups of people created organizations with inclusive-sounding names, like the "National Coalition Against Racism." Whenever a television network aired an offensive movie or television episode, a protester could google the contact information of corporate sponsors, and threaten to have the National Coalition Against Racism initiate a boycott. The letter-writer might opt to assume a forceful title, signing the complaint as the "East Coast Regional Director" of the anti-racism alliance. The same protester might also consider starting several organizations with the same handful of members. That way, letters could include a list of the coalition's member groups. Corporate sponsors would take this type of letter more seriously than if they simply heard from one irate individual writing on behalf of his or her family. There is no law against a lone guy in his parent's basement declaring himself the executive director of an anti-racism alliance. It would be easy to get a small organization with a big-sounding name to act against a particular corporate sponsor if doing so only involved getting the permission of a handful of family members and friends. Sponsors are less likely to continue purchasing commercial airtime if doing so incurs the wrath of impressive-sounding groups who threaten to boycott them for funding xenophobic programming. Since network executives are dependent on advertising revenues, they would be unlikely to continue airing controversial broadcasting if corporate sponsors express concern about community protests.

63) Launch Educational Campaigns

The 9/11 backlash showed that many Americans were ignorant about Arab, Muslim, and South Asian ethnic communities in the U.S. To combat hate crimes, minority organizations launched educational campaigns to explain who they were and how they had nothing to do with the terrorist attacks. A few weeks after 9/11, Sikh Americans attempted to educate their fellow citizens about the differences between their turbans and those worn by Islamic fundamentalists. According to the

September 26, 2001 issue of the *Wall St. Journal*, Sikhs distributed flyers explaining that their turbans are larger, pointier, and more colorful than those worn by Muslim fundamentalists.[242] Since racist misconceptions facilitate hate crimes, the Department of Homeland Security and the FBI should launch anti-discrimination educational campaigns so that Americans do not terrorize and assault their fellow citizens. Because the federal government does not undertake large-scale anti-racism work, community organizations are compelled to shoulder this burden.

Despite the best efforts of Sikh, Muslim, and Arab-American organizations, many Americans continued to view minority groups with suspicion years after 9/11. In the September 16, 2002 issue of the *Arab American News*, Ray Hannania describes seeing a confrontational car sign in his neighborhood, declaring, "If you want to see jahad or ala, mess with an American."[243] The sign's two misspellings and hostile message indicate the need for cultural programs to combat bigotry. In the same newspaper, Hannania recounted that one of his neighbors sent him a threatening email during the 9/11 backlash, informing him that he would be punished for what his people did.[244] Apparently, the neighbor was not aware that Hannania was a Vietnam vet, and that his father had fought for the U.S. in World War II. The neighbor's assumption that Arabs could not be U.S. patriots shows that more citizens need to be made aware of the accomplishments of Arab-American veterans, like WWII. General Omar Bradley. Throughout the country, public schools should offer more inclusive U.S. history classes that celebrate the contributions of diverse ethnic and religious groups.

Researchers have found that many Americans are ignorant about the cultural practices of their fellow citizens, and view minorities with distrust and suspicion. According to the *Washington Post*, a November 2005 poll found that 10% of Americans believe Muslims worship a moon god, presumably because of the crescent symbol on the Islamic flag.[245] Other newspapers published equally-disturbing survey results. A June 2006 *Los Angeles Times* poll reported that only 46% of respondents said they would be willing to vote for a Muslim candidate for president.[246] The same poll reported that 85% of respondents said they would vote for a Jewish presidential candidate, and 79% would support an evangelical Christian for top office. Other polls indicated that years after 9/11, Americans were still willing to restrict the civil liberties of vulnerable minority communities. A *USA Today* Gallup poll of 1,007 Americans, conducted between July 28-30, 2006, found that 39% of respondents thought that Muslims should be required to carry a special ID, even if they were U.S. citizens, as a means of preventing future terrorist attacks.[247] A third of respondents believed that U.S. Muslims were sympathetic to al-Qaeda, and said that they would feel more nervous flying if there was a Muslim on the plane.[248]

Governmental officials also need to launch educational campaigns about Sikhs so they will no longer be confused with members of the Taliban. Without such outreach efforts, Sikhs might continue to be unfairly associated with the 9/11 hijackers. John Manherz Singh, a Sikh in his 50s, told the *Los Angeles Times* that he was frequently singled out by bigoted community members, and was even called "Osama bin Lennon" on occasion, in reference to his long hair and Beatles-style glasses.[249]

Sikh children were also bullied throughout the U.S. in the months and years following 9/11. In some parts of the country, educators and elected officials took steps to address the widespread harassment of Sikh and Muslim youth in public schools. In 2003, California Lt. Gov. Cruz Bustamante introduced a new program to educate elementary school students about Sikh beliefs and practices. This program involved the distribution of a coloring book, "The Boy with Long Hair," intended to demystify Sikhs.[250] At the beginning of the story, students at a bus stop ask questions about a Sikh classmate, wondering about his appearance and gender.[251] The other characters eventually cast aside their prejudices, understanding and accepting this new student. By promoting educational materials spreading awareness about diversity, governmental officials can curb community xenophobia.

64) Promote Community Tolerance by Building Interfaith Bridges

To promote cultural awareness, it is important for Americans to join interfaith organizations and dialogue with people with different viewpoints. In 1993, Rabbi Sheldon Lewis of the Palo Alto Congregation Kol Emeth formed the Jewish Arab Muslim American working group to combat religious bigotry and ethnic discrimination.[252] After 9/11, members of this organization worked together to curb the nativist backlash, and held discussions about whether the terrorist attacks should be used to justify the Iraq War.

Unless community groups encourage this type of interfaith dialogue and cultural exchange, Americans will continue to view minority communities with suspicion. In the aftermath of the terrorist strikes, minority Americans turned on one another. In New Jersey, African-Americans verbally lashed out at black Muslims in the days following 9/11. According to the New Orleans *Times-Picayune*, African-American Muslims in Teaneck were surprised that much of the backlash bigotry they were experiencing was coming from other blacks.[253] In other parts of the country, African-Americans singled out South Asians and other vulnerable ethnic groups. A month after 9/11, *India Abroad* reported that some blacks used 9/11 as an opportunity to vent xenophobia and religious bigotry, with some African-Americans publicly demanding that brown-skinned immigrants be rounded up and shipped back home.[254]

Some minorities responded to the backlash by distancing themselves from other "suspect" religious communities. As the 9/11 backlash intensified, some Sikhs tried to prove their patriotism by distinguishing themselves from Muslims. Shortly after the terrorist strikes, the *Washington Post* noted that one website advised Sikhs to carry placards explaining that Sikhs were not Muslims.[255] Many Sikhs were outraged that members of their faith were stepping away from other groups under attack during the 9/11 backlash. About a week after 9/11, Inderpreet Singh told the *New York Times* that it was antithetical to Sikhism for its practitioners to distance themselves from Muslims, who needed the support of the entire community.[256]

Despite Interpreet Singh's admonishment, many of his fellow Sikhs continued to emphasize that they were not followers of Islam. Some Sikhs suggested launching educational campaigns spelling out how they were different from Muslims. A month after 9/11, *India Abroad* published a controversial letter-to-the-editor, written by a Sikh, suggesting that South Asians should explain to Latino and white Americans that Hindus and Sikhs were peaceful, loyal, and law-abiding citizens who were different from Muslims.[257] Many *India Abroad* readers were upset with the writer's assumption that Muslims were unpatriotic and violence-prone community members.

Many South Asians were also outraged when the Indian consul general exacerbated religious rifts by suggesting that Hindu women wear bindis as a means of differentiating themselves from Muslims. *India Abroad* published a letter-to-the editor criticizing this suggestion, noting that Muslim women also wore bindis, and that hate groups like the Dot-Busters targeted immigrants from diverse religious backgrounds.[258] To curb American nativism and religious scapegoating, advocates need to promote tolerance and build interfaith bridges in the U.S.

65) Air Effective PSAs

In the aftermath of the terrorist strikes, many television and radio stations aired PSAs in the hopes of stemming community xenophobia. Listening to some of these PSAs, I wondered whether their platitudes about tolerance actually changed a single bigot's mind. Like Nancy Reagan's admonishments to "Just Say No to Drugs," vague anti-racism PSAs admonishing listeners to "Stop the Hate" might be ineffective.

It might be more worthwhile to do an anti-racism television PSA featuring video clips of famous minority Americans, with patriotic music in the background. While listening to Ray Charles' raspy voice singing "America the Beautiful," viewers could watch a montage of clips of famous Arab-Americans, showing Lakers girl Paula Abdul cheering, Baywatch lifeguard Yasmin Bleeth jogging in the famous red swimsuit, artificial heart creator Michael DeBakey operating, computer pioneer Steve Jobs tinkering, child star Kristie McNichol and Vince Vaughn acting, Quarterback Doug Flutie throwing his famous Heismannwinning catch, and New Hampshire teacher Krista MacAuliffe waving as she boarded the ill-fated Challenger. The bottom of the screen could contain the message that America's diversity is her greatest natural resource, with an ending caption about the need to fight anti-Arab racism. By invoking iconic symbols of America – the cheerleader, the quarterback, the movie star, the research pioneer, and the astronaut – the ad would convey the message that Arab-Americans are as familiar as apple pie. Other PSAs could focus on the contributions of famous American Sikhs, Muslims, and Hindus.

When preparing anti-bigotry PSAs, advocates might consider avoiding the terms, "Islamophobia" or "Hinduphobia," since they suggest a passive or benign fear instead of a malicious and active contempt for a faith. Civil rights groups should find more forceful words to convey vicious sentiments, like anti-Muslim bigotry or anti-Hindu hatred. PSAs discussing anti-Arab attacks might consider using the term, "anti-Semitism," since it is a powerful and inclusive term recognizing that attacks on Middle Easterners and Jews are two manifestations of the same ugliness.

Since many of the 9/11 backlash crimes were committed by Latinos, it might be beneficial to air Spanish-language PSAs to explain that turban-wearing Sikhs have no connection to the Taliban, and that the majority of American Muslims are peace-loving patriotic citizens. Other PSAs could educate Latinos about Arabs, perhaps reminding listeners that Mexican actress Salma Hayek and Columbian pop singer Shakira are of Middle Eastern ancestry. These PSAs could be aired on Spanish-language stations or ethnic programs.

Other PSAs could focus on educating African-Americans about South Asians, perhaps drawing upon Martin Luther King, Jr.'s views on the importance of combating discrimination and celebrating ethno-racial differences.

66) Promote Academic Diversity and Overturn State Laws Preventing Sikhs From Teaching in Public Schools

To promote tolerance, it is important to encourage minority students to enter the teaching profession, to increase ethnic and religious diversity on American campuses. It is also imperative to challenge laws aimed at keeping minorities out of the classroom. In the 1920s, some states, fueled by anti-Catholic sentiment, passed laws prohibiting the wearing of sectarian clothing, including priestly garb and nun's habits, in public school classrooms. As of January 2010, these laws were still being enforced in three states, barring turbaned Sikhs or veiled Muslims from teaching positions and other jobs in the education sector.[259] By repealing antiquated laws, Americans can make campuses more diverse places and allow children to be exposed to Sikh and Muslim teachers and school administrators.

67) Advocate for Textbook Reform

Educators and activists need to lobby text book publishers and teachers' associations to improve the information students are given about 9/11, the Iraq War, and the history of minority communities in America. In chapter one, I mentioned Michael Romanowski's essay, "Textbook Omissions and 9/11."[260] In this article, Romanowski argues that school children are not given information on the wave of hate crimes that followed the terrorist strikes. He notes that the texts fail to mention that Muslims in the U.S. and around the world quickly condemned the hijackings, an omission that leaves American school children with the mistaken assumption that all Muslims might be dangerous. Romanowski finds that the majority of textbooks he examined inaccurately claimed that coalition forces defeated the Taliban in just two or three short months.[261] He also noted that U.S. textbooks failed to explore the ethics of Abu Ghraib, the issue of oil in their discussion of the Iraq War, or the reasons why the government was willing to believe that Saddam Hussein had WMDs.[262] By addressing these omissions, educators and advocates can ensure that American school children have a better understanding of U.S. history.

Educators and activists should also consider writing text book publishers and asking them to include more information about the history of Arab-Americans, Muslims, and South Asians in the U.S. For example, U.S. textbooks fail to mention that Kahlil Gibran, a Christian Lebanese immigrant, organized a literary group in New York in the 1920s. Feminists, poets, artists, and novelists joined this "Pen Bond," which met regularly for more than a decade and produced a school of modern Arabic poetry known throughout the Middle East.[263] By including information about this literary community in U.S. textbooks, educators can give students a more comprehensive understanding of Arab-Americans.

68) Teach Science in Schools to Counter Outdated Racial Paradigms

An indirect way of combating backlash bigotry is by teaching science in public schools. In the 2009 documentary, *Prom Night in Mississippi*, actor Morgan Freeman asks students from his hometown why they continue to have two racially-segregated proms: one for white students and another for blacks. Throughout the movie, the students repeatedly reify the concept of race, believing it to be a scientific reality. By the 21st century, geneticists have overwhelmingly rejected the idea of a handful disparate races. In his public television documentary and book, Journey of Man, Stanford professor Spencer Wells traces the path of genetic mutations across continents.[264] He acknowledges the existence of dozens of distinct genetic populations in Africa, a land mass with more DNA diversity than all of the other continents combined. He then uses forensic analysis to trace the path of human migrations into Asia, Europe, and the Americas, arguing that small genetic changes took place at various points along the way. If nativists understood 21st-century genetic evidence pointing to the common origin of all people, it might be more difficult for them to adhere to outmoded racial paradigms like those expressed by the Mississippi teenagers in Freeman's documentary. This might be an important step in getting U.S. bigots to stop lashing out at darker-skinned community members.

69) Read Diverse Ethnic Publications and Consider Different Perspectives

To combat post-9/11, it is important for different ethnic and religious groups to understand each other's experiences. For that reason, it is crucial that individuals make an effort to access other communities' formal and informal news sources. Arab-Americans read the *ADC Newsletter*, and hear about hate crimes targeting Middle Easterners. Sikhs read *India Abroad*, and learn about crimes targeting South Asians. GLBT activists hear about gay bashings, and conclude that members of their community are the most likely to experience bias crimes. Because minority communities are particularly likely to hear of bigotry-motivated attacks affecting their friends and relatives, some groups might have difficulty understanding the extent to which other communities are also under siege in the U.S. It is important for individuals to make an effort to access new information channels to broaden their worldviews. By increasing inter-group communications and accessing different information channels, minority communities can assist one another and create a more just America.

When I was in graduate school at Brandeis, a professor once made a comment about how great it was that there were no racial problems on the campus. Shocked by this instructor's naiveté, I silently reflected on a recent discussion I had the week before with a Japanese-American faculty member who spent about an hour talking to me about the racism he had personally experienced at the university. The conflicting experiences of the two teachers reminded me of the parable of the elephant and the blind men, who felt different body parts of the animal and arrived at different conclusions about its shape. If there is one minority woman and nine white students in a discussion seminar, she looks around the room and sees nine white faces and one fewer female. From her minority perspective, the class looks 100% white. Any other student looking around the same room would see one fewer white face and one more minority female one. From this majority perspective, the class looks somewhat integrated, appearing only 8/9ths (89%) white.

At some point in their lives, it is important for all Americans to have the experience of being a visible minority, so they can obtain insight into the intolerance some community members are forced to endure in many parts of the U.S. Many Arab-Americans, particularly those with non-Arabic surnames, are invisible minorities, and often have trouble relating to the life experiences of people who confront racism on a daily basis. By reading ethnic periodicals and visiting different neighborhoods, Americans can achieve a heightened understanding of the perspectives of others.

70) Organize Community Events and Volunteer to Address Hate Crimes

Americans can promote tolerance by volunteering to combat bias-motivated crimes. In response to the 9/11 backlash, Washington state activist Pramila Jayapal organized the Hate Free Zone campaign in November 2001, to address problems facing Seattle's immigrant community. According to *Colorlines*, the HFZ's six employees and 75 volunteers ran a helpline to log calls related to hate crimes, employment discrimination, and FBI interrogations and detentions.[265] HFZ also brought legal challenges to free innocent people locked up for months, and organized 'know your rights' seminars to inform immigrants of their legal options. By volunteering to help at-risk immigrant groups, Americans can help curb 'War on Terror' xenophobia.

Minority communities should also perform community service, simultaneously helping their neighbors and combating pernicious stereotypes. On occasion, bigoted Americans barred minorities from participating in civic activities. Shortly after 9/11, Asha Mohammed was prohibited from donating blood in Seattle by a volunteer who took issue with her Muslim-sounding name.[266] By organizing philanthropic events, minority groups can improve their standing in the community and ensure that event staffers treat all participants with dignity and respect. Rajwant Singh, the national director of SCORE, told *India Abroad* that blood drives were an important way of showing that the Sikhs were civic-minded community members.[267] He also felt that participation in interfaith events was an important way of educating others about Sikh beliefs and practices. This helps build a more tolerant society.

71) Resist both the Sanctification and the Commercialization of the Flag

Whereas some Americans regard the flag and the Statue of Liberty as sacred symbols, others opted to commercialize these icons. In the years following 9/11, marketers took advantage of America's collective grief and desire for patriotic consumer goods, selling red, white, and blue popsicles and lawn chairs. Some Americans undermined the spirit of patriotic rituals by making them compulsory. When displaying the American flag or pledging allegiance ceases to be voluntary, these rituals lose their true meaning. American school children also need to be taught a true understanding of the Constitution rather than embrace superficial trappings of patriotism. This would help curtail nativist jingoism and promote a more just society.

72) Use Humor and Charm to Bridge Ethno-Cultural Barriers

Some Arabs, Muslims, and South Asians relied on humor to cope with intolerance and ignorance. On September 8, 2002, the *Boston Globe* reported that some Sikh-Americans learned to use humor to defuse community tensions. Dr. Gurcharan Singh Khalsa told the *Boston Globe* that when people would ask him about his turban, he would smile and say that he thought it looked pretty good.[268]

Responding to 'War on Terror' excesses, a small group of minority comedians formed the 'Axis of Evil Comedy Tour,' entertaining American audiences with their experiences coping with bigotry and racism in the U.S. These shows provided an opportunity for audiences to laugh about the lunacy of the 9/11 backlash, and the idiocy of racial stereotypes.

73) Engage in Personal Acts of Courage and Commitment

Activists can also stem the 9/11 backlash by taking steps to promote interfaith understanding. To spread awareness about his faith and make an international gesture of peace, 92-year old Sikh marathoner Fauja Singh ran 26 miles in seven hours in 2003 in front of New York race audiences. According to the *News India-Times*, the British runner endured taunts over the course of the race, with spectators comparing him to Osama bin Laden and Saddam Hussein.[269] After winning the over 90 category in five hours and 40 minutes, Singh was presented with the Bob Hope International Peace Award for taking such a creative and brave stand against bigotry. He was also featured in Adidas' 'Impossible is Nothing' campaign.[270] Singh's example shows how individuals can take unconventional paths to challenge racial and religious stereotypes.

74) Support Artistic Responses

Many artists and dramatists channeled their creativity into raising awareness about the 9/11 backlash. Alarmed by discussions of Arab-American internment, some Japanese American artists, playwrights, and actors took action to protect the liberties of their fellow citizens. In her show, "Big Head," performance artist Denise Uyehara explored the fragile nature of civil liberties in wartime, drawing upon her family's internment camp experiences in Arkansas and the more recent experiences of Arab-Americans and South East Asians in the U.S.[271] After interviewing activists and hate crime victims, Uyehara weaved together their narratives, showing audiences how different communities were affected by the backlash. Community members should support playwrights, poets, and painters who challenge xenophobia through their creative work.

75) Help Other Americans

While bigots were lashing out at their fellow citizens, tolerant Americans were assisting Arabs, Muslims, and South Asians under attack in the U.S. On September 15, 2001, Adisa Jittipun, a 23-year old Muslim senior at George Mason University, went to eat at Chason's Country Buffet in Winchester, Virginia, accompanied by two non-Muslim girlfriends.[272] Because Jittipun wore her hijab to the restaurant, she became concerned when a waitress walked up to the table after serving their food. Jittipun told the *Washington Post* that she was moved when the waitress paid for their meal, expressing sympathy for the reprehensible ways in which Muslims were being scapegoated and admiration for women who had the courage to wear their veils.[273] The waitress' kindness shows the compassion that many Americans displayed in the aftermath of 9/11.

Other Americans also reached out to minority groups under attack. Shortly after 9/11, students from Manhattan brought teddy bears and cards to Muslim children, delivering the message that Americans from all faiths were outraged by backlash hate crimes.[274] In Sacramento, California, Japanese-Americans expressed solidarity with Muslim community members by folding thousands of origami paper cranes and covering the windows of a local Islamic school with these symbols of peace.[275]

In many parts of the country, empathetic students reached out to their Arab and Muslim classmates. Karim Baz, an Egyptian high school senior at Rockville's Magruder High School, told the *Washington Post* that many of his peers offered to come to his aid if anyone hassled him or blamed him for 9/11.[276] Instructors at the school also helped Muslims under attack. According to the *Post*, English teacher Linda Jasper was so bothered by the increase in hate crimes that she joined a group standing guard at night outside the Islamic Center of Maryland.[277] In Oakland, California, Latino women dropping their children off at Garfield Elementary School protectively encircled hijab-wearing mothers, shielding them from community bigots in the days immediately following the terrorist strikes.[278]

To combat post-9/11 bigotry, Americans of all faiths began volunteering to assist targeted minority students in the U.S. The *Los Angeles Times* reported that shortly after the terrorist strikes, community members began helping out at an Islamic school in Pomona, escorting Muslim children home.[279]

Hollywood celebrities – including Patricia Arquette, Whoopi Goldberg, Ben Stiller, Lucy Liu, and Benecio del Toro – also took action to curb the backlash, filming PSAs and speaking out against bigotry.[280]

Hate crime victims sometimes received support from strangers, particularly after national newspapers published their stories. In chapter three, I discussed a September 2001 attack on the Old Town Islamic Bookstore in Alexandria. A few weeks after his store window was smashed, Palestinian store manager Hazim Barakat told the *Washington Post* that he had received 15 bouquets of flowers and 50 sympathy cards from Americans outraged about what had happened.[281] He also said that people from distant states like Nebraska and Tennessee called with condolences, making him feel part of the American family.

On many occasions, strangers put themselves in danger to help minorities under attack. *India Abroad* reported a particularly uplifting story of a group of people coming to the aid of a Sikh American unfairly targeted by an inebriated bigot on a Long Island commuter train.[282] On March 1, 2003, Gurpreet Singh, a 24-year old technology consultant, was traveling home when another commuter began harassing him. According to *India Abroad*, Singh walked to the other end of the car to avoid a confrontation, but the drunk followed him and began shoving him with his chest, repeatedly ordering him to leave the train.[283] Singh was dismayed that a fellow American was harassing him simply because he was a Sikh, particularly since he had fled Afghanistan at age six with his family in search of religious freedom. Worried that the drunk might try to grab his turban, Singh began preparing to defend himself, drawing on his faith for inspiration. To Singh's surprise, another passenger came to his aid, offering him a seat and telling him not to worry about the drunk. The good Samaritan was off-duty NYPD officer Captain Stephen Hughes.

In response to the intervention, the drunk turned on Hughes, asking him why he was defending a Muslim since his people were murderers.[284] Hughes told the inebriated man that he was willing to fight anyone who unfairly targeted innocent people, explaining that the minority passenger had nothing to do with 9/11.[285] When the drunk became increasingly belligerent, Hughes grabbed him by the waist and attempted to move him into the next car.

At that point, an African-American man came to Hughes' assistance, promising to help him protect the targeted commuter.[286] Once the disruptive bully was arrested in Hicksville, the two good Samaritans and three other witnesses signed statements about the bias-motivated assault. Singh told *India Abroad* that he was deeply moved that two strangers were willing to put themselves in harm's way to protect his rights, seeing it as the embodiment of what he loved most about his adopted country.[287]

Despite witness testimony indicating that Brand acted out of bias, responding officers initially refused to file hate crime charges until they were pressured into doing so by Sikh civil rights advocates. Rather than demand that Thomas Brand go to jail for aggravated harassment, a bias crime, Singh requested that his assailant be sentenced to community service so that he could overcome his xenophobia by interacting with local South Asians.

Brand completed his mandatory 20 hours at the Sikh Coalition, where he collected hate crime reports at area gurdwaras and served food to members of the congregation. Standing next to Gurpreet Singh at a Sikh gathering in New York, Brand sincerely apologized for his egregious behavior and acknowledged that he had grown from the experience of interacting with people of other faiths.[288] He also described his compulsory community service as a blessing in disguise, since it gave him an opportunity to learn about Sikh beliefs and culture, which he characterized as beautiful.

This story captures the America I long to live in all the time.

We don't need "barbarians" anymore.

AFTERWORD:

THE AUGUST 5, 2012
WISCONSIN SIKH TEMPLE MASSACRE

Despite all the hundreds of hate crimes I encountered while researching this project, I hoped to finish this book on a positive note, highlighting the diverse communities that came together to overcome post-9/11 bigotry. I intended to use Cavafy's famous poem about intolerance in the book's beginning and ending, since the narrative verse commences with a society in the grips of xenophobia and concludes with a provocative question on the function that fear serves in a community. Unfortunately, hate crimes taking place after the ten-year anniversary of 9/11 have eliminated the possibility of an optimistic ending.

More than a decade after the terrorist strikes, minority groups in the U.S. continue to be scapegoated. On February 5, 2012, a vandal attacked a gurdwara in Sterling Heights, Michigan, defacing the house of worship with profanities and references to 9/11.[1] The graffiti included the misspelled words, "Fcuk you," "Air Mohmed," and "Don't Builed," blaming local Sikhs for the terrorist strikes and the decision to construct an Islamic center near the World Trade Center site.[2]

A few months later, on Sunday morning, August 5, 2012, neo-Nazi gunman Wade Michael Page approached the Sikh Temple of Wisconsin and began shooting at worshippers. The hate crime took place at approximately 10:25 a.m., when some congregants were meditating and others were cooking a communal meal.

Several hundred South Asian families belong to this gurdwara, which was established in Milwaukee in 1997 and rebuilt in Oak Creek in 2007.[3] At the time of the attack, there were between 20 and 30 people inside the 17,000-ft. facility, including young children.[4] Scores of congregants were expected to arrive later for 11:30 a.m. religious services.

Since visitors are welcome at the house of worship, the presence of an unknown person entering the temple's parking lot in an SUV raised no eyebrows. What happened next, however, was totally shocking. A bald, tattooed gunman walked up to two Sikh worshippers and, without speaking, abruptly shot them.[5] He then reloaded and entered the gurdwara.

Nine-year old Amanat Singh and her eleven-year old brother Abhay were sitting outside the building when the attack began.[6] Earlier that morning, their parents had left them inside the gurdwara's kitchen while they went to buy paper plates for Amanat's birthday party luncheon, which was to be held at the temple later that day.[7] Although their mother had instructed them not to leave the building, the children decided to play outside. The kitchen had become hot from the grilling of samosas and chapattis, and the siblings wanted to get a little air. Soon after they exited the building, they saw an armed man go into the gurdwara. With little concern for their own safety, Abhay and Amanat Singh ran inside to warn the adults that there was a gunman on the premises.[8]

After entering the house of worship, Page continued his bloody rampage, firing a 9 mm weapon at the Sikh worshippers. In an incredible act of bravery, 65-year old Satwant Singh Kaleka found a butter knife in the kitchen and tried to stab the intruder with it, hoping to protect the people on the premises.[9] At this point, Page shot Kaleka twice in the hip and upper leg, causing him to collapse onto the floor. Kaleka's decision to take on the shooter gave other congregants a chance to escape or hide. Some barricaded themselves in closets, bathrooms and prayer rooms, texting desperate pleas for help.[10] Kaleka's wife Satpal and 12 other women were cooking in the kitchen when they heard the shots. Soon thereafter, they encountered Abhay and Amanat, who informed them that there was a gunman on the loose. The 13 women, two children, and a male congregation member all hid in a small pantry, listening in terror to the sound of gunfire.[11] They huddled there for over an hour while the food they had been preparing began smoking on the stove. Another large group of Sikhs took refuge in the basement, hoping desperately that they would not be discovered.

A few worshippers inadvertently ran toward the shooter while trying to get out of the building. Witnesses reported that the gunman was targeting South Asian men with turbans and religiously-proscribed beards.[12] Some people at the scene claimed that he had a 9/11 tattoo on his arm.[13]

When 40-year old Jatinder Mangat first learned of the shooting on his way to the temple, he tried to call his uncle, temple president Satwant Singh Kaleka.[14] Mangat was surprised when Gurmail Singh answered his relative's phone. With the sound of cries and screams in the background, Singh told Mangat that his uncle had been shot and that they were frantically waiting for an ambulance to arrive.[15] After speaking with Mangat, Singh called the priest's son Amardeep to inform him about the armed attack.[16] Satwant Kaleka bled out while Gurmail Singh was cradling him on the floor of the temple.

Shortly after the gunfire began, Lt. Brian Murphy arrived on the scene. Although some frightened congregants had told the 911 dispatcher that there might be more than one shooter, Murphy courageously raced to the front of the building, attempting to help a gunshot victim. At this point, Page ambushed the 51-year old police officer and shot him approximately eight or nine times.[17]

When other officers arrived, they observed Page walking through the parking lot. They ordered him to drop his weapon and put his hands up.[18] Rather than comply, Page responded with gunfire, spraying two police vehicles with bullets.[19]

Soon thereafter, sharpshooter Sam Lenda shot page in the stomach, causing the gunman to commit suicide by means of a self-inflicted gunshot wound to the head.[20] By the time the attack ended, there were five dead men and one dead woman on the temple grounds. When other law enforcement personnel arrived, Murphy told them to attend to the Sikh victims before assisting him.[21] Crime scene investigators spent hours sweeping the premises, and recovered two semi-automatic handguns that had belonged to the gunman.

Emergency responders used a nearby bowling alley as a makeshift shelter, treating the injured and gathering witness statements until late in the evening.[22] Congregation members began frantically searching for relatives and friends, hoping that they were not among the dead. The parents of Abhay and Amanat were incredibly relieved to learn that their children had not been killed or physically wounded by the gunman. While the massacre was still underway, their 36-year old mother, Kamwal Singh, had been hysterical, begging authorities to turn off the gas at the temple so that the food on the stove would not cause a kitchen fire while the intruder was inside the building.[23]

Many area Sikhs expressed shock and disbelief at the attack. According to the *New York Times*, Harpreet Singh was on the way to the temple with his wife and two children when they were stopped outside the parking lot.[24] At first, they thought that the commotion was due to some kids setting off a fire alarm as a prank. Once Singh and his wife understood the extent of the bloodbath, they felt overcome with sorrow at the magnitude of the crime.

Community members were grateful for the courageous actions of police officers and congregation members. Police chief John Edwards credited these heroes for preventing additional deaths. Shortly after the attacks, FBI agents and area police surrounded Page's rented apartment in Cudahy, another Milwaukee suburb.[25] Although they found no grand manifesto explaining his actions, they reported having no doubt that he was a white supremacist who belonged to organized hate groups advocating the extermination of minority groups.

According to the *Los Angeles Times*, FBI agents reported that their agency failed to track Page because federal law prohibited them from collecting information on U.S. citizens not suspected of committing a crime.[26] Some civil libertarians found this stance hypocritical, pointing out that the Department of Homeland Security and the FBI had no qualms about monitoring the movements, conversations, and activities of innocent Arab-Americans and Muslims in the years since 9/11.

Because federal agents was too busy wire-tapping the phones of ethnic minorities to pay close attention to Page, civil rights groups shouldered the burden of chronicling his activities. Both the ADL and the SPLC had been closely watching Page for years, researching his hate-filled writings, monitoring his whereabouts, and compiling photos of him alongside Confederate and Nazi symbols.

Page played bass guitar at the neo-Nazi music festival Hammerfest.[27] Some of the songs his hate rock band performed called for the murder of all Jews and non-white people.[28] According to ABC News, one of his music group's album covers depicted a white arm punching an African-American man.[29] Page also belonged to the racist terrorist group, the Hammerskins, and posted hundreds of times on neo-Nazi websites under the aliases 'Jack Boot' and 'End Apathy,' which was also the name of his band.[30] On many occasions, he urged other whites to take action against minorities instead of just complaining about the browning of America.

According to the ADL, Page had a number of racist tattoos, including a Nazi Death head, a Celtic cross, and a Hammerskins insignia.[31] He also had a drawing of a German soldier on his calf, and a tattoo of the number 14, referring to the white power slogan, "We must secure the existence of our people and a future for white children."[32]

After learning of the massacre, Page's stepmother Laura claimed that he had been given a kind and loving upbringing in Colorado.[33] She noticed a change in his personality after he enlisted in the army in 1992 and spent time at Fort Bliss, Texas and Fort Bragg, North Carolina. In the service, he worked as a psychological ops specialist and a repairman for the Hawk surface-to-air missile system. Page once told researcher Pete Simi that he had become significantly more racist as a result of his 6× years in the military.[34] Page was eventually demoted for getting drunk while on duty and going AWOL. He also got in trouble for drunk driving and for kicking holes in a bar. After his discharge, he worked as a trucker and factory worker. He had difficulty staying employed, and had recently been fired from a job at a metal works company.

Page's girlfriend, convicted felon Misty Cook, broke up with him in June 2012. Investigators believe that she had nothing to do with the gurdwara shooting even though she was in possession of an illegal firearm at the time of the attack and belonged to at least two neo-Nazi groups.[35]

Page's victims were all active members of the temple. Prakash Singh, a 39-year old Sikh priest, performed daily religious services at the gurdwara and gave lectures on Sikhism.[36] He enjoyed working in the kitchen and making tea for congregants and visitors. His friends and relatives described him as a fun-loving man who often told jokes.[37] After moving to the U.S. nine years ago and obtaining his green card, he brought over his wife and teenage children from India. The family was temporarily living at the temple and making preparations to move into a nearby apartment they had rented.[38] His daughter was in high school, and his son had recently graduated from middle school. Prakash Singh's family members were horrified and dismayed by his bias-motivated murder.

Brothers Sita Singh, 41, and Ranjit Singh, 49, were also killed in the Sikh temple massacre. Ranjit Singh worked at a grocery store and helped out at the gurdwara, where he occasionally played the drum during religious services.[39] He immigrated to the U.S. from India 16 years ago, hoping to get a green card and bring over his wife, his two daughters, and his son. According to the New York Times, when he first came to America, he promised them that they would not be separated for too long.[40] As soon as he found a job working at a convenience store, he began wiring them money on a monthly basis. He would also call them every few days, sending them his love.[41] Due to visa issues and financial considerations, he had never had an opportunity to return home to Delhi, where his family lived in a modest two-story home. He felt particularly broken-hearted about missing his daughters' weddings. Shortly before he was killed, Ranjit Singh had made plans to travel to India in November 2012 to see his family and celebrate the Diwali festival with them.[42] His son Dhillon was only seven months old when he last saw his father, and the teenager was eagerly awaiting their reunion. His youngest daughter, Jaspreet, told the Times that she wanted so desperately to see her dad again, who departed for America when she was only four years old.[43] Despite the distance, she said, he remained an important part of her life, doing so much for the family. She noted that she was going to miss him terribly.

Like his brother Ranjit, Sita Singh was also a temple priest and devoted family man with relatives back in India. About six months prior to his death, he had moved to Wisconsin from New York City to help out at the gurdwara and be closer to his brother.[44] He would routinely wake up between 4:30 and 5:00 a.m. to ensure that all gurdwara visitors had prasad, the traditional food offered at the end of every prayer session.

Interjeet Singh Dhillon, the secretary of the Sikh Temple of Wisconsin, remembers that Sita Singh would often gesture with his hands to make guests feel welcome, conveying the message that there was always plenty of food for everyone. He would often mentored younger Sikhs, telling many of them that singing loudly was an excellent means of lifting their depressed spirits.[45]

Indian television showed footage of Ranjit and Sita Singh's relatives in India weeping uncontrollably in response to their deaths.[46] Viewers around the world saw images of Ranjit Singh's son Dhillon grieving forlornly while staring at a photo of his father.

Like the other victims of the massacre, Satwant Singh Kaleka was another devout member of the temple. He immigrated to the U.S. with only $35 in his pocket, after being sponsored by his elder brother, Jagit Singh Kaleka.[47] After years of hard work, Satwant Singh Kaleka became the owner of several gas stations. His nephew, Jatinder Mangat, said that his uncle routinely worked hard to help others, even if it meant dirtying his own clothes in the process.[48] To give back to the Sikh community, Satwant Singh Kaleka became the founder of the temple and one of the lead contributors to the building's construction. Jagit Singh Kaleka told the *Los Angeles Times* that his brother loved America even though he encountered discrimination "on a daily basis."[49]

Satwant Singh Kaleka's children were devastated by their father's murder and the attack on their beloved gurdwara. His sons, 34-year old Pardeep and 36-year old Amandeep, remembered him as a loving parent who stressed the importance of community service.[50] Satwant Singh Kaleka's daughter, Ritu Sharma, told reporters that it was important that the relatives of all the shooting victims support one another in the aftermath of the hate-motivated attack.[51]

The eldest victim of the massacre was 84-year old Suveg Singh Khattra. For most of his life, he had worked as a dairy farmer in Patiala, a city in the Punjab region of India.[52] In 2004, he and his wife, Nachattra Kaur Khattra, immigrated to the U.S. to be with their son Balginder. Sandeep Kaur Khattra said her grandfather, Suveg Singh Khattra, spent most of his days at the temple, particularly after his wife died in 2010.[53] Usually, his son would give him a ride to the gurdwara, which was located two miles from his residence. When Balinger was busy, Suveg Singh Khattra would walk to the temple so he could volunteer in the kitchen. Mandeep Khattra remembered his grandfather as an honest, humble, and devout person who enjoyed making tea for everyone.[54] Suveg Singh Khattra's relatives were upset by his death, and wished they could have done something to save his life. On the morning of the massacre, Suveg Singh Khattra's daughter-in-law Kulwant Kaur was in the temple, hiding with the other women in the pantry.[55] When she was finally evacuated, she saw her father-in-law's bloody body on the floor. She tried to touch him to determine if he was conscious, but was told by police officers to keep moving so that emergency responders could attend to the survivors.[56]

The only woman killed in the temple attack was 42-year old Paramjit Kaur, who had immigrated to the U.S. with her husband in 2007.[57] Her sons, 18 and 20, remembered her as a sweet and loving woman who was devoted to her family and her faith.[58] She worked long hours, six days a week, at B.D. Medical Systems, helping to provide for her family. Her co-worker, Baljit Kaur, remembered her as a talkative and friendly person who was always willing to help others.[59] Manpreet Kaur characterized Paramjit Kaur as a wonderful and reliable friend who brought her food after the birth of her son.[60] Paramjit Kaur usually prayed for at least an hour a day, and had just finished her morning meditations when Page shot her in the front hallway of the temple.

In addition to murdering five men and one woman, Page injured other Sikhs. These surviving victims were rushed to Froedtert hospital in Wauwatosa, Wisconsin. Although 50-year old Santokh Singh was only hit with one bullet, the wound affected his chest, diaphragm, stomach, and liver.[61] The other critically-injured South Asian victim, 65-year old Punjab Singh, suffered injuries to his face and abdomen.[62] He required two surgeries just to stay alive.

Along with the Sikh survivors, Lt. Brian Murphy was also hospitalized. Because he was wearing a bullet-proof vest, the 51-year old police officer survived the attack but had a serious neck wound. According to Dr. Gary Seabrook, all three shooting victims were listed in critical condition as a result of their multiple gunshot wounds.[63] Another congregation member was also treated at the medical center, but was released shortly thereafter.[64]

Sikhs across the country were terrified by the massacre in Wisconsin. In the immediate aftermath of the shootings, NYPD commissioner Raymond Kelly dispatched law enforcement personnel to gurdwaras in New York City, in case Page's skinhead associates were planning on attacking other houses of worship.[65] Since xenophobia had escalated considerably in New York in the years after 9/11, Sikhs in this city felt particularly vulnerable. Police officers in Chicago also took steps to protect area gurdwaras.

Days after the shooting, Punjab Singh remained in critical condition, suffering a stroke as a result of his injuries. Singh was a resident of India who had been volunteering at different gurdwaras in the U.S. His son, Raghuvinder Singh, was a priest at the Sri Singh Sabha Sikh Temple in Glen Rock, New Jersey, and had often enlisted his father to serve as a guest prayer leader and caretaker.[66] In addition to helping out at the Glen Rock temple, Punjab Singh acted as a "sevador," or religious assistant, at other gurdwaras. On the day of the massacre, he was visiting the Oak Creek temple, helping other Sikhs translate different hymns used in prayer services.[67] His son was in India at the time of the massacre, and became distraught at the horrifying news.

While Punjab Singh was barely clinging to life, other shooting victims were faring better. After two surgeries, Santokh Singh showed enough improvement that his health status was upgraded from critical to serious.[68] Like Punjab Singh, he was also a traveling priest, dividing his time between gurdwaras in Canada and the U.S. while his family remained in India.[69]

Along with updating reporters on the condition of the Sikh survivors, physicians at Froedtert Hospital issued a statement declaring that Lt. Murphy was out of danger. Many members of the Oak Creek police department were pleased that their wounded colleague was ambulatory, even though he still had a bullet lodged in his neck. The Sikh community hailed Murphy as a hero, risking his life to protect others. The group, Sikhs for Justice, awarded him $10,000 in appreciation for his valiant efforts to protect innocent civilians. According to ABC News, Murphy was a seasoned police officer with more than 20 years on the force.[70] He was born in Brooklyn, but moved to Wisconsin to be closer to his wife's family. He was also a loving father who was close to his daughter and two stepchildren. Terry Murphy, a recently-retired NYPD officer, said that his brother had no plans to retire, and was looking forward to resuming his professional duties.[71]

Community members were also grateful to Lenda, the tactical weapons expert who shot Page with a squad rifle from a distance of 75 yards.[72] Lenda, a 32-year veteran of the Oak Creek Police department, was a SWAT instructor at Milwaukee Area Technical College. FBI agents and other law enforcement personnel characterized Lenda's precision as incredible.

In the aftermath of the massacre, visitors from many parts of the country dropped by the targeted Sikh temple to express their condolences, leaving stuffed animals and flowers as gestures of solidarity. Hundreds of well-wishers attended vigils to pray for peace and tolerance. Similar gatherings took place at Sikh temples and other venues across the U.S.[73] Many Sikhs traveled hundreds of miles to attend the memorial service, which was held at the Oak Creek high school gymnasium on August 10, 2012. Some of the victim's relatives, including Ranjit Singh's wife Lokinder Kaur, traveled from India to attend the funeral.[74] At the gathering, Wisconsin governor Scott Walker told mourners that people throughout the state shared in the families' grief.[75] On this occasion, he observed that the Sikh community lived the words of the Rev. Martin Luther King, Jr., who urged others to respond to acts of unspeakable bigotry with love and kindness. U.S. Attorney General Eric Holder also addressed the crowd, characterizing the bias-motivated shooting as an act of domestic terrorism.[76] Some activists were encouraged by Holder's words, since the government must believe that a suspect has broken federal law before opening up a domestic terrorism investigation. Some civil rights activists were hopeful that authorities might use the Oak Creek shooting as an opportunity to look into neo-Nazi organizations, since Page had been an active member of these groups.

In the aftermath of the attack, congregants worked hard to clean up their prayer center. Although they replaced the blood-stained carpet, they deliberately left one bullet hole in a door jamb as a memorial to the shooting victims.[77]

News of the massacre prompted angry protests in India. In New Delhi and Jammir, Sikhs held up signs denouncing the bigotry-motivated killing of their countrymen in Wisconsin.[78] Although most of the demonstrators were peaceful, a few upset people destroyed American flags in front of reporters, hoping that their actions might prompt U.S. authorities to take more steps to protect vulnerable Sikhs.

Despite the best efforts of community activists to promote awareness of their faith, Sikhs were dismayed that many public figures continued to confuse them with Arab Muslims. At a gathering at the West Des Moines Country Club shortly after the Oak Creek massacre, Republican Presidential candidate Mitt Romney mentioned participating in a moment of silence in honor of the victims of the "sheik" temple shooting.[79] American journalists called attention to the gaff, lamenting the fact that Romney was confusing "Sikhs" with "sheikhs," the Arabic word for tribal leaders. Other prominent Americans also showed a stunning lack of awareness of Sikhism in the aftermath of the tragedy. In an interview with the nephew of one of the shooting victims, Fox News host Gregg Jarritt asked if there had been any previous incidents of anti-Semitism at the temple, apparently confusing the gurdwara with a synagogue and Sikhs with Jews.[80]

Civil rights activists attempted to correct misperceptions about Sikhs and inform others about the discrimination they regularly encountered. Abraham Foxman, the national director of the ADL, issued a statement condemning the Oak Creek massacre, which he viewed in the context of post-9/11 hate crimes targeting Muslims, Sikhs, and Arab-Americans.[81] Other watchdog groups also viewed the August 5th shooting as a manifestation of the ongoing backlash. In an interview with CNN, Mark Potok of the SPLC described Page as a fool who thought he was murdering Muslims.[82] In the United Kingdom, news sources like the *Daily Mail* drew attention to earlier instances of backlash-related discrimination in Wisconsin, reporting that Sikh businesses in Milwaukee had been targeted prior to the August 5, 2012 shootings.[83]

Some investigative journalists uncovered information showing that Page had long been an anti-Arab bigot. The *Huffington Post* drew attention to the fact that that shortly after 9/11, Page scapegoated all overseas Muslims for the terrorist attacks.[84] He had angrily responded to September 11th by asserting in writing that Americans should go over to the Middle East and bomb everyone there.[85]

Throughout the country, national newspapers and television stations – including CNN, ABC, the *Journal-Sentinel*, the *New York Post*, and the *New Yorker* – reported that Page had a 9/11 tattoo, based on the recollections of his neighbor Amber Young and temple survivors.[86] News accounts of this 9/11 tattoo spread internationally in publications like the *Daily Mail*.[87]

Oak Creek police chief John Edwards said that although Page's arms were covered with white supremacist graffiti, he was unable to find a 9/11 tattoo on the gunman's body.[88] It is possible that nervous neighbors and traumatized massacre survivors might have made a mistake, misreading Page's intricate racist body art.

Although he may not have had a 9/11 tattoo, Page was clearly a violence-prone neo-Nazi. Ignoring the considerable evidence that the Oak Creek shooting was a product of Page's rabid bigotry, Edwards seemed reluctant to characterize the attack as a hate crime, telling reporters that there was no information about why Page opted to gun down people at the Oak Creek gurdwara. Edwards told the *Los Angeles Times* that he knew of no reason why Page would attack the Sikh house of worship, commenting that the reason for the shootings may have died with the gunman.[89] Edwards also cautioned against assuming that Page's body art could reveal the cause of the massacre, telling journalists that they might never know what prompted the temple attack.[90]

Other law enforcement officials were equally reluctant to state that the Oak Creek killings were bias-motivated. Shortly after the shootings, federal investigators made public statements asserting that they might never figure out why Page targeted the building. Steven Conley, the FBI agent in charge of national security, told reporters that the possibility of obtaining answers about why the gurdwara was targeted "may have died with Page."[91] Teresa Carlson, the special agent in charge of the FBI's Milwaukee division, also hesitated to label the attack a hate crime, telling the *New York Times* and CNN that investigators had been unable to discern Page's motive.[92]

Many news commentators and politicians characterized the Oak Creek shooting as an inexplicable incident committed by a lone gunman, comparing it to the *Dark Knight* massacre in Colorado.[93] In an opinion piece in *U.S. News and World Report*, journalist Teresa Welsh lamented the fact that many American newspapers and television stations were not covering the Oak Creek massacre with the same depth that they gave to the July 2012 attack in Aurora.[94] In this editorial, she suggested that the minimal attention given to the Sikh temple shooting may have been a result of the fact that the victims were of a relatively-unknown religion and were praying in a non-Christian house of worship, making it somewhat difficult for many Americans to relate to the tragedy.

Rather than regard the Oak Creek massacre as an example of yet another random shooting, South Asians in the U.S. linked the crime to the rise in xenophobia that began after 9/11. According to the *New York Times*, Sikhs in Oak Creek reported that the killings revived bitter memories of the period just after September 11th when they were confused with Islamic terrorists.[95] Manjit Singh told the *Times* that area Sikhs viewed the attack as a hate crime, triggered by the widely-held misperception that they were Muslims.[96] Other Sikhs concurred. Discussing the August 5, 2012 attack, 65-year old Ravi Chawli told the *Times* that in the years prior to the massacre, many people in Oak Creek would look at his turban and assume that he was a member of the Taliban.[97] Many South Asians in Wisconsin reported that strangers often confused them with members of al-Qaeda. Jeji Shergill, a 62-year old gas station owner, told the *Guardian* that he was frequently called 'Osama bin Laden' by Oak Creek residents.[98] When he would try to explain that Indian Sikhs were not Middle Eastern Muslims, they would ignore him and continue to taunt him, referring to him as the September 11th mastermind.[99] In an August 7, 2012 interview with CNN's Carol Costello, Kanwardeep Singh Kaleka, the nephew of slain temple member Satwant Singh Kaleka, also viewed the gurdwara massacre in the context of the 9/11 backlash, suggesting that Page had targeted the house of worship because he mistakenly thought that its congregants were followers of Islam.[100]

Sikhs in other states also viewed the Wisconsin shootings in the context of post-9/11 intolerance. At an August 8, 2012 Las Vegas vigil for the Wisconsin victims, Teji Malik, a Sikh member of the Interfaith Council of Southern Nevada, spoke about the discrimination he routinely encountered in the years after 9/11, describing how angry Americans often gave him the finger because they thought he was a turban-wearing Arab.[101] Commenting on the Oak Creek massacre, Sikh Coalition activist Amardeep Singh reported that many South Asians were tired of the harassment: "We've had 11 years where the turban is equated with terrorism."[102]

Instead of putting the crime in the context of post-9/11 bigotry, both President Barack Obama and Republican presidential candidate Mitt Romney characterized the assault on the Sikh Temple of Wisconsin as a "senseless act of violence."[103] Unfortunately, the enduring misperception that American Sikhs are Muslim terrorists make the Oak Creek shooting far from inexplicable.

Along with Sikhs, American Muslims continued to face discrimination more than a decade after the terrorist strikes. In one seven-day period in early August 2012, there were six different anti-Muslim attacks that took place in various parts of the U.S. On August 4, 2012, four teenage boys, ranging in age from 13 to 16, attacked a mosque in Hayward, California, throwing oranges and lemons at the American Muslim Association.[104] One worshipper was hit by a projectile. Shortly after the attack, the assailants were arrested and charged with interfering with a religious community's right to worship.

The following day, an intruder smashed the sign of the Masjid al-Islam in North Smithfield, Rhode Island. The *Providence Journal* reported that the mosque's surveillance camera showed a man knocking down the sign at 3:30 a.m., putting it in his car, and driving away.[105] The hate crime frightened area Muslims, particularly since it happened the same day as the Oak Creek massacre.

Exactly 24 hours after the Rhode Island attack, a Missouri mosque was burned to the ground in a suspicious fire. According to Imam Lahmuddin, area Muslims had been using the Islamic Center of Joplin until 11:20 p.m., conducting Ramadan prayer services and engaging in social activities.[106] A few hours later, at approximately 3:40 a.m., drivers in the area called in the blaze. The *Joplin Globe* reported that 15-year old Omar Ahmed was stunned by the destruction, surveying the charred remains of the mosque when he arrived at 5:00 a.m. for daybreak prayers.[107] Congregation members were shaken by the destruction, which they viewed in the context of other attacks against Muslims.

The previous month, on July 4, 2012, an arsonist had tried to burn down the same house of worship, which had opened in 2007. Because the attack took place on Independence Day, area Muslims speculated that the perpetrator was trying to send them the message that their faith was un-American. According to the *Boston Globe*, surveillance cameras captured footage of the July 4th intruder throwing an incendiary device on the roof, igniting the structure but failing to burn it down completely.[108]

Federal agents were investigating both fires, but were pessimistic about solving the cases. According to fire chief Bill Dunn, the strength of the August 6th blaze suggested that an accelerant might have been used, but the totality of the destruction likely eliminated any physical evidence.[109] To complicate matters, the Jasper County Sheriff's Office reported that the mosque's security camera had been severely damaged in the fire, making it unlikely that it could aid in the investigation.[110]

The 50 families who prayed at the Islamic Center of Joplin were shaken by the fires. Many congregation members urged federal authorities to increase police protection at area mosques, especially in light of the recent massacre at the Oak Creek gurdwara.

Also on August 6, 2012, a van belonging to a Muslim man was vandalized in Detroit. Fox News reported that the hate-filled drawings left at the scene were too vulgar to be televised.[111] The owner of the damaged vehicle, Shafik Shoaib, was extremely frightened by the bias-motivated attack, particularly since he had been viciously beaten by a group of bigoted men outside his home in 2006. When he discovered the ugly graffiti, he feared that his assailants were targeting him once again. Because he suspected that one of his neighbors might have been involved in the hate crime, he wanted desperately to move out of the area.

The following day, a mosque was attacked in Ontario, California. The *Press-Enterprise* reported that at approximately 10:00 p.m., two women in a white truck threw pigs' legs at the Al-Nur Islamic Center, which was under construction.[112] The dead animal parts hit the house of worship in three separate places, desecrating it. A security guard witnessed the attack and filed a report with the San Bernardino County sheriff's department. The August 7th hate crime frightened area Muslims, who had been using an adjacent house as their prayer center while builders were finishing up the mosque. A few days after the attack, congregation members became impatient with the failure of the U.S. attorney's office in Los Angeles to open an investigation into the bias-motivated incident, which took place during Ramadan. According to the *Press-Enterprise*, the prayer center was used by approximately 70 Muslims, most of whom were of Bangladeshi descent.[113]

Three days later, on the evening of August 10, 2012, a shooter with an air rifle fired two shots at a mosque in Illinois.[114] Congregation members believed that a neighbor may have been involved, since he had a long history of opposition to the prayer center. The gunfire damaged a brick wall at the Muslim Education Center of Morton Grove. Police and federal agents were investigating the attack.

The frequency of hate crimes against Sikhs and Muslims indicates that post-9/11 xenophobia has not abated. In a February 2002 lecture on the 'War on Terror,' Noam Chomsky declared that only those who were entirely ignorant of modern history could be surprised by the course of current events.[115] As Chomsky so aptly recognized, knowledge of the past provides valuable insights into the present.

America's inadequate response to the ongoing 9/11 backlash is somewhat similar to the actions of the Army Corps of Engineers in the aftermath of Hurricane Katrina. I recently watched the 2010 documentary, *The Big Uneasy*, exploring how New Orleans' levees collapsed in 2005 due to faulty design. When the levees were under construction, one of the builders actually filed a lawsuit to point out the folly of building safety structures on top of sand, arguing that digging deeper was imperative for the barriers to work. He lost, and was ordered to proceed with the unsafe project. The documentary called attention to the fact that the Army Corps of Engineers was rebuilding the levees and pumps without addressing all of the reasons why they had failed when they were most needed. The reconstruction of structurally-unsound levees by the same agency that screwed them up in the first place can serve as a metaphor for the ongoing mishandling of hate crimes by federal and local authorities in the U.S.

Unless we address the various reasons why the post-9/11 wave of xenophobia was able to drown out America's commitment to pluralism, the country will remain at risk of another surge of bias attacks. We must do better.

ENDNOTES:

Chapter One:

[1] Constantine Cavafy. "Waiting for the Barbarians," in <u>Complete Poems of Cavafy</u>, translated by Rae Dalven. (New York: Harcourt, Brace, and World, 1961). Constantine Cavafy. <u>C.P. Cavafy: Collected Poems</u>, translated by Edmund Keeley and Philip Sherrard. (Princeton: Princeton University Press, 1975).

[2] Guillermo Contreras. "Getting Tough," *San Antonio Express-News*. San Antonio, TX May 8, 2007, pg. 1A.

[3] Roma Khanna. "Hate Crimes Peak After Sept. 11," *Houston Chronicle*. Houston, TX Dec. 14, 2001, pg. A37.

[4] "Protests at Mosque," *Arab-American View*. Orlando Park, IL. Nov. 5, 2001, v. 2, Iss. 11, pg. 1.

[5] Somini Sengupta. "Sept. 11 Attack," *New York Times*. New York, NY Oct. 10, 2001 pg. B1.

[6] Duncan Campbell. "American Muslims Fear Reprisals," *Guardian*. Manchester, UK, Sept. 12, 2001, pg. 1, 16.

[7] Bernice Jackson. "The Fire Next Time," *Oakland Post*. Oakland, CA Sept. 26, 2001, v. 38, iss 29, pg. 4.

[8] Richard Serrano. "Deluge of Hate Crimes," *Los Angeles Times*. Los Angeles, CA July 6, 2002, pg. A8.

[9] Greg Winter. "Some Mideast Immigrants, Shaken," *New York Times*, New York, NY Nov. 23, 2001, pg. B1.

[10] Ibid.

[11] Annie Nakao. "Sikhs Say They're Being Made Targets," *San Francisco Chronicle*, San Francisco, CA Sept. 19, 2001, pg. A11.

[12] Ruben Navarrette. "Ugliness," *San Antonio Express-News* San Antonio, TX Oct. 8, 2001, pg. 5B.

[13] Ahan Kim. "58% in Poll Want Special Security," *Austin American Statesman*. Austin, TX. Sept. 19, 2001, pg. A6.

[14] Ibid.

[15] "Detention Camps for Arab Americans?" *Arab American News*. Dearborn, MI Aug. 2, 2001, v. 19, iss 859, pg. 4.

[16] Ibid.

[17] Moustafa Bayoumi. "For Muslims," *Milwaukee Journal Sentinel*. Milwaukee, WI. Sept. 9, 2001, pg. 13A.; Moustafa Bayoumi. "Congressional Ground Has Been Lost," *Times Union*. Albany, NY Sept. 8, 2002, pg. B2.

[18] Ibid.

[19] "Detention Camps for Arab Americans?" pg. 4.

[20] Mona Eltahawy. "Bracing for a Backlash," *Washington Post*. DC. March 24, 2003, pg. A13.

[21] Sam McManis. "Protective Coloring," *San Francisco Chronicle*. San Francisco, CA Oct. 6, 2001, pg. A13.

[22] Hugh Hart. "Art of Urgency." *Los Angeles Times*. Los Angeles, CA Feb. 18, 2003, pg. E1.

[23] Jodi Wilgoren. "Going by 'Joe,' Not 'Yussef,'" *New York Times*. New York, NY Sept. 11, 2002, pg. G15.

[24] Sam McManis. "Protective Coloring," pg. A13.

[25] Katrice Franklin. "Punjabi Society Cancels Festival," *Virginia Pilot*. Norfolk, VA Oct. 6, 2001, pg. B2.

[26] Theola Labbe. "Muslims Endure Season of Suspicion," *Times Union*. Albany, NY. Sept. 30, 2001, pg. A9.

[27] Tamar Lewin, Gustav Niebuhr. "Attacks," *New York Times*. New York, NY. Sept. 18, 2001, pg. B5.

[28] Jo Becker, Phuong Ly. "Sikhs Campaign Against Hate," *Washington Post*. DC Sept. 24, 2001, pg. B1.

[29] Ibid.

[30] Todd Hartman. "Immigrants Find Kindness," *Rocky Mountain News*. Denver, CO Sept. 19, 2001, pg. 28A.

[31] Mary Beth Sheridan. "Backlash Changes Form," *Washington Post*. DC March 4, 2002, pg. B1.

[32] Lisa Tsering. "Bay Area Businesses," *India-West*. San Leandro, CA Oct. 5, 2001, v. 26, Iss. 48, pg. B5.

[33] Vik Jolly. "Hate Crimes," *Orange County Register*. Orange County, CA Sept. 5, 2002, pg. 1.

[34] Ibid.

[35] Moustafa Bayoumi. "Congressional Ground Has Been Lost," pg. B2.

[36] Ibid.

[37] Ibid.

[38] Ian Callaghan. "War on Terrorism," *Yakima Herald-Republic*. Yakima, WA, July 23, 2002, C1.

[39] Michelle Malkin. In Defense of Internment: The Case for 'Racial Profiling' in World War II and the War on Terror, (DC: Regnery Pub., 2004.)

[40] Douglas Brown. "In Disgrace or in Defense?" *Denver Post*. Denver, CO Sept. 2, 2004, pg. F1.

[41] Ibid.

[42] Ibid.

[43] John Iwasaki. "Book Defends Internment," *Seattle Post-Intelligencer*. Seattle, WA Aug. 6, 2004, pg. B3.

[44] Ibid.

[45] Ibid.

[46] Paul Campos. "A Dangerous Argument," *Rocky Mountain News*. Denver, CO Jan. 4, 2005, pg. 31A.

[47] Douglas Brown. "In Disgrace or in Defense?" pg. F1.

[48] Sam McManis. "Protective Coloring," pg. A13.

[49] Ibid.

[50] Richard J. Riordan, David A. Lehrer. "Commentary: We Can All Just Get Along: A Major Hate-Crime Backlash Against Muslims and Arab-Americans Failed to Materialize Despite Ominous Warnings," *Los Angeles Times*, Los Angeles, CA May 8, 2003, pg. B15.

[51] Ibid.

[52] Michelle Malkin. "Fake Muslim Hate Crimes: Where's the Apology, CAIR?" www.michellemalkin.com, October 3, 2004.

[53] Editorial. "Never Mind," *Richmond Times-Dispatch*. Richmond, VA July 24, 2005, pg. E2.

[54] Deborah Bulkeley. "Muslims in U.S. See Little 9/11 Backlash," *Deseret Morning News*, Salt Lake City, UT Sept. 9, 2006, pg. E1.

[55] "Cabby Attack," *New York Post*. New York, NY Aug. 26, 2010, pg. 34.

[56] "The Predicted Anti-Islam Backlash Never Occurred," *Corpus Christi Caller Times*. Corpus Christi, TX Aug. 27, 2010, pg. A9.

[57] Jonah Goldberg. "The Supposed Anti-Muslim Backlash Among Americans is Mostly a Myth," *Vancouver Sun*. Vancouver, BC Aug. 30, 2010, pg. A9.

[58] Jeff Jacoby. "The 'Islamophobia' Myth," *Boston Globe*. Boston, MA Dec. 8, 2010, pg. A17.

[59] Michael Romanowski. "Textbook Omissions and 9/11," *Clearinghouse*. DC. July 2009. v. 82, iss 6, pg. 290-6.

[60] Ibid.

[61] "Hate Crimes on Increase," *Arab American News*. Dearborn, MI. Sept. 21, 2001, v. 18, iss. 814, pg. 15.

[62] Saeed Ahmed. "Retaliation," *Atlanta Constitution*. Atlanta, GA Sept. 18, 2001, pg. B4.

[63] Anna Whitney. "Terror in America: Race Tensions – Three Held After Attack on Afghan Taxi Driver," *The Independent*. London, UK Sept. 18, 2001, pg. 2.

[64] Ibid.

[65] Ibid.

[66] "Hate Crimes on Increase," pg. 15.

[67] Vasantha Arora. "Brother of Hate Crime," *News India Times*. New York, NY. Aug. 16, 2002, v. 33, iss. 33, pg. 52.

[68] Angie Chuang. "Expressions of Hate," *Oregonian*. Portland, OR. Sept. 19, 2001, pg. A6.

[69] Annie Nakao. "Sikhs Say They're Being Made Targets," *San Francisco Chronicle*, San Francisco, CA Sept. 19, 2001, pg. A11.

[70] Kavita Chhibber. "The Sikhs in the Shadows of 9/11." *Little India*. Reading: April 2005, v. 14, iss. 4, pg. 37.

[71] Larry Stammer. "Turbans Make Sikhs Innocent Targets," *Los Angeles Times*. Sept. 20, 2001, pg. A21.

[72] Richard Fausset. "Sikhs Mark New Year," *Los Angeles Times*, Los Angeles, CA, April 14, 2003, pg. B1.

[73] Nadia Malik. "Faith and Fitting In," *Daily Herald*. Arlington Heights, IL. May 27, 2007, pg. 1.

[74] Charles McCarthy. "Leaders Condemn Defacing of Temple," *Fresno Bee*. Fresno, CA March 17, 2004, pg. B1.

[75] "Hindu American Foundation," www.hafsite.org.

[76] Harry Bruinius. "Muslims Deal With Grief," *Christian Science Monitor*. Boston, MA. Sept. 18, 2001, pg. 3.

[77] Ibid.

[78] Robert Marquand. "The Hurricane that Swirls," *Christian Science Monitor*, Boston, MA, Feb. 12,1996, pg. 10.

[79] Allan Austin. African Muslims in Antebellum America: A Sourcebook. (New York: Garland, 1984); Allan Austin. African Muslims in Antebellum America. (New York: Rutledge, 1997).

[80] James Brooke. "Attacks on U.S. Muslims Surge," *New York Times*, New York, NY. Aug. 28, 1995, pg. A1.

[81] Tanmaya Nanda. "There Are No Boundaries for Hate Crimes," *India Abroad*. New York, NY Oct. 4, 2002, v. 33, iss 1, pg. A12.

[82] Joseph Pereira, William Bulkeley. "US Arab, Religious Groups Want More Police Protection," *Wall St. Journal* Europe. Brussels, Sept. 20, 2001, pg. 27.

[83] Ibid.

[84] Ibid.

[85] "Survey of Iranian Americans," conducted in 2008 by Zogby International for the Public Affairs of Iranian Americans.

[86] Lynda Gorov. "Afghan Community in Fremont Angry." *Boston Globe*. Boston, MA Sept. 24, 2001, pg. A11.

Chapter Two:

[1] Sheryl Thomas. "Hate Crimes," *News India-Times*. New York, NY. Sept. 21, 2007, v. 38, iss. 38, pg. 8.

[2] Allan Austin. African Muslims in Antebellum America: A Sourcebook. (New York: Garland, 1984); Allan Austin. African Muslims in Antebellum America. (New York: Rutledge, 1997).

[3] Lawrence O'Kane. "Muslim Negroes Suing the State," *New York Times*. New York, NY March 19, 1961.

[4] M.S. Handler. "Malcolm X Flees Firebomb Attack," *New York Times*. New York, NY, Feb. 15, 1965, pg.1.

[5] Robert Lipsyte. "Other Muslims Fear For Their Lives," *New York Times*. New York, NY, Feb. 22, 1965, pg. 10; Donald Johnson. "Inmate Killed," *New York Times*. New York, NY Oct. 17, 1975, pg. 39.

[6] Don Jelinek. Attica Justice. (Berkeley: Jelinek, 2011): 397. Jelinek references *New York Times* articles published on July 22, 1976 and May 22, 1977.

[7] "Campus Life; Swarthmore New Orientation," *New York Times*. New York, NY, Sept. 8, 1991, pg. A51.

[8] Ibid.

[9] August Miller. "Racist Fliers Distributed," *Orange County Register*. Santa Ana, March 19, 1992, pg. B9.

[10] Ibid.

[11] Yusuf Salaam. "Attorney for Muslim," *NY Amsterdam News*, New York, NY Feb. 6, 1993, v. 84, iss 6 pg. 6.

[12] Ibid.

[13] Ibid.

[14] Ibid.

[15] Yawu Miller. "Muslim Minister Settles Suit," *Bay State Banner*. Boston, MA March 20, 1997, v. 32 iss 24, pg. 3.

[16] Ibid.

[17] Russell Walker. "CMHA Officer Alleges Beating," *Call and Post*. Cleveland OH Sept. 26, 1996, pg. A1.

[18] Ibid.

[19] Dequendre Neeley. "Hackers," *NY Amsterdam News*. New York, NY Oct. 28, 1995, pg. 8.

[20] Jim Hughes, Sheba Wheeler. "Denver Marchers Decry Acts," *Denver Post*. Denver, CO Nov. 23, 1997, pg. A23.

[21] Ibid.

[22] Herb Boyd. "The Diallos Visit Mosque No. 7," *NY Amsterdam News*. New York, NY April 15, 1999, pg. 3:3.

[23] Arthur Pais. "Fear of the Dark," *India Abroad*, New York, NY Oct. 5, 2007, v. 38, iss 1 pg. M3.

[24] "Hindus Hounded from the City," *Bellingham Herald*, Sept. 5, 1907, pg. 1, discussed in Nayan Shah. Stranger Intimacy. (Berkeley: University of California Press, 2011): 27.

[25] *U.S. vs. Bhagat Singh Thind*. 261 US 204 (1923).

[26] Nayan Shah. Stranger Intimacy, pg. 246.

[27] Tom Mooney. "False Arrest Begins Journey," *Providence Journal*. Providence, RI Feb. 20, 2003, pg. 1.

[28] Kavita Chhibber. "The Sikhs in the Shadows of 9/11," *Little India*. Reading: April 2005, v. 15, iss 4, pg. 37.

[29] Ibid.

[30] Viji Sundaram. "Vandals Paint Swastikas," *India-West*. San Leandro, CA. Sept. 21, 1990, v. 15, iss 45, pg. 1.

[31] "Dot-busters in New Jersey," in "Dot-busters," www.wikipedia.org.

[32] Arthur Pais. "When Will We Learn?" *India Abroad*. New York, NY. Oct. 5, 2007, v. 38, issue 1 pg. M3-4.

[33] Paul Murphy. "Mody's Father," *India Abroad*. New York, NY April 3, 1992, v. 22, iss 27, pg. 34; Arthur Pais. "Fear of the Dark," pg. M3-4; Arthur Pais. "When Will We Learn?" pg. M3-4.

[34] Ibid.

[35] Anuradha Kher. "Hate Crimes Against Hindus," *Noticias Financieras*. Miami, FL Nov. 21, 2007 pg. 1.

[36] Paul Murphy. "Mody's Father," pg. 34.

[37] Arthur Pais. "Fear of the Dark," pg. M3-4.

[38] Ibid.

[39] Ibid.

[40] Vasantha Arora. "Study Details Wide Scope," *India-West*. San Leandro, CA April 29, 1994, v. 19, iss 24, pg. 29.

[41] "Indians Protest in Dotbuster City," *News India*. New York, NY May 8, 1992, v. 22, iss 19, pg. 1.

[42] Arthur Pais. "Fear of the Dark," pg. M3-4.

[43] Aseem Chhabra. *India Abroad*. New York: NY. Oct. 5, 2007, v. 38, iss. 1 pg. M12.

[44] Viji Sundaram. "Vandals Paint Swastikas," pg. 1.

[45] Ibid.

[46] Ibid.

[47] Ibid.

[48] Francis Assisi. "Community Target of Harassment," *India-West*. San Leandro, CA Feb. 1991, v. 16, iss 11, pg. 1.

[49] Anita Wadhwani. "Campaign Launched," *Asianweek*. San Francisco, CA Jan. 28, 1998, v. 19, iss 22, pg. 14.

[50] Francis Assisi. "Community Target of Harassment," pg. 1.

[51] Ibid.

[52] Ibid.

[53] Ibid.

[54] Ibid.

[55] Ibid.

[56] Ibid.

[57] Tracey Eaton. "Anti-Arab Acts," *Orange County Register*. Santa Ana, CA March 15, 1991, pg. B8.

[58] Ibid.

[59] Vasantha Arora. "Study Details Wide Scope," pg. 29.

[60] Ibid.

[61] Anita Wadhwani. "Campaign Launched," pg. 14.

[62] Ibid.

[63] Ibid.

[64] Ibid.

[65] Arthur Pais. "Fear of the Dark," pg. M3.

[66] Ibid.

[67] Ibid.

[68] "Anti-Sikh Bias," *News India-Times*. New York, NY Sept. 10, 1999, v. 29 iss 37, pg. 8.

[69] Ibid.

[70] Ibid.

[71] Ibid.

[72] Ravi Adhikari. "Thanksgiving Ordeal," *News India Times*, New York, NY Dec. 3, 1999, v. 29 iss 49 pg. 1.

[73] Ibid.

[74] Ibid.

[75] Ibid.

[76] Ibid.

[77] "School Badgering," *Hinduism Today*. Kapaa, India. Feb. 28, 2001, pg. 62.

[78] Carl Campanile. "Bias Eyed in Beating of Muslim," *New York Post*. New York, NY Feb. 8, 2002, pg. 19.

[79] "Masters of Mendicants," *New York Times*. New York, NY Feb. 21, 1888, pg. 3.

[80] Ibid.

[81] Carl Hansmann. "Asiatic Whites," *New York Times*. New York, NY Nov. 15, 1909, pg. 8.

[82] Ibid.

[83] Sarah Gualtieri. "Strange Fruit?" *Arab Studies Quarterly*. Belmont. Summer 2004. v. 26, iss. 3 pg. 63-86.

[84] Ibid.

[85] The Editor. "Syrian and Wife Killed in Florida," *Syrian World*, New York, NY: (June 1929): 45-8.

[86] Ibid.

[87] Ibid.

[88] "Has the Syrian Become a Negro?" from *As-Shab*, (June 1929), reprinted in the *Syrian World*, New York, NY: (June 1929): 42.

[89] Gregory Gross. "9/11 Cited in 15% Rise in Hate Crimes," *San Diego Union Tribune*. San Diego, CA Sept. 19, 2002, pg. B1.

[90] Thanassis Cambanis. "Threat to Arab American Admitted," *Boston Globe*. Boston, MA June 7, 2002, pg. B1.

[91] James Brooke. "Attacks on US Muslims Surge," *New York Times*, New York, NY. Aug. 28, 1995, pg. A1.

[92] Ibid.

[93] Patricia Edmonds. "Coping on the Home Front," *Orange County Register*. Santa Ana, CA Feb 7, 1991 pg. A5.

[94] Tracey Eaton. "Anti-Arab Acts," pg. B8; Patricia Edmonds. "Coping on the Home Front," pg. A5; Jesse Katz. "Gulf Tensions," *Los Angeles Times*. Los Angeles, CA March 2, 1991, pg. 3. "FBI Interviews of Arab-Americans," *Los Angeles Times*, Los Angeles, CA. Feb. 3, 1991, pg. 6.

[95] "FBI Interviews of Arab-Americans," *Los Angeles Times*, Los Angeles, CA. Feb. 3, 1991, pg. 6.

[96] Tracey Eaton. "Anti-Arab Acts," pg. B8.

[97] Patricia Edmonds. "Coping on the Home Front," pg. A5.

[98] Ibid.

[99] Ibid.

[100] Riad Ibrahim. "A War Spawns Misguided Rage," *San Diego Union*. San Diego, CA. Jan. 30, 1991, pg. B7.

[101] Ibid.

[102] Ibid.

[103] Francis Assisi. "Community Target of Harassment," pg. 1.

[104] Riad Ibrahim. "A War Spawns Misguided Rage," pg. B7.

[105] Ibid.

[106] Ibid.

[107] Patricia Edmonds. "Coping on the Home Front," pg. A5.

[108] Pat Twair. "Hate Crimes," *Washington Report*. DC March 1991, v. 9, iss. 10, pg. 71.

[109] Riad Ibrahim. "A War Spawns Misguided Rage," pg. B7.

[110] Ibid.

[111] Sarah Okeson. "Judge Dismisses Suit Filed by Muslim Group; Vandalism at Area Mosque Not Subjected to Hate Crime Laws," *Journal Star*. Peoria, IL Aug. 27, 1992, pg. B4.

[112] Stephanie Chavez. "Hate Crimes," *Los Angeles Times*. Los Angeles, CA March 26, 1992, pg. 3.

[113] Pat Sullivan. "Police Say Alleged Stoning of Muslims not a Hate Crime," *Boston Herald*. Boston, MA April 21, 1992, pg. 8.

[114] David Schutz. "W. Springfield Police Faulted," *Boston Globe*. Boston, MA April 21, 1992, pg. 20; Pat Sullivan. "Police Say Alleged Stoning of Muslims not a Hate Crime," pg. 8.

[115] Ibid.

[116] David Schutz. "W. Springfield Police Faulted," pg. 20.

[117] Pat Sullivan. "Police Say Alleged Stoning of Muslims not a Hate Crime," pg. 8.

[118] Ibid.

[119] Ibid.

[120] Betty Liu Ebron. "Arabs Feel Blast Effect," *Oregonian*. Portland, OR March 12, 1993, pg. A22.

[121] Jack Shaheen. Reel Bad Arabs. (New York: Olive Branch Press, 2001): 504.

[122] Ibid.

[123] "Attacks on American Islamic Centers Increase," *Arab American News*. Dearborn, MI. Aug. 11, 1995, v. 11, issue 518, pg. 3.

[124] Ibid.

[125] "Hate Crimes Reported Up;" "Muslim Group Denounces Terror Attacks." *New York Beacon*. New York, NY Sept. 26, 2001, v. 8, iss 38 pg. 23.

[126] James Brooke. "Attacks on U.S. Muslims Surge," pg. A1.

[127] "Bombing Anniversary," *Arab American News*. Dearborn, MI April 28, 2000 v. 16 iss. 743 pg. 8; Jason Piscia. "Area Muslim Community," *State Journal Register*. Springfield, IL Sept. 12, 2001, pg. 21.

[128] Hamzi Moghrabi. "A Rush to Judgment," *Plain Dealer*. Cleveland, OH. April 23, 1995, pg. 3C.

[129] Felix Hoover. "Arab, Muslim Organizations," *Columbus Dispatch*. Columbus, OH Sept. 12, 2001, pg. 14A.

[130] James Brooke. "Attacks on U.S. Muslims Surge," pg. A1.

[131] Hamzi Moghrabi. "A Rush to Judgment," pg. 3C.

[132] Ann Rodgers-Melnick. "Muslims Condemn Terrorism, Urge Halt to Bigotry," *Pittsburgh Post-Gazette*. Pittsburgh, PA, April 21, 1995, pg. A21.

[133] Ibid.

[134] Charles Sennott. "After Bombings, American Faces Up to Prejudice," *Boston Globe*, Boston: MA June 21, 1995, pg. 1; Mofeed Ismael. "Baby Salam was 169th Victim of Oklahoma City Bombing," Middle East News Online, Durham. June 11, 2001.

[135] Ibid.

[136] Ibid.

[137] Ibid.

[138] Ibid.

[139] Ibid.

[140] Ibid.

[141] Mofeed Ismael. "Baby Salam was 169th Victim of Oklahoma City Bombing," Middle East News Online, Durham. June 11, 2001.

[142] Charles Sennott. "After Bombings, American Faces Up to Prejudice," pg. 1.

[143] Jane Lampman. "Moving Beyond Stereotypes," *Christian Science Monitor*. Boston, MA June 18, 1998, pg. B4.

[144] James Brooke. "Attacks on US Muslims Surge," pg. A1

[145] Ibid.

[146] Laura Outerbridge. "American Muslims Articulate Fear," *Washington Times*, DC, April 21, 1995, pg. A16.

[147] Rhett Morgan. "Oklahoma Reacts," *Tulsa World*. Tulsa, OK Sept. 13, 2001, pg. 9.

[148] Ibid.

[149] "Attacks on American Islamic Centers Increase," pg. 3.

[150] Shonda McLain. "Muslims Terrorized," *Recorder*. Indianapolis, IN May 6, 1995, v. 100, iss 18 pg. A1.

[151] Ibid.

[152] James Brooke. "Attacks on US Muslims Surge," pg. A1.

[153] Ibid.

[154] Ibid.

[155] Ed Bierschenk. "Muslim Leaders Meet," *State Journal Register*. Springfield IL June 14, 1995, pg. 9.

[156] Ibid.

[157] Kevin McDermott. "Mosque Arson," *St. Louis Post Dispatch*, St. Louis, MO June 17, 1995, pg. 13B.

[158] James Brooke. "Attacks on US Muslims Surge," pg. A1.

[159] Ibid.

[160] Frank Fuhrig. "Simon Visits Burned-Out Mosque," *State Journal Register*. Springfield, IL Oct. 9, 1995, pg. 17.

[161] Tricia Haugen. "Islamic Society May Rebuild Mosque," *State Journal Register*. Springfield, IL April 2, 1996, pg. 7.

[162] Ibid.

[163] "Attacks on American Islamic Centers Increase," pg. 3.

[164] Ibid.

[165] Ibid.

[166] "Report," *Arab American News*. Dearborn, MI. Sept. 12, 2003, v. 20, iss. 917, pg. 11.

[167] Wiley McKellar III. "Cheer and Jeers," *Patriot*. Harrisburg, PA July 27, 1996, pg. A9.

[168] *Arab American News*. Dearborn, MI. April 24, 1997, v. 13, iss 606, pg. 9.

[169] "Bombing Anniversary," pg. 8.

[170] Jan Barry. "Hate Crimes Intolerable," *Record*. Bergen County, NJ Oct. 5, 1992, pg. A4.

[171] Jim Zamora. "California Study," *Oregonian*. Portland, OR July 19, 1996, pg. A12.

[172] Ibid.

[173] Jim Zamora, Larry Hatfield. "State's First Compilation Lists 1,754 Hate Crimes," *San Francisco Examiner*. San Francisco, CA July 18, 1996, pg. A2.

[174] Virginia Culver. "4 Charged in Anthem Incident," *Denver Post*. Denver, CO March 23, 1996, pg. A1.

[175] "Radio Stunt Could Lead to Charges," *Milwaukee Journal Sentinel*. Milwaukee, WI March 22, 1996, pg. 1.

[176] "Radio Show Prank," *New York Times*. New York, NY March 22, 1996, pg. A16.

[177] Virginia Culver. "4 Charged in Anthem Incident," pg. A1.

[178] Ibid.

[179] Ibid.

[180] Genghis Khan. "Media Has a Responsibility," *Times Union*. Albany, NY March 11, 1997 pg. A10.

[181] Ilene Lelchuk. "In Peril at the Projects," *San Francisco Chronicle*. San Francisco, CA Jan. 24, 2002, A17.

[182] Ibid.

[183] Katharine Seelye. "Desecration of Crescent and Star," *New York Times*, New York, NY, Dec. 29, 1997, pg. 12.

[184] Ibid.

[185] "Groups Replace Islamic Symbols Hit By Vandals," *Washington Post*. DC Jan. 4, 1998, pg. B6.

[186] Jonathan Salant. "This is a Case of Hatred," *Houston Chronicle*. Houston, TX Dec. 29, 1997, pg. 3.

[187] "Swastika Spray-Painted on Islamic Symbol," *Fort-Worth Star Telegram*, Fort Worth, TX Dec. 29, 1997, pg. 6.

[188] Coleman Cornelius. "Muslim Worshipers Fear Hate," *Denver Post*. Denver, CO Jan. 29, 1008, pg. B8.

[189] Ibid.

[190] Ibid.

[191] Tony Horwitz. "Saudi School Tests Limits of Diversity," *Wall St. Journal*. New York: NY Feb. 18, 1998, pg. A1.

[192] Matthew Strozier. "Muslim Community Leaders," *India in NY*. New York, NY Feb. 20, 1998, v.1 iss 34, pg. 6.

[193] "Animal Heads Found on Fence," *Austin American Statesman*. Austin, TX May 29, 1998, pg. B5.

[194] Richard Cardona. "Mosque Desecration," *Austin American Statesman*. Austin, TX June 3, 1998, pg. A10.

[195] Bob Reeves. "Can't We All Get Along?" *Lincoln Star Journal*. Lincoln, NB July 4, 1998, pg. 1.

[196] Ibid.

[197] Mary Abbe. "Wellstone Inspects Burned Mosque," *Star Tribune*. Minneapolis, MN March 14, 1999, pg. 1B.

[198] Ibid.

[199] Ibid.

[200] Ibid.

[201] Jim Adams. "Suspicious Fires Gut Mosque," *Star Tribune*. Minneapolis, MN March 6, 1999 pg. 1A.

[202] Ibid.

[203] Ibid.

[204] Raeed Tayeh. "Chicago-Area Mosque Vandalized," *Washington Report*. DC Aug. 31, 1999 v. 17, iss 5 pg. 67.

[205] Ibid.

[206] Noreen Ahmed-Ullah. "Mosque May Have Suspect," *Daily Herald*. Arlington Heights, IL May 18, 1999, pg. 4.

[207] "Editorials," *Daily Herald*. Arlington Heights, IL May 19, 1999, pg. 12.

[208] Noreen Ahmed-Ullah. "Mosque May Have Suspect," pg. 4.

[209] Ibid.

[210] Ibid.

[211] Raeed Tayeh. "Chicago-Area Mosque Vandalized," pg. 67.

[212] "Pullman Police Investigate Fire Outside Mosque," *Columbian*. Vancouver, WA June 18, 1999, pg. B5.

[213] "White Supremacist Sentenced to Federal Prison," Middle East Online. Durham. Nov. 29, 2000.

[214] Margaret Ramirez. "Security Tightened," *Los Angeles Times*, Los Angeles, CA Nov. 9, 2000, pg. B1.

[215] Ibid.

[216] Ibid.

[217] Ibid.

[218] Martin Griffith. "2 Muslims Attacked," *San Diego Union Tribune*. San Diego, CA March 18, 2001, pg. A3.

[219] Ibid.

[220] Ibid.

[221] Jennifer Chambers. "Group Calls Attack Hate Crime," *Detroit News*. Detroit, MI May 10, 2001, pg D1.

[222] Ibid.

[223] "CAIR Objects to Falwell," *Arab American News*. Dearborn, MI March 16, 2001, v. 15, iss 786, pg. 5.

[224] Ibid.

[225] Aziz Haniffa. "Muslim Prayer Rug Vandalized," *India Abroad*, New York, NY May 4, 2001, v. 31 iss 31 pg. 48.

[226] Yolanda Jones and Chris Conley. "Ambush at Mosque," *Commercial Appeal*. Memphis, TN June 21, 2001 pg. A1.

[227] Ibid.

[228] Ibid.

[229] Ibid.

[230] Ibid.

[231] Ibid.

[232] Ibid.

[233] Ibid.

[234] Susan Ives. "Our People," *San Antonio Express-News*. San Antonio, TX April 17, 2004, pg. 11B.

[235] Ibid.

[236] Jack Shaheen. <u>Reel Bad Arabs</u>. Throughout my book, I have relied extensively on Shaheen's descriptions of 20th century anti-Arab movies. Many of the films I discuss appear on Shaheen's "Worst List," pg. 550-551.

[237] Ibid, 6.

[238] Ibid.

[239] Ibid, 8.

[240] Tim Jon Semmerling. <u>'Evil' Arabs in American Popular Film</u>. (Austin: University of Texas Press, 2006).

[241] Jack Shaheen. <u>Reel Bad Arabs</u>, pg. 450.

[242] Ibid.

[243] Ibid, 91.

[244] Ibid, 92.

[245] Ibid, 91.

[246] Ibid.

[247] Jack Shaheen. <u>Reel Bad Arabs.</u>

[248] Ibid, 41.

[249] Ibid.

[250] Ibid.

[251] Ibid, 179.

[252] Ibid.

[253] Ibid, 204.

[254] Ibid, 205.

[255] Ibid.

[256] Tim Jon Semmerling. <u>'Evil' Arabs in American Popular Film</u>, pg. 255.

[257] Ibid, 30.

[258] Ibid, 31.

[259] Ibid, 104.

[260] Ibid.

[261] Ibid.

[262] Ibid, 123.

[263] Ibid.

[264] Jack Shaheen. Reel Bad Arabs, pg. 266-267.

[265] Ibid.

[266] Ibid, pg. 262.

[267] Ibid, pg. 476.

[268] Ibid.

[269] Ibid, pg. 501.

[270] Nicci Gerrard, "Jamie Lee Curtis," Newswire Sept. 21, 1994, in Jack Shaheen. Reel Bad Arabs, pg. 504.

[271] Jack Shaheen. Reel Bad Arabs, pg. 252.

[272] Tim Jon Semmerling. 'Evil' Arabs in American Popular Film, pg. 124.

[273] Ibid, 125

[274] Ibid, 162.

[275] Jack Shaheen. Guilty. (Northampton, MA: Olive Branch Press, 2008): 150.

Chapter Three:

[1] "Casualties of the September 11 Attacks," www.wikipedia.org, Aug. 25, 2011.

[2] "Casualties of the September 11 Attacks;" Asfaque Swapan. "South Asians Reflect," *India-West*. San Leandro, CA Sept. 15, 2006, v. 31 iss. 43 pg. A1.

[3] Carolee Walker. "Five-year 9/11 Remembrance Honors Victims from 90 Countries," www.america.gov, Aug. 11, 2006.

[4] Asfaque Swapan. "South Asians Reflect," pg. A1.

[5] Shankar Vendatam. "For Some In U.S., Grief Over Attacks," *Washington Post*, DC, Sept. 22, 2001 pg. A16; Shankar Vendatam. *Washington Post*. DC. Sept. 23, 2001, pg. A14.

[6] Ela Dutt. "The Effort to Cope with Loss," *News India Times*. New York, NY Jan. 4, 2002, v. 33, iss 1 pg. 14.

[7] Shankar Vendatam. "For Some In U.S., Grief Over Attacks." A16.

[8] Ibid.

[9] "9/11 Family Mourns, Rejects War on Terror," NBC News. www.msnbc.msn.com, Sept. 11, 2004.

[10] Ibid.

[11] Ibid.

[12] Ibid.

[13] Ibid.

[14] Asfaque Swapan. "South Asians Reflect," pg. A1.

[15] David Usborne. "Collateral Damage," *The Independent*. London, UK. Oct. 11, 2001, pg. 1.

[16] Ibid.

[17] Ibid.

[18] Raja Mishra. "Arab and Asian Immigrants Find Hostility," *Boston Globe*, Boston, MA Sept. 18, 2001 pg. A13.

[19] Shankar Vendatam. "For Some In U.S., Grief Over Attacks," pg. A16.

[20] Ibid.

[21] Rick Olanoff. "Bombing, Ground Troops No Solution," *Post-Standard*. Syracuse, NY Nov. 5, 2001 pg. A9.

[22] Ibid.

[23] Ibid.

[24] David Usborne. "Collateral Damage," pg. 1.

[25] Tom Berg. "Sept. 11 One Year Later," *Orange County Register*. Santa Ana, CA Sept. 9, 2002, cover.

[26] Ibid.

[27] David Usborne. "Collateral Damage," pg. 1.

[28] Joyce Purnick. "Our Daily Tribute to Differences," *New York Times*. New York, NY Sept. 20, 2001, pg. A20.

[29] Ibid.

[30] David Usborne. "Collateral Damage," pg. 1.

[31] Ibid.

[32] Ibid.

[33] Ibid.

[34] Teresa Mask. "Arab-American Lawyers," *Daily Herald*. Arlington Heights, IL Sept. 27, 2001, pg. 14.

[35] Richard Winton. "Hate Crimes Soar," *Los Angeles Times*, Los Angeles, CA Dec. 21, 2001, pg. B1.

[36] "Protests at Mosque," *Arab-American View*. Orlando Park: IL Nov. 5, 2001, v. 2 Iss. 11, pg. 1.

[37] Ibid.

[38] Ibid.

Chapter Four:

[1] Shankar Vendatam. "For Some in U.S., Grief Followed by Fear," *Washington Post*. DC Sept. 22, 2001, pg. A16.

[2] Ibid.

[3] Ibid.

[4] Ibid.

[5] Ibid.

[6] Adrian Leung. "South Asian Journalists Discuss Backlash," *Asianweek*. Sept. 26, 2001, v. 23, iss 5 pg. 9.

[7] Editorial. "Misplaced Anger," *Boston Globe*. Boston, MA Sept. 14, 2001, pg. A22.

[8] Maki Becker. "Sikhs Facing Anti-Muslim Harassment," *New York Daily News*. New York, NY Sept. 29, 2001, pg. 20.

[9] Nicole Marshall. "Assaults, Hit-And-Run Possible Hate Crimes," *Tulsa World*. Tulsa, OK Sept. 16, 2001, pg. 13.

[10] Ibid.

[11] Rhett Morgan. "Support Flows for Beaten Pakistani," *Tulsa World*. Tulsa, OK Sept. 15, 2001, pg. 14.

[12] Ibid.

[13] Mark Bixler. "FBI Probes Attack on Sudanese," *Atlanta Constitution*. Atlanta, GA Sept. 20, 2001, pg. G4.

[14] Ibid.

[15] Ibid.

[16] Ibid.

[17] Ibid.

[18] Tom Mooney. "False Arrest Begins Journey," *Providence Journal*. Providence, RI Feb. 20, 2003, pg. 1.

[19] Ibid.

[20] Ibid.

[21] Ibid.

[22] Ibid.

[23] Jo Becker, Phuong Ly. "Sikhs Campaign Against Hate," *Washington Post*. DC Sept. 24, 2001, pg. B1.

[24] Thomas Edsall. "Anti-Muslim Violence Assailed," *Washington Post*. DC Sept. 15, 2001, pg. A9.

[25] Ela Dutt. "The Effort to Cope with Loss," *News India Times*. New York, NY Jan. 4, 2002, v. 33, iss 1 pg. 14.

[26] Chris Jenkins. "Deliveryman who Beat Immigrant," *Washington Post*, DC March 8, 2002, pg. B1.

[27] Ibid.

[28] Ibid.

[29] Ibid.

[30] "Arab Americans Targets of Hate Crimes," *San Francisco Chronicle*, San Francisco, CA Sept. 18, 2001, pg. A13.

[31] Ibid.

[32] Ibid.

[33] Laurie Goodstein, Tamar Lewin. "Victims of Mistaken Identity," *New York Times*. New York, NY Sept. 19, 2001, pg. A1.

[34] Roma Khanna. "Hate Crimes Peak After Sept. 11," *Houston Chronicle*. Houston, TX Dec. 14, 2001, pg. A37.

[35] Suman Mozumder. "Oregon Woman Gets Jail," *India Abroad*. New York, NY Jan. 4, 2002, v. 32, iss 14, pg. 6.

[36] Ibid.

[37] Bryan Denson. "Incidents Targeting Muslims," *Oregonian*. Portland, OR Nov. 26, 2002, pg. C1.

[38] Ibid.

[39] Ibid.

[40] Bill Bishop. "Woman Gets Jail Time," *Register-Guard*. Eugene, OR Dec. 15, 2001, pg. 1.

[41] Ibid.

[42] Ibid.

[43] Ibid.

[44] Suman Mozumder. "Oregon Woman Gets Jail," pg. 6.

[45] Ellen Silberman, Marie Szaniszlo. "Mayor: Ethnic Attacks," *Boston Herald*. Boston, MA Sept. 19, 2001, pg. 18.

[46] Ibid.

[47] Ibid.

[48] Ed Hayward. "Hub Attack," *Boston Herald*. Boston, MA Sept. 18, 2001, pg. 28.

[49] Ibid.

[50] "Hate Hurts Driver," *Plain Dealer*. Cleveland, OH Sept. 19, 2001 pg. B10.

[51] L.A. Johnson. "Standing Up to Racism," *Pittsburgh Post-Gazette*. Pittsburgh, PA Nov.1, 2001, C1.

[52] Ibid.

[53] Ibid.

[54] Ibid.

[55] Ibid.

[56] Ashok Easwaran. "Hate Crimes Grip Chicago," *India Abroad*. New York, NY Sept. 28, 2001, v. 31, iss 52, pg. 4.

[57] Sam McManis. "Protective Coloring," *San Francisco Chronicle*. San Francisco, CA Oct. 6, 2001, pg. A13.

[58] Maki Becker. "Sikhs Facing Anti-Muslim Harassment," pg. 20.

[59] Tara Tuckwiller. "Worries Return," *Sunday Gazette-Mail*. Charleston, WV Sept. 8, 2002, pg. 1B.

[60] Annah Dumas-Mitchell. "America Seeks to Recover From Attacks," *Chicago Defender*, Chicago, IL Sept. 13, 2001, pg. 3

[61] "List of Hate Crimes from Sept. 11, 2001 to Jan. 8, 2002," www.realsikhism.com

[62] Richard Winton. "Suspected Hate Crimes Rise," *Los Angeles Times*. Los Angeles, CA Sept. 10, 2002, pg. B3.

[63] Dina Gerdeman. "Reality Check," *Patriot-Ledger*. Quincy, MA March 1, 2002, pg. 1.

[64] Debi Wilgoren and Ann O'Hanlon. "Mosques' Days of Worship," *Washington Post*. DC Sept. 23, 2001, pg. C1.

[65] Ibid.

[66] Kavita Kumar. "Sikhs are Targets of Harassment," *Star Tribune*. Minneapolis, MN Oct. 2, 2001, pg. 7B.

[67] Ibid.

[68] Ibid.

[69] "9/11: A Year After," *Los Angeles Times*, Los Angeles, CA Sept. 11, 2002, pg. S14.

[70] Ibid.

[71] Troy Anderson. "Hate Crimes Up," *Daily News*, Los Angeles, CA Dec. 21, 2001, pg. N3.

[72] "9/11: A Year After," pg. S14.

[73] Joe Hughes. "Hate-Crime Victim," *San Diego Union Tribune*. San Diego, CA Dec. 18, 2001, pg. B2.

[74] "9/11: A Year After," pg. S14.

[75] Ibid.

[76] Ibid.

[77] Ibid.

[78] Silja Talvi. "And Justice for All," *Colorlines*. Winter 2002/2003. Oakland, CA Jan. 31, 2003 v. 5 iss 4 pg. 18.

[79] Ibid.

[80] Ibid.

[81] David Connerty-Marin. "Maine Not Immune to Intolerance," *Portland Press Herald*. Portland, OR Dec. 22, 2002, pg. 1A.

[82] Pedro Perez. "Northwest Sees Onslaught of Racist Attacks," *Columbian*. Vancouver, WA Sept. 19, 2001 pg. C2.

[83] Ibid.

[84] Ibid.

[85] Raja Mishra. "Arab and Asian Immigrants Find Hostility," *Boston Globe*, Boston, MA Sept. 18, 2001 pg. A13.

[86] Alan Cooper. "Sikh Receives Oliver Hill Law Award," pg. B5.

[87] Wayne Coffey. "Fever Pitch," *New York Daily News*, New York, NY Sept. 23, 2001, pg. 85

[88] Ibid.

[89] "Arab Americans Targets of Hate Crimes," *San Francisco Chronicle*, San Francisco, CA Sept. 18, 2001, pg. A13.

[90] Khalil Osman. "Muslims Come Under Attack," Middle East Online. Durham. Oct. 6, 2001.

[91] Anindita Ramaswamy. "Sikhs and Muslims," *News India-Times*. New York. Sept. 21, 2001, v. 32, iss 34, pg. 10.

[92] Viji Sundaram. "Reports of Hate Crimes," *India-West*. San Leandro, CA Sept. 28, 2001, v. 26, iss 47 pg. A1.

[93] Ibid.

[94] Kristen Convery. "Forum Offers Insights," *Dayton* Daily News. Dayton, OH Oct. 31, 2001, pg. 2B.

[95] Julia Angwin. "Aftermath: A Changing Society," *Wall St. Journal*. New York, NY Sept. 26, 2001, pg. A6.

[96] Ibid.

[97] Lisa Kocian. "Millis Sikhs," *Boston Globe*. Boston, MA Sept. 8, 2002, pg. 1.

[98] Richard Winton. "Hate Crimes Soar," *Los Angeles Times*. Los Angeles, CA Dec. 21, 2001, pg. B1.

[99] Ibid.

[100] Karen Maeshiro. "Not Guilty Plea in Beating Case," *Daily News*. Los Angeles, CA Oct. 3, 2001, pg. A2.

[101] Ibid.

[102] Ibid.

[103] Richard Winton. "Suspected Hate Crimes Rise," B3.

[104] "Ontario; Window Screen Foils Molotov," *Los Angeles Times*. Los Angeles, CA Oct. 3, 2001, pg. B6.

[105] Lenora Chu. "Hate Around the Nation," *Asianweek*. San Francisco, CA Oct 3, 2001 v. 23, iss 6 pg. 9.

[106] Aldrin Brown. "Hate Crimes," *Orange County Register*. Santa Ana, CA April 12, 2002, pg. A3.

[107] Alan Cooper. "Sikh Receives Oliver Hill Law Award," pg. B5.

[108] Ibid.

[109] Ibid.

[110] Kimi Yoshino. "Mistake Leads to Assault," *Los Angeles Times*, Los Angeles, CA Oct. 23, 2001, pg. B3.

[111] In articles about the assault, the victim asked journalists to protect his identity by concealing his last name.

[112] Michael Potts. "$1,000 Reward Offered," *India-West*. San Leandro, CA Dec. 28, 2001, v. 27 iss 8 pg. A32.

[113] Ibid.

[114] Ibid.

[115] Ibid.

[116] Ibid.

[117] Ann Pepper. "OC's Hate Spike," *Orange County Register*. Santa Ana, CA Sept. 19, 2002, pg. A3.

[118] Kimi Yoshino. "Mistake Leads to Assault," pg. B3.

[119] Ibid.

[120] Michael Potts. "$1,000 Reward Offered," pg. A32.

[121] Somini Sengupta. "Beaten in Pakistan," *New York Times*, New York, NY Oct. 24, 2001, pg. B10

[122] Ibid.

[123] Judith Browne. "Racial Profiling," *Atlanta Inquirer*, Atlanta, GA Nov. 17, 2001, v. 41, iss 16, pg. 4.

[124] Evelyn Alsultany. "Representations of Arabs and Muslims in Post-9/11 TV Dramas," in <u>Arab and Muslim Civil Rights and Identity</u>. (DC: ADC Research Institute, 2011): 183-190.

[125] Jack Shaheen. <u>Guilty</u>. (Northampton, MA: Olive Branch Press, 2008).

[126] Ibid, pg. 120

[127] Ibid, pg. 140.

[128] Allan Turner and Dale Lezon. "Our Changed World," *Houston Chronicle*. Houston, TX Sept. 8, 2002, pg. A33.

[129] Ibid.

[130] Ibid.

[131] Ibid.

[132] Matt Volz. "Muslims Hope to Curb Backlash," *Commercial Appeal*. Memphis, TN March 21, 2003, pg. DS6.

[133] Jaclyn O'Malley. "Loud Crowd Intolerant of Hate," *Omaha World*. Omaha, NB Oct. 4, 2002, pg. 4B

[134] Ibid.

[135] David Connerty-Marin. "Maine Not Immune to Intolerance," pg. 1A.

[136] Ibid.

[137] Mona Eltahawy. "Bracing For a Backlash," *Washington Post*. DC March 24, 2003, pg. A13.

[138] Ann Pepper. "Yorba Linda Brothers File Suit," *Orange County Register*. Santa Ana, CA April 24, 2003, pg. C; Christine Hanley. "Beaten Muslim Teen's Suit," *Los Angeles Times*. Los Angeles, CA April 24, 2003, pg. B6.

[139] Zaheera Wahid. "A Burning Question," "Apparent Hate Crimes in O.C.," *Orange County Register*. Santa Ana, CA March 19, 2003, pg. 1.

[140] William Lobdell and Christine Hanley. *Los Angeles Times*. Los Angeles, CA March 4, 2003, pg. B1.

[141] Ibid.

[142] Ibid.

[143] Ibid.

[144] Ibid.

[145] Ibid.

[146] Ibid.

[147] Ibid.

[148] Ibid.

[149] Ann Pepper. "Yorba Linda Brothers File Suit," pg. C.

[150] Ibid.

[151] William Lobdell and Christine Hanley. *Los Angeles Times*. pg. B1.

[152] Ann Pepper. "Yorba Linda Brothers File Suit," pg. C.

[153] Ibid.

[154] Ibid.

[155] Ibid.

[156] Ibid.

[157] Ibid.

[158] Alisa Solomon. "From Baghdad to Brooklyn," *Village Voice*. New York, NY April 2, 2003, v. 48 iss 14, pg. 26-8.

[159] *Arab American News*. Dearborn, MI. March 14, 2003, v. 19, iss 891, pg. 15.

[160] "Mass. Man Thought to Be Muslim," US Newswire. DC June 25, 2003, pg. 1.

[161] Ibid.

[162] "U.S. Cartoonist's Sorry to Sikhs for 'Insensitivity'," *Press Trust of India*, www.indianexpress.com, October 19, 2003.

[163] Dave Carlin. "Hate Crimes Committed Against 2 NJ Sikhs," WCBS TV, October 31, 2008.

[164] Jack Shaheen. Guilty. 115.

[165] Lona O'Connor. "Islamic Schoolgirl Assaulted," *Palm Beach Post*. West Palm Beach, FL April 13, 2004, pg. 1B.

[166] Mary Beth Sheridan. "Bias Against Muslims Up 70%," *Washington Post*. DC May 3, 2004, pg. A12.

[167] PR Newswire. "CAIR: Muslims Assaulted," New York. June 30, 2004, pg. 1.

[168] Jay Tokasz. "Group Calls Harassment Hate Crime," *Buffalo News*. Buffalo, NY July 28, 2004, pg. B6.

[169] Ibid.

[170] Pauline Repard. "Muslim Beaten," *San Diego Union Tribune*. San Diego, CA July 1, 2004 pg. B12-7.

[171] Ibid.

[172] Jack Shaheen. Guilty, pg. 158.

[173] Jack Shaheen. Guilty.

[174] Ibid, pg. 118.

[175] Suman Mozumder. "5 Convicted," *India Abroad*. New York, NY Dec. 16, 2005, v. 36, iss 11, pg. A10.

[176] Ibid.

[177] Ibid.

[178] Scott Shifrel. "Sikh Man Testifies," *New York Daily News*. New York, NY Nov. 15, 2005, pg. 31.

[179] "Metro Briefing," *New York Times*. New York, NY Aug. 10, 2004, pg. B6.

[180] Scott Shifrel. "Sikh Man Testifies," pg. 31.

[181] Thomas Lueck. "L.I. Man Charged in Bias Assault," *New York Times*, New York, NY July 13, 2004, pg. B4.

[182] Jyotirmoy Datta. "5 Sentenced," *India-Times*. Dec. 30, 2005, v. 36, iss 52, pg. 8.

[183] Tanmaya Nanda. "Two Sikhs Attacked," *India Abroad*. New York, NY July 23, 2004, v. 24, iss 43, pg. A10.

[184] "Metro Briefing," pg. B6.

[185] Alex Ginsberg. "Dirty Linen' Aired," *New York Post*. New York, NY Nov. 1, 2005, pg. 19.

[186] Alex Ginsberg. "Turban Wrap Unravels," *New York Post*. New York: NY Dec. 6, 2005, pg. 30.

[187] Jyotirmoy Datta. "5 Sentenced," pg. 8.

[188] Alex Ginsberg. "Turban Wrap Unravels," pg. 30.

[189] Ibid.

[190] Scott Shifrel. "2 Guilty of Beating Sikh," *New York Daily News*, New York, NY. Dec. 6, 2005, pg. 36.

[191] Ibid.

[192] "Virginia Muslim Attacked By Men Shouting Racist Slurs," US Newswire. DC Aug 8, 2005, pg. 1.

[193] Ibid.

[194] Jack Shaheen. Guilty, pg. 109.

[195] Moinuddin Naser. "9/11 Anniversary Sparks Hate Crimes Against Bangladeshis," *Bangla Patrika*, Sept. 16, 2005. Reprinted in English in *New York Community Media Alliance*. www.indypressny.org. Sept. 22, 2005.

[196] Ibid.

[197] Ibid.

[198] Ibid.

[199] Lisa Tsering. "80 Year old Victim," *India-West*. San Leandro, CA Feb. 10, 2006, v. 31, iss 13, pg. A26.

[200] George Joseph. "In City of Earliest Sikhs," *India Abroad*. New York, NY Feb. 10, 2006, v. 36, iss 19 pg. C6.

[201] Lisa Tsering. "80 Year Old Victim," pg. A26.

[202] Ibid.

[203] Ibid.

[204] George Joseph. "In City of Earliest Sikhs," pg. C6.

[205] Ibid.

[206] Jack Shaheen. Guilty, pg. 141.

[207] Kerry Burke, Nancie Katz. "Muslim Beating," *New York Daily News*, New York, NY Nov. 3, 2006 pg. 23.

[208] Ibid.

[209] Ibid.

[210] Ibid.

[211] Ibid.

[212] Ibid.

[213] Ibid.

[214] Kerry Burke, Nancie Katz. "Muslim Beating," pg. 23.

[215] Nathaniel Popper. "Jewish-Muslim Incident Rocks Ethnic Balance," *Forward*. New York, NY. Nov. 10, 2006, v. 110, iss 31627, pg. A1, A8.

[216] "Slurs Used in Attacks on Muslims," US Newswire. DC. Dec. 7, 2006.

[217] "Hate Crimes," *Arab American News*. Dearborn, MI Jan. 27, 2007, v. 23, iss 1094, pg. 8.

[218] Tamara El-Khoury. "Man Claims Racial Harassment," *St. Petersburg Times*. St. Petersburg, FL Jan. 31, 2007, pg. 1.

[219] Ibid.

[220] Ibid.

[221] "Federal Charges," *Arab American News*. Dearborn, MI May 5, 2007, v. 23, iss 1108, pg. 14.

[222] Tony Bridges. "Bay School Bus Driver Charged," *News Herald*. Panama City, FL June 13, 2007, pg. 1

[223] Ibid.

[224] Ibid.

[225] Ibid.

[226] Ibid.

[227] Ibid.

[228] Ibid.

[229] Ibid.

[230] Tony Bridges. "Muslims Want Bay Bus Driver Prosecuted," *News Herald*. Panama City, FL July 6, 2007, pg. 1.

[231] David Angier. "Hate Crime Charges Dropped," *News Herald*. Panama City, FL Jan. 6, 2009.

[232] Asfaque Swapan. "Outrage in Lake Tahoe Hate Crime," *India-West*. Aug. 31, 2007, v. 32, iss 41, pg. A1, A32.

[233] Beleza Chan. "Dropped Hate Crime," *Asianweek*. San Francisco, CA Aug. 22, 2008, v. 4, iss. 53, pg. 7.

[234] Sunita Sohrabji. "Federal Charges Filed," *India-West*. San Leandro, CA March 13, 2009, v. 34, iss 16, pg. A22.

[235] George Joseph. "Hate Crime Charges," *India Abroad*. New York, NY March 20, 3009, v. 39, iss 25, pg. A15.

[236] Asfaque Swapan. "Outrage in Lake Tahoe Hate Crime," pg. A1, A32.

[237] Sunita Sohrabji. "Felony & Hate," *India-West*. San Leandro, CA Aug. 8, 2008, v.33, iss 35, pg. A28.

[238] George Joseph. "Hate Crime Charges," pg. A15.

[239] "Three Charged with Hate Crime Against Sikh," *India-West*. San Leandro, CA Nov. 30, 2007, v. 33, iss 1 pg. A4.

[240] US Newswire. "Sikh Coalition Disappointed," March 21, 2008.

[241] Ibid.

[242] Asfaque Swapan. "2 Sikhs Attacked," *India-West*. San Leandro, CA Sept. 28, 2007, v. 32, iss 44 pg. A1, A30.

[243] Ibid.

[244] Asfaque Swapan. "Sept. 11 Continues," *India-West*. San Leandro, CA Oct. 5, 2007, v. 32 iss 45 pg. A10.

[245] Ibid.

[246] Ibid.

[247] Ibid.

[248] "Turban Grabber Avoids Hate Crime," *India-West*. San Leandro, CA April 11, 2008, v. 33, iss 19 pg. A12.

[249] Ibid.

[250] Ibid.

[251] Ibid.

[252] George Joseph. "One Charged," *India Abroad*. New York, NY Feb. 15, 2008, v. 38, iss 20, pg. A14.

[253] Brendan Bosh. "Hate Attack Charged," *New York Daily News*. New York, NY Jan. 18, 2008, pg. 32.

[254] "Queens Man Charged," *Culvert Chronicles*. Laurelton, NY Jan. 24, 2008, v. 3 iss 2 pg. 8.

[255] "Sikh Grad Student Attacked in Texas," *India-West*. San Leandro, CA. May 9, 2008, v. 33 iss 23 pg. B14.

[256] "CAIR Urges Hate Crime Probe of Ohio Shooting," PR Newswire. New York, NY June 24, 2008.

[257] Edgar Sandoval, Alison Gendar, John Marzulli. "Hate Crime Outrage: Probers Link Election Night Beating of Muslim Teen and Brutal Hit and Run in SI," *New York Daily News*. New York, NY Dec. 23, 2008, pg. 5.

[258] John Marzulli. "Hate Attacker Wants a Favor," *Daily News*. New York, NY March 25, 2009, pg. 14.

[259] "Guilty Plea in Election Night Attacks," *New York Times*. New York, NY Feb. 3, 2009, pg. A25.

[260] John Doyle. "Bronx Hate Spree," *New York Post*. New York, NY Aug. 11, 2009, pg. 6.

[261] Joseph Mallia. "Cops: Man Tried to Run Down Muslim Mom, Daughter," *McClatchy-Tribune Business News*. DC. Aug. 27, 2009.

[262] Ibid.

[263] Patrik Jonsson. "Woman Charged," *Christian Science Monitor*. Boston, MA Nov. 20, 2009, pg. 8.

[264] "Illinois: Hate Crime Alleged," *New York Times*, New York, NY Nov 28, 2009, pg A13.

[265] "CAIR: Anti-Muslim Slurs Used in Attack on Oregon Muslim Inmate," PR Newswire. NY Dec. 1, 2010.

[266] Ibid.

[267] "Minneapolis Man Pleads Guilty to Hate Grime in Assault on Somali Man," *Minneapolis Star-Tribune*. Minneapolis, MN Aug. 10, 2011.

[268] Ibid.

[269] Ryan Foley. "Man Who Beat Muslim Teen: I'd Do It Again," *Telegraph-Herald*. Dubuque, IA March 11, 2011, pg. B5.

[270] "CAIR: Racial Slurs Used During Attack on Iowa Muslim," US Newswire. DC June 18, 2010.

[271] Ibid.

[272] Ibid.

[273] Ryan Foley. "Man Who Beat Muslim Teen: I'd Do It Again," pg. B5.

[274] Ibid.

[275] "CAIR Calls for FBI Probe of Attack," *McClatchy-Tribune Business News*. DC June 13, 2010.

[276] Lisa Fernandez. "Sunnyvale: Man Attacked for Being Muslim," *Oakland Tribune*. Oakland, CA June 14, 2010.

[277] Ibid.

[278] Ibid.

[279] "Washington State: Attack Called a Hate Crime," *Los Angeles Times*. Los Angeles, CA Oct. 22, 2010, pg. 25.

[280] Ibid.

[281] Ibid.

[282] Janet Tu. "Woman Charged." *Seattle Times*. *McClatchy-Tribune News Service*. DC Oct. 21, 2010.

[283] Melissa Grace, Jonathan Lemire, Corky Siemaskzo, Pete Donahue, Lia Colangelo. "Transit Cop, Pal Held in Beatdown of Imam." *New York Daily News*. New York, NY Dec. 10, 2010, pg. 14.

[284] Ibid.; "CAIR Asks that Bias Assault on NY Imam be Prosecuted as Hate Crime," *Arab American News*. Dearborn, MI. Dec. 11, 2010, v. 26, iss 1296, pg. 14.

[285] "Man Accused of NY Hate Attack on Imam is Cleared," *Daily News*. Midland, MI Dec. 16, 2010.

[286] "New York: Officer Cleared in Hate Crime," *Los Angeles Times*. Los Angeles, CA Dec. 17, 2010, pg. AA2.

[287] Jose Girona. "Muslim Man Tells of Attack in St. Petersburg," *Tampa Tribune*. Tampa, FL Feb. 8, 2011, pg. 6.

[288] Ibid.

[289] Ibid.

[290] Drew Harwell. "Hate Crime Suspect Out of Jail," *St. Petersburg Times*. St. Petersburg, FL Feb. 7, 2011, pg. B3.

[291] Ibid.

[292] Ibid.

[293] "Sikh Man Attacked," *News India-Times*. New York, NY June 17, 2011, v. 42, iss 24, pg. 11.

[294] Jineta Raval. "Sikh Attacked," *India Abroad*. New York, NY June 17, 2001, v. 41, iss 38, pg. A23.

[295] "Sikh Man Attacked," pg. 11.

[296] Jineta Raval. "Sikh Attacked," pg. A23.

[297] Ibid.

[298] "Wisconsin Sikh Temple Shooting Dredges Up Memories of Long History of Bias Crimes Against Sikhs." ABC News. www. abcactionnews.com. August 6, 2012.

[299] Jamie Schram, Maura O'Connor. *New York Post*. New York, NY July 8, 2011, pg. 17.

[300] Ibid.

[301] Vanessa Ho. "Being Muslim on 9/11 Anniversary," *Seattle Post-Intelligencer*. Seattle, WA. Seattle www.pi.com, Sept. 8, 20011.

[302] Ibid.

Chapter Five:

[1] Lou Grieco, James Cummings. "Hate Crimes Reported in Valley," *Dayton Daily News*. Dayton, OH Sept. 14, 2001, pg. 2A.

[2] Nicholas Geranios. "Most Hate Crimes Happened After 9/11," *Columbian*. Vancouver, WA March 6, 2002, pg. C2.

[3] Gaiutra Bahadur. "Rush to Judgment," *Austin American Statesman*. Austin, TX Sept. 13, 2001, pg. B7.

[4] Ibid.

[5] Ibid.

[6] Jennifer Levitz. "One Year After," *Providence Journal*. Providence, RI. Sept. 14, 2002, pg. A1.

[7] Ibid.

[8] Robert Tomsho. "Changing Winds," *Asian Wall St. Journal*. New York, NY Sept. 20, 2001, pg. 1.

[9] Dan DeLeo. "Sept. 11, 2001; Sept 11, 2003," *Patriot-Ledger*. Quincy, MA Sept. 10, 2003, pg. 1.

[10] Ibid.

[11] Pat Sullivan. "Police Say Alleged Stoning of Muslims not a Hate Crime," *Boston Herald*. Boston, MA April 21, 1992, pg. 8.

[12] Robert Tomsho. "Changing Winds," pg. 1.

[13] "Group Hatred is Un-American," *ADL On the Frontline*. New York, NY Fall 2001, v. 11 iss 7,8,9 pg. S1.

[14] "Roundup," Xinhua News Agency. CEIS. Woodside. Sept. 14, 2001, pg. 1.

[15] Johnny Edwards. "Hate Criminals," *Augusta Chronicle*. Augusta, GA Sept. 16, 2001, pg. A14.

[16] Ibid.

[17] Ibid.

[18] Hanna Rosin. "For Arab Americans, A Familiar Backlash," *Washington Post*. DC Sept. 13, 2001, pg. A26.

[19] Ibid.

[20] Harry Bruinius. "Muslims Deal with Grief," *Christian Science Monitor*. Boston, MA Sept. 18, 2001, pg. 3.

[21] Florangela Davila. "Hate Crime Response Criticized." *Seattle Times*, Seattle, WA Nov. 14, 2002, pg. B2.

[22] Armando Villafranca. "Attack Slightly Damages Nation of Islam Mosque," *Houston Chronicle*. Houston, TX Sept. 18, 2001, pg. 16.

[23] "Group Hatred is Un-American," pg. S1.

[24] Ibid.

[25] Maureen Hayden. "'We Feel Safe,'" *Evansville Courier and Press*. Evansville, IN March 20, 2003, pg. A4.

[26] Ibid.

[27] Jonathan Osborne. "Austin Mosque Is Attacked," *Austin American Statesman*. Austin, TX Sept. 18, 2001, pg. B1.

[28] Ibid.

[29] Richard A. Serrano. "Response to Terror," *Los Angeles Times*. Los Angeles, CA Sept. 28, 2001, pg. A19.

[30] Sam Skolnik. "Man Sentenced to Six Years," *Seattle Post Intelligencer*. Seattle, WA Dec. 18, 2002, pg. B1.

[31] Richard A. Serrano. "Response to Terror," pg. A19.

[32] Sam Skolnik. "Man Sentenced to Six Years," pg. B1.

[33] Richard Serrano. "Deluge of Hate Crimes," *Los Angeles Times*. Los Angeles, CA July 6, 2002, pg. A8.

[34] Ibid.

[35] Sam Skolnik. 'Man Sentenced to Six Years," pg. B1.

[36] Ibid.

[37] Ibid.

[38] Ibid.

[39] Ibid.

[40] Pedro Perez. "Northwest Sees Onslaught of Racist Attacks," *Columbian*. Vancouver, WA Sept. 19, 2001, pg. C2.

[41] Florangela Davila. "Hate Crime Response Criticized." pg. B2.

[42] Stephen Hegarty. "9/11 Fuels Hate Crimes," *St. Petersburg Times*. St Petersburg, Fla. Aug. 30, 2002, pg 1A.

[43] Ibid.

[44] Ibid.

[45] Hanna Rosin. "For Arab Americans, A Familiar Backlash," pg. A26.

[46] "Hate Crimes on Increase," *Arab American News*. Dearborn, MI Sept. 21, 2001, v. 18, iss 814, pg. 15.

[47] Melissa Knopper. "Fallout of Hatred," *Rocky Mountain News*. Denver, CO Dec. 12, 2002, pg. 6A.

[48] Teresa Mask. "Arab-American Lawyers," *Daily Herald*. Arlington Heights, IL Sept. 27, 2001, pg. 14.

[49] Jonathan Osborne. "Carpet Store Torched," *Austin American Statesman*, Austin, TX Sept. 25, 2001, pg. B1.

[50] Jonathan Osborne. "Austin Mosque Is Attacked," pg. B1.

[51] Ibid.

[52] Armando Villafranca. "Attack Slightly Damages Nation of Islam Mosque," p. 16.

[53] Jonathan Osborne. "Austin Mosque Is Attacked." pg. B1.

[54] Ibid.

[55] "Hate Crimes Reported Up;" "Muslim Group Denounces Terror Attacks." *New York Beacon*. New York, NY Sept. 26, 2001, v. 8, iss 38, pg. 23.

[56] Saeed Ahmed. "Retaliation," *Atlanta Constitution*. Atlanta, GA Sept. 18, 2001, pg. B4.

[57] Robert Eckhart. "Fire Set at Mosque," *Sarasota Herald Tribune*. Sarasota, FL Sept. 20, 2001, pg. A3.

[58] Ibid.

[59] Ibid.

[60] Ibid.

[61] Ibid.

[62] Tamar Lewin, Gustav Niebuhr. "Attacks," *New York Times*, New York, NY Sept. 18, 2001, pg. B5.

[63] Bernice Jackson. "The Fire Next Time," *Oakland Post*. Oakland, CA Sept. 26, 2001, v. 38, iss 29, pg. 4.

[64] "Hate Crimes on Increase," *Arab American News*. Dearborn, MI Sept. 21, 2001, v. 18, iss 814, pg. 15.

[65] Teresa Mask. "Arab-American Lawyers," pg. 14.

[66] Ibid.

[67] "Hate Crimes on Increase," *Arab American News*. Dearborn, MI Sept. 21, 2001, pg. 15.

[68] Peter Reichard. "Muslim-Owned," *New Orleans City Business*. Metaire, LA Sept. 24, 2001, v. 22, iss 13, pg. 4.

[69] Ela Dutt. "The Effort to Cope with Loss," *News India Times*. New York, NY Jan. 4, 2002, v. 33, iss 1 pg. 14.

[70] Annie Nakao. "Sikhs Say They're Being Made Targets," *San Francisco Chronicle*, San Francisco, CA Sept. 19, 2001, pg. A11.

[71] "9/11 Hate Crime Victim Not Sore Any More." *Hindustan Times*. New Delhi, India. Aug. 29. 2008.

[72] "Hate Crimes Reported Up," pg. 23.

[73] Angie Chuang. "Expressions of Hate," *Oregonian*. Portland, OR Sept. 19, 2001, pg. A6.

[74] Adrian Leung. "South Asian Journalists Discuss Backlash," *Asianweek*. Sept. 26, 2001, v. 23, iss 5 pg. 9.

[75] Zay Smith. "No Lights, Camera, Action?" *Chicago Sun-Times*. Chicago, IL Oct. 1, 2001, pg. 36.

[76] Ibid.

[77] "Synagogue Hit by Hate Crimes After Sept. 11," *Charleston Daily Mail*. Charlestom. WV Sept. 14, 2002, pg. 6A.

[78] Nicholas Geranios. "Tacoma Synagogue Set Ablaze," *Columbian*. Vancouver, WA March 6, 2002, pg. C2.

[79] Lee Hammel. "Arson Attempt Not Seen as a Hate Crime," *Telegram & Gazette*. Worcester, MA June 4, 2001, pg. A5.

[80] Jacob Fries. "Bronx: Muslim Clergyman Attacked," *New York Times*. New York, NY Oct. 11, 2001, pg. 9.

[81] Daniel Chacon. "Stabbing of Muslim," *San Diego Union-Tribune*. San Diego, CA Oct. 26, 2001, pg. 3.

[82] Ibid.

[83] Ibid.

[84] Greg Winter. "Two Held in Plot," *New York Times*. New York, NY Dec. 13, 2001, pg. A22.

[85] Ibid.

[86] Ibid.

[87] Ibid.

[88] Ibid.

[89] Jerry Seper. "Two Leaders of Jewish Group Arrested," *Washington Times*. DC Dec. 13, 2001, pg. A1.

[90] Greg Winter. "Two Held in Plot," pg. A22

[91] Ibid.

[92] Jerry Seper. "Two Leaders of Jewish Group Arrested," pg. A1

[93] Greg Winter. "Two Held in Plot," pg. A22.

[94] Ibid.

[95] Thanassis Cambanis. "Threat to Arab American Admitted," *Boston Globe*. Boston, MA June 7, 2002, pg. B1.

[96] Daniel Kurtzman. "FBI Reportedly Investigating Threat to Muslims in America," *Jewish Telegraphic Agency*, New York, NY May 9, 1996, pg. 3.

[97] Ibid.

[98] Nicholas Geranious. "Most Hate Crimes Happened After 9/11," *Columbian*. Vancouver, WA March 6, 2002, C2.

[99] Catie O'Toole. "3 Arrested in Sikh Temple Fire," *Post-Standard*. Syracuse, NY. Dec. 15, 2001, pg. A1.

[100] Chris Iven. "4th Teen Charged," *Post-Standard*. Syracuse, NY Feb. 22, 2002, pg. B1.

[101] Ibid.

[102] Hope Reeves. "Palermo," *New York Times*. Nov. 22, 2001, pg. 6.

[103] AP. "No Sign of Arson in Fire at Temple," *Times Union*. Albany, NY Nov. 24, 2001, pg. B2.

[104] Ibid.

[105] Chris Iven. "Officials Say Sikh Fire Was Arson," *Post-Standard*. Syracuse, NY. Nov. 20, 2001, pg. A1.

[106] Ibid.

[107] Ibid.

[108] Ibid.

[109] Ibid.

[110] Viji Sundaram. "NY Sikh Temple Fire," *India-West*. San Leandro, CA Nov. 30, 2001, v. 27 iss 4, pg. A30.

[111] Catie O'Toole. "3 Arrested In Sikh Temple Fire," pg. A1.

[112] Catie O'Toole. "Oswego: Teen to Plead Guilty," *Post-Standard*. Syracuse, NY April 13, 2002, pg. A1.

[113] Ibid.

[114] Ibid.

[115] Catie O'Toole. "3 Arrested in Sikh Temple Fire," pg. A1.

[116] Ibid.

[117] Ibid.

[118] Catie O'Toole. "Oswego: Teen to Plead Guilty," pg. A1.

[119] Suman Mozumder. "Arsonists Mistake," *India Abroad*. New York, NY Dec. 28, 2001, v. 32, iss 13, pg. 4.

[120] Chris Iven. "Federal Agents Probe," *Post-Standard*. Syracuse, NY. Nov. 20, 2001, pg. A1.

[121] Mary Beth Sheridan. "Cleaning Up After Attack," *Washington Post*. DC Dec. 23, 2001, pg. C3.

[122] Ibid.

[123] Ibid.

[124] Ibid.

[125] Ruth Krause. "Mosque Shootings," *Post-Tribune*. Gary, IN Dec. 13, 2001, pg. A4.

[126] David Zahniser. "Hate Crimes Against Muslims Rise," *Daily Breeze*. Torrance, CA Dec. 21, 2001, pg. A3.

[127] Ibid.

[128] Jeb Phillips. "Columbus Hate Crimes," *Columbus Dispatch*. Columbus, OH Dec. 9, 2002, pg. 1B.

[129] "Muslims Suspect Hate Crime," *Cincinnati Post*. Cincinnati, OH Dec. 31, 2001.

[130] Ibid.

[131] Ibid.

[132] "Neighbors Reach Out to Mosque," *Columbus Dispatch*. Columbus, OH Jan. 1, 2002.

[133] Ibid.

[134] Ibid.

[135] "Muslims Suspect Hate Crime," *Cincinnati Post*. Cincinnati, OH Dec. 31, 2001.

[136] Jeb Phillips. "Columbus Hate Crimes," pg. 1B.

[137] "Neighbors Reach Out to Mosque," *Columbus Dispatch*. Columbus, OH Jan. 1, 2002.

[138] Dave Ghose. "Support Buoys City," *Arab American News*. Dearborn, MI Jan. 25, 2002, v. 18, iss. 832, pg. 7.

[139] "Neighbors Reach Out to Mosque," *Columbus Dispatch*. Columbus, OH Jan. 1, 2002.

[140] Ibid.

[141] Dave Ghose. "Support Buoys City," pg. 7.

[142] Ibid; *Christian Science Monitor*, "Tides of Support," Boston, MA Jan. 15, 2002.

[143] Alice Thomas. "Forum Advises Local Muslims," *Columbus Dispatch*. Columbus, OH Jan. 27, 2002, pg. 4B.

[144] Suzanne Herel. "Fire at Arab Americans' Church Ruled Arson," *San Francisco Chronicle*. San Francisco, CA April 12, 2002, pg. A19.

[145] Ibid.

[146] Ibid.

[147] "Successful Hate Crime Persecutions," *ADC Times*. DC Winter 2002. v. 21, iss 9, pg. 10.

[148] Guy Taylor. "Hate Acts Against Muslims Subside," *Washington Times*. DC June 25, 2002, pg. B1.

[149] Matthew Stannard. "Site for Mosque Hit," *San Francisco Chronicle*. San Francisco, CA June 14, 2002, pg. A27.

[150] Ibid.

[151] Seamus McGraw. "Mystery Surrounds Florida Doc Who Plotted Mosque Bombing," *Forward*. New York, NY June 27, 2003, v. CVI iss 31, pg. 1.

[152] Ibid.

[153] Ibid.

[154] Ibid.

[155] Ibid.

[156] Ibid.

[157] Ibid.

[158] Ibid.

[159] Moustafa Bayoumi. "Constitutional Ground Has Been Lost," *Times Union*. Albany, NY Sept. 8, 2002, pg. B2.

[160] Seamus McGraw. "Mystery Surrounds Florida Doc Who Plotted Mosque Bombing," pg. 1.

[161] Ibid.

[162] Michelle Mundy. "BOCA Man Arrested," *Palm Beach Post*. West Palm Beach, FL Sept. 6, 2002, pg. 3B.

[163] Ibid.

[164] Susan Spencer-Wendel. "Man Who Burned Sign," *Palm Beach Post*. West Palm Beach, FL Feb. 25, 2003, pg. 1B.

[165] Ibid.

[166] Ibid.

[167] Ibid.

[168] Ibid.

[169] Ibid.

[170] Richard Winton. "Suspected Hate Crimes Rise," *Los Angeles Times*. Los Angeles, CA Sept. 10, 2002, pg. B3.

[171] Ibid.

[172] Abhi Raghunathan. "2 Charged in Damage to Mosque," *Washington Post*. DC Nov. 14, 2002, pg. T14.

[173] Ibid.

[174] Ibid.

[175] Ibid.

[176] Michael Scott. "Several Bullets Fired," *Plain Dealer*. Cleveland, OH Sept. 16, 2002, pg. B3.

[177] Ibid.

[178] Ibid.

[179] Jack Shaheen. Guilty. (Northampton, MA: Olive Branch Press, 2008)· 118-9.

[180] Ibid.

[181] "Hawaii: Threats Against Muslims," *New York Times*, New York, NY Oct. 23, 2002, pg. A20.

[182] Rod Antone. "FBI and Police Probe Hate Leaflets," *Honolulu Star Bulletin*. Honolulu, HA Oct. 22, 2002.

[183] Ibid.

[184] Ibid.

[185] Ibid.

[186] Philip O'Connor. "FBI Looks into Firebombing," *St. Louis Post-Dispatch*. St. Louis, MO March 4, 2003, pg. B1.

[187] Ibid.

[188] Ibid.

[189] Ibid.

[190] Ibid.

[191] Ibid.

[192] Ibid.

[193] Ibid.

[194] "Teens Charged In Temple Firebombing," *Tulsa World*. Tulsa, OK March 25, 2003, pg A11.

[195] Philip O'Connor. "FBI Looks into Firebombing," pg. B1.

[196] Deborah Kong. "Arabs, Muslims Try and Prevent Backlash," *Arab American News*. Dearborn, MI March 28, 2003, v. 19, iss 893, pg. 8.

[197] Kathryn Grondin. "Family of Muslim Marine," *Daily Herald*. Arlington Heights, IL March 13, 2003, pg. 1.

[198] Jack Shaheen. Guilty, pg. 172.

[199] Ibid.

[200] Kathryn Grondin. "Family of Muslim Marine," pg. 1.

[201] Ibid.

[202] Ibid.

[203] Ibid.

[204] Michael Janofsky. "War Brings New Surge of Anxiety," *New York Times*. New York, NY March 29, 2003, pg. B15.

[205] Beth Sneller. "Religious Groups Unite," *Daily Herald*. March 17, 2003, pg. 3.

[206] Atique Mahmood. "Home Grown Act of Terror," *Muslim Journal*. Chicago, IL April 4, 2003, pg. A1.

[207] Mona Eltahawy. "Bracing for a Backlash," *Washington Post*. DC March 24, 2003, pg. A13.

[208] Alisa Solomon. "From Baghdad to Brooklyn," *Village Voice*. New York, NY April 2, 2003, v. 48, iss 14 pg. 26-8.

[209] "Hate Crimes: Anti-Muslim Incidents on the Rise," *Arab-American News*. Dearborn, Michigan, March 28, 2003, v. 19, iss 893, pg. 16.

[210] Annie Nakao. "Muslims in America," *San Francisco Chronicle*. San Francisco, CA April 1, 2003, pg. D8.

[211] "Metro: In Brief," *Washington Post*. DC April 6, 2003, pg. C3.

[212] Trinity Hartman. "Sikh Temple Vandalism Probed," *Spokesman Review*. Spokane, WA April 22, 2003, pg. A1.

[213] Ibid.

[214] Ibid.

[215] Jack Shaheen. Guilty, pg. 95.

[216] Ibid.

[217] Dan DeLeo. "Sept. 11, 2001; Sept. 11, 2003," *Patriot-Ledger*. Quincy, MA Sept. 10, 2003, pg.1.

[218] Ibid.

[219] Ibid.

[220] "Police and Fire Reports," *Press Enterprise*. Riverside, CA July 23, 2003, pg. B4.

[221] Jeet Thayil. "Cross-burning," *India Abroad*, New York, NY Aug. 8, 2003, v. 33, iss 45 pg. A12.

[222] Ibid.

[223] Jingle Davis. "Mosque Fire," *Atlanta Journal-Constitution*. Atlanta, GA Aug. 29, 2003, pg C1.

[224] Ibid.

[225] Anne Hart, Eric Williamson. "Investigators Search for Answers in Mosque Fire," *Savannah Morning News*, Savannah, GA Aug. 20, 2003, pg. 1A.

[226] Ibid.

[227] Jingle Davis. "Mosque Fire," pg C1.

[228] Anne Hart. "Islamic Center." *Savannah Morning News*. Savannah, GA Aug. 26, 2003, pg. 1A.

[229] Ibid.

[230] Ibid.

[231] Ann Stifter. "Muslims Keep Praying," *Savannah Morning News*. Savannah, GA Aug. 30, 2003, pg. A1.

[232] Ibid.

[233] Ibid.

[234] Ibid.

[235] "Anti-Muslim Bomber Gets Probation," *Arab American News*. Dearborn MI Oct. 3, 2003, v. 20 iss 920 pg. 2.

[236] Mary Beth Sheridan. "Bias Against Muslims Up 70%," *Washington Post*. DC May 3, 2004, pg. A12.

[237] "FBI Probe Sought," *US Newswire*. DC July 27, 2004, pg. 1.

[238] Elizabeth Langton. "Mosque Vandals Receive Probation," *Augusta Chronicle*. Augusta, GA May 6, 2004, pg. A6.

[239] Ibid.

[240] Ibid.

[241] Ibid.

[242] Ibid.

[243] "Arundel Digest," *Capital*. Annapolis, MD. April 12, 2004. pg. B1.

[244] "Repeated Vandalism of Mosque," *New York Times*. New York, NY April 24, 2004, pg. B6.

[245] Ibid.

[246] Ibid.

[247] Wayne Parry. "Anti-Muslim Bias Rose Sharply." *Record*. Bergen County, NJ May 12, 2005, pg. A4.

[248] Andrew Ryan. "Muslims Urge Hate-Crime Inquiry," *South Florida Sun-Sentinel*. Ft. Lauderdale, FL May 30, 2005, pg. 3B.

[249] Ibid.

[250] Lisa Martinez. "Racist Groups Pass Out Fliers," *The Gazette*. Colorado Springs, CO May 18, 2004, pg. 3.

[251] Heather Radcliffe. "Vandal Paints Swastika," *St. Louis Post Dispatch*. St. Louis, MO June 22, 2004, pg. B2.

[252] Ibid.

[253] Ibid.

[254] "FBI Probe Sought," pg. 1.

[255] Ibid.

[256] Ibid.

[257] "Two U.S. Mosques Burned in One Week," US Newswire. Dec. 9, 2004, pg. 1.

[258] Waleed Muhammed. "Al-Baqi Islamic Center Fire," *Muslim Journal*. Chicago, IL Jan. 7, 2005, pg. 5.

[259] "Two U.S. Mosques Burned in One Week," pg. 1.

[260] Charles McCarthy. "Vandals Deface Temple," *Fresno Bee*. Fresno, CA March 15, 2004, pg. B1.

[261] Ibid.

[262] Ibid.

[263] Suman Mozumder. "Fresno Gurdwara Defiled," *India Abroad*. New York, NY. March 26, 2004 v. 34, iss 26, C2.

[264] Vanessa Colon. "Sikh Temple Stands Despite Defacement," *Fresno Bee*. Fresno, CA April 18, 2004, pg. A16.

[265] Ibid.

[266] Ron Orozco. "Calm After the Storm," *Fresno Bee*. Fresno, CA Sept. 11, 2004, pg. H1

[267] George Joseph. "Bullet Attacks," *India Abroad*. New York, NY June 25, 2004, v. 34, iss 39, pg. A8.

[268] Ibid.

[269] Ibid.

[270] Ibid.

[271] Andrew Ryan. "Muslims Urge Hate Crime Inquiry," pg. 3B.

[272] Ginelle Torres. "Islamic School Vandalized," *South Florida Sun-Sentinel*. Ft. Lauderdale, FL June 8, 2005, pg. 4B.

[273] Lance Pugmire. "Desert Mosque Burns to Ground," *Los Angeles Times*. Los Angeles, CA June 4, 2005, pg. B4.

[274] Ibid.

[275] Ibid.

[276] Kelly Rush. "Muslims Hope to Rebuild Mosque," *Inland Valley Daily Bulletin*. Ontario, CA July 17, 2005.

[277] Gina Tenorio. "Interfaith Peace Rally," *The Sun*. San Bernardino, CA July 18, 2005.

[278] Andrew Wang. "Muslims Feel Targeted," *Los Angeles Times*. Los Angeles, CA July 30, 2005, pg. B4.

[279] Ibid.

[280] "FBI Investigates Mosque Fire," *Chicago Tribune*. Chicago, IL July 10, 2005 pg. 12.

[281] William Porter. "Bloomington, Indiana." *Denver Post*. Denver, CO Sept. 10, 2006, pg. 7.

[282] Chrystian Tejedor. "Boca Mosque Vandalized," *South Florida Sun-Sentinel*. Ft. Lauderdale, FL Sept. 16, 2005, pg. 4B.

[283] Danielle Smith. "Islamic House of Worship Vandalized," *Arab American News*. Dearborn, MI Sept. 17, 2005, v. 21 iss 1023, pg. 10.

[284] Ibid.

[285] Aatif Bokhari. "Muslims, Mosques," *Arab American News*. Dearborne, MI July 15, 2006, v. 22, iss 1066, pg. 16.

[286] Larry Fish. "Gunfire Riddles Cars at Mosque," *Philadelphia Inquirer*. Philadelphia, PA Nov. 10, 2005, pg. B7.

[287] John Chadwick. "Hate Letters," *Record*. Bergen County, NJ Feb. 2, 2007, pg. A3.

[288] Lisa Tsering. "Pigs' Heads Tossed at Gurdwara," *India-West*. Jan. 6, 2006, v. 31, iss 9, pg A1.

[289] Ibid.

[290] Ibid.

[291] Ibid.

[292] Ibid.

[293] Ibid.

[294] Aatif Bokhari, "Muslims, Mosques," pg. 16.

[295] Ibid.

[296] Ibid.

[297] "Video Shows Bullet-Ridden Quran Thrown at Tenn. Mosque," PR Newswire. New York. July 10, 2006.

[298] Rosanna Ruiz. "Muslims Say Sign Left Near Mosque," *Houston Chronicle*. Houston, TX Feb. 8, 2006, pg. 3.

[299] Ibid.

[300] Ibid.

[301] Ibid.

[302] Ibid.

[303] David Hench. "Prosecutors Have Options," *Portland Press Herald*. Portland, ME Aug. 8, 2006, pg. A1; "Video Shows Bullet-Ridden Quran Thrown at Tenn. Mosque."

[304] Ibid.

[305] Aatif Bokhari. "Muslims, Mosques," pg. 16.

[306] Lindsay Tice. "Mosque Incident Suspect Arrested," *Sun Journal*. Lewiston, ME July 5, 2006, pg. A1.

[307] Justin Ellis. "Muslims Urge Respect," *Portland Press Herald*. Portland, ME July 6, 2006, A1.

[308] Ibid.

[309] David Hench. "Prosecutors Have Options," pg. A1.

[310] Lindsay Tice. "Mosque Incident Suspect Arrested," pg. A1.

[311] David Hench. "Prosecutors Have Options," pg. A1.

[312] Ibid.

[313] Ibid.

[314] H.D.S. Greenway. "Standing Up to Prejudice," *Boston Globe*. Boston, MA Aug. 1, 2006, pg. A13.

[315] David Hench. "Prosecutors Have Options," pg. A1.

[316] H.D.S. Greenway. "Standing Up to Prejudice," pg. A13.

[317] Ibid.

[318] Ziad Hamzeh. "The Letter: An American Town and the Somali Invasion," 2003.

[319] Dana Felty. "Man Rolls Pig's Head," *Savannah Morning News*, Savannah, GA July 22, 2006, pg. 13.

[320] David Hench. "Prosecutors Have Options," pg. A1.

[321] Sandy Mazza. "FBI: Mosque Damage Not Hate Crime," *Whittier Daily News*. Whittier, CA Aug. 18, 2006.

[322] Giselle Sotelo. "Mosque Vandalism Stirs Hate Fears," *Whittier Daily News Service*. Whittier, CA Aug. 12, 2006.

[323] Ibid.

[324] Bethania Palma. "Mosque Targeted Again," *Pasadena Star-News*. Pasadena, CA Aug. 15, 2006.

[325] Ibid.

[326] Ibid.

[327] Giselle Sotelo. "Vandalism Stirs Hate Fears."

[328] Ibid.

[329] Bethania Palma. "Mosque Targeted Again."

[330] Ibid.

[331] "Slurs Used in Attacks on Muslims," *US Newswire*. DC Dec. 7, 2006.

[332] Nirmal Singh. "Sikh's Appearance Leads to Confusion," *Patriot-News*. Harrisburg, PA Oct. 9, 2006, pg. A13.

[333] Jack Shaheen. Guilty, pg. 139.

[334] Ibid, pg. 140.

[335] "Hate Crimes Against Arabs," *Arab American News*. Dearborn, MI Jan. 27, 2007, v. 23, iss 1094, pg. 8.

[336] Ibid.

[337] "New Jersey Imams Receive Threatening Letters," US Newswire. DC Feb. 1, 2007.

[338] John Chadwick. "Hate Letters," pg. A3.

[339] Cassandra Braun. "Local Muslims Fear Islamic Center Target of Hate Crimes," *Oakland Tribune*. Oakland, CA Jan. 30, 2007 pg. 1.

[340] Ibid.

[341] Ibid.

[342] Ibid.

[343] Ibid.

[344] Ibid.

[345] "Hate Crimes Against Arabs," pg. 8.

[346] Gregg Krupa. "FBI Probes Mosque Vandalism," *Detroit News*. Detroit, MI May 18, 2007, pg. B3.

[347] Ibid.

[348] "Hate Crimes Against Arabs," pg. 8.

[349] Ibid.

[350] Lisa Tserling. "California Sikhs," *India-West*. San Leandro, CA April 13, 2007, v. 32, iss 21, pg. A20.

[351] Ibid.

[352] Abbie Vansickle. "Mosque Burns," *St. Petersburg Times*. St. Petersburg, FL April 13, 2007, pg. 1B.

[353] Ibid.

[354] Ibid.

[355] Keith Morelli. "Islamic Center Set Afire," *Tampa Tribune*. Tampa, FL April 15, 2007, pg. 1.

[356] Ibid.

[357] Ibid.

[358] Andriy Pazuniak. "CAIR Director Condemns Church Vandalism," *Tampa Tribune*, Tampa FL June 27, 2007, pg. 5.

[359] Ibid.

[360] Ibid.

[361] "Federal Charges," *Arab American News*. Dearborn, MI. May 5, 2007, v. 23, iss 1108, pg. 14.

[362] Jack Shaheen. Guilty, pg. 104.

[363] Ibid.

[364] Ibid, pg. 166.

[365] Ibid, pg. 165.

[366] Ibid.

[367] Henry Lee, Marisa Lagos. "Previously-Vandalized Mosque Hit by Arson," *San Francisco Chronicle*. San Francisco, CA Aug. 14, 2007, pg. B3.

[368] Ibid.

[369] Ibid.

[370] Ibid.

[371] Ibid.

[372] Ibid.

[373] Meredith Heagney. "Rock Throwers Hit," *Columbus Dispatch*. Columbus, OH Sept. 19, 2007, pg. 1B.

[374] Ibid.

[375] "Slurs Used During Attack," PR Newswire. NY Oct. 9, 2007.

[376] Patrik Jonsson. "Bacon Attack," *Christian Science Monitor*. Boston, MA Oct. 15, 2010.

[377] "New Yorker Charged," *Hindustan Times*. New Delhi, India. Jan. 28, 2008.

[378] Ibid.

[379] Ibid.

[380] "Tennessee Man Sentenced to 183 Months in Prison for Burning Islamic Center," www.justice.gov. March 25, 2010.

[381] Erik Ose. "Pro-McCain Group Dumping 28 Million Terror Scare DVDs in Swing States," *Tennessee Tribune*. Nashville, TN Oct. 9. 2008, v. 19, iss 39, pg. 6A.

[382] Ibid.

[383] Ibid.

[384] Ibid.

[385] Ibid.

[386] "CAIR: California," PR Newswire. New York: July 2, 2009.

[387] "California Imam Killed," *Arab American News*. Dearborn, MI July 4, 2009, v. 25, iss 1221 pg. 14.

[388] "FBI Asked to Probe Latest Vandalism," US Newswire. DC: July 2, 2009.

[389] Yonat Shimron. "Fayetteville Street Mosque Vandalized," *News & Observer*. Raleigh, NC Nov. 7, 2009, pg. A3.

[390] Ibid.

[391] Ibid.

[392] Ibid.

[393] My-Thuan Tran. "Cypress Mosque's Walls Painted," *Los Angeles Times*. Los Angeles, CA June 5, 2009, pg. A9.

[394] "CAIR: California," PR Newswire. New York: July 2, 2009.

[395] "CAIR Asks for Probe of Bias Motive in Shooting at Maine Mosque," PR Newswire. New York, NY Sept. 1, 2009.

[396] Lindsay Wise. "Man Admits Vandalizing," *Houston Chronicle*. Houston, TX Oct. 17, 2009, pg. B11.

[397] Ellyn Pak. "Police Consider Torched Koran," *Orange County Register*. Santa Ana, CA Jan. 18, 2010.

[398] Claire Webb. "Religious Groups," *Orange County Register*. Santa Ana, CA Jan. 10, 2010.

[399] Barbara Abel, Julia Lieblich. "Rural Controversy: A Mosque in Sheboygan." www.time.com, Aug. 19, 2010.

[400] "CAIR: Tenn. Mosque Vandalism," US Newswire. DC Feb. 10, 2010.

[401] Jeff Brumley, Dana Treen. "FBI: Mosque Video," *Florida Times Union*. Jacksonville, FL May 12, 2010, pg. A1.

[402] Larry Hannan. "Investigators Ask for Help," *Florida Times Union*. Jacksonville, FL May 13, 2010, pg. C2.

[403] Jeff Brumley, Dana Treen. "FBI: Mosque Video," *Florida Times Union*. Jacksonville, FL May 12, 2010, pg. A1.

[404] Dana Hertneky. "Suspect in 2010 Florida Mosque Bombing Killed in Oklahoma," www.news9.com, May 4, 2001.

[405] "CAIR Seeks Probe of Vandalism," *Arab American News*. Dearborn, MI May 22, 2010, b. 26, iss 1267, pg. 16.

[406] Eugene Robinson. "Pandering Over a Mosque," *Oakland Tribune*. Oakland, CA Aug. 17, 2010, pg. A8.

[407] Ibid.

[408] Ibid.

[409] Ibid.

[410] Patrik Jonsson. "Bacon Attack," *Christian Science Monitor*. Boston, MA Oct. 15, 2010.

[411] Moises Mendoza. "Berry Under Fire for Mosque Comment," *Houston Chronicle*. Houston, TX www.khou.com, May 28, 2010.

[412] Kristin Hall. "Feds File Legal Brief in Support of Tenn. Mosque," *Daily News*. Midland, MI Oct. 18, 2010.

[413] Andrew Grossman. "For Strippers Near Ground Zero, It's Business As Usual Amid Mosque Uproar," *Wall Street Journal*. New York, NY Aug. 19, 2010.

[414] Scott Shane. "Killings in Norway Spotlight Anti-Muslim Thought in U.S." *New York Times*. New York, NY July 24, 2011, pg. A1.

[415] Thomas Tracy. "What Kind of America?" *Brooklyn Paper*. Brooklyn, NY. June 28, 2010.

[416] "A Little Intolerant, but Good Reason to Be," *Newsweek* video, www. Newsweek.com, Aug. 27, 2010.

[417] Thomas Tracy. "What Kind of America?"

[418] Ibid.

[419] Amy Padnani. "No Midland Beach Mosque – Convent Sale Canceled," www.silive.com, July 23, 2010.

[420] Ibid.

[421] "CAIR WA: Van with Islam Ads Smeared with Feces," US Newswire, DC June 24, 2010.

[422] Phil Willon. "Islamic Group Denounces Planned Temecula Mosque," *Los Angeles Times*. Los Angeles, CA July 28, 2010.

[423] "CAIR-WA" Van with Islam Ads Smeared with Feces."

[424] Kristin Hall. "Feds File Legal Brief in Support of Tenn. Mosque," *Daily News*. Midland, MI Oct. 18, 2010.

[425] Cristina Breem. "Muslims Plan for Protests," *Charlotte Observer*. Charlotte, NC. Article without publication date found on website www.operationsaveamerica.org.

[426] "CAIR: Calf. Muslim Called a 'Raghead,' Assaulted by Fourth of July Revelers," US Newswire. DC July 7, 2010.

[427] Ibid.

[428] "US Attorney for the Northern District of Texas, in Texas Man Pleads Guilty to Federal Hate Crime in Connection with Mosque Arson in Arlington, Texas," *Targeted News Service*. DC Feb. 23, 2011.

[429] Ibid.

[430] "CAIR-CT Seeks Protection," US Newswire. DC Aug. 7, 2010.

[431] Ben Dobbin. "New Charges for 5 Accused of Harassing NY Mosque," *Daily News*. Midland, MI Sept. 13, 2010.

[432] Ibid.

[433] Ibid.

[434] "CAIR: No Mosque in NYC Pig," US Newswire. DC Aug. 29, 2010.

[435] "CAIR Welcomes Arrest in Attack on California Mosque," PR Newswire. NY March 10, 2011.

[436] Eugene Robinson. "Pandering Over a Mosque," pg. A8.

[437] Patrik Jonsson. "Bacon Attack," *Christian Science Monitor*. Boston, MA Oct. 15, 2010.

[438] Oralandar Brand-Williams. "No Charges Filed," *Detroit News*. Detroit, MI Sept. 23, 2010, pg. A9.

[439] "Burned Quran," *Chicago Tribune*. Chicago, IL Sept. 15, 2010, pg. 11.

[440] Deepa Bharath. "Blacks Most Targeted," *Orange County Register*. Santa Ana, CA Sept. 26, 2010.

[441] Patrik Jonsson. "Bacon Attack."

[442] "CAIR: No Mosque in NYC Pig."

[443] Patrik Jonsson. "Bacon Attack."

[444] Ibid.

[445] "CAIR Seeks Protection for NY Mosque Vandalized for 4th Time," US Newswire. DC: Oct. 26, 2010.

[446] Jerry Wofford. "Jury Says Hospitalization Not Needed for Man Charged with Hate Crime," *Tulsa World*. Tulsa, OK Jan. 14, 2011.

[447] Ibid.

[448] Ibid.

[449] "CAIR: Anti-Muslim Slurs Used in Attack on Oregon Muslim Inmate," PR Newswire. NY Dec. 1, 2010.

[450] Ibid.

[451] "CAIR: Missouri Mosque Vandalized with Hate Graffiti," PR Newswire. NY Jan. 13, 2011.

[452] "Calif. Mosque Fire Ruled Arson," *Arab American News*. Dearborn, MI March 28, 2011, v. 27 iss 1320, pg. 15.

[453] "CAIR: Missouri Mosque Targeted with 'Terrorist Threat,' Desecrated Qurans," PR Newswire, NY April 14, 2011.

[454] Ibid.

[455] "CAIR: Michigan Muslim's Car Defaced with Sand N*gger," US Newswire, DC May 14, 2011.

[456] "CAIR Seeks Hate Crime Charges for Attack on Fla. Worker." US Newswire, DC April 29, 2011.

[457] Ibid.

[458] Mauricio Guerrero. "Clear Lake Muslims Feel Safe," *Houston Chronicle*. Houston, TX May 12, 2011, pg. 1.

[459] Stephen Magagnini. "Stockton Mosque Fire an Arson," *Sacramento Bee*. Sacramento, CA May 26, 2011, pg. 4B.

[460] David Hench. "Graffiti on Portland Mosque Under Investigation," *Portland Press Herald*. Portland, ME May 2, 2011; Susan Hogan. "Star Tribune, Minneapolis, Susan Hogan Column," *McClatchy-Tribune Business News*. DC May 3, 2011; "Portland Mosque Vandalized in Wake of bin Laden Death," *Maine Public Broadcast Network*, May 2, 2011.

[461] Lalit K. Jha. "Sikhs in U.S. Apprehensive," *Press Trust of India*. Delhi, India. May 4, 2011.

[462] "CAIR Asks FBI to Probe Texas Mosque Arson as Hate Crime," US Newswire. DC May 16, 2011.

[463] Jay Tokasz. "Lawn Sign Advances Feud Between Mosque, Neighbor," *Buffalo News*. Buffalo, NY May 9, 2011.

[464] Ibid.

[465] Brittany Pieper. "Bossier Mosque Vandalized." *KSLA News 12*. Shreveport, LA May 9, 2011.

[466] Larry Flowers. "Mosque's Adopt a Highway Sign Vandalized 5-25-2011," *WSMV* TV. Murfreesboro, TN May 25, 2011.

[467] Ibid.

[468] "Mosque Lawsuit Plaintiffs to Get June 27 Motion Hearing," *Daily News Journal*. Murfreesboro, TN June 14, 2011.

[469] Scott Croteau. "Set Fire Singes Greater Worcester Islamic Society," *Telegram & Gazette*, Worcester, MA, June 1, 2011; Lee Hammel. "Arson Attempt Not Seen as a Hate Crime," pg. A5.

[470] Ibid.

[471] Tony Gonzalez. "Work on Murfreesboro Mosque Delayed," *Tennessean*. Nashville, TN Sept. 14, 2011.

[472] Ibid.

[473] "Arson Reported at Tennessee Mosque Construction Site," *USA Today*. www.USAToday.com. Aug. 29, 2010.

[474] Tony Gonzalez. "Work on Murfreesboro Mosque Delayed."

[475] WABC news channel 7 video posted online in "CAIR Concerned About 9/11 Spike in Anti-Muslim Incidents," www.turntoislam.com/forum, Sept. 14, 2011.

[476] Ibid.

[477] "New York Mosque Sign Smashed on 9/11 Anniversary," WIVB channel 4 News, Buffalo, Sept. 12, 2011.

[478] Ibid.

Chapter Six:

[1] Jack Shaheen. <u>Reel Bad Arabs</u>. (New York: Olive Branch Press, 2001).

[2] Ibid, pg. 103.

[3] Ibid.

[4] Ibid, pg. 103-4.

[5] Ibid.

[6] Ibid, pg. 83.

[7] Ibid.

[8] Ibid, pg. 260.

[9] Ibid, pg. 476.

[10] Ibid.

[11] Ibid.

[12] Ibid, pg. 66-67.

[13] Ibid, pg. 51.

[14] Ibid, pg. 446.

[15] Ibid, pg. 52.

[16] Ibid, pg. 272.

[17] Tim Jon Semmerling. 'Evil' Arabs in American Popular Film. (Austin: University of Texas Press, 2006): 253.

[18] Ibid, pg. 254.

[19] Rachel Gordon. "Victims of Hate," *San Francisco Chronicle*, San Francisco, CA Jan. 11, 2002, pg. A1.

[20] Education Outlook," *ADC Times*. DC Oct./Nov. 2001 v. 21 iss 5 pg. 1-5.

[21] Silja Talvi. "And Justice for All," *Colorlines*. Winter 2002/2003. Oakland, CA. Jan. 31, 2003 v. 5, iss 4 pg. 18.

[22] Dina Gerdeman. "Reality Check," *Patriot-Ledger*. Quincy, MA March 1, 2002, pg. 1.

[23] Ibid.

[24] Ibid.

[25] "Education Outlook," pg. 1-5.

[26] Teresa Watanabe. "Feeling Like the Enemy," *Los Angeles Times*. Los Angeles, CA Sept. 20, 2001, pg. A1.

[27] Ibid.

[28] Ibid.

[29] Ibid.

[30] Tamar Lewin, Gustav Niebuhr. "Attacks," *New York Times*. New York, NY Sept. 18, 2001, pg. B5.

[31] Gaiutra Bahadur. "Rush to Judgment," *Austin American Statesman*. Austin, TX Sept. 13, 2001, pg. B7.

[32] "Education Outlook," pg. 1-5.

[33] Ibid.

[34] Viji Sundaram. "Bay Area Muslims," *India-West*. San Leandro, CA Sept. 21, 2001, v. 26, iss 46, pg. A26.

[35] Ibid.

[36] Maureen Nolan. "An Anniversary," *Post-Standard*. Syracuse, NY Sept. 10, 2002, pg. B6.

[37] Ibid.

[38] Jo Becker, Phuong Ly. "Sikhs Campaign Against Hate," *Washington Post*. DC Sept. 24, 2001, pg. B1.

[39] Shelby Oppel. "Muslims Take on Role," *Oregonian*. Portland, OR Oct. 11, 2001, pg. B1.

[40] Silja Talvi. "And Justice for All," pg. 18.

[41] Lynda Gorov. "Afghan Community in Fremont Angry." *Boston Globe*. Boston, MA Sept. 24, 2001, pg. A11.

[42] "Education Outlook," pg. 1-5.

[43] Aisha Sultan. "Muslims in the St. Louis Area," *Post-Dispatch*. St. Louis, MO Sept. 13, 2001, pg. B2.

[44] Robert Smith. "Local Arab-Americans ," *Plain Dealer*. Cleveland, OH Sept. 14, 2001, pg. A15.

[45] Ibid.

[46] Deborah Bulkeley. "Muslims in U.S. See Little 9/11 Backlash," *Deseret Morning News*, Salt Lake City, UT Sept. 9, 2006, pg. E1.

[47] "Education Outlook," pg. 1-5.

[48] Ibid.

[49] Nery Ynclan. "Middle Eastern Teens," *Seattle Times*. Seattle, WA April 28, 2003, pg. F7.

[50] Ibid.

[51] Tanya Weinberg. "Many Muslims No Longer Feel Safe in the U.S." *South Florida Sentinel*. Sept. 5, 2002, pg. 1.

[52] "Education Outlook," pg. 1-5.

[53] Mary Leonard. "Arab-Americans Feel Sting of Profiling," *Boston Globe*. Boston, MA Oct. 19, 2001, pg. A20.

[54] Ibid.

[55] Ibid.

[56] "Education Outlook," pg. 1-5

[57] Theola Labbe. "Muslims Endure Season of Suspicion." *Times Union*. Albany, NY Sept. 30, 2001, pg. A9.

[58] Ibid.

[59] Richard Fausset. "Sikhs Mark New Year," *Los Angeles Times*. Los Angeles, CA April 14, 2003, pg. B1.

[60] Karen MacPherson. "Activists," *Pittsburgh Post-Gazette*. Pittsburg, PA Sept. 20, 2001, pg. A9.

[61] "Education Outlook," pg. 1-5.

[62] Ibid.

[63] Ibid.

[64] "Where, Exactly, Are We?" *Times-Picayune*. New Orleans, LA Sept. 14, 2001, pg. B6.

[65] Ibid.

[66] James Ridgeway. "John Ashcroft's New America," *Village Voice*. New York, NY Oct. 2, 2001, v 46 iss 39, pg. 41.

[67] "Volunteers Escort Muslims Fearing Attack," *Charleston Daily Mail*. Charleston, WV Oct. 4, 2001, pg. 3A.

[68] Ibid.

[69] "Education Outlook," pg. 1-5.

[70] Teresa Mask. "Arab-American Lawyers," *Daily Herald*. Arlington Heights, IL Sept. 27, 2001, pg. 14.

[71] Larry Stammer, Teresa Watanabe. "Muslims," *Los Angeles Times*. Los Angeles, CA Sept. 12, 2001, pg. A38.

[72] Lynda Gorov. "Afghan Community in Fremont Angry." pg. A11.

[73] Kendra Hamilton. "Campuses Unite," *Black Issues in Higher Education*. Reston. Oct. 11, 2001, v. 16, iss. 17 pg. 32-4, pg. 3.

[74] Aisha Sultan. "Muslims in the St. Louis Area," pg. B2.

[75] Ibid.

[76] Annah Dumas-Mitchell. "America Seeks to Recover From Attacks," *Chicago Defender*. Chicago, IL Sept. 13, 2001, pg. 3.

[77] Norm Parish. "Immigrants Here Fear Violence," *St. Louis Post-Dispatch*. St. Louis, MO Sept. 18, 2001, pg. D1.

[78] "We the People," *Times-Picayune*. New Orleans, LA Sept. 19, 2001, pg. B6.

[79] Jocelyn Wiener. "Lessons in Patience," *St. Petersburg Times*. St. Petersburg, FL Sept. 29, 2002, pg. 1F.

[80] Ibid.

[81] Carri Thevenot. "Nevadans Fear Rise in Hate," *Las Vegas Review Journal*. Las Vegas, NV Sept. 18, 2001, pg. 1A.

[82] Lou Grieco, James Cummings. "Hate Crimes Reported in Valley," *Dayton Daily News*. Dayton, OH Sept. 14, 2001, pg. 2A.

[83] Allison Foreman. "UNCG Staff and Students," *Greensboro News Record*. Greensboro, NC Sept. 25, 2001, pg. B1.

[84] "Lebanese Student Attacked in US," *Middle East News Online*. Durham. Sept. 20, 2001.

[85] Phillip Reese. "Two Men Beat UNCG Student From Lebanon," *Greensboro News Record*. Greensboro, NC Sept. 19, 2001, pg. B1.

[86] Allison Foreman. "UNCG Staff and Students," pg. B1.

[87] Ibid.

[88] William Porter. "Bloomington, Indiana." *Denver Post*. Denver, CO Sept. 10, 2006, pg. 7.

[89] Barbara Karkabi. "Learning from the Pain," *Houston Chronicle*. Houston, TX Oct. 7, 2001, pg. E1.

[90] Patrick Smyth. "U.S. Muslims Suffer Spate of Hate Attacks," *Irish Times*. Dublin, Ire Sept. 19, 2001, pg. 10.

[91] Rick Orlov, Orith Goldberg. "Officials Worried," *Daily News*. Los Angeles, CA Sept. 14, 2001, pg. N11.

[92] Viji Sundaram. "Bay Area Muslims," pg. A26.

[93] Brian Kluepfel. "Upswing in Hate Crimes," *Asianweek*. San Francisco, CA April 9, 2003, v. 24, iss 32 pg. 14.

[94] Ibid.

[95] Ibid.

[96] Ibid.

[97] Michael Potts. "ASU Police Investigating," *India-West*. San Leandro, CA Oct. 5, 2001, v. 26, iss 48, pg. A30.

[98] Ibid.

[99] Ibid.

[100] Ibid.

[101] Christine Tamer. "Arab-Americans, Affirmative Action, and a Quest for Racial Identity," in *Texas Journal on Civil Liberties & Civil Rights*, (Fall 2010): 101-127.

[102] Viji Sundaram. "Sikh Store Owner Beaten Up," *India-West*. San Leandro, CA Sept. 21, 2001, v. 26, iss 46 pg. 1.

[103] Robert Smith. "Local Arab-Americans," pg. A15.

[104] Ibid.

[105] "Education Outlook," pg. 1-5.

[106] Ashok Easwaran. "Hate Crimes Grip Chicago Too," *India Abroad*. New York, NY Sept. 28, 2001, v. 31, iss 52, pg. 4.

[107] Ellen Silberman, Marie Szaniszlo. "War on Terrorism," *Boston Herald*. Boston, MA Sept. 19, 2001, pg. 18.

[108] Ibid.

[109] Julie Buzbee. "War of Words," *St. Joseph News-Press*. St. Joseph, MO Sept. 21, 2001.

[110] Ibid.

[111] Dave Curtin. "Arab Students Leaving Campus," *Denver Post*. Denver, CO Oct. 1, 2001.

[112] Edward Hegstrom. "Foreign Student Tells of Beating," *Houston Chronicle*. Houston, TX Sept. 29, 2001, pg. 31

[113] Ibid.

[114] Ibid.

[115] Ibid.

[116] Ibid.

[117] Ibid.

[118] Ibid.

[119] Ibid.

[120] Hanna Rosin. "For Arab-Americans, A Familiar Backlash," *Washington Post*. DC Sept. 13, 2001, pg. A26.

[121] Dave Curtin. "Arab Students Leaving Campus."

[122] Ibid.

[123] Jocelyn Wiener. "Lessons in Patience," pg. 1F.

[124] Roma Khanna. "Hate Crimes Peak After 9/11," *Houston Chronicle*. Houston, TX Dec. 14, 2001, pg. A37.

[125] Mary Sanchez. "A Look at Kansas City Area Muslims," *Kansas City Star*. Kansas City, MO Sept. 20, 2001 pg. A6

[126] Cynthia Yeldell. "Local Muslims Pray," *News Sentinel*. Knoxville, TN March 22, 2003, pg. A7.

[127] Martha Irvine. "Ethnic Backlash." *Denver Post*. Denver, CO Sept. 18, 2001, pg. A12.

[128] Viji Sundaram. "Hate Crime Fears Rise," *India-West*. San Leandro, CA Sept. 28, 2001, v. 26, iss 47 pg. A1.

[129] Samara Derby. "Forum Targets Hate Crimes Here," *Capital Times*. Madison, WI May 3, 2006, pg. C1.

[130] Ibid.

[131] Ibid.

[132] "Metro Digest." *Denver Post*. Denver, CO Oct. 24, 2001, pg. B2.

[133] Melissa Knopper. "Fallout of Hatred," *Rocky Mountain News*. Denver, CO Dec. 12, 2002, pg. 6A.

[134] Ibid.

[135] Ibid.

[136] Meeta Kaur. "Pushed Too Far," *Asianweek*. San Francisco, CA Feb. 26, 2003, v. 24, iss 26, pg. 20.

[137] Jocelyn Wiener. "Lessons in Patience," pg. 1F.

[138] "Home Front," *Dayton Daily News*. Dayton, OH Oct. 25, 2001, pg. 14A.

[139] Ibid.

[140] "Education Outlook," pg. 1-5.

[141] Ibid.

[142] Jack Shaheen. <u>Guilty</u>. (Northampton, MA: Olive Branch Press, 2008): 119.

[143] "Education Outlook," pg. 1-5.

[144] Ibid.

[145] Ibid.

[146] Ibid.

[147] Ibid.

[148] Judith Browne. "Racial Profiling," *Atlanta Inquirer*, Atlanta, GA Nov. 17, 2001, v. 41, iss 16, pg. 4.

[149] Paul Wood. "Muslim Student Beaten," *News Gazette*. Champaign, IL Dec. 20, 2001, pg. B1.

[150] Ibid.

[151] Ibid.

[152] Ibid.

[153] Ibid.

[154] Greg Winter. "Some Mideast Immigrants, Shaken," *New York Times*, New York, NY Nov. 23, 2001, pg. B1.

[155] Carl Campanile. "Bias Eyed in Beating of Muslim," *New York Post*. New York, NY Feb. 8, 2002, pg. 19.

[156] Ibid.

[157] Ibid.

[158] Jocelyn Wiener. "Lessons in Patience," pg. 1F.

[159] Ibid.

[160] Meeta Kaur. "Pushed Too Far," pg. 20.

[161] Ibid.

[162] Ibid.

[163] Ibid.

[164] Ibid.

[165] Ibid.

[166] Ibid.

[167] Ibid.

[168] Ibid.

[169] Ibid.

[170] Ibid.

[171] Ibid.

[172] Ibid.

[173] Susan Spencer-Wendel. "Student Pleads Guilty," *Palm Beach Post*. West Palm Beach, FA Feb. 27, 2003, pg. 3B.

[174] Ibid.

[175] Ibid.

[176] Ibid.

[177] Ibid.

[178] Ibid.

[179] Vik Jolly, Ann Pepper. "State's Muslims," *Orange County Register*. Santa Ana, CA May 4, 2002, pg. 1.

[180] Ibid.

[181] Jodi Wilgoren. "Going by 'Joe,' not 'Yussef,'" *New York Times*. New York, NY Sept. 11, 2002, pg. G15.

[182] Ibid.

[183] Tara Tuckwiller. "Worries Return," *Sunday Gazette-Mail*. Charleston, WV Sept. 8, 2002, pg. 1B.

[184] Ibid.

[185] Ibid.

[186] Ibid.

[187] Ibid.

[188] Ibid.

[189] Ibid.

[190] Jocelyn Wiener. "Lessons in Patience," pg. 1F.

[191] Ibid.

[192] Cynthia Yeldell. "Local Muslims Pray," pg. A7.

[193] Jocelyn Wiener. "Lessons in Patience," pg. 1F.

[194] Ibid.

[195] Michael May and Lisa Tobin. "9/11 Stories: Hate Crime Victim Doesn't Hate Attackers," WBUR 90.9 Boston, MA www.wbur.org, Sept. 8, 3011.

[196] Jack Minch article from *Lowell Sun* discussed in Vanita Shastri. "Press Release in Response to the Lowell Hate Crimes." *Indian-American Forum for Political Education*. Lexington, MA www.iafpe-ma.org. Dec. 6, 2002.

[197] Ibid.

[198] Tyche Hendricks. "Muslim Kids," *San Francisco Chronicle*, San Francisco, CA March 25, 2003, pg. A15.

[199] Ibid.

[200] Richard Fausset. "Sikhs Mark New Year," pg. B1.

[201] Ibid.

[202] Tyche Hendricks. "Muslim Kids," pg. A15.

[203] Nery Ynclan. "Middle Eastern Teens," pg. F7.

[204] Ibid.

[205] Ibid.

[206] Ibid.

[207] Ibid.

[208] "Ariz. Sikh Shot, Penn Iraqi Teen Assaulted," US Newswire. DC May 21, 2001, pg. 1.

[209] Ibid.

[210] Tyche Hendricks. "Muslim Kids," pg. A15.

[211] Nery Ynclan. "Middle Eastern Teens," pg. F7.

[212] Mary Sanchez. "American Muslims Fear," *Kansas City Star*. Kansas City, MO April 27, 2003, pg. 1.

[213] Ibid.

[214] Annie Nakao. "Muslims in America," *San Francisco Chronicle*. San Francisco, CA April 1, 2003, pg. D8; "Muslim University Students," *Arab American News*. Dearborn, MI March 21, 2003, v. 19, iss 892, pg. 17.

[215] "Muslim University Students," *Arab American News*. Dearborn, MI March 21, 2003, v. 19, iss 892, pg. 17.

[216] Nahal Toosi. "Muslim Student Group," *Milwaukee Journal Sentinel*. Milwaukee, WI May 1, 2004, pg. 3B

[217] Ibid.

[218] Nora Achrati. "Hate Crimes Follow," *Atlanta Journal-Constitution*. Atlanta, GA March 30, 2003, pg. A5.

[219] "Pig's Blood Poured on Prayer Rugs," *Arab American News*. Dearborn, MI May 9, 2003. v. 19, iss 899 pg. 12.

[220] "Muslim Prayer Rug Defaced," *Los Angeles Times*. Los Angeles, CA April 25, 2003, pg. B4.

[221] "Pig's Blood Poured on Prayer Rugs," pg. 12.

[222] Anne Hart, Eric Williamson. "Investigators Search for Answers in Mosque Fire," *Savannah Morning News*, Savannah, GA Aug. 20, 2003, pg. 1A.

[223] Moni Basu. "Sept. 11 Changed Lives," *Atlanta Journal-Constitution*. Atlanta, GA Sept. 10, 2003, pg. F3.

[224] Ibid.

[225] Ibid.

[226] Mary Beth Sheridan. "Bias Against Muslims Up 70%," *Washington Post*. DC May 3, 2004, pg. A12.

[227] Lornet Turnball. "Group Cites Rising Violence," *Seattle Times*. Seattle, WA May 4, 2004, pg. B4.

[228] Ibid.

[229] "Anti-Muslim Bomber Gets Probation," *Arab American News*. Dearborn, MI. Oct. 3, 2003, v. 20, iss 920, pg. 2.

[230] Ibid.

[231] Curt Anderson. "US, Muskogee Schools Agree to Scarf Settlement," *Commercial Appeal*. Memphis, TN May 20, 2004, pg. A14.

[232] Ibid.

[233] "Coalition Joins Groups Issuing letter to GMU President to Urge Investigation into Abusive Treatment of South Asian Muslim Student," *Sikh Coalition Newsletter*. www.sikhcoalition.org, Sept. 30, 2003.

[234] Gary Grass, Ammar Askari. "U.S. Must Recognize Loyalty of Citizens of Arab Descent," *Capital Times*. Madison, WI Sept. 11, 2003, pg. 12A.

[235] "Sikh Boy's Turban Set Alight in School," US Newswire. DC May 12, 2008.

[236] Ashok Jethanandani. "Proof of Allegiance," *India Currents*. San Jose, CA Oct. 2004. v. 18, iss 7 pg. 1.

[237] Jack Shaheen. Guilty, pg. 158.

[238] Ibid, pg. 137.

[239] Ibid, pg. 181.

[240] Lona O'Connor. "Islamic Schoolgirl Assaulted," *Palm Beach Post*. West Palm Beach, FL April 13, 2004, pg. 1B.

[241] Ibid.

[242] Ibid.

[243] Ibid.

[244] Marc Freeman. "Florida Hate Crime May Have Been Horseplay," *Knight Ridder Tribune News Service*. DC April 14, 2004, pg. 1

[245] Ibid.

[246] Ibid.

[247] Ibid.

[248] Ibid.

[249] Nahal Toosi. "Muslim Student Group," pg. 3B

[250] Ibid.

[251] Ibid.

[252] Susan Anasagasti. "Arab Students at UCI," *Los Angeles Times*. Los Angeles, CA May 26, 2004, pg. B3.

[253] Ibid.

[254] Ibid.

[255] AP. "Fire Destroys UCI Protest Wall," *Daily Breeze*. Torrance, CA May 23, 2004, pg. A5.

[256] Susan Anasagasti. "Arab Students at UCI," pg. B3

[257] Mary Shibata. "8 Female Muslims Victims of Hate Crime," *Daily Californian*. Berkeley, CA Sept. 20, 2004.

[258] Jack Shaheen. Guilty, pg. 96.

[259] "Another Campus Dealing With Alleged Hate Crime," WCVB Boston Channel 5. www.thebostonchannel.com, May 4, 2005.

[260] Ibid.

[261] Ibid.

[262] Jack Shaheen. Guilty, pg. 151.

[263] Ibid.

[264] Ibid, 179.

[265] Marilyn Elias. "USA's Muslims Are Under Fire," *USA Today*, McLean, VA Aug. 10, 2006, pg. D1.

[266] Ibid.

[267] Terri Jo Ryan. "Muslim BU Student," *Waco Tribune-Herald*. Waco, TX April 7, 2006.

[268] Ibid.

[269] Ibid.

[270] Ibid.

[271] Ibid.

[272] Sidney Blumental. "Meek, Mild, and Menacing," *Salon*. June 12, 2006, www.politics.salon.com.

[273] Ibid.

[274] Jack Shaheen. Guilty, pg. 164.

[275] Ibid, pg. 114.

[276] Ibid, pg. 135.

[277] Ibid, pg. 157.

[278] Ibid.

[279] Tim Woods. "Muslim Student," *Waco Tribune-Herald*. Waco, TX April 5, 2006.

[280] Ibid.

[281] Ibid.

[282] Ibid.

[283] Ibid.

[284] Ibid.

[285] Ibid.

[286] Monica Ortiz Uribe. "FBI Joins Baylor Police," *Waco Tribune-Herald*. Waco, TX April 6, 2006.

[287] Terri Jo Ryan. "Muslim BU Student." *Waco Tribune-Herald*. Waco, TX April 7, 2006.

[288] Sushama Subramanian. "Graffiti Victim," *Orange County Register*. Santa Ana, CA July 6, 2006, pg. 1.

[289] Ibid.

[290] Aseem Chhabra. *India Abroad*. New York: NY. Oct. 5, 2007, v. 38, iss. 1 pg. M12.

[291] Marilyn Elias. "USA's Muslims are Under Fire," pg. D1.

[292] Deborah Bulkeley. "Muslims in U.S. See Little 9/11 Backlash," pg. E1.

[293] Ibid.

[294] "Muslim Buildings Attacked," *Arab American News*. Dearborn, MI Sept. 30, 2006, v. 22, iss 1077, pg. 10.

[295] Karen Arenson. "Bias Episodes," *New York Times*. New York, NY Oct. 21, 2006, pg. B2.

[296] Ibid.

[297] Ibid.

[298] Audrey Hudson. "Koran Abuse Draws Hate-Crime Charge," *Washington Times*. DC July 31, 2007, pg. A3.

[299] Ibid.

[300] Ibid.

[301] Jack Shaheen. Guilty, pg. 123-4.

[302] "Hate Crimes Against Arabs," *Arab American News*. Dearborn, MI Jan. 27, 2007, v. 23, iss 1094, pg. 8.

[303] Ibid.

[304] Ibid.

[305] Ibid.

[306] Ibid.

[307] Ibid.

[308] Jack Shaheen. Guilty, pg. 49.

[309] Jada Yuan. "The White-Castle Ceiling," *New York*. New York, NY. March 4, 2007. For a helpful discussion of pre-9/11 dramatic roles that demean South Asians, see Kavita Daswani, "South Asian Actors Find Little Support, Lots of Stereotype," *Los Angeles Times*. Los Angeles, CA. July 27, 2001.

[310] Ruth Morris. "Leader of Muslim Group," *Knight Ridder Tribune News Service*. DC May 2, 2007, pg. 1.

[311] "Federal Charges," *Arab American News*. Dearborn, MI May 5, 2007, v. 23, iss 1108, pg. 14.

[312] Ibid.

[313] Ikimulisa Livingston. "Teen Guilty," *New York Post*. New York, NY March 8, 2008, pg. 12.

[314] Ibid.

[315] Ibid.

[316] Elaine Chan. "Harassment Ordeal," *New York Daily News*. New York, NY June 6, 2007, pg. 1.

[317] Ikimulisa Livingston. "Teen Guilty," pg. 12.

[318] Nicole Bode. "Teen Gets No Jail," *New York Daily News*. New York, NY June 6, 2008, pg. 16.

[319] Ibid.

[320] "Khalsa Kids," *India-West*. San Leandro, CA Oct. 12, 2007, v. 32 iss 46 pg. B25.

[321] "Attacks Against Sikh Students in NY Schools," *Hindustan Times*. New Delhi, India. June 11, 2007.

[322] "CA School District to Apologize for Hijab Incident," PR Newswire. New York. Oct. 26, 2007.

[323] Jack Shaheen. Guilty, pg. 174.

[324] "Dispute Between Muslim Couple, Neighbors," *Brattleboro Reformer*. Brattleboro, VT. July 26, 2007.

[325] Will Youmans. "Fear of Arabs," *Arab American News*. Dearborn, MI Aug. 18, 2007 v. 23, iss 1123, pg. 12.

[326] Kareem Fahim. "Girl's Beating Not Reported," *New York Times*. New York, NY Oct. 17, 2007, pg. B7.

[327] Ibid.

[328] Ibid.

[329] Ibid.

[330] Thomas Tobin. "Harassment of Muslim Sixth-Grader," *St. Petersburg Times*. St. Petersburg, Fla. Nov. 13, 2007.

[331] Ibid.

[332] Ibid.

[333] Ibid.

[334] Doug Guthrie. "Admission on Nooses," *Detroit News*. Detroit, MI Nov. 19, 2007, pg. B1.

[335] Ibid.

[336] Sarah Lemagie. "Muslim Civil Liberties Group," *Star Tribune*. Minneapolis, MN April 15, 2008, pg. B4.

[337] Ibid.

[338] Ibid.

[339] Julianne Hing. "War on Terror Fuels Racial Bullying," *Colorlines*. Oakland, CA March 2009 v. 12, iss 2, pg. 15.

[340] "Sikh Boy's Turban Set Alight in School," US Newswire. DC May 12, 2008.

[341] Ibid.

[342] Julianne Hing. "War on Terror Fuels Racial Bullying," pg. 15.

[343] Monika Joshi. "Sikh Students," *India Abroad*. New York, NY June 20, 2008 v. 38, iss. 38, pg. A12.

[344] Sunita Sohrabji. "Student Found Guilty," *India-West*. San Leandro, CA July 31, 2009, v. 34, iss 36, pg. A32.

[345] Ibid.

[346] Julianne Hing. "War on Terror Fuels Racial Bullying," pg. 15.

[347] Arthur Pais. "Student Doe Found Guilty," *India Abroad*. New York, NY July 31, 2009, v. 39, iss 44, pg. A20.

[348] Julianne Hing. "War on Terror Fuels Racial Bullying," pg. 15.

[349] Ibid.

[350] Peggy O'Hare. "Most Defend Friendswood Principal," *Houston Chronicle*. Houston, TX June 11, 2008, pg. 1.

[351] Ibid.

[352] "Texas School District Exempts Sikh Boy," *India Abroad*. New York, NY Oct. 22, 2010, v.41, iss 4, pg. A22.

[353] Deepa Bharath. "Blacks Most Targeted," *Orange County Register*. Santa Ana, CA Sept. 26, 2010.

[354] Oralandar Brand-Williams. "Rights Office Looks at Beating," *Detroit News*. Detroit, MI Sept. 12, 2009 pg A3.

[355] Nick Meyer. "No Local Hate Crime," *Arab American News*. Dearborn, MI, Oct. 16, 2009, v. 25, iss 1235, pg. 19.

[356] Ibid.

[357] Ibid.

[358] Oralandar Brand-Williams. "Rights Office Looks at Beating," pg A3.

[359] Nick Meyer. "No Local Hate Crime," pg. 19.

[360] Ibid.

[361] Ibid.

[362] "National Briefing/New York; Bullying," *Los Angeles Times*. Los Angeles, CA Oct. 12, 2010, pg. A11.

[363] Ibid.

[364] Ibid.

[365] Ibid.

[366] "Four Teens Face Hate Charges," *AM New York*. New York, NY Oct. 12, 2010, pg. 3.

[367] Ibid.

[368] Marvin Scott. "Brief: 4 Teens Charged," *McClatchy-Tribune Business News*. DC Oct. 11, 2010.

[369] "CAIR: Texas Muslim Student," US Newswire. DC Feb. 4, 2010.

[370] Patrik Jonsson. "Bacon Attack," *Christian Science Monitor*. Boston, MA Oct. 15, 2010.

[371] Jason Woods. "Chaplains Decry Vandalism," *Boston Globe*. Boston, MA March 11, 2010, pg. B4.

[372] James Twitchwell. Branded Nation. (New York: Simon & Schuster, 2004): 109-192.

[373] Lisa Fernandez. "Sunnyvale: Man Attacked For Being Muslim," *Oakland Tribune*. Oakland, CA June 14, 2010.

[374] Ibid.

[375] Jeremy Gorner. "Muslim Student's Exhibit Defaced," *Chicago Tribune*. Chicago, IL May 13, 2010, pg. 1.7.

[376] Ali estimates that 9/11 backlash caused a 1700% increase in hate crimes in the U.S. Although many scholars find this figure to be reasonable, writers seeking to trivialize the 9/11 backlash dramatically underestimated the numbers of bias-motivated hate crimes triggered by the terrorist attacks. Without any evidence, *Florida Ledger* writer Nadine Smith estimates that the U.S. Muslim community experienced a 50% increase in hate crimes in the aftermath of 9/11. (See: Nadine Smith. "Polk Murder Points to Hate Crime," *Ledger*. Lakeland, FL Feb. 27, 2009.) Other writers have arrived at much higher estimates of the increase in hate crimes following 9/11. Gregory Elder, a history professor at Riverside Community College, estimates that hate crimes against Muslims

rose 7,000% since 2001. (See Gregory Elder. "Sept. 11, Eight Years Later," *Redlands Daily Facts*. Redlands, CA Sept. 9, 2009.)

[377] Natasha Dado. "Chicago Muslim," *Arab American News*. Dearborn, MI May 15, 2010 v. 26, iss 1266 pg. 18.

[378] Jessica Simeone. "Bye, Bye Birdie," *New York Post*. New York, NY April 6, 2011, pg. 10.

[379] "11 Year Old American Schoolboy Charged with anti-Muslim Hate Crime," *Hindustan Times*. New Delhi, India April 4, 2011.

[380] Edgar Sandoval, Matthew Lysiak, Rich Shapiro, and Meredith Kolodner. "Called Her a Terrorist: Muslim Girl Tells of Attacks by Her Two S.I. Schoolmates," *New York Daily News*. New York, NY April 1, 2011, pg. 12.

[381] Anthony Destefano. "NYC In Brief," *Newsday*. Long Island, New York. April 6, 2011, pg. A41.

[382] Jessica Simeone. "Bye, Bye Birdie," pg. 10.

[383] Ibid.

[384] "11 Year Old American Schoolboy Charged with anti-Muslim Hate Crime,"

[385] Hannah Rappleye, Doug Auer, Dan Mangan. "Li'l Angry Bird," *New York Post*. New York, NY April 1, 2011, pg. 7.

[386] "11 Year Old American Schoolboy Charged with anti-Muslim Hate Crime,"; "Child Arrested in Attack on Muslim Girl," *Jakarta Post*. Jakarta, Indonesia. April 12, 2011.

[387] Mauricio Guerrero. "Clear Lake Muslims Feel Safe," *Houston Chronicle*. Houston, TX May 12, 2011, pg. 1.

[388] Ibid.

[389] Ellyn Fortino. "Garfield Park School Marks 9/11 Anniversary: Chicago Firefighters Share Their Grief With Students," *Austin Weekly News*. Austin, TX Sept. 14, 2011.

[390] David Hurst. "School Changes Play Plans," *Tribune-Democrat*. Johnstown, PA Sept. 19, 2011.

[391] Adam Hetrick. "Western Pennsylvania School Cancels *Kismet* in Wake of 9/11 Anniversary," www.playbill.com, Sept. 20, 2011. "School Pulls Musical 'Kismet' After 9/11 Complaints," MSNBC, www.msnbc.msn.com, Sept. 20, 2011.

[392] Ibid.

[393] "10th Anniversary of Sept. 11, 2001: USC Experts Available to Discuss Aspects of 9/11 and U.S. Response," USC News Release, Sept. 2, 2011. www.usc.edu/usnews/newsroom.

Chapter Seven:

[1] Karen Robinson-Jacobs. "Emerging Community," *Los Angeles Times*. Los Angeles, CA Sept. 24, 2001, pg. C1.

[2] Ibid.

[3] Ibid.

[4] Jack Shaheen. *Reel Bad Arabs*. (Media Education Foundation, 2006).

[5] Tim Jon Semmerling. 'Evil' Arabs in American Popular Film. (Austin: University of Texas Press, 2006): 60.

[6] Ibid.

[7] Jack Shaheen. Reel Bad Arabs, pg. 243-4.

[8] Ibid.

[9] Ibid, pg. 356.

[10] Ibid.

[11] Ibid.

[12] Troy Anderson. "Hate Crimes Up," *Daily News*. Los Angeles, CA Dec. 21, 2001, pg. N3.

[13] Thanassis Cambanis. "UPS Sued over 9/11 Hate Crime," *Boston Globe*. Boston, MA May 17, 2002, pg. B2.

[14] Ibid.

[15] Ellen Barry. "Reilly Puts Focus on Hate Crimes," *Boston Globe*. Boston, MA Sept. 25, 2001, pg. B1.

[16] Ibid.

[17] Ellen Barry. "Tensions High," *Boston Globe*. Boston, MA Sept. 17, 2001, pg. B1.

[18] Ibid.

[19] Ed Hayward. "Attack on America," *Boston Herald*. Boston, MA Sept. 29, 2001, pg. 6.

[20] Editorial. "Misplaced Anger," *Boston Globe*. Boston, MA Sept. 14, 2001, pg. A22.

[21] Ellen Barry. "Reilly Puts Focus on Hate Crimes," pg. B1.

[22] Ellen Barry. "Tensions High," pg. B1.

[23] Ibid.

[24] Ibid.

[25] Ellen Barry. "Reilly Puts Focus on Hate Crimes," pg. B1.

[26] Ibid.

[27] Richard Louv. "Security Experts," *San Diego Union-Tribune*. San Diego, CA Oct. 14, 2001, pg. A12.

[28] Michael Laris. "Supervisors Try Getting Back to Work," *Washington Post*. DC Sept. 20, 2001, pg. T1.

[29] Pat Burson. "Terrorist Attacks," *Newsday*. Long Island, NY Sept. 13, 2001, pg. W53.

[30] Ellen Barry. "Reilly Puts Focus on Hate Crimes," pg. B1.

[31] Elizabeth Crowley. "Shafts of Hate," *Patriot-Ledger*. Quincy, MA Sept. 19, 2001, pg. 9.

[32] Dina Gerdeman. "Reality Check," *Patriot-Ledger*. Quincy, MA March 1, 2002, pg. 1.

[33] Ibid.

[34] Ibid.

[35] Ibid.

[36] Ibid.

[37] Elizabeth Crowley. "Shafts of Hate," pg. 9.

[38] Editorial. "Misplaced Anger," pg. A22.

[39] Ibid.

[40] Elizabeth Crowley. "Shafts of Hate," pg. 9.

[41] Dianne Williamson. "City People," *Telegram and Gazette*. Worcester, MA Sept. 18, 2001, pg. B1.

[42] Somini Sengupta. "Sept. 11 Attack," *New York Times*. New York, NY, Oct. 10, 2001, pg. B1.

[43] "Roundup," *Xinhua News Agency*. CEIS. Woodside, Sept. 14, 2001, pg. 1.

[44] Editorial. "Misplaced Anger," pg. A22.

[45] Somini Sengupta. "Sept. 11 Attack," pg. B1.

[46] "Advice to Educators," *ADC Times*. DC Sept. 30, 2001, v. 21, iss 4 pg. 3.

[47] Kieran Crowley, Angela Allen, and Brad Hunter. "Arabs Under Siege Here," *New York Post*. New York, NY Sept. 13, 2001, pg. 37.

[48] Ibid.

[49] Viji Sundaram. "Reports of Hate Crimes," *India-West*. San Leandro, CA Sept. 28, 2001, v. 26, iss 47 pg. A1.

[50] Adrian Leung. "South Asian Journalists Discuss Backlash," *Asianweek*. Sept. 26, 2001, v. 23, iss 5 pg. 9.

[51] Ibid.

[52] Jennifer Levitz. "One Year After," *Providence Journal*. Providence, RI Sept. 14, 2002, pg. A1; Tanya Weinberg. "Many Muslims No Longer Feel Safe in the U.S." *South Florida Sentinel*. Sept. 5, 2002, pg. 1.

[53] Ibid.

[54] Ibid.

[55] Jennifer Levitz. "One Year After," pg. A1.

[56] Ibid.

[57] Ibid.

[58] Ibid.

[59] Ibid.

[60] Lenora Chu. "Hate Around the Nation," *Asianweek*. San Francisco, CA Oct. 3, 2001, v 23, iss 6 pg. 9.

[61] Ibid.

[62] Ibid.

[63] *ADC Times*. DC Sept. 30, 2001, v. 21, iss 4 pg. 3.

[64] Hanna Rosin. "For Arab-Americans, A Familiar Backlash," *Washington Post*. DC Sept. 13, 2001, pg. A26.

[65] Ibid.

[66] James Gill. "Boycott is Hateful," *Times-Picayune*. New Orleans, LA Sept. 28, 2001, pg. B7.

[67] Thanassis Cambanis. "Threat to Arab-American Admitted," *Boston Globe*. Boston, MA June 7, 2002, pg. B1.

[68] Ibid.

[69] "Attack Backlash Fades," *Washington Times*. DC Feb. 11, 2002.

[70] Ibid.

[71] Ibid.

[72] Ibid.

[73] Jo Becker, Phyong Ly. "Sikhs Campaign Against Hate," *Washington Post*. DC Sept. 24, 2001, pg. B1.

[74] Stephen Hegarty. "9/11 Fuels Hate Crimes," *St. Petersburg Times*. St. Petersburg, FL Aug. 30, 2002, pg. 1A.

[75] Tanya Weinberg. "Many Muslims No Longer Feel Safe in the U.S." pg. 1.

[76] Ibid.

[77] "We the People," *Times-Picayune*. New Orleans, LA Sept. 19, 2001, pg. B6.

[78] Peter Reichard. "Muslim Owned," *New Orleans City Business*. Metairie, LA Sept. 24, 2001, v. 22 iss 13, pg. 4.

[79] Ibid.

[80] Ibid.

[81] Ibid.

[82] Ibid.

[83] Bob Anderson. "Attack on Café," *Advocate*. Baton Rouge, LA Sept. 26, 2001, pg. 8A.

[84] Ibid.

[85] Ibid.

[86] Ibid.

[87] James Gill. "Boycott is Hateful," pg. B7.

[88] Ibid.

[89] Ibid.

[90] Aisha Sultan. "Muslims in the St. Louis Area," *Post-Dispatch*. St. Louis, MO Sept. 13, 2001, pg. B2.

[91] Ibid.

[92] Editorials. "Americans Must Take Time," "Hate Hurts," *Plain Dealer*. Cleveland, OH Sept. 19, 2001, pg. B10.

[93] Ibid.

[94] Robert Smith. "Local Arab Americans," *Plain Dealer*. Cleveland, OH Sept. 14, 2001, pg. A15.

[95] Lou Grieco, James Cummings. "Hate Crimes Reported in Valley," *Dayton Daily News*. Dayton, OH Sept. 14, 2001, pg. 2A.

[96] Ibid.

[97] Ibid.

[98] Ibid.

[99] "Protests at Mosque," *Arab-American View*. Orlando Park, IL Nov. 5, 2001, v. 2, iss 11 pg. 1.

[100] Ashok Easwaran. "Hate Crimes Grip Chicago," *India Abroad*. New York, NY. Sept. 28, 2001, v. 31, iss 52, pg. 4.

[101] William Porter. "Bloomington, Indiana." *Denver Post*. Denver, CO Sept. 10, 2006, pg. 7.

[102] Tonya Weger. "Arson Raises Questions," *South Bend Tribune*. South Bend, IN Oct. 2, 2001.

[103] Ibid.

[104] Ibid.

[105] Ibid.

[106] Gary Grass, Ammar Askari. "U.S. Must Recognize Loyalty of Citizens of Arab Descent,'" *Capital Times*. Madison, WI Sept. 11, 2003, pg. 12A.

[107] Ibid.

[108] Nicole Marshall. "Assaults, Hit-and-Run possible Hate Crimes," *Tulsa World*. Tulsa, OK Sept. 16, 2001, pg. 13.

[109] Ibid.

[110] Ibid.

[111] Ibid.

[112] Richard Serrano. "Deluge of Hate Crimes," *Los Angeles Times*. Los Angeles, CA July 6, 2002, pg. A8.

[113] Deborah Bulkeley. "Muslims in U.S. See Little 9/11 Backlash," *Deseret Morning News*, Salt Lake City, UT Sept. 9, 2006, pg. E1.

[114] Ibid.

[115] Richard Serrano. "Deluge of Hate Crimes," pg. A8.

[116] Ibid.

[117] Jeff Gettleman. "Response to Terror," *Los Angeles Times*. Los Angeles, CA Oct. 25, 2001, pg A12.

[118] Deborah Bulkeley. "Muslims in U.S. See Little 9/11 Backlash," pg. E1.

[119] Jeannine Relly. "Immigrants and Hostility," *Arizona Daily Star*. Tucson, AZ Oct. 2, 2001, pg. D1.

[120] Ibid.

[121] Lenora Chu. "Hate Around the Nation," pg. 9.

[122] K.C. Mason. "Hate Crimes," *Albuquerque Journal*. Albuquerque, NM Sept. 26, 2001, pg. 1.

[123] Ibid.

[124] Ahan Kim. "58% in Poll Want Special Security," *Austin American Statesman*. Austin, TX Sept. 19, 2001, pg. A6.

[125] Emanuel Gonzales. "Tri-Faith Group," *San Antonio Express-News*. San Antonio, TX. Oct. 4, 2001, pg. 5B.

[126] Ibid.

[127] "Group Hatred is Un-American," *ADL On the Frontline*. New York, NY Fall 2001, v. 11 iss 7,8,9 pg. S1.

[128] Dale Lezon. "America Responds," *Houston Chronicle*. Houston, TX Sept. 19, 2001, pg. A27.

[129] Ibid.

[130] Roma Khanna. "Hate Crimes Peak After 9/11," *Houston Chronicle*. Houston, TX Dec. 14, 2001, pg. A37.

[131] Richard Serrano. "Deluge of Hate Crimes," pg. A8.

[132] Jonathan Osborne. "Carpet Store Torched," *Austin American Statesman*. Austin, TX Sept. 25, 2001, pg. B1.

[133] Ibid.

[134] Ibid.

[135] Aretha Williams. "Fighting Arab Stereotypes," *San Antonio Express-News*. San Antonio, TX March 9, 2003, pg. 1K.

[136] Larry Stammer. "Turbans," *Los Angeles Times*. Los Angeles, CA Sept. 12, 2001, pg. A38.

[137] Ibid.

[138] Scott Farwell, Sharyn Obsatz, and Mark Acosta. "Two Weeks Later," *Press Enterprise*. Riverside, CA Sept. 25, 2001, pg. A1.

[139] Ibid.

[140] Anna Gorman. "2 Men are Charged," *Los Angeles Times*. Los Angeles, CA Sept. 29, 2001, pg. B6.

[141] Ibid.

[142] Lynda Gorov. "Afghan Community in Fremont Angry." *Boston Globe*. Boston, MA Sept. 24, 2001, pg. A11.

[143] Ibid.

[144] Ibid.

[145] Jose Arballo, Jr. "No Spike in Hate Crime," *Press Enterprise*. Riverside, CA Sept. 27, 2001, pg. 11A.

[146] "Group Hatred is Un-American," pg. S1.

[147] Kathleen Sullivan. "Battling Backlash," *Chronicle*. San Francisco, CA Sept. 19, 2001, pg. A15.

[148] Ibid.

[149] Ibid.

[150] Kristen Green. "Arab-Americans' Routine," *San Diego Union-Tribune*. San Diego, CA Oct. 21, 2001, pg. B1.

[151] Ibid.

[152] Barbara Kingsley, Charles Adamson, and Vik Jolly. "Restaurant Fire Fuels Hate," *Orange County Register*. Santa Ana, CA Sept. 28, 2001, pg. 1.

[153] Ibid.

[154] Ibid.

[155] Ibid.

[156] Jerry Hicks. "Fire Guts Part of a Pakistani Eatery," *Los Angeles Times*. Los Angeles, CA Sept. 28, 2001, pg. B8.

[157] Barbara Kingsley, Charles Adamson, and Vik Jolly. "Restaurant Fire Fuels Hate," pg. 1.

[158] Jerry Hicks. "Fire Guts Part of a Pakistani Eatery," pg. B8

[159] Ibid.

[160] Ibid.

[161] Ibid.

[162] Ibid.

[163] Ibid.

[164] Ibid.

[165] Vik Jolly. "Hate Crimes," *Orange County Register*. Orange County, CA Sept. 5, 2002, pg. 1.

[166] Jerry Hicks. "Fire Guts Part of a Pakistani Eatery," pg. B8.

[167] Ibid.

[168] Vik Jolly. "Hate Crimes," pg. 1.

[169] Larry Welborn. "Man Pleads Guilty," *Orange County Register*. Santa Ana, CA June 15, 2002, pg. 1.

[170] Elizabeth Bell. "Second Yemeni Shot in Valley," *San Francisco Chronicle*. San Francisco, CA Dec. 8, 2001, pg. A9.

[171] Lisa Tsering. "Bay Area Businesses," *India-West*. San Leandro, CA Oct. 5, 2001, v. 26, Iss. 48, pg. B5.

[172] Peter Callaghan. "Those Who React By Targeting," *Tacoma News Tribune*. Tacoma, WA Sept. 16, 2001, pg. A1.

[173] "Attack on America," *Yakima Herald*. Yakima, WA Sept. 19, 2001, pg. C4.

[174] Peter Callaghan. "Those Who React By Targeting," pg. A1.

[175] Lenora Chu. "Hate Around the Nation," pg. 9.

[176] Ibid.

[177] Ibid.

[178] Ibid.

[179] Saeed Ahmad. "Retaliation," *Atlantic Constitution*. Atlanta, GA Sept. 18, 2001, pg. B4.

[180] Deborah Kong. "Anti-Muslim Backlash May Have Peaked." *Columbian*. Vancouver, WA Sept. 30, 2001, pg. A5.

[181] Peter Reichard. "Muslim Owned," pg. 4.

[182] Ibid.

[183] Ibid.

[184] Ibid.

[185] Pat Burson. "Terrorist Attacks," pg. W53.

[186] Editorial. "Misplaced Anger," pg. A22.

[187] Ellen Barry. "Tensions High," pg. B1.

[188] Ibid.

[189] Alex Taylor. "Area Mideast Business People," *Austin American Statesman*. Austin, TX Sept. 22, 2001 G1.

[190] Nicole Marshall. "Assaults, Hit-and Run Possible Hate Crimes," pg. 13.

[191] Ibid.

[192] Kendra Hamilton. "Campuses Unite," *Black Issues in Higher Education*. Reston. Oct. 11, 2001, v. 18, iss 17, pg. 32-4.

[193] Ruth Krause. "Shootings Seen as Possible Hate Crime," *Post-Tribune*. Gary, IN Dec. 13, 2001, pg. A1, 4.

[194] Ibid.

[195] Ibid.

[196] Ibid.

[197] Mike Nichols. "In United Stand," *Milwaukee Journal Sentinel*. Milwaukee, WI Sept. 20, 2001,pg. 1B.

[198] Ibid.

[199] Ibid.

[200] Anna Gorman. "2 Men are Charged," pg. B6.

[201] Ibid.

[202] Jenifer Hanrahan. "Two Families Cope," *San Diego Union Tribune*. San Diego, CA Sept. 29, 2001, pg. E1.

[203] Ibid.

[204] Ibid.

[205] Ibid.

[206] Ibid.

[207] Ibid.

[208] Jeannine Relly. "Immigrants and Hostility," pg. D1.

[209] Ibid.

[210] Ibid.

[211] Ibid.

[212] Anindita Ramaswamy. "Sikhs and Muslims," *News India-Times*. New York. Sept. 21, 2001, v. 32, iss 34, pg. 10.

[213] Sukhjit Purewal. "We are Sikh," *India Abroad*. New York, NY Sept. 28, 2001, v. 31, iss 52, pg. 37.

[214] Ibid.

[215] Viji Sundaram. "Hate Crime Fears Rise," *India-West*. San Leandro, CA Sept. 28, 2001, v. 26, iss 47, pg. A1.

[216] Jeannine Relly. "Immigrants and Hostility," pg. D1.

[217] Ibid.

[218] Richard Louv. "Security Experts," pg. A12.

[219] Ibid.

[220] David Zahniser. "Hate Crimes Against Muslims Rise," *Daily Breeze*. Torrance, CA Dec. 21, 2001, pg. A3.

[221] Randy Kennedy. "Drivers Say They Risk Violence," *New York Times*. New York, NY Sept. 24, 2001, pg. B8.

[222] Ibid.

[223] Ibid.

[224] Ibid.

[225] Ibid.

[226] Ibid.

[227] Ibid.

[228] Ibid.

[229] Ibid.

[230] Ibid.

[231] "Sikhs and Immigration Reform," *India-West*. San Leandro, CA June 2, 2006, v. 31, iss 28, pg. A5.

[232] Ibid.

[233] Ibid.

[234] Ibid.

[235] Somini Sengupta. "Sept. 11 Attack," *New York Times*. New York, NY, Oct. 10, 2001, pg. B1.

[236] Michael Winerip. "The High Cost," *New York Times*. New York, NY Oct. 21, 2001, pg. 1.33.

[237] Ibid.

[238] Ibid.

[239] Ibid.

[240] Diana Fishlock. "Hate Crimes Increase," *Patriot-News*. Harrisburg, PA Oct. 12, 2001, pg. B1.

[241] Gary Grass, Ammar Askari. "U.S. Must Recognize Loyalty of Citizens of Arab Descent,"' pg. 12A.

[242] "California Man Charged With Assaulting Cabbie," *Post Intelligencer*. Seattle, WA Sept. 19, 2001, pg. B2.

[243] Ibid.

[244] Guy Taylor. "Hate Acts Against Muslims Subside," *Washington Times*. DC June 25, 2002, pg. B1.

[245] Saeed Ahmad. "Retaliation," pg. B4.

[246] Karen Robinson-Jacobs. "Emerging Community," pg. C1.

[247] Laurie Goodstein, Tamar Lewin. "Victims of Mistaken Identity," *New York Times*. New York, NY Sept. 19, 2001, pg. A1.

[248] Tomoeh Murakami. "Arab-American Cabbies," *Plain Dealer*. Cleveland, OH Sept. 19, 2001, pg. A18.

[249] Ibid.

[250] Ibid.

[251] Randy Kennedy. "Drivers Say They Risk Violence," pg. B8.

[252] Geoff Boucher. "Crossover Dreams Grounded." *Los Angeles Times*. Los Angeles, CA Sept. 21, 2001, pg. F1.

[253] Johnny Edwards. "Hate Criminals," *Augusta Chronicle*. Augusta, GA Sept. 16, 2001, pg. A14.

[254] "DOJ Announces Successful Hate Crime Prosecutions," *ADC Times*. DC April 30, 2002, vol 21 iss 7 pg. 13.

[255] John Iwasaki. "Hateful Assault," *Seattle Post-Intelligencer*. Seattle, WA Sept. 11, 2003, pg. A10.

[256] Ibid.

[257] Ibid.

[258] Ibid.

[259] Ibid.

[260] Ibid.

[261] Ibid.

[262] Marsha Ginsburg. "Shattered Dream," *San Francisco Chronicle*. San Francisco, CA Dec. 29, 2001.

[263] Ibid.

[264] Ibid.

[265] Ibid.

[266] Beth Shuster. "U.S. Strikes Back," *Los Angeles Times*. Los Angeles, CA Oct. 11, 2001, pg. A1.

[267] Jerry Seper. "Two Leaders of Jewish Group Arrested," *Washington Times*. DC Dec. 13, 2001, pg. B1.

[268] Tom Droege. "Doctor Enters Innocent Plea," *Tulsa World*. Tulsa, OK Nov. 7, 2001, pg. 13.

[269] Kristen Green. "Afghan Cabbie Says He Was Beaten," *San Diego Union-Tribune*. San Diego, CA Oct. 25, 2001, pg. B2.

[270] Aldrin Brown. "Hate Crimes," *Orange County Register.* Santa Ana, CA April 12, 2002, pg. A3

[271] Ibid.

[272] Teresa Watanabe. "Immigration Stories," *Los Angeles Times.* Los Angeles, CA Sept. 14, 2003, pg. B1.

[273] "2 Men Sentenced to Prison for Hate Crimes," *New York Times.* New York, NY Jan. 9, 2002, pg. A12.

[274] Sukhjit Purewal. "We Are Sikh," pg. 4.

[275] Ibid.

[276] Ibid.

[277] Ibid.

[278] Ibid.

[279] Viji Sundaram. "Misplaced Anger," *India-West.* San Leandro, CA Dec. 14, 2001, v. 27, iss 6, pg. A22.

[280] Orith Goldberg. "Valley Sikh's Beating," *Daily News.* Los Angeles, CA Dec. 8, 2001, pg. N1.

[281] Elizabeth Bell. "Second Yemeni Shot in Valley," pg. A9.

[282] Ibid.

[283] Ibid.

[284] Eric Lichtblau. "Bias Against U.S. Arabs," *Los Angeles Times.* Los Angeles, CA Feb. 10, 2002.

[285] Ibid.

[286] Barbara Karkabi. "Learning from the Pain," *Houston Chronicle.* Houston, TX Oct. 7, 2001, pg. E1.

[287] Allan Turner and Dale Lezon. "Our Changed World," *Houston Chronicle.* Houston, TX Sept. 8, 2002, pg. A33.

[288] Ibid.

[289] Ibid.

[290] Ibid.

[291] Roma Khanna. "Hate Crimes Peak After 9/11," pg. A37.

[292] Rachel Gordon. "Victims of Hate," *San Francisco Chronicle.* San Francisco, CA Jan. 11, 2002, pg. A1

[293] Ibid.

[294] Ibid.

[295] Ibid.

[296] Jack Shaheen. Guilty. (Northampton, MA: Olive Branch Press, 2008): 175.

[297] Tom Ramstack. "Attack Backlash Fades," *Washington Times.* DC Feb. 11, 2002.

[298] Ibid.

[299] Ryan Kim. "Cops Call Rape a Hate Crime," *San Francisco Chronicle.* San Francisco, CA Sept. 5, 2002, pg. A19.

[300] Ibid.

[301] Interfaith tensions South Asian immigrants in the U.S. have persisted for decades. A particularly vicious hate crime took place on August 15, 1993, when Muhammed Ashraf opened fire on Sikh and Hindu participants at a New York celebration of India's 47th year of Independence. See "Pakistani Shoots at India Day Parade," *News India-Times.* New York, NY Aug. 20, 1993, v. 23, iss. 34, pg. 1.

[302] Ryan Kim. "Cops Call Rape a Hate Crime," pg. A19.

[303] Suleman Din. "California Drug Store Rape," *India Abroad.* New York, NY Sept. 27, 2002, v. 32, iss 52, pg. A14.

[304] Ibid.

[305] Ibid.

[306] Tanya Weinberg. "Many Muslims No Longer Feel Safe in the U.S.," pg. 1.

[307] Ibid.

[308] Sheila Poole. "Showdown with Iraq," *Atlanta Journal-Constitution*. Atlanta, GA March 19, 2003, pg. A14.

[309] Ibid.

[310] Mary Beth Sheridan. "Bias Against Muslims Up 70%," *Washington Post*. DC May 3, 2004, pg. A12.

[311] Ibid.

[312] Silja Talvi. "And Justice for All," *Colorlines*. Winter 2002/2003. Oakland, CA Jan. 31, 2003, v. 5, iss 4, pg. 18.

[313] Ibid.

[314] Aretha Williams. "Take Steps to Fight," *San Antonio Express-News*. San Antonio, TX March 9, 2003, pg. 11C.

[315] Jeff Jardine. "Some 'Patriots' Are Merely Bigots," *Modesto Bee*. Modesto, CA Sept. 14, 2003, pg. B1.

[316] Ibid.

[317] Ibid.

[318] Michael Janofsky. "War Brings New Surge of Anxiety," *New York Times*. New York, NY March 29, 2003, pg. B15. "Indiana Muslim Burned," *Muslim Journal*. Chicago, IL April 11, 2003, pg. 3.

[319] Brian Kluepfel. "Upswing in Hate Crimes," *Asianweek*. San Francisco, CA April 9, 2003, v. 24, iss 32, pg. 14.

[320] Ibid.

[321] Michael Potts. "Sikh Still Fearful," *India-West*. San Leandro, CA Aug. 18, 2006, v. 31 iss 39 pg. A42.

[322] Ibid.

[323] Mantoshe Devji. "Sikh Shot," *India-West*. San Leandro, CA May 23, 2003 v. 28, iss 29 pg. A1.

[324] Ibid.

[325] Michael Potts. "Sikh Still Fearful," pg. A42.

[326] Ibid.

[327] George Joseph. "Phoenix Hate Crime," *India Abroad*. May 30, 2005, v. 33 iss 35, pg. A4.

[328] Mantoshe Devji. "Sikh Shot," pg. A1.

[329] Greg Frost. "No Discrimination," *Birmingham Post*. Birmingham, UK. July 24, 2003, pg. 11.

[330] Ibid.

[331] Arthur Pais. "'I Thought They Were Taking Me to the Sea to Dump Me,' Saurabh Bhalerao Recalls Hate Attack," *India Abroad*. New York, NY July 11, 2003, v. 33, iss 41, pg. A1

[332] Anuradha Kher. "Hate Crimes Against Hindis," *Noticias Financieras*. Miami, FL Nov. 21, 2007, pg. 1.

[333] Greg Frost. "No Discrimination," pg. 11.

[334] Arthur Pais. "'I Thought They Were Taking Me to the Sea to Dump Me,'" pg. A1.

[335] Ibid.

[336] Ibid.

[337] Ibid.

[338] Ibid.

[339] Ibid.

[340] Arthur Pais. "New Bedford Rallies," *India Abroad*. New York, NY July 11, 2003, v. 33, iss 41, pg. A5.

[341] Ibid.

[342] Greg Frost. "No Discrimination," pg. 11.

[343] Arthur Pais. "7 × Years in Jail for Bhalerao Attacker," *India Abroad*. New York, NY April 16, 2004, v. 34, iss 29, pg. A4.

[344] Ibid.

[345] Teresa Watanabe. "Immigration Stories," pg. B1.

[346] Jeet Thayil. "Third Sikh Shot in Arizona," *India Abroad*. New York, NY Oct. 3, 2003, v. 34, iss 1 pg. A1.

[347] Ibid.

[348] Ibid.

[349] "Sikh Taxi Driver Assaulted in Seattle," *Sikh Coalition Newsletter*. www.sikhcoalition.org, Nov. 2, 2003.

[350] Ibid.

[351] "Seattle Taxi Cab Attack," *Sikh Coalition Newsletter*. www.sikhcoalition.org, Nov. 18, 2003.

[352] Hardeep Rekhi. "Outraged Sikh," *Northwest Asian Weekly*. Seattle, WA Dec. 8, 2007, v. 26, iss 50 pg. 11-12.

[353] Arvind Padmanabhan. "16 Year Old Arrested in California," *News India-Times*. New York, NY Feb. 13, 2004, v. 35, iss 7 pg. 10.

[354] Ibid.

[355] Kathy Steele. "Sikhs Fight Post-Attack Prejudice," *Tampa Tribune*. Tampa, FL March 1, 2004, pg. 4.

[356] Ibid.

[357] Ibid.

[358] Ibid.

[359] Kevin Graham. "Police Seek Three," *St. Petersburg Times*. St. Petersburg, FL April 9, 2004, pg. 3B.

[360] Ibid.

[361] Maro Robbins. Sonja Garza, Tracy Hamilton. "Suspect Arrested at Scene of Fire," *San Antonio Express-News*. San Antonio, TX April 10, 2004, pg. 1A.

[362] Ibid.

[363] Ibid.

[364] Ibid.

[365] Ibid.

[366] Ibid.

[367] Ibid.

[368] Ibid.

[369] Ibid.

[370] AP. "Arson Suspect is Arrested At the Scene of a San Antonio Blaze," *Corpus Christi Caller-Times*. Corpus Christi, TX April 11, 2004, pg. A12.

[371] Maro Robbins, Sonja Garza, Tracy Hamilton. "Suspect Arrested at Scene of Fire," pg. 1A.

[372] Aretha Williams. "More Ideas," *San Antonio Express-News*. San Antonio, TX June 14, 2004, pg. 9C.

[373] Guillermo Contreras. "Getting Tough," *San Antonio Express-News*. San Antonio, TX May 8, 2007, pg. 1A.

[374] Ryan Kim. "Attacked for Art," *San Francisco Chronicle*. San Francisco, CA May 30, 2004, pg. B2.

[375] Michael Romanowski. "Textbook Omissions and 9/11," *Clearinghouse*. DC July 2009, v. 82, iss 6, pg. 290-6.

[376] Ryan Kim. "Attacked for Art," pg. B2.

[377] Ibid.

[378] Lisa Leff. "Painting of Prisoner Abuse," *Chicago Sun-Times*. Chicago, IL May 30, 2004, pg. 58.

[379] Ryan Kim. "Attacked for Art," pg. B2.

[380] Ibid.

[381] "Reaction to Colwell Painting Forces Owner to Quit," *Comics Reporter*. www.comicsreporter.com, May 26, 2004. Updated in June 2004.

[382] Ibid.

[383] Zachary Mider. "New School," *Providence Journal*. Providence, RI Aug. 20, 2004, pg. B1.

[384] US Newswire. DC July 27, 2004, pg. 1.

[385] Ron Orozco. "Calm After the Storm," *Fresno Bee*. Fresno, CA Sept. 11, 2004, pg. H1.

[386] Arun Venugopal. "Vandals Set Fire," *India Abroad*. New York, NY Dec. 10, 2004, v. 35, iss 11, pg. A6.

[387] Ibid.

[388] Meredith Bonny. "Enon Arson Probed," *Richmond Times-Dispatch*. Richmond, VA Dec. 1, 2004, pg. B2.

[389] Arun Venugopal. "Vandals Set Fire," pg. A6.

[390] Sushma Subramanian. "Graffiti Victim," *Orange County Register*. Santa Ana, CA July 6, 2006, pg. 1.

[391] Ibid.

[392] Ibid.

[393] Jack Shaheen. Guilty, pg. 106.

[394] Ibid, pg. 109.

[395] Tom Gordon. "Man of Arab Descent Shot; Suspect Held," *Birmingham News*. Birmingham, AL Feb. 25, 2006.

[396] Ibid.

[397] Ibid.

[398] Jack Shaheen. Guilty, pg. 136-7.

[399] Ibid, pg. 104.

[400] Mike Salinero. "2 Charged in Hate Crime," *Tampa Tribune*. Tampa, FL Sept. 23, 2006, pg. 4.

[401] Ibid.

[402] Ibid.

[403] Larry Miller. "Anti-Muslim Attacks Subdued," *Tribune*. Philadelphia, PA Sept. 11, 2007, v. 123, iss 85, pg. 4A.

[404] "Philadelphia Woman Sentenced," PR Newswire. New York. Oct. 24, 2007.

[405] Shelley Murphy. "Man Charged With Making Threats," *Boston Globe*. Boston, MA May 1, 2008, pg. B1.

[406] Ibid.

[407] Ibid.

[408] Jack Shaheen. Guilty, pg. 113.

[409] Ibid, pg. 105.

[410] Ibid, pg. 125.

[411] Ibid.

[412] "NY Man Faces Hate Crime Charges," *India-West*. San Leandro, CA March 30, 2007, v. 32, iss 19, pg. A32.

[413] Ibid.

[414] "Neighbor: Store's Owner Has Been Target Before," KETV Channel 7, Omaha, NB www.ketv.com, Feb. 19, 2007.

[415]"Robbery, Explosion May Be Hate Crime, Police Say," KETV Channel 7, Omaha, NB www.ketv.com, Feb. 20, 2007.

[416] "NAACP Asks Police to Investigate Possible Hate Crime," KETV Channel 7, Omaha, NB www.ketv.com, Feb. 21, 2007.

[417] "North Omaha Store Torn Down After Fire," KETV Channel 7, Omaha, NB www.ketv.com, March 14, 2007.

[418] Jennifer Maloney. "Victim of Hatred," *Newsday*. Long Island, NY Sept. 17, 2007, pg. A3.

[419] Michael Frazier. "2 Men Sought in Nail Salon Bias Attack," *Newsday*. Long Island, NY Sept. 18, 2007, A18.

[420] Jennifer Maloney. "Victim of Hatred," pg. A3.

[421] Lisa Tsering. "Cab Driver Victim," *India-West*. San Leandro, CA Nov. 30, 2007, v. 33, iss 1, pg. A1, A28.

[422] Ibid.

[423] Ibid.

[424] Hardeep Rekhi. "Outraged Sikh," pg. 11-12.

[425] Tracy Johnson. "Taxi Driver Forgives," *Seattle Post-Intelligencer*. Seattle, WA April 19, 2008, pg. B3.

[426] Christine Clarridge. "Remorse, Forgiveness," *Seattle Times*. Seattle, WA April 19, 2008, pg. B3.

[427] Tracy Johnson. "Taxi Driver Forgives," pg. B3.

[428] Ibid.

[429] Ibid.

[430] Tim Harlow. "Hate Crime," *Star Tribune*. Minneapolis, MN Feb. 9, 2008.

[431] Ibid.

[432] "Kansas Muslim Attacked With Molotov Cocktail," PR Newswire. NY. April 17, 2008.

[433] Ibid.

[434] Ibid.

[435] Mary Warner. "Graffiti Dismays Plant Workers," *Patriot-News*. Harrisburg, PA Aug. 30, 2008.

[436] Cindy Wolf. "Cash, Lives for Taking at City's Gritty Convenience Stores, Where 2 Were Slain Saturday," *Commercial Appeal*. www.commercialappeal.com, Feb, 3, 2009.

[437] Joyce Peterson. "Middle Eastern Clerks Shot in Memphis: Robberies or Hate Crimes?" My Eyewitness News, Feb. 2, 2009. "Hate Crimes Against Arab Americans, Muslims, and Sikhs," The Leadership Conference. www.civilrights.org, Aug. 8, 2012.

[438] Ibid.

[439] "Hate Crimes Against Arab Americans, Muslims, and Sikhs," The Leadership Conference; "Crime Report." *Commercial Appeal*. www.commercialappeal.com, Jan. 2, 2009.

[440] Robert Moran. "Store Trashed," *Philadelphia Inquirer*. Philadelphia, PA Aug. 21, 2009, pg. B11.

[441] Ibid.

[442] Sophia Kazmi. "Two Face Battery Charges," *Oakland Tribune*. Oakland, CA Sept. 24, 2009.

[443] Sunita Sohrabji. "No Hate Crime Charges," *India-West*. San Leandro, CA Oct. 9, 2009, v. 34, iss 46, pg. A18.

[444] Ibid, A28, 31.

[445] Ibid, A18.

[446] Ibid, A28, 31.

[447] *St. Cloud Times*, reported in Kari Petrie. *McClatchy-Tribune Business News.* DC Dec. 10, 2009.

[448] "CAIR: Hate Crime Charges Sought in Attack on Calif. Muslim," *US Newswire.* DC May 15, 2010.

[449] Michael Feenley. "Muslim's Beating," *New York Daily News.* New York, NY May 25, 2010, pg. 12.

[450] Ibid.

[451] Dave Aeikens. "St. Cloud Somali Store Vandalized," *McClatchy-Tribune Business News.* DC July 9, 2010.

[452] Sean Gardiner, Tamer El-Ghobashy. "Student Charged," *Wall St. Journal.* New York, NY Aug. 26, 2010, pg. A17.

[453] John Elilgon. "$500,000 Bail in Slashing," *New York Times.* New York, NY Oct. 14, 2010, pg. A34.

[454] "Man Accused of Slashing Cabby" *New York Times.* New York, NY Oct. 20, 2010, pg. A22.

[455] Jennifer Peltz. "Student Indicted in Muslim Cabbie Attack," *Daily News.* Midland, MI Aug. 30, 2010.

[456] "Cabby Attack," *New York Post.* New York, NY Aug. 26, 2010, pg. 34.

[457] Jennifer Peltz. "Student Indicted in Muslim Cabbie Attack."

[458] "City News: Accused Cab Slasher," *Wall St. Journal.* New York, NY Oct. 20, 2010, pg. A25.

[459] Cathy Locke. "Two Arrested," *Sacramento Bee.* Sacramento, CA Dec. 3, 2010, pg. B3.

[460] Sunita Sohrabji. "Two Suspects Arrested," *India-West.* San Leandro, CA Dec. 10, 2010, v. 36, iss 3, pg. A12.

[461] "Two Plead Guilty to Attack on Sikh," *News India-Times.* New York, NY March 18. 2011, v. 42 iss 11 pg. 8.

[462] Cathy Locke. "Two Arrested," pg. B3.

[463] Ritu Jha. "Man Gets 13 Years in Jail for Hate Attack On Cab Driver," *India Abroad.* New York, NY June 17, 2011, v. 41, iss 38, pg. A22.

[464] Rowena Lugtu-Shaddox. *McClatchy-Tribune Business News.* DC Dec. 6, 2010.

[465] "Two Plead Guilty to Attack on Sikh," pg. 8.

[466] Cathy Locke. "Man Draws 13 Years in Sikh Cabbie Attack." *Merced Star,* www.mercedstar.com, June 7, 2011.

[467] Kieran Crowley. "Ex-Cop Charged in Flag Assault," *New York Post.* New York, NY Nov. 4, 2010.

[468] Ibid.

[469] Ibid.

[470] "Sikh Youth Attacked in Texas," *Hindustan Times.* New Delhi, India Dec. 19, 2009.

[471] Ibid.

[472] Ibid.

[473] "Pizza Delivery Man Attacked in Texas," *India-West.* San Leandro, CA Jan. 8, 2010 v. 35, iss 7 pg. A18.

[474] Ibid.

[475] "Sikh Youth Attacked in Texas."

[476] "Pizza Delivery Man Attacked in Texas," pg. A18.

[477] Eric Heisig. "Busted Glass Door Yields Hate-Crime Charges," *Courier.* Houma, LA April 19, 2011.

[478] Ibid.

[479] Rita Farlow. "Clearwater Police Investigate Whether Crash Was Racially Motivated." *St. Petersburg Times.* St. Petersburg, Fla. April 29, 2011.

[480] Ibid.

[481] "CAIR: Michigan Muslim's Car Defaced with Sand N*gger," US Newswire, DC May 14, 2011.

[482] "Fire Targeted Sikh-Owned Shop in Clay County," *Asheville Citizen-Times*. www.citizen-times.com. Sept. 12, 2011.

[483] Ibid.

[484] "Dry Cleaning Fire Investigated As Possible Hate Crime," KCRA Channel 3 News, Sacramento, www.kcra.com, Sept. 14, 2011.

[485] Ibid.

[486] Ibid.

[487] Stephen Magagnini. "Orangevale Arson Attack Nation's Only Confirmed Federal Hate Crime Since 9/11 Anniversary," *Sacramento Bee*. Sacramento, CA Sept. 15, 2011, pg. 1B.

[488] Ibid.

[489] "Dry Cleaning Fire Investigated As Possible Hate Crime."

[490] Stephen Magagnini. "Orangevale Arson Attack Nation's Only Confirmed Federal Hate Crime Since 9/11 Anniversary," pg. 1B.

[491] Ibid.

[492] Ibid.

[493] Ibid.

[494] Vanessa Ho. "Being Muslim on 9/11 Anniversary," *Seattle Post-Intelligencer*. Seattle, WA. Seattle PI.com. Sept. 8, 2011.

Chapter Eight:

[1] Jack Shaheen. <u>Reel Bad Arabs</u>. (New York: Olive Branch Press, 2001).

[2] Ibid, pg. 193.

[3] Roger Ebert. *Chicago Sun Times*. Chicago, IL Nov. 6, 1998, quoted in Jack Shaheen, <u>Reel Bad Arabs</u>. (New York: Olive Branch Press, 2001): 6.

[4] Larry Stammer, Teresa Watanabe. "America Attacked," *Los Angeles Times*. Los Angeles, CA Sept. 12, 2001, pg. A38.

[5] Editorial. "Misplaced Anger," *Boston Globe*. Boston, MA Sept. 14, 2001, pg. A22.

[6] Nicholas Geranios. "Most Hate Crimes Happened After 9/11," *Columbian*. Vancouver, WA March 6, 2002, pg. C2.

[7] "Aiding the Enemy," *Roanoke Times and World News*. Roanoke, VA Sept. 26, 2001, pg. A14.

[8] Alex Tizon. "Muslim Family Feels at Home," *Seattle Times*. Seattle, WA Sept. 21, 2001, pg. A1.

[9] Ibid.

[10] Ibid.

[11] Ibid.

[12] Marie Szaniszlo. "War on Terrorism," *Boston Herald*. Boston, MA Sept. 26, 2001, pg. 6.

[13] Theola Labbe. "Muslims Endure Season of Suspicion," *Times Union*. Albany, NY Sept. 30, 2001, pg. A9.

[14] Jo Becker. "Sikhs Campaign Against Bigotry," *Washington Post*. DC Sept. 24, 2001, pg. 6.

[15] "Letters," *Gazette*. Colorado Springs, CO Sept. 18, 2001, pg. Metro 5.

[16] "List of Hate Crimes from Sept. 11, 2001 to Jan. 8, 2002," www.realsikhism.com.

[17] Viji Sundaram. "Sikh Store Owner Beaten Up," *India-West*. San Leandro, CA Sept. 21, 2001, v. 26, iss 46, pg. 1.

[18] Ibid.

[19] Ibid.

[20] Nicole Marshall. "Assaults, Hit-and-Run Possible Hate Crimes," *Tulsa World*. Tulsa, OK Sept. 16, 2001, pg. 13.

[21] Ibid.

[22] Ibid.

[23] Barbara Karkabi. "Learning from the Pain," *Houston Chronicle*. Houston, TX Oct. 7, 2001, pg. E1.

[24] Ibid.

[25] Ibid.

[26] Ibid.

[27] Edward Hegstrom, Peggy O'Hare. "Houston Area Muslims Detail Alleged Hate Crimes," *Houston Chronicle*, Houston, TX Oct. 3, 2001, pg. A28.

[28] Barbara Karkabi. "Learning from the Pain," pg. E1.

[29] Terry Saucier. "Un-American Responses," *Los Angeles Times*. Los Angeles, CA Sept. 22, 2001, pg. B20.

[30] Ibid.

[31] Diana Fishlock. "Hate Crimes Increase," *Patriot-News*. Harrisburg, PA Oct. 12, 2001, pg. B1

[32] Ibid.

[33] Ibid.

[34] Jocelyn Wiener. "Lessons in Patience," *St. Petersburg Times*. St. Petersburg, FL Sept. 29, 2002, pg. 1F.

[35] Ibid.

[36] Ibid.

[37] Ibid.

[38] Ibid.

[39] Ibid.

[40] Barbara Karkabi. "Learning from the Pain," pg. E1.

[41] "Successful Hate Crime Persecutions," *ADC Times*. DC Winter 2002. v. 21, iss 9, pg. 10.

[42] Mary Leonard. "Arab-Americans Feel Sting of Profiling," *Boston Globe*. Boston, MA Oct. 19, 2001, pg. A20.

[43] Ilene Lelchuk. "In Peril at the Projects," *San Francisco Chronicle*. San Francisco, CA Jan. 24, 2002, pg. A17.

[44] Ibid.

[45] Ibid.

[46] Ibid.

[47] Ibid.

[48] Ibid.

[49] Ibid.

[50] Ibid.

[51] Lisa Hill. "Number of Hate Crimes Reported Decreases," *Press-Enterprise*. Riverside, CA Dec. 12, 2001, pg. B1.

[52] Nicholas Geranios. "Most Hate Crimes Happened After 9/11," pg. C2.

[53] Jack Shaheen. Guilty. (Northampton, MA: Olive Branch Press, 2008): 174.

[54] Edward Park. "Increase in Hate Incidents," *Asianweek*. San Francisco, CA Jan. 2, 2002, v. 23, iss 19, pg. 11.

[55] Imran Vittachi. "Homeland Insecurities," *Post-Dispatch*. St. Louis, MO June 3, 2002, pg. B1.

[56] Ibid.

[57] Allan Turner and Dale Lezon. "Our Changed World," *Houston Chronicle*. Houston, TX Sept. 8, 2002, pg. A33.

[58] Ibid.

[59] Ibid.

[60] Ibid.

[61] Roger Miller. "Local Muslims Apprehensive," *Pantagraph*. Bloomington, IL March 22, 2003, pg. A7.

[62] Mark Bowes. "Attacks on Muslims," *Richmond Times-Dispatch*. Richmond, VA Dec. 11, 2002, pg. B1.

[63] Alisa Solomon. "From Baghdad to Brooklyn," *Village Voice*. New York, NY April 2, 2003, v. 48, iss 14, pg. 26-8; Albor Ruiz. "Hate Crimes Target Arabs," *New York Daily News*. New York, NY April 16, 2003, pg. 8.

[64] Albor Ruiz. "Hate Crimes Target Arabs," pg. 8.

[65] Alisa Solomon. "From Baghdad to Brooklyn," pg. 26-8.

[66] Ibid.

[67] Ibid.

[68] Ibid.

[69] Ibid.

[70] Suleman Din. "Scratches That Don't Go," *India Abroad*. New York, NY Jan. 10, 2003, v. 33, iss 15, pg. M7.

[71] Ibid.

[72] Ibid.

[73] Ibid.

[74] Ibid.

[75] Inger Sandal. "Arabs Form Anti-Bias Chapter Here," *Arizona Daily Star*. Tucson, AZ March 20, 2003, pg. B1.

[76] Ibid.

[77] "Beating of Muslim," *Arab American News*. Dearborn, MI March 14, 2003, v. 19, iss 891 pg. 15.

[78] Nora Achrati. "Hate Crimes Follow," *Atlanta Journal-Constitution*. Atlanta, GA March 30, 2003, pg. A5.

[79] "Anti-Muslim Bomber Gets Probation," *Arab American News*. Dearborn, MI Oct. 3, 2003 v. 20 iss 920 pg. 2.

[80] Michael Janofsky. "War Brings New Surge of Anxiety," *New York Times*. New York, NY March 29, 2003, pg. B15.

[81] "Anti-Muslim Bomber Gets Probation," pg. 2.

[82] Ibid.

[83] Nora Achrati. "Hate Crimes Follow," pg. A5.

[84] Brian Kluepfel. "Upswing in Hate Crimes," *Asianweek*. San Francisco, CA April 9, 2003, v. 24, iss 32, pg. 14.

[85] Jack Shaheen. <u>Guilty</u>, pg. 158.

[86] Ibid.

[87] Patrick Healy. "3 Indians Attacked," *New York Times*. New York, NY Aug. 5, 2003, pg. B3.

[88] Tanmaya Nanda. "Sikh Family Attacked," *India Abroad*. New York, NY Aug. 15, 2003, v. 33, iss 46, pg. A10.

[89] Ibid.

[90] Ibid.

[91] Ibid.

[92] Patrick Healy. "3 Indians Attacked," pg. B3.

[93] Lisa Tsering. "Sikh Family in New York," *India-West*. San Leandro, CA Aug. 8, 2003, v. 28, iss 40, pg. A1.

[94] Patrick Healy. "3 Indians Attacked," pg. B3.

[95] *New York Post* quoted in Lisa Tsering. "Sikh Family in New York," pg. A1

[96] Tanmaya Nanda. "Sikh Family Attacked," pg. A10.

[97] Aziz Haniffa. "Sikh Group Forms Forum," *India Abroad*. New York, NY. Sept. 26, 2003, v. 33 iss 52 pg. A8.

[98] "Sikh Family Harassed by Neighbor," *Sikh Coalition Newsletter*. www.sikhcoalition.org, Nov. 18, 2003.

[99] Lisa Tsering. "Congress Members," *India-West*. San Leandro, CA April 11, 2003, v. 28, iss 23, pg. A31.

[100] Ibid.

[101] Jack Shaheen. Guilty, pg. 98.

[102] Ibid, pg. 120.

[103] Editorial. "Anti-American Violence," *Patriot-News*. Harrisburg, PA July 14, 2004, pg. A12.

[104] Chris Lau. "Police Say Attacks on Fremont Family Not a Hate Crime," *Oakland Tribune*. Oakland, CA April 20, 2005, pg. 1.

[105] Ibid.

[106] Ibid.

[107] Ibid.

[108] Kavita Chhibber. "The Sikhs in the Shadows of 9/11," *Little India*. Reading: April 2005. v. 15, iss 4 pg. 37.

[109] Jeannie Nuss. "3 Charged with Committing a Hate Crime," *Boston Globe*. Boston, MA Sept. 26, 2008, pg. B2.

[110] Ibid.

[111] "Values Briefs," *Lincoln Star Journal*. Lincoln, NB Aug. 20, 2005, pg. 1.

[112] Jada Yuan. "The White-Castle Ceiling," *New York*. New York, NY. March 4, 2007.

[113] Ibid.

[114] "FBI Asked to Probe Attack on Georgia Muslim Family," PR Newswire. New York. April 26, 2006.

[115] Jack Shaheen. Guilty, pg. 93.

[116] Ibid, pg. 110.

[117] "Indian Family in US Target of Racial Vandalism," *Hindustan Times*. New Delhi, India. June 2, 2006.

[118] Ibid.

[119] Ibid.

[120] Sushma Subramanian. "Graffiti Called Hate Crime," *Orange County Register*. Santa Ana, Ca. June 29, 2006, pg. 1.

[121] Ibid.

[122] Ibid.

[123] John Cot. "Hate Crime Alleged in Stabbing," *San Francisco Chronicle*. San Francisco, CA Aug. 2, 2006, pg. B10.

[124] Ketaki Gohkhale. "Sikh Stabbed," *India-West*. San Leandro, CA Aug. 11, 2006, v. 31, iss 38, pg. A1.

[125] "Another Sikh Becomes Hate Crime Victim in US," *Hindustan Times*. New Delhi, India. Aug. 2, 2006.

[126] Ibid.

[127] John Cot. "Hate Crime Alleged in Stabbing," pg. B10.

[128] Yudhvir Rana. "Sikh Falls Victim to US Hate Crime," *Times of India*. New Delhi, India. Aug. 3, 2006.

[129] Ibid.

[130] Aatif Al Bokhari. "No Hate Crime," *Arab American News*. Dearborn, MI Dec. 2, 2006, v. 22, iss 1086, pg. 19.

[131] Ibid.

[132] Ibid.

[133] Ibid.

[134] Ibid.

[135] Ibid.

[136] Ibid.

[137] Detroit News quoted in Aatif Al Bokhari. "No Hate Crime," *Arab American News*. Dearborn, MI Dec. 2, 2006, v. 22, iss 1086, pg. 19.

[138] Aatif Al Bokhari. "No Hate Crime," pg. 19.

[139] Jack Shaheen. "'24' Glorifies Torture, Foments Hate," *Augusta Chronicle*. Augusta, GA Feb. 26, 2007, pg. A5.

[140] Tom Lyons. "Movie Matters," *Sarasota Herald Tribune*. Sarasota, FL Oct. 21, 2007, pg. BS1.

[141] Latisha Gray. "Action Sought on Hate Crime," *Sarasota Herald Tribune*. Sarasota, FL July 14, 2007, pg. BS1.

[142] Ibid.

[143] Ibid.

[144] Ibid.

[145] Ibid.

[146] Ibid.

[147] Guillermo Contreras. "Vandalism," *San Antonio Express-News*. San Antonio, TX July 18, 2007, pg. B1.

[148] Ibid.

[149] Ibid.

[150] "Dispute Between Muslim Couple, Neighbors," *Brattleboro Reformer*. Brattleboro, VT July 26, 2007.

[151] Ibid.

[152] Ibid.

[153] Katherine Shaver. "9/11 Brings a Return of Vandalism," *Washington Post*. DC Sept. 12, 2007, pg. B4.

[154] Ibid.

[155] Steve Vogel. "Muslim Family Seeks Answers to Violence," *Washington Post*. DC Sept. 18, 1997, pg. M1.

[156] Ibid.

[157] David Montgomery. "Vandalism Kindles Support," *Washington Post*, DC May 2, 1994, pg. D1.

[158] Ibid.

[159] Ibid.

[160] Steve Vogel. "Muslim Family Seeks Answers to Violence," pg. M1.

[161] Katherine Shaver. "9/11 Brings a Return of Vandalism," pg. B4.

[162] Ibid.

[163] "Hate Crime Draws Five Days in Jail," *Washington Post*. DC. May 27, 1998, pg. B7.

[164] Ibid.

[165] Ibid.

[166] Delinda Hanley. "Muslim Family Endures Hate," *Washington Report*. DC Nov. 2007, v. 26, iss 8, pg. 53.

[167] "CAIR Condemns Cross Burning on Lawn of NJ Obama Supporters," PR Newswire. NY Nov. 7, 2008.

[168] "CAIR Seeks Probe into Harassment of NC Muslim," US Newswire. DC: May 10, 2009.

[169] Christina Lane. "Assault on Muslim." *Longview News-Journal*. Longview, TX June 13, 2009.

[170] Ibid.

[171] Ben Aguirre Jr. "Vandalism Probe Sought," *Oakland Tribune*. Oakland, CA Oct 16, 2009.

[172] Ibid.

[173] "CAIR – Fla. Muslim Receives White Powder in Mail," PR Newswire. NY June 8, 2010.

[174] "CAIR – Anti-Muslim Okla. Lawn Signs," US Newswire. DC June 26, 2010.

[175] "Rochester/ Muslims Ask for FBI Investigation," *Saint Paul Pioneer Press*. Saint Paul, MN May 6, 2011.

[176] Ibid.

[177] Rocco Parascandola, Kerry Burke, Bill Hutchinson. "Neighbor's A Terror. B'klyn Haid Charged with Felony Hate Crime After Attacking 'F—ing Arabs,'" *New York Daily News*. New York: NY June 28, 2011, pg. 3.

[178] Ibid.

[179] Ibid.

[180] Ibid.

[181] Ibid.

[182] Ibid.

[183] Ibid.

[184] Ibid.

[185] "Fremont Police Say Soaring Gold Prices Make South Asians a Target." KCBS News, Fremont, CA Sept. 30. 2011.

[186] Lauren Fitzpatrick. "Chicago Muslim, Age 10 on 9/11, No Longer Scared of Hate Crimes," *Chicago Sun-Times*. Chicago, IL Sept. 8, 2011.

[187] Steve Huntley. "Radicals Shape American Views of Islam," *Chicago Sun-Times*. Chicago, IL Sept. 14, 2011.

Chapter Nine:

[1] Jack Shaheen. <u>Reel Bad Arabs</u>. (New York: Olive Branch Press, 2001): 11.

[2] Jack Shaheen. <u>Reel Bad Arabs</u>.

[3] Ibid, pg. 211.

[4] Ibid, pg. 212.

[5] Ibid.

[6] Chris Bull. "Gay, Muslim, and Scared," *The Advocate*. Los Angeles, CA Oct. 23, 2001, iss 849, pg. 54.

[7] Ibid.

[8] Diane Dietz. "Suspicion Makes for Fearful Patriots," *Register Guard*. Eugene, OR March 5, 2003, pg. 1.

[9] Carri Thevenot. "Nevadans Fear Rise in Hate," *Las Vegas Review-Journal*. Las Vegas, NV Sept. 18, 2001, pg. 1A.

[10] Ibid.

[11] "List of Hate Crimes from Sept. 11, 2001 to Jan. 8, 2002," www.realsikhism.com

[12] Jose Arballo Jr. "Hate Crime Case Filed," *Press Enterprise*. Riverside, CA Sept. 19, 2001, pg. B1.

[13] Jose Arballo Jr. "Guilty Plea in Anti-Muslim Case," *Press Enterprise*. Riverside, CA Oct. 2, 2001, pg. B3.

[14] Jose Arballo Jr. "Hate Crime Case Filed," pg. B1.

[15] Jose Arballo Jr. "Guilty Plea in Anti-Muslim Case," pg. B3.

[16] Saeed Ahmed. "Retaliation," *Atlanta Constitution*. Atlanta, GA Sept. 18, 2001, pg. B4.

[17] Angie Chuang. "Expressions of Hate," *Oregonian*. Portland, OR Sept. 19, 2001, pg. A6.

[18] Ibid.

[19] Nicholas Geranios. "Most Hate Crimes Happened After 9/11," *Columbian*. Vancouver, WA March 6, 2002, pg. C2.

[20] Ibid.

[21] Ashok Easwaran. "Hate Crimes Grip Chicago," *India Abroad*. New York, NY Sept. 28, 2001, v. 31, iss 52, pg. 4.

[22] Viji Sundaram. "Reports of Hate Crimes," *India-West*. San Leandro, CA Sept. 28, 2001, v. 26, iss 47, pg. A1.

[23] Jose Arballo Jr. "No Spike in Hate Crime," *Press Enterprise*. Riverside, CA Sept. 27, 2001, pg. B1.

[24] Monte Morin and Mai Tran. "The Region; Man Held in Post-9/11 Hate Crime," *Los Angeles Times*. Los Angeles, CA May 31, 2002, pg. B7.

[25] "Apparent Hate Crimes in OC," *Orange County Register*. Santa Ana, CA March 19, 2003, pg. 1.

[26] Gaiutra Bahadur, Kim Perkes. "Arabs in Central Texas," *Austin American Statesman*. Austin, TX Sept. 13, 2001, pg. B7.

[27] Kieran Crowley, Angela Allen, and Brad Hunter. "Arabs Under Siege Here," *New York Post*. New York, NY Sept. 13, 2001, pg. 37.

[28] Wayne Coffey. "Fever Pitch," *New York Daily News*, New York, NY Sept. 23, 2001, pg. 85

[29] Ibid.

[30] Pedro Perez. "Northwest Sees Onslaught of Racist Attacks," *Columbian*. Vancouver, WA Sept. 19, 2001, pg. C2.

[31] Johnny Edwards. "Hate Criminals," *Augusta Chronicle*. Augusta, GA Sept. 16, 2001, pg. A14.

[32] Ibid.

[33] Ibid.

[34] Tina Griego. "Intolerance Makes Innocents Casualties of Fear," *Denver Post*. Denver, CO Sept. 19, 2001, pg. B1.

[35] Ibid.

[36] Johnny Edwards. "Hate Criminals," pg. A14.

[37] Anna Gorman. "2 Men are Charged," *Los Angeles Times*. Los Angeles, CA Sept. 29, 2001, pg. B6.

[38] Ibid.

[39] Ibid.

[40] "Police Reports." *Daily Herald*. Arlington Heights, IL Nov. 1, 2001, pg. 4.

[41] Editorial. *Daily Herald*. Arlington Heights, IL Nov. 6, 2001, pg. 6.

[42] Somini Sengupta. "Sept. 11 Attack," *New York Times*. New York, NY Oct. 10, 2001, pg. B1.

[43] Teresa Mask. "Not All Can Share a Feeling of Unity," *Daily Herald*. Arlington Heights, IL Sept. 11, 2002, pg. 12.

[44] Tanya Weinberg. "Not Safe at Home," *South Florida Sun Sentinel*. Ft. Lauderdale, FL Sept. 5, 2002, pg. 1.

[45] Ibid.

[46] Ibid.

[47] Ibid.

[48] Ibid.

[49] Ibid.

[50] Ibid.

[51] Ibid.

[52] Teresa Mask. "Not All Can Share a Feeling of Unity," pg. 12.

[53] Inara Verzemnieks and Katy Muldoon. "9/11: One Year Later," *Oregonian*. Portland, OR Sept. 11, 2002, pg. A9.

[54] Jack Shaheen. Guilty. (Northampton, MA: Olive Branch Press, 2008).

[55] Ibid.

[56] Cynthia Yeldell. "Local Muslims Pray," *News Sentinel*. Knoxville, TN March 22, 2003, pg. A7.

[57] Mary Sanchez. "American Muslims Fear," *Kansas City Star*. Kansas City, MO April 27, 2003, pg. 1.

[58] Michael Janofsky. "War Brings New Surge of Anxiety," *New York Times*. New York, NY March 29, 2003, pg. B15.

[59] "Hate Crime Charge in Singing," *San Diego Union Tribune*. San Diego, CA March 26, 2003, pg. A14.

[60] *Arab American News*. Dearborn, MI March 28, 2003, v. 19, iss 893, pg. 16.

[61] Aziz Haniffa. "Minority Groups," *India Abroad*. New York, NY April 4, 2003, v. 32, iss 27, pg. A4.

[62] Matt Cooper. "Local Leaders Decry Crimes of Hate," *Register Guard*. Eugene, OR March 26, 2003, pg. A1.

[63] Alice Tallmadge. "Muslims Keeping Low Profile," *Oregonian*. Portland, OR March 27, 2003, pg. C3.

[64] Ibid.

[65] Matt Cooper. "Local Leaders Decry Crimes of Hate," pg. A1.

[66] Alice Tallmadge. "Muslims Keeping Low Profile," pg. C3.

[67] Erik Ortiz. "North Jersey Sikhs fight Bigotry," *Record*. Bergen County, NJ. May 22, 2003, pg. L6.

[68] Ibid.

[69] Wayne Parry. "Anti-Muslim Bias Rose Sharply," *Record*. Bergen County, NJ. May 12, 2005, pg. A4.

[70] Ali Moossavi. "Professor Debunks Myths in Hostile Atmosphere," *Arab American News*. Dearborn, MI Nov. 12, 2005, v. 21, iss 1031, pg. 15.

[71] Jack Shaheen. Guilty, pg. 106.

[72] Ibid, pg. 163.

[73] "Virginia Muslim Attacked by Men Shouting Racist Slurs," US Newswire. DC Aug 9, 2005, pg. 1.

[74] Jack Shaheen. Guilty, pg. 153.

[75] Jack Shaheen. Guilty.

[76] Larry Fish. "Gunfire Riddles Cars at Mosque," *Philadelphia Inquirer*. Philadelphia, PA Nov. 10, 2005, pg. B7.

[77] Marilyn Elias. "USA's Muslims are Under Fire," *USA Today*. McLean, VA Aug. 10, 2006, pg. D1.

[78] Ibid.

[79] Ibid.

[80] Ibid.

[81] Deborah Ziff. "Muslims in Area Feel Bullied," *Tampa Tribune*. Tampa, FL Aug. 16, 2006, pg. 1.

[82] Ibid.

[83] Ibid.

[84] Ibid.

[85] Ibid.

[86] Jack Shaheen. Guilty, pg. 125.

[87] Ibid, pg. 125.

[88] Ibid, pg. 177.

[89] "FL Web Host Asked to Drop 'Kill All Muslim Kids' Site," US Newswire. DC Dec. 14, 2006.

[90] Ibid.

[91] US Newswire. DC Dec. 7, 2006.

[92] Alison Gendar. "Hate-Crime Rap," New York Daily News. New York, NY March 8, 2007, pg. 34.

[93] Ibid.

[94] Ibid.

[95] Eric Leach. "Baisakhi Celebrated," Daily News. Los Angeles, CA April 9, 2007, pg. N3.

[96] Jack Shaheen. Guilty, pg. 109.

[97] Ibid, pg. 115.

[98] Chrissie Thompson. "Hate Crime Charged," Buffalo News. Buffalo, NY July 7, 2007, pg. D3.

[99] Ibid.

[100] "Muslim Candidate for Irvine City Council Gets Death Threat," Los Angeles Times, in "CAIR: Calif. Muslim Candidate Receives Death Threats," PR Newswire. New York Oct. 10, 2008.

[101] Ibid.

[102] "CAIR: Muslim Woman Verbally Assaulted at NC Wal-Mart," US Newswire, DC Oct. 28, 2010.

[103] Ibid.

[104] Andrea Elliott. "Generation 9/11," New York Times. New York, NY Sept. 8, 2011.

[105] Ibid.

[106] "CAIR-LA Seeks Hate Crime Charges for Vandalism," PR Newswire. NY March 12, 2011.

[107] Ibid.

[108] Ibid.

[109] "CAIR: Michigan Muslim's Car Defaced with Sand N*gger," US Newswire, DC May 14, 2011.

[110] Vivian Ho. "Abercrombie & Fitch Sued Over Hijab Firing," San Francisco Chronicle. www.sfgate.com, June 28, 2011.

[111] Ibid.

[112] "Muslim Fired from Abercrombie and Fitch Received Death Threats," CNN video posted on CAIR website.

[113] "21-Year old Muslim Woman Says She Was the Victim of Hate Crime in Ann Arbor," WXYZ Action News, Ann Arbor, MI Aug. 7, 2011.

[114] Ibid.

[115] Ibid.

[116] Amy Crawford. "9/11 Anniversary Makes Some Muslims and Sikhs Wary," Examiner. San Francisco, CA Sept. 8, 2011.

[117] "CAIR Concerned About 9/11 Spike in Anti-Muslim Incidents," www.turntoislam.com/forum, Sept. 14, 2011.

[118] Philip Caulfield. "Muslim Man Says Houston Bar Wished Him 'Happy Sept. 11th' On To-Go Order," New York Daily News. New York, NY Sept. 14, 2011.

[119] Ibid.

Chapter Ten:

[1] Jack Shaheen. <u>Reel Bad Arabs</u>. (New York: Olive Branch Press, 2001): 404.

[2] Ibid.

[3] Ibid, pg. 405.

[4] Ibid, pg. 183.

[5] Ibid, pg. 254.

[6] Kavita Chhibber. "The Sikhs in the Shadows of 9/11," *Little India*. Reading: April 2005. v. 15, iss 4, pg. 37.

[7] Ibid.

[8] Ibid.

[9] Richard Louv. "Security Experts," *San Diego Union-Tribune*. San Diego, CA Oct. 14, 2001, pg. A12.

[10] Maki Becker. "Sikhs Facing Anti-Muslim Harassment," *New York Daily News*. New York, NY Sept. 29, 2001, pg. 20.

[11] Jeet Thayil. "Balbir Singh Killer's Trial," *India Abroad*. New York, NY July 25, 2003, v. 33, iss 43, pg. A10.

[12] Ibid.

[13] Lynda Gorov. "Man's Death is Laid to Homegrown Hate," *Boston Globe*. Boston, MA Sept. 18, 2001, pg. A12

[14] Ibid.

[15] Ibid.

[16] "Thousands Mourn Sikh Killed in Hate Rampage," *Houston Chronicle*. Houston, TX Sept. 23, 2001, pg. 26.

[17] Kavita Chhibber. "The Sikhs in the Shadows of 9/11," pg. 37.

[18] Robert Pierre. "Victims of Hate," *Washington Post*. DC Sept. 14, 2002, pg. A1.

[19] "Hate Crimes on Increase," *Arab American News*. Dearborn, MI Sept. 21, 2001, v. 18, iss 814, pg. 15.

[20] Richard Louv. "Security Experts," pg. A12.

[21] "Hate Crimes on Increase," pg. 15.

[22] Lynda Gorov. "Man's Death is Laid to Homegrown Hate," pg. A12

[23] Ibid.

[24] Ibid.

[25] Ibid.

[26] Ibid.

[27] Ibid.

[28] Ibid.

[29] "Thousands Mourn Sikh Killed in Hate Rampage," pg. 26.

[30] Anindita Ramaswamy. "Sikhs and Muslims," *News India-Times*. New York, Sept. 21, 2001, v. 32, iss 34, pg. 10.

[31] Jeet Thayil. "Balbir Singh Killer's Trial," pg. A10.

[32] Jeet Thayil. "Sodhi Killer May Get Death," *India Abroad*. New York, NY Oct. 10, 2003, v. 34, iss 2 pg. A1.

[33] Michael Potts. "Frank Roque Gets Death," *India-West*. San Leandro, CA Oct. 17, 2003, v. 27, iss 50 pg. A26.

[34] Jeet Thayil. "Balbir Singh Killer's Trial," pg. A10.

[35] Jeet Thayil. "Killer Roque Says He's Sorry," *India Abroad*. New York, NY Oct. 24, 2003, v. 34, iss 4, pg. A8.

[36] Ibid.

[37] Suman Mozumder. "Balbir Sodhi," *India Abroad*. New York, NY Aug. 25, 2006, v. 36, iss 47, pg. A6.

[38] Jeet Thayil. "9/11 Hate Crime Victim's Brother Killed," *India Abroad*. New York, NY Aug. 16, 2002, v. 32, iss 46, pg. A1.

[39] Ray Hanania. "Now that We've Remembered 9/11," *Arab American News*. Dearborn, MI Sept. 16, 2006, v. 22, iss 1075, pg. 4.

[40] Joe Mozingo. "Slain Egyptian Was a Fixture," *Los Angeles Times*. Los Angeles, CA Sept. 19, 2001, pg. B3.

[41] Tamar Lewin. "Sikh Owner of Gas Station," *New York Times*. New York, NY Sept. 17, 2001, pg. B16.

[42] Beth Shuster. "U.S. Strikes Back," *Los Angeles Times*. Los Angeles, CA Oct. 11, 2001, pg. A1.

[43] Ruby Gonzales. "Slain San Gabriel Grocer," *Whittier Daily News*. Whittier, CA Sept. 11, 2010.

[44] Joe Mozingo. "Slain Egyptian Was a Fixture," pg. B3.

[45] Ibid.

[46] Ibid.

[47] Ibid.

[48] Ibid.

[49] Ibid.

[50] Ibid.

[51] Ibid.

[52] Ruby Gonzales. "Slain San Gabriel Grocer."

[53] Ibid.

[54] Ibid.

[55] Ibid.

[56] Ibid.

[57] Tamar Lewin. "Sikh Owner of Gas Station," pg. B16.

[58] Helen Teitelbaum. "Jewish Community Fights Deportation of Muslim Family Victimized by Hate Crime," *Jewish News*. Whappany, NJ May 1, 2003, v. LVII, iss 18, pg. 9.

[59] Tamar Lewin. "Sikh Owner of Gas Station," pg. B16.

[60] Ibid.

[61] Anand Vaishnav. "Bias Probed," *Boston Globe*. Boston, MA Sept. 17, 2001, pg. A12.

[62] Ibid.

[63] Lenora Chu. "Hate Around the Nation," *Asianweek*. San Francisco, CA Oct. 3, 2001 v. 23 iss 6 pg. 9.

[64] Ibid.

[65] Richard Serrano. "Deluge of Hate Crimes," *Los Angeles Times*. Los Angeles, CA July 6, 2002, pg. A8.

[66] Ibid.

[67] Ibid.

[68] Ibid.

[69] Ibid.

[70] Robert Pierre. "Victims of Hate," pg. A1.

[71] Ibid.

[72] Ibid.

[73] Ibid.

[74] Ibid.

[75] Ibid.

[76] Ibid.

[77] Richard Serrano. "Deluge of Hate Crimes." pg. A8.

[78] Helen Teitelbaum. "Jewish Community Fights Deportation of Muslim Family Victimized by Hate Crime," pg. 9.

[79] Richard Serrano. "Deluge of Hate Crimes," pg. A8.

[80] Ibid.

[81] Ibid.

[82] Ibid.

[83] Robert Pierre. "Victims of Hate," pg. A1.

[84] Richard Serrano. "Deluge of Hate Crimes." pg. A8.

[85] Robert Pierre. "Victims of Hate," pg. A1.

[86] Ibid.

[87] Ibid.

[88] Ibid.

[89] Ibid.

[90] Ibid.

[91] Ibid.

[92] Helen Teitelbaum. "Jewish Community Fights Deportation of Muslim Family Victimized by Hate Crime," pg. 9.

[93] Ela Dutt. "NCPA Urges to Save Family," *News India-Times*. New York, NY May 9, 2003, v. 34, iss 19, pg. 10.

[94] Robin Keats. "200 Defy Rain in Milltown," *Jewish News*. Whippany, NJ Sept. 18, 2003, v. LVII, iss 38, pg. 11.

[95] Ibid.

[96] Helen Teitelbaum. "Jewish Community Fights Deportation of Muslim Family Victimized by Hate Crime," pg. 9.

[97] Robin Keats. "200 Defy Rain in Milltown," pg. 11.

[98] Lenora Chu. "Hate Around the Nation," pg. 9.

[99] Jodi Wilgoren. "Going by 'Joe,' not 'Yussef,'" *New York Times*. New York, NY Sept. 11, 2002, pg. G15.

[100] Middle East Online. Durham. Sept. 23, 2001.

[101] Robin Keats. "200 Defy Rain in Milltown," pg. 11.

[102] Jodi Wilgoren. "Going by 'Joe,' not 'Yussef,'" pg. G15.

[103] "Fourth Murder Victim," *Arab American News*. Dearborn, MI Sept. 28, 2001, v. 18, iss 815, pg. 11.

[104] Jodi Wilgoren. "Going by 'Joe,' not 'Yussef,'" pg. G15.

[105] Ibid.

[106] Karen de Sa. "Local Muslims," *San Jose Mercury News*. San Jose, CA Dec. 5, 2001, pg. 1.

[107] Ibid.

[108] Ibid.

[109] Ibid.

[110] Ibid.

[111] Ibid.

[112] Ibid.

[113] Richard Louv. "Security Experts," pg. A12.

[114] Evelyn Nieves. "Slain Arab-American May Be Hate Crime Victim," *New York Times*. New York, NY Oct. 6, 2001, pg. A8.

[115] Ibid.

[116] Elizabeth Bell. "Yemeni Immigrant Mourned," *San Francisco Chronicle*. San Francisco, CA Oct. 5, 2001, pg. A7.

[117] Karen de Sa. "Local Muslims," pg. 1.

[118] Ibid.

[119] Elizabeth Bell. "Yemeni Immigrant Mourned," pg. A7.

[120] Ibid.

[121] "300 Attend Funeral," *San Diego Union Tribune*. San Diego, CA Oct. 5, 2001, pg. A9.

[122] Evelyn Nieves. "Slain Arab-American May Be Hate Crime Victim," pg. A8.

[123] Karen de Sa. "Local Muslims," pg. 1.

[124] Ibid.

[125] Elizabeth Bell. "Second Yemeni Shot in Valley," *San Francisco Chronicle*. San Francisco, CA Dec. 8, 2001, pg. A9.

[126] Ibid.

[127] Karen de Sa. "Local Muslims," pg. 1.

[128] Valeria Godines. "Slain Muslim Interred," *Orange County Register*. Santa Ana, CA Oct. 11, 2001, pg. B.

[129] Hector Becerra. "A New Ambiguity," *Los Angeles Times*. Los Angeles, CA Oct. 13, 2001, pg. B18.

[130] Valeria Godines. "Slain Muslim Interred," pg. B.

[131] Ibid. Biographical information about Nimer and his family come from the *Orange County Register*.

[132] Hector Becerra. "A New Ambiguity," pg. B18.

[133] Ibid.

[134] Ibid.

[135] Ibid.

[136] Ibid.

[137] Ibid.

[138] Ibid.

[139] "Palestinian Man Killed," *Sentinel*. Los Angeles, CA Oct. 17, 2001, v. 67, iss 29, pg. A1.

[140] Hector Becerra. "A New Ambiguity," pg. B18.

[141] Richard Winton. "Suspected Hate Crimes Rise," *Los Angeles Times*. Los Angeles, CA Sept. 10, 2002, pg. B3.

[142] Tony Anderson. "Hate Crimes Up Since 9/11," *Daily News*. Los Angeles, CA Dec. 21, 2001, pg. N3.

[143] Bernice Jackson. "Murder of a Native American Girl in Oklahoma," *Oakland Post*. Oakland, CA Sept. 26, 2001, v. 38, iss 29 pg. 4.

[144] "List of Hate Crimes from Sept. 11, 2001 to Jan. 8, 2002," www.realsikhism.com

[145] Jim Gray. "Murdered Native American Found Not to be Victim of Hate Crime," *Native American Times*. Tulsa, OK Oct. 1, 2001, v 7, iss 12, pg. 1.

[146] Nicole Marshall. "Assaults, Hit-and-Run Possible Hate Crimes," *Tulsa World*. Tulsa, OK Sept. 16, 2001, pg. 13.

[147] Jim Gray. "Murdered Native American Found Not to be Victim of Hate Crime," pg. 1.

[148] "Driving Death lands Tulsan Behind Bars," *Tulsa World*. Tulsa, OK Dec. 18, 2001, pg. 15.

[149] List of Hate Crimes from Sept. 11, 2001 to Jan. 8, 2002."

[150] David Chanen, Joy Powell. "Somali Man," *Star Tribune*. Minneapolis, MN Oct 27, 2001, pg. 3B

[151] Ibid.

[152] Ibid.

[153] Kavita Kumar. "Somalis Discuss Freedom and Fear," *Star Tribune*. Minneapolis, MN Oct. 25, 2001, pg. 1B.

[154] David Chanen, Joy Powell. "Somali Man," pg. 3B.

[155] Ibid.

[156] Ibid.

[157] Ibid.

[158] Ibid.

[159] Ibid.

[160] David Chanen. "Man Assaulted at Bus Stop Dies," *Star Tribune*. Minneapolis, MN Oct. 25, 2001, pg. 7B.

[161] David Chanen, Joy Powell. "Somali Man," pg. 3B.

[162] Ibid.

[163] Ibid.

[164] Ibid.

[165] Ibid.

[166] Ibid.

[167] Kavita Kumar. "Somalis Discuss Freedom and Fear," pg. 1B.

[168] Ibid.

[169] Ibid.

[170] Ibid.

[171] Ibid.

[172] Ibid.

[173] David Chanen. "Bus Stop Assault Ruled Homicide," *Star Tribune*. Minneapolis, MN Jan. 9, 2002, pg. 1B.

[174] Ibid.

[175] Ibid.

[176] Ibid.

[177] Ibid.

[178] Jennifer Langston. "Questions Remain in Death of Somali," *Herald*. Everett, WA Oct. 26, 2001, pg. B1.

[179] Mark Bowen. <u>Black Hawk Down</u>. (Berkeley: Atlantic Monthly Press, 1999).

[180] Jack Shaheen. <u>Guilty</u>. (Northampton, MA: Olive Branch Press, 2008): 100.

[181] Ibid.

[182] Jim Doyle. "Cabbie's Shooting," *San Francisco Chronicle*. San Francisco, CA Aug. 5, 2002, pg. B1.

[183] Ibid.

[184] Ibid.

[185] Kavita Chhibber. "The Sikhs in the Shadows of 9/11," pg. 37.

[186] Jeet Thayil. "9/11 Hate Crime Victim's Brother Killed," pg. A1.

[187] Ibid.

[188] Ibid.

[189] Ibid.

[190] Ibid.

[191] "Hate Crime Victim's Brother Shot," *Statesman*. New Delhi, India. Aug. 7, 2002, pg. 1.

[192] Jim Doyle. "Cabbie's Shooting," pg. B1.

[193] Ibid.

[194] Jeet Thayil. "9/11 Hate Crime Victim's Brother Killed," pg. A1.

[195] Ibid.

[196] Gloria Suhasini. "2 Arrested," *News India-Times*, New York, NY Aug. 23, 2002, v. 22, iss 34, pg. 37.

[197] Ibid.

[198] Ibid.

[199] Ibid.

[200] Albor Ruiz. "Hate Crimes Target Arabs," *New York Daily News*. New York, NY April 16, 2003, pg. 8.

[201] Alisa Solomon. "From Baghdad to Brooklyn," *Village Voice*. New York, NY April 2, 2003, v. 48, iss 14 pg. 26-8.

[202] Albor Ruiz. "Hate Crimes Target Arabs," pg. 8.

[203] Larry Celona, Ikimulisa Sockwell-Mason, Roosevelt Joseph. "9/11 Made 'Psycho' Slayer Go Nuts: Mom," *New York Post*. New York, NY Mar. 31, 2003, pg. 17.

[204] Melanie Lefkowitz, Sean Gardiner. "Slayings Attributed to Sept. 11 Hate," *Cincinnati Post*. Cincinnati, Ohio. April 1, 2003, pg. A2.

[205] Nancie Katz. "Thrill Kill Confession," *New York Daily News*. New York, NY. May 2, 2003, pg. 18.

[206] Ibid.

[207] Larry Celona, Ikimulisa Sockwell-Mason, Roosevelt Joseph. "9/11 Made 'Psycho' Slayer Go Nuts: Mom," pg. 17.

[208] Ibid.

[209] Ibid.

[210] Nancie Katz, Owen Moritz. "It's Life for Killer," *New York Daily News*. New York, NY Feb. 12, 2004, pg. 38.

[211] Ibid.

[212] Nancie Katz. "Thrill Kill Confession," pg. 18.

[213] Ibid.

[214] Albor Ruiz. "Hate Crimes Target Arabs," pg. 8.

[215] Nancie Katz. "Thrill Kill Confession," pg. 18.

[216] Ikimulisa Sockwell-Mason, Roosevelt Joseph. "I Hope He Gets the Death Penalty," *New York Post*. New York, NY Mar 31, 2003, pg. 17.

[217] Amy McLaughlin. "Cab Driver's Last Rider Charged," *Daily Herald*. Arlington Heights, IL May 3, 2003, pg. 1.

[218] Ibid.

[219] Dan Rozek. "Cabdriver's Friend, Kin Say Death May Be Hate Crime; Family Fears Pakistani Immigrant's Muslim Faith Spurred Killer," *Chicago Sun-Times*. Chicago, IL April 20, 2003, pg. 13.

[220] Ibid.

[221] Amy McLaughlin. "Cab Driver's Last Rider Charged," pg. 1.

[222] George Joseph. "Sikh Cabbies," *India Abroad*. New York, NY July 18, 2003, v. 33, iss 42, pg. A1.

[223] Ibid.

[224] Ibid.

[225] Jeet Thayil. "Redwood City Cabbies," *India Abroad*. New York, NY Sept. 26, 2003, v. 33 iss 52, pg. A4.

[226] George Joseph. "Sikh Cabbies," pg. A1.

[227] Ibid.

[228] Ibid.

[229] Ibid.

[230] Ibid.

[231] Jeet Thayil. "Redwood City Cabbies," pg. A4.

[232] Ibid.

[233] Diana Walsh. "Hate Crime Feared," *San Francisco Chronicle*. San Francisco, CA Sept. 16, 2003, pg. A19.

[234] Rupal Shah. "N.Y. Man Faces Hate," *India-West*. San Leandro, CA Sept. 19, 2003, v. 28, iss 46, pg. A32.

[235] Ibid.

[236] Diana Walsh. "Hate Crime Feared," pg. A19.

[237] Ibid.

[238] US Newswire. DC Sept. 17, 2003, pg. 1.

[239] Jason Dearen. "Cab Driver Mourned at Funeral," *Oakland Tribune*. Oakland, CA Sept. 19, 2003, pg. 1.

[240] Ibid.

[241] Ibid.

[242] Ibid.

[243] Ibid.

[244] Ibid.

[245] Ibid.

[246] Ibid.

[247] Ibid.

[248] Shaun Bishop. "Menlo Park Man Faces Trial," *Oakland Tribune*. Oakland, CA Feb. 5, 2010.

[249] Jeet Thayil. "Third Sikh Shot Since 9/11," *India Abroad*. New York, NY Oct. 3, 2003, v. 34, iss 1, pg. A1.

[250] Jyotirmoy Datta. "Sukhvir 'Sonny' Singh," *News India-Times*. New York, NY Oct. 3, 2003, v. 34, iss 40, pg. 29.

[251] Ibid.

[252] Jeet Thayil. "Third Sikh Shot Since 9/11," pg. A1.

[253] Ibid.

[254] Jeet Thayil. "Sukhvir 'Sonny' Singh," *India Abroad*. New York, NY Oct. 3, 2003, v. 34, iss 1, pg. A1.

[255] Ibid.

[256] Ibid.

[257] Ibid.

[258] Ibid.

[259] Ibid.

[260] Ibid.

[261] Ibid.

[262] Jack Shaheen. Guilty, pg. 22.

[263] George Joseph. "Police Clueless," *India Abroad*. New York, NY March 11, 2005, v. 35, iss 24, pg. A6.

[264] Ibid.

[265] Ibid.

[266] Ibid.

[267] M. Chooki. "Clipboard," *News India-Times*. New York, NY March 25, 2005, v. 36, iss 12, pg. 13.

[268] Ibid.

[269] Viji Sundaram. "$5,000 Reward Offered," *India-West*. San Leandro, CA Jan. 13, 2006, v. 31, iss 10, pg. 32.

[270] Jack Shaheen. Guilty, pg. 101.

[271] Henry Lee. "Memorial Service," *San Francisco Chronicle*. San Francisco, CA Oct. 28, 2006, pg. B6.

[272] Ibid.

[273] Ibid.

[274] Ibid.

[275] Henry Lee. "Slain Woman's Daughter," *San Francisco Chronicle*. San Francisco, CA Feb. 8, 2005, pg. B8.

[276] Ibid.

[277] Henry Lee. "50 Years for Killing," *San Francisco Chronicle*. San Francisco, CA April 15, 2008, pg. B3.

[278] Ibid.

[279] Jack Shaheen. Guilty, pg. 154.

[280] Suman Mozumder. "Alleged Hate Crime," *India Abroad*. New York, NY July 27, 2007 v. 37, iss 43, pg. A17.

[281] Ibid.

[282] Ibid.

[283] Ibid.

[284] Ibid.

[285] Ibid.

[286] Ibid.

[287] Ibid.

[288] Christopher Lisotta. "Killed in Broad Daylight," *Advocate*. Los Angeles, CA Dec. 4, 2007, iss 998 pg. 29-33.

[289] Ibid.

[290] Ibid.

[291] Ibid.

[292] Ibid.

[293] Vanessa Colon. "Sikhs Oppose New Turban Rules," *Sacramento Bee*. Sacramento, CA Sept. 22, 2007, pg. A3.

[294] Kenneth Turan. "The Kingdom," *Los Angeles Times*, September 28, 2007, in Jack Shaheen. Guilty. (Northampton, MA: Olive Branch Press, 2008): 128.

[295] Jack Shaheen. Guilty, pg. 128.

[296] Carolyn Jones. "Indian Brothers Shot," *San Francisco Chronicle*. San Francisco, CA Dec. 29, 2007, pg. B1.

[297] Ibid.

[298] Ibid.

[299] "FBI to Probe Sikh Brothers' Murder," *Hindustan Times*. New Delhi, India Jan. 9, 2008.

[300] Carolyn Jones. "Indian Brothers Shot," pg. B1.

[301] Fernanda Santos. "Man is Found Dead near a Sikh Temple in Queens," *New York Times*. New York, NY Aug. 9, 2008, pg. B4.

[302] Ibid.

[303] "Man with Children in Hand Kills," *India-West*. San Leandro, CA Aug. 15, 2008, v. 33 iss 36 pg. 32.

[304] Ibid.

[305] Meriana Alrabadi. "Did Police Kill Palestinian-American Shehada for Speaking Arabic?" *Washington Report*. DC: Sept/Oct 2009, v. 28, iss. 7, pg. 30.

[306] Ibid.

[307] Ibid.

[308] Ibid.

[309] David Kelly. "FBI Probes Fatal Blast," *Los Angeles Times*. Los Angeles, CA July 10, 2009, pg. A6.

[310] "California Imam Killed," *Arab American News*. Dearborn, MI July 4, 2009, v. 25, iss. 1221 pg. 14.

[311] Ibid.

[312] Ibid.

[313] David Kelly. "FBI Probes Fatal Blast," pg. A6.

[314] Ibid.

[315] Ibid.

[316] Ibid.

[317] "California Imam Killed," pg. 14.

[318] Jack Shaheen. Guilty, pg. 115-6.

[319] Cindy Horswell. "Was Liberty Shooting a Hate Crime? Officials Review Slaying of a Muslim Store Owner," *Houston Chronicle*. Houston, TX Dec. 30, 2009, pg. B2.

[320] Ibid.

[321] Suman Mozumder. "All For One," *India Abroad*. New York, NY July 30, 2010 v.40, iss 44, pg. A6.

[322] Ibid.

[323] Lee Romney. "Attack Shakes Community," *Los Angeles Times*. Los Angeles, CA April 11, 2011, pg. A1.

[324] "Reward Offered in Killing of Two Sikhs in U.S.," *Hindustan Times*. New Delhi, India April 16, 2011.

[325] Ritu Jha. "Sacramento Comes Together," *India Abroad*. New York, NY March 18, 2011 v 41 iss 25 pg. A15.

[326] Lee Romney. "Attack Shakes Community," pg. A1.

[327] Ibid.

[328] Ibid.

[329] "California Lawmaker, Officials Don Turban." *The Pioneer.* New Delhi, India. March 15, 2011.

[330] Cynthia Hubert. "Funeral: 2nd Sikh Shooting Victim Mourned," *Sacramento Bee.* Sacramento, CA April 24, 2011, pg. B1; "Reward Offered in Killing of Two Sikhs in U.S."

[331] Stephen Magagnini. "Second Sikh Man Dies," *Sacramento Bee.* McClatchy-Tribune Business News. DC April 17, 2011.

[332] "Reward Offered in Killing of Two Sikhs in U.S."

[333] Jessica Jenkins. "Sikhs Still Targets of Hate Crimes 10 Years After 9/11, AP Reports," www.groundswell-movement.org, July 11, 2011.

Chapter Eleven:

[1] Tanmaya Nanda. "There Are No Boundaries for Hate Crimes," *India Abroad.* New York, NY Oct. 4, 2002, v. 33, iss 1, pg. A12.

[2] Ibid.

[3] Lee Romney. Attack Shakes Community," *Los Angeles Times.* Los Angeles, CA April 11, 2011, pg. A1.

[4] Jeff Jacoby. "The 'Islamophobia' Myth." *Boston Globe.* Boston, MA Dec. 8, 2010, pg. A17.

[5] Ibid.

[6] Ibid.

[7] Beth Shuster. "US Strikes Back," *Los Angeles Times.* Los Angeles, CA Oct. 11, 1001, pg. A1.

[8] Ibid.

[9] Ibid.

[10] J. Zamga Browne. "With Guns Drawn, Police Invade Mosque on Suspicious Pretext," *NY Amsterdam News.* New York, NY Jan. 15, 1994, v. 85, iss 3 pg. 3.

[11] Yusuf Salaam. "What Muslims Want," *NY Amsterdam News.* New York, NY Jan. 22, 1994, v. 85, iss 4, pg. 1.

[12] Yusef Salaam. "Police Storm Troop Muslims' Ramadan," *NY Amsterdam News.* March 2, 1996 v. 87, iss 9, pg. 1.

[13] Ibid.

[14] Ibid.

[15] Charles Baillou. "Muslims Seek Answers," *NY Amsterdam News.* New York, NY. Feb. 19, 1994, v. 85 iss 3, pg. 3.

[16] Ibid.

[17] Ibid.

[18] Frank Fuhrig. "Simon Visits Burned-Out Mosque," *State Journal Register.* Springfield, IL Oct. 9, 1995, pg. 17.

[19] Martha Irvine. "Ethnic Backlash," *Denver Post.* Denver, CO Sept. 18, 2001, pg. A12.

[20] Ibid.

[21] Mary Leonard. "Arab-Americans Feel Sting of Profiling," *Boston Globe.* Boston, MA Oct. 19, 2001 pg. A20.

[22] Ibid.

[23] Ibid.

[24] Ibid.

[25] Allan Turner and Dale Lezon. "Our Changed World," *Houston Chronicle.* Houston, TX Sept. 8, 2002, pg. A33.

[26] Ibid.

[27] Lisa Tsering. "Cab Driver Victim," *India-West*. San Leandro, CA Nov. 30, 2007, v. 33, iss 1, pg. A1, A28.

[28] Jennifer Sullivan. "Hate Crime Charge Filed in Cab Attack," *Seattle Times*. Seattle, WA Nov. 28, 2007, pg. B1.

[29] Interview with human rights attorney Hamdy Zeidan, Alexandria, Egypt, May 1, 2002.

[30] "New York Police Man's Son Not Charged With Hate Crime in Racial Attack," www.leosigh.com, Nov. 5, 2010.

[31] Albor Ruiz. "Positive Steps Attack Negative Bias," *New York Daily News*. New York, NY July 18, 2004, pg. 1.

[32] Troy Anderson. "Hate Crimes Up," *Daily News*. Los Angeles, CA Dec. 21, 2001, pg. N3.

[33] Joe Hughes. "Hate-Crime Victim," *San Diego Union Tribune*. San Diego, CA Dec. 18, 2001, pg. B2.

[34] Daniel Chacon. 'Stabbing of Muslim," *San Diego Union-Tribune*. San Diego, CA Oct. 26, 2001, pg. 3.

[35] Arun Venugopal. "Vandals Set Fire," *India Abroad*. New York, NY Dec. 10, 2004, v. 35, iss 11, pg. A6.

[36] Cassandra Braun. "Local Muslims Fear Islamic Center Target of Hate Crimes," *Oakland Tribune*. Oakland, Ca. Jan. 30, 2007, pg. 1.

[37] Tanmaya Nanda. "Two Sikhs Attacked," *India Abroad*. New York, NY July 23, 2004, v. 24, iss 43, pg. A10.

[38] Elizabeth Langton. "Mosque Vandals Receive Probation," *Augusta Chronicle*. Augusta, GA May 6, 2004, pg. A6.

[39] "News Roundup," *San Antonio Express-News*. San Antonio, TX May 6, 2004, pg. 2B.

[40] Tamara El-Khoury. "Man Claims Racial Harassment," *St. Petersburg Times*. St. Petersburg, FL Jan. 31, 2007, pg. 1.

[41] Tony Bridges. "Bay School Bus Driver Charged," *News Herald*. Panama City, FL June 13, 2007, pg. 1

[42] Ibid.

[43] "Protests at Mosque," *Arab-American View*. Orland Park: IL Nov. 5. 2001 v 2 Issue 11, pg. 1.

[44] Ibid.

[45] Ibid.

[46] Ibid.

[47] Beth Shuster. "U.S. Strikes Back," pg. A1.

[48] Jose Arballo Jr. "Guilty Plea in Anti-Muslim Case," *Press Enterprise*. Riverside, CA Oct. 2, 2001, pg. B3.

[49] Ibid.

[50] James Zogby. "Arab Americans," *Arab American News*. Dearborn, MI April 10, 1998, v. 13, iss 652, pg. 4.

[51] Ibid.

[52] Ibid.

[53] Greg Winter. "Some Mideast Immigrants, Shaken," *New York Times*, New York, NY Nov. 23, 2001, pg. B1.

[54] Ibid.

[55] Kelly Thornton. "Local Muslims Feel Eyes," *San Diego Union Tribune*, San Diego, CA Sept. 10, 2002 pg. A1.

[56] Asfaque Swapan. "Sept. 11 Continues," *India-West*. San Leandro, CA Oct. 5, 2007, v. 32, iss 45 pg. A10.

[57] Silja Talvi. "And Justice for All," *Colorlines*. Winter 2002/2003. Oakland, CA Jan. 31, 2003 v. 5 iss 4 pg. 18.

[58] Ibid.

[59] Ibid.

[60] Chris Newton. "FBI Widens Sleeper Terrorist Search," *Charleston Gazette*. Charleston, WV July 12, 2002, pg. 32.

[61] Ibid.

[62] Bina Ahmad. "People of Color," *San Diego Union Tribune*. San Diego, CA June 23, 2002, pg. G6.

[63] "FBI Searching for Al-Qaeda's Hidden US Support Network," *Philadelphia Daily News*, Philadelphia, PA July 12, 2002, pg. 22.

[64] Annie Nakao. "Muslims in America," *San Francisco Chronicle*. San Francisco, CA April 1, 2003, pg. D8.

[65] Michael Potts. "Racial Harassment Persists," *India-West*. San Leandro, CA Sept. 15, 2006, v. 31, iss 43 pg. A1.

[66] Lynette Clemetson. "FBI Tries to Dispel Surveillance Concerns," *New York Times*, New York, NY Jan. 12, 2006, pg. A18.

[67] Ibid.

[68] Paloma Esquivel. "FBI Losing Trust," *Los Angeles Times*. Los Angeles, CA April 20, 2009, pg. A3.

[69] Ibid.

[70] Ibid.

[71] Ibid.

[72] Matthai Kuruvila. "US Muslims Debate," *San Francisco Chronicle*. San Francisco, CA April 6, 2009, pg. A1.

[73] "CAIR: Calif. Muslim to Sue FBI for Secret GPS Surveillance," PR Newswire. New York, NY March 1, 2011.

[74] Ibid.

[75] Jerry Markon. "Mosque Infiltration Feeds Muslims' Distrust of FBI," *Washington Post*. DC Dec. 5, 2010, pg. A1.

[76] Ibid.

[77] Ibid.

[78] Sunita Sohrabji. "S. Asian Groups," *India-West*. San Leandro, CA Jan. 9, 2009 v. 34, iss 7, pg. A10.

[79] Michelle Boorstein. "Surge in Anti-Muslim Incidents Reported," *Washington Post*. DC Sept. 19, 2006, pg. B3.

[80] Aziz Haniffa. "Dr. Singh's Daughter," *India Abroad*. New York, NY June 15, 2007, v. 37, iss 37, pg. A1

[81] Silja Talvi. "And Justice for All," pg. 18.

[82] Ibid.

[83] Ibid.

[84] Asfaque Swapan. "South Asians Reflect," *India-West*. San Leandro, CA Sept. 15, 2006 v. 31, iss 43 pg. A1

[85] Ibid.

[86] Ibid.

[87] "Muslims Mull Over Law Suits," *India Abroad*. New York, NY. Oct. 12, 2001, v. 32 iss. 2, pg. 1.

[88] Tanmaya Nanda. "Two Sikhs Attacked," pg. A10.

[89] Steve Miller. "Rights Panel," *Washington Times*. DC Oct. 13, 2001, pg. A2.

[90] Ibid.

[91] Ibid.

[92] Ibid.

[93] Eleanor Lee. "Hate Crimes," *Northwest Asian Weekly*. Seattle, WA Dec. 8, 2007, v. 26, iss 50, pg. 11.

[94] Cassandra Braun. "Local Muslims Fear Islamic Center Target of Hate Crimes," pg. 1.

[95] Chris Bull. "Gay, Muslim, and Scared," *The Advocate*. Los Angeles, CA Oct. 23, 2001 iss 849, pg. 54.

[96] Chris Lisotta. "Killed in Broad Daylight," *The Advocate*. Los Angeles, CA Dec. 4, 2007 iss 998 pg. 29-33.

[97] Robert Salladay, "Northern California Protests War," *San Francisco Chronicle*. San Francisco, CA Feb. 16, 2003.

[98] Arun Venugopal. "Vandals Set Fire," pg. A6.

[99] Aziz Haniffa. "Asian Groups Dispute FBI," *India Abroad*. New York, NY Dec. 10, 2004, v. 35, iss 11, pg. A6.

[100] Ibid.

[101] Sher Singh. "They Said I Was a Terrorist," *The Record*. Bergen County, NJ March 21, 2002, pg. L11.

[102] Carri Thevenot. "Nevadans Fear Rise in Hate Crimes," *Las Vegas Review-Journal*. Sept. 18, 2001, pg. 23.

[103] Alberta Phillips. "When Racism is No Longer Somebody Else's Problem," *Austin American Statesman*. Austin, TX March 31, 2002, pg. J3.

[104] Ibid.

[105] Ibid.

[106] Keith Morelli. "Islamic Center Set Afire," *Tampa Tribune*. Tampa, FL April 13, 2007, pg. 1.

[107] Susan Ives. "Our People," *San Antonio Express-News*. San Antonio, TX April 17, 2004, pg. 11B.

[108] Ibid.

[109] "Reporting Hate Crimes Against Muslims," *Washington Times*. DC May 15, 2004, pg. A14.

[110] Ibid.

[111] Deborah Bulkeley. "Muslims in U.S. See Little 9/11 Backlash," *Deseret Morning News*. Salt Lake City, UT Sept. 9, 2006, E1.

[112] Ibid.

[113] Cassandra Braun. "Local Muslims Fear Islamic Center Target of Hate Crimes," pg. 1.

[114] "Prosecutor Wisely Passes on Hate Crimes," *Honolulu Star Bulletin*. Honolulu, HI March 23, 2007, v. 12, iss 82.

[115] Ibid.

[116] Michelle Malkin. "Fake Muslim Hate Crimes: Where's the Apology, CAIR?" www.michellemalkin.com, October 3, 2004.

[117] Ibid.

[118] "Swastika Spray-Painted on Islamic Symbol," *Fort-Worth Star Telegram*, Fort Worth, TX Dec. 29, 1997 pg. 6.

[119] Marc Freeman. "Florida Hate Crime May Have Been Horseplay," *Knight Ridder Tribune News Service*. DC April 14, 2004, pg. 1.

[120] Ibid.

[121] Cassandra Braun. "Local Muslims Fear Islamic Center Target of Hate Crimes," pg. 1.

[122] Ibid.

[123] Georgett Roberts. "Hair Tomorrow," *New York Post*. New York, NY May 28, 2007, pg. 13.

[124] Sarah Okeson. "Judge Dismisses Suit Filed by Muslim Group; Vandalism at Area Mosque Not Subjected to Hate Crime Laws," *Journal Star*. Peoria, IL Aug. 27, 1992, pg. B4.

[125] Ibid.

[126] Alex Ginsberg. "Turban Rap Unravels," *New York Post*. New York, NY Dec. 6, 2005, pg. 30.

[127] George Joseph. "Khalsa's Case," *India Abroad*. New York, NY July 22, 2005, v. 35, iss 43, pg. A12.

[128] "Judge Tells Sikh He Can Not Wear Turban in Court," *Sikh Coalition Newsletter*. www.sikhcoalition.org, Nov. 18, 2003.

[129] Rebecca Rosen Lum. "Reports of Anti-Muslim Bias," *Oakland Tribune*. Oakland, CA July 6, 2007, pg. 1.

[130] Gary Grass, Ammar Askari. "U.S. Must Recognize Loyalty of Citizens of Arab Descent,'" *Capital Times*. Madison, WI Sept. 11, 2003, pg. 12A.

[131] "Muslims Mull Over Law Suits," pg. 1.

[132] Ibid.

[133] Chris Jenkins. "Immigrant's Assailant Sentenced." *Washington Post*. DC March 8, 2002, pg. B9.

[134] Ibid.

[135] Ibid.

[136] Ibid.

[137] Ibid.

[138] Ibid.

[139] Ibid.

[140] Ibid.

[141] Susan Ives. "Our People," pg. 11B.

[142] Karen de Sa. "Local Muslims," *San Jose Mercury News*. San Jose, CA, Dec. 5, 2001, pg. 1.

[143] H.G. Reza. "San Diego Muslims Criticize Mayor," *Los Angeles Times*, Los Angeles, CA Oct. 12, 2001, pg. B8.

[144] Kristen Green. "Murphy Shuns Meeting," *San Diego Union Tribune*. San Diego, CA. Oct. 13, 2001, B2:6,7; B3:1.

[145] Riad Abdelkarim. "Arab and Muslim Americans," *Washington Report*. May 2003, vol 22, iss 4, pg. 55-6.

[146] Shaun Sutner. "Activists Say Glodis Flier Amounted to Hate Crime," *Telegram and Gazette*, Worcester, MA July 5, 2003, pg. A3.

[147] Cliff Cheng. "Hate-Crime Prevention," *Daily News*. Los Angeles, CA March 17, 2003, pg. N13.

[148] Khalil Osman. "Muslims Come Under Attack," *Middle East Online*. Durham. Oct. 6, 2001.

[149] Dan Eggen. "Alleged Remarks on Islam," *Washington Post*, DC February 14, 2002, pg. A31.

[150] Ibid.

[151] Ibid.

[152] Edward Park. "Increase in Hate Incidents," *Asianweek*. San Francisco, CA Jan. 2, 2002, v. 23, iss 19, pg. 11.

[153] Jack Shaheen. Guilty. (Northampton, MA: Olive Branch Press, 2008): 101.

[154] Nahal Toosi. "Muslim Student Group," *Milwaukee Journal Sentinel*. Milwaukee, WI May 1, 2004, pg. 3B

[155] Gregory Gross. "9/11 Cited in 15% Rise in Hate Crimes," *San Diego Union Tribune*. San Diego, CA Sept. 19, 2002, pg. B1.

[156] Guillermo Contreras. "Getting Tough," *San Antonio Express-News*. San Antonio, TX May 8, 2007, pg. 1A.

[157] Beth Shuster. "U.S. Strikes Back," pg. A1.

[158] Kevin Rothstein. "Mass. Fourth in Hate Crimes," *Boston Herald*. Boston, MA Nov. 26, 2002, pg. 3.

[159] Jim Llim. "We Are Not the Enemy," *Asianweek*. San Francisco, CA Sept. 4, 2002, v. 24, iss 2, pg. 10.

[160] Ibid.

[161] Ibid.

[162] Beth Shuster. "U.S. Strikes Back," pg. A1.

[163] Mary Beth Sheridan. "Backlash Changes Form," *Washington Post*. DC March 4, 2002, pg. B1.

[164] Ibid.

165 Guillermo Contreras. "Vandalism," *San Antonio Express-News*. San Antonio, TX July 18, 2007, pg. B1.

166 Aziz Haniffa. "Asian Groups Dispute FBI," pg. A6.

167 Curt Anderson. "Muslims in the U.S." *Seattle Times*. Seattle, WA Nov. 26, 2002, pg. A5.

168 Ryan Kim. "Cops Call Rape a Hate Rape," *San Francisco Chronicle*. San Francisco, CA Sept. 5, 2002, pg. A19.

169 Tim Zorn. "Feds Handle Most Hate Crime Cases," *Post Tribune*. Gary, IN Jan. 22, 2002, pg. A3.

170 Ruth Morris. "Leader of Muslim Group," *Knight Ridder Tribune News Service*. DC May 2, 2007, pg. 1.

171 Ibid.

172 Laylan Connelly. "Sikhs Encouraged to Wear Turbans," *Orange County Register*. Santa Ana, Ca. April 10, 2006, pg. 1.

173 Sushma Subramanian. "Graffiti Called Hate Crime," *Orange County Register*. Santa Ana, Ca. June 29, 2006 pg. 1.

174 "Apparent Hate Crimes in OC," *Orange County Register*. Santa Ana, CA March 19, 2003, pg. 1.

175 Ibid.

176 Meredith Heagney. "Rock Throwers Hit Local Mosque," *Columbus Dispatch*. Columbus, OH Sept. 19, 2007, pg. 1B.

177 George Joseph. "Bullet Attacks," *India Abroad*. New York, NY June 25, 2004, v. 34, iss 39, pg. A8.

178 Ahan Kim. "Computer Hackers Hit U.S. Muslim Council," *Palm Beach Post*. West Palm Beach, FL Nov. 15, 2001, pg. 15A.

179 Ruth Morris. "Leader of Muslim Group," pg. 1.

180 Tom Ramstack. "Attack Backlash Fades," *Washington Times*. DC Feb. 11, 2002.

181 *Los Angeles Times*. Los Angeles, CA Feb. 2, 2002.

182 Joe Hughes. "Hate-Crime Victim," pg. B2.

183 Catie O'Toole. "Oswego: Teen to Plead Guilty," *Post-Standard*. Syracuse, NY April 13, 2002, pg. A1.

184 Ibid.

185 Margaret Kimberly. "Professor is Turning His Back on His Ancestors' Trial," *Seattle Skanner*. Portland, OR June 21, 2006, v. 28, iss 35, pg. 5.

186 Ibid.

187 Randall Kennedy. Nigger: The Strange Career of a Troublesome Word. (New York: Pantheon, 2002).

188 Margaret Kimberley. "Professor is Turning His Back On His Ancestors' Trial," pg. 5.

189 Arthur Pais. "Fear of the Dark," *India Abroad*. New York, NY Oct. 5, 2007, v. 38, iss 1, pg. M3, 4.

190 "Education Outlook," *ADC Times*. Oct./Nov. 2001, v. 21, iss 5 pg. 1-5.

191 Arthur Pais. "Fear of the Dark," pg. M3, 4.

192 Chris Lau. "Police Say Attacks on Fremont Family Not a Hate Crime," *Oakland Tribune*. Oakland, CA April 20, 2005, pg. 1.

193 David Arenberg. "A Jew in Prison," *Utne Reader*. Topeka, KS no. 159 (May-June 2010). pg. 34.

194 Hanna Rosin. "For Arab Americans, a Familiar Backlash," *Washington Post*. DC Sept. 13, 2001, pg. A26.

195 Raja Mishra. "Arab and Asian Immigrants Find Hostility," *Boston Globe*, Boston, MA Sept. 18, 2001 pg. A13.

196 Pat Sullivan. "Police Say Alleged Stoning of Muslims Not a 'Hate Crime,'" *Boston Herald*. Boston, MA April 21, 1992, pg. 8.

197 "No Place for Hate," *Post-Standard*. Syracuse, NY Nov. 23, 2001, pg. A16.

198 Ibid.

Chapter Twelve:

[1] Constantine Cavafy. "Waiting for the Barbarians," in <u>Complete Poems of Cavafy</u>, translated by Rae Dalven. (New York: Harcourt, Brace, and World, 1961). Constantine Cavafy. <u>C.P. Cavafy: Collected Poems</u>, translated by Edmund Keeley and Philip Sherrard. (Princeton: Princeton University Press, 1975). This excerpt is a variation of previous translations.

[2] "US Muslims, Arab-Americans," *Hindustan Times*. New Delhi, India, Sept. 6, 2006.

[3] "UC Berkeley Co-Sponsored Report Finds Islamophobia on the Rise," *Oakland Tribune*. Oakland, CA June 24, 3011.

[4] "Muslim Buildings Attacked," *Arab American News*. Dearborn, MI Sept. 30, 2006, v. 22 iss 1077 pg. 10.

[5] Ibid.

[6] "Hate Crime Against Arabs," *Arab American News*. Dearborn, MI Jan. 27, 2007, v. 23, iss 1094, pg. 8.

[7] Patrik Jonsson. "Bacon Attack," *Christian Science Monitor*. Boston, MA Oct 15, 2010.

[8] "Pig's Head on Pole," *Nottingham Evening Post*. Nottingham, UK June 29, 2011, pg. 8.

[9] Brendan Manning. "Forum," *Northwest Asian Weekly*. Seattle, WA Oct. 4, 2002, v. 21, iss 39, pg. 1.

[10] Anju Kaur. "TSA: Body Scanners Cannot See Through Turbans," SikhNN. January 13, 2011.

[11] Ibid.

[12] Ibid.

[13] "Sikh Coalition Responds to the TSA," US Newswire. DC Oct. 16, 2007.

[14] Viji Sundaram. "Reports of Hate Crimes," *India-West*. San Leandro, CA Sept. 28, 2001, v. 26, iss 47, pg. A1.

[15] Ibid.

[16] Teresa Mask. "Arab-American Lawyers," *Daily Herald*. Arlington Heights, IL Sept. 27, 2001, pg. 14.

[17] Ibid.

[18] "Lawsuits Accuse 4 Airlines of Bias," *Washington Post*. DC June 5, 2002, pg. A2.

[19] "Coalition Endorses Airline Discrimination Suit Against Delta," *Sikh Coalition Newsletter*, www.sikhcoalition.org, Sept. 30, 2003; "Delta Airlines Reaches Agreement with Sikh American Alleging Harassment, Profiling," www.saldelf.org.

[20] Ibid.

[21] "Discrimination Lawsuit Filed," *Arab American News*. Dearborn, MI Oct. 27, 2007, v. 23, iss 1133, pg. 22.

[22] Ibid.

[23] Ibid.

[24] Ibid.

[25] Susan Ferriss. "Sikh Musicians Protest Order," *Sacramento Bee*. Sacramento, CA Nov. 27, 2008, pg. B5.

[26] Larry Gordon. "Arabic Language Flash Cards Don't Fly With the TSA," *Los Angeles Times*. Los Angeles, CA Feb. 11, 2010.

[27] Ibid.

[28] Steve Crump. "Imams Plan to File Suit After Removal From Flight," *WBTV*. Charlotte, NC May 6, 2011.

[29] Ibid.

[30] Ibid.

[31] Kay Johnson. "Third Imam Says He was Not Allowed to Board Flights," *WBTV* online. Charlotte, NC May 8, 2011.

[32] Niraj Warikoo. "Ohio Woman Says That Detainment After 9/11 Flight Was Ethnic Profiling," *Detroit Free Press*. Detroit, MI Sept. 14, 2011.

[33] Ibid.

[34] Andrew Gumbel. "Ohio Woman Shoshana Hebshi Tells of Detention After Removal From Plane." *Guardian*. London, UK. www.guardian.co.uk, Sept. 14, 2011.

[35] Ibid.

[36] Niraj Warikoo. "Ohio Woman Says That Detainment After 9/11 Flight Was Ethnic Profiling."

[37] Oralandar Brand-Williams. "Muslims Urge Probe of Border Treatment," *Detroit News*. Detroit, MI March 25, 2011, pg. A1.

[38] Ibid.

[39] Ibid.

[40] Imad Hamad. "Civil Remedies," *Arab American News*. Dearborn, MI March 18, 2006, v. 22, iss 1049, pg. 5.

[41] Ibid.

[42] Kate Long. "FBI Tries to Reassure Muslims," *Charleston Gazette*. Charleston, WV March 22, 2003, pg. 5A.

[43] Robert Salladay, "Northern California Protests War," *San Francisco Chronicle*. San Francisco, CA Feb. 16, 2003.

[44] Riad Abdelkarim. "Surge in Hate Crimes," *Washington Report*. DC April 2003, v. 22, iss 3 pg. 51.

[45] Michael Potts. "CAIR Reports," *India-West*. San Leandro, CA May 7, 2004, v. 29, iss 27, pg. A28.

[46] Ibid.

[47] Riad Abdelkarim. "Surge in Hate Crimes," pg. 51.

[48] Michael Potts. "CAIR Reports." pg. A28.

[49] Ibid.

[50] Alisa Solomon. "From Baghdad to Brooklyn," *Village Voice*. New York, NY April 2, 2003, v. 48 iss 14, pg. 26-8.

[51] Ibid.

[52] Teresa Watanabe. "Anti-Muslim Incidents Rise," *Los Angeles Times*. Los Angeles, CA May 3, 2004, pg. B1.

[53] Allan Turner and Dale Lezon. "Our Changed World," *Houston Chronicle*. Houston, TX Sept. 8, 2002, pg. A33.

[54] Ibid.

[55] Kelly Brewington. "FBI's Mosque-Counting Policy," *Orlando Sentinel*. Orlando, FL Feb. 12, 2003, pg. 1.

[56] "Mosque Census Order Ignored," *Tulsa World*. Tulsa, OK Feb. 22, 2003, pg. A15.

[57] Ibid.

[58] Ibid.

[59] Kelly Brewington. "Anti-Terrorism," *Augusta Chronicle*. Augusta, GA Feb. 22, 2003, pg. D5.

[60] Ibid.

[61] Ibid.

[62] Spencer Ackerman. "FBI Teaches Agents: 'Mainstream' Muslim are 'Violent, Radical,'" *Wired*. www.wired.com. Sept. 14, 2011; Janet Smith. "Anti-Muslim Hate Crime Rash Reported Around 9/11 Anniversary," *Hatewatch*. Southern Poverty Law Center. www.splc.org, Sept. 14, 2011.

[63] Teresa Watanabe. "Anti-Muslim Incidents Rise," pg. B1.

[64] Ibid.

[65] Albor Ruiz. "Hate Crimes Target Arabs," *New York Daily News*. New York, NY April 16, 2003, pg. 8.

[66] "Election 2004," *Arab American News*. Dearborn, MI May 8, 2004, v. 20, iss 952, pg. 11.

[67] Ibid.

[68] Ibid.

[69] Ibid.

[70] Riad Abdelkarim. "Surge in Hate Crimes," pg. 51.

[71] Albor Ruiz. "Hate Crimes Target Arabs," pg. 8.

[72] Ibid.

[73] Deborah Kong. "Arabs, Muslims Try and Prevent Backlash," *Arab American News*. Dearborn, MI March 28, 2003, v. 19, iss 893, pg. 8.

[74] Michael Potts. "CAIR Reports" pg. A28.

[75] Annie Nakao. "Muslims in America," *San Francisco Chronicle*. San Francisco, CA April 1, 2003, pg. D8.

[76] Loudres Leslie. "Muslim, Arabs," *Star Tribune*. Minneapolis, MN Sept. 9, 2002, pg. 8A.

[77] Mary Beth Sheridan. "Muslims in the U.S. Feel Targeted," *Washington Post*. DC July 9, 2003, pg. A1.

[78] "Anti-Muslim Bomber Gets Probation," *Arab American News*. Dearborn, MI Oct. 3, 2003, v. 20, iss 920, pg. 2.

[79] Ibid.

[80] Mary Beth Sheridan. "Muslims in the U.S. Feel Targeted," pg. A1.

[81] Sunita Sohrabji. "S. Asian Groups," *India-West*. San Leandro, CA Jan. 9, 2009 v. 34, iss 7, pg. A10.

[82] Tanmaya Nanda. "There Are No Boundaries for Hate Crimes," *India Abroad*. New York, NY Oct. 4, 2002, v. 33, iss 1, pg. A12.

[83] Ibid.

[84] Ed Hayward. "Attack on America," *Boston Herald*. Boston, MA Sept. 29, 2001, pg. 6.

[85] "Two More Kirpan Prosecutions Dropped in Montana," *Sikh Coalition Newsletter*. www.sikhcoalition.org, May 18, 2004.

[86] Ibid.

[87] Ibid.

[88] "California Passes Bill on the Sikh Symbol Kirpan," *Hindustan Times*. New Delhi, India June 3, 2009.

[89] Jim Zamora. "California Study," *Oregonian*. Portland, OR July 19, 1996, pg. A12.

[90] Florangela Davila. "Hate Crime Response Criticized." *Seattle Times*, Seattle, WA Nov. 14, 2002, pg. B2.

[91] Gregory Gross. "9/11 Cited in 15% Rise in Hate Crimes," *San Diego Union Tribune*. San Diego, CA Sept. 19, 2002, pg. B1.

[92] Ibid.

[93] "Sikh to Sue Police Over His Turban and Beard," *New York Times*, New York, NY March 4, 2003; Susan Saulny. "State Lawyer to Aid Sikh Suing in Bias Case," *New York Times*, New York, NY June 5, 2004.

[94] "The Sikh Coalition Ensures that the LA County Police Department Welcomes Sikhs," "Washington DC Police Chief Welcomes Sikhs into DC Police Force," *Sikh Coalition Newsletter*. www.sikhcoalition.org, April 12, 2002.

[95] "MTA Proposes Turban Policy," *Sikh Coalition Newsletter*. www.sikhcoalition.org, Nov. 4, 2004.

[96] "Stranded Passenger with Kirpan," *Sikh Coalition Newsletter*. www.sikhcoalition.org, April 5, 2002.

[97] Ibid.

[98] "Sikh Given Criminal Citation for Wearing Kirpan," *Sikh Coalition Newsletter*. www.sikhcoalition.org, March 1, 2005.

[99] Andrea Elliott. "Generation 9/11," *New York Times*. New York, NY Sept. 8, 2011.

[100] Sara Goo. "Sen. Kennedy Flagged by No-Fly List," *Washington Post*. Washington, DC Aug. 20, 2004, pg. A1.

[101] Ronald Smothers. "Steadfast in His Turban, a Lawyer Raises Awareness," *New York Times* online. Jan. 28, 2003.

[102] Ibid.

[103] Francis Assisi. "Community Target of Harassment," *India-West*. San Leandro, CA Feb. 1991, v. 16, iss 11, pg. 1.

[104] Jodi Wilgoren. "Going by 'Joe,' not 'Yussef,'" *New York Times*. New York, NY Sept. 11, 2002, pg. G15.

[105] Ibid.

[106] Rachel Zoll. "Interest in Muslim Products," *San Francisco Chronicle*. San Francisco, CA Dec. 27, 2010, pg. D3.

[107] Viji Sundaram. "Hate Crime Fears Rise," *India-West*. San Leandro, CA Sept. 28, 2001, v. 26, iss 47, pg. A1.

[108] Ibid.

[109] Mona Eltahawy. "USA's Muslims Are Under Fire," *Washington Post*. DC March 24, 2003, pg. A13.

[110] Colin McNickle. "A Few Notes," *Pittsburgh Tribune-Review*. Greensburg, PA June 1, 2008.

[111] Timothy Williams. "Business Bias," *Los Angeles Times*. Los Angeles, CA Oct. 4, 1992, pg. 5.

[112] Ibid.

[113] Deborah Kong. "Anti-Muslim Backlash May Have Peaked," *Columbian*. Vancouver, WA Sept. 30, 2001, pg. A5.

[114] Dana Hedgpeth. "Marriott to Pay $115,000," *Washington Post*. DC Aug. 16, 2002, pg. E1.

[115] Ibid.

[116] Mackenzie Carpenter. "Sikh's Turban," *Pittsburgh Post-Gazette*. Pittsburgh, PA July 30, 2003, pg. B1.

[117] Ibid.

[118] "Pittsburgh Club Amends 'No Hats' Policy." *Sikh Coalition Newsletter*. www.sikhcoalition.org, Sept. 30, 2003.

[119] "Restaurant Agrees to Change Admissions Policy," *Sikh Coalition Newsletter*. www.sikhcoalition.org, Nov. 2, 2003.

[120] "Sikh Denied Entry to Club in Decatur, Georgia," *Sikh Coalition Newsletter*. www.sikhcoalition.org, March 26, 2004.

[121] Mary Beth Sheridan. "Muslims in the U.S. Feel Targeted," pg. A1.

[122] "Sikh Subway Franchise Owner," *Sikh Coalition Newsletter*. www.sikhcoalition.org, March 1, 2005.

[123] "Sikh States He Was Told Not To Work While Wearing Kara," Sikh *Coalition Newsletter*. www.sikhcoalition.org, March 1, 2005.

[124] Vivian Ho. "Abercrombie & Fitch Sued Over Hijab Firing," *San Francisco Chronicle*. www.SFGate.com, June 28, 2011.

[125] David Harper. "Jury Awards $20,000 in Suit," *Tulsa World*. Tulsa, OK www.tulsaworld.com. July 21, 2011.

[126] Sushma Subramanian. "Graffiti Victim," *Orange County Register*. Santa Ana, CA July 6, 2006, pg. 1.

[127] Ray Hanania. "Now That We've Remembered 9/11," *Arab American News*. Dearborn, MI Sept. 16, 2006, v. 22, iss 1075, pg. 4. There is 'halal food,' the Muslim equivalent to kosher cuisine, but this is distinct from 'Muslim food.'

[128] Ibid.

[129] Ibid.

[130] Ibid.

[131] Arthur Pais. "Fear of the Dark," *India Abroad.* New York, NY Oct. 5, 2007, v. 38 iss 1 pg. M3.

[132] Jodi Wilgoren. "Going by 'Joe,' not 'Yussef,'" pg. G15.

[133] Ibid.

[134] Deborah Kong. "Anti-Muslim Backlash May Have Peaked," pg. A5.

[135] Jodi Wilgoren. "Going by 'Joe,' not 'Yussef,'" pg. G15.

[136] Mary Sanchez. "American Muslims Fear," *Kansas City Star.* Kansas City, MO April 27, 2003, pg. 1.

[137] Ibid.

[138] Mary Beth Sheridan. "Backlash Changes Form," *Washington Post.* DC March 4, 2002, pg. B1.

[139] "Coalition Combats Kirpan Ban with IBM," "Coalition Resolves Kirpan Conflict with Accenture," in *Sikh Coalition Newsletter.* www.sikhcoalition.org, July 14, 2002; "Employer Allows Sikh Woman to wear Kirpan at Work," *Sikh Coalition Newsletter.* www.sikhcoalition.org, March 26, 2004.

[140] Momo Chang. "9/11 Bias Threatens Muslims' Careers," *Oakland Tribune,* Oakland, CA Sept. 19, 2005, pg. 1.

[141] Ibid.

[142] Marilyn Elias. "USA's Muslims Are Under Fire," *USA Today.* McLean, VA Aug. 10, 2006, pg. D1.

[143] Momo Chang. "9/11 Bias Threatens Muslims' Careers," pg. 1.

[144] "Coalition Assists Sikh Student Denied Admission," *Sikh Coalition Newsletter.* www.sikhcoalition.org, March 26, 2003.

[145] Momo Chang. "9/11 Bias Threatens Muslims' Careers," pg. 1.

[146] Christine Tamer. "Arab-Americans, Affirmative Action, and a Quest for Racial Identity," in *Texas Journal on Civil Liberties & Civil Rights,* (Fall 2010): 101-127.

[147] Lynette Celetson. "Homeland Security Given Data on Arab Americans," *New York Times.* New York, NY July 30, 2004.

[148] Ibid.

[149] Ibid.

[150] Ibid.

[151] Ibid.

[152] Nicoletta Karam. "Census Data and Security." *New York Times.* New York, NY Aug. 3, 2004.

[153] Jeb Phillips. "Columbus Hate Crimes," *Columbus Dispatch.* Columbus, OH Dec. 9, 2002, pg. 1B.

[154] Ruth Morris. "Leader of Muslim Group," *Knight Ridder Tribune News* Service. DC May 2, 2007, pg. 1.

[155] Teresa Watanabe. "Immigration Stories," *Los Angeles Times.* Los Angeles, CA Sept. 14, 2003, pg. B1.

[156] Ibid.

[157] Tamar Lewin, Gustav Niebuhr. "Attacks," *New York Times.* New York, NY. Sept. 18, 2001, pg. B5.

[158] Aziz Haniffa. "Muslim, Arab, and Sikh," *India Abroad.* New York, NY March 28, 2003, v. 32, iss 26, pg. A4.

[159] "CAIR: Anti-Muslim Okla. Lawn Signs," *US Newswire.* DC June 26, 2010.

[160] David Nakamura. "Hearings Stir Japanese Empathy," *Journal-Gazette.* Ft. Wayne, IN March 11, 2011, pg. A7.

[161] Ibid.

[162] Aziz Haniffa. "Obama Appoints," *India Abroad.* New York, NY Sept. 24, 2010, v. 40, iss 52, pg. A19.

[163] Josh Poltilove. "Anti-Muslim Bias," *Tampa Tribune.* Tampa, FL June 21, 2007, pg. 1.

[164] Ibid.

[165] Geneive Abdo and E.A. Torriero. "Army Chaplain's Case Has Left Many U.S. Muslims Distrustful," *Chicago Tribune*. Chicago, IL Knight Ridder Tribune News Service. DC May 6, 2004, pg. 1.

[166] Ibid.

[167] Will Youmans. "ADC," *Arab American News*. Dearborn, MI Dec. 6, 2008, v. 24, iss 1191, pg. 18.

[168] Aziz Haniffa. "Lawmakers Pledge," *India Abroad*. New York, NY May 29, 2009, v. 39, iss 35, pg. A23.

[169] Ibid.

[170] Sunita Sohrabji. "S. Asian Groups," pg. A10.

[171] Gerald Seib. "Attacks Enhance Role of Religion," *Wall St. Journal*. (Europe) Brussels, Sept. 19, 2001, pg. 2.

[172] Ibid.

[173] Jocelyn Wiener. "Lessons in Patience," *St. Petersburg Times*. St. Petersburg, FL Sept. 29, 2002, pg. 1F.

[174] Ibid.

[175] Hanna Rosin. "For Arab-Americans, A Familiar Backlash," *Washington Post*. DC Sept. 13, 2001, pg. A26.

[176] Jeff Sharlet. "Junkets for Jesus," *Mother Jones*. San Francisco, CA Dec. 2010.

[177] Richard Morin. "Babies, Bigotry, and 9/11," *Washington Post*. DC March 23, 2006, pg. A2.

[178] Ibid.

[179] Solana Pyne. "Making Enemies," *Village Voice*. New York, NY July 9, 2003, v. 48, iss 28, pg. 48.

[180] Ibid.

[181] Ibid.

[182] Ibid.

[183] Ibid.

[184] Ibid.

[185] Richard Rhodes. Why They Kill. (New York: Knopf, 1999).

[186] Suman Mozumder. "FBI Says Hate Crimes Against Muslims Were Up in 2001," *India Abroad*. New York, NY Dec. 6, 2002, v. 33, iss 10, pg. A3.

[187] Solana Pyne. "Making Enemies," pg. 48.

[188] Jessica Jenkins. "Sikhs Still Targets of Hate Crimes 10 Years After 9/11, AP Reports," www.groundswell-movement.org. July 11, 2011.

[189] Martin Seligman. Learned Optimism. (New York: Knopf, 1991).

[190] Marilyn Elias. "USA's Muslims Are Under Fire," pg. D1.

[191] Ibid.

[192] Ibid.

[193] Ibid.

[194] Ibid.

[195] "Case Update: Lodi Youths Fabricate Bias Crime Attack," *Sikh Coalition Newsletter*. www.sikhcoalition.org, March 26, 2004.

[196] Imad Hamad. "Climate of Fear," *Arab American News*. Dearborn, MI March 18, 2006, v. 22, iss 1049, pg. 5.

[197] Ibid.

[198] Amy Goodman. "Did CIA Destroy Tapes Showing Waterboarding and Involvement of Psychologists in Torture?" *Democracy Now*. www.democracynow.org. Dec. 10, 2007.

[199] David Goodman. "The Enablers: The Psychology Industry's Long and Shameful History with Torture." *Mother Jones.* www.motherjones.com. March 1. 2008.

[200] Ibid.

[201] Ibid.

[202] Andrew Welsh-Huggins. "APA Wants James Mitchell, Psychologist Who Helped CIA Torture, Stripped of His License," *Huffington Post.* www.huffingtonpost.com July 10, 2010.

[203] Ela Dutt. "Study Released," *India-Times.* New York, NY Sept. 22, 2006, v. 37, iss 38, pg. 6.

[204] Asfaque Swapan. "South Asians Reflect," *India-West.* San Leandro, CA Sept. 15, 2006 v. 31, iss 43 pg. A1.

[205] Lisa Martinez. "Racist Groups Pass Out Fliers," *The Gazette.* Colorado Springs, CO May 18, 2004, pg. 3 metro

[206] Ibid.

[207] Guillermo Contreras. "Getting Tough," *San Antonio Express-News.* San Antonio, TX May 8, 2007, pg. 1A.

[208] Ibid.

[209] Ibid.

[210] Ibid.

[211] Sheryl Thomas. "645 Bias Incidents," *News India Times.* New York, NY. Sept. 21, 2007, v. 38, iss 38, pg. 8.

[212] Margaret Kimberley. "Professor is Turning His Back On His Ancestors' Trial," *Seattle Skanner.* Portland, OR June 21, 2006, v. 28, iss 35 pg. 5.

[213] Elaine Chan. "Harassment Ordeal," *New York Daily News.* New York, NY June 6, 2007, pg. 1.

[214] Ly Phuong. "Montgomery Steps Up Its Fight Against Hate," *Washington Post.* DC Oct. 3, 2001, pg. B4.

[215] Brian Kluepfel. "Upswing in Hate Crimes," *Asianweek.* San Francisco, CA April 9, 2003, v. 24, iss 32, pg. 14.

[216] Jeet Thayil. "9/11 Hate Crime Victim's Brother Killed," *India Abroad.* New York, NY Aug. 16, 2002, v. 32, iss 46, pg. A1.

[217] Tamara Lush. "9/11 Memorial's Words," *Charleston Gazette.* Charleston, WV May 30, 2011, pg. A2

[218] Susan Ives. "Our People," *San Antonio Express-News.* San Antonio, TX April 17, 2004, pg. 11B.

[219] Ian Kilroy. "Muslim Group," *Irish Times.* Dublin, Ireland. May 3, 2004, pg. 11.

[220] Jessica Bennett. "Islamic Group Sees Firing of Radio Host," *Boston Globe.* Boston, MA April 25, 2004, pg. B3.

[221] Ibid.

[222] Richard Dujardin. "Religion," *Providence Journal.* Providence, RI March 22, 2003, pg. D1.

[223] Ibid.

[224] Ela Dutt. "WNEW Radio Relents," *News India-Times.* New York, NY Feb. 22, 2002, v. 33, iss 8, pg. 10.

[225] "RJ Compares Turban to Diaper," *Hindustan Times.* New Delhi, India. Sept. 21, 2007.

[226] David Folkenflik. "NPR Ends Williams' Contract After Muslim Remarks," National Public Radio. www.npr.org. Oct. 21, 2010.

[227] Jack Shaheen. "'24' Glorifies Torture, Foments Hate," *Augusta Chronicle.* Augusta, GA Feb. 26, 2007, pg. A5.

[228] Ibid.

[229] Ibid.

[230] Ibid.

[231] Patrik Jonsson. "Bacon Attack."

[232] Lisa Tsering. "Congress Members," *India-West.* San Leandro, CA April 11, 2003, v. 28, iss 23, pg. A31.

[233] Asfaque Swapan. "Irate Sikhs," *India-West*. San Leandro, CA Oct. 25, 2002, v. 27, iss 51, pg. A30.

[234] Ibid.

[235] "CAIR Asks Wal-Mart to Drop Game," PR Newswire. NY Dec. 19, 2006.

[236] Ibid.

[237] Ibid.

[238] Ilene Lelchuk. "Convert or Die Game," *San Francisco Chronicle*, San Francisco, CA Dec. 12, 2006.

[239] Anuradha Kher. "Hate Crimes Against Hindus," *Noticias Financieras*. Miami, FL Nov. 21, 2007, pg. 1.

[240] Ibid.

[241] Ed Condran. "Kathy Griffin," *Bucks County Courier Times*. Bucks County, PA June 2, 2008.

[242] Julia Angwin. "Aftermath: A Changing Society," *Wall St. Journal*. New York, NY Sept. 26, 2001, pg. A6.

[243] Ray Hanania. "Now That We've Remembered 9/11," pg. 4.

[244] Marilyn Elias. "USA's Muslims Are Under Fire," pg. D1

[245] Michelle Boorstein. "Surge in Anti-Muslim Incidents Reported," *Washington Post*. DC Sept. 19, 2006, pg. B3.

[246] Marilyn Elias. "USA's Muslims Are Under Fire," pg. D1.

[247] Ibid.

[248] Ibid.

[249] Richard Fausset. "Sikhs Mark New Year," *Los Angeles Times*. Los Angeles, CA April 14, 2003, pg. B1.

[250] Ibid.

[251] Ibid.

[252] Lesley Pearl. "Student Joins Jewish-Muslim Battle Against Backlash," *Jewish Bulletin of Northern California*. San Francisco, CA April 28, 1995, v. 144, iss 17 pg. 19.

[253] "Backlash Stings Muslims," *Times-Picayune*. New Orleans, LA Sept. 19, 2001, pg. 9.

[254] S. Ali. "Ship Them Back Home!" *India Abroad*. New York, NY Oct. 12, 2001, v. 32, iss 2, pg. M7.

[255] Jo Becker, Phuong Ly. "Sikhs Campaign Against Hate," *Washington Post*. DC Sept. 24, 2001, pg. B1.

[256] Laurie Goodstein, Tamar Lewin. "Victims of Mistaken Identity," *New York Times*. New York, NY Sept. 19, 2001, pg. A1.

[257] S. Ali. "Ship Them Back Home!" pg. M7.

[258] Ibid.

[259] "Sikhs Hopeful Oregon Will Overturn Turban Ban," *India-West*. San Leandro, CA Jan. 22, 2010, v.35, iss 9, pg. A16.

[260] Michael Romanowski. "Textbook Omissions and 9/11," *Clearinghouse*. DC July 2009, v. 82, iss 6, pg. 290-6.

[261] Ibid.

[262] Ibid.

[263] Nicoletta Karam. "Kahlil Gibran's Pen Bond: Modernism and the Manhattan Renaissance of Arab-American Literature," Ph.D. Dissertation, Brandeis University, May 2005.

[264] Spencer Wells. Journey of Man. (Princeton, New Jersey: Princeton University Press, 2002.)

[265] Silja Talvi. "And Justice for All," *Colorlines*. Winter 2002/2003. Oakland, CA Jan. 31, 2003, v. 5, iss 4 pg. 18.

[266] Ibid.

[267] Aziz Haniffa. "Sikh Group Forms Forum," *India Abroad*. New York, NY Sept. 26, 2003, v. 33, iss 52, pg. A8.

[268] Lisa Kocian. "Millis Sikhs," *Boston Globe*. Boston, MA Sept. 8, 2002, pg. 1.

[269] Ganesh Lakshman. "Faruja Singh," *News India-Times*. New York, NY Nov. 21, 2003, v. 34, iss 47, pg. 37.

[270] "Fauja Singh Inspires Through Adidas' 'Impossible is Nothing' Ad Campaign," *Sikh Coalition Newsletter*. www.sikhcoalition.org, May 18, 2004.

[271] Hugh Hart. "Art of Urgency." *Los Angeles Times*. Los Angeles, CA Feb. 18, 2003, pg. E1.

[272] Carlye Murphy. "For Muslims," *Washington Post*. DC Oct. 6, 2001, pg. A1.

[273] Ibid.

[274] Eric Lenkowitz. "Kids Reach Out to Muslims," *New York Post*. New York, NY Oct. 11, 2001, pg. 27.

[275] David Nakamura. "Hearings Stir Japanese Empathy," pg. A7.

[276] Carlye Murphy. "For Muslims," pg. A1.

[277] Ibid.

[278] Interview with instructor Deborah Messersmith, Garfield elementary school, Oakland, CA, Apr. 16, 2012.

[279] Kenneth Reich. "Hate-Crimes Hotline Launched," *Los Angeles Times*. Los Angeles, CA Oct. 5, 2001, pg. B8.

[280] Richard Winton. "Hate Crimes Soar," *Los Angeles Times*, Los Angeles, CA Dec. 21, 2001, pg. B1.

[281] Carlye Murphy. "For Muslims," pg. A1.

[282] Tanmaya Nanda. "Samaritans on a Train," *India Abroad*. New York, NY March 14, 2003, v. 32, iss 24, pg. A15.

[283] Ibid.

[284] Ibid.

[285] Ibid.

[286] Ibid.

[287] Ibid.

[288] "Judge Orders Attacker to Perform Community Service," *Sikh Coalition Newsletter*. www.sikhcoalition.org, April 28, 2004.

Afterword:

[1] "Group Calls For Investigation," CBS News. www.detroit.cbslocal.com, Feb. 7, 2012.

[2] Ibid.

[3] Laura Pullman, Michael Zennie, and Louis Boyle. "Neo-Nazi Shooter Who Gunned Down Six at Sikh Temple was Former Soldier who was Leader of a Racist White Power Band." *Daily Mail*. www.dailymail.com, Aug. 7, 2012.

[4] Ibid.

[5] Tom Schalmo and Leonard Green. "'9/11' Tattoo Skinhead Responsible for Massacre in Wisconsin," *New York Post*. www.nypost.com, Aug. 6, 2012.

[6] "Wisconsin Siblings Tell of Running to Warn Others As Temple Shooting Erupted," CNN. www.cnn.com, Aug. 9, 2012.

[7] "At Temple, Children's Warning Saved Others," *Boston Globe*. www.articles.boston.com, Aug. 8, 2012.

[8] Ibid.

[9] "Sikh Temple Shooting Victims," *Los Angeles Times*. www.graphics.latimes.com, Aug. 8, 2012.

[10] "Gunman Kills 6 at Sikh Temple in Wisconsin," *New York Times*. www.nytimes.com, Aug. 6, 2012.

[11] Dinesh Ramde. "Wisconsin Sikhs Leave Bullet Hole to Mark Mass Shooting," *Kansas City Star*. www.kansascity.com, Aug. 10, 2012.

[12] Tom Schalmo and Leonard Green. "'9/11' Tattoo Skinhead Responsible for Massacre in Wisconsin."

[13] Ibid.

[14] Cathy Lynn Grossman. "Sikh Temple Shooting Victims Remembered for their Kindness," *Washington Post.* www.washingtonpost.com, Aug. 8, 2012.

[15] Ibid.

[16] "Victim: Satwant Singh Kaleka," NBC News. www.nbc15.com, Aug. 8, 2012.

[17] "Wounded Cop Murphy, One Other Victim Upgraded After Sikh Temple Shooting," WTAQ News. www.wtaq.com, Aug. 9, 2012.

[18] Kevin Dolak. "Wisconsin Temple Shooting Hero Cop Brian Murphy Shot 8 Times, Waved Off Aid," ABC News, www.abcnews.go.com, Aug. 8, 2012.

[19] Ibid.

[20] Molly Hennessy-Fiske. "Before Suicide, Sikh Temple Gunman was Felled by 'Amazing Shot'," *Los Angeles Times.* www.latimes.com, Aug. 8, 2012.

[21] Amy Davidson. "Terror in Oak Creek," *New Yorker.* www.newyorker.com, Aug. 6, 2012.

[22] "Sikh Temple Shooting," www.huffingtonpost.com, Aug. 9, 2012.

[23] "At Temple, Children's Warning Saved Others," *Boston Globe.* www.articles.boston.com, Aug. 8, 2012.

[24] Steven Yaccino, Michael Schwirtz, and Marc Santora. "Gunman Kills 6 at a Sikh Temple Near Milwaukee," *New York Times.* www.nytimes.com, Aug. 6, 2012.

[25] "7 Shot Dead at Sikh Temple Near Milwaukee," *Chicago Tribune.* www.chicagotribune.com, Aug. 6, 2012.

[26] Brian Bennett. "Sikh Temple Shooting: Gunman Had Been on Investigators' Radar," *Los Angeles Times.* www.latimes.com, Aug. 6, 2012.

[27] "Temple Shooter Thrived as Neo-Nazi Musician," *USA Today.* www.usatoday.com, Aug. 6, 2012.

[28] Ibid.

[29] "2 of 3 Critical Sikh Temple Shooting Victims Upgraded." ABC News. www.abclocal.go.com, Aug. 9, 2012.

[30] "Cracking Wisconsin Gunman's Secret Racist Tattoo Code," ABC News. www.abcnews.go.com, Aug. 7, 2012.

[31] Abraham Foxman. "ADL Deplores Shooting at Sikh Temple," ADL Statement, www.adl.org, Aug. 6, 2012.

[32] Amy Davidson. "Terror in Oak Creek," *New Yorker.* www.newyorker.com, Aug. 6, 2012.

[33] "Sikh Temple Gunman had 'Kind and Gentle and Loving' Childhood, Stepmom Says," Fox News. www.foxnews.com, Aug. 6, 2012.

[34] "Exclusive: Interview with Professor Who Extensively Studied Alleged Wisconsin Mass Killer," *Huffington Post.* www.huffingtonpost.com, Aug. 10, 2012.

[35] "Wisconsin Siblings Tell of Running to Warn Others As Temple Shooting Erupted," CNN. www.cnn.com, Aug. 9, 2012.

[36] Gretchen Ehlke and Dinesh Ramde. "Sikh Temple Shooting Victims Described by Friends," *Huffington Post.* www.huffingtonpost.com, Aug. 8, 2012.

[37] Ibid.

[38] "Sikh Temple Shooting Victims," *Los Angeles Times.* www.graphics.latimes.com, Aug. 8, 2012.

[39] Jim Yardley and Sruthi Gottipati. "For Victim in Sikh Temple Shooting, a Life of Separation," *New York Times.* www.nytimes.com, Aug. 9, 2012.

[40] Ibid.

[41] Ibid.

[42] "Sikh Temple Shooting Victims," *Los Angeles Times.*

[43] Jim Yardley and Sruthi Gottipati. "For Victim in Sikh Temple Shooting, a Life of Separation."

[44] "Sikh Temple Shooting Victims," *Los Angeles Times.*

[45] Gretchen Ehlke and Dinesh Ramde. "Sikh Temple Shooting Victims Described by Friends."

[46] "Sikh Temple Shooting Victims," *Los Angeles Times.*

[47] Ibid.

[48] "The Sikh Temple Shooting Victims," CBS News. www.cbsnews.com, Aug. 6, 2012.

[49] "Sikh Temple Shooting Victims," *Los Angeles Times.*

[50] "Son Honors Father Killed in Fatal Shooting," *Examiner.* www.examiner.com, Aug. 10, 2012.

[51] Annysa Johnson and Aisha Qidwae. "Slain Temple President's Family Organizing Community Service," *Milwaukee Journal Sentinel.* www.jsonline.com, Aug. 6, 2012.

[52] "Victim: Suveg Singh Khattra," NBC News. www.nbc15.com, Aug. 8, 2012.

[53] "Sikh Temple Shooting Victims," *Los Angeles Times.*

[54] Dinesh Ramde. "Relatives Speak of Those Killed in Temple Shooting," www.boston.com, Aug. 6, 2012.

[55] Gretchen Ehlke and Dinesh Ramde. "Sikh Temple Shooting Victims Described by Friends."

[56] Cathy Lynn Grossman. "Sikh Temple Shooting Victims Remembered for their Kindness," *Washington Post.* www.washingtonpost.com, Aug. 8, 2012.

[57] "Sikh Temple Shooting Victims," *Los Angeles Times.*

[58] Ibid.

[59] Gretchen Ehlke and Dinesh Ramde. "Sikh Temple Shooting Victims Described by Friends," *Huffington Post.* www.huffingtonpost.com, Aug. 8, 2012.

[60] "Sikh Temple Shooting Victims," *Los Angeles Times.*

[61] "Son Honors Father Killed in Fatal Shooting," www.examiner.com, Aug. 10, 2012.

[62] "7 Shot Dead at Sikh Temple Near Milwaukee," *Chicago Tribune.* www.articles.chicagotribune.com, Aug. 6, 2012.

[63] Ibid.

[64] "Wounded Cop Murphy, One Other Victim Upgraded After Sikh Temple Shooting," WTAQ News. www.wtaq.com, Aug. 9, 2012.

[65] Linda Spice, Maggie Hayes, and Bill Hutchinson. "Gunman who Killed Six at Sikh Temple of Wisconsin in Suburban Milwaukee May Have been Army Veteran and Reportedly was 'Skinhead' or 'White Supremacist'," *New York Daily News.* www.nydailynews.com, Aug. 6, 2012.

[66] Monsy Alvarado. "Guest Preacher at Glen Rock Sikh Temple Among Wounded in Wisconsin Shooting," www.northjersey.com, Aug. 6, 2011.

[67] Ibid.

[68] "Wounded Cop Murphy, One Other Victim Upgraded After Sikh Temple Shooting," WTAQ News.

[69] Jim Yardley and Sruthi Gottipati. "For Victim in Sikh Temple Shooting, a Life of Separation," *New York Times.* www.nytimes.com, Aug. 9, 2012.

[70] Kevin Dolak. "Wisconsin Temple Shooting Hero Cop Brian Murphy Shot 8 Times, Waved Off Aid," www.abnews.go.com. Aug. 8, 2012.

[71] Matthew Lysiak and Corky Siemaszko. "Stunning New Revelations in Sikh Massacre Probe," *New York Daily News.* www.nydailnews.com, Aug. 8, 2012.

[72] Molly Hennessy-Fiske. "Before Suicide, Sikh Temple Gunman was Felled by 'Amazing Shot'," *Los Angeles Times.* www.latimes.com, Aug. 8, 2012.

[73] Andrea Domanick. "Candlelight Vigil in Las Vegas Honors Victims of Sikh Temple Shooting," *Las Vegas Sun.* www.lasvegassun.com, Aug. 8, 2012.

[74] Jim Yardley and Sruthi Gottipati. "For Victim in Sikh Temple Shooting, a Life of Separation."

[75] "At Service, Holder Calls Sikh Temple Shooting a Hate Crime." CNN. www.CNN.com, Aug. 10, 2012.

[76] Ibid.

[77] Ibid.

[78] Laura Pullman, Michael Zennie, and Louis Boyle. "Neo-Nazi Shooter Who Gunned Down Six at Sikh Temple was Former Soldier who was Leader of a Racist White Power Band." *Daily Mail.* www.dailymail.com. Aug. 7, 2012.

[79] Emily Friedman. "Romney Slips, Refers to Shooting Site as 'Sheik' Temple," ABC News. abcnews.go.com. Aug. 7, 2012.

[80] Dylan Byers. "Fox News: Anti-Semitism at Temple?" www.politico.com, Aug. 6, 2012.

[81] Abraham Foxman. "ADL Deplores Shooting at Sikh Temple," ADL Statement, www.adl.org, Aug. 6, 2012.

[82] Christina Hartman. "U.S. News: Was Sikh Temple Targeting Muslims? Does it Matter?" www.newsy.com. Aug. 8, 2012.

[83] Laura Pullman, Michael Zennie, and Louis Boyle. "Neo-Nazi Shooter Who Gunned Down Six at Sikh Temple was Former Soldier who was Leader of a Racist White Power Band."

[84] "Exclusive: Interview with Professor Who Extensively Studied Alleged Wisconsin Mass Killer," *Huffington Post*. www.huffingtonpost.com, Aug. 10, 2012.

[85] Ibid.

[86] Amy Davidson. "Terror in Oak Creek," *New Yorker*. www.newyorker.com, Aug. 6, 2012; Tom Schalmo and Leonard Green. "'9/11' Tattoo Skinhead Responsible for Massacre in Wisconsin," *New York Post*. www.nypost.com, Aug. 6, 2012.

[87] Laura Pullman, Michael Zennie, and Louis Boyle. "Neo-Nazi Shooter Who Gunned Down Six at Sikh Temple was Former Soldier who was Leader of a Racist White Power Band."

[88] Mitchell Landsberg. "Motive Uncertain in Sikh Temple Shooting, Police Say," *Los Angeles Times*. www.latimes.com, Aug. 6, 2012.

[89] Ibid.

[90] Ibid.

[91] Matthew Lysiak and Corky Siemaszko. "Stunning New Revelations in Sikh Massacre Probe," *New York Daily News*. www.nydailnews.com, Aug. 8, 2012.

[92] "Gunman Kills 6 at Sikh Temple in Wisconsin," *New York Times*. www.nytimes.com, Aug. 6, 2012; "Wisconsin Siblings Tell of Running to Warn Others As Temple Shooting Erupted," CNN. www.cnn.com, Aug. 9, 2012.

[93] Linda Spice, Maggie Hayes, and Bill Hutchinson. "Gunman who Killed Six at Sikh Temple of Wisconsin in Suburban Milwaukee May Have been Army Veteran and Reportedly was 'Skinhead' or 'White Supremacist'," *New York Daily News*. www.nydailynews.com, Aug. 6, 2012.

[94] Teresa Welsh. "Is the Media Undercovering the Wisconsin Sikh Temple Shooting? The Tragedy is not Receiving the Same National Attention as a Recent Shooting in Colorado." *U.S. News and World Report*. www.usnews.com, Aug. 8. 2012.

[95] Ethan Bronner. "Mourning Victims, Sikhs Lament Being Mistaken for Radicals or Militants," *New York Times*. www.nytimes.com, Aug. 7, 2012.

[96] "Gunman Kills 6 at Sikh Temple in Wisconsin," *New York Times*.

[97] Ibid.

[98] Chris McGreal. "Sikhs Say Attacks on Community are 'Collateral Damage' of 9/11," *Guardian*. www.guardian.co.uk, Aug. 8, 2012.

[99] Ibid.

[100] CNN Newsroom, with Carol Costello. Aug. 7, 2012.

[101] Andrea Domanick. "Candlelight Vigil in Las Vegas Honors Victims of Sikh Temple Shooting," *Las Vegas Sun*. www.lasvegassun.com, Aug. 8, 2012.

[102] Lakshimi Chaudhy. "Sacred Symbol, Shorthand for Terror." www.firstpost.com, Aug. 8, 2012.

[103] "Gunman Kills 6 at Sikh Temple in Wisconsin," *New York Times*.

[104] "California Muslims Want Federal Probe of Pig-Leg Vandalism," Associated Press, Aug. 10, 2012.

[105] Richard Dujardin. "Muslims in North Smithfield Ask for Protection After Sign Vandalism." *Providence Journal*. www.news.providencejournal.com, Aug. 7, 2012.

[106] Kelsey Ryan. "Suspicious Fire Leads to Destruction of Joplin Mosque," *Joplin Globe*. www.joplinglobe.com, Aug. 6, 2012.

[107] Ibid.

[108] Maria Sudenkum. "Joplin Mosque Razed in Fire; 2nd Blaze This Summer," *Boston Globe*. www.boston.com, Aug. 7, 2012.

[109] Kelsey Ryan. "Suspicious Fire Leads to Destruction of Joplin Mosque."

[110] "Missouri: After Arson a Month Ago, a Second Fire Destroys Joplin Mosque," *New York Times*, www.nytimes.com, Aug. 6, 2012.

[111] Alexis Wiley. "Detroit Man Fears He'll Be Attacked Again After Van Vandalism," Fox News. www.myfoxdetroit.com, Aug. 8, 2012.

[112] Ben Goad and David Olson. "Ontario: Pig Parts Dumped As Muslims Pray," *Press-Enterprise*. www.pe.com, Aug. 10, 2012.

[113] Ibid.

[114] "CAIR: Shots Fired at Illinois Mosque," PR Newswire. Aug. 11, 2012.

[115] Noam Chomsky. "Distorted Morality," lecture at Kennedy School of Government, Cambridge, MA, Feb. 6, 2002.

9781478230953